QUICK REFERENCE GUIDE

READINGS

LOOKING AT DIVERSITY PROFILES

IN REAL LIFE TRANSCRIPTS

ETHICAL CHALLENGES

INVITATIONS TO INSIGHT

SKILL BUILDERS

ON THE JOB BOXES

Looking Out, Looking In

13th Edition

Ronald B. Adler | Russell F. Proctor II

CENGAGE
Learning™

Australia • Brazil • Japan • Korea • Mexico • Singapore • Spain • United Kingdom • United States

CENGAGE
Learning™

Looking Out, Looking In: 13th Edition

Executive Editors:
Maureen Staudt
Michael Stranz

Senior Project Development Manager:
Linda deStefano

Marketing Specialist:
Courtney Sheldon

Senior Production/Manufacturing
Manager:
Donna M. Brown

PreMedia Manager:
Joel Brennecke

Sr. Rights Acquisition Account Manager:

Todd Osborne

Cover Image:
Getty Images*

*Unless otherwise noted, all cover images used by
Custom Solutions, a part of Cengage Learning,
have been supplied courtesy of Getty Images with
the exception of the Earthview cover image, which
has been supplied by the National Aeronautics and
Space Administration (NASA).

Looking Out, Looking In, 13th Edition
Ronald B. Adler | Russell F. Proctor II

© 2011, 2007, 2005 Wadsworth Cengage Learning. All rights reserved.

For product information and technology assistance, contact us at
Cengage Learning Customer & Sales Support, 1-800-354-9706

For permission to use material from this text or product,
submit all requests online at **cengage.com/permissions**
Further permissions questions can be emailed to
permissionrequest@cengage.com

This book contains select works from existing Cengage Learning resources and
was produced by Cengage Learning Custom Solutions for collegiate use. As such,
those adopting and/or contributing to this work are responsible for editorial
content accuracy, continuity and completeness.

Compilation © 2010 Cengage Learning

ISBN-13: 978-1-111-39738-8

ISBN-10: 1-111-39738-4

Cengage Learning
5191 Natorp Boulevard
Mason, Ohio 45040
USA

Cengage Learning is a leading provider of customized learning solutions with
office locations around the globe, including Singapore, the United Kingdom,
Australia, Mexico, Brazil, and Japan. Locate your local office at:
international.cengage.com/region

Cengage Learning products are represented in Canada by Nelson Education, Ltd.
For your lifelong learning solutions, visit **www.cengage.com /custom**
Visit our corporate website at **www.cengage.com**

Printed in the United States of America

To Neil Towne, whose legacy endures in these pages.

BRIEF CONTENTS

CONTENTS

CHAPTER TEN

IMPROVING COMMUNICATION CLIMATES   338

CHAPTER ELEVEN

MANAGING INTERPERSONAL CONFLICTS   376

PREFACE

Professors who teach the first course in interpersonal communication and the students who study the subject are lucky people. They get to explore a topic with obvious relevance to their own personal lives, and great potential for personal benefit.

The success of *Looking Out/Looking In* over almost four decades suggests that this book does justice to this important subject. We think you will find that this new edition continues this tradition.

What's Familiar

The defining characteristic of *Looking Out/Looking In* continues to be a user-friendly approach that highlights the connection between scholarship and everyday life. Virtually every page spread contains an attention-grabbing assortment of materials that support the text: quotations, poetry, music lyrics, articles from print and online sources, cartoons, and photography. A prominent treatment of ethical issues helps readers explore how to communicate in a principled manner. An extensive package of ancillary resources (described in detail in the following pages) aims at helping students learn and instructors teach efficiently and effectively.

This edition of *Looking Out/Looking In* continues to emphasize the transactional nature of interpersonal relationships. It presents communication not as a collection of techniques we use *on* others, but as a process we engage in *with* them. Readers also learn that even the most competent communication doesn't always seek to create warm, fuzzy relationships, and that even less personal interaction usually has the best chance of success when handled in a constructive, respectful manner.

The discussion of gender and culture is integrated throughout the book, rather than being isolated in separate chapters. The treatment of these important topics is non-ideological, citing research that shows how other variables are often at least as important in shaping interaction. The basic focus of the chapters has remained constant, and Chapters 2 through 11 can be covered in whatever order works best for individual situations.

New to This Edition

Long-time users of *Looking Out/Looking In* will find that this new edition has been improved in several ways.

UPDATED AND EXPANDED COVERAGE Updates begin with the text itself. Almost 20 percent of the 1,200 references are new to this edition, demonstrating to readers that principles and prescriptions offered in *Looking Out/Looking In* are grounded in scholarly research. These citations reflect developments in the discipline of communication, including emotion labor, privacy management, reappraisal, listening fidelity, and relational commitment. Many other topics have been expanded and updated. For example, there is expanded coverage of deception, the nature of mediated interpersonal relationships, interpersonal perception, argumentativeness, and social support.

ENHANCED CAREER FOCUS New "On the Job" sidebars in every chapter highlight the importance of interpersonal communication in the workplace. Grounded in scholarly research, these sidebars equip readers with communication strategies that will enhance career success. Topics include managing emotions on the job, effective nonverbal communication in employment interviews, avoiding negative self-fulfilling prophecies in the workplace, integrating newcomers into an organization's culture, dealing with workplace romances, and leaving a job on a positive note.

EXAMPLES FROM POPULAR MEDIA This edition integrates references to popular culture throughout the book in the form of photos, quotes, and in-text discussions. Lyrics of musical artists including Beyonce, Gavin DeGraw, Destiny's Child, Chris Cagle, Alison Krauss, and Diamond Rio echo themes from the text. Illustrations from television programs include *House*, *Ugly Betty*, *The Office*, and *Hell's Kitchen*. References to films include *The Pursuit of Happyness*, *Legally Blonde*, *Star Trek*, *The Breakfast Club*, and *I Love You, Man*. Even popular commercials reinforce the notion that the media are filled with examples that illustrate the principles of interpersonal communication.

Along with the in-chapter references to popular culture, new profiles of feature films and television programs wrap up each chapter, showing how entertainment can illustrate concepts from the text. New films discussed in this edition include *Into the Wild* (the necessity of communication), *Lars and the Real Girl* (shared narratives), *Yes Man* (emotional fallacies), *Hitch* (nonverbal cues), *The Devil Wears Prada* (poor listening), *The Break-Up* (relational deterioration), and *Borat* (incompetence in intercultural communication). Television series include *MADE* (self-improvement), *Lie to Me* (deception), *CSI / Law & Order* (listening), *Everybody Loves Raymond* (confirming/disconfirming communication), and *30 Rock* (conflict styles).

INCREASED EMPHASIS ON MEDIATED RELATIONSHIPS This edition recognizes the growing importance of mediated communication via social networking sites, blogging, email, instant messages, text messaging, and other forms of electronic media. In addition to presenting scholarship on mediated communication, this edition is loaded with sidebar material that illustrates how it operates in relationships. For example, Chapter 1 describes how friends and strangers in cyberspace helped one man prevail in his battle with substance abuse. Chapter 2 explores the way gamers create new identities and rich relationships that supplement their "real" ones. Chapter 7 describes how some businesses enhance listening by reducing the distractions of laptops and PDAs.

Chapter 8 presents a story of one loving couple whose long-distance relationship flourishes in cyberspace. Chapter 9 explores the world of PostSecret, a blog where people escape from the constraints of everyday privacy management by anonymously disclosing very personal information.

UPDATED VARIETY OF RELEVANT, INTERESTING READINGS Beyond mediated communication, this edition features a new lineup of sidebar readings that show how principles in the text operate in a wide range of settings and relationships. In Chapter 3, a Korean-American woman describes her resentment at being confused with other Asian women—and how she made the same mistake herself. The same chapter explores how workers in a retirement home gain empathy for their clients by simulating old age. Chapter 5 includes a plea discouraging the casual use of the B-word to describe women (and men). In Chapter 7, a young writer whose father recently died offers advice on how to let mourners grieve for their loss. Chapter 9 describes the challenges of "friends with benefits" relationships.

NEW COVERAGE OF DIVERSITY Throughout the book, "Looking at Diversity" profiles—many new to this edition—provide first-person accounts by communicators from a wide range of backgrounds. In Chapter 6, a person who is blind describes the challenges of interpreting others' nonverbal cues. In Chapter 7, an inmate explains how communication skills learned in a prison program helped her become a better listener. In Chapter 9, a Latina discusses the impact of culture and gender on communication with her African American husband and others. In Chapter 11, an international business consultant describes the challenges of cross-cultural communication.

Enhanced "Making the Grade" Pedagogy

Whatever else they bring to the interpersonal communication course, virtually all students want to earn a grade that reflects success. (Instructors are just as eager to see their students succeed.) The "Making the Grade" pedagogy in this edition features a variety of devices to help students learn concepts and develop skills most effectively.

CHAPTER-OPENING OBJECTIVES A list of learning outcomes opens each chapter, giving students a clear idea of the concepts and skills they need to learn in order to succeed. These objectives also help instructors focus class time, out-of-class assignments, and examinations on the outcomes that are clearly identified.

"IN REAL LIFE" DIALOGUES These transcripts, based on actual situations, describe how the skills and concepts from the text sound when used in everyday life. Seeing real people use the skills in familiar situations gives students both the modeling and confidence to try them in their own relationships. Dramatized versions of many of these transcripts are featured in the *Looking Out/Looking In* online resources described in the following pages.

ACTIVITIES Every chapter contains activities that help readers take a closer look at important concepts. They are labeled by type: "Invitations to Insight" help readers understand how theory and research applies to their own lives. "Skill Builders" help them improve their communication skills. "Ethical Challenges" highlight some challenges communicators face as they pursue their own goals.

END-OF-CHAPTER RESOURCES The "Making the Grade" section at the end of each chapter provides more resources to help students succeed. Along with the familiar chapter summary and key terms, students will find lists of search terms gleaned from online databases. These terms will help readers uncover scholarship that explains and extends the concepts they have learned in *Looking Out/Looking In*.

The "Making the Grade" section also directs students to the Premium Website for *Looking Out/Looking In*, where they will find digital resources that accompany this edition.

Teaching and Learning Resources

Along with the text itself, *Looking Out/Looking In* is accompanied by an extensive array of materials that will make teaching and learning more efficient and effective. **Note to faculty:** If you want your students to have access to the online resources for this handbook, please be sure to order them for your course. The content in these resources can be bundled with every new copy of the text or ordered separately. If you do not order them, your students will not have access to the online resources. *Contact your local Wadsworth Cengage Learning sales representative for more details.*

- The **Premium Website for *Looking Out/Looking In*** provides students with one-stop access to all the integrated technology resources that accompany the book. These resources include an enhanced eBook; Audio Study Tools chapter downloads; InfoTrac College Edition; interactive versions of the Invitation to Insight, Skill Builder, and Ethical Challenge exercises; interactive video activities; web links; and self-assessments. All resources are mapped to show both key discipline learning concepts as well as specific chapter learn lists.

- ***Looking Out/Looking In* interactive video activities** feature the **"In Real Life" communication scenarios**, which allow students to read, watch, listen to, and analyze videos of communication encounters that illustrate concepts discussed in the book. In addition, interactive **video simulations** ask students to consider the consequences of their choices in hypothetical interpersonal situations.

- **Audio Study Tools for *Looking Out/Looking In*** provide a fun and easy way for students to review chapter content whenever and wherever. For each chapter, students will have access to a brief interpersonal scenario example and a five- to seven-minute review consisting of a brief summary of the main points in the text and three review questions. Students can purchase the Audio Study Tools through iChapters (see below) and download files to their computers, iPods, or other MP3 players.

- The **Advantage Edition of *Looking Out/Looking In*** is available for instructors who are interested in an alternate version of the book. Part of the Cengage Learning Advantage Series, this version of the book is paperback and black-and-white, and it offers a built-in student workbook at the end of each chapter that has perforated pages so material can be submitted as homework.

- The **Interactive eBook for *Looking Out/Looking In*** provides students with interactive exercises, highlighting and bookmarking tools, a printing option, search tools, and an integrated online text-specific workbook.

- The **Student Activity Manual and Study Guide** has been revised by Shannon Doyle, San Jose State University. It contains a wealth of resources to help students understand and master concepts and skills introduced in the text.

- **Video Skillbuilder college success videos** provide unscripted clips of students talking about their struggles and successes in college. Topics covered include taking notes to improve your grades, time management, and learning styles.

- **InfoTrac College Edition with InfoMarks** is a virtual library featuring more than 18 million reliable, full-length articles from 5,000 academic and popular periodicals that can be retrieved almost instantly. Students also have access to InfoMarks—stable URLs that can be linked to articles, journals, and searches to save valuable time when doing research—and to the InfoWrite online resource center, where they can access grammar help, critical thinking guidelines, guides to writing research papers, and much more.

- **iChapters.com** is an online store that provides students with exactly what they've been asking for: choice, convenience, and savings. A 2005 research study by the National Association of College Stores indicates that as many as 60 percent of students do not purchase all required course material; however, those who do are more likely to succeed. This research also tells us that students want the ability to purchase "à la carte" course material in the format that suits them best. Accordingly, iChapters.com is the only online store that offers eBooks at up to 50 percent off, eChapters for as low as $1.99 each, and new textbooks at up to 25 percent off, plus up to 25 percent off print and digital supplements that can help improve student performance.

- A comprehensive **Instructor's Resource Manual**, revised by Justin Braxton-Brown, Kentucky Community and Technical College System, and Heidi Murphy, Central New Mexico Community College, provides tips and tools for both new and experienced instructors. The manual also contains hard copy of over 1,200 class-tested exam questions, indexed by page number and level of understanding.

- The **PowerLecture** CD-ROM contains an electronic version of the Instructor's Resource Manual, ExamView® Computerized Testing, predesigned Microsoft PowerPoint presentations, and JoinIn® classroom quizzing. The PowerPoint presentations contain text, images, and videos of student speeches and can be used as they are or customized to suit your course needs.

- **Communication Scenarios for Critique and Analysis Videos** include the communication scenarios included in the *Looking Out/Looking In* interactive videos as well as additional scenarios covering interviewing and group work. *Contact your Wadsworth Cengage Learning sales representative for details.*

- **BBC News and CBS News DVD:** *Interpersonal Communication* provides footage of news stories that relate to current topics in interpersonal communication, such as adult sibling rivalry, communicating with your mom, and teen texting codes. Available Spring 2010.

- *Communication in Film III: Teaching Communication Courses Using Feature Films* by Russell F. Proctor II, Northern Kentucky University, expands on the film tips in each chapter of *Looking Out/Looking In*. This guide provides detailed suggestions for using both new and classic films to illustrate communication principles introduced in the text.

- *Media Guide for Interpersonal Communication* by Charles G. Apple, University of Michigan–Flint, provides faculty with media resource listings focused on general interpersonal communication topics. Each listing provides compelling examples of how interpersonal communication concepts are illustrated in particular films, books, plays, websites, or journal articles. Discussion questions are provided.

- *The Teaching Assistant's Guide to the Basic Course* by Katherine G. Hendrix, University of Memphis, is based on leading communication teacher training programs and covers general teaching and course management topics, as well as specific strategies for communication instruction, such as providing effective feedback on performance, managing sensitive class discussions, and conducting mock interviews.

- *A Guide to the Basic Course for ESL Students* by Esther Yook, Mary Washington College, is available bundled with the text and assists the nonnative English speaker. It features FAQs, helpful URLs, and strategies for accent management and overcoming speech apprehension.

- *The Art and Strategy of Service Learning* by Rick Isaacson and Jeff Saperstein can be bundled with the text and is an invaluable resource for students in a basic course that integrates a service-learning component. The handbook provides guidelines for connecting service learning work with classroom concepts and advice for working effectively with agencies and organizations. The handbook also provides model forms and reports and a directory of online resources.

- **TeamUP technology training and support** can help you get trained, get connected, and get the support you need for seamless integration of technology resources into your course with Cengage Learning's TeamUP Program. This unparalleled technology service and training program provides robust online resources, peer-to-peer instruction, personalized training, and a customizable program you can count on. Visit http://academic.cengage.com/tlc to sign up for online seminars, first day of class services, technical support, or personalized face-to-face training. Our online or onsite training sessions are frequently led by one of our lead teachers, faculty members who are experts in using Wadsworth Cengage Learning technology and can provide the best practices and teaching tips.

- As part of our **Flex-Text customization program**, you can add your personal touch to *Looking Out/Looking In* with a course-specific cover and up to 32 pages of your own content, at no additional cost. Create a text as unique as your course: quickly, simply, and affordably. A bonus chapter unique to *Looking Out/Looking In* about computer-mediated communication is available now.

Acknowledgments

The success of *Looking Out/Looking In* is due to the contributions of many people. First and foremost are our families, who tolerated our absences and distractions over the year that we worked on this book. We also thank our students, who over the years have helped us understand how to present material in ways that make sense and make a difference. We are especially grateful to Jenny Prigge at Northern Kentucky University, who supplied us with numerous popular media illustrations of communication concepts.

We are also grateful for the ideas of colleagues whose reviews helped shape this new edition: Alicia Alexander, Southern Illinois University, Edwardsville; Evelyn Dufner, International Academy of Design and Technology; Clark Friesen, Lone Star College, Tomball; Frank Giannotti, Gibbs College; Carrie Harrison, Pittsburgh Technical Institute; Jacob Isaacs, Ivy Tech Community College, Lafayette; Carrie Johnson, National-Louis University; Sarah Riley, University of Kentucky; and Joseph Valenzano, University of Nevada, Las Vegas.

Our thanks also go to the talented and hard-working team at Wadsworth Cengage Learning who have played a role in this edition from start to finish: Greer Lleuad, Monica Eckman, Erin Mitchell, Bryant Chrzan, Rebekah Matthews, Colin Solan, Jessica Badiner, Michael Lepera, Jill Haber, Linda Helcher, Margaret Chamberlain-Gaston, Bob Kauser, Robyn Young, Bill Jentzen, Audrey Pettengill, Christine Dobberpuhl, and Lyn Uhl. In addition, we are grateful to the publishing professionals whose fingerprints are all over this edition: Rita Dienst, Ginjer Clarke, Kathy Deselle, Yvo Riezebos, Jennifer Bonnar, Beth Minick, Eric Zeiter, Raquel Sousa, and Tim Herzog. As always, we are indebted to Sherri Adler for selecting the photos that help make this book a standout.

About the Authors

Since this is a book about interpersonal communication, it seems appropriate for us to introduce ourselves to you, the reader. The "we" you'll be reading throughout this book isn't just an editorial device: It refers to two real people—Ron Adler and Russ Proctor.

Ron Adler lives in Santa Barbara, California, with his wife, Sherri, an artist and photo researcher who selected most of the images in this book. Their three adult children were infants when early editions of *Looking Out / Looking In* were conceived, and they grew up as guinea pigs for the field testing of many concepts in this book. If you asked them, they would vouch for the value of the information between these covers.

Ron spends most of his professional time writing about communication. In addition to helping create *Looking Out / Looking In*, he has contributed to six other books about topics including business communication, public speaking, small group communication, assertiveness, and social skills. Besides writing and teaching, Ron teaches college courses and helps professional and business people improve their communication on the job. Cycling and hiking help keep Ron physically and emotionally healthy.

Russ Proctor is a professor at Northern Kentucky University, where his sons R. P. and Randy both attended. Russ's wife, Pam, is an educator too, training teachers, students, and businesses to use energy more efficiently.

Russ met Ron at a communication conference in 1990, where they quickly discovered a shared interest in using feature films as a teaching tool. They have written and spoken extensively on this topic over the years, and they have also co-authored several textbooks and articles. When Russ isn't teaching, writing, or presenting, his hobbies include sports (especially baseball), classic rock music (especially Steely Dan), and cooking (especially for family and friends on his birthday each year).

A FIRST LOOK AT INTERPERSONAL COMMUNICATION

✔+ MAKING THE GRADE

Here are the topics discussed in this chapter:

After studying the topics in this chapter, you should be able to:

1. Assess the needs (physical, identity, social, and practical) that communicators are attempting to satisfy in a given situation or relationship.

2. Apply the transactional communication model to a specific situation.

3. Describe how the communication principles on pages 13–15 and misconceptions on pages 15–16 are evident in a specific situation.

4. Describe the degree to which communication (in a specific instance or a relationship) is qualitatively impersonal or interpersonal, and describe the consequences of this level of interaction.

5. Diagnose the effectiveness of various communication channels in a specific situation.

6. Use the criteria on pages 27–31 to determine the level of communication competence in a specific instance or a relationship.

The Silencing

As his name was called, James J. Pelosi, the 452nd West Point cadet of the class of '73, drew in his breath and went to the podium—steeling himself for one last moment of humiliation. The slender, bespectacled young man accepted his diploma, then turned to face the rows of starched white hats and—so he expected—a chorus of boos. Instead, there was only silence. But when he returned to his classmates, the newly fledged lieutenant was treated to something new—a round of handshakes. "It was just as if I were a person again," he said. Thus ended one of the strangest and most brutal episodes in the long history of the corps.

A year earlier, the Long Island cadet was hauled up before the West Point Honor Committee and charged with cheating on an engineering exam. In spite of conflicting testimony given at his trial and his own determined plea of innocence, the third-year cadet, one of the most respected in his company and himself a candidate for the Honor Committee, was convicted. Pelosi's case was thrown out by the Academy superintendent after his military lawyer proved there had been undue influence over the proceeding by the Honor Committee adviser, but that wasn't the end of it. The Academy honor code reserves a special fate for those thought by the majority to be guilty even when there is insufficient evidence to convict. It is called "silencing."

Pelosi's fellow cadets voted to support the Honor Committee sentence. And so for most of his third and all of

© Bettye Lane/Photo Research

his fourth year at West Point, Pelosi was ostracized. He was transferred by the Academy to what one friend called a "straight-strict" company— "one of the toughest in the corps." He ate alone each day at a table for ten; he lived by himself in a room meant for two or three; he endured insult and occasional brickbats tossed in his direction; he saw his mail mutilated and his locker vandalized. And hardly anyone, even a close friend who wept when he heard the silencing decision, would talk to him in public. Under those conditions, most cadets resign. But even though he lost 26 pounds, Pelosi hung tough. "When you're right," he said later, "you have to prove yourself. . . . I told myself I didn't care."

And in the end, James Pelosi survived—one of only a handful of Academy cadets in history to graduate after silencing. Now that he is out, Lieutenant Pelosi is almost dispassionate in his criticism of the Academy and his fellow cadets. About as far as he will go is to say that "Silencing should be abolished. It says cadets are above the law. This attitude of superiority bothers me." As for his own state of mind during the ordeal, he told *Newsweek*'s Deborah Beers, "I've taken a psychology course and I know what isolation does to animals. No one at the Academy asks how it affects a person. Doesn't that seem strange?"

Newsweek

*P*erhaps you played this game as a child. The group of children chooses a victim—either as punishment for committing a real or imagined offense or just for "fun." Then for a period of time, that victim is given the silent treatment. No one speaks to him or her, and no one responds to anything the victim says or does.

If you were the subject of this silent treatment, you probably experienced a range of emotions. At first you might have felt—or at least acted—indifferent. But after a while the strain of being treated as a nonperson probably began to grow. If the game went on long enough, it's likely you found yourself either retreating into a state of depression or lashing out with hostility—partly to show your anger and partly to get a response from the others.

Adults, as well as children, have used the silent treatment in virtually every society throughout history as a powerful tool to express displeasure and for social control.[1] We all know intuitively that communication—the company of others—is one of the most basic human needs, and that lack of contact is among the cruelest punishments a person can suffer.

Besides being emotionally painful, being deprived of companionship is so serious that it can affect life itself. Fredrick II, emperor of Germany from 1196 to 1250, may have been the first person to prove the point systematically. A medieval historian described one of his significant, if inhumane, experiments:

> He bade foster mothers and nurses to suckle the children, to bathe and wash them, but in no way to prattle with them, for he wanted to learn whether they would speak the Hebrew language, which was the oldest, or Greek, or Latin, or Arabic, or perhaps the language of their parents, of whom they had been born. But he labored in vain because all the children died. For they could not live without the petting and joyful faces and loving words of their foster mothers.[2]

Fortunately, contemporary researchers have found less barbaric ways to illustrate the importance of communication. In one study of isolation, subjects were paid to remain alone in a locked room. Of the five subjects, one lasted for eight days. Three held out for two days, one commenting, "Never again." The fifth subject lasted only two hours.[3]

The need for contact and companionship is just as strong outside the laboratory, as individuals who have led solitary lives by choice or necessity have discovered. W. Carl Jackson, an adventurer who sailed across the Atlantic Ocean alone in fifty-one days, summarized the feelings common to most loners:

> I found the loneliness of the second month almost excruciating. I always thought of myself as self-sufficient, but I found life without people had no meaning. I had a definite need for somebody to talk to, someone real, alive, and breathing.[4]

Why We Communicate

You might object to stories like this, claiming that solitude would be a welcome relief from the irritations of everyday life. It's true that all of us need solitude, often more than we get, but each of us has a point beyond which we do not want to be alone. Beyond this point, solitude changes from a pleasurable to a painful condition. In other words, we all need relationships. We all need to communicate.

PHYSICAL NEEDS

Communication is so important that its presence or absence affects physical health. In extreme cases, communication can even become a matter of life or death. When he was a Navy pilot, U.S. Senator John McCain was shot down over North Vietnam and held as a prisoner of war for six years, often in solitary confinement. He describes how POWs set up clandestine codes in which they sent messages by tapping on walls to laboriously spell out words. McCain describes the importance of keeping contact and the risks that inmates would take to maintain contact with one another:

> We must love one another or die.
>
> —W. H. Auden

> The punishment for communicating could be severe, and a few POWs, having been caught and beaten for their efforts, had their spirits broken as their bodies were battered. Terrified of a return trip to the punishment room, they would lie still in their cells when their comrades tried to tap them up on the wall. Very few would remain uncommunicative for long. To suffer all this alone was less tolerable than torture. Withdrawing in silence from the fellowship of other Americans . . . was to us the approach of death.[5]

Other prisoners have also described the punishing effects of social isolation. Reflecting on his seven years as a hostage in Lebanon, former news correspondent Terry Anderson said flatly, "I would rather have had the worst companion than no companion at all."[6]

The link between communication and physical well-being isn't restricted to prisoners. Medical researchers have identified a wide range of health threats that can result from a lack of close relationships. For instance:

- A lack of social relationships jeopardizes coronary health to a degree that rivals cigarette smoking, high blood pressure, blood lipids, obesity, and lack of physical activity.[7]

- Socially isolated people are four times more susceptible to the common cold than are those who have active social networks.[8]

- Social isolates are two to three times more likely to die prematurely than are those with strong social ties. The type of relationship doesn't seem to matter: Marriage, friendship, religious ties, and community ties all seem to increase longevity.[9]

- The likelihood of death increases when a close relative dies. In one Welsh village, citizens who had lost a close relative died within one year at a rate more than five times greater than the rate of those who had not lost a relative.[10]

By contrast, a life that includes positive relationships created through communication leads to better health. As little as ten minutes per day of socializing improves memory and boosts intellectual function.[11] Communicators who are willing to acknowledge their possible limitations have lower blood pressure than those who are more defensive.[12] Stress hormones decline the more often people hear expressions of affection from loved ones.[13]

Research like this demonstrates the importance of having satisfying personal relationships. Not everyone needs the same amount of contact, and the quality of communication is almost certainly as important as the quantity. The important point is that personal communication is essential for our well-being.

IDENTITY NEEDS

Communication does more than enable us to survive. It is the way—indeed, the *only* way—we learn who we are. As Chapter 2 explains, our sense of identity comes from the way we interact with other people. Are we smart or stupid, attractive or ugly, skillful or inept? The answers to these questions don't come from looking in the mirror. We decide who we are based on how others react to us.

Deprived of communication with others, we would have no sense of ourselves. In his book *Bridges Not Walls*, John Stewart dramatically illustrates this fact by citing the case of the famous "Wild Boy of Aveyron," who spent his early childhood without any apparent human contact. The boy was discovered in January 1800 digging for vegetables in a French village garden. He showed no behaviors that one would expect in a social human. The boy could not speak but rather uttered only weird cries. More significant than this lack of social skills was his lack of any identity as a human being. As author Roger Shattuck put it, "The boy had no human sense of being in the world. He had no sense of himself as a person related to other persons."[14] Only with the influence of a loving "mother" did the boy begin to behave—and, we can imagine, think of himself—as a human.

Like the boy of Aveyron, each of us enters the world with little or no sense of identity. We gain an idea of who we are from the way others define us. As Chapter 2 explains, the messages we receive in early childhood are the strongest, but the influence of others continues throughout life.

SOCIAL NEEDS

Besides helping to define who we are, communication provides a vital link with others. Researchers and theorists have identified a whole range of social needs that we satisfy by communicating. These include pleasure, affection, companionship, escape, relaxation, and control.[15]

Research suggests a strong link between effective interpersonal communication and happiness. In one study of more than 200 college students, the happiest 10 percent described themselves as having a rich social life. (The very happy people were no different from their classmates in any other measurable way such as amount of sleep, exercise, TV watching, religious activity, or alcohol consumption.)[16] In another study, women reported that "socializing" contributed more to a satisfying life than virtually any other activity, including relaxing, shopping, eating, exercise, TV, or prayer.[17] Married couples who are effective communicators report happier relationships than less skillful husbands and wives—a finding that has been supported across cultures.[18]

Despite knowing that communication is vital to social satisfaction, a variety of evidence suggests that many people aren't very successful at managing their interpersonal relationships. For example, one study revealed that one-quarter of the more than 4,000 adults surveyed knew more about their dogs than they did about their neighbors' backgrounds.[19] Research also suggests that the number of friendships is in decline. One widely recognized survey reported that, in 1985, Americans had an average of 2.94 close friends. Twenty years later, that number had dropped to 2.08. In other words, Americans are

> Two are better than one, because they have a good reward for their labor. For if they fall, one will lift up his companion. But woe to him who is alone when he falls, for he has no one to help him up.
>
> —*Ecclesiastes 4:9, 10*

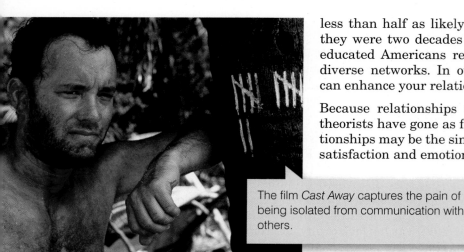

The film *Cast Away* captures the pain of being isolated from communication with others.

20th Century Fox/Dreamworks/The Kobal Collection/Duhamel, Francois

less than half as likely to have close friends now than they were two decades earlier.[20] It's worth noting that educated Americans reported having larger and more diverse networks. In other words, a higher education can enhance your relational life as well as your intellect.

Because relationships with others are so vital, some theorists have gone as far as to argue that positive relationships may be the single most important source of life satisfaction and emotional well-being in every culture.[21]

If you pause now and make a mental list of your own relationships, you'll probably see that, no matter how successful your relationships at home, with friends, at school, and at work, there is plenty of room for improvement in your everyday life. The information that follows will help you improve the way you communicate with the people who matter most to you.

PRACTICAL GOALS

Besides satisfying social needs and shaping our identity, communication is the most widely used approach to satisfying what communication scholars call **instrumental goals**: getting others to behave in ways we want. Some instrumental goals are quite basic: Communication is the tool that lets you tell the hair stylist to take just a little off the sides, lets you negotiate household duties, and lets you convince the plumber that the broken pipe needs attention *now*!

Other instrumental goals are more important. Career success is the prime example. As the On the Job box on page 9 shows, communication skill is essential in virtually every career. On-the-job communication skills can even make the difference between life and death. The Los Angeles Police Department cited "bad communication" among the most common reasons for errors in shooting by its officers.[22] Communication skills are just as essential for doctors, nurses, and other medical practitioners.[23] Researchers discovered that "poor communication" was the root of more than 60 percent of reported medical errors—including death, serious physical injury, and psychological trauma.[24] Research published in the *Journal of the American Medical Association* and elsewhere revealed a significant difference between the communication skills of physicians who had no malpractice claims against them and those with previous claims.[25]

Psychologist Abraham Maslow suggested that the physical, identity, social, and practical needs we have been discussing fall into five hierarchical categories, each of which must be satisfied before we concern ourselves with the less fundamental needs.[26] The most basic of these needs are *physical*: sufficient air, water, food, and rest, and the ability to reproduce as a species. The second of Maslow's needs is *safety*: protection from threats to our well-being. Beyond physical and safety needs are the *social needs* we have mentioned already. Beyond these, Maslow suggests, each of us

ON THE JOB

Communication and Career Success

No matter what the field, research confirms what experienced workers already know—that communication skills are crucial in finding and succeeding in a job. Communication skills often make the difference between being hired and being rejected. In one widely followed annual survey, employers list the skills and qualities for their ideal candidate. Communication skills always top the list, ranking ahead of technical skills, initiative, analytical ability, and computer skills.[a]

In another survey, managers across the country rated the abilities to speak and listen effectively as the two most important factors in helping college graduates find jobs in a competitive workplace—more important than technical competence, work experience, and specific degree earned.[b] When 170 well-known business and industrial firms were asked to list the most common reasons for *not* offering jobs to applicants, the most frequent replies were "inability to communicate" and "poor communication skills."[c]

Once you have been hired, the need for communication skills is important in virtually every career.[d] Engineers spend the bulk of their working lives speaking and listening, mostly in one-to-one and small-group settings.[e] Accounting professionals spend 80 percent of their time on the job communicating with others, individually and in groups.[f] One executive at computer giant Sun Microsystems made the point forcefully: "If there's one skill that's required for success in this industry, it's communication skills."[g] Writing in *The Scientist*, a commentator echoed this sentiment: "If I give any advice, it is that you can never do enough training around your overall communication skills."[h]

has *self-esteem* needs: the desire to believe that we are worthwhile, valuable people. The final category of needs described by Maslow is *self-actualization*: the desire to develop our potential to the maximum, to become the best person we can be. As you read on, think about the ways in which communication is often necessary to satisfy each level of need.

The Process of Communication

We have been talking about *communication* as though the meaning of this word were perfectly clear. Before going further, we need to explain systematically what happens when people exchange messages with one another. Doing so will introduce you to a common working vocabulary and, at the same time, preview some of the topics that are covered in later chapters.

A LINEAR VIEW

In the early days of studying communication as a social science, researchers created models to illustrate the communication process. Their first attempts resulted in a **linear communication model**, which depicts communication as something a sender "does to" a receiver. According to the linear model in Figure 1.1,

> A **sender** (the person creating the message)
> **encodes** (puts thoughts into symbols, usually words) a
> **message** (the information being transmitted), sending it through a
> **channel** (the medium through which the message passes) to a
> **receiver** (the person attending to the message) who

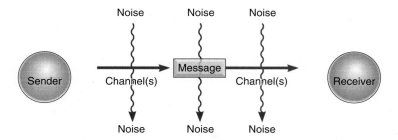

Figure 1.1
Linear Communication Model

decodes (makes sense of the message), while contending with
noise (distractions that disrupt transmission).

Notice how the appearance of and vocabulary in Figure 1.1 represent how radio and television broadcasting operate. This isn't a coincidence: The scientists who created it were primarily interested in electronic media. The widespread use of this model has affected the way we think and talk about communication. There is a linear, machine-like quality to familiar phrases, such as "We're having a communication breakdown" and "I don't think my message is getting through." While this is sometimes the case in mediated forms of communication, these familiar phrases (and the thinking they represent) obscure some important features of human communication. Does interpersonal communication really "break down," or are people still exchanging information even when they're not talking to each other? Is it possible to "get a message through" to someone loudly and clearly, but still not get the desired reaction? Here are some other questions to consider about the shortcomings of the linear model:

- When you're having a face-to-face conversation with a friend, is there only one sender and one receiver, or do both of you send and receive messages simultaneously?

- Do you purposely encode every message you send, or do you engage in some behaviors unconsciously that still communicate messages to others?

- Does communication take place in a vacuum, or is a message's meaning affected by larger factors such as culture, environment, and relational history?

These and other questions have led scholars to create models that better represent interpersonal communication. We will look at one of these models now.

A TRANSACTIONAL VIEW

A **transactional communication model** (Figure 1.2) updates and expands the linear model to better capture communication as a uniquely human process. Some concepts and terms from the linear model are retained in the transactional model, whereas others are enhanced, added, or eliminated.

The transactional model uses the word *communicator* instead of *sender* and *receiver*. This term reflects the fact that people send and receive messages simultaneously and not in a unidirectional or back-and-forth manner, as suggested by the linear model. Consider, for example, what might happen when you and a housemate negotiate how to handle household chores. As soon as you begin to hear (receive) the words sent by your housemate, "I want to talk about cleaning the kitchen . . . ," you grimace and

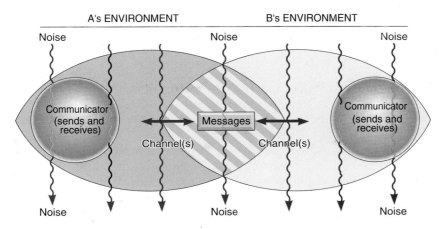

Figure 1.2
Transactional Communication Model

clench your jaw (sending a nonverbal message of your own while receiving the verbal one). This reaction leads your housemate to interrupt herself defensively, sending a new message: "Now wait a minute . . ."

A transactional model also shows that communicators often occupy different **environments**—fields of experience that affect how they understand others' behavior. In communication terminology, *environment* refers not only to a physical location but also to the personal experiences and cultural background that participants bring to a conversation.

Consider just some of the factors that might contribute to different environments:

- Person A might belong to one ethnic group and person B to another.

- A might be rich and B poor.

- A might be rushed and B have nowhere to go.

- A might have lived a long, eventful life and B might be young and inexperienced.

- A might be passionately concerned with the subject and B indifferent to it.

> Like paths and alleys overgrown with hardy, rank-growing weeds, the words we use are overgrown with our individual, private, provincial associations, which tend to choke the meaning.
>
> —*Stefan Themerson*

Notice how the model in Figure 1.2 shows that the environments of individuals A and B overlap. This area represents the background that the communicators have in common. As the shared environment becomes smaller, communication becomes more difficult. Consider a few examples in which different perspectives can make understanding difficult:

- Bosses who have trouble understanding the perspectives of their employees will be less effective managers, and workers who do not appreciate the challenges of being a boss are more likely to be uncooperative (and probably less suitable for advancement).

- Parents who have trouble recalling their youth are likely to clash with their children, who have never known and may not appreciate the responsibility that comes with parenting.

- Members of a dominant culture who have never experienced how it feels to be "different" may not appreciate the concerns of people from minority co-cultures, whose own perspectives make it hard to understand the cultural blindness of the majority.

Communication channels retain a significant role in the transactional model, as they did in the linear model. Although it's tempting to see channels simply as neutral conduits for delivering a message, a closer look reveals the important role they play. For instance, should you say "I love you" in person? Over the phone? By renting space on a billboard? By sending flowers and a card? With a singing telegram? Via email? In a voice mail? Channel selection matters just as much when sending breakup messages. A recent study of 1,000 cell phone users found that 45 percent had used their mobile phone to end a relationship (usually by text).[27] Obviously, this way of delivering bad news runs the risk of wounding and infuriating the person being dumped ("She didn't even have the guts to tell me to my face").

The transactional model also retains the concept of noise but with a broader focus. In the linear model, the focus is on noise in the channel—what is known as *external noise*. For instance, loud music or too much cigarette smoke in a crowded room might make it difficult for you to pay attention to another person. The transactional model shows that noise also resides *within* communicators. This includes *physiological noise*, which involves biological factors that interfere with accurate reception: illness, fatigue, hearing loss, and so on. Communicators can also encounter *psychological noise*: forces within that interfere with the ability to understand a message accurately. For instance, a student might become so upset upon learning that she failed a test that she would be unable (perhaps *unwilling* is a better word) to understand clearly where she went wrong. Psychological noise is such an important communication problem that we have devoted much of Chapter 10 to investigating its most common form, defensiveness.

For all the insights they offer, models can't capture some important features of interpersonal communication. A model is a "snapshot," while communication more closely resembles a "motion picture." In real life it's difficult to isolate a single discrete "act" of communication from the events that precede and follow it.[28] Consider the "Zits" cartoon on this page. If you read only the final frame, it appears that Jeremy is the victim of his mother's nagging. If you then read the first three frames, you might conclude that if Jeremy were more responsive to his mother, she might not need to be so persistent. And if you watched the two of them interact over the days and weeks preceding the incident in this cartoon, you would have a larger (but still incomplete) picture of the relational history that contributed to this event. In other words, the communication pattern that Jeremy and his mother have created together contributes to the quality of their relationship.

Comparing and Contrasting Communication Models

Visit the Pragmatic Communication Model website. You can find the link to this site through your Premium Website for *Looking Out/Looking In*. Read the explanation and then, in your own words, summarize the similarities and differences between the Pragmatic Model at this site and the Transactional Model in your textbook. What does each have in common? What does one model explain better than the other? Which one do you prefer and why?

This leads to another important point: Transactional communication isn't something that we do *to* others; rather, it is an activity that we do *with* them. In this sense, person-to-person communication is rather like dancing—at least the kind of dancing we do with partners. Like dancing, communication depends on the involvement of a partner. And like good dancing, successful communication doesn't depend only on the person who takes the lead. A great dancer who forgets to consider and adapt to the skill level of his or her partner can make both people look bad. In communication and dancing, even having two talented partners doesn't guarantee success. When two skilled dancers perform without coordinating their movements, the results feel bad to the dancers and look foolish to an audience. Finally, relational communication—like dancing—is a unique creation that arises out of the way in which the partners interact. The way you dance probably varies from one partner to another. Likewise, the way you communicate almost certainly varies from one partner to another.

Now we can summarize the definition of *communication* that we have been developing. **Communication** is a transactional process involving participants who occupy different but overlapping environments and create relationships through the exchange of messages, many of which are affected by external, physiological, and psychological noise. Whether or not you memorize this definition is a matter for you and your instructor to decide. In any case, notice how it reflects a more sophisticated view of the process than you might have had before reading this far.

Communication Principles and Misconceptions

Before we look at the qualities that distinguish interpersonal communication, it's important to define what communication is and what it isn't and to discuss what it can and can't accomplish.

COMMUNICATION PRINCIPLES

It's possible to draw several important conclusions about communication from what you have already learned in this chapter.

COMMUNICATION CAN BE INTENTIONAL OR UNINTENTIONAL Some communication is clearly intentional: You probably plan your words carefully before asking the boss for a raise or offering constructive criticism. Some scholars argue that only intentional messages like these qualify as communication. Others argue that even unintentional behavior is communicative. Suppose, for instance, that a friend overhears you muttering complaints to yourself. Even though you didn't intend for her to hear your remarks, they certainly did carry a message. In addition to these slips of the tongue, we unintentionally send many nonverbal messages. You might not be aware of your sour expression, impatient shifting, or sigh of boredom, but others view them nonetheless. Scholars have debated without reaching consensus about whether unintentional behavior should be considered communication, and it's unlikely that they will ever settle this issue.[29] In *Looking Out / Looking In*, we will look at the communicative value of both intentional and unintentional behavior.

COMMUNICATION IS IRREVERSIBLE We sometimes wish that we could back up in time, erasing words or acts and replacing them with better alternatives. As the cartoon on this page points out, such reversal is impossible. Sometimes, further explanation can clear up another's confusion, or an apology can mollify another's hurt feelings, but other times no amount of explanation can erase the impression you have created. It is no more possible to "unreceive" a message than to "unsqueeze" a tube of toothpaste. Words said and deeds done are irretrievable.

"We can pause, Stu—we can even try fast-forwarding—
but we can never rewind."

IT'S IMPOSSIBLE NOT TO COMMUNICATE Because both intentional and unintentional behaviors send a message, many theorists agree that it is impossible not to communicate. Whatever you do—whether you speak or remain silent, confront or avoid, act emotional or keep a poker face—you provide information to others about your thoughts and feelings. In this sense we are like transmitters that can't be shut off.

Of course, the people who decode your message may not interpret it accurately. They might take your kidding seriously or underestimate your feelings, for example. The message that you intend to convey may not even resemble the one that others infer from your actions. Thus, when we talk about "a communication breakdown" or "miscommunication," we rarely mean that communication has ended. Instead, we mean that it is inaccurate, ineffective, or unsatisfying.[30]

This explains why the best way to boost understanding is to discuss your intentions and your interpretations of the other person's behavior until you have negotiated a shared meaning. The perception-checking skills described in Chapter 3, the tips on clear language offered in Chapter 5, and the listening skills introduced in Chapter 7 will give you tools to boost the odds that the meanings of messages you send and receive are understandable to both you and others.

COMMUNICATION IS UNREPEATABLE Because communication is an ongoing process, it is impossible to repeat the same event. The friendly smile that worked so well when meeting a stranger last week might not succeed with the person you meet tomorrow: It might feel stale and artificial to you the second time around, or it might be wrong for the new person or occasion. Even with the same person, it's impossible to re-create an event. Why? Because neither you nor the other person is the same person. You've both lived longer. Your feelings about each other may have changed. You need not constantly invent new ways to act around familiar people, but you should realize that the "same" words and behavior are different each time they are spoken or performed.

COMMUNICATION HAS A CONTENT AND A RELATIONAL DIMENSION   Practically all exchanges operate on two levels. The **content dimension** involves the information being explicitly discussed: "Turn left at the next corner." "You can buy that for less online." "You're standing on my foot." In addition to this sort of obvious content, all messages also have a **relational dimension** that expresses how you feel about the other person: whether you like or dislike the other person, feel in control or subordinate, feel comfortable or anxious, and so on.[31] For instance, consider how many different relational messages you could communicate by simply saying, "I'm busy tonight, but maybe some other time" in different ways.

Sometimes the content dimension of a message is all that matters. For example, you probably don't care much about how the customer service rep feels about you as long as you get a technician scheduled to fix your car. At other times, though, the relational dimension of a message is more important than the content under discussion. This explains why arguments can develop over apparently trivial subjects such as whose turn it is to wash the dishes or how to spend the weekend. In cases like this, what's really being tested is the nature of the relationship. Who's in control? How important are we to each other? Chapter 8 will explore these key relational issues in detail.

COMMUNICATION MISCONCEPTIONS

It's just as important to know what communication is *not* as to know what it is.[32] Avoiding the following misconceptions can save you a great deal of personal trouble.

MORE COMMUNICATION IS NOT ALWAYS BETTER   Whereas not communicating enough can cause problems, there are also situations when *too much* communication is a mistake. Sometimes excessive communication is simply unproductive, as when two people "talk a problem to death," going over the same ground again and again without making progress. As one communication book puts it, "More and more negative communication merely leads to more and more negative results."[33] Even when you aren't being critical, too much communication can backfire. Pestering a prospective employer after your job interview or texting too many "call me" messages can generate the opposite reaction from what you're seeking.

MEANINGS ARE NOT IN WORDS   The biggest mistake we can make is to assume that *saying* something is the same thing as *communicating* it. As Chapter 3 explains, the words that make perfect sense to you can be interpreted in entirely different ways by others. Chapter 5 describes the most common types of verbal misunderstandings and suggests ways to minimize them. Chapter 7 introduces listening skills that help ensure that the way you receive messages matches the ideas that a speaker is trying to convey.

SUCCESSFUL COMMUNICATION DOESN'T ALWAYS INVOLVE SHARED UNDERSTANDING   George Bernard Shaw once remarked, "The problem with communication . . . is the illusion that it has been accomplished." This observation may sound cynical, but research (and most likely your personal experience) demonstrates that misunderstandings are common.[34] In fact, evidence suggests that people who are well acquainted may be more likely to misunderstand one another than relative strangers.[35]

Mutual understanding can be one measure of successful communication,[36] but there are times when success comes from *not* completely understanding one another. For example, we are often deliberately vague in order to spare another's feelings. Imagine how you might reply when a friend asks, "What do you think about my new tattoo?" You might tactfully say, "Wow—that's really unusual," instead of honestly and clearly answering, "I think it's grotesque." In cases like this we sacrifice clarity for the sake of kindness and to maintain our relationships.

"My wife understands me."

Some research suggests that satisfying relationships depend in part on flawed understanding. As the cartoon on this page suggests, couples who *think* their partners understand them are more satisfied with each other than those who *actually* understand what the other says and means.[37] In other words, more satisfying relationships can sometimes come from less-than-perfect understanding. Chapter 9 describes in detail the way we sometimes sacrifice clarity for the sake of maintaining relationships.

NO SINGLE PERSON OR EVENT CAUSES ANOTHER'S REACTION Although communicative skill can often make the difference between satisfying and unsatisfying outcomes, it's a mistake to suggest that any single thing we say or do causes an outcome. Many factors play a role in how others will react to your communication in a single situation. Suppose, for example, that you lose your temper and say something to a friend that you regret as soon as the words escape your lips. Your friend's reaction will depend on a whole host of events besides your unjustified remark: her frame of mind at the moment (uptight or mellow), elements of her personality (judgmental or forgiving), your relational history (supportive or hostile), and her knowledge of any factors in your life that might have contributed to your unjustified remark. Because communication is a transactional, ongoing, collaborative process, it's usually a mistake to think that any event occurs in a vacuum.

COMMUNICATION WILL NOT SOLVE ALL PROBLEMS Sometimes even the best-planned, best-timed communication won't solve a problem. Imagine, for example, that you ask an instructor to explain why you received a poor grade on a project that you believe deserved top marks. The instructor clearly outlines the reasons why you received the poor grade and sticks to that position after listening thoughtfully to your protests. Has communication solved the problem? Hardly.

Sometimes clear communication is even the *cause* of problems. Suppose, for example, that a friend asks you for an honest opinion of the $200 outfit she has just bought. Your clear and sincere answer, "I think it makes you look fat," might do more harm than good. Deciding when and how to self-disclose isn't always easy. See Chapter 9 for suggestions.

The Nature of Interpersonal Communication

Now that you have a better understanding of the overall process of human communication, it's time to look at what makes some types uniquely interpersonal.

TWO VIEWS OF INTERPERSONAL COMMUNICATION

Scholars have characterized **interpersonal communication** in a number of ways.[38] The most obvious definition focuses on the number of people involved. A **quantitative** definition of interpersonal communication includes any interaction between two people, usually face to face. Social scientists call two people interacting a **dyad**, and they often use the adjective *dyadic* to describe this type of communication. So, in a quantitative sense, the terms *dyadic communication* and *interpersonal communication* can be used interchangeably. Using a quantitative definition, a salesclerk and customer or a police officer ticketing a speeding driver would be examples of interpersonal acts, whereas a teacher and class or a performer and audience would not.

You might object to the quantitative definition of interpersonal communication. For example, consider a routine transaction between a salesclerk and customer or the rushed exchange when you ask a stranger on the street for directions. Communication of this sort hardly seems interpersonal—or personal in any sense of the word. In fact, after transactions like this, we commonly remark, "I might as well have been talking to a machine."

The impersonal nature of some two-person exchanges and the personal nature of others have led some scholars to argue that *quality*, not quantity, is what distinguishes interpersonal communication.[39] Using a **qualitative** definition, interpersonal communication occurs when people treat one another as unique individuals, regardless of the context in which the interaction occurs or the number of people involved. When quality of interaction is the criterion, the opposite of interpersonal communication is **impersonal communication**, not group, public, or mass communication.

Several features distinguish qualitatively interpersonal communication from less-personal communication.[40] The first feature is *uniqueness*. Communication in impersonal exchanges is determined by social *rules* (e.g., laugh politely at others' jokes, don't dominate a conversation) and by social *roles* (e.g., the customer is always right, be especially polite to senior citizens). Qualitatively interpersonal relationships are characterized by the development of unique rules and roles. For example, in one relationship you might exchange good-natured insults, whereas in another you are careful never to offend your partner. Likewise, you might handle conflicts with one friend or family member by expressing disagreements as soon as they arise, whereas the unwritten rule in another relationship is to withhold resentments until they build up and then clear the air periodically. One communication scholar coined the term *relational culture* to describe people in close relationships who create their own unique ways of interacting.[41]

A second feature of qualitatively interpersonal relationships is *irreplaceability*. Because interpersonal relationships are unique, they can't be replaced. This explains why we usually feel so sad when a close friendship or love affair cools down. We know that no matter how many other relationships fill our lives, none of them will ever be quite like the one that just ended.

Image Source/Jupiter Images

Even the "closest" relationships can become impersonal over time.

Interdependence is a third feature of qualitatively interpersonal relationships. At the most basic level, the fate of the partners is connected. You might be able to brush off the anger, affection, excitement, or depression of someone you're not involved with personally, but in an interpersonal relationship the other's life affects you. Sometimes interdependence is a pleasure, and at other times it is a burden. In either case, it is a fact of life in qualitatively interpersonal relationships. Interdependence goes beyond the level of joined fates. In interpersonal relationships, our very identity depends on the nature of our interaction with others. As psychologist Kenneth Gergen puts it: "One cannot be 'attractive' without others who are attracted, a 'leader' without others willing to follow, or a 'loving person' without others to affirm with appreciation."[42]

A fourth feature of interpersonal relationships is often (though not always) the amount of *disclosure* of personal information. In impersonal relationships we don't reveal much about ourselves, but in interpersonal relationships we feel more comfortable sharing our thoughts and feelings. This doesn't mean that all interpersonal relationships are warm and caring, or that all self-disclosure is positive. It's possible to reveal negative, personal information: "I'm really angry with you."

A fifth feature of interpersonal communication is *intrinsic rewards*. In impersonal communication we seek payoffs that have little to do with the people involved. You listen to professors in class or talk to potential buyers of your used car in order to reach goals that have little to do with developing personal relationships. By contrast, you spend time in qualitatively interpersonal relationships with friends, lovers, and others because you find the time personally rewarding. It often doesn't matter *what* you talk about: The relationship itself is what's important.

Because relationships that are unique, irreplaceable, interdependent, disclosing, and intrinsically rewarding are rare, qualitatively interpersonal communication is relatively scarce. We chat pleasantly with shopkeepers or fellow passengers on the bus or plane; we discuss the weather or current events with most classmates and neighbors; we enjoy bantering with online acquaintances on social networking websites; but considering the number of people with whom we communicate, personal relationships are by far in the minority.

Some observers argue that communicators who strive to acquire a large number of "friends" on social networking websites like Facebook and Twitter are engaging in superficial, impersonal relationships. As one critic put it:

> The idea . . . is to attain as many of these not really-friends as possible. . . . Like cheap wine, "friends" provide a high that can only be sustained by acquiring more and more of them. Quantity trumps quality.[43]

Most of us don't have the time or energy to create highly personal relationships with everyone we encounter, either in person or via mediated channels. In fact, the scarcity of qualitatively interpersonal communication contributes to its value. Like precious jewels and one-of-a-kind artwork, interpersonal relationships are special because of their scarcity.

MEDIATED INTERPERSONAL COMMUNICATION

As you've read by now, face-to-face conversation isn't the only way people create and maintain personal relationships. Along with the telephone and old-fashioned correspondence, **mediated communication** channels provide many other ways to interact. Instant messaging, emailing, blogging, Twittering, and participating on social networking websites like Facebook and MySpace are some of the many ways that acquaintances—and strangers—can communicate through mediated channels. In fact, research suggests that the difference between face-to-face and virtual relationships is eroding.[44]

BENEFITS OF MEDIATED COMMUNICATION A growing body of research reveals that mediated communication isn't the threat to relationships that some critics once feared. Most Internet users—both adults and children—report the time they spend online has no influence on the amount of time they spend with their family or friends. More than three-quarters of these people say they never feel ignored by another

Social Networking, Survival, and Healing

If you dig enough, you'll find little bits and pieces of my life scattered across the 'Net. For many people, this sort of transparency is unnerving. For me, it's always been a source of comfort in the storm that has been my life. Throughout 20 years of drinking and drugs, I've always had cyber-friends who, for reasons I can't explain, have stayed up late and saved me more times than I can count.

James Gritz/Photodisc/Getty Images

When I made the decision—or more accurately, when the decision smashed down upon me—to get sober, I was terrified, embarrassed, and angry. I certainly didn't think I needed anyone to help me. Sometime near the end of the third month, the last bits of my sanity were gone. I couldn't function any longer. That's when I turned to the Web. I began to post what I've been told was an ever-increasing series of erratic blurbs—some directly to FriendFeed and others on Twitter, Facebook, and MySpace.

Those messages started a dialogue that took on a life of its own. I began to get e-mails, phone calls, text messages, tweets and other digital notes from people around the world. Some offered kind words. Some offered support. Many people shared their own stories of addiction. In my darkest times, these notes would come. And always, without question, they pulled me back from the brink. Many of these messages were from people I have known for years. Another handful came from childhood friends and people I'd grown up with. Some I had known well; many I had not. Others came from complete strangers. I

have no idea how they found me.

The moment when I knew I'd be okay came one night, during a cross-country drive. The phone rang as I blew through Tennessee, but I didn't recognize the number so I let it go to voice mail. When I pulled into a gas station, I listened to the message. The woman on the phone didn't leave her name, and to this day I have no idea who she was. She told me about her father and his drinking. She told me that she was proud of me for getting sober and that she wanted me to keep trying. Already tenuous with my emotions, I sat on the side of the road crying. I listened to that message dozens of times, over and over.

The encouragement kept coming: strangers leaving messages about their lives, encouraging me to keep going. Throughout the next few months, my life became a 24-hour shower of love. There wasn't one free moment that wasn't taken up by someone making sure that my dumb ass wasn't back at the bar, that I wasn't looking for ways to die, and that I was doing the right thing. I still couldn't bring myself to leave the house. I rarely left my couch. I couldn't communicate with most people. But I was never alone.

AA keeps me sane. But social media got me there. Without that far-reaching network of people—friends and strangers alike—I wouldn't be here today.

Brad K.

household member spending time online.[45] In fact, the majority of Internet users said that IMing, email, websites, and chat rooms had a "modestly positive impact" on their ability to communicate with family members and make new friends. More than half of the people surveyed stated that the number of their personal relationships has grown since they started to use the Internet.[46] Families that use mediated communication—particularly cell phones—stay in touch more regularly.[47]

More recent studies are similarly positive about the role that mediated communication plays in people's relationships and decision making.[48] They show that mediated communication enriches social networks. This is especially true among teens and younger adults who have grown up using the Internet, but findings prove true across generations. For example:

- Internet users have more social networks than nonusers.

- Mediated communication is a source of "glocalization," connecting people to distant friends and relatives as well as to those who live nearby.

- Computer-based communication encourages offline interaction with close friends by keeping relationships alive and active.

- The text-only format of email and instant messages can bring people closer by minimizing the perception of differences due to gender, social class, ethnicity, and age.

- Text-only messages have the power to stimulate both self-disclosure and direct questioning between strangers, resulting in greater interpersonal attraction.[49]

It's important to note that mediated communication isn't a replacement for face-to-face interaction. One study of college students who frequently use instant messaging concluded that "nothing appears to compare to face-to-face communication in terms of satisfying individuals' communication, information, and social needs."[50] Rather than diminishing other forms of relating, mediated communication actually promotes and reinforces them. Furthermore, there is an interactive relationship between

✔+ INVITATION TO INSIGHT

How Networked Are You?

The studies cited in this section suggest that mediated communication can enhance interpersonal relationships and networking. See if you agree or disagree by answering the following questions.

Can you identify a relationship that . . .

1 has been enhanced by regular mediated interactions, such as IMing, emailing, or texting?

2 was created through mediated channels, perhaps on social networking websites or online dating services?

3 would suffer or perhaps end if mediated channels weren't available?

What do your answers tell you about the impact of mediated communication on interpersonal relationships? Can you think of times when mediated communication has hurt or hindered relationships?

computer-based messages, phone contact, and in-person communication. In other words, if you regularly communicate with friends and family online, it is likely that you will also call them and try to see them more often.[51]

There are several reasons why mediated interaction can increase both the quantity and quality of interpersonal communication. For one thing, mediated communication makes it easier to maintain relationships.[52] Busy schedules and long distances can make quality time in face-to-face contact difficult or impossible. The challenge of finding time is especially tough for people who are separated by long distances and multiple time zones. In relationships like this, the *asynchronous* nature of email provides a way to share information that otherwise would be impossible. Communicators can create their own message and respond to one another without having to connect in real time. Instant messaging is another way to keep in touch: Discovering that a friend or relative is online and starting an electronic conversation is "like walking down the street and sometimes running into a friend," says Laura Balsam, a New York computer consultant.[53]

Even when face-to-face communication is convenient, some people find it easier to share personal information via mediated channels. Sociolinguist Deborah Tannen describes how email transformed the quality of two relationships:

> E-mail deepened my friendship with Ralph. Though his office was next to mine, we rarely had extended conversations because he is shy. Face to face he mumbled so, I could barely tell he was speaking. But when we both got on e-mail, I started receiving long, self-revealing messages; we poured our hearts out to each other. A friend discovered that e-mail opened up that kind of communication with her father. He would never talk much on the phone (as her mother would), but they have become close since they both got on line.[54]

Experiences like these help explain why Steve Jobs, the cofounder of Apple Computer, suggested that personal computers be renamed "*inter*personal computers."[55]

CHALLENGES OF MEDIATED COMMUNICATION Despite its benefits, mediated communication also presents several challenges.

Leaner Messages Social scientists use the term **richness** to describe the abundance of nonverbal cues that add clarity to a verbal message. Face-to-face communication is rich because it abounds with nonverbal cues that help clarify the meanings of one another's words and offer hints about their feelings.[56] By comparison, most mediated communication is a much leaner channel for conveying information.

To appreciate how message richness varies by medium, imagine you haven't heard from a friend in several weeks, and you decide to ask "Is anything wrong?" Your friend replies, "No, I'm fine." Would that response be more or less descriptive depending on whether you received it via text message, over the phone, or in person? You almost certainly would be able to tell a great deal more from a face-to-face response, because it would contain a richer array of cues: facial expressions, vocal tone, and so on. By contrast, a text message contains only words. The phone message—containing vocal, but no visual cues—would probably fall somewhere in between.

Because most mediated messages are leaner than the face-to-face variety, they can be more difficult to interpret with confidence. Irony and attempts at humor can easily be misunderstood; so as a receiver, it's important to clarify your interpretations before jumping to conclusions. And as a sender, think about how to send unambiguous messages so you aren't misunderstood.

The leanness of mediated messages presents another challenge. Without nonverbal cues, online communicators can create idealized—and sometimes unrealistic—images of one another. The absence of nonverbal cues allows cybercommunicators to carefully manage their identities. After all, it's a world without bad breath, unsightly blemishes, or stammering responses. Such conditions encourage participants to engage in what Joseph Walther calls "hyperpersonal" communication, accelerating the discussion of personal topics and relational development beyond what normally happens in face-to-face interaction.[57] This may explain why communicators who meet online sometimes have difficulty shifting to a face-to-face relationship.[58]

Disinhibition Sooner or later, most of us speak before we think, blurting out remarks that embarrass ourselves and offend others. The tendency to transmit messages without considering their consequences can be especially great in online communication, where we don't see, hear, or sometimes even know the target of our remarks. This **disinhibition** can take two forms.

Sometimes online communicators volunteer personal information that they would prefer to keep confidential from at least some receivers. Consider the example of social networking sites like Facebook, MySpace, and Friendster. A quick scan of home pages there shows that many users post text and images about themselves that could prove embarrassing in some contexts: "Here I am just before my DUI arrest"; "This is me in Cancun on spring break." This is not the sort of information most people would be eager to show a prospective employer or certain family members.

Along with mediated communication being more personal than the face-to-face variety, it also is more expressive. A growing body of research shows that communicators are more direct—often in a critical way—when using mediated channels than in face-to-face contact.[59] Sometimes communicators take disinhibition to the extreme, blasting off angry—even vicious—emails, text messages, and website postings. The common term for these outbursts is *flaming*. (See the reading on page 133 for a first-person account of being flamed.)

Permanence Common decency aside, the risk of hostile e-messages—or any inappropriate mediated messages—is their permanence. It can be bad enough to blurt out a private thought or lash out in person, but at least there is no permanent record of your indiscretion. By contrast, a regrettable text message, email, or web posting can be archived virtually forever. Even worse, it can be retrieved and forwarded in ways that can only be imagined in your worst dreams. The best advice, then, is to take the same approach with mediated messages that you do in person: Think twice before saying something you may later regret.

PERSONAL AND IMPERSONAL COMMUNICATION: A MATTER OF BALANCE

Now that you understand the differences between qualitatively interpersonal and impersonal communication, we need to ask some important questions: Is interpersonal communication better than impersonal communication? Is more interpersonal communication the goal?

ETHICAL CHALLENGE

Martin Buber's *I and Thou*

Martin Buber is arguably the most influential advocate of qualitatively interpersonal communication, as defined on pages 17–18. His book *Ich und Du (I and Thou)* is a worldwide classic, selling millions of copies since its publication in 1922.

Buber states that "I-It" and "I-Thou" represent two ways in which humans can relate to one another. "I-It" relationships are stable, predictable, detached. In an "I-It" mode we deal with people because they can do things for us: pump gas, laugh at our jokes, buy products we are selling, provide information or amusement. "I-It" is also the approach of science, which attempts to understand what makes people tick in order to explain, predict, and control their behavior. Buber would have regarded advertisers as operating in an "I-It" mode, crafting messages that lead people to buy their products or services. "I-It" relationships exist in personal relationships as well as impersonal ones: On an everyday basis, parents and children, bosses and employees, service providers and customers—even lovers—deal with one another as objects ("I wish she would leave me alone." "Can you pick me up after work?" "How can I get him/her to love me?").

In profound contrast to "I-It" relationships, Buber described an "I-Thou" way of interacting. "I-Thou" relationships are utterly unique. Because no two teachers or students, parents or children, husbands or wives, bosses or employees are alike, we encounter each person as an individual and not as a member of some category. An "I-Thou" posture goes further: Not only are people different from one another, but also they change from moment to moment. An "I-Thou" relationship arises out of how we are now, not how we might have been yesterday or even a moment ago. In an "I-Thou" relationship, persuasion and control are out of the question: We certainly may explain our point of view, but ultimately we respect the fact that others are free to act.

Buber acknowledges that it is impossible to create and sustain pure "I-Thou" relationships. But without this qualitatively interpersonal level of contact, our lives are impoverished. To paraphrase Buber, without "I-It" we cannot exist, but if we live only with "I-It," we are not fully human.

Think of your most important relationships:

1. To what degree can they be described as "I-Thou" or "I-It"?

2. How satisfied are you with this level of relating?

3. What obligation do you have to treat others in an "I-Thou" manner?

Based on your answers to these questions, how might you change your style of communication?

An English translation of Martin Buber's I and Thou *was published in 1970 by Scribner's. For useful descriptions of its central themes, see J. Stewart (2006). "A Philosopher's Approach." In J. Stewart (Ed.), Bridges Not Walls, 9th ed. New York: McGraw-Hill; and H. J. Paton (1955). "Martin Buber." In The Modern Predicament. London: Allen & Unwin.*

Most relationships aren't *either* interpersonal *or* impersonal. Rather, they fall somewhere on a continuum between these two extremes. Your own experience probably reveals that there is often a personal element in even the most impersonal situations. You might appreciate the unique sense of humor of a grocery checker or connect on a personal level with the person cutting your hair. And even the most tyrannical, demanding, by-the-book boss might show an occasional flash of humanity.

Just as there's a personal element in many impersonal settings, there is also an impersonal element in our relationships with the people we care most about. There are occasions when we don't want to be personal: when we're distracted, tired, busy, or just not interested. In fact, interpersonal communication is rather like rich food—it's fine in moderation, but too much can make you uncomfortable.

The personal-impersonal mixture of communicating in a relationship can change over time. The communication between young lovers who talk only about their feelings may change as their relationship develops, so that several years later, their communication has become more routine and ritualized, and the percentage of time they spend on personal, relational issues drops and the conversation about less intimate topics increases. Chapter 8 discusses how communication changes as relationships pass through various stages and also describes the role of self-disclosure in keeping those relationships strong. As you read this information, you will see even more clearly that, although interpersonal communication can make life worth living, it isn't possible or desirable all the time.

It's clear that there is a place in our lives for both impersonal and interpersonal communication. Each type has its uses. The real challenge, then, is to find the right balance between the two types.

✔+ INVITATION TO INSIGHT

How Personal Are Your Relationships?

Use the characteristics of qualitatively interpersonal communication described on pages 17–18 to think about your own relationships.

1 Make a list of several people who are close to you (e.g., family members, people you live with, friends, coworkers, and so on).

2 Use the scales that follow to rate each relationship. To distinguish the relationships from one another, use a different color of ink for each one.

3 Consider comparing your results with those of classmates or friends.

After completing the exercise, ask yourself the important question: How satisfied are you with the answers you have found?

Uniqueness

1	2	3	4	5

Standardized, habitual ———————————————————————————— Unique

Replaceability

1	2	3	4	5

Replaceable ———————————————————————————— Irreplaceable

Dependence

1	2	3	4	5

Independent ———————————————————————————— Interdependent

Disclosure

1	2	3	4	5

Low disclosure ———————————————————————————— High disclosure

Intrinsic rewards

1	2	3	4	5

Unrewarding ———————————————————————————— Rewarding

What Makes an Effective Communicator?

It's easy to recognize good communicators and even easier to spot poor ones, but what characteristics distinguish effective communicators from their less successful counterparts? Answering this question has been one of the leading challenges for communication scholars.[60] Although all of the answers aren't yet in, research has identified a great deal of important information about communication competence.

COMMUNICATION COMPETENCE DEFINED

Defining **communication competence** isn't as easy as it might seem. Although scholars are still struggling to agree on a precise definition, most would agree that competent communication involves achieving one's goals in a manner that, in most cases, maintains or enhances the relationship in which it occurs.[61] Put another way, competence seeks to be both *effective* and *appropriate*. You can probably think of people who achieve one of these goals at the expense of the other, such as the high-achieving businessperson who regularly ruffles feathers, or the kind and gracious person who doesn't stand up for her or himself. Competence is a balancing act that requires looking out both for yourself and for others—sometimes a challenging task. The following characteristics typify a competent communicator.

THERE IS NO IDEAL WAY TO COMMUNICATE   Your own experience shows that a variety of communication styles can be effective. Some very successful communicators are serious, whereas others use humor; some are gregarious, whereas others are quieter; and some are more straightforward, whereas others hint diplomatically. Just as there are many kinds of beautiful music or art, there are many kinds of competent communication. It certainly is possible to learn new, effective ways of communicating from observing models, but it would be a mistake to try to copy others in a way that doesn't reflect your own style or values.

COMPETENCE IS SITUATIONAL   Even within a culture or relationship, the specific communication that is competent in one setting might be a colossal blunder in another. The joking insults you routinely trade with one friend might offend a sensitive family member, and last Saturday night's romantic approach would most likely be out of place at work on Monday morning.

Because competent behavior varies so much from one situation and person to another, it's a mistake to think that communication competence is a trait that a person either has or does not have. As television character Dr. Gregory House demonstrates, it's more accurate to talk about *degrees* or *areas* of competence.[62] You might deal quite skillfully with peers, for example, but feel clumsy interacting with people much older or younger, wealthier or poorer, more or less attractive than yourself. In fact, your competence with one person may vary from situation to situation. This means that it's an

Fox-TV/The Kobal Collection

When it comes to communication competence, TV character Dr. Gregory House (Hugh Laurie) is good at achieving professional goals but weaker at maintaining relationships.

overgeneralization to say in a moment of distress, "I'm a terrible communicator!" when it's more accurate to say, "I didn't handle this situation very well, even though I'm better in others."

COMPETENCE IS RELATIONAL Because communication is transactional—something we do with others rather than to others—behavior that is competent in one relationship isn't necessarily competent in others. One important measure of competence is whether the people with whom you are communicating view your approach as effective.[63] For example, researchers have uncovered a variety of ways by which people deal with jealousy in their relationships.[64] The ways include keeping closer tabs on the partner, acting indifferent, decreasing affection, talking the matter over, and acting angry. The researchers concluded that approaches that work in some relationships would be harmful to others. Findings like these demonstrate that competence arises out of developing ways of interacting that work for you and for the other people involved.[65]

> You did the best that you knew how.
>
> Now that you know better, you'll do better.
>
> —Maya Angelou

COMPETENCE CAN BE LEARNED To some degree, biology is destiny when it comes to communication style.[66] Studies of identical and fraternal twins suggest that traits including sociability, anger, and relaxation seem to be partially a function of our genetic makeup. Chapter 2 will have more to say about the role of neurobiology in communication traits.

Fortunately, biology isn't the only factor that shapes how we communicate. Communication competence is, to a great degree, a set of skills that anyone can learn. Skills training has been found to help communicators in a variety of ways, ranging from overcoming speech anxiety[67] to becoming more perceptive in detecting deception.[68] Research also shows that college students typically become more competent communicators over the course of their undergraduate studies.[69] In other words, your level of competence can improve through education and training, which means that reading this book and taking this course can help you become a more competent communicator.[70]

✔+ INVITATION TO INSIGHT

Assessing Your Communication Skills

How effective are you as a communicator? You can get a clearer answer to this question by taking an online self-assessment. You can find the link to this site through your Premium Website for *Looking Out/ Looking In*.

This self-test measures your abilities in the following interpersonal communication areas:

adaptability, conversational involvement, conversation management, empathy, effectiveness, and appropriateness. This test requires an honest self-assessment. Even if you don't like what you learn about yourself, you will find the self-test is a good way to set goals for improving your communication.

CHARACTERISTICS OF COMPETENT COMMUNICATORS

Although competent communication varies from one situation to another, scholars have identified several common denominators that characterize effective communication in most contexts.

A WIDE RANGE OF BEHAVIORS   Effective communicators are able to choose their actions from a wide range of behaviors.[71] To understand the importance of having a large communication repertoire, imagine that someone you know repeatedly tells jokes—perhaps racist or sexist ones—that you find offensive. You could respond to these jokes in a number of ways:

- You could decide to say nothing, figuring that the risks of bringing the subject up would be greater than the benefits.

- You could ask a third party to say something to the joke teller about the offensiveness of the jokes.

- You could hint at your discomfort, hoping your friend would get the point.

- You could joke about your friend's insensitivity, counting on humor to soften the blow of your criticism.

- You could express your discomfort in a straightforward way, asking your friend to stop telling the offensive jokes, at least around you.

- You could even demand that your friend stop.

With this choice of responses at your disposal (and you can probably think of others as well), you could pick the one that has the best chance of success. But if you were able to use only one or two of these responses when raising a delicate issue—always keeping quiet or always hinting, for example—your chances of success would be much smaller. Indeed, many poor communicators are easy to spot by their limited range of responses. Some are chronic jokers. Others are always belligerent. Still others are quiet in almost every situation. Like a piano player who knows only one tune or a chef who can prepare only a few dishes, these people are forced to rely on a small range of responses again and again, whether or not they are successful.

Many people with disabilities have learned the value of having a repertoire of options available to manage unwanted offers of help.[72] Some of those options include performing a task quickly, before anyone has the chance to intervene; pretending not to hear the offer; accepting a well-intentioned invitation to avoid seeming rude or ungrateful; using humor to deflect a bid for help; declining a well-intentioned offer with thanks; and assertively refusing help from those who won't take no for an answer.

ABILITY TO CHOOSE THE MOST APPROPRIATE BEHAVIOR   Simply possessing a large range of communication skills is no guarantee of success. It's also necessary to know which of these skills will work best in a particular situation. This ability to choose the best approach is essential, because a response that works well in one setting would flop miserably in another one.

Although it's impossible to say precisely how to act in every situation, you should consider at least three factors when choosing a response. The first factor is the communication *context*. The time and place will almost always influence how you act. Asking your boss for a raise or your lover for a kiss might produce good results if the

LOOKING AT DIVERSITY

Daria Muse: Competent Communication in Suburbia and the Inner City

In this profile, Daria Muse describes how effective communication varies in two strikingly different environments: her home neighborhood of South-Central Los Angeles and her school in the suburban San Fernando Valley. This account demonstrates some of the elements of communication competence introduced in Chapter 1: a wide range of behaviors, the ability to choose the best behavior for a given situation, and skill at performing that behavior.

Photo courtesy of Daria Muse

During my elementary and middle-school years, I was a well-behaved, friendly student at school and a tough, hard-nosed "bad girl" in my neighborhood. This contrast in behavior was a survival tool, for I lived in a part of South-Central Los Angeles where "goody-goodies" aren't tolerated, and I attended school in Northridge, where troublemakers aren't tolerated.

Beckford Ave. Elementary School was in the heart of middle-class suburbia, and I, coming from what has been described as the "urban jungle," was bused there every day for six years. In a roundabout way, I was told from the first day of school that if I wanted to continue my privileged attendance in the hallowed classrooms of Beckford, I would have to conform and adapt to their standards. I guess I began to believe all that they said, because slowly I began to conform.

Instead of wearing the tight jeans and T-shirt that were the style in South-Central at the time, I wore schoolgirl dresses like those of my female classmates. I even changed my language. When asking a question, instead of saying, "Boy! Gimme those scissors before I knock you up you head!" in school, I asked, "Excuse me, would you please hand me the scissors?" When giving a compliment in school I'd say, "You look very nice today," instead of "Girl, who do you think you are, dressin' so fine, Miss Thang."

This conformation of my appearance and speech won me the acceptance of my proper classmates at Beckford Elementary School, but after getting out of the school bus and stepping onto the sidewalks of South-Central, my appearance quit being an asset and became a dangerous liability. One day, when I got off the school bus, a group of tough girls who looked as though they were part of a gang approached me, looked at my pink and white lace dress, and accused me of trying to "look white." They surrounded me and demanded a response that would prove to them that I was still loyal to my black heritage. I screamed, "Lay off me, girl, or I'll bust you in the eyes so bad that you'll need a telescope just to see!" The girls walked away without causing any more trouble.

From then on, two personalities emerged. I began living a double life. At school I was prim and proper in appearance and in speech, but during the drive on the school bus from Northridge to South-Central, my other personality emerged. Once I got off the bus I put a black jacket over my dress, I hardened my face, and roughened my speech to show everyone who looked my way that I was not a girl to be messed with. I led this double life throughout my six years of elementary school.

Now that I am older and can look back at that time objectively, I don't regret displaying contrasting behavior in the two different environments. It was for my survival. Daria, the hard-nosed bad girl, survived in the urban jungle and Daria, the well-behaved student, survived in the suburbs.

As a teenager in high school I still display different personalities: I act one way in school, which is different from the way I act with my parents, which is different from the way I act with my friends, which is different from the way I act in religious services. But don't we all? We all put on character masks for our different roles in life. All people are guilty of acting differently at work than at play and differently with coworkers than with the boss. There's nothing wrong with having different personalities to fit different situations; the trick is knowing the real you from the characters.

time is right, but the identical request might backfire if your timing is poor. Likewise, the joke that would be ideal at a bachelor party would probably be inappropriate at a funeral.

Your *goal* will also shape the approach you take. Inviting a new neighbor over for a cup of coffee or dinner could be just the right approach if you want to encourage a friendship, but if you want to maintain your privacy, it might be wiser to be polite but cool. Likewise, your goal will determine your approach in situations in which you want to help another person. As you will learn in Chapter 7, sometimes offering advice is just what is needed. But when you want to help others develop the ability to solve problems on their own, it's better to withhold your own ideas and function as a sounding board to let them consider alternatives and choose their solutions.

Finally, your *knowledge of the other person* should shape the approach you take. If you're dealing with someone who is very sensitive or insecure, your response might be supportive and cautious. With an old and trusted friend, you might be blunt. The social niche of the other party can also influence how you communicate. For instance, you would probably act differently toward an 80-year-old person than you would toward a teenager. Likewise, there are times when it's appropriate to treat a man differently than a woman, even in this age of gender equity.

SKILL AT PERFORMING BEHAVIORS   After you have chosen the most appropriate way to communicate, it's still necessary to perform the required skills effectively.[73] There is a big difference between knowing *about* a skill and being able to put it into practice. Simply being aware of alternatives isn't much help unless you can skillfully put these alternatives to work.

Just reading about communication skills in the following chapters won't guarantee that you can start using them flawlessly. As with any other skills—playing a musical instrument or learning a sport, for example—the road to competence in communication is not a short one. As you learn and practice the communication skills in the following pages, you can expect to pass through several stages,[74] shown in Figure 1.3 on page 30.

COGNITIVE COMPLEXITY   Social scientists use the term **cognitive complexity** to describe the ability to construct a variety of frameworks for viewing an issue.[75] To understand how cognitive complexity can increase competence, imagine that a long-time friend seems to be angry with you. One possible explanation is that your friend is offended by something you've done. Another possibility is that something has happened in another part of your friend's life that is upsetting. Or perhaps nothing at all is wrong, and you're just being overly sensitive. Considering the issue from several angles might prevent you from overreacting or misunderstanding the situation, increasing the odds of finding a way to resolve the problem constructively. Chapter 3 discusses cognitive complexity—and ways to improve it—in much greater detail.

✔+ SKILL BUILDER

Stages in Learning Communication Skills

Learning any new skill requires moving through several levels of competence:

1. *Beginning Awareness.* This is the point at which you first learn that there is a new and better way of behaving. If you play tennis, for example, awareness might grow when you learn about a new way of serving that can improve your power and accuracy. In the area of communication, *Looking Out/Looking In* should bring this sort of awareness to you.

2. *Awkwardness.* Just as you were awkward when you first tried to ride a bicycle or drive a car, your initial attempts at communicating in new ways may also be awkward. As the saying goes, "You have to be willing to look bad in order to get good."

3. *Skillfulness.* If you keep working at overcoming the awkwardness of your initial attempts, you'll be able to handle yourself well, although you will still need to think about what you're doing. As an interpersonal communicator, you can expect the stage of skillfulness to be marked by a great deal of thinking and planning, and also by increasingly good results.

4. *Integration.* Integration occurs when you're able to perform well without thinking about it. The behavior becomes automatic, a part of your repertoire.

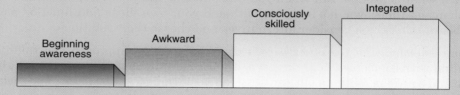

Figure 1.3
Stages in Learning Communication Skills

EMPATHY   Seeing a situation from multiple points of view is important, but there's another step that goes beyond understanding different perspectives. *Empathy* involves feeling and experiencing another person's situation, almost as they do. This ability is so important that some researchers have labeled empathy the most important aspect of communication competence.[76] Chapters 3 and 7 introduce you to a set of skills that can boost your ability to empathize. For now, it's enough to note that getting a feel for how others view the world is a useful and important way to become a more effective communicator.

SELF-MONITORING   Whereas increased cognitive complexity and empathy help you understand others better, self-monitoring is one way to understand *yourself* better. Psychologists use the term **self-monitoring** to describe the process of paying close attention to one's behavior and using these observations to shape the way one behaves. Self-monitors are able to separate a part of their consciousness and observe their behavior from a detached viewpoint, making observations such as:

"I'm making a fool out of myself."

"I'd better speak up now."

"This approach is working well. I'll keep it up."

Although too much self-monitoring can be problematic (see Chapter 2), people who are aware of their behavior and the impression it makes are more skillful communicators than people who are low self-monitors.[77] For example, they are more accurate in judging others' emotional states, better at remembering information about others, less shy, and more assertive. By contrast, low self-monitors aren't able even to recognize their incompetence. One study revealed that poor communicators were blissfully ignorant of their shortcomings and more likely to overestimate their skill than were better communicators.[78] For example, experimental subjects who scored in the lowest quartile on joke-telling skills were more likely than their funnier counterparts to grossly overestimate their sense of humor.

Whereas low self-monitors may blunder through life, succeeding or failing without understanding why, high self-monitors have the detachment to ask themselves the question "How am I doing?" and to change their behavior if the answer isn't positive.

COMMITMENT   One feature that distinguishes effective communication—at least in qualitatively interpersonal relationships—is commitment. In other words, people who seem to care about relationships communicate better than those who don't.[79] This care shows up in at least two ways. The first is *commitment to the other person*. Concern for the other person is revealed in a variety of ways: a desire to spend time with him or her instead of rushing, a willingness to listen carefully instead of doing all the talking, the use of language that makes sense to the other person, and openness to change after hearing the other person's ideas. Effective communicators also care about *the message*. They appear sincere, seem to know what they are talking about, and demonstrate through words and deeds that they care about what they say.

How do you measure up as a competent communicator? Competence isn't a trait that people either have or do not have. Rather, it's a state that we achieve more or less frequently. A realistic goal, then, is not to become perfect but rather to boost the percentage of time when you communicate in ways outlined in this section.

✔+ SKILL BUILDER

Check Your Competence

Other people are often the best judges of your competence as a communicator. They can also offer useful information about how to improve your communication. Find out for yourself by following these steps:

1. Choose a person with whom you have an important relationship.

2. In cooperation with this person, identify several contexts in which you communicate. For example, you might choose different situations such as "handling conflicts," "lending support to friends," or "expressing feelings."

3. For each situation, have your friend rate your competence by answering the following questions:
   a. Do you have a wide repertoire of response styles in this situation, or do you always respond in the same way?
   b. Are you able to choose the most effective way of behaving for the situation at hand?

c. Are you skillful at performing behaviors? (Note that knowing how you *want* to behave isn't the same as being *able* to behave.)
   d. Do you communicate in a way that leaves others satisfied?

4. After reviewing your partner's answers, identify the situations in which your communication is most competent.

5. Choose a situation in which you would like to communicate more competently, and with the help of your partner:
   a. Determine whether your repertoire of behaviors needs to be expanded.
   b. Identify the ways in which you need to communicate more skillfully.
   c. Develop ways to monitor your behavior in the key situation to get feedback on your effectiveness.

COMPETENCE IN INTERCULTURAL COMMUNICATION

Throughout history, most people lived and died within a few miles of where they were born. They rarely had much to do with people from different backgrounds. Today is a different story. To use a familiar metaphor, we live in a global village, our lives intertwined with people from very different personal histories and communication styles.

Hans Neleman/Getty Images

As our world becomes more multicultural, the likelihood of interacting with people from different parts of the world is greater than ever. Given this fact, it's important to realize that what qualifies as competent behavior in one culture might be completely inept, or even offensive, in another.[80]

On an obvious level, customs like belching after a meal or appearing nude in public that might be appropriate in some parts of the world would be considered outrageous in others. But there are more subtle differences in competent communication. For example, qualities like self-disclosing and speaking clearly that are valued in the United States are likely to be considered overly aggressive and insensitive in many Asian cultures, where subtlety and indirectness are considered important.[81]

Even within a single society, members of various co-cultures may have different notions of appropriate behavior. One study revealed that ideas of how good friends should communicate varied from one ethnic group to another.[82] As a group, Latinos valued relational support most highly, whereas African Americans valued respect and acceptance. Asian Americans prized a caring, positive exchange of ideas, and Anglo Americans prized friends who recognized their needs as individuals. Findings like these mean that there can be no surefire list of rules or tips that will guarantee your success as a communicator. They also mean that competent communicators are able to adapt their style to suit the individual and cultural preferences of others.[83]

National and ethnic differences aren't the only dimensions of culture. Within a society **co-cultures** have different communication practices. Consider just a few co-cultures:

> age (e.g., teen, senior citizen)
> occupation (e.g., fashion model, long-distance trucker)
> sexual orientation (e.g., lesbian, gay male)
> physical disability (e.g., wheelchair user, hearing-impaired)
> religion (e.g., evangelical Christian, Muslim)
> activity (e.g., biker, gamer)

Some scholars have even characterized men and women as belonging to different co-cultures, claiming that each gender's style of communication is distinct. We'll have more to say about that topic throughout this book.

Communicating successfully with people from different cultural backgrounds calls for the same elements of competence outlined in the pages you have just read. But beyond these basic qualities, communication researchers have identified several other especially important ingredients of successful intercultural communication.[84]

Most obviously, it helps to know the rules of a specific culture. For example, the kind of self-deprecating humor that Americans are likely to find amusing is likely to fall flat among Arabs from the Middle East.[85] But beyond knowing the specific rules of an individual culture, there are also attitudes and skills called "culture-general" that help communicators build relationships with people from other backgrounds.[86]

To illustrate the ingredients of culture-general communication competence, imagine you've just been hired to work in a Japanese-owned company in the United States that has manufacturing operations in Mexico and customers around the world. In your new job, you are surrounded by coworkers, supervisors, and clients who come from cultures and co-cultures that are different from your own. You are also required to make occasional trips abroad. How will you handle the communication demands of this position? Ideally, you'll possess the following attributes.

MOTIVATION The desire to communicate successfully with strangers is an important start. For example, people who are high in willingness to communicate with people from other cultures report a greater number of friends from different backgrounds than those who are less willing to reach out.[87] Having the proper motivation is important in all communication, but particularly so in intercultural interactions, because they can be quite challenging.

In your multinational company, you'll need motivation to reach out to people whose communication style is different from yours. For example, during visits to China you might first be pleased, and then exhausted to discover that parties and banquets, typically with much alcohol, are part of the business scene. Even if you are a seasoned partygoer, you may need to draw on a deep well of motivation to spend yet another evening of jovially toasting strangers when you would rather be recovering from jet lag and hard work.

TOLERANCE FOR AMBIGUITY Communicating with people from different backgrounds can be confusing. A tolerance for ambiguity makes it possible to accept, and even embrace, the often equivocal and sometimes downright incomprehensible messages that characterize intercultural communication.

If you happen to work with colleagues raised in traditional Native American co-cultures, you may find them much quieter and less outgoing than you are used to. Your first reaction might be to chalk up this reticence to a lack of friendliness. However, it may just be a reflection of a co-culture in which reticence is valued more than extroversion, and silence more than loquacity. In cross-cultural situations like this, ambiguity is a fact of life, and a challenge.

OPEN-MINDEDNESS It's one thing to tolerate ambiguity; it's another thing to become open-minded about cultural differences. There is a natural tendency to view others' communication choices as "wrong" when they don't match our cultural upbringing. In some parts of the world, you may find that women are not regarded with the same attitude of equality that is common in the West. Likewise, in other cultures, you may be aghast at the casual tolerance of poverty beyond anything at home, or with practices of bribery that don't jibe with homegrown notions of what is ethical. In situations like these, principled communicators aren't likely to compromise deeply held beliefs about what is right. At the same time, competence requires an attitude that recognizes that people who behave differently are most likely following rules that have governed their whole lives. Chapter 3 will offer more guidance on the challenges of viewing the world from others' perspectives.

KNOWLEDGE AND SKILL The rules and customs that work with one group might be quite different from those that succeed with another. For example, when traveling in Latin America, you are likely to find that meetings there usually don't begin or end at their scheduled time, and that it takes the participants quite awhile to "get down to business." Rather than viewing your hosts as irresponsible and unproductive, you'll want to recognize that the meaning of time is not the same in all cultures. Likewise, the gestures others make, the distance they stand from you, and the eye contact they maintain have ambiguous meanings that you'll need to learn and follow.

At your new job, you'll want to engage in *mindfulness*—awareness of your own behavior and that of others.[88] Communicators who lack this quality blunder through intercultural encounters *mindlessly*, oblivious of how their own behavior may confuse or offend others and how behavior that they consider weird may be simply different. When you're in a mindful state, you can use three strategies for moving toward a more competent style of intercultural communication[89]:

1. *Passive observation* involves noticing what behaviors members of a different culture use and using these insights to communicate in ways that are most effective.
2. *Active strategies* include reading, watching films, asking experts and members of the other culture how to behave, as well as taking academic courses related to intercultural communication and diversity.[90]
3. *Self-disclosure* involves volunteering personal information to people from the other culture with whom you want to communicate.

One type of self-disclosure is to confess your cultural ignorance: "This is very new to me. What's the right thing to do in this situation?" This approach is the riskiest of the three described here, because some cultures may not value candor and self-disclosure as much as others. Nevertheless, most people are pleased when strangers attempt to learn the practices of their culture, and they are usually more than willing to offer information and assistance.

✔+ MAKING THE GRADE

Summary

Communication is essential on many levels. Besides satisfying practical needs, effective communication can enhance physical health and emotional well-being. As children, we learn about our identity via the messages sent by others, and as adults our self-concept is shaped and refined through social interaction. Communication also satisfies social needs: involvement with others, control over the environment, and giving and receiving affection.

The process of communication is not a linear one that people *do* to one another. Rather, communication is a transactional process in which participants create a relationship by simultaneously sending and receiving messages, many of which are distorted by various types of noise.

Interpersonal communication can be defined quantitatively by the number of people involved or qualitatively by the nature of interaction between them. In a qualitative sense, interpersonal relationships are unique, irreplaceable, interdependent, and intrinsically rewarding. Qualitatively interpersonal communication can occur in mediated contexts as well as in traditional ones (there are both benefits and challenges to communicating through mediated channels). Qualitatively interpersonal communication is relatively infrequent, even in the strongest relationships. Both personal and impersonal communications are useful, and most relationships have both personal and impersonal elements.

All communication, whether personal or impersonal, content or relational, follows the same basic principles. Messages can be intentional or unintentional. It is impossible not to communicate. Communication is irreversible and unrepeatable. Messages have both a content and a relational dimension. Some common misconceptions should be avoided when thinking about communication: meanings are not in words, but rather in people; more communication does not always make matters better; communication will not solve all problems; communication—at least effective communication—is not a natural ability.

Communication competence is the ability to get what you are seeking from others in a manner that maintains the relationship on terms that are acceptable to all parties. Competence doesn't mean behaving the same way in all settings and with all people; rather, competence varies from one situation to another. The most competent communicators have a wide repertoire of behaviors, and they are able to choose the best behavior for a given situation and perform it skillfully. They are able to understand others' points of view and respond with empathy. They also monitor their own behavior and are committed to communicating successfully. In intercultural communication, competence involves having the right motivation, a tolerance for ambiguity, open-mindedness, and the knowledge and skill to communicate effectively.

Key Terms

channel (9)
co-culture (32)
cognitive complexity (29)
communication (13)
communication competence
   (25)
content dimension (15)
decode (10)
disinhibition (22)
dyad (17)

encode (9)
environment (11)
impersonal communication
   (17)
instrumental goals (8)
interpersonal communication
   (quantitative and qualitative) (17)
linear communication model
   (9)

mediated communication (18)
message (9)
noise (10)
receiver (9)
relational dimension (15)
richness (21)
self-monitoring (30)
sender (9)
transactional communication
   model (10)

Online Resources

Now that you have read this chapter, use your Premium Website for *Looking Out/ Looking In* for quick access to the electronic resources that accompany this text. Your Premium Website gives you access to:

- **Study tools** that will help you assess your learning and prepare for exams (*digital glossary, key term flash cards, review quizzes*).

- **Activities and assignments** that will help you hone your knowledge, understand how theory and research applies to your own life (*Invitation to Insight*), consider ethical challenges in interpersonal communication (*Ethical Challenge*), and build your interpersonal communication skills throughout the course (*Skill Builder*). If requested, you can submit your answers to your instructor.

- **Media resources** that will allow you to watch and critique news video and videos of interpersonal communication situations (*In Real Life*, *interpersonal video simulations*) and download a chapter review so you can study when and where you'd like (*Audio Study Tools*).

This chapter's key terms and search terms for additional reading are featured in this end-of-chapter section, and you can find this chapter's Invitation to Insight, Ethical Challenge, and Skill Builder activities in the body of the chapter.

Search Terms

When searching online databases to research topics in this chapter, use the following terms (along with this chapter's key terms) to maximize the chances of finding useful information:

communication & technology
communication models
communicative competence

information theory
interpersonal relations

quality of life
social networks

Film and Television

You can see the communication principles described in this chapter portrayed in the following films and television programs:

THE IMPORTANCE OF INTERPERSONAL COMMUNICATION

Into the Wild (2007) Rated R

Armed with a few books about survival and a fierce streak of independence, 20-year-old college graduate Christopher McCandless (Emile Hirsch) literally turns his back on civilization and heads into the Alaskan wilderness. McCandless dismisses the advice of wiser and more experienced people, convinced that he doesn't need anyone to survive and thrive. As film critic Roger Ebert puts it, "He sees himself not as homeless, but as a man freed from homes."

The last part of the film reconstructs McCandless's final harrowing weeks. More than simply a wilderness adventure, this story provides an extreme example of the human need for contact and support. The self-sufficient loner may be a romantic stereotype, but in real life we can't survive—physically or emotionally—without others.

THE NATURE OF INTERPERSONAL COMMUNICATION

The Visitor (2008) Rated PG-13

The dull, predictable world of college professor Walter Vale (Richard Jenkins) is shaken when he finds a beautiful young African woman named Zainab (Danai Gurira) soaking in the bathtub of his Manhattan apartment. When Vale learns that Zainab and her Syrian boyfriend Tarek (Haaz Sleiman) were victims of a scam artist, he reluctantly allows them to stay until they find a new home.

From this shaky beginning, a rich set of relationships develops. Tarek teaches Vale the joys of drumming, and the professor slowly finds new joy in making music and building community with the drummers in Central Park. Zainab is initially wary of Vale, but as trust grows between them, their friendship develops. When Tarek is imprisoned on immigration charges, Vale meets Tarek's mother Mouna (Hiam Abbass), and we see the beginning of a special relationship between two people who had given up on such things.

This bittersweet film demonstrates how qualitatively interpersonal relationships can transcend differences in age, economic status, nationality, and cultural background.

Babel (2006) Rated R

The film's promotional materials proclaim that this complicated story "demonstrates the necessity and importance of human communication." It also demonstrates the difference between impersonal and qualitatively interpersonal communication. In the course of this tale, some relationships shift from impersonal to intensely personal: An American (Brad Pitt) bonds with a generous Moroccan villager (Mohamed Akhzam). A rebellious deaf Japanese teenager (Rinko Kikuchi) lets go of her hostility and connects with both her father and a kind police investigator. Other communication is heartbreakingly impersonal: U.S. Border Patrol officers dispassionately pursue a loving nanny (Adriana Barraza), and the Moroccan police abuse a naive and unsophisticated family. Despite the cultural differences, the film illustrates the importance and value of interpersonal relationships for people from all backgrounds.

TRANSACTIONAL COMMUNICATION

Friends (1994–2004) Rated TV-14

This long-running television series chronicles the interconnected lives of six twenty-something (and later thirty-something) New Yorkers. Over ten seasons, dedicated viewers followed the many changes in the relationships of this group. Knowledge of their complex relational history helps viewers understand and appreciate each episode. This series illustrates the principle that communication is a transactional process. For example, the other characters' affection for Joey and Phoebe leads them to regard their simpleminded statements with affection; Rachel's relationship with Ross influences their friendship; and everyone's knowledge of Monica's need for order and cleanliness allows them to not take her neurotic comments personally.

COMMUNICATION COMPETENCE

The Office (2005–) Rated TV-14

This TV mock documentary portrays the world of the cubicle jockeys at Dunder Mifflin Paper Supply Company in Scranton, Pennsylvania. Most of the action centers on the exploits of regional manager Michael Scott (Steve Carrell). Michael believes he is funny, a fountain of business wisdom, and revered by his staff. In truth, his misguided sense of humor and bumbling management style make him an object of ridicule. From a communication perspective, Michael is a paragon of poor self-monitoring and incompetent communication.

COMMUNICATION AND IDENTITY:
Creating and
Presenting the Self

✔+ MAKING THE GRADE

Here are the topics discussed in this chapter:

✔ **Communication and the Self**

Self-Concept and Self-Esteem

Biological and Social Roots of the Self

Characteristics of the Self-Concept

Culture, Gender, and Identity

The Self-Fulfilling Prophecy and
Communication

Changing Your Self-Concept

✔ **Presenting the Self: Communication as Identity
Management**

Public and Private Selves

Characteristics of Identity Management

Why Manage Identities?

How Do We Manage Identities?

Identity Management and Honesty

✔ **Making the Grade**

Summary

Key Terms

Online Resources

Search Terms

Film and Television

After studying the topics in this chapter, you should be able to:

1. Describe the relationship between self-concept, self-esteem, and communication.

2. Explain how self-fulfilling prophecies shape the self-concept and influence communication.

3. Demonstrate how the principles on pages 60–62 can be used to change the self-concept, and hence communication.

4. Compare and contrast the perceived self and the presenting self as they relate to identity management.

5. Describe the role that identity management plays in both face-to-face and mediated relationships.

Who are you? Take a moment now to answer this question. You'll need the following list as you read the rest of this chapter, so be sure to complete it now. Try to include all the characteristics that describe you:

> Your moods or feelings (e.g., happy, angry, excited)
> Your appearance (e.g., attractive, short)
> Your social traits (e.g., friendly, shy)
> Talents you have or do not have (e.g., musical, nonathletic)
> Your intellectual capacity (e.g., smart, slow learner)
> Your strong beliefs (e.g., religious, environmentalist)
> Your social roles (e.g., parent, girlfriend)
> Your physical condition (e.g., healthy, overweight)

Now look at what you've written. How did you define yourself? As a student? A man or woman? By your age? Your religion? Your occupation? There are many ways of identifying yourself. List as many ways as you can. You'll probably see that the words you've chosen represent a profile of what you view as your most important characteristics. In other words, if you were required to describe the "real you," this list ought to be a good summary.

Communication and the Self

You might be wondering how this self-analysis is related to interpersonal communication. The short answer is that who you are both reflects and affects your communication with others. The long answer involves everything from biology to socialization to culture to gender. We'll begin with a look at two terms that are basic to the relationship between the self and communication.

It has become something of a cliché to observe that if we do not love ourselves, we cannot love anyone else. This is true enough, but it is only part of the picture. If we do not love ourselves, it is almost impossible to believe fully that we are loved by someone else. It is almost impossible to accept love. It is almost impossible to receive love. No matter what our partner does to show that he or she cares, we do not experience the devotion as convincing because we do not feel lovable to ourselves.

—*Nathaniel Branden,* The Psychology of Romantic Love

SELF-CONCEPT AND SELF-ESTEEM

The list you created attempted to answer the question "Who do you think you are?" It's likely that the phrases you chose generated some emotional responses—perhaps terms like "happy" or "sad," "confident" or "nervous." Replies like these show that how you *feel* about yourself is a big part of who you think you are. What we think and feel about ourselves are important components of the self that we'll examine now.

SELF-CONCEPT   Who you think you are can be described as your **self-concept**: the relatively stable set of perceptions you hold of yourself. If a special mirror existed that reflected not only your physical features but also other aspects of yourself—emotional states, talents, likes, dislikes, values, roles, and so on—the reflection you'd see would be your self-concept. You probably recognize that the self-concept list you recorded earlier is only a partial one. To make the description complete, you'd have to keep adding items until your list ran into hundreds of words.

Take a moment now to demonstrate the many parts of your self-concept by simply responding to the question "Who am I?" over and over again. Add these responses to

✔+ INVITATION TO INSIGHT

Take Away

1 Look over the list of words you've just used to describe yourself. If you haven't already done so, pick the ten words that describe the most fundamental aspects of who you are. Be sure that you've organized these words so that the most fundamental one is in first place and the one that is least central to your identity is number 10, arranging the words or phrases in between in their proper order.

2 Now find a comfortable spot where you can think without being interrupted. You can complete this exercise in a group with the leader giving instructions, or you can do it alone by reading the directions yourself when necessary.

3 Close your eyes and get a mental picture of yourself. Besides visualizing your appearance, you should also include in your image your less-observable features: your disposition, your hopes, your concerns, including all of the items you described in step 1.

4 Keep this picture in mind, but now imagine what would happen if the tenth item on your list disappeared from your makeup. How would you be different? Does the idea of giving up that item leave you feeling better or worse? How hard was it to let go of that item?

5 Now, without taking back the item you just abandoned, give up the ninth item on your list, and see what difference this makes to you. After pausing to experience your thoughts and feelings, give up each succeeding item on your list one by one.

6 After you've abandoned the number-one feature of who you are, take a few minutes to add back the parts of yourself that you abandoned, and then read on.

You can complete this activity at your Premium Website for *Looking Out/Looking In* and, if requested, email your responses to your instructor.

---

the list you started earlier. Of course, not every item on your self-concept list is equally important. For example, the most significant part of one person's self-concept might consist of social roles, and for another person it might be physical appearance, health, friendships, accomplishments, or skills.

You can discover how much you value each part of your self-concept by rank-ordering the items on your list. Try it now: Place a "1" next to the most fundamental item about you, a "2" next to the second-most fundamental item, and continue in this manner until you've completed your list. This self-concept you've just described is extremely important. To see just how important it is, try the "Take Away" exercise above.

For most people this exercise dramatically illustrates just how fundamental the concept of self is. Even when the item being abandoned is an unpleasant one, it's often hard to give it up. And when asked to let go of their most central feelings or thoughts, most people balk. "I wouldn't be *me* without that," they insist. Of course, this proves our point: The concept of self is perhaps our most fundamental possession. Knowing who we are is essential, because without a self-concept it would be impossible to relate to the world.

SELF-ESTEEM   While your self-concept describes who you think you are, **self-esteem** involves evaluations of self-worth. A hypothetical communicator's self-concept might include being quiet, argumentative, or self-controlled. His or her self-esteem would be determined by how he or she *felt* about these qualities. Consider these differing evaluations:

Quiet	"I'm a coward for not speaking up."
	versus
	"I enjoy listening more than talking."
Argumentative	"I'm pushy, and that's obnoxious."
	versus
	"I stand up for my beliefs."
Self-controlled	"I'm too cautious."
	versus
	"I think carefully before I say or do things."

Table 2.1 summarizes some important differences between communicators with high and low self-esteem. Differences like these make sense when you realize that people who dislike themselves are likely to believe that others won't like them either. Realistically or not, they imagine that others are constantly viewing them critically, and they accept these imagined or real criticisms as more proof that they are indeed unlikable people. Sometimes this low self-esteem is manifested in hostility toward others, because the communicator takes the approach that the only way to look good is to put others down.

As Table 2.1 shows, high self-esteem has obvious benefits, but it doesn't guarantee interpersonal success.[1] People with exaggerated self-esteem may *think* they make better impressions on others and have better friendships and romantic lives, but neither

Table 2.1

Differences between Communicators with High and Low Self-Esteem

People with High Self-Esteem
Likely to think well of others.
Expect to be accepted by others.
Evaluate their own performance more favorably than people with low self-esteem.
Perform well when being watched; not afraid of others' reactions.
Work harder for people who demand high standards of performance.
Inclined to feel comfortable with others they view as superior in some way.
Able to defend themselves against negative comments of others.

People with Low Self-Esteem
Likely to disapprove of others.
Expect to be rejected by others.
Evaluate their own performance less favorably than people with high self-esteem.
Perform poorly when being watched; sensitive to possible negative reaction.
Work harder for undemanding, less-critical people.
Feel threatened by people they view as superior in some way.
Have difficulty defending themselves against others' negative comments; more easily influenced.

Summarized by D. E. Hamachek (1982). Encounters with the Self, 2nd ed. (pp. 3–5). New York: Holt, Rinehart, and Winston.

✔+ INVITATION TO INSIGHT

Your Self-Esteem

Take a self-guided tour of your self-esteem provided by the National Association of Self-Esteem. As you explore, consider how the past and present have shaped your current level of self-esteem. Additionally, speculate about how your current level of self-esteem affects your own communication style and interpersonal relationships. You can find the link to this site through your Premium Website for *Looking Out/Looking In*. The test will take about 10 to 15 minutes.

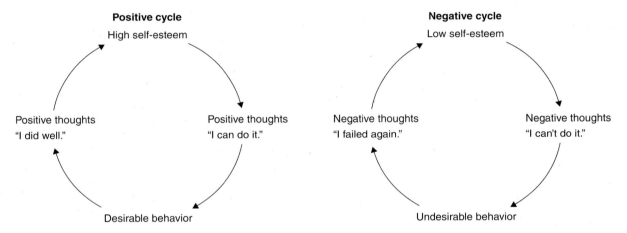

Figure 2.1
The Relationship between Self-Esteem and Communication Behavior

impartial observers nor objective tests verify these beliefs. It's easy to see how people with an inflated sense of self-worth could irritate others by coming across as condescending know-it-alls, especially when their self-worth is challenged.[2]

Despite these cautions, self-esteem *can* be the starting point for positive behaviors and interactions. Figure 2.1 shows the cycles that may begin from both positive and negative self-evaluations. These patterns often become self-fulfilling prophecies, as we'll discuss later in this chapter.

BIOLOGICAL AND SOCIAL ROOTS OF THE SELF

How did you become the kind of communicator you are? Were you born that way? Are you a product of your environment? As you'll now see, the correct answer to both of these questions is "yes."

BIOLOGY AND THE SELF   Take another look at the "Who am I?" list you developed at the beginning of this chapter. You will almost certainly find some terms that describe your **personality**—characteristic ways that you think and behave across a variety of situations. Your personality tends to be stable throughout your life, and often it grows

more pronounced over time.[3] Research suggests that personality is, to a large degree, part of our genetic makeup.[4] For example, people who were judged shy as children still show a distinctive reaction in their brains as adults when they encounter new situations.[5]

In fact, biology accounts for as much as half of some communication-related personality traits, including extroversion,[6] shyness,[7] assertiveness,[8] verbal aggression,[9] and overall willingness to communicate.[10] In other words, to some degree, we come programmed to communicate in characteristic ways. You can get a rough measure of your personality by taking the online test described in the Invitation to Insight, "Your Personality Profile," on page 45.

Social scientists have grouped personality traits into five primary categories, which are outlined in Table 2.2.[11] These trait categories seem to be universal, and they are recognized in cultures as diverse as German and Chinese.[12] Take a look at that table now, and identify the terms that best describe your personality. Although labels like "neurotic" and "antagonistic" can be difficult to acknowledge, the descriptors underneath them may be more typical of you than the words under their "stable" and "agreeable" counterparts. You will notice that several dimensions of these personality types relate to communication. How does your communication reflect your personality?

Before you become distressed about being stuck with a personality that makes communication difficult, keep two important points in mind. First, realize that these traits are a matter of degree, not an either-or matter. It's an oversimplification to think of yourself as shy *or* sociable, argumentative *or* agreeable, self-controlled *or* spontaneous.

Table 2.2

The "Big Five" Personality Traits

Extroverted	Introverted	Agreeable	Antagonistic
Sociable	Reserved	Courteous	Rude
Fun-loving	Sober	Selfless	Selfish
Talkative	Quiet	Trusting	Suspicious
Spontaneous	Self-controlled	Cooperative	Uncooperative
Open	**Not Open**	**Neurotic**	**Stable**
Imaginative	Unimaginative	Worried	Calm
Independent	Conforming	Vulnerable	Hardy
Curious	Incurious	Self-pitying	Self-satisfied
Broad interests	Narrow interests	Impatient	Patient
Conscientious	**Undirected**		
Careful	Careless		
Reliable	Undependable		
Persevering	Lax		
Ambitious	Aimless		

Your Personality Profile

You can get an idea of your personality and how it affects your communication by taking a self-test online. You can find the link to this site through your Premium Website for *Looking Out/ Looking In*. The test will take approximately 20 minutes.

It's more accurate to realize that almost everyone's personality fits at some point on a spectrum for each trait. You may be somewhat shy, a little argumentative, or moderately self-controlled.

Second, while you may have a disposition toward traits like shyness or aggressiveness, you can do a great deal to control how you actually communicate. More and more research suggests that personality is flexible, dynamic, and shaped by experiences.[13] Even shy people can learn how to reach out to others, and those with aggressive tendencies can learn to communicate in more-sociable ways. One author put it this way: "Experiences can silence genes or activate them. Even shyness is like Silly Putty once life gets hold of it."[14] Throughout this book you will learn about communication skills that, with practice, you can build into your repertoire.

SOCIALIZATION AND THE SELF-CONCEPT   How important are others in shaping our self-concept? Imagine growing up on a deserted island, with no one to talk to or share activities. How would you know how smart you are—or aren't? How would you gauge your attractiveness? How would you decide if you're short or tall, kind or mean, skinny or fat? Even if you could view your reflection in a mirror, you still wouldn't know how to evaluate your appearance without appraisals from others or people with whom to compare yourself. In fact, the messages we receive from the people in our lives play the most important role in shaping how we regard ourselves. To gain an appreciation for this role, try the exercise on page 46.

> We are not only our brother's keeper; in countless large and small ways, we are our brother's maker.
>
> —*Bonaro Overstreet*

As early as 1912, sociologist Charles Cooley used the metaphor of a mirror to identify the process of **reflected appraisal**: the fact that each of us develops a self-concept that reflects the way we believe others see us.[15] In other words, we are likely to feel less valuable, lovable, and capable to the degree that others have communicated ego-busting signals; and we will probably feel good about ourselves to the degree that others affirm our value.[16] The principle of reflected appraisal will become clear when you realize that the self-concept you described in the list at the beginning of this chapter is a product of the positive and negative messages you have received throughout your life.

To illustrate this point further, let's start at the beginning. Children aren't born with any sense of identity. They learn to judge themselves only through the way others treat them. As children learn to speak and understand language, verbal messages contribute to a developing self-concept. Every day a child is bombarded with scores of messages about him or herself. Some of these are positive: "You're so cute!" "I love you." "What a big girl." Other messages are negative: "What's the matter with you?" "Can't you do anything right?" "You're a bad boy." "Leave me alone. You're driving me

✔+ INVITATION TO INSIGHT

"Ego Boosters" and "Ego Busters"

1 Either by yourself or with a partner, recall someone you know or once knew who was an "ego booster"—who helped enhance your self-esteem by acting in a way that made you feel accepted, competent, worthwhile, important, appreciated, or loved. This person needn't have played a crucial role in your life as long as the role was positive. Often your self-concept is shaped by many tiny nudges as well as by a few giant events. A family member with whom you've spent most of your life can be an "ego booster," but so can the stranger on the street who spontaneously offers you an unexpected compliment.

2 Now recall an "ego buster" from your life—someone who acted in a large or small way to reduce your self-esteem. As with ego-booster messages, ego-buster messages aren't always intentional. The acquaintance who forgets your name after you've been introduced or the friend who yawns while you're describing an important problem can diminish your feelings of self-worth.

3 Now that you've thought about how others shape your self-concept, recall a time when you were an ego booster to someone else—when you intentionally or unintentionally boosted another's self-esteem. Don't merely settle for an instance in which you were nice: Look for a time when your actions left another person feeling valued, loved, needed, and so on. You may have to ask the help of others to answer this question.

4 Finally, recall a recent instance in which you were an ego buster for someone else. What did you do to diminish another's self-esteem? Were you aware of the effect of your behavior at the time? Your answer might show that some events we intend as boosters have the effect of busters. For example, you might joke with a friend in what you mean as a friendly gesture, only to discover that your remarks are received as criticism.

After completing the exercise (you *did* complete it, didn't you?), you should begin to see that your self-concept is shaped by those around you. This process of shaping occurs in two ways: reflected appraisal and social comparison.

You can complete this activity at your Premium Website for *Looking Out/Looking In* and, if requested, email your responses to your instructor.

crazy!" Evaluations like these are the mirror by which we know ourselves. Because children are trusting souls who have no other way of viewing themselves, they accept at face value both the positive and negative evaluations of the apparently all-knowing and all-powerful adults around them.

These same principles in the formation of the self-concept continue in later life, especially when messages come from what sociologists term **significant others**—people whose opinions we especially value. (See the story "Cipher in the Snow" on pages 50–51 for an example.) A look at the ego boosters and ego busters you described in the previous exercise will show that the evaluations of a few especially important people can be powerful. Family members are the most obvious type of significant other, and their ego busters can be particularly hurtful as a result.[17] Others, though, can also be significant others: a special friend, a teacher, or perhaps an

"Now look what you've done!"

acquaintance whose opinion you value can leave an imprint on how you view yourself. To see the importance of significant others, ask yourself how you arrived at your opinion of yourself as a student, as a person attractive to others, as a competent worker, and you'll see that these self-evaluations were probably influenced by the way others regarded you.

The impact of significant others remains strong during adolescence. Inclusion in (or exclusion from) peer groups is a crucial factor in self-concept development for teenagers.[18] The good news is that parents who are understanding of their children's self-concepts during the adolescent years typically have better communication with their teens and can help them create a strong self-concept.[19] The influence of significant others becomes less powerful as people grow older. After most people approach the age of thirty, their self-concepts don't change radically, at least without a conscious effort.[20]

So far we have looked at the way in which others' messages shape our self-concept. In addition to these messages, each of us forms our self-image by the process of **social comparison**: evaluating ourselves in terms of how we compare with others.

Two types of social comparison need highlighting. In the first, we decide whether we are *superior* or *inferior* by comparing ourselves to others. Are we attractive or ugly? A success or failure? Intelligent or stupid? It depends on those against whom we measure ourselves.[21] For instance, research shows that young women who regularly compare themselves with ultra-thin media models develop negative appraisals of their own bodies.[22] In one study, young women's perceptions of their bodies changed for the worse after watching just thirty minutes of televised images of the "ideal" female form.[23] Men, too, who compare themselves to media-idealized male physiques, evaluate their bodies negatively.[24] Even popular TV makeover shows—with their underlying message of "you must improve your appearance"—can lead viewers to feel worse about themselves.[25]

> I walk a tightrope of unique design.
> I teeter, falter, recover and bow.
> You applaud.
> I run forward, backward, hesitate and bow.
> You applaud.
> If you don't applaud I'll Fall.
> Cheer me! Hurray me!
> Or you push me
> Down.
>
> —*Lenni Shender Goldstein*

King Features © Zits Partnership

> In order to get at any truth about myself, I must have contact with another person. The other is indispensable to my own existence, as well as to my knowledge about myself.
>
> —*Jean-Paul Sartre*

You'll probably never be as beautiful as a Hollywood star, as agile as a professional athlete, or as wealthy as a millionaire. When you consider the matter logically, these facts don't mean you're worthless. Nonetheless, many people judge themselves against unreasonable standards and suffer accordingly.[26] These distorted self-images can lead to serious behavioral disorders, such as depression, anorexia nervosa, and bulimia.[27] You'll read more about how to avoid placing perfectionistic demands on yourself in Chapter 4.

In addition to feelings of superiority and inferiority, social comparison provides a way to decide if we are the *same as* or *different from* others. A child who is interested in ballet and who lives in a setting where such preferences are regarded as weird will start to accept this label if there is no support from others. Likewise, adults who want to improve the quality of their relationships but are surrounded by friends and family who don't recognize or acknowledge the importance of these matters may think of themselves as oddballs. Thus, it's easy to recognize that the **reference groups** against which we compare ourselves play an important role in shaping our view of ourselves.

You might argue that not every part of one's self-concept is shaped by others, insisting that certain objective facts are recognizable by self-observation. After all, nobody needs to tell a person that he is taller than others, speaks with an accent, has acne, and so on. These facts are obvious. Though it's true that some features of the self are immediately apparent, the *significance* we attach to them—the rank we assign them in the hierarchy of our list and the interpretation we give them—depends greatly on the opinions of others. After all, many of your features are readily observable, yet you don't find them important at all, because nobody has regarded them as significant.

We once heard a woman in her eighties describing her youth. "When I was a girl," she declared, "we didn't worry about weight. Some people were skinny and others were plump, and we pretty much accepted the bodies God gave us." In those days it was unlikely that weight would have found its way onto the self-concept list you constructed, because it wasn't considered significant. Compare this attitude with what you find today: It's seldom that you pick up a popular magazine or visit a bookstore without reading about the latest diet fads, and television ads are filled with scenes of slender, happy people. As a result you'll rarely find a person who doesn't complain about the need to "lose a few pounds." Obviously, the reason for such concern comes from the attention paid to fitness. We generally see slimness as desirable, because others tell us it is. In a society where obesity is the ideal, a person who regards herself as extremely heavy would be a beauty. In the same way, the fact that one is single or married, solitary or sociable, aggressive or passive takes on meaning depending on the interpretation that society attaches to those traits (see the discussion of *Bridget Jones's Diary* on page 77 as an illustration of the issues raised in this paragraph).

The namesake of the TV series *Ugly Betty* is smart, kind, and diligent. But she isn't as thin or beautiful as the coworkers at the high-fashion magazine where she works. Social comparison leads to Betty's ongoing struggle with shyness and low self-esteem.

George Napolitano/FilmMagic/Getty Images

By now you might be thinking, "It's not my fault that I've always been shy or insecure. Because I developed a picture of myself as a result of the way others have treated me, I can't help being what I am." Though it's true that to a certain extent you are a product of your environment, to believe that you are forever doomed to a poor self-concept would be a big mistake. Having held a poor self-image in the past is no reason for continuing to do so in the future. You *can* change your attitudes and behaviors, as you'll soon read.

CHARACTERISTICS OF THE SELF-CONCEPT

Now that you have a better idea of how your self-concept has developed, we can look closer at some of its characteristics.

THE SELF-CONCEPT IS SUBJECTIVE   Although we tend to believe that our self-concept is accurate, in truth it may well be distorted. Some people view themselves more favorably than objective facts would merit. For example, researchers have found that there is no relationship between the way college students rate their ability as interpersonal communicators, public speakers, or listeners and their true effectiveness.[28] In all cases, the self-reported communication skill is higher than actual performance. In another study, a random sample of men were asked to rank themselves on their ability to get along with others.[29] Defying mathematical laws, all subjects—every last one— put themselves in the top half of the population. Sixty percent rated themselves in the top 10 percent of the population, and an amazing 25 percent believed they were in the top 1 percent. The men had similarly lofty appraisals of their leadership and athletic abilities. Other research shows that these perceptions of superiority tend to increase over time.[30] Similarly, online daters often have a "foggy mirror"—that is, they see themselves more positively than others do.[31] This leads to inflated self-descriptions that don't always match what an objective third party might say about them.

> Self-love, My liege, is not so vile a sin as self-neglecting.
>
> —*Shakespeare,* King Henry V

Not all distortion of the self-concept is positive. Many people view themselves more harshly than the objective facts warrant. We have all experienced a temporary case of the "uglies," convinced that we look much worse than others assure us we really look. Research confirms what common sense suggests: People are more critical of themselves when they are experiencing these negative moods than when they are feeling more positive.[32] Although we all suffer occasional bouts of self-doubt that affect our communication, some people suffer from long-term or even permanent states of excessive self-doubt and criticism.[33] It's easy to understand how this chronic condition can influence the way they approach and respond to others.

Distorted self-evaluations like these can occur for several reasons. One reason is *obsolete information*. The effects of past failures in school or social relations can linger long after they have occurred, even though such events don't predict failure in the future. Likewise, your past successes don't guarantee future success. Perhaps your jokes used to be well received or your work was superior, but now the facts have changed.

Distorted feedback also can create a self-image that is worse or better than the facts warrant. Overly critical parents are one of the most common causes of a negative self-image. In other cases the remarks of cruel friends, uncaring teachers, excessively demanding employers, or even memorable strangers can have a lasting effect. Other distorted

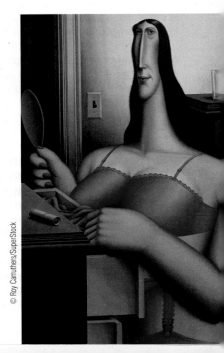

> I am not what I think I am. I am not what you think I am. I am what I think you think I am.
>
> —*Aaron Bleiberg and Harry Leubling*

A final reason why people often sell themselves short is connected to *social expectations*. Curiously, the perfectionist society to which we belong rewards those people who downplay the strengths we demand that they possess (or pretend to possess). We term these people "modest" and find their behavior agreeable. On the other hand, we consider those who honestly appreciate their strengths to be "braggarts" or "egotists," confusing them with the people who boast about accomplishments they do not possess.[34] This convention leads most of us to talk freely about our shortcomings while downplaying our accomplishments. It's all right to proclaim that you're miserable if you have failed to do well on a project, but it's considered boastful to express your pride at a job well done.

After a while we begin to believe the types of statements we repeatedly make. The disparaging remarks are viewed as modesty and become part of our self-concept, and the strengths and accomplishments go unmentioned and are thus forgotten. And in the end we see ourselves as much worse than we are. One way to avoid falling into the trap of becoming overly critical is to recognize your strengths. The following exercise will give you a chance to suspend the ordinary rules of modesty and appreciate yourself publicly for a change.

✔+ INVITATION TO INSIGHT

Recognizing Your Strengths

1 This exercise can be done either alone or with a group. If you are with others, sit in a circle so that everyone can see one another.

2 Each person should share three personal strengths or accomplishments. These needn't feature areas in which you are an expert, and they don't have to be concerned with momentous feats. On the contrary, it's perfectly acceptable to talk about some part of yourself that leaves you feeling pleased or proud. For instance, you might say that, instead of procrastinating, you completed a school assignment before the last minute, that you spoke up to a friend even though you were afraid of disapproval, or that you baked a fantastic chocolate cake.

3 If you're at a loss for items, ask yourself:
   a. What are some ways in which you've grown in the past year? How are you more skillful, wiser, or a better person than you previously were?

   b. Why do certain friends or family members care about you? What features do you possess that make them appreciate you?

4 After you've finished, consider the experience. Did you have a hard time thinking of things to share? Would it have been easier to list the things that are *wrong* with you? If so, is this because you are truly a wretched person, or is it because you are in the habit of stressing your defects and ignoring your strengths? Consider the impact of such a habit on your self-concept, and ask yourself whether it wouldn't be wiser to strike a better balance distinguishing between your strengths and weaknesses.

You can complete this activity at your Premium Website for *Looking Out/Looking In* and, if requested, email your responses to your instructor.

THE SELF-CONCEPT RESISTS CHANGE Although we all change, there is a tendency to cling to an existing self-concept, even when evidence shows that it is obsolete. This tendency to seek and attend to information that conforms to an existing self-concept has been labeled **cognitive conservatism**.

This tendency toward cognitive conservatism leads us to seek out people who support our self-concept. For example, both college students and married couples with high self-esteem seek out partners who view them favorably, whereas those with negative self-esteem are more inclined to interact with people who view them unfavorably.[35] It appears that we are less concerned with learning the "truth" about ourselves than with reinforcing a familiar self-concept.

It's understandable why we're reluctant to revise a previously favorable self-concept. A student who did well in earlier years but now has failed to study might be unwilling to admit that the label "good scholar" no longer applies. Likewise, a previously industrious worker might resent a supervisor's mentioning increased absences and low productivity. These people aren't *lying* when they insist that they're doing well despite the facts to the contrary; they honestly believe that the old truths still hold, precisely because their self-concepts are so resistant to change.

Curiously, the tendency to cling to an outmoded self-perception also holds when the new self-perception would be more favorable than the old one. We recall a former student whom almost anyone would have regarded as beautiful, with physical features attractive enough to appear in any glamour magazine. Despite her appearance, in a class exercise this woman characterized herself as "ordinary" and "unattractive." When questioned by her classmates, she described how as a child her teeth were extremely crooked and how she had worn braces for several years in her teens to correct this problem. During this time she was often teased by her friends, who never let her forget her "metal mouth," as she put it. Even though the braces had been off for two years, our student reported that she still saw herself as ugly and brushed aside our compliments by insisting that we were just saying these things to be nice—she knew how she *really* looked.

Examples like this show one problem that occurs when we resist changing an inaccurate self-concept. Our student denied herself a much happier life by clinging to an obsolete picture of herself. In the same way, some communicators insist that they are less talented or less worthy of friendship than others would suggest, thus creating their own miserable world when it needn't exist. These unfortunate souls probably resist changing because they aren't willing to go through the disorientation that comes from redefining themselves, correctly anticipating that it *is* an effort to think of oneself in a new way. Whatever their reasons, it's sad to see people in such an unnecessary state.

A second problem arising from the persistence of an inaccurate self-concept is self-delusion and lack of growth. If you hold an unrealistically favorable picture of yourself, you won't see the real need for change that may exist. Instead of learning new talents, working to change a relationship, or improving your physical condition, you'll stay with the familiar and comfortable delusion that everything is all right. As time goes by, this delusion becomes more difficult to maintain, leading to a third type of problem: defensiveness.

To understand this problem, you need to remember that communicators who are presented with information that contradicts their self-perception have two choices: They can either accept the new data and change their perception accordingly, or they can keep their original perception and in some way refute the new information. Because most communicators are reluctant to downgrade a favorable image of themselves, their tendency is to opt for refutation, either by discounting the information and rationalizing it away or by counterattacking the person who transmitted it. The problem of defensiveness is so great that we will examine it in detail in Chapter 10.

CULTURE, GENDER, AND IDENTITY

We have already seen how experiences in the family, especially during childhood, shape our sense of who we are. Along with the messages we receive at home, many other forces shape our identity, and thus our communication, including age, physical ability/disability, sexual orientation, and socioeconomic status. Along with these forces, culture and gender are powerful forces in shaping how we view ourselves and others and how we communicate. We will examine each of these forces now.

CULTURE   Although we seldom recognize the fact, our sense of self is shaped, often in subtle ways, by the culture in which we have been reared.[36] Most Western cultures are highly individualistic, whereas other traditional cultures—most Asian ones, for example—are much more collective. When asked to identify themselves, individualistic people in the United States, Canada, Australia, and Europe would probably respond by giving their first name, surname, street, town, and country. Many Asians do it the other way around.[37] If you ask Hindus for their identity, they will give you their caste and village as well as their name. The Sanskrit formula for identifying one's self begins with lineage and goes on to state family, house, and ends with one's personal name.[38] When members of different cultures were asked to create an "I am" list similar to the one you completed earlier in this chapter, those from collectivist cultures made far more group references than those from individualistic cultures.[39]

These conventions for naming aren't just cultural curiosities: They reflect a very different way of viewing one's self and of what kinds of relationships are important. In collective cultures, a person gains identity by belonging to a group. This means that the perceived degree of interdependence among members of the society and its subgroups is high. Feelings of pride and self-worth are likely to be shaped not only by what the individual does but also by behavior of other members of the community. This linkage to others explains the traditional Asian denial of self-importance—a strong contrast to the self-promotion that is common in individualistic Western cultures.[40] In Chinese written language, for example, the pronoun *I* looks very similar to the word for selfish.[41] Table 2.3 summarizes some differences between individualistic cultures and more collective ones.

In Japan, in fact, everything had been made level and uniform—even humanity. By one official count, 90 percent of the population regarded themselves as middle-class; in schools, it was not the outcasts who beat up the conformists, but vice versa. Every Japanese individual seemed to have the same goal as every other—to become like every other Japanese individual. The word for "different," I was told, was the same as the word for "wrong." And again and again in Japan, in contexts varying from the baseball stadium to the watercolor canvas, I heard the same unswerving, even maxim: "The nail that sticks out must be hammered down."

—*Pico Iyer,* Video Night in Katmandu

This sort of cultural difference isn't just a matter of interest to anthropologists. It shows up in the level of comfort or anxiety that people feel when communicating. In collective societies, there is a higher degree of communication apprehension. For example, as a group, residents of China, South Korea, and Japan exhibit a significantly higher degree of anxiety about speaking out than do members of individualistic cultures, such as the United States and Australia.[42] It's important to realize that

Table 2.3

The Self in Individualistic and Collectivistic Cultures

Individualistic Cultures
Self is separate, unique individual; should be independent, self-sufficient.
Individual should take care of him or herself and immediate family.
Many flexible group memberships; friends based on shared interests and activities.
Reward for individual achievement and initiative; individual decisions encouraged; individual credit and blame assigned.
High value on autonomy, change, youth, individual security, equality.

Collectivistic Cultures
People belong to extended families or in-groups; "we" or group orientation.
Person should take care of extended family before self.
Emphasis on belonging to a very few permanent in-groups that have a strong influence over the person.
Reward for contribution to group goals and well-being; cooperation with in-group members; group decisions valued; credit and blame shared.
High value on duty, order, tradition, age, group security, status, and hierarchy.

Adapted by S. Sudweeks from material in H. C. Triandis (1990). "Cross-Cultural Studies of Individualism and Collectivism." In J. Berman (Ed.), Nebraska Symposium on Motivation, 37 (pp. 41–133). Lincoln: University of Nebraska Press.

different levels of communication apprehension don't mean that shyness is a "problem" in some cultures. In fact, just the opposite is true: In these societies reticence is valued. To avoid being a standout, it's logical to feel nervous when you make yourself appear different by calling attention to yourself. A self-concept that includes "assertive" might make a Westerner feel proud, but in much of Asia it would more likely be cause for shame.

The difference between individualism and collectivism shows up in everyday interaction. Communication researcher Stella Ting-Toomey has developed a theory that explains cultural differences in important norms, such as honesty and directness.[43] She suggests that in individualistic Western cultures where there is a strong "I" orientation, the norm of speaking directly is honored, whereas in collectivistic cultures, where the main desire is to build connections between the self and others, indirect approaches that maintain harmony are considered more desirable. "I gotta be me" could be the motto of a Westerner, but "If I hurt you, I hurt myself" is closer to the Asian way of thinking.

You don't need to travel overseas to appreciate the influence of culture on the self. Within societies, co-cultural identity plays an important role in how we see ourselves and others. For example, ethnicity can have a powerful effect on how people think of themselves and how they communicate. Recall how you described yourself in the "Who Am I?" list you created when you began this chapter. If you are a member of a nondominant ethnic group, it's likely that you included your ethnicity in the most important parts of who you are. There's no surprise here: If society keeps reminding you that your ethnicity is important, then you begin to think of yourself in those terms. If you are part of the dominant majority, you probably aren't as conscious of your ethnicity. Nonetheless, it plays an important part in your self-concept. Being part of the majority increases the chances that you have a sense of belonging to the society in which you live and of entitlement to being treated fairly. Members of less privileged ethnic groups often don't have these feelings.

SEX AND GENDER   One way to appreciate the tremendous importance of gender on your sense of self is to imagine how your identity would be different if you had been born as a member of the opposite sex. Would you express your emotions in the same way? Deal with conflict? Relate to friends and strangers? The answer is almost certainly a resounding "no."

From the earliest months of life, being male or female shapes the way others communicate with us, and thus how they shape our sense of self. Think about the first questions most people ask when a child is born. One of them is almost always "Is it a boy or a girl?" As the "Cathy" cartoon on this page shows, after most people know what the baby "is," they often behave accordingly.[44] They use different pronouns and often choose gender-related nicknames. With boys, comments often focus on size, strength, and activity; comments about girls more often address beauty, sweetness, and facial responsiveness. It's not surprising that these messages shape a child's sense of identity and how he or she will communicate. The implicit message is that some ways of behaving are masculine and others feminine. Little girls, for example, are more likely to be reinforced for acting "sweet" than are little boys. The same principle operates in adulthood: A man who stands up for his beliefs might get approval for being "tough" or "persistent," whereas a woman who behaves in the same way could be described by critics as a "nag" or "bitch."[45] It's not hard to see how the gender roles and labels like these can have a profound effect on how men and women view themselves and on how they communicate.

Self-esteem is also influenced by gender. In a society that values competitiveness more in men than in women, it isn't surprising that the self-esteem of adolescent young men is closely related to having abilities that are superior in some way to those of their peers, whereas teenage women's self-worth is tied more closely to the success of their social relationships and verbal skills.[46] Research also suggests that young women struggle more with self-esteem issues than do young men. For example, the self-esteem of about two-thirds of the males in one study (ages 14 to 23) increased.[47]

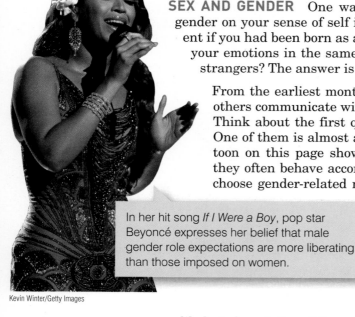

In her hit song *If I Were a Boy*, pop star Beyoncé expresses her belief that male gender role expectations are more liberating than those imposed on women.

Kevin Winter/Getty Images

The same study revealed that about 57 percent of females in the same age group grew to feel *less* good about themselves.

Don't resign yourself to being a prisoner of expectations about your gender. Research demonstrates that our sense of self is shaped strongly by the people with whom we interact and by the contexts in which we communicate.[48] For example, a nonaggressive young man who might feel unwelcome and inept in a macho environment might gain new self-esteem by finding others who appreciate his style of communicating. A woman whose self-esteem is stifled by the limited expectations of bosses and coworkers can look for more hospitable places to work. Children usually can't choose the reference groups that shape their identities, but adults can.

THE SELF-FULFILLING PROPHECY AND COMMUNICATION

The self-concept is such a powerful force on the personality that it not only determines how you see yourself in the present but also can actually influence your future behavior and that of others. Such occurrences come about through a phenomenon called the self-fulfilling prophecy.

A **self-fulfilling prophecy** occurs when a person's expectations of an event, and his or her subsequent behavior based on those expectations, make the event more likely to occur than would otherwise have been true. A self-fulfilling prophecy involves four stages:

1. Holding an expectation (for yourself or for others)
2. Behaving in accordance with that expectation
3. The expectation coming to pass
4. Reinforcing the original expectation

You can see how this process operates by considering an example. Imagine you're scheduled to interview for a job you really want. You are nervous about how you'll do, and not at all sure you are really qualified for the position. You share your concerns with a professor who knows you well and a friend who works for the company. Both assure you that you're perfect for the job and that the firm would be lucky to have you as an employee. Based on these comments, you come to the interview feeling good about yourself. As a result, you speak with authority and sell yourself with confidence. The employers are clearly impressed, and you receive the job offer. Your conclusion: "My friend and professor were right. I'm the kind of person an employer would want!"

This example illustrates the four stages of a self-fulfilling prophecy. Thanks to the assurances of your professor and friend, your expectations about the interview were upbeat (Stage 1). Because of your optimistic attitude, you communicated confidently in the interview (Stage 2). Your confident behavior—along with your other qualifications—led to a job offer (Stage 3). Finally, the positive results reinforced your positive self-assessment, and you'll probably approach future interviews with greater assurance (Stage 4).

It's important to recognize the tremendous influence that self-fulfilling prophecies play in our lives. To a great extent we become what we believe. In this sense, we and those around us constantly create and re-create our self-concepts.

TYPES OF SELF-FULFILLING PROPHECIES   There are two types of self-fulfilling prophecies. *Self-imposed prophecies* occur when your own expectations influence your behavior. In sports you've probably psyched yourself into playing either better

a doctor believes that a patient will improve, the patient may do so precisely because of this expectation, whereas another person for whom the doctor has little hope often fails to recover.[57] Apparently the patient's self-concept as sick or well—as shaped by the doctor—plays an important role in determining the actual state of health.

Notice that the observer must do more than just *believe* to create a self-fulfilling prophecy for the person who is the target of the expectations. The observer also must *communicate* that belief in order for the prediction to have any effect. If parents have faith in their children, but the kids aren't aware of that confidence, they won't be affected by their parents' expectations. If a boss has concerns about an employee's

or worse than usual, so that the only explanation for your unusual performance was your attitude. Similarly, you've probably faced an audience at one time or another with a fearful attitude and forgotten your remarks, not because you were unprepared, but because you said to yourself, "I know I'll blow it."

Research has demonstrated the power of self-imposed prophecies.[49] In one study, communicators who believed they were incompetent proved less likely than others to pursue rewarding relationships

A self-fulfilling prophecy occurs when expectations of an event influence a person's behavior, which in turn influences the event's outcome. One type of prophecy consists of predictions by others, whereas another type is self-imposed. Self-fulfilling prophecies can be both positive and negative.

It is possible to change one's self-concept in ways that lead to more effective communication. It is necessary to have realistic expectations about how much change is possible and a realistic assessment of oneself. Willingness to exert the effort to change is important, and in some cases change requires new information or skill.

Identity management consists of strategic communication designed to influence others' perceptions of an individual. Identity management aims at presenting to others one or more faces, which may be different from private, spontaneous behavior that occurs outside of others' presence. Some communicators are high self-monitors who are highly conscious of their own behavior, whereas others are less aware of how their words and actions affect others.

Identity management occurs for two reasons. Many times it aims at following social rules and conventions. At other times it aims at achieving a variety of content and relational goals. In either case, communicators engage in creating an identity by managing their manner, appearance, and the settings in which they interact with others. Identity management occurs both in face-to-face and mediated communication. Although identity management might seem manipulative, it can be an authentic form of communication. Because each person has a variety of faces that he or she can reveal, choosing which one to present need not be dishonest.

Key Terms

cognitive conservatism (53)
face (64)
identity management (62)
perceived self (64)
personality (43)

presenting self (64)
reference groups (48)
reflected appraisal (45)
self-concept (40)

self-esteem (41)
self-fulfilling prophecy (57)
significant others (46)
social comparison (47)

Online Resources

Now that you have read this chapter, use your Premium Website for *Looking Out/ Looking In* for quick access to the electronic resources that accompany this text. Your Premium Website gives you access to:

- **Study tools** that will help you assess your learning and prepare for exams (*digital glossary, key term flash cards, review quizzes*).

- **Activities and assignments** that will help you hone your knowledge, understand how theory and research applies to your own life (*Invitation to Insight*), consider ethical challenges in interpersonal communication (*Ethical Challenge*), and build your interpersonal communication skills throughout the course (*Skill Builder*). If requested, you can submit your answers to your instructor.

- **Media resources** that will allow you to watch and critique news video and videos of interpersonal communication situations (*In Real Life, interpersonal video* *simulations*) and download a chapter review so you can study when and where you'd like (*Audio Study Tools*).

This chapter's key terms and search terms for additional reading are featured in this end-of-chapter section, and you can find this chapter's Invitation to Insight, Ethical Challenge, and Skill Builder activities in the body of the chapter.

Search Terms

When searching online databases to research topics in this chapter, use the following terms (along with this chapter's key terms) to maximize the chances of finding useful information:

impression management	self-evaluation	self-perception
self-awareness	self-monitoring	self-presentation
self-congruence		

Film and Television

You can see the communication principles described in this chapter portrayed in the following films and television programs:

INFLUENCES ON THE SELF-CONCEPT

Akeelah and the Bee (2006) Rated PG

Eleven-year-old Akeelah Anderson (Keke Palmer) is a really good speller—maybe good enough to win the national championship. But she is also desperately afraid of being ridiculed as a brainiac by her classmates at their inner-city middle school. Akeelah is encouraged to excel by her teachers, her principal, and her new mentor, UCLA professor Dr. Joshua Larabee (Laurence Fishburne). Will Akeelah hide her talents to fit in, or will she think and act like a potential champion? This film illustrates how struggles of self-definition are shaped by both our own desires and the messages we receive from significant others.

Bridget Jones's Diary (2001) Rated R

Unmarried and in her early thirties, Bridget Jones (Renée Zellweger) measures her self-worth by whether men pay attention to her. She worries about dying "fat and alone." Bridget's obsession with losing weight and finding a partner are due in part to the media appraisals and comparisons that surround her. She has photos of thin models on her refrigerator, self-help books (*What Men Want*) on the shelf, glamour magazines on her coffee table, and cry-in-your-beer music ("All By Myself") blaring on the stereo. These media messages scream that she has been weighed in the balance and found wanting.

After years of self-loathing, Bridget finds a suitor named Mark (Colin Firth), who offers an appraisal that is water on the desert of Bridget's self-concept: "I like you very much, just as you are." She has spent much of her life trying to live up to social expectations of attractiveness, but Mark accepts her imperfections and appreciates her many positive attributes. Bridget finally embraces the notion that she is fine "just as she is."

CHANGING THE SELF

MADE (2003–) Rated TV-PG

In this long-running MTV reality show, teens with goals that would be impossible under normal circumstances get a little help from their *MADE* coach to realize their dreams. While most of us don't have the support of a major TV network and personal coaches, the show does demonstrate that it's possible to become more of the person you hope to be, especially when you have the will and skill to change.

SELF-FULFILLING PROPHECIES

Stand and Deliver (1988) Rated PG-13

Jaime Escalante (Edward James Olmos) is a mild-mannered math teacher who is commissioned to the tough classrooms of Garfield High. He is soft-spoken, cerebral, and demanding—in other words, the kind of teacher street-hardened students would normally despise and ignore. Although the students do, in fact, regard him suspiciously at first, by the story's end they adore him. Perhaps more important, they achieve top-flight scores on their advanced-placement calculus exam, which is their ticket to a college education.

How can we account for the students' success? The film suggests that the key is not Escalante's knowledge of math, his lecture techniques, or his classroom charisma. The key is that he believes in his students, who hadn't been believed in before. Because he believes in them, they stop thinking of themselves as losers. Escalante helps them master a subject they thought was impossible, and in so doing radically changes their self-concepts. Based on a true story, this movie offers contemporary support for the Pygmalion theory of the self-fulfilling prophecy.

IDENTITY MANAGEMENT

Brokeback Mountain (2005) Rated R

In the summer of 1963, Ennis Del Mar (Heath Ledger) and Jack Twist (Jake Gyllenhaal) are hired to tend sheep on the slopes of Montana's Brokeback Mountain. In their remote campsite, the two men surprise themselves by becoming lovers. After the summer ends, they return to their separate lives. Both marry and have children, managing to ignore their feelings for one another until they meet again. This tragic story of denial shows the extent to which people are willing to go to hide parts of their identity in order to avoid social disapproval.

Catch Me If You Can (2003) Rated PG-13

Frank Abagnale (Leonardo DiCaprio) learns to escape his family's financial and interpersonal woes by creating false identities. He impersonates a teacher, a pilot, a doctor, and a lawyer. These false fronts allow him to become rich, admired, and respected—and very lonely. The more faces and façades he constructs, the more he loses his sense of self. More significantly, his unwillingness to disclose his real identity isolates him from significant others, including his fiancée.

The person who knows Frank best is FBI agent Carl Hanratty (Tom Hanks), who is trying to capture and arrest him. By film's end, Carl becomes something of a father figure to Frank, helping him reestablish a legitimate identity. Based on a true story, this movie illustrates how identity management, when used unethically, can lead to strained relationships and a loss of self.

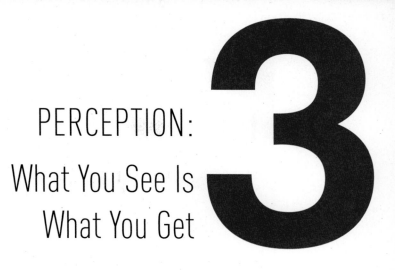

PERCEPTION:
What You See Is What You Get

3

After studying the topics in this chapter, you should be able to:

1. Describe how the processes of selection, organization, interpretation, and negotiation shape communication in a given situation.

2. Explain how the influences on perception listed on pages 93–101 affect communication in a specific situation.

3. Analyze how the tendencies described on pages 101–103 have distorted your perceptions of another person, and hence your communication.

Use this information to present a more accurate alternative set of perceptions.

4. Demonstrate how you might use the skill of perception checking in a significant relationship.

5. Enhance your cognitive complexity by applying the "pillow method" in a significant disagreement. Explain how your expanded view of this situation might affect your communication with the other(s) involved.

*S*tudy M. C. Escher's drawing *Relativity* on this page. It pictures a strange universe in which the inhabitants of each world exist at right angles, using the same staircase but oblivious to one another's existence. Each has his or her own conception of up and down, right and left. If these characters were introduced to the residents of other worlds, they would find them odd, defying the rule of gravity.

This surreal vision provides a useful metaphor for challenges we encounter every day. Each of us experiences a different reality, and failing to understand other people's point of view can lead to problems on both practical and relational levels. But perceptual differences can enhance as well as interfere with relationships. By seeing the world through others' eyes, you can gain insights that are different—and often more valuable—than those arising out of your own experiences.

This chapter will help you deal with the challenge of communicating in the face of perceptual differences. We will begin by looking at some of the reasons why the world appears different to each of us. In our survey we'll explore several areas: how our psychological makeup, personal needs, interests, and biases shape our perceptions; the physiological factors that influence our view of the world; the social roles that affect our image of events; and the role that culture plays in creating our ideas of what behavior is proper. In doing so, we'll cover many of the types of physiological and psychological noise you read about in Chapter 1. After examining the perceptual factors that can drive us apart, we will look at two useful skills for bridging the perceptual gap.

I've always admired those reporters who can descend on an area, talk to key people, ask key questions, take samplings of opinions, and then set down an orderly report very much like a road map. I envy this technique and at the same time do not trust it as a mirror of reality. I feel that there are too many realities. What I set down here is true until someone else passes that way and rearranges the world in his own style. In literary criticism the critic has no choice but to make over the victim of his attention into something the size and shape of himself. . . . So much there is to see, but our morning eyes describe a different world than do our afternoon eyes, and surely our wearied evening eyes can only report a weary evening world.

—*John Steinbeck,* Travels with Charley

The Perception Process

We need to begin our discussion of perception by examining the gap between "what is" and what we know. At one time or another, you've probably seen photos of sights invisible to the unaided eye: perhaps an infrared photo of a familiar area or the vastly enlarged image of a minute object taken by an electron microscope. You've also noticed how certain animals are able to hear sounds and smell odors that are not apparent to humans. Experiences like these remind us that there is much more going on in the world than we are able to experience with our limited senses, that our idea of reality is in fact only a partial one.

Even within the realm of our senses, we're aware of only a small part of what is going on around us. A simple walk in the park would probably be a different experience for companions with different interests. A botanist might notice the vegetation; a fashion designer might pay attention to the way people are dressed; and an artist might be aware of the colors and forms of the people and surroundings. On a personal level, we've all had the experience of failing to notice something unusual about a friend—perhaps a new hairstyle or a sad expression—until it's called to our attention. Sometimes our failure to recognize some events while recognizing others comes from not paying attention to important information. But in other cases it's simply impossible to be aware of everything, no matter how attentive we might be. There is just too much going on.

Psychologist William James said, "To the infant the world is just a big blooming, buzzing confusion." One reason for this is the fact that infants are not yet able to sort out the myriad impressions with which we're all bombarded. As we grow, we learn to manage all this data, and as we do so, we begin to make sense out of the world.

Because this ability to organize our perceptions in a useful way is such a critical factor in our ability to function, we need to begin our study of perception by taking a closer look at this process. We can do so by examining the four steps by which we attach meaning to our experiences: selection, organization, interpretation, and negotiation.

SELECTION

Because we're exposed to more input than we can possibly manage, the first step in perception is the **selection** of which impressions we will attend to. Several factors cause us to notice some things and ignore others.

Stimuli that are *intense* often attract our attention. Something that is louder, larger, or brighter stands out. This explains why—other things being equal—we're more likely to remember extremely tall or short people, and why someone who laughs or talks loudly at a party attracts more attention (not always favorable) than do quiet guests.

> We usually see only the things we are looking for—so much that we sometimes see them where they are not.
>
> —*Eric Hoffer*

Repetitious stimuli, repetitious stimuli, repetitious stimuli, repetitious stimuli, repetitious stimuli, repetitious stimuli also attract attention.[1] Just as a quiet but steadily dripping faucet can come to dominate our awareness, people to whom we're frequently exposed become noticeable.

ATTENTION IS ALSO FREQUENTLY RELATED TO contrast OR change IN STIMULATION. Put differently, unchanging people or things become less noticeable. This principle gives an explanation (excuse?) for why we take wonderful people for granted when we interact with them frequently. It's only when they stop being so wonderful or go away that we appreciate them.

Motives also determine what information we select from our environment. If you're anxious about being late for a date, you'll notice whatever clocks may be around you; and if you're hungry, you'll become aware of any restaurants, markets, and billboards advertising food in your path. Motives also determine how we perceive people. For example, someone on the lookout for a romantic adventure will be especially aware of attractive potential partners, whereas the same person at a different time might be oblivious to anyone but police or medical personnel in an emergency.

Selection isn't just a matter of attending to some stimuli: It also involves ignoring other cues. If, for example, you decide that someone is a terrific person, you may overlook his or her flaws. If you are focused on examples of unfair male bosses, you might not recognize unfair female bosses.

ORGANIZATION

Along with selecting information from the environment, we must arrange it in some meaningful way. You can see how the principle of **organization** works by looking at Figure 3.1. You can view the picture either as one of a vase or as one of two twins, depending on whether you focus on the light or the dark areas. In instances such as this, we make sense of stimuli by noticing some data that stand out as a *figure* against a less striking *ground*. The "vase-face" drawing is interesting, because it allows us to choose between two sets of figure-ground relationships.

This principle of figure-ground organization operates in communication, too. Recall, for instance, how certain speech can suddenly stand out from a babble of voices. Sometimes the words are noticeable because they include your name, whereas at other times they might be spoken by a familiar voice.

The vase-face drawing suggests that there are only two ways to organize impressions. In fact, there are usually many more. Consider, for example, Figure 3.2. How many ways can you view the boxes? One? Two? Three? Keep looking. If you're stumped, Figure 3.3 will help.

Figure 3.1

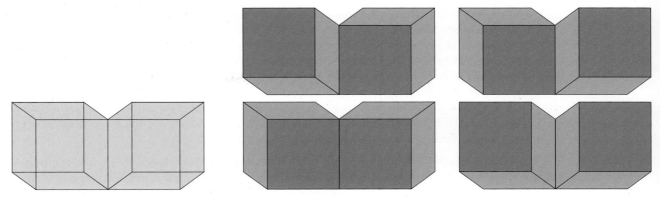

Figure 3.2   Figure 3.3

Just as you were inclined to view these boxes in one way, each of us can organize our impressions of other communicators using a number of schemes (called *perceptual schema* by social scientists). Sometimes we classify people according to their *appearance*: male or female, beautiful or ugly, heavy or thin, young or old, and so on. At other times we classify people according to their *social roles*: student, attorney, wife, and so on. Another way we classify people is by their *interaction style*: friendly, helpful, aloof, and sarcastic are examples. In other cases we classify people by their *psychological traits*: curious, nervous, insecure, and so on. Finally, we can use others' *membership*, classifying them according to the group to which they belong: Democrat, immigrant, Christian, and so on.

The perceptual schemas we use shape the way we think about and communicate with others. If you've classified a professor, for example, as "friendly," you'll handle questions or problems one way; if you've classified a professor as "mean," your behavior will probably be quite different. What constructs do you use to classify the people you encounter in your life? Consider how your relationship might change if you used different schemas.

✔+ INVITATION TO INSIGHT

Your Perceptual Filters

1 Identify the perceptual schema described in this section that you would use to classify people in each of the following contexts:
 a. Spending time with new acquaintances at a party
 b. Socializing with fellow workers on the job
 c. Choosing teammates for an important class project
 d. Offering help to a stranded motorist

Describe both the general type of organizing scheme (e.g., "physical," "membership") and the specific

category within each type (e.g., "attractive," "roughly the same age as me").

2 Consider:
 a. Other schema you might use in each context.
 b. The different consequences of using the schema you originally chose and the alternative you identified in the preceding step.
 c. How your relationships might change if you used different constructs.

STEREOTYPING   After we have chosen an organizing scheme to classify people, we use that scheme to make generalizations and predictions about members of the groups who fit the categories we use. For example, if you were especially aware of gender, you might be alert to the differences between the way men and women behave or the way they are treated. If religion played an important part in your life, you might think of members of your faith differently from others. If ethnicity was an important issue for you, you would probably tune in to the differences between members of various ethnic groups. There's nothing wrong with generalizations as long as they are accurate. In fact, it would be impossible to get through life without them.

But when generalizations lose touch with reality, they lead to **stereotyping**—exaggerated generalizations associated with a categorizing system.[2] Stereotypes may be based on a kernel of truth, but they go beyond the facts at hand and make claims that usually have no valid basis.

You can begin to get a sense of your tendency to make generalizations and to stereotype by completing the following sentences:

1. Women are   _____
2. Men are   _____
3. Republicans are   _____
4. Vegetarians are   _____
5. Muslims are   _____
6. Older people are   _____

It's likely that you were able to complete each sentence without much hesitation. Does this mean you were stereotyping? You can answer this question by deciding whether your generalizations fit the three characteristics of stereotypes (we'll use "older people" as an example):

- *You often categorize people on the basis of an easily recognized characteristic.* Age is relatively simple to identify, so if you see someone who appears to be in her eighties, you might quickly categorize her as "elderly."

- *You ascribe a set of characteristics to most or all members of a category.* Based on your (limited) experiences with some elderly relatives, you conclude that older people have trouble hearing and are not mentally alert.

- *You apply the set of characteristics to any member of the group.* When you run into an elderly person at the store, you talk very loudly and slowly. Of course, that can be extremely annoying to energetic and sprightly older people who do not fit your stereotype.

Once we buy into stereotypes, we often seek out isolated behaviors that support our inaccurate beliefs. For example, men and women in conflict often remember only behaviors of the opposite sex that fit their gender stereotypes.[3] They then point to these behaviors—which might not be representative of how the other person typically behaves—as "evidence" to suit their stereotypical and inaccurate claims: "Look! There you go criticizing me again. Typical for a woman!"

Consider how Reese Witherspoon's character in the *Legally Blonde* films both adheres to and refutes common stereotypes.

Stereotypes can plague interracial communication.[4] Surveys of college student attitudes show

MGM/The Kobal Collection/Emerson, Sam

that many blacks characterize whites as "demanding" and "manipulative," whereas many whites characterize blacks as "loud" and "ostentatious." Stereotypes like these can hamper professional relationships as well as personal ones. For example, doctor–patient communication in the United States—particularly between white physicians and minority patients—can suffer from stereotyping on both sides. Physicians may fail to provide important information because they think their patients won't understand, and patients may not ask important questions because they believe their doctors don't have time for them. These kinds of expectations lead to self-fulfilling spirals and poorer health care.[5]

Stereotyping doesn't always arise from bad intentions. In some cases, careless generalizations can grow from good intentions, and even from a little bit of knowledge. For example, knowing that people raised in collectivistic cultures (see pages 54–56 in Chapter 2) tend to conform to group norms may lead you to mistakenly assume that anyone you meet from such a background is likely to be a selfless team player. But not all members of a group are equally collectivistic, or individualistic, for that matter. For example, a close look at Americans of European and Latin descent showed differences within each group.[6] Some Latinos were more independent than

THE INVESTIGATION

John Jonik

some Euro Americans, and vice versa. Moreover, teens in Japan (a traditionally collectivist culture) say they often feel torn between individualism and collectivism, between time-honored traditions and contemporary trends.[7] As our world's "global village" becomes more connected by technology and media, generalizations about specific cultures are likely to become less accurate.

Stereotypes don't always lead to communication problems. If the person with whom you are interacting happens to fit the pattern in your mind, there may be no difficulties. But if your mental image does not happen to match the characteristics of the other person, problems can arise. A fascinating series of experiments on perceptions of prejudice and gender bias illustrates this point.[8] In one phase of the experiments, white and black students were presented with stories in which a prejudicial act might or might not have taken place. For example, a man who has been promised a hotel room over the phone is later denied the room when he shows up in person. Four race combinations were used for each story: white perpetrator/black victim, white perpetrator/white victim, black perpetrator/white victim, and black perpetrator/black victim. In almost all instances, participants were more likely to label white-on-black behavior (white perpetrator and black victim) as prejudice than any other combination.

LOOKING AT DIVERSITY

Christa Kilvington: Socioeconomic Stereotyping

Courtesy of Christa Kilvington

What comes to mind when you hear the description "4.0 college student"? How about when you hear "welfare mom"? Most likely you get two very different mental pictures. Perhaps you imagine those kinds of people as complete opposites. And yet, I am both: A college student with straight-A grades who is also a single mother on public assistance. To some people, the combination doesn't fit. They figure that anyone smart enough to earn a 4.0 GPA shouldn't have ended up on welfare, or that anybody on welfare is probably too dumb and lazy to be in college and have straight-A grades.

The stereotypes people use to classify me shape the way they communicate. Most people who only know me from school and have no idea of my economic situation think of me as intelligent and ambitious—an academic standout. They speak to me formally and respectfully. Those who know me only by my income level—caseworkers, healthcare workers, grocery store clerks—tend to communicate with me in quite a different way. When I go to the welfare office, present my Medicaid card for a prescription, or pay for groceries with food stamps I am often treated as unintelligent, lazy, and dishonest. People speak to me in condescending and disrespectful tones.

Why do some people equate income level with intelligence? Why do they treat me and others differently based on our economic status? Why is it all right to treat people disrespectfully just because they are poor? Stereotypes exist for a reason, but it's important to go beyond them to find out each person's unique story. When you leave your mind open to the possibility that there is more to a person than meets the eye, that is when you grow as a person yourself.

In addition, females were more likely than males, and blacks were more likely than whites, to label an action as prejudiced.

From these results, the researchers conclude that a prototypic or "model" stereotype exists regarding racism (whites oppress blacks, men oppress women, and not the reverse) and that "participants who belong to traditionally oppressed groups (blacks, women) may be more sensitive to potential prejudice." In other words, we select, organize, and interpret behavior in ways that fit our existing notions about others' motives. (See the description of the movie *Crash* on page 118 for an example of how stereotyping can lead to myriad personal and interpersonal problems.)

One way to avoid the kinds of communication problems that come from excessive stereotyping is to decategorize others, giving yourself a chance to treat them as individuals instead of assuming that they possess the same characteristics as every other member of the group to which you assign them.

✔+ INVITATION TO INSIGHT

Exploring Your Biases

You can explore your hidden biases toward race, gender, age, disability, and other issues by taking a series of self-tests online. You can find the link to these tests through your Premium Website for *Looking Out/Looking In.*

The Magic Wand

Quick-change artist extraordinaire,

I whip out my folded cane and change from black man to blind man with a flick of the wrist.

It is a profound metamorphosis

From God gifted wizard of roundball dominating backboards across America,

To God-gifted idiot savant pounding out chart-busters on a cock-eyed whim;

From sociopathic gangbanger with death for eyes

To all seeing soul with saintly spirit;

From rape deranged misogynist to poor motherless child;

From welfare-rich pimp to disability-rich gimp;

And from "white man's burden" to every man's burden.

It is always a profound metamorphosis.

Whether from cursed by man to cursed by God or from scripture condemned to God ordained, my final form is never of my choosing.

I only wield the wand; you are the magician.

—*Lynn Manning*

Photodisc/Getty Images

PUNCTUATION The process of organizing goes beyond our generalized perceptions of people. We also can organize our interactions with others in different ways, and these differing organizational schemas can have a powerful effect on our relationships with others. Communication theorists use the term **punctuation** to describe the determination of causes and effects in a series of interactions.[9] You can begin to understand how punctuation operates by visualizing a running quarrel between a husband and wife. The husband accuses the wife of being too critical, whereas she complains that he is withdrawing from her. Notice that the order in which each partner punctuates this cycle affects how the quarrel looks. The husband begins by blaming the wife: "I withdraw because you're so critical." The wife organizes the situation differently, starting with the husband: "I criticize because you withdraw." After the cycle gets rolling, it is impossible to say which accusation is accurate. The answer depends on how the sentence is punctuated. Figure 3.4 illustrates how this process operates.

Punctuation #1

Nagging ⟶ Withdrawing ⟶ Nagging ⟶ Withdrawing

Punctuation #2

Withdrawing ⟶ Nagging ⟶ Withdrawing ⟶ Nagging

Figure 3.4
The Same Event Can Be Punctuated in More Than One Way

Differing punctuations can lead to a variety of communication problems. Notice how the following situations seem different depending on how they're punctuated:

"I don't like your friend because he never has anything to say."

"He doesn't talk to you because you act like you don't like him."

"I keep talking because you interrupt so much."

"I interrupt because you don't give me a chance to say what's on my mind."

The kind of finger-pointing that goes along with arguing over which punctuation scheme is correct will probably make matters worse. It's far more productive to recognize that a dispute can look different to each party and then move on to the more important question of "What can we do to make things better?"

✔+ SKILL BUILDER

Punctuation Practice

You can appreciate how different punctuation patterns can influence attitudes and behavior by following these directions.

1. Use the format pictured in Figure 3.4 to diagram the following situations:
   a. A father and daughter are growing more and more distant. The daughter withdraws because she interprets her father's coolness as rejection. The father views his daughter's aloofness as a rebuff and withdraws further.
   b. The relationship between two friends is becoming strained. One jokes to lighten up the tension, and the other becomes more tense.
   c. A dating couple is on the verge of breaking up. One partner frequently asks the other to show more affection. The other withdraws physical contact.

2. Identify two punctuating schemes for each of the situations described in step 1. Consider how the differing schemes would affect the way the two people in each situation respond to one another.

Now identify a difficult communication issue in your own life. Punctuate it in two ways: how you would punctuate it and how the other person might punctuate it. Discuss how seeing the issue from the other person's point of view might change the way you communicate as you discuss the issue.

INTERPRETATION

After we have selected and organized our perceptions, we interpret them in a way that makes some sort of sense. **Interpretation** plays a role in virtually every interpersonal act. Is the person who smiles at you across a crowded room interested in romance or simply being polite? Is a friend's kidding a sign of affection or irritation? Should you take an invitation to "drop by any time" literally or not?

Several factors cause us to interpret an event in one way or another:

Degree of involvement with the other person. We sometimes view people with whom we have or seek a relationship more favorably than those whom we observe from a detached perspective.[10] One study revealed how this principle operates in everyday life. A group of male subjects was asked to critique presentations by women who allegedly owned restaurants. Half of these presentations were designed to be competent and half to be incompetent. The men who were told they would be having a casual date with the female speakers judged their presentations—whether competent or not—more highly than those who didn't expect any involvement with the speakers.[11]

Personal experience. What meaning have similar events held? If, for example, you've been gouged by landlords in the past, you might be skeptical about an apartment manager's assurances that careful housekeeping will assure you the refund of your cleaning deposit.

Assumptions about human behavior. "People generally do as little work as possible to get by." "In spite of their mistakes, people are doing the best they can." Beliefs like these will shape the way we interpret another's actions.

Attitudes. The attitudes we hold shape the way we make sense of others' behaviors. For example, what would you think if you overheard one man say "I love you" to another? In one study, people with a high degree of homophobia (the fear of or discrimination against homosexuals) were likely to interpret this comment as an indication that the speaker was gay. Those with lower levels of homophobia were more likely to regard the affectionate statement as platonic rather than romantic.[12]

Expectations. Anticipation shapes interpretations. Suppose you took a class and were told in advance that the instructor is terrific. Would this affect the way you perceive the teacher? Research shows that it almost certainly would. In one study, students who read positive comments about instructors on a website viewed those teachers as more credible and attractive than did students who were not exposed to the same comments.[13] In situations like these and others, our expectations influence our perceptions.

Knowledge. If you know that a friend has just been jilted by a lover or been fired from a job, you'll interpret his aloof behavior differently than you would if you were unaware of what had happened. If you know that an instructor speaks sarcastically to all students, you won't be as likely to take her remarks personally.

Self-concept. When you're feeling insecure, the world is a very different place from the world you experience when you're feeling secure. For example, the recipient's self-concept has proven to be the single greatest factor in determining whether people who are on the receiving end of being teased interpret the teaser's motives as being friendly or hostile, and whether they respond with comfort or defensiveness.[14] The same goes for happiness and sadness or any other opposing emotions. The way we feel about ourselves strongly influences how we interpret others' behavior.

> We don't see things as they are.
> We see things as we are.
>
> —Anaïs Nin

Relational satisfaction. The behavior that seems positive when you are happy with a partner might seem completely different when you are unhappy with a partner. For example, unsatisfied partners in a couple are more likely than satisfied partners to blame one another when things go wrong.[15] They are also more likely to believe that their partners are selfish and have negative intentions. Unhappy spouses are more likely than happy ones to make negative interpretations of their mate's behavior.

Although we have talked about selection, organization, and interpretation separately, the three phases of perception can occur in differing sequences. For example, a parent or babysitter's past interpretations (such as "Jason is a troublemaker") can influence future selections (his behavior becomes especially noticeable) and the organization of events (when there's a fight, the assumption is that Jason started it). As with all communication, perception is an ongoing process in which it is difficult to pin down beginnings and endings.

NEGOTIATION

So far our discussion has focused on the components of perception—selection, organization, and interpretation—that take place in each individual's mind. But perception isn't just a solitary activity: A big part of sense-making occurs between and among people as they influence one another's perceptions and try to achieve a shared perspective. This process is known as **negotiation**.

One way to understand how negotiation operates is to view interpersonal communication as an exchange of stories. Scholars call the stories we use to describe our personal worlds **narratives**.[16] Virtually every interpersonal situation can be described by more than one narrative. These narratives often differ. Ask two quarreling children why they're fighting, and they'll each describe how the other person is responsible for launching the conflict. Likewise, courtrooms are filled with opponents who tell very different narratives about who is the "villain" and who is the "hero." Even happy families have stories that place members in particular roles. (Think of the roles in some families you know: "scatterbrain," "the smart one," "athlete," and so on.) In best-case scenarios, family storytelling can actually enhance perspective-taking and lead to family satisfaction and functioning.[17]

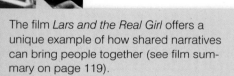

The film *Lars and the Real Girl* offers a unique example of how shared narratives can bring people together (see film summary on page 119).

Sidney Kimmel Entertainment/The Kobal Collection

When our narratives clash with those of others, we can either hang on to our own point of view and refuse to consider anyone else's (usually not productive), or we can try to negotiate a narrative that creates at least some common ground. Shared narratives provide the best chance for smooth communication. For example, romantic partners who celebrate their successful struggles against relational obstacles are happier than those who don't have this shared appreciation.[18] Likewise, couples that agree about the important turning points in their relationships are more satisfied than those who have different views of what incidents were most important.[19]

Shared narratives don't have to be accurate to be powerful. Couples who report being happily married after fifty or more years seem to collude in a relational narrative that doesn't jibe with the facts.[20] They agree that they rarely have conflict, although objective analysis reveals that they have had their share of struggles. Without overtly agreeing to do so, they choose to blame outside forces or unusual circumstances for problems instead of blaming each other. They offer the most charitable interpretations of each other's behavior, believing that their spouse acts with good intentions when things don't go well. They seem willing to forgive, or even forget, transgressions. Communication researcher Judy Pearson evaluates these findings:

> Should we conclude that happy couples have a poor grip on reality? Perhaps they do, but is the reality of one's marriage better known by outside onlookers than by the players themselves? The conclusion is evident. One key to a long happy marriage is to tell yourself and others that you have one and then to behave as though you do![21]

Influences on Perception

Now that we've explored the processes by which we perceive, it's time to look at some of the influences that cause us to select, organize, interpret, and negotiate information.

PHYSIOLOGICAL INFLUENCES

The first set of influences we need to examine involves our physical makeup. Within the wide range of human similarities, each of us perceives the world in a unique way because of physiological factors. In other words, although the same events exist "out there," each of us receives different images because of our unique perceptual hardware. Consider the long list of physiological factors that shapes our views of the world: the senses, age, health and fatigue, hunger, biological cycles, and psychological challenges.

THE SENSES The differences in how each of us sees, hears, tastes, touches, and smells stimuli can affect interpersonal relationships. Consider the following everyday situations:

"Turn down that radio! It's going to make me go deaf."

"It's not too loud. If I turn it down, it will be impossible to hear it."

"It's freezing in here."

"Are you kidding? We'll suffocate if you turn up the heat!"

"Why don't you pass that truck? The highway is clear for a mile."

"I can't see that far, and I'm not going to get us killed."

> To a Laplander, a temperature of fifty-eight degrees may be "hot," to a South African it may be "cold." The statement "It is hot (or cold)" is a statement about what is going on inside one's body. The statement "The temperature is now ninety degrees (or fifty-eight degrees)" is a statement about what is going on outside one's body. . . .
>
> This distinction is by no means trivial. . . . I can never prove to a Laplander that fifty-eight degrees is "cool," but I can prove to him that it is fifty-eight degrees. In other words, there is no paradox in two different people's concluding that the weather is both "hot" and "cold" at the same time. As long as they both know that each of them is talking about a different reality, their conversation can proceed in a fairly orderly way.
>
> *From Neil Postman,* Crazy Talk, Stupid Talk

These disputes aren't just over matters of opinion. The sensory data we receive are different. Differences in vision and hearing are the easiest to recognize, but other differences exist as well. There is evidence that identical foods taste differently to different individuals.[22] Scents that please some people repel others. Likewise, temperature

King Features © Zits Partnership

Simulating Age 85

What does it feel like to be old in America? At the Westminster Thurber Retirement Community here, Heather Ramirez summed it up in two words. "Painful," she said. "Frustrating." Mrs. Ramirez is only 33, but on a recent morning she was taking part in a three-hour training program called Xtreme Aging, designed to simulate the diminished abilities associated with old age.

Along with 15 colleagues and a reporter, Mrs. Ramirez, a social worker at the facility, put on distorting glasses to blur her vision; stuffed cotton balls in her ears to reduce her hearing, and in her nose to dampen her sense of smell; and put on latex gloves with adhesive bands around the knuckles to impede her manual dexterity. Everyone put kernels of corn in their shoes to approximate the aches that come from losing fatty tissue. They had become, in other words, virtual members of the 5.3 million Americans age 85 and older, the nation's fastest-growing age group—the people the staff at the facility work with every day.

As the population in the developing world ages, simulation programs like Xtreme Aging have become a regular part of many nursing or medical school curriculums, and have crept into the corporate world, where knowing what it is like to be elderly increasingly means better understanding one's customers or even employees—how to design

Tetra Images/Jupiter Images

signs or instrument panels, how to make devices more usable.

"I must say, you look lovely," said Vicki Rosebrook, executive director of the Macklin Intergenerational Institute in Findlay, Ohio, which developed Xtreme Aging as a sensitivity training program for schools, churches, workplaces and other groups that have contact with the elderly.

Then Dr. Rosebrook put the group through a series of routine tasks, including buttoning a shirt, finding a number in a telephone book, dialing a cellphone and folding and unfolding a map. The result was a domestic obstacle course. Some tasks were difficult, some impossible. The type in the telephone book appeared microscopic, the buttons on the cellphone even smaller. And forget about refolding a map or handling coins from a zippered wallet.

Dr. Rosebrook told the group an anecdote about being in a department store behind a slow-moving older woman, when an impatient customer behind her called the woman a "Q-Tip head."

"The next time you're in line at the grocery store and you're thinking, 'You old geezer, hurry up,' just think about how this felt," she said.

John Leland

variations that leave some of us uncomfortable are inconsequential to others. Recognizing these differences won't eliminate them, but it will make it easier to remember that the other person's preferences aren't crazy, just different.

AGE   Older people often view the world differently from younger ones, because they have a greater scope and number of experiences. There are also developmental differences that shape perceptions. Swiss psychologist Jean Piaget described a series of stages that children pass through on their way to adulthood.[23] According to Piaget, younger children are incapable of performing mental feats that are natural to the rest of us. Until they approach the age of seven, for example, they aren't able to take another person's point of view. This fact helps explain why children often seem egocentric, selfish, and uncooperative. A parent's exasperated plea, "Can't you see I'm too tired to play?" just won't make sense to a four-year-old who is full of energy and imagines that everyone else must feel the same way.

HEALTH AND FATIGUE   Recall the last time you came down with a cold, flu, or some other ailment. Do you remember how different you felt? You probably had much less energy. It's likely that you felt less sociable and that your thinking was slower than usual. These kinds of changes have a strong impact on how you relate to others. It's good to realize that someone else may be behaving differently because of illness. In the same way, it's important to let others know when you feel ill so that they can give you the understanding you need.

Just as being ill can affect your relationships, so can being overly tired. Again it's important to recognize the fact that you or someone else may behave differently when fatigued. Trying to deal with important issues at such a time can get you into trouble.

HUNGER   People often get grumpy when they haven't eaten and get sleepy after stuffing themselves. Several physiological changes occur as we eat and become hungry again. Research confirms our own experience that being hungry (and getting grumpy) or having overeaten (and getting tired) affects how we interact with others. In one study, teenagers who reported that their family did not get enough food to eat were almost three times as likely to have been suspended from school, almost twice as likely to have difficulty getting along with others, and four times as likely to have no friends.[24]

BIOLOGICAL CYCLES   Are you a "morning person" or a "night person"? Most of us can answer this question easily, and there's a good physiological reason behind our answer. Each of us is in a daily cycle in which all sorts of changes constantly occur, including body temperature, sexual drive, alertness, tolerance to stress, and mood.[25] Most of these changes are caused by hormonal cycles. For instance, adrenal hormones, which affect feelings of stress, are secreted at higher rates during some hours. In the same manner, the male and female sex hormones enter our systems at variable rates. We often aren't conscious of these changes, but they surely influence the way we relate to one another. After we're aware that our own daily cycles and those of others govern our feelings and behavior, it becomes possible to manage our lives so that we deal with important issues at the most effective times.

✔+ INVITATION TO INSIGHT

New Body, New Perspective

You can get a clearer idea of how physiology influences perception by trying the following exercise.

1 Choose one of the following situations:
   a.   An evening in a singles bar.
   b.   A volleyball game.
   c.   A doctor's physical examination.

2 How would the event you chose seem different if:
   a.   Your eyesight were much worse (or better).

   b.   You had a hearing loss.
   c.   You were eight inches taller (or shorter).
   d.   You were coming down with a serious cold.
   e.   You were a member of the other sex.
   f.   You were ten years older (or younger).
   g.   You had AD/HD.

PSYCHOLOGICAL CHALLENGES   Some differences in perception are rooted in neurology. For instance, people with AD/HD (attention-deficit/hyperactivity disorder) are easily distracted from tasks and have difficulty delaying gratification. It's easy to imagine how those with AD/HD might find a long lecture boring and tedious, while other audience members are fascinated by the same lecture. People with bipolar disorder experience significant mood swings in which their perceptions of events, friends, and even family members shift dramatically. The National Institute of Mental Health estimates that between five and seven million Americans are affected by these two disorders alone—and many other psychological conditions influence people's perceptions.[26] It's important to remember that when others see and respond to the world differently than we do, there may be causes beyond what we immediately recognize.

CULTURAL DIFFERENCES

So far you have seen how physical factors can make the world a different place for each of us. But there's another kind of perceptual gap that often blocks communication—the gap between people from different backgrounds. Every culture has its own worldview, its own way of looking at the world. Keeping in mind these differing cultural perspectives can be a good way of learning more about both ourselves and others, but at times it's easy to forget that people everywhere don't see things the way we do.

The power of culture to shape perceptions was demonstrated in studies more than fifty years ago exploring the domination of vision in one eye over the other.[27] Researchers used a binocular-like device that projects different images to each eye. The subjects were twelve natives of the United States and twelve Mexicans. Each was presented with ten pairs of photographs, each pair containing one picture from U.S. culture (e.g., a baseball game) and one from Mexican culture (e.g., a bullfight). After viewing each pair of images, the subjects reported what they saw. The results clearly indicated the power of culture to influence perceptions: Subjects had a strong tendency to focus on the image from their own background.

The range of cultural differences is wide. In Middle Eastern countries, personal scents play an important role in interpersonal relationships. Arabs consistently breathe on people when they talk. As anthropologist Edward Hall explains:

> To smell one's friend is not only nice, but desirable, for to deny him your breath is to act ashamed. Americans, on the other hand, trained as they are not to breathe in people's faces, automatically communicate shame in trying to be polite. Who would expect that when our highest diplomats are putting on their best manners they are also communicating shame? Yet this is what occurs constantly, because diplomacy is not only "eyeball to eyeball" but breath to breath.[28]

Even beliefs about the very value of talk differ from one culture to another.[29] Western cultures view talk as desirable and use it for social purposes as well as for task performance. Silence has a negative value in these cultures. It is likely to be interpreted as lack of interest, unwillingness to communicate, hostility, anxiety, shyness, or a sign of interpersonal incompatibility. Westerners are uncomfortable with silence, which they find embarrassing and awkward.

On the other hand, Asian cultures perceive talk differently. For thousands of years, Asian cultures have discouraged the expression of thoughts and feelings. Silence is valued, as Taoist sayings indicate: "In much talk there is great weariness," or "One who speaks does not know; one who knows does not speak." Unlike most North Americans, who are uncomfortable with silence, Japanese and Chinese believe that remaining quiet is the proper state when there is nothing to be said. In Asian cultures, a talkative person is often considered a show-off or insincere.

It's easy to see how these different views of speech and silence can lead to communication problems when people from different cultures meet. Both the talkative American and the silent Asian are behaving in ways they believe are proper, yet each views the other with disapproval and mistrust. This may require them to recognize and deal with their **ethnocentrism**—the attitude that one's own culture is superior to others. An ethnocentric person thinks—either privately or openly—that anyone who does not belong to his or her in-group is somehow strange, wrong, or even inferior. Travel writer Rick Steves describes how an ethnocentric point of view can interfere with respect for other cultural practices:

> ... we [Americans] consider ourselves very clean and commonly criticize other cultures as dirty. In the bathtub we soak, clean, and rinse, all in the same water. (We would never wash our dishes that way.) A Japanese visitor, who uses clean water for each step, might find our way of bathing strange or even disgusting. Many cultures spit in public and blow their nose right onto the street. They couldn't imagine doing that into a small cloth, called a hanky, and storing that in their pocket to be used again and again. Too often we think of the world in terms of a pyramid of "civilized" (us) on the top and "primitive" groups on the bottom. If we measured things differently (maybe according to stress, loneliness, heart attacks, hours spent in traffic jams, or family togetherness) things stack up differently.[30]

The way we communicate with strangers can reflect ethnocentric thinking. Author Anne Fadiman explains why Hmong immigrants from the mountains of Laos prefer their traditional shamanistic healers, called *txiv neeb*, to American doctors. Notice that both perspectives make sense, and that neither the American physicians nor the Hmong immigrants were able to get beyond their familiar set of perceptions to see the encounter from the other culture's point of view:

> A *txiv neeb* might spend as much as eight hours in a sick person's home; doctors forced their patients, no matter how weak they were, to come to the hospital, and then might spend only twenty minutes at their bedsides. *Txiv neebs* were polite and never needed to ask questions; doctors asked about their sexual and excretory habits. *Txiv neebs* could render an immediate diagnosis; doctors often demanded samples of blood (or even urine or feces, which they liked to keep in little bottles), took X rays, and waited for days for the results to come back from the laboratory—and then, after all that, sometimes they were unable to identify the cause of the problem. *Txiv neebs* never undressed their patients; doctors asked patients to take off all their clothes, and sometimes dared to put their fingers inside women's vaginas. *Txiv neebs* knew that to treat the body without treating the soul was an act of patent folly; doctors never even mentioned the soul.[31]

It isn't necessary to travel overseas to encounter differing cultural perspectives. Within this country there are many subcultures, and the members of each one have backgrounds that cause them to see things in different ways. Failure to recognize these differences can lead to unfortunate and unnecessary misunderstandings. For example, an uninformed Anglo teacher or police officer might interpret the downcast expression of a Latina as a sign of avoidance, or even dishonesty, when in fact this is the proper behavior in her culture for a female being addressed by an older man. To make direct eye contact in such a case would be considered undue brashness or even a sexual come-on.

Along with ethnicity, geography also can influence perception. A fascinating series of studies revealed that climate and geographic latitude are remarkably accurate predictors of communication predispositions.[32] People living in southern latitudes of the United States are more socially isolated, less tolerant of ambiguity, higher in self-esteem, more likely to touch others, and more likely to verbalize their thoughts and feelings. This sort of finding helps explain why communicators who travel from one part of a country to another find that their old patterns of communicating don't work as well in their new location. A southerner whose relatively talkative, high-touch style seemed completely normal at home might be viewed as pushy and aggressive in a new northern home.

It's encouraging to know that open-minded communicators can overcome preexisting stereotypes and learn to appreciate people from different backgrounds as individuals. In one study, college students who were introduced to strangers from different cultural backgrounds developed attitudes about their new conversational partners based more on their personal behavior than on preexisting expectations about how people from those backgrounds might behave.[33]

SOCIAL ROLES

So far you have seen how physiological and cultural differences can affect communication. Along with these differences, another set of perceptual factors can lead to communication difficulties. From almost the time we're born, each of us is indirectly taught a whole set of roles that we'll be expected to play. In one sense this set of prescribed parts is necessary, because it enables a society to function smoothly and provides the security that comes from knowing what's expected of you. But in another sense, having roles defined in advance can lead to wide gaps in understanding. When roles become unquestioned and rigid, people tend to see the world from their own viewpoint, having no experiences that show them how other people see it. Naturally, in such a situation communication suffers.

GENDER ROLES Although people use the terms *sex* and *gender* as if they were identical, there is an important difference. *Sex* refers to biological characteristics of a male or female, whereas *gender* refers to the social and psychological dimensions of masculine and feminine behavior. A large body of research shows that males and females do perceive the world differently, for reasons ranging from genes to neurology to hormones.[34] However, even cognitive researchers who focus on biological differences between males and females acknowledge that societal gender roles and stereotypes affect perception dramatically.[35]

Gender roles are socially approved ways that men and women are expected to behave. Children learn the importance of gender roles by watching other people and by being exposed to media, as well as by receiving reinforcement.[36] After members of a society learn these customary roles, they tend to regard violations as unusual—or even undesirable.

Some theorists have suggested that stereotypical masculine and feminine behaviors are not opposite poles of a single continuum, but rather two separate sets of behavior.[37] With this view, an individual can act in a masculine manner or a feminine manner or exhibit both types of characteristics. The male–female dichotomy, then, is

Table 3.1
Gender Roles

	Male	Female
Masculine	Masculine males	Masculine females
Feminine	Feminine males	Feminine females
Androgynous	Androgynous males	Androgynous females
Undifferentiated	Undifferentiated males	Undifferentiated females

replaced with four psychological sex types: masculine, feminine, **androgynous** (combining masculine and feminine traits), and undifferentiated (neither masculine nor feminine). Combining the four psychological sex types with the traditional physiological sex types produces the eight categories listed in Table 3.1.

Each of these eight psychological sex types perceives interpersonal relationships differently. For example, masculine males may be likely to see their interpersonal relationships as opportunities for competitive interaction, as opportunities to win something. Feminine females probably see their interpersonal relationships as opportunities to be nurturing, to express their feelings and emotions. Androgynous males and females, on the other hand, differ little in their perceptions of their interpersonal relationships.

Androgynous individuals tend to see their relationships as opportunities to behave in a variety of ways, depending on the nature of the relationships themselves, the context in which a particular relationship takes place, and the myriad other variables affecting what might constitute appropriate behavior. These variables are usually ignored by the sex-typed masculine males and feminine females, who have a smaller repertoire of behaviors.

OCCUPATIONAL ROLES   The kind of work we do often influences our view of the world. Imagine five people taking a walk through the park. One, a botanist, is fascinated by the variety of trees and other plants. Another, a zoologist, is looking for interesting

✔+ INVITATION TO INSIGHT

Role Reversal

Walk a mile in another person's shoes. Find a group that is foreign to you, and try to become a member of it for a while.

1 If you're down on the police, see if your local department has a ride-along program where you can spend several hours on patrol with one or two officers.

2 If you think the present state of education is a mess, become a teacher yourself. Maybe an instructor will give you the chance to plan one or more classes.

3 If you're a political conservative, try getting involved in a progressive organization; if you're a progressive, check out the conservatives.

Whatever group you join, try to become part of it as best you can. Don't just observe. Get into the philosophy of your new role and see how it feels. You may find that all those weird people aren't so weird after all.

ON THE JOB

Changing Roles, Changing Perceptions

An old adage says, "When you're a fence painter, all you see are fences." That saying reflects a truth verified by social science: Occupational roles can alter the way we view others, sometimes in harmful ways.

Perhaps the most dramatic illustration of how jobs can shape perception occurred in a classic study by Stanford psychologist Philip Zimbardo.[a] He recruited a group of middle-class, well-educated young men, randomly assigning half of them to serve as "guards" in a mock prison. He issued the guards uniforms, handcuffs, whistles, and billy clubs. The remaining subjects became "prisoners" and were placed in rooms with metal bars, bucket toilets, and cots.

Zimbardo let the guards establish their own regulations for the inmates. The rules were tough: No talking during meals, rest periods, or after lights-out. Head counts at 2:30 A.M. Troublemakers received short rations.

Within a short time the experiment had become reality for both prisoners and guards. Several inmates developed stomach cramps and lapsed into uncontrollable weeping. Others suffered from headaches, and one broke out in a head-to-toe rash after his request for early "parole" was denied by the guards.

The experiment was scheduled to go on for two weeks, but after six days Zimbardo realized that the simulation had become too intense. "I knew by then that they were thinking like prisoners and not like people," he said. "If we were able to demonstrate that pathological behavior could be produced in so short a time, think of what damage is being done in 'real' prisons. . . ."

Rhetorician Kenneth Burke and others have called the tendency to view the world through the lens of one's job an "occupational psychosis."[b] Most role-based perceptions are less dramatic than the prison experiment, but they still create problems. Workers who deal with the public every day can grow cynical and unsympathetic, viewing their clientele as unreasonable and demanding. Bosses who see the big picture may come to regard employees as lazy and self-centered, and workers who haven't been managers may regard supervisors as unappreciative and power hungry.

The best antidote to occupational psychosis is to step outside one's role and regard others as you would independent of your job—or try the role-reversal exercise described in the Invitation to Insight on page 99.

animals. The third, a meteorologist, keeps an eye on the sky, noticing changes in the weather. The fourth companion, a psychologist, is totally unaware of nature, instead concentrating on the interaction among the people in the park. The fifth person, being a pickpocket, quickly takes advantage of the others' absorption to make some money. There are two lessons in this little scenario. The first, of course, is to watch your wallet carefully. The second is that our occupational roles shape our perceptions.

Even within the same occupational setting, the different roles that participants have can affect their perceptions. Consider a typical college classroom, for example. The experiences of the instructor and students often are dissimilar. Having dedicated a large part of their lives to their work, most instructors see their subject matter—whether French literature, physics, or communication—as vitally important. Students who are taking the course to satisfy a general education requirement may view the subject differently: maybe as one of many obstacles that stand between them and a degree, maybe as a chance to meet new people. Another difference centers on the amount of knowledge possessed by the parties. To an instructor who has taught the course many times, the material probably seems extremely simple, but to students encountering it for the first time, it may seem strange and confusing. We don't need to spell out the interpersonal strains and stresses that come from such differing perceptions (see the On The Job box on page 100 for other examples of stresses and strains arising from occupational roles).

RELATIONAL ROLES   Think back to the "Who am I?" list you made in Chapter 2 (page 40). It's likely your list included roles you play in relation to others: daughter, roommate, husband, friend, and so on. Roles like these don't just define who you are—they also affect your perception.

Take, for example, the role of parent. As most new mothers and fathers will attest, having a child alters the way they see the world. They might perceive their crying baby as a helpless soul in need of comfort, while nearby strangers have a less charitable appraisal. As the child grows, parents often pay more attention to the messages in the child's environment. One father we know said he never noticed how much football fans curse and swear until he took his six-year-old to a game with him. In other words, his role as father affected what he heard and how he interpreted it.

The roles involved in romantic love can also dramatically affect perception. These roles have many labels: partner, spouse, boyfriend/girlfriend, sweetheart, and so on. There are times when your affinity biases the way you perceive the object of your affection. You may see your sweetheart as more attractive than other people do, and perhaps you overlook some faults that others notice.[38] Your romantic role can also change the way you view others. One study found that when people are in love, they view other romantic candidates as less attractive than they normally would.[39]

Perhaps the most telltale sign of the effect of "love goggles" is when they come off. Many people have experienced breaking up with a romantic partner and wondering later, "What did I ever see in that person?" The answer—at least in part—is that you saw what your relational role led you to see.

Common Tendencies in Perception

By now it's obvious that many factors affect the way we interpret the world. Social scientists use the term **attribution** to describe the process of attaching meaning to behavior. We attribute meaning both to our own actions and to the actions of others, but we often use different yardsticks. Research has uncovered several perceptual tendencies that can lead to attribution errors.[40]

WE JUDGE OURSELVES MORE CHARITABLY THAN OTHERS

In an attempt to convince ourselves and others that the positive face we show to the world is true, we tend to judge ourselves in the most generous terms possible. Social scientists have labeled this tendency the **self-serving bias**.[41] On the one hand, when others suffer, we often blame the problem on their personal qualities. On the other hand, when we suffer, we blame the problem on forces outside ourselves. Consider a few examples:

> I have heard students say things like, "It was John's fault, his speech was so confusing nobody could have understood it." Then, two minutes later, the same student remarked, "It wasn't my fault, what I said could not have been clearer. John must be stupid." Poor John! He was blamed when he was the sender and when he was the receiver. John's problem was that he was the other person, and that's who is always at fault.
>
> —*Stephen W. King*

When *they* botch a job, we might think they weren't listening well or trying hard enough; when *we* botch a job, the problem was unclear directions or not enough time.

"The truth is, Cauldwell, we never see ourselves as others see us."

When *he* lashes out angrily, we say he's being moody or too sensitive; when *we* lash out angrily, it's because of the pressure we've been under.

When *she* gets caught speeding, we say she should have been more careful; when *we* get caught speeding, we deny that we were driving too fast or we say, "Everybody does it."

When *she* uses profanity, it's because of a flaw in her character; when *we* swear, it's because the situation called for it.[42]

WE CLING TO FIRST IMPRESSIONS

Labeling people according to our first impressions is an inevitable part of the perception process. These labels are a way of making interpretations: "She seems cheerful." "He seems sincere." "They sound awfully conceited." If such first impressions are accurate, they can be useful ways of deciding how to respond best to people in the future. Problems arise, however, when the labels we attach are inaccurate; after we form an opinion of someone, we tend to hang on to it and make any conflicting information fit our opinion.

Social scientists have coined the term **halo effect** to describe the tendency to form an overall positive impression of a person on the basis of one positive characteristic. Most typically, the positive impression comes from physical attractiveness, which can lead people to attribute all sorts of other virtues to the good-looking person.[43] For example, employment interviewers rate mediocre but attractive job applicants higher than their less attractive candidates.[44] And once employers form positive impressions, they often ask questions that confirm their image of the applicant.[45] For example, when an interviewer forms a positive impression, she might ask leading questions aimed at supporting her positive views ("What lessons did you learn from that setback?"), interpret answers in a positive light ("Ah, taking time away from school to travel was a good idea!"), encourage the applicant ("Good point!"), and sell the company's virtues ("I think you would like working here"). Likewise, applicants who create a negative first impression are operating under a cloud that may be impossible to dispel—a phenomenon sometimes referred to as "the devil effect."[46]

The power of first impressions is also important in personal relationships. A study of college roommates found that those who had positive initial impressions of each other were likely to have positive subsequent interactions, manage their conflicts constructively, and continue living together.[47] The converse was also true: Roommates who got off to a bad start tended to spiral negatively. This reinforces the wisdom and importance of the old adage, "You never get a second chance to make a first impression."

Given the almost unavoidable tendency to form first impressions, the best advice we can give is to keep an open mind and to be willing to change your opinion as events prove it mistaken.

WE ASSUME THAT OTHERS ARE SIMILAR TO US

In Chapter 2 you read one example of this principle: that people with low self-esteem imagine that others view them unfavorably, whereas people with high self-esteem imagine that others view them favorably, too. The frequently mistaken assumption that others' views are similar to our own applies in a wide range of situations:

- You've heard a slightly raunchy joke that you think is pretty funny. You assume that it won't offend a somewhat straitlaced friend. It does.

- You've been bothered by an instructor's tendency to get off the subject during lectures. If you were an instructor, you'd want to know if anything you were doing was creating problems for your students, so you decide that your instructor will probably be grateful for some constructive criticism. Unfortunately, you're wrong.

- You lost your temper with a friend a week ago and said some things you regret. In fact, if someone said those things to you, you'd consider the relationship finished. Imagining that your friend feels the same way, you avoid making contact. In fact, your friend has avoided you because she thinks *you're* the one who wants to end things.

Examples like these show that others don't always think or feel the way we do and that assuming that similarities exist can lead to problems.[48] How can you find out the other person's real position? Sometimes by asking directly, sometimes by checking with others, and sometimes by making an educated guess after you've thought the matter out. All these alternatives are better than simply assuming that everyone would react as you do.

WE ARE INFLUENCED BY THE OBVIOUS

The error of being influenced by what is most obvious is understandable. As you read at the beginning of this chapter, we select stimuli from our environment that are noticeable: intense, repetitious, unusual, or otherwise attention-grabbing. The problem is that the most obvious factor is not necessarily the only one—or the most significant one for an event. For example:

- When two children (or adults, for that matter) fight, it may be a mistake to blame the one who lashes out first. Perhaps the other one was at least equally responsible, teasing or refusing to cooperate.

- You might complain about an acquaintance whose malicious gossiping or arguing has become a bother, forgetting that by putting up with such behavior in the past you have been at least partially responsible.

- You might blame an unhappy working situation on the boss, overlooking other factors beyond her control, such as a change in the economy, the policy of higher management, or demands of customers or other workers.

Perception Checking

Serious problems can arise when people treat interpretations as if they were matters of fact. Like most people, you probably resent others jumping to conclusions about the reasons for your behavior.

"Why are you mad at me?" (Who said you were?)

"What's the matter with you?" (Who said anything was the matter?)

"Come on now. Tell the truth." (Who said you were lying?)

As you'll learn in Chapter 10, even if your interpretation is correct, a dogmatic, mind-reading statement is likely to generate defensiveness. The skill of **perception checking** provides a better way to handle your interpretations.[49]

I'm Not Who You Think I Am

Being confused for every other Asian woman used to be maddening—until I fell into the same trap.

I'm tired of being confused with people who really, objectively, don't look like me. I am short, and have been mistaken for people who are quite tall. I tend to wear jeans and loose sweaters; I have been mistaken for people who wear fur and tulle. I don't wear makeup—well, I could go on and on. Given the vast array of those I've been told I look exactly like who have neither my facial structure nor my body shape nor my demeanor, I have always felt justified in assuming that people who make these mistakes are, at some level, racist. Meaning that when they see me, their normal powers of observation switch off so that the only information their brains receive is: Asian. These people see a type, not a person.

But then.

My husband and I host an annual barbecue for the associates at his law firm. This group changes every few years, so it never seems worthwhile to really get to know them, and I must confess that they are virtually indistinguishable to me except that each year's batch seems younger than the one before. Once a year, though, I make an effort to be pleasant. I know they work hard, and I appreciate what they do.

Among those who were to attend last time were a young couple who stood out in my mind because they had brought their infant to the prior year's party, and also because the wife was Korean-American, like me. I remembered having had a conversation with her, and that she was very nice.

When the guests started to arrive, I shook hands with and smiled at a half-dozen or so people, and then I noticed the Korean-American woman. I was somewhat relieved to see someone I had met before, so I approached her in a friendly way and said, "Hello! So you're taking a little holiday from the baby today?"

She sort of nodded but did not say anything, and that instant was all it took for me to realize she was a different

Scout Tufankjian/Polaris

Asian-American woman. One who did not have a baby. I also realized that she looked nothing like the woman I had mistaken her for. I believe I muttered something under my breath, so that maybe she would think I was just crazy, as bosses' wives often are. Or drunk, perhaps. Mostly I thought: thank God I'm Asian. Whatever else she may think of me, at least she can't accuse me of being racist.

A few months after that I was with my 10-year-old daughter at a horse show. Her hair, like all the other young riders' hair, was in two braids, as dictated by horse-show convention. We were waiting in a very slow line to buy soft drinks. Bored, I left the line to pick up a magazine from a nearby table. I leafed through it and walked back, looking down at a picture I had found. I nudged my daughter to show her the picture. She didn't respond, so I nudged her again, and that was when I saw it was not my daughter I was nudging, but a different Asian child.

Even though I knew that this could not mean I was a racist—racist toward my own daughter?—I was mortified nonetheless.

"Oh, I'm sorry! You all look the same from the top!" I said.

By which I meant, all little girls with dark pigtails look similar to a taller person who is not really paying attention. The girl's mother smiled pleasantly enough. To further complicate the matter, at least in my roiling brain, the mother was Caucasian. I wondered, confusedly, whether this changed the situation. If she and I were not from the same ethnic group, did this mean I really was a racist?

A plea, then, for all of us to take the time to look more carefully. For those who see the race and not the individual: look harder. And for those who, like me, may be hypersensitive after years of not being properly seen, keep in mind that while there are people who are racist, many others are merely distracted, overeager, careless, tired, old. We, the thin-skinned, also need to avoid applying the easy label.

Carol Paik

ELEMENTS OF PERCEPTION CHECKING

A complete perception check has three parts:

1. A description of the behavior you noticed
2. At least two possible interpretations of the behavior
3. A request for clarification about how to interpret the behavior

Perception checks for the preceding three examples would look like this:

"Of course I care about how you imagined I thought you perceived I wanted you to feel."

> "When you stomped out of the room and slammed the door," (*behavior*) "I wasn't sure whether you were mad at me" (*first interpretation*) "or just in a hurry." (*second interpretation*) "How *did* you feel?" (*request for clarification*)

> "You haven't laughed much in the last couple of days." (*behavior*) "It makes me wonder whether something's bothering you" (*first interpretation*) "or whether you're just feeling quiet." (*second interpretation*) "What's up?" (*request for clarification*)

> "You said you really liked the job I did." (*behavior*) "On the other hand, there was something about your voice that made me think you may not like it." (*first interpretation*) "Maybe it's just my imagination, though." (*second interpretation*) "How do you really feel?" (*request for clarification*)

Perception checking is a tool for helping you understand others accurately instead of assuming that your first interpretation is correct. Because its goal is mutual understanding, perception checking is a cooperative approach to communication. Besides leading to more accurate perceptions, it minimizes defensiveness by preserving the other person's face. Instead of saying, in effect, "I know what you're thinking . . . ," a perception check takes the more respectful approach that states or implies, "I know I'm not qualified to judge you without some help."

PERCEPTION CHECKING CONSIDERATIONS

Like every communication skill outlined in *Looking Out/Looking In*, perception checking isn't a mechanical formula that will work in every situation. As you develop the ability to check your perceptions, consider the following factors in deciding when and how to use this approach.

COMPLETENESS Sometimes a perception check won't need all of the parts listed earlier to be effective:

> "You haven't dropped by lately. Is anything the matter?" (*single interpretation combined with request for clarification*)

> "I can't tell whether you're kidding me about being cheap or if you're serious." (*behavior combined with interpretations*) "Are you mad at me?"

> "Are you sure you don't mind driving? I can use a ride if it's no trouble, but I don't want to take you out of your way." (*no need to describe behavior*)

Sometimes even the most skimpy perception check—a simple question like "What's going on?"—will do the job. You might also rely on other people to help you make sense

✔+ IN REAL LIFE

Perception Checking in Everyday Life

Perception checking only works if it is sincere and fits your personal style. The following examples show how perception checking sounds in everyday life and may help you find ways to use it when you are faced with ambiguous messages.

My Texting Student

I'm a teacher who likes to have my class's complete attention when I'm talking. During a lecture last week, one of my students was typing away on her PDA, fast and furiously. I assumed she was texting a friend, so I asked her to put the device away immediately. She looked a bit hurt, but she slipped it into her bookbag.

After class, the student approached me and said she wasn't using her PDA to talk with friends—she was using it to take notes. I found myself doubting the student until she pulled out the PDA and showed me several screens of information she had taken from my lecture.

I was really embarrassed and offered a sincere apology. A perception check sure would have helped in this case. I could have pulled her aside after class and said, "I noticed you were typing on your PDA a lot during my lecture. I assumed you were using it for personal reasons, but maybe you were just taking class notes. Could you please let me know, because your attention in class means a lot to me."

To be honest, I think a lot of students do use PDAs in class for personal reasons—but I want to be careful not to jump to that conclusion without checking the facts.

My Boss's Jokes

I get confused by my boss's sense of humor. Sometimes he jokes just to be funny, but other times he uses humor to make a point without coming right out and saying what's on his mind. Last week he was talking about the upcoming work schedule and he said with a laugh, "I own you all weekend!" I have a life besides work, so his comment left me worried.

I used a perception check to figure out what he meant: "Brad, when you told me 'I own you all weekend,' I wasn't sure whether you were kidding or whether you really expect me to work Saturday and Sunday. Were you serious?"

He kind of smiled and said, "No, I was just kidding. You only have to work Saturday and Sunday."

I still couldn't be sure whether or not he was serious, so I checked again: "You're kidding, right?"

My boss replied, "Well, I do need you at least one day, and two would be better." Once I figured out what he really meant, we worked out a schedule that had me work Friday evening and Saturday morning, which gave me the time off I needed.

If I hadn't used the perception check, I would have wound up worrying about being tied up all weekend, and getting mad at my boss for no good reason. I'm glad I spoke up.

My Nervous Friend

My friend and I have been planning to spend a month in Europe next summer. We've had fun surfing the

of confusing behavior: "Rachelle has been awfully quiet lately. Do you know what's up?" A complete perception check is most necessary when the risk of sounding judgmental is highest.

NONVERBAL CONGRUENCY   A perception check can succeed only if your nonverbal behavior reflects the open-mindedness of your words. An accusing tone of voice or a hostile glare will contradict the sincerely worded request for clarification, suggesting that you have already made up your mind about the other person's intentions.

CULTURAL RULES   The straightforward approach of perception checking has the best chance of working in what Chapter 5 identifies as *low-context cultures*: ones in which members use language as directly as possible. The dominant cultures of North America and Western Europe fit into this category, and members of these groups are most likely to appreciate the kind of straight talking that perception checking embodies. Members

web for sites and getting the advice of people we know who have gone to places we want to visit.

We decided it would be simpler for one of us to handle all the reservations, and that's been my job. I really don't mind doing this, except my friend started to interrogate me about every detail. "Did you lock in the airfare?" "Did you remember to get the Eurail passes?" "What about a hotel in Rome?" "What about phone cards so we can call home?"

I kept my growing irritation inside, but finally it got to be more than I could handle. Fortunately, I used a perception check instead of attacking my friend: "Look, you've been asking me about every detail of our plan, even though I told you I would take care of everything. Do you think I'm going to mess up the planning? Do you want to take over the planning? What's going on?"

When I confronted her, my friend was embarrassed. She said she trusts me completely, but she is so excited that she has a hard time controlling herself. She told me that having the reservations made will leave her feeling like the trip is more of a reality and less of a dream. Since we've talked, my friend still asks me how the plans are coming. But now that I know why she is so insistent, I find it more amusing than annoying.

My Dad's Affection
My father and I have a great relationship. A while back I picked him up at the airport after a week-long business trip and a long cross-country flight. On the

way home, he was quiet—not his usual self. He said he was exhausted, which I understood. When we got home, he brightened up and started joking and playing with my younger brother. This left me feeling unhappy. I thought to myself, "Why is he so happy to see my brother when he hardly said a word to me?" I didn't say anything at the time. The next day I found myself feeling resentful toward my dad, and it showed. He said, "What's up with you?" But I was too embarrassed to say anything.

After learning this approach in class, I tried a perception check. I said, "Dad—when you were quiet on the way home after your business trip and then you perked up when you got home and saw Jaime, I wasn't sure what was up. I thought maybe you were happier to see him than me, or that maybe I'm imagining things. How come you said you were tired with me and then you perked up with Jaime?"

My dad felt awful. He said he was tired in the car, but once he got back to the house he was glad to be home and felt like a new man. I was too wrapped up in my mind to consider this alternative. Because I didn't use a perception check, I was unhappy and I started an unnecessary fight.

Using your Premium Website for Looking Out/ Looking In, *access "In Real Life Communication Scenarios" and then select "Perception Checking in Everyday Life" to watch and analyze video examples of perception checking.*

of *high-context cultures* (more common in Latin America and Asia), however, value social harmony over directness. High-context communicators are more likely to regard candid approaches like perception checking as potentially embarrassing, preferring instead less-direct ways of understanding one another. Thus, a "let's get this straight" perception check that might work well with a Euro American manager who was raised to value directness could be a serious mistake with a Mexican American or Asian American boss who has spent most of his or her life in a high-context culture.

FACE SAVING Along with clarifying meaning, perception checking can sometimes be a face-saving way to raise an issue without directly threatening or attacking the other person. Consider these examples:

"Are you planning on doing those dishes later, or did you forget that it's your turn?"
"Am I boring you, or do you have something else on your mind?"

In the first case, you might have been quite confident that the other person had no intention of doing the dishes, and in the second that the other person was bored. Even so, a perception check is a less threatening way of pointing out their behavior than direct confrontation. Remember: One element of competent communication is the ability to choose the best option from a large repertoire, and perception checking can be a useful strategy at times.

✔+ SKILL BUILDER

Perception Checking Practice

Practice your perception-checking ability by developing three-part verifications for the following situations:

1. You made what you thought was an excellent suggestion to an instructor. The instructor looked uninterested but said she would check on the matter right away. Three weeks have passed, and nothing has changed.

2. A neighbor and good friend has not responded to your "Good morning" for three days in a row. This person is usually friendly.

3. You haven't received the usual weekly phone call from the folks back home in over a month. The last time you spoke, you had an argument about where to spend the holidays.

4. An old friend with whom you have shared the problems of your love life for years has recently changed behavior when around you.: The formerly casual hugs and kisses have become longer and stronger, and the occasions where you "accidentally" brush up against each other have become more frequent.

Empathy, Cognitive Complexity, and Communication

Perception checking is a valuable tool for clarifying ambiguous messages, but ambiguity isn't the only cause of perceptual problems. Sometimes we understand what people mean without understanding why they believe as they do. At times like this, we are short on the vital ability to empathize.

EMPATHY

Empathy is the ability to re-create another person's perspective, to experience the world from the other's point of view. It may be impossible to ever experience another person's perspective completely, but with enough effort we can certainly gain a better idea of how the world appears to him or her. As we'll use the term here, empathy involves three dimensions.[50] In one dimension, empathy involves *perspective taking*—an attempt to take on the viewpoint of another person. This requires a suspension of judgment so that for the moment you set aside your own opinions and try to understand the other person. Empathy also has an *emotional* dimension that helps us get closer to experiencing others' feelings: to gain a sense of their fear, joy, sadness, and so on. A third dimension of empathy is a genuine *concern* for the welfare of the other person. When we empathize, we go beyond just thinking and feeling as others do and genuinely care about their well-being.

Scores of recent studies show that humans are hardwired to empathize with others—it's built into our brains.[51] Best-selling author Daniel Goleman believes that cultivating this natural tendency toward empathy is the essence of "social intelligence."[52] The ability to empathize seems to exist in a rudimentary form in even the youngest children. Research sponsored by the National Institute of Mental Health revealed what many parents know from experience: Virtually from birth, infants become visibly upset when they hear another baby crying, and children who are a few months old cry when they observe another child in tears. Young children have trouble distinguishing others' distress from their own. If, for example, one child hurts its finger, another baby might put its own finger into her mouth as if she were feeling pain. Researchers report cases in which children who see their parents in tears wipe their own eyes, even though they are not crying.

Although children may have a basic capacity to empathize, studies with twins suggest that the degree to which we are born with the ability to sense how others are feeling seems to vary according to genetic factors.[53] Although some people may have an inborn edge, environmental experiences are the key to developing the ability to understand others. Specifically, the way in which parents communicate with their children seems to affect their ability to understand others' emotional states.[54] When parents point out to children the distress that others feel from their misbehavior ("Look how sad Jessica is because you took her toy. Wouldn't you be sad if someone took away your toys?"), those children gain a greater appreciation that their acts have emotional consequences than when parents simply label such behavior as inappropriate ("That was a mean thing to do!"). Studies also show that allowing children to experience and manage frustrating events can help increase their empathic concern for others later in life.[55]

Culture plays an important role in our ability to understand the perspectives of others. Research shows that people raised in individualist cultures (which value independence) are often less adept at perspective-taking than those from collectivist cultures (which value interdependence).[56] In one study, Chinese and American players were paired together in a communication game that required the participants to take on the perspective of their partners. In all measures, the collectivist Chinese had greater success in perspective-taking than did their American counterparts. This isn't to suggest that one cultural orientation is better than the other; it only shows that culture shapes the way we perceive, understand, and empathize with others.

It is easy to confuse empathy with **sympathy**, but the concepts are different. With sympathy, you view the other person's situation from *your* point of view. With empathy, you view it from *the other person's* perspective. Consider the difference between sympathizing and empathizing with an unwed mother or a homeless person. When you sympathize, it is the other person's confusion, joy, or pain. When you empathize, the experience becomes your own, at least for the moment. It's one thing to feel bad (or good) *for* someone; it's more profound to feel bad (or good) *with* someone. Nonetheless, empathy doesn't require you to *agree* with the other person. You can empathize with a difficult relative or a rude stranger

"How would you feel if the mouse did that to you?"

without endorsing their behavior. Ultimately, all of us can profit from putting ourselves in others' shoes to better understand their worlds, as the reading on page 94 illustrates.

COGNITIVE COMPLEXITY

By now you can probably appreciate the value of empathy in boosting understanding and enhancing relationships. But how can we become more empathic? To answer that question, let's return to a feature of communication competence: cognitive complexity.

COGNITIVE COMPLEXITY AND COMMUNICATION   As noted in Chapter 1 (page 29), cognitive complexity is the ability to construct a variety of frameworks for viewing an issue. Researchers have found that cognitive complexity increases the chances of satisfying communication in a variety of contexts, including marriage,[57] helping others who are feeling distressed,[58] being persuasive,[59] and career advancement.[60]

Not surprisingly, studies show a connection between cognitive complexity and empathy.[61] The relationship makes sense: The more ways you have to understand others and interpret their behaviors, the greater is the likelihood that you can see the world from their perspective. Cognitive complexity can also help people describe situations more thoroughly and less simplistically.[62] Interestingly, one study showed that cognitive complex people are better able to identify and understand when others are using sarcasm—an abstract form of communication that is sometimes lost on those with less mental acumen.[63] The good news is that cognitive complexity can be enhanced through training.[64] With that in mind, let's look at a skill that can help you achieve that goal.

INCREASING YOUR COGNITIVE COMPLEXITY: THE PILLOW METHOD   The skill of perception checking discussed earlier in this chapter (pages 103–108) is a relatively quick, easy tool for clarifying potential misunderstandings, but some issues are too complex and serious to be handled with this approach. Writer Paul Reps describes a tool for boosting empathy when finding merit in another's position seems impossible.[65]

Developed by a group of Japanese schoolchildren, the **pillow method** gets its name from the fact that a problem has four sides and a middle, just like a pillow (Figure 3.5). As the examples on pages 114–115 show, viewing the issue from each of these

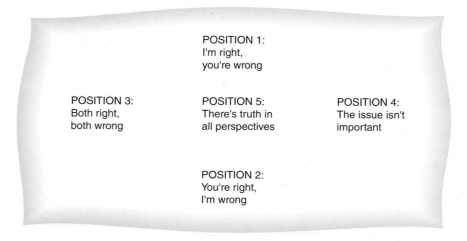

POSITION 1:
I'm right,
you're wrong

POSITION 3:
Both right,
both wrong

POSITION 5:
There's truth in
all perspectives

POSITION 4:
The issue isn't
important

POSITION 2:
You're right,
I'm wrong

Figure 3.5
The Pillow Method

perspectives almost always leads to valuable insights—and in so doing enhances cognitive complexity.

Position 1: I'm Right, You're Wrong This is the perspective that we usually take when viewing an issue. We immediately see the virtues in our position and find fault with anyone who happens to disagree with us. Detailing this position takes little effort and provides little new information.

Position 2: You're Right, I'm Wrong At this point you switch perspectives and build the strongest possible arguments to explain how another person can view the issue differently from you. Besides identifying the strengths in the other's position, this is the time to play the devil's advocate and find flaws in your position. Finding flaws in your position and trying to support the other's position requires discipline and a certain amount of courage, even though this is only an exercise, and you will

ETHICAL CHALLENGE

Empathy and the Golden Rule

Virtually everyone is familiar with the Golden Rule, which most of us learned in the form "Do unto others as you would have them do unto you." By obliging us to treat others as well as we would treat ourselves, this maxim seems to offer the foundation for a civil society in which everyone would behave with consideration.

Some ethicists have pointed out that the Golden Rule doesn't work well in situations where others don't want to be treated the same way you would. You may like to blast hip-hop music at top volume at 3 A.M., but appeals to the Golden Rule probably won't placate your neighbors who don't share your musical tastes or late-night hours. Likewise, just because you enjoy teasing banter, you aren't entitled to banter with others who might find this type of humor offensive or hurtful.

The Golden Rule presents special problems in cases of intercultural contacts, where norms for what is desirable vary dramatically. For example, most speakers from low-context cultures where English is the first language value honesty and explicit communication, but this level of candor would be offensive in the high-context cultures of Asia or the Middle East. A naive communicator following the Golden Rule might justify social blunders by claiming, "I was just communicating the way I'd like to be treated." This sort of ethnocentrism is a recipe for unsuccessful communication and perhaps for very unpleasant consequences.

In response to the challenge of differing wants, Milton Bennett proposed a "Platinum Rule": "Do unto others as they themselves would have done unto them." Unlike the Golden Rule, this rule requires us to understand how others think and what they want before we can determine how to act ethically. Put differently, the Platinum Rule implies that empathy is a prerequisite for moral sensitivity.

Despite its initial appeal, the Platinum Rule poses its own problems. There are certainly cases where doing unto others what they want might compromise our own needs or even our ethical principles. It is easy to imagine cases in which the Platinum Rule would oblige us to cheat, steal, or lie on others' behalf.

Even if acting on the Platinum Rule is problematic, the benefit of thinking about it seems clear. An essential requirement for benign behavior is the ability to empathize, helping us recognize that what others want may be different than what we would want under the same circumstances.

Describe how applying the Golden Rule and the Platinum Rule would affect one of your important interpersonal relationships.

1. What communication is necessary before you could put each rule into practice?

2. Which rule seems to be preferable?

For a discussion of the Golden and Platinum rules, see M. Bennett (1979). "Overcoming the Golden Rule: Sympathy and Empathy." In D. Nimmo (Ed.), Communication Yearbook 3 *(pp. 407–422). New Brunswick, NJ: Transaction Books; and R. L. Johannesen (2002). Ethics in Human Communication. Prospect Heights, IL: Waveland Press.*

soon be able to retreat to position 1 if you choose. But most people learn that switching perspectives reveals there is some merit to the other person's perspective.

There are some issues where it seems impossible to call the other position "right." Criminal behavior, deceit, and disloyalty often seem beyond justification. At times like these, it is possible to arrive at position 2 by realizing that the other person's behavior is understandable. For example, without approving, you may be able to understand how someone would resort to violence, tell lies, or cheat. Whatever the particulars, the goal of position 2 is to find some way of comprehending how anyone could behave in a way that you originally found impossible to defend.

Position 3: Both Right, Both Wrong From this position, you acknowledge the strengths and weaknesses of each person's arguments. If you have done a good job with position 2, it should be clear that there is some merit in both points of view, and that each side has its demerits. Taking a more evenhanded look at the issue can lead you to be less critical and more understanding of another's point of view.

> The test of a first-rate intelligence is the ability to hold two opposed ideas in mind at the same time and still retain the ability to function.
>
> —*F. Scott Fitzgerald*

Position 3 can also help you find the commonalities between your position and the other's. Perhaps you've both been right to care so much about the issue, but both wrong to fail to recognize the other person's concerns. Perhaps there are underlying values that you both share and similar mistakes that you've both made. In any case, the perspective of position

✔+ SKILL BUILDER

Pillow Talk

Try using the pillow method in your life. It isn't easy, but after you begin to understand it, the payoff in increased understanding is great.

1. Choose a person or viewpoint with whom or which you strongly disagree. If you've chosen a person, it's best to have him or her there with you, but if that's not possible, you can do it alone.

2. What disagreement should you choose? No doubt there are many in your life:

Parent–child	Friend–friend
Teacher–student	Nation–nation
Employer–employee	Republican–Democrat
Brother–sister	

3. For each disagreement you choose, really place yourself in each position on the pillow as you encounter it:
   a. Your position is correct, and your opponent's is wrong.
   b. Your opponent's position is correct, and yours is wrong.
   c. Both your positions are correct, and both are wrong.
   d. It isn't important which position is right or wrong.
   e. Finally, affirm the fact that there is truth in all four positions.

4. The more important the disagreement is to you, the harder it will be to accept positions 2 through 5 as valid, but the exercise will work only if you can suspend your present position and imagine how it would feel to hold the other ones.

5. How can you tell if you've been successful with the pillow method? The answer is simple: If, after going over all the steps, you can understand—not necessarily accept, but just understand—the other person's position, you've done it. After you've reached this *understanding*, do you notice any change in how you feel about the other person?

It was six men of Indostan
To learning much inclined,
Who went to see the elephant
Though all of them were blind
That each by observation
Might satisfy his mind.
The first approached the elephant
And, happening to fall
Against the broad and sturdy side,
At once began to bawl:
"Why, bless me! But the elephant
Is very much like a wall!"
The second, feeling of the tusk,
Cried: "Ho! What have we here
So very round and smooth and sharp?
To me, 'tis very clear,
This wonder of an elephant
Is very like a spear!"
The third approached the animal,
And, happening to take
The squirming trunk within his hands
Thus boldly up he spake:
"I see," quoth he, "the elephant
Is very like a snake!"
The fourth reached out his eager hand
And felt about the knee:
"What most this wondrous beast is like
Is very plain," quoth he:
"'Tis clear enough the elephant
Is very like a tree!"
The fifth who chanced to touch the ear

Said: "E'en the blindest man
Can tell what this resembles most—
Deny the fact who can:
This marvel of an elephant
Is very like a fan!"
The sixth no sooner had begun
About the beast to grope
Than, seizing on the swinging tail
That fell within his scope,
"I see," quoth he, "the elephant
Is very like a rope!"
And so these men of Indostan
Disputed loud and long,
Each in his own opinion
Exceeding stiff and strong;
Though each was partly in the right,
And all were in the wrong.

—*John G. Saxe*

Library of Congress, LC-USZC4-8702

3 should help you see that the issue isn't as much a matter of complete right and wrong as it first appeared to be.

Position 4: The Issue Isn't as Important as It Seems This perspective will help you realize that the issue isn't as important as you thought. Although it is difficult to think of some issues as unimportant, a little thought will show that most aren't as important as we make them out to be. The impact of even the most traumatic events—the death of a loved one or the breakup of a relationship, for example—usually lessens over time. The effects may not disappear, but we learn to accept them and get on with

✔+ IN REAL LIFE

The Pillow Method in Action

My Mother and Facebook

Background

My mother recently opened a Facebook account and sent me an invitation to become her friend. I ignored her request for a couple of weeks until she finally asked why I hadn't responded. The talk turned into an argument. She couldn't understand why I didn't want her as a Facebook friend. I couldn't understand why she wanted to butt into my personal life.

Position 1: I'm Right, She's Wrong

Facebook was created for college students, not middle-aged parents. The fact that my mom wants access to my personal world feels like an invasion of privacy—like reading my diary or rummaging through my belongings. If she wants to keep up with her friends on Facebook, that's her business—but leave me out of it.

Position 2: She's Right, I'm Wrong

When I objected to my mom snooping, she said she would stop looking at my page if it makes her uncomfortable. So she's right in saying that I don't need to worry about her judgments. When I told her I'd be embarrassed to have her commenting on my life, she promised not to write on my Wall, tag embarrassing pictures of me, or do anything else visible.

Position 3: Both of Us Are Right, and Both Are Wrong

I'm justified to be concerned about my mom being freaked out by some things on my Facebook page. She's justified in wanting to know more about my life and how my generation communicates. I'm probably overreacting when I worry about her reactions or demand that she keep her nose out of my business. She's wrong not to appreciate my desire for privacy.

Position 4: The Issue Isn't Important

I don't think anything I or my friends post on my Facebook page would change my relationship with my mom. Turning this into a major issue is probably not worth the hurt feelings that have resulted from this mini-crisis.

Position 5: There Is Truth In All Perspectives

Viewing this issue from several angles calmed me down and made it easier for my mother and me to have a good talk. We decided that I would friend her for a trial period. If I decide her looking at my page becomes a problem, she agreed to willingly remove herself from my friends list.

Planning a Wedding

Background

Who would have thought that planning a wedding would be such a nightmare? My fiancé and I are struggling to decide whether we should have a large, festive wedding or a small, intimate one. I'm in favor of having a big, expensive ceremony and party. He wants a smaller, more affordable one.

Position 1: I'm Right, He's Wrong

I have a big family, and I would feel guilty not inviting everyone. Also, we have lots of friends who would really miss not being present to celebrate our special day. If we invite one friend or relative, I say we have to invite them all to avoid hurting anybody's feelings. Otherwise, where do you draw the line? As far as money goes, I say that you get married only once, and this is no time to scrimp. My parents are willing to help pay the expenses, because they want our entire family to be there at the wedding.

Position 2: He's Right, I'm Wrong

My fiancé is right to say that we really don't have the funds to spend on a fancy wedding. Every dollar we spend on a lavish event will be one less dollar we have to buy a house, which we hope to do soon. My fiancé is right to say that a big wedding could postpone our house purchase for a year or two—maybe even longer, if real estate prices go up before we can buy. Even if my parents help pay for the event, our portion would still be more than we can afford. He's also right to say that no matter how many people we invite, someone is always going to be left out. It's just a case of where we draw the line. Finally, he's right to say that planning a big wedding will be a very stressful process.

Position 3: Both of Us Are Right, and Both Are Wrong

Both of us are right, and both are wrong. I'm right to want to include our extended families and friends on this joyous day, and I'm right to say that a special wedding would be a lifetime memory. He's right that doing so could still leave some hurt feelings and that it will postpone our house purchase. He also has a good point when he says that planning a big event could drive us crazy and distract us from the real importance of joining our lives.

Position 4: The Issue Isn't Important

After thinking about it, I've realized that getting married is different from being married. The decision about what kind of ceremony to have is important, but ultimately it won't affect the kind of marriage we have. How we behave after we're married will be much more important. And we are going to face a lot of decisions together—about children and jobs, for example—that will have much bigger consequences than this ceremony.

Position 5: There Is Truth In All Perspectives

Before using the pillow method to think through all sides of this issue, I was focused on getting my way. This attitude was creating some feelings between my fiancé and me that were not what we should be having as we faced this most important event. I've realized that if one or the other of us "wins" but the result is injured feelings, it won't be much of a victory. I don't know what kind of ceremony we will finally decide to have, but I'm determined to keep my focus on the really important goal of keeping our relationship positive and respectful.

Example 3: Exotic Dancing

Background

My best friend is an exotic dancer. I have tried to persuade her to find a less degrading way to earn a living, but she doesn't see the need to stop yet. She knows I don't agree with her decision to dance for money, but she tells me it's the only way she can make a decent income at this point in her life.

Position 1: I'm Right, She's Wrong

My friend is exaggerating when she says this job is the only way she can get the money to put herself through school. She could get a job that doesn't pay as well and make it through until she graduates. It wouldn't be perfect, but other people manage this way, and so can she. My friend is wrong to say this

job doesn't intrude into her life away from work. When we lived together, she had some arguments with her boyfriend about a strange man who would send her gifts at the club where she dances. This was really affecting their relationship. Also, sometimes she comes home at 4 A.M. after eight hours of dancing. I don't see how she can go on like this.

Position 2: She's Right, I'm Wrong

She is right to say that there is no other job where she can make this much money in so little time, at her age, and with her credentials. No one else provides financial support for my friend. She earns enough money to cover rent, food, and pay off some of her loans. She is still physically okay. She is a straight-A student, so it's true that the job isn't affecting her school work. The club where she works is clean and safe.

Position 3: Both of Us Are Right, and Both Are Wrong

I'm right to worry about her and encourage her to think about other options besides exotic dancing. She's right when she says there's no other job that pays so well. She's also right to say that her family doesn't support her in any way, which puts additional pressure on her that I can't imagine.

Position 4: The Issue Isn't Important

My friend and I both love each other and won't let this disagreement affect that. My friend hasn't let the dancing affect her self-worth. The dancing is just a chapter in her life, and it will be over soon.

Position 5: There Is Truth In All Perspectives

Now I can see that this dispute has many sides. I still wish my friend would quit her dancing job, and I'm still going to keep trying to persuade her to stop. But this method makes it easier for us to talk about the issue without either of us shutting down or rejecting the other.

Using your Premium Website for Looking Out/Looking In, *access "In Real Life Communication Scenarios" and then select either "Pillow Method: Wedding" or "Pillow Method: Dancing" to watch and analyze video examples of the pillow method.*

> The belief that one's own view of reality is the only reality is the most dangerous of all delusions.
>
> —*Paul Watzlawick*

life. The importance of a dispute can also fade when you realize that you've let it overshadow other equally important parts of your relationship. It's easy to become so wrapped up in a dispute about one subject that you forget about the other ways in which you are close to the other person.

Position 5: There Is Truth in All Four Perspectives After completing the first four positions, a final step is to recognize that each of them has some merit. Although logic might suggest that it's impossible for a position to be both right and wrong, both important and unimportant, your own experience will show that there is some truth in each of the positions you have explored. This fifth is very different from the "I'm right and you're wrong" attitude that most people bring to an issue. After you have looked at an issue from these five perspectives, it is almost certain that you will gain new insights. These insights may not cause you to change your mind or even solve the problem at hand. Nonetheless, they can increase your tolerance for the other person's position and thus improve the communication climate.

✔+ MAKING THE GRADE

Summary

There is more to the world "out there" than any person is capable of understanding. We make sense of our environment by the four-step process of selecting certain stimuli from the environment, organizing them into meaningful patterns, interpreting them in a manner that is shaped by a variety of factors, and negotiating them through narratives we share with others.

Many factors affect the way we select, organize, interpret, and negotiate information. Physiological factors such as our senses, age, and health play an important role. Cultural background also influences the way we view the world, as do social roles. In addition to these factors, some common tendencies affect the way we assign meaning to others' behavior.

Perception checking can be a useful tool for verifying interpretations of others' behavior, instead of assuming that the first hunch is correct. A complete perception check includes a description of the other's behavior, at least two plausible interpretations of its meaning, and a request for clarification about what the behavior does mean.

Empathy is the ability to experience another person's point of view. Empathy differs from sympathy, because it involves seeing the situation from the other person's perspective rather than your own. Cognitive complexity is the ability to construct a variety of frameworks for understanding an issue. One means for boosting both empathy and cognitive complexity is the pillow method, which involves viewing an issue from five different perspectives.

Key Terms

androgynous (99)
attribution (101)
empathy (108)
ethnocentrism (97)
gender role (98)
halo effect (102)

interpretation (90)
narrative (92)
negotiation (92)
organization (84)
perception checking (103)
pillow method (110)

punctuation (89)
selection (83)
self-serving bias (101)
stereotyping (86)
sympathy (109)

Online Resources

Now that you have read this chapter, use your Premium Website for *Looking Out/Looking In* for quick access to the electronic resources that accompany this text. Your Premium Website gives you access to:

- **Study tools** that will help you assess your learning and prepare for exams (*digital glossary*, *key term flash cards*, *review quizzes*).

- **Activities and assignments** that will help you hone your knowledge, understand how theory and research applies to your own life (*Invitation to Insight*), consider ethical challenges in interpersonal communication (*Ethical Challenge*), and build your interpersonal communication skills throughout the course (*Skill Builder*). If requested, you can submit your answers to your instructor.

- **Media resources** that will allow you to watch and critique news video and videos of interpersonal communication situations (*In Real Life, interpersonal video simulations*) and download a chapter review so you can study when and where you'd like (*Audio Study Tools*).

This chapter's key terms and search terms for additional reading are featured in this end-of-chapter section, and you can find this chapter's Invitation to Insight, Ethical Challenge, Skill Builder, and In Real Life activities in the body of the chapter.

Search Terms

When searching online databases to research topics in this chapter, use the following terms (along with this chapter's key terms) to maximize the chances of finding useful information:

attribution error
cognition
cognitive complexity

emotional intelligence
intercultural communication

sense-making
social perception

Film and Television

You can see the communication principles described in this chapter portrayed in the following films and television programs:

STEREOTYPING

Crash (2004) Rated R

Over the course of thirty-six hours in Los Angeles, the lives of several strangers collide. Because they come from such different backgrounds, this diverse group of people relies on stereotypes—usually relating to race—to form snap judgments of each other. Unfortunately, their judgments are almost always wrong.

Again and again, the characters' assumptions keep them from understanding the human beings they are encountering. Matt Dillon plays an angry cop who goes out of his way to humiliate a black citizen. An upper-class housewife (Sandra Bullock) believes a Mexican American locksmith (Michael Peña) is a gangbanger who plans to burgle her home, even though he is actually a gentle man struggling to build a safe life for his family. An Iranian businessman (Shaun Toub) keeps being misidentified as an Arab. Two clean-cut young black men (Larenz Tate and Ludacris) bemoan the fact that they are regarded with fear by whites in an upscale neighborhood.

Since childhood, most of us have been reminded not to judge a book by its cover. *Crash* provides a dramatic example of the problems that can result from ignoring this maxim.

Lost (2004–2010) Rated TV-14

This television series chronicles the mostly desperate lives of survivors of a plane crash that left forty-eight passengers stranded on a remote island in the South Pacific. The survivors include a doctor, a former prisoner, a rock semi-star, an Iraqi military vet, a mysterious man named Locke, and plenty of others.

The show's first few seasons offer numerous illustrations of the problems of jumping to quick conclusions about strangers. Just about the time the characters—and the viewers—are ready to vilify one of the survivors, a backstory helps explain the character's motives and provides a measure of empathy for that person. Conversely, some survivors who are initially seen as heroic become less so after their life stories are told. To paraphrase an old adage, *Lost* illustrates that people are typically more than their worst moments, and often less than their best ones.

NARRATIVES

Lars and the Real Girl (2007) Rated PG-13

Lars (Ryan Gosling) is a kind and decent but painfully shy 27-year-old. By choice, he lives alone in a garage and avoids conversation and contact with others as much as possible. Everyone in his small, close-knit town is stunned when Lars introduces his new girlfriend, Bianca—an anatomically correct silicone mannequin. Understandably worried about Lars's mental health, his brother and sister-in-law seek the help of their family doctor, who advises them to play along with his delusion and see what happens. Soon the entire town buys into the shared narrative that Bianca and Lars are a real couple. Bianca volunteers at the local hospital, "reads" stories to schoolchildren, and even wins a seat on the school board.

While this plot might seem far-fetched, critics and moviegoers have agreed that this tender drama-comedy showcases the power of a community to support one of its own. The obvious fiction they conspire to construct takes on its own reality, illustrating how communication can be a powerful tool for creating shared narratives.

BUILDING EMPATHY

The Doctor (1991) Rated PG-13

Jack McKee (William Hurt) is an ace surgeon and a first-class egotist. He treats his patients with a breezy self-assurance, brushing aside their concerns with jokes and indifference. It's not that McKee is mean-spirited: He just views his patients as objects upon which he can practice his skill and not as human beings with feelings.

McKee receives a major attitude adjustment when his nagging cough is diagnosed as throat cancer, and his surgeon treats him with the same mechanical indifference that he had bestowed on his patients. As McKee suffers the indignities of a hospital patient and confronts his mortality, his attitude toward the human side of medical care predictably changes. The film should become a part of the medical school curriculum, but it also shows other viewers how walking a mile in another person's shoes can lead to greater tolerance and understanding.

EMOTIONS:
Feeling, Thinking, and Communicating

✔+ MAKING THE GRADE

Here are the topics discussed in this chapter:

✔ **What Are Emotions?**
- Physiological Factors
- Nonverbal Reactions
- Cognitive Interpretations
- Verbal Expression

✔ **Influences on Emotional Expression**
- Personality
- Culture
- Gender
- Social Conventions
- Fear of Self-Disclosure
- Emotional Contagion

✔ **Guidelines for Expressing Emotions**
- Recognize Your Feelings
- Recognize the Difference between Feeling, Talking, and Acting
- Expand Your Emotional Vocabulary

- Share Multiple Feelings
- Consider When and Where to Express Your Feelings
- Accept Responsibility for Your Feelings
- Be Mindful of the Communication Channel

✔ **Managing Difficult Emotions**
- Facilitative and Debilitative Emotions
- Sources of Debilitative Emotions
- Irrational Thinking and Debilitative Emotions
- Minimizing Debilitative Emotions

✔ **Making the Grade**
- Summary
- Key Terms
- Online Resources
- Search Terms
- Film and Television

After studying the topics in this chapter, you should be able to:

1. Describe how the four components listed on pages 122–126 affect your emotions, and hence your communication, in an important situation.

2. Describe how the influences on emotional expression listed on pages 126–132 have affected your communication in an important relationship.

3. Apply the guidelines for effectively communicating emotions (pages 132–141) in an important situation.

4. Identify and dispute the fallacies (pages 145–150) that are creating debilitative emotions in an important situation. Explain how more rational thinking can lead to more constructive communication.

*I*t's impossible to talk about communication without acknowledging the importance of emotions. Think about it: Feeling confident can assist you in everything from giving a speech to asking for a date, whereas feeling insecure can ruin your chances. Feeling angry or defensive can spoil your time with others, whereas feeling and acting calm will help prevent or solve problems. The way you share or withhold your feelings of affection can affect the future of your relationships. On and on goes the list of feelings: appreciation, loneliness, joy, insecurity, curiosity, irritation. The point is clear: Communication shapes our feelings, and feelings shape our communication.

Consider how emotional intelligence is— and isn't—exhibited by the characters in the TV show *The Office.*

© NBC/Everett Collection

The role of emotions in human affairs is apparent to social scientists and laypeople alike. Researcher Daniel Goleman coined the term *emotional intelligence* to describe the ability to understand and manage one's own emotions and be sensitive to others' feelings.[1] Studies show that emotional intelligence is positively linked with self-esteem, life satisfaction, and self-acceptance,[2] as well as with healthy conflict management and relationships.[3] Emotional intelligence is unquestionably vital to both personal and interpersonal success.

Because emotions play such an important role in virtually all types of relationships, this chapter looks closer at analyzing and expressing them. The following pages will clarify what feelings are and how to recognize them. You'll read guidelines about when and how to best share your feelings with others. Finally, we will explore what causes feelings and how to enhance ones that make communication more rewarding and decrease ones that interfere with effective relationships. In later chapters we'll discuss how to interpret others' emotional states, but for now we'll focus on identifying and expressing your own emotions.

What Are Emotions?

Suppose that an extraterrestrial visitor asked you to explain emotions. How would you answer? You might start by saying that emotions are things that we feel. But this doesn't say much, because in turn you would probably describe feelings as synonymous with emotions. Social scientists generally agree that there are several components to the phenomena we label as feelings.[4]

PHYSIOLOGICAL FACTORS

When a person has strong emotions, many bodily changes occur.[5] For example, the physical components of fear include an increased heart rate, a rise in blood pressure, an increase in adrenaline secretions, an elevated blood sugar level, a slowing of digestion, and a dilation of the pupils. Marriage researcher John Gottman notes that symptoms like these also occur when couples are in intense conflicts.[6] He calls the condition "flooding" and has found that it impedes effective problem-solving. Some physiological changes are recognizable to the person having them: a churning stomach or tense jaw, for example. These cues can offer a significant clue to your emotions after you become aware of them.

NONVERBAL REACTIONS

Not all physical changes that accompany emotions are internal. Feelings are often apparent by observable changes. Some of these changes involve a person's appearance: blushing, sweating, and so on. Other changes involve behavior: a distinctive facial expression, posture, gestures, different vocal tone and rate, and so on.

"Emo" artists like Dashboard Confessional have both fans and critics of their emotionally expressive music. Clearly, however, *all* music and lyrics offer a means for expressing feelings.

©NBC/Courtesy Everett Collection/Everett Collection

Although it's reasonably easy to tell when someone is feeling a strong emotion, it's more difficult to be certain exactly what that emotion might be. A slumped posture and sigh may be a sign of sadness, or they may be a sign of fatigue. Likewise, trembling hands might indicate excitement, or they may indicate fear. As you'll learn in Chapter 6, nonverbal behavior is usually ambiguous, and it's dangerous to assume that it can be read with much accuracy.

Although we usually think of nonverbal behavior as the reaction to an emotional state, there may be times when the reverse is true—when nonverbal behavior actually *causes* an emotional state. In one study, experimental subjects were able to create various emotional states by altering their facial expressions.[7] When subjects were coached to move their facial muscles in ways that appeared afraid, angry, disgusted, amused, sad, surprised, and contemptuous, the subjects' bodies responded as if they were having these feelings. In another experiment, subjects who were coached to smile actually reported feeling better, and when they altered their expressions to look unhappy, they felt worse than before.[8]

COGNITIVE INTERPRETATIONS

Although there may be situations in which physical behavior and emotional states are directly connected, in most situations the mind plays an important role in determining emotional states. As you read earlier, some physiological components of fear are a racing heart, perspiration, tense muscles, and elevated blood pressure. Interestingly enough, these symptoms are similar to the physical changes that accompany excitement, joy, and other emotions. In other words, if we were to measure the physical condition of someone having a strong emotion, we would have a hard time knowing whether that person was trembling with fear or quivering with excitement. The recognition that the bodily components of most emotions are similar led some psychologists to conclude that the experience of fright, joy, or anger comes primarily from the label we give to the same physical symptoms at a given time.[9] Psychologist Philip Zimbardo offers a good example of this principle:

> I notice I'm perspiring while lecturing. From that I infer I am nervous. If it occurs often, I might even label myself a "nervous person." Once I have the label, the next question I must answer is "Why am I nervous?" Then I start to search for an appropriate explanation. I might notice some students leaving the room, or being inattentive. I am nervous because I'm not giving a

good lecture. That makes me nervous. How do I know it's not good? Because I'm boring my audience. I am nervous because I am a boring lecturer and I want to be a good lecturer. I feel inadequate. Maybe I should open a delicatessen instead. Just then a student says, "It's hot in here, I'm perspiring and it makes it tough to concentrate on your lecture." Instantly, I'm no longer "nervous" or "boring."[10]

Zimbardo found that changing his interpretation of the event affected the way he felt about it. Social scientists refer to this process as **reappraisal**—rethinking the meaning of emotionally charged events in ways that alter their emotional impact.[11] Research shows that reappraisal is vastly superior to suppressing one's feelings: It often leads to lower stress, higher self-esteem, and increased productivity.[12] Here are two examples:

- Your self-esteem has been shattered since you lost your job, particularly because some of your less-ambitious coworkers were not fired. You lack confidence as you look for new employment. You could reappraise the event as an opportunity to find a new position (or career) where your hard work and contributions will be better appreciated.

- A friend of yours says some malicious things about you behind your back. Although you are hurt, you decide her actions are a statement about *her* character, not yours—and that you'll demonstrate your character by not speaking poorly about her to others.

It's important to note that reappraisal is not about denying your feelings. Recognizing and acknowledging emotions such as anger, hurt, and grief (as well as happiness, love, and relief) are vital to psychological and relational health. However, when you're ready to move past difficult emotions, reappraisal can help. We'll take a closer look at using reappraisal to reduce debilitative emotions later in this chapter.

VERBAL EXPRESSION

As you will read in Chapter 6, nonverbal behavior is a powerful way of communicating emotion. In fact, nonverbal actions are better at conveying emotions than they are at conveying ideas. But sometimes words are necessary to express feelings. Is your friend's uncharacteristically short temper a sign of anger at you, or does it mean something less personal? Is a lover's unenthusiastic response a sign of boredom with you or the result of a long workday? Is a new acquaintance mistaking your friendliness as a come-on? There are times—especially in our low-context culture—when you can't rely on perceptiveness to be sure that a message is communicated and understood accurately.

Emotional Weather Report

Late night and early morning low clouds
with a chance of fog;
Chance of showers into the afternoon
with variable high cloudiness and gusty winds, gusty winds . . .
Things are tough all over
when the thunderstorms start;
Increasing over the southeast and south central portions
of my apartment.
I get upset and a line of thunderstorms
was developing in the early morning,
ahead of a slow moving cold front.
Cold blooded, with tornado watches issued
shortly before noon Sunday
for the areas including the western region
of my mental health and the northern portions of my
ability to deal rationally with my
disconcerted precarious emotional situation.

—Tom Waits

Some researchers believe there are several basic or primary emotions.[13] However, there isn't much agreement among scholars about what those emotions are, or about what makes them basic.[14] Moreover, emotions that are primary in one culture may not be primary in others, and some emotions have no direct equivalent in other cultures.[15] For example, "shame" is a central emotion in the Chinese experience,[16] whereas it's much less familiar to most people from Western cultures. Despite this debate, most scholars acknowledge that *anger*, *joy*, *fear*, and *sadness* are common and typical human emotions.

We experience most emotions with different degrees of intensity, and it's important to use language that represents these differences. Figure 4.1 illustrates this point clearly. To say you're "annoyed" when a friend breaks an important promise, for example, would probably be an understatement. In other cases, people chronically overstate the strength of their feelings. To them, everything is "wonderful" or "terrible." The problem with this sort of exaggeration is that when a truly intense emotion comes along, they have no words left to describe it adequately. If chocolate chip cookies from the local bakery are "fantastic," how does it feel to fall in love?

Researchers have identified a wide range of problems that arise for people who aren't able to talk about emotions constructively,

Annoyed	**Angry**	**Furious**
Pensive	Sad	**Grieving**
Content	**Happy**	**Ecstatic**
Anxious	**Afraid**	**Terrified**
Liking	**Loving**	**Adoring**

Figure 4.1
Intensity of Emotions

✔+ INVITATION TO INSIGHT

Recognizing Your Emotions

Keep a three-day record of your feelings. You can do this by spending a few minutes each evening recalling what emotions you felt during the day, what other people were involved, and the circumstances in which the emotions occurred.

At the end of the three-day period, you can understand the role that emotions play in your communication by answering the following questions:

1 How did you recognize the emotions you felt: through physiological stimuli, nonverbal behaviors, or cognitive processes?

2 Did you have any difficulty deciding which emotions you were feeling?

3 What emotions do you have most often? Are they primary or mixed? Mild or intense?

4 In what circumstances do you or don't you show your feelings? What factors influence your decision to show or not show your feelings? The type of feeling? The person or persons involved? The situation (time, place)? The subject that the feeling involves (money, sex, and so on)?

5 What are the consequences of the type of communicating you just described in step 4? Are you satisfied with these consequences? If not, what can you do to become more satisfied?

including social isolation, unsatisfying relationships, feelings of anxiety and depression, and misdirected aggression.[17] Furthermore, the way parents talk to their children about emotions has a powerful effect on the children's development.[18] The researchers identified two distinct parenting styles: "emotion coaching" and "emotion dismissing." They show how the coaching approach gives children skills for communicating about feelings in later life that lead to much more satisfying relationships. Children who grow up in families where parents dismiss emotions are at higher risk for behavior problems than those who are raised in families that practice emotion coaching.[19] Later in this chapter you will find some guidelines for effectively communicating about emotions.

Influences on Emotional Expression

Most people rarely express their emotions, at least verbally. People are generally comfortable making statements of fact and often delight in expressing their opinion, but they rarely disclose how they feel. Why do people fail to express their emotions? Let's look at several reasons.

PERSONALITY

There is an increasingly clear relationship between personality and the way we experience and communicate emotions.[20] For example, extraverted people—those with a tendency to be upbeat, optimistic, and to enjoy social contact—report more positive emotions in everyday life than less extraverted individuals.[21] Likewise, people with neurotic personalities (those with a tendency to worry, feel anxious, and be apprehensive) report more negative emotions in everyday life than less neurotic individuals. These personality traits are at least partially biological in nature. Psychologists have used magnetic imaging to measure the relationship between personality type and brain activity.[22] People who tested high on measures of extraversion had greater brain reactivity to positive stimuli than did less extraverted people. Those who scored high on the neuroticism measures had more brain reactions to negative stimuli. Research like this confirms the familiar belief that some people see the cup being half (or more) full, whereas others see it as being more empty.

"I'm not an emotional person myself. Fortunately, Georgine feels things for both of us."

Personality can be a powerful force, but it doesn't have to govern your communication satisfaction. Consider shyness, which can be considered the opposite of extraversion. Introverted people can devise comfortable and effective strategies for reaching out. For example, the Internet has proven to be an effective way for reticent communicators to make contact. Chat rooms, instant messaging, email, and computer dating services all provide a low-threat way to approach others and get acquainted.[23]

CULTURE

People around the world generally experience the same emotions, but the same events can generate quite different feelings in different cultures.[24]

The notion of eating snails might bring a smile of delight to some residents of France, whereas it would cause many North Americans to grimace in disgust. More to the point of this book, research has shown that fear of strangers and risky situations is more likely to frighten people living in the United States and Europe than those living in Japan, whereas Japanese are more apprehensive about relational communication than Americans and Europeans.[25] Culture also has an effect on how emotions are valued. One study found that Asian Americans and Hong Kong Chinese value "low arousal positive affect" (such as "calm") more than do European Americans, who tend to value "high arousal positive affect" (such as "excitement").[26]

LOOKING AT DIVERSITY

Todd Epaloose: A Native American Perspective on Emotional Expression

Todd Epaloose was raised on the Zuñi pueblo in New Mexico. He spent part of his childhood on the reservation and part attending school in the city. He now lives in Albuquerque. As an urbanite who still spends time with his family on the reservation, Todd alternates between two worlds.

Todd Epaloose

Zuñi and Anglo cultures are as different as night and day in the ways they treat communication about emotions. In mainstream U.S. culture, speaking up is accepted, or even approved. This is true from the time you are a child. Parents are proud when their child speaks up—whether that means showing affection, being curious, or even expressing unhappiness in a way that the parents approve. Being quiet gets a child labeled as "shy," and is considered a problem. Assertiveness is just as important in school, at work, and in adult relationships.

In Zuñi culture, emotions are much less public. We are a private people, who consider a public display of feelings embarrassing. Self-control is considered a virtue. I think a lot of our emotional reticence comes from a respect for privacy. Your feelings are your own, and showing them to others is just as wrong as taking off your clothes in public. It's not that traditional Zuñis have fewer or less intense feelings than people in the city: It's just that there is less value placed on showing them in obvious ways.

The way we express affection is a good example of Zuñi attitudes and rules for sharing emotions. Our families are full of love. But someone from the city might not recognize this love, since it isn't displayed

very much. There isn't a lot of hugging and kissing, even between children and parents. Also, there isn't a lot of verbal expression: People don't say "I love you" to one another very much. We show our emotions by our actions: by helping one another, by caring for the people we love when they need us. That's enough to keep us happy.

Which approach is best? I think both cultures have strengths. Many Zuñis and other Native Americans who want to join the mainstream culture are at a disadvantage. They aren't very good at standing up for their rights, and so they get taken advantage of. Even at home, there are probably times when it's important to express feelings to prevent misunderstandings. On the other hand, I think some Native American emotional restraint might be helpful for people who are used to Anglo communication styles. Respecting others' privacy can be important: Some feelings are nobody else's business, and prying or demanding that they open up seems pushy and rude. Native American self-control can also add some civility to personal relationships. I'm not sure that "letting it all hang out" is always the best way.

One final word: I believe that in order to really understand the differences between emotional expression in Native American and Anglo cultures you have to live in both. If that isn't possible, at least realize that the familiar one isn't the only good approach. Try to respect what you don't understand.

There are also differences in the degree to which people in various cultures display their feelings. For example, social scientists have found support for the notion that people from warmer climates are more emotionally expressive than those who live in cooler climates.[27] More than twenty-nine hundred respondents representing twenty-six nationalities reported that people from the southern part of their countries were more emotionally expressive than were northerners.

One of the most significant factors that influences emotional expression is the position of a culture on the individualism-collectivism spectrum. Members of collectivistic cultures (such as Japan and India) prize harmony among members of their in-group and discourage expression of any negative emotions that might upset relationships among people who belong to it. By contrast, members of highly individualistic cultures (such as the United States and Canada) feel comfortable revealing their emotions to people with whom they are close.[28] Individualists and collectivists also handle emotional expression with members of out-groups differently: Whereas collectivists are frank about expressing negative emotions toward outsiders, individualists are more likely to hide emotions such as dislike.[29] It's easy to see how differences in display rules can lead to communication problems. For example, individualistic North Americans might view collectivistic Asians as less than candid, whereas Asians could easily regard North Americans as overly demonstrative.[30]

The phrase "I love you" offers an interesting case study of cultural differences in emotion expression. Researchers found that Americans say "I love you" more frequently (and to more people) than do members of most other cultures.[31] It's not that love isn't a universal experience; rather, there are significant cultural differences about when, where, how often, and with whom the phrase should be used. For instance, Middle Easterners in the study said that "I love you" should only be expressed between spouses, and they warned that American men who use the phrase cavalierly with Middle Eastern women might be misinterpreted as making a marriage proposal. They were not alone: study participants from a variety of backgrounds (e.g., Eastern Europe, India, Korea) said they use the phrase quite sparingly, believing that its power and meaning would be lost if used too often. However, one factor was consistent across cultures: Women tend to say "I love you" more often than men. For more examples of the effect that gender has on emotion expression, read on.

GENDER

Even within a culture, biological sex and gender roles often shape the ways in which men and women experience and express their emotions.[32] In fact, biological sex is the best predictor of the ability to detect and interpret emotional expressions—better than academic background, amount of foreign travel, cultural similarity, or ethnicity.[33] For example, research suggests that women are more attuned to emotions than men,[34] both within and across cultures.[35] A team of psychologists tested men's and women's recall of emotional images and found that females were 10 to 15 percent more accurate in remembering them. Furthermore, women's reactions to these emotion-producing stimuli were significantly more intense than men's.

Research on emotional expression suggests that there is at least some truth to the cultural stereotype of the unexpressive male and the more expressive female.[36] As a group, women are more likely than men to express both positive emotions (e.g., love, liking, joy, and contentment) and feelings of vulnerability (including fear, sadness, loneliness, and embarrassment). Men, however, are less bashful about revealing their strengths.[37] On the Internet, the same differences between male and female emotional expressiveness apply. For example, women were more likely than men to use emoticons, such as the symbol ☺, to express their feelings than were men.[38] Chapter 9 will discuss how men often express their feelings through actions and activities rather than in words.

One's gender isn't the only factor that affects emotional sensitivity. A second factor is whether the other person is of the same or different sex. For example, men are more likely to express feelings (especially positive ones) with women than with other men.[39] Of course, these gender differences are statistical averages, and many men and women don't fit these profiles.

A third factor that influences sensitivity to others' emotions is the person or people with whom we are communicating. For example, dating and married couples are significantly better at recognizing each other's emotional cues than are strangers, just as people from the same culture seem to be better at recognizing each other's emotions.[40] Not surprisingly, people in close relationships are likely to experience and express more emotions than those in less-close relationships.[41] For example, we have stronger feelings about romantic partners than about people we're less involved with. Of course, not all of those emotions are positive. The potential for feeling hurt and neglected is stronger in romantic relationships than in other types of relationships.[42]

Emoticons (from the words "emotion" and "icons") are a way to express and clarify feelings in mediated messages.

© William Whitehurst/CORBIS

A final factor is the difference in power between the two parties. People who are less powerful learn—probably from necessity—to read the more powerful person's signals. One experiment revealed that "women's intuition" should be relabeled "subordinate's intuition." In opposite-sex twosomes, the person with less control—regardless of sex—was better at interpreting the leader's nonverbal signals than vice versa.[43]

SOCIAL CONVENTIONS

In mainstream U.S. society, the unwritten rules of communication discourage the direct expression of most emotions.[44] Count the number of genuine emotional expressions that you hear over a two- or three-day period and you'll discover that emotional expressions are rare.

Not surprisingly, the emotions that people *do* share directly are usually positive. Communicators are reluctant to send messages that embarrass or threaten the "face" of others.[45] This is particularly true in the early stages of a new relationship, when a high ratio of positive-to-negative emotions is crucial to the relationship's development.[46] By contrast, historians offer a detailed description of the ways in which contemporary society discourages expressions of anger.[47] When compared to past centuries, Americans today strive to suppress this unpleasant emotion in almost every context, including child-raising, the workplace, and personal relationships. Research supports this analysis. One study

© The New Yorker Collection 1991 Jack Ziegler

"It was a time when men regularly performed great feats of valor but were rarely in touch with their feelings."

"It's not a word I can put into feelings."

each other." You can recognize the absence of emotion in each case by adding a genuine word of feeling to it. For instance, "I'm *bored*, and I want to go to a show" or "I think we've been seeing too much of each other, and I feel *confined*."

Relying on a small vocabulary to describe feelings is as limiting as relying on a small vocabulary to describe colors. To say that the ocean in all its moods, the sky as it varies from day to day, and the color of your true love's eyes are all "blue" tells only a fraction of the story. Likewise, it's overly broad to use a term like *good* or *great* to describe how you feel in situations as different as earning a high grade, finishing a marathon, and hearing the words "I love you" from a special person.

There are several ways to express a feeling verbally[68]:

- By using *single words*: "I'm angry" (or "excited," "depressed," "curious," and so on).

- By describing what's happening *to you*: "My stomach is tied in knots," "I'm on top of the world."

- By describing what you'd like *to do*: "I want to run away," "I'd like to give you a hug," "I feel like giving up."

Sometimes communicators inaccurately minimize the strength of their feelings: "I'm a *little* unhappy" or "I'm *pretty* excited" or "I'm *sort of* confused." Of course, not all feelings are strong ones. We do feel degrees of sadness and joy, for example, but some people have a tendency to discount almost every feeling. Do you?

In other cases, communicators express feelings in a coded manner. This happens most often when the sender is uncomfortable about revealing the feeling in question. Some codes are verbal ones, as when the sender hints more or less subtly at the message. For example, an indirect way to say "I'm lonesome" might be "I guess there's not much going on this weekend, so if you don't have any plans maybe you could text me and we could hang out." Such a message is so indirect that your real feeling may not be recognized. For this reason, people who send coded messages stand less of a chance of having their feelings understood—and their needs met.

If you do decide to express your feeling, you can be most clear by making sure that both you and your partner understand that your feeling is centered on a specific set of

✔+ INVITATION TO INSIGHT

Expanding Your Emotional Vocabulary

Use the online activity "Expressing Emotions by Expanding Your Feelings Vocabulary" to expand your emotional vocabulary. (For more suggestions, see Table 4.2 on page 135.) Using the guidelines for expressing emotions on pages 132–141, practice

describing your feelings by writing statements for each of the hypothetical situations listed at the website. You can find the link to this site at your Premium Website for *Looking Out/Looking In.*

circumstances rather than being indicative of the whole relationship. Instead of saying "I resent you," say "I resent you when you don't keep your promises." Rather than saying "I'm bored with you," say "I'm bored when you talk about your money."

SHARE MULTIPLE FEELINGS

The feeling you express often isn't the only one you're experiencing. For example, you might often express your anger but overlook the confusion, disappointment, frustration, sadness, or embarrassment that preceded it. To understand why, consider the following examples. For each one, ask yourself two questions: "How would I feel? What feelings might I express?"

> An out-of-town friend has promised to arrive at your place at six o'clock. When he hasn't arrived by nine, you are convinced that a terrible accident has occurred. Just as you pick up the phone to call the police and local hospitals, your friend breezes in the door with an offhand remark about getting a late start.

> You and your companion have a fight just before leaving for a party. Deep inside, you know that you were mostly to blame, even though you aren't willing to admit it. When you arrive at the party, your companion leaves you to flirt with several other attractive guests.

In situations like these, you would probably feel mixed emotions. Consider the case of the overdue friend. Your first reaction to his arrival would probably be relief: "Thank goodness, he's safe!" But you would also be likely to feel anger: "Why didn't he phone to tell me he'd be late?" The second example would probably leave you with an even greater number of mixed emotions: guilt at contributing to the fight, hurt and perhaps embarrassment at your companion's flirtations, and anger at this sort of vengefulness.

Despite the commonness of mixed emotions, we often communicate only one feeling—usually the most negative one. In both of the preceding examples, you might show only your anger, leaving the other person with little idea of the full range of your feelings. Consider the different reaction you would get by showing *all* of your emotions in these cases and in others.

CONSIDER WHEN AND WHERE TO EXPRESS YOUR FEELINGS

Often the first flush of a strong feeling is not the best time to speak out. If you're awakened by the racket caused by a noisy neighbor, storming over to complain might result in your saying things you'll regret later. In such a case, it's probably wiser to wait until you have thought out carefully how you might express your feelings in a way that would most likely be heard. Research shows that "imagined interactions" in advance of actual conversations can enhance relationships by allowing communicators to rehearse what they will say and to consider how others might respond.[69]

Even after you've waited for the first wave of strong feeling to subside, it's still important to choose the time that's best suited to the message. Being rushed or tired or disturbed by some other matter is probably a good reason for postponing the expression of your feeling. Often, dealing with your emotions can take a great amount of time and effort, and fatigue or distraction will make it difficult

> Anyone can become angry. That is easy. But to be angry with the right person to the right degree, at the right time for the right purpose, and in the right way: This is not easy.
>
> —*Aristotle*

ago, and the decision about when to use mediated channels—such as email, instant messaging, cell phones, social media sites, PDAs, and blogging—call for a level of

✔+ IN REAL LIFE

Guidelines for Emotional Expression

After a long and frustrating search, Logan thinks he has found the ideal job that he wants and needs. The interview went well. As Logan was leaving, the interviewer said he was "very well qualified" and promised "You'll be hearing from us soon." That conversation took place almost two weeks ago, and Logan hasn't heard a word from the company.

The two transcripts below reflect very different ways of responding to this difficult situation. The first one ignores and the second one follows the Guidelines for Expressing Emotions described on pages 132–141. In each, Logan begins by ruminating (page 142) about the employer's failure to get in touch as promised.

IGNORING GUIDELINES FOR EMOTIONAL EXPRESSION

Logan doesn't explicitly recognize a single emotion he is experiencing (page 134), let alone any mixed emotions (page 137). Rather than accepting responsibility for his own feelings, he blames the employer for "driving me crazy" (page 138).	"I can't believe those inconsiderate idiots! Who do they think they are, promising to call soon and then doing nothing? They're driving me crazy."
Logan jumps to the conclusion that a job offer isn't forthcoming, and lashes out without considering any alternatives.	"I give up. Since they aren't going to hire me, I'm going to call that interviewer and let her know what a screwed-up company they're running. I'll probably get her voice mail, but that's even better: That way I can say what's on my mind without getting nervous or being interrupted. They have no right to jerk me around like this, and I'm going to tell them just that." (*Angrily dials phone.*)

FOLLOWING GUIDELINES FOR EMOTIONAL EXPRESSION

Logan identifies his mixture of feelings as a starting point for deciding what to do (page 137).	"I'm mad at the company for not keeping in touch like they promised. I'm also confused about whether I'm as qualified as I thought I was, and I'm starting to worry that maybe I didn't do as well in the interview as I thought. I'm also sorry I didn't ask her for a more specific time than 'soon.' And I'm really unsure about whether to give up, wait for them to call me, or reach out to the company and ask what's going on."
He recognizes the difference between what he would like to do (chew out the interviewer) and what is more appropriate and effective (pages 134–135).	"If I'm not going to get the job, I'd like to chew out that interviewer for promising to call. But that would probably be a bad idea—burning my bridges, as my family would say."
Logan uses a perception check (pages 103–108) and considers sharing his feelings with the employer in a nonblaming way. He deliberately considers when and how to express himself (pages 137–138), choosing email as the best channel to achieve his goals (pages 139–141).	"Maybe I'll call her and say something like 'I'm confused. You said at the interview that I'd hear from you soon, but it's been almost two weeks now with no word.' I could ask whether I misunderstood (although I doubt that), or whether they need some more information from me. Let me think about that overnight. If the idea still sounds good in the morning, I'll call them."
Having decided to email the employer, Logan could use the face-saving methods described in Chapter 10 (pages 355–370) to compose his message. He could begin by speaking positively about his continued interest in the company, then raise his concern about not having heard from them, and then close by saying that he's looking forward to hearing back from them.	"Actually, an email would be better: I could edit my words until they're just right, and an email wouldn't put the interviewer on the spot like a phone call would."

analysis that wasn't required in the past.[73] For instance, is it appropriate to signal your desire to end a relationship in a voice-mail message? When is it acceptable to use CAPITAL LETTERS in an instant message to express displeasure? If you're excited about some good news, should you first tell your family and friends in person before publishing it in your blog?

Most people intuitively recognize that the selection of a channel depends in part on the kind of message they're sending. In one survey, students identified which channel they would find best for delivering a variety of messages.[74] Most respondents said they would have little trouble expressing positive messages in person, but preferred mediated channels for negative messages.

"Flaming" is an extreme example of how mediated channels lend themselves to expressing negative emotions. As the reading on page 133 points out, the kind of civility that most people honor in other communication channels seems to have less of a hold on the Internet—certainly among strangers, but even among people who belong to the same personal networks. Before saying something you may later regret, it's worth remembering the principle stated in Chapter 1 that communication is irreversible. Once you hit the "Send" button, you can't retract an emotional outburst.

Managing Difficult Emotions

Although feeling and expressing many emotions add to the quality of interpersonal relationships, not all feelings are beneficial. For instance, rage, depression, terror, and jealousy do little to help you feel better or improve your relationships. The following pages will give you tools to minimize these unproductive emotions.

FACILITATIVE AND DEBILITATIVE EMOTIONS

First, we need to make a distinction between **facilitative emotions**, which contribute to effective functioning, and **debilitative emotions**, which detract from effective functioning.

One difference between the two types is their *intensity*. For instance, a certain amount of anger or irritation can be constructive, because it often provides the stimulus that leads you to improve the unsatisfying conditions. Rage, however, usually makes matters worse—especially when driving, as illustrated by the problems associated with "road rage."[75] The same holds true for fear. A little bit of fear before an important athletic contest or job interview might give you the boost that will improve your performance.[76] (Mellow athletes or employees usually don't do well.) But total terror is something else. Even a

Difficult emotions can spoil the quality of a relationship.

© Blend Images/SuperStock

little suspicion can make people more effective communicators. One study revealed that mates who doubted that their relational partners were telling the truth were better at detecting deception than were trusting mates.[77] Of course, an extreme case of paranoia would have the opposite and debilitative effect, reducing the ability to interpret the partner's behavior accurately.

> I can't choose how I feel, but I can choose what I do about it.
>
> —Andy Rooney

Not surprisingly, debilitative emotions like communication apprehension can lead to a variety of problems in personal, business, educational, and even medical settings.[78] When people become anxious, they generally speak less, which means that their needs aren't met; and when they do manage to speak up, they are less effective at communicating than their more confident counterparts.[79]

A second characteristic that distinguishes debilitative feelings from facilitative ones is their extended *duration*. Feeling depressed for a while after the breakup of a relationship or the loss of a job is natural, but spending the rest of your life grieving over your loss would accomplish nothing. In the same way, staying angry at someone for a wrong inflicted long ago can be just as punishing to you as to the wrongdoer. Social scientists call this **rumination**—dwelling persistently on negative thoughts that, in turn, intensify negative feelings. A substantial body of research confirms that rumination increases feelings of sadness, anxiety, and depression.[80] Just as bad, people who ruminate are more likely to lash out with displaced aggression at innocent bystanders.[81]

Many debilitative emotions involve communication. Here are a few examples, offered by readers of *Looking Out/Looking In*:

> When I first came to college, I had to leave my boyfriend. I was living with three girls, and for most of the first semester I was so lonesome and unhappy that I was a pretty terrible roommate.

> I got so frustrated with my overly critical boss that I lost my temper and quit one day. I told him what a horrible manager he was and walked off the job right then and there. Now I'm afraid to list my former boss as a reference, and I'm afraid my temper tantrum will make it harder for me to get a new job.

> I've had ongoing problems with my family, and sometimes I get so upset that I can't concentrate on my work or school, or even sleep well at night.

In the following pages you will learn a method for dealing with debilitative feelings like these that can improve your effectiveness as a communicator. This method is based on the idea that one way to minimize debilitative feelings is to minimize unproductive thinking.

SOURCES OF DEBILITATIVE EMOTIONS

For most people, feelings seem to have a life of their own. You wish you could feel calm when approaching strangers, yet your voice quivers. You try to appear confident when asking for a raise, yet your eye twitches nervously. Where do feelings like these come from?

PHYSIOLOGY   One answer lies in our genetic makeup. As you read in Chapter 2, temperament is, to a large degree, inherited. Communication traits like shyness, verbal aggressiveness, and assertiveness are rooted in biology. Fortunately, biology isn't destiny. As you'll soon read, it is possible to overcome debilitative feelings.

Beyond heredity, cognitive scientists tell us that the cause of some debilitative feelings—especially those involving fight-or-flight responses—lies deep inside the brain, in an almond-sized cluster of interconnected structures called the amygdala (pronounced uh-MIG-duh-luh). The amygdala acts as a kind of sentinel that scans every experience, looking for threats. In literally a split second, it can sound an alarm that triggers a flood of physiological reactions: speeding heart rate, elevating blood pressure, heightening the senses, and preparing the muscles to react.[82]

> In the words of a broken heart
>
> It's just emotion taking me over
>
> —*Destiny's Child*

This defense system has obvious value when we are confronted with real physical dangers, but in social situations the amygdala can hijack the brain, triggering emotions like fear and anger when there is no real threat. You might find yourself feeling uncomfortable when somebody stands too close to you or angry when someone cuts in front of you in line. As you'll soon read, thinking clearly is the way to avoid overreacting to nonthreats like these.

EMOTIONAL MEMORY   The source of some threats lies in what neuroscientists have termed our *emotional memory*. Seemingly harmless events can trigger debilitative feelings if they bear even a slight resemblance to troublesome experiences from the past. A few examples illustrate the point:

- Ever since being teased when he moved to a new elementary school, Trent has been uncomfortable in unfamiliar situations.

- Alicia feels apprehensive around men, especially those with deep, booming voices. As a child, she was mistreated by a family member with a loud baritone voice.

- Paul feels a wave of insecurity whenever he is around women who use the same perfume worn by a former lover who jilted him.

SELF-TALK   Beyond neurobiology, what we think can have a profound effect on how we feel. It's common to say that strangers or your boss make you feel nervous, just as you would say that a bee sting makes you feel pain. The apparent similarities between physical and emotional discomforts become clear if you look at them in the following way:

TATION TO INSIGHT

...ng to Yourself

...become better at understanding how your thoughts shape your feelings by completing the following steps...

1 Take a few minutes to listen to the inner voice you use when thinking. Close your eyes now and listen to it. . . . Did you hear the voice? Perhaps it was saying, "What voice? I don't have any voice. . . ." Try again, and pay attention to what the voice is saying.

2 Now think about the following situations, and imagine how you would react in each. How would you interpret them with your inner voice? What feelings would follow from each interpretation?

   a. While sitting on a bus, in class, or on the street, you notice an attractive person sneaking glances at you.

   b. During a lecture your professor asks the class, "What do you think about this?" and looks toward you.

   c. You are telling friends about your vacation, and one yawns.

   d. You run into a friend on the street and ask how things are going. "Fine," she replies, and rushes off.

3 Now recall three recent times when you felt a strong emotion. For each one, recall the activating event and then the interpretation that led to your emotional reaction.

Event	*Feeling*
Bee sting	physical pain
Meeting strangers	nervous feelings

When looking at your emotions in this way, you seem to have little control over how you feel. However, this apparent similarity between physical pain and emotional discomfort (or pleasure) isn't as great as it seems to be. Cognitive psychologists argue that it is not *events* such as meeting strangers or being jilted by a lover that cause people to feel bad, but rather the *beliefs they hold* about these events. As discussed earlier in the chapter, *reappraisal* involves changing our thoughts to help manage our emotions.

Albert Ellis, who developed an approach to reappraisal called *rational-emotive therapy*, tells a story that makes this point clear. Imagine yourself walking by a friend's house and seeing your friend stick his head out of a window and call you a string of vile names. (You supply the friend and the names.) Under these circumstances it's likely that you would feel hurt and upset. Now imagine that instead of walking by the house you were passing a mental institution when the same friend, who was obviously a patient there, shouted the same vile names at you. In this case, your feelings would probably be quite different—most likely sadness and pity. You can see that in this story the activating event of being called names was the same in both cases, yet the emotional consequences were very different. The reason for your different feelings has to do with your thinking in each case. In the first case, you would most likely think that your friend was very angry with you; further, you might imagine that you must have done something terrible to deserve such a response. In the second case, you would probably assume that your friend had some psychological difficulty, and most likely you would feel sympathetic.

From this example you can start to see that it's the *interpretations* that people make of an event, during the process of **self-talk**, that determine their feelings.[83] Thus, the model for emotions looks like this:

Event	*Thought*	*Feeling*
Being called names	"I've done something wrong."	hurt, upset
Being called names	"My friend must be sick."	concern, sympathy

The same principle applies in more common situations. In job interviews, for example, people who become nervous are likely to use negative self-talk when they think about their performance: "I won't do well," "I don't know why I'm doing this."[84] In romantic relationships, thoughts shape satisfaction. The words "I love you" can be interpreted in a variety of ways. They could be taken at face value as a genuine expression of deep affection:

Event	*Thought*	*Feeling*
Hearing "I love you"	"This is a genuine statement."	delight (perhaps)

The same words might be decoded as a sincere but mistaken declaration uttered in a moment of passion, an attempt to make the recipient feel better, or an attempt at manipulation. For example,

Hearing "I love you"	"S/he's just saying this to manipulate me."	anger

One study revealed that women are more likely than men to regard expressions of love as genuine statements rather than attribute them to some other cause.[85] Other research shows the importance of self-talk in relationships. Members of couples who are unhappy with one another have more negative self-talk about their partner and fewer positive thoughts about their partner and the relationship.[86]

IRRATIONAL THINKING AND DEBILITATIVE EMOTIONS

Focusing on the self-talk that we use to think is the key to understanding debilitative emotions. Many debilitative emotions come from accepting a number of irrational thoughts—we'll call them *fallacies* here—that lead to illogical conclusions and in turn to debilitative emotions. We usually aren't aware of these thoughts, which makes them especially powerful.[87]

1. THE FALLACY OF PERFECTION People who accept the **fallacy of perfection** believe that a worthwhile communicator should be able to handle every situation with complete confidence and skill.

If you accept the belief that it's desirable and possible to be a perfect communicator, you'll probably assume that people won't appreciate you if you are imperfect. Admitting your mistakes, saying "I don't know," and sharing feelings of uncertainty seem like social defects when viewed in this manner. Given the desire to be valued and appreciated, it's tempting to try to *appear* to be perfect, but the costs of such deception are high. If others ever find you out,

Carol and Mike Werner/Jupiter Images

Most emotions come from the way we think. When thoughts are irrational, unwelcome emotions can interfere with effective communication.

they'll see you as a phony. Even when your act isn't uncovered, such an act uses up a great deal of psychological energy, and thus makes the rewards of approval less enjoyable.

> The mind is its own place, and in itself can make a Heav'n of Hell, a Hell of Heav'n.
>
> —*John Milton,* Paradise Lost

Subscribing to the myth of perfection not only can keep others from liking you, but also can act as a force to diminish your own self-esteem. How can you like yourself when you don't measure up to the way you ought to be? How liberated you become when you can comfortably accept the idea that you are not perfect! That,

Like everyone else, you sometimes have a hard time expressing yourself.

Like everyone else, you make mistakes from time to time, and there is no reason to hide this.

You are honestly doing the best you can to realize your potential, to become the best person you can be.

2. THE FALLACY OF APPROVAL   The **fallacy of approval** is based on the idea that it is not only desirable but also vital to get the approval of virtually every person. People who accept this idea go to incredible lengths to seek approval from others, even when they have to sacrifice their own principles and happiness to do so. Accepting this fallacy can lead to some ludicrous situations:

Feeling nervous because people you really don't like seem to disapprove of you

Feeling apologetic when others are at fault

Feeling embarrassed after behaving unnaturally to gain another's approval

In addition to the obvious discomfort that arises from denying your own principles and needs, the fallacy of approval is irrational, because it implies that others will respect and like you more if you go out of your way to please them. Often this simply isn't true. How is it possible to respect people who have compromised important values just to gain acceptance? How is it possible to think highly of people who repeatedly deny their own needs as a means of buying approval? Though others may find it tempting to use these individuals to suit their ends, these individuals hardly deserve genuine affection and respect.

Striving for universal approval is irrational because it's simply not possible. Sooner or later a conflict of expectations is bound to occur; one person will approve if you behave only in a certain way, but another will accept only the opposite behavior. What are you to do then?

Don't misunderstand: Abandoning the fallacy of approval doesn't mean living a life of selfishness. It's still important to consider the needs of others and to meet them whenever possible. It's also pleasant—we might say even necessary—to strive for the respect of those people you value. The point here is that when you must abandon your own needs and principles in order to seek these goals, the price is too high—as Jim Carrey's character learned in the movie *Yes Man* (see discussion on page 157).

In the film *Yes Man,* Jim Carrey's character discovers the problems that arise from trying to please everybody.

3. THE FALLACY OF SHOULDS The **fallacy of shoulds** is the inability to distinguish between what is and what should be. You can see the difference by imagining a person who is full of complaints about the world:

> "There should be no rain on weekends."
>
> "People ought to live forever."
>
> "Money should grow on trees."
>
> "We should all be able to fly."

> I never was what you would call a fancy skater—and while I seldom actually fell, it might have been more impressive if I had. A good resounding fall is no disgrace. It is the fantastic writhing to avoid a fall which destroys any illusion of being a gentleman. How like life that is, after all!
>
> —*Robert Benchley*

Complaints like these are obviously foolish. However pleasant wishing may be, insisting that the unchangeable should be changed won't affect reality one bit. And yet many people torture themselves by engaging in this sort of irrational thinking when they confuse *is* with *should*. They say and think things like this:

> "My friend should be more understanding."
>
> "She shouldn't be so inconsiderate."
>
> "They should be more friendly."
>
> "You should work harder."

The message in each of these cases is that you would *prefer* people to behave differently. Wishing that things were better is perfectly legitimate, and trying to change them is, of course, a good idea; but it's unreasonable to *insist* that the world operate just as you want it to or to feel cheated when things aren't ideal.

Imposing the fallacy of shoulds on yourself can also lead to unnecessary unhappiness. Psychologist Aaron Beck points out some unrealistic self-imposed "shoulds"[88]:

> "I should be able to find a quick solution to every problem."
>
> "I should never feel hurt; I should always be happy and serene."
>
> "I should always demonstrate the utmost generosity, considerateness, dignity, courage, unselfishness."

Becoming obsessed with "shoulds" like these has three troublesome consequences. First, it leads to unnecessary unhappiness, because people who are constantly dreaming about the ideal are seldom satisfied with what they have or who they are. Second, merely complaining without acting can keep you from doing anything to change unsatisfying conditions. Third, this sort of complaining can build a defensive

> A man said to the universe:
> "Sir, I exist!"
> "However," replied the universe,
> "The fact has not created in me
> A sense of obligation."
>
> —*Stephen Crane*

climate with others, who will resent being nagged. It's much more effective to tell people about what you'd like than to preach. Say, "I wish you'd be more punctual" instead of "You should be on time." We'll discuss ways of avoiding defensive climates in Chapter 10.

4. THE FALLACY OF OVERGENERALIZATION The **fallacy of overgeneralization** comprises two types. The first occurs when we base a belief on a limited amount of evidence. For instance, how many times have you found yourself saying something like this:

> "I'm so stupid! I can't even figure out how to download music on my iPod."
>
> "Some friend I am! I forgot my best friend's birthday."

In cases like these, we focus on a limited type of shortcoming as if it represented everything about us. We forget that along with encountering our difficulties we have solved tough problems and that though we're sometimes forgetful, at other times we're caring and thoughtful.

A second type of overgeneralization occurs when we *exaggerate* shortcomings:

"You *never* listen to me."
"You're *always* late."
"I can't think of *anything*."

On closer examination, absolute statements like these are almost always false and usually lead to discouragement or anger. You'll feel far better when you replace overgeneralizations with more accurate messages to yourself and others:

"You often don't listen to me."
"You've been late three times this week."
"I haven't had any ideas I like today."

5. THE FALLACY OF CAUSATION   The **fallacy of causation** is based on the irrational belief that emotions are caused by others rather than by one's own self-talk.

> No one can make you feel inferior without your consent.
>
> —*Eleanor Roosevelt*

This fallacy causes trouble in two ways. The first plagues people who become overly cautious about communicating because they don't want to "cause" any pain or inconvenience for others. This attitude occurs in cases such as:

Visiting friends or family out of a sense of obligation rather than a genuine desire to see them

Keeping quiet when another person's behavior is bothering you

Pretending to be attentive to a speaker when you are already late for an appointment or feeling ill

Praising and reassuring others who ask for your opinion, even when your honest response would be negative

There's certainly no excuse for going out of your way to say things that will result in pain for others, and there will be times when you choose to inconvenience yourself to make life easier for those you care about. It's essential to realize, however, that it's an overstatement to say that you are the one who causes others' feelings. It's more accurate to say that they *respond* to your behavior with feelings of their own. For example, consider how strange it sounds to suggest that you make others fall in love with you. Such a statement simply doesn't make sense. It would be closer to the truth to say that you act in one way or another, and some people might fall in love with you as a result of these actions, whereas others wouldn't. In the same way, it's incorrect to say that you *make* others angry, upset—or happy, for that matter. It's better to say that others create their own responses to your behavior.

The fallacy of causation also operates when we believe that others cause *our* emotions. Sometimes it certainly seems as if they do, either raising or lowering our spirits by their actions. But think about it for a moment: The same actions that will cause you happiness or unhappiness one day have little effect at other times. The insult or compliment that affected your mood strongly yesterday leaves you unaffected today. Why? Because in the latter case you attached less importance to either. You certainly wouldn't feel some emotions without others' behavior, but your reaction, not their actions, determines how you feel.

6. THE FALLACY OF HELPLESSNESS The **fallacy of helplessness** suggests that satisfaction in life is determined by forces beyond your control. People who continuously see themselves as victims make such statements as:

> "There's no way a woman can get ahead in this society. It's a man's world, and the best thing I can do is to accept it."

> "I was born with a shy personality. I'd like to be more outgoing, but there's nothing I can do about that."

> "I can't tell my boss that she is putting too many demands on me. If I did, I might lose my job."

The mistake in statements like these becomes apparent after you realize that you can do many things if you really want to. As you read in Chapter 2, most "can't" statements can be more correctly rephrased either as "won't" ("I can't tell him what I think" becomes "I won't be honest with him") or as "don't know how" ("I can't carry on an interesting conversation" becomes "I don't know what to say"). After you've rephrased these inaccurate "can'ts," it becomes clear that they're either a matter of choice or an area that calls for your action—both quite different from saying that you're helpless.

When viewed in this light, it's apparent that many "can'ts" are really rationalizations to justify not wanting to change. Lonely people, for example, tend to attribute their poor interpersonal relationships to uncontrollable causes. "It's beyond my control," they think. Also, they expect their relational partners to reject them. Notice the self-fulfilling prophecy in this attitude: Believing that your relational prospects are dim can lead you to act in ways that make you an unattractive prospect, whereas acknowledging that there is a way to change—even though it may be difficult—puts the responsibility for your predicament on your shoulders. You *can* become a better communicator—this book is one step in your movement toward that goal. Don't give up or sell yourself short.

7. THE FALLACY OF CATASTROPHIC EXPECTATIONS Fearful communicators who subscribe to the irrational **fallacy of catastrophic expectations** operate on the assumption that if something bad can possibly happen, it will. Typical catastrophic expectations include:

> "If I invite them to the party, they probably won't want to come."

> "If I speak up in order to try to resolve a conflict, things will probably get worse."

> "If I apply for the job I want, I probably won't be hired."

> "If I tell them how I really feel, they'll probably laugh at me."

Imagining the worst possible outcome can create unnecessary debilitative feelings.

© Hans Neleman/Corbis

After you start expecting catastrophic consequences, a self-fulfilling prophecy can begin to build. One study revealed that people who believed that their romantic partners would not change for the better were likely to behave in ways that contributed to the breakup of the relationship.[89]

✔+ INVITATION TO INSIGHT

How Irrational Are You?

1 Return to the situations described in the exercise "Talking to Yourself" on page 144. Examine each one to see whether your self-talk contains any irrational thoughts.

2 Keep a two- or three-day record of your debilitative emotions. Are any of them based on irrational thinking? Examine your conclusions,

and see if you repeatedly use any of the fallacies described in the preceding section.

3 Take a class poll to see which fallacies are most popular. Also, discuss what subjects seem to stimulate most of this irrational thinking (e.g., schoolwork, dating, jobs, family).

Although it's naive to assume that all of your interactions with others will meet with success, it's just as naive to assume that you'll fail. One way to escape from the fallacy of catastrophic expectations is to think about the consequences that would follow even if you don't communicate successfully. Keeping in mind the folly of trying to be perfect and of living only for the approval of others, realize that failing in a given instance usually isn't as bad as it might seem. What if people do laugh at you? Suppose you don't get the job? What if others do get angry at your remarks? Are these matters really *that* serious?

Before moving on, we need to add a few thoughts about thinking and feeling. First, you should realize that thinking rationally won't completely eliminate debilitative emotions. Some debilitative emotions, after all, are very rational: grief over the death of someone you love, euphoria over getting a new job, and apprehension about the future of an important relationship after a serious fight, for example. Thinking rationally can eliminate many debilitative emotions from your life, but not all of them.

MINIMIZING DEBILITATIVE EMOTIONS

How can you overcome irrational thinking? Social scientists and therapists have developed a simple yet effective approach.[90] When practiced conscientiously, it can help you cut down on the self-defeating thinking that leads to many debilitative emotions.

1. *Monitor your emotional reactions.* The first step is to recognize when you're feeling debilitative emotions. (Of course, it's also nice to recognize pleasant emotions when they occur!) As we suggested earlier, one way to recognize emotions is through proprioceptive stimuli: butterflies in the stomach, racing heart, hot flashes, and so on. Although such stimuli might be symptoms of food poisoning, more often they are symptoms of a strong emotion. You can also recognize certain ways of behaving that suggest your feelings: stomping instead of walking normally, being unusually quiet, or speaking in a sarcastic tone of voice are some examples.

   It may seem strange to suggest that it's necessary to look for emotions—they ought to be immediately apparent. The fact is, however, that we often suffer from debilitative emotions for some time without noticing them. For example, at the end of a trying day you've probably caught yourself frowning and realized that you've been wearing that mask for some time without noticing it.

2. *Note the activating event.* After you're aware of how you're feeling, the next step is to figure out what activating event triggered your response. Sometimes it is obvious. For instance, a common source of anger is being accused unfairly (or fairly) of foolish behavior; a common source of hurt is being rejected by somebody important to you. In other cases, however, the activating event isn't so apparent.

    Sometimes there isn't a single activating event but rather a series of small events that finally builds toward a critical mass and triggers a debilitative emotion. This happens when you're trying to work or sleep and are continually interrupted by a string of interruptions, or when you suffer a series of small disappointments.

    The best way to begin tracking down activating events is to notice the circumstances in which you have debilitative emotions. Perhaps they occur when you're around *specific people*. In other cases, you might be bothered by certain *types of individuals* because of their age, role, background, or some other factor. Or perhaps certain *settings* stimulate unpleasant emotions: parties, work, school. Sometimes the *topic* of conversation is the factor that sets you off, whether it be politics, religion, sex, or some other topic.

3. *Record your self-talk.* This is the point at which you analyze the thoughts that are the link between the activating event and your feeling. If you're serious about getting rid of debilitative emotions, it's important to actually write down your self-talk when first learning to use this method. Putting your thoughts on paper will help you see whether they make any sense.

    Monitoring your self-talk might be difficult at first. This is a new activity, and any new activity seems awkward. If you persevere, however, you'll find that you will be able to identify the thoughts that lead to your debilitative emotions. After you get in the habit of recognizing this internal monologue, you'll be able to identify your thoughts quickly and easily.

4. *Reappraise your irrational beliefs.* Reappraising your irrational beliefs is the key to success in the rational-emotive approach. Use the list of irrational fallacies on pages 145–150 to discover which of your internal statements are based on mistaken thinking.

    You can do this most effectively by following three steps. First, decide whether each belief you've recorded is rational or irrational. Next, explain why the

The thought manifests as the word;

The word manifests as the deed;

The deed develops into habit; And the habit hardens into character.

So watch the thought and its ways with care . . .

As we think, so we become.

—*From the* Dhammapada
(The sayings of the Buddha)

"So, when he says, 'What a good boy am I,' Jack is really reinforcing his self-esteem."

belief is rational or irrational. Finally, if the belief is irrational, you should write down an alternative way of thinking that is more rational and that can leave you feeling better when faced with the same activating event in the future.

Replacing self-defeating self-talk with more constructive thinking is an especially effective tool for improving self-confidence and relational communication.[91] Nonetheless, this approach triggers objections from some readers:

"The rational-emotive approach sounds like nothing more than trying to talk yourself out of feeling bad." This accusation is totally correct. After all, because we talk ourselves into feeling bad, what's wrong with talking ourselves out of feeling bad, especially when such feelings are based on irrational thoughts? Rationalizing may be an excuse and a self-deception, but there's nothing wrong with being rational.

"The kind of reappraising we just read sounds phony and unnatural. I don't talk to myself in sentences and paragraphs." There's no need to dispute your irrational beliefs in any special literary style. You can be just as colloquial as you want. The important thing is to clearly understand what thoughts led you into your debilitative emotions so that you can clearly reappraise them. While the approach is new to you, it's a good idea to write or talk out your thoughts in order to make them clear. After you've had some practice, you'll be able to do these steps in a quicker, less formal way.

"This approach is too cold and impersonal. It seems to aim at turning people into calculating, emotionless machines." This is simply not true. A rational thinker can still dream, hope, and love. There's nothing necessarily irrational about feelings like these. Basically rational people even indulge in a bit of irrational thinking once in a while, but they usually know what they're doing. Like healthy eaters who occasionally allow themselves a snack of junk food, rational thinkers occasionally indulge in irrational thoughts, knowing that they'll return to their healthy lifestyle soon with no real damage done.

"This technique promises too much. There's no chance I could rid myself of all unpleasant feelings, however nice that might be." We can answer this objection by assuring you that rational-emotive thinking probably won't totally solve your emotional problems. What it can do is to reduce their number, intensity, and duration. This method is not the answer to all your problems, but it can make a significant difference—which is not a bad accomplishment.

✔+ IN REAL LIFE

Rational Thinking in Action

The following scenarios demonstrate how the rational thinking method described on pages 150–152 applies in everyday challenges. Notice that thinking rationally doesn't eliminate debilitative emotions. Instead, it helps keep them in control, making effective communication more possible.

Situation 1: Dealing with Annoying Customers

Activating Event
I work in a shopping mall that swarms with tourists and locals. Our company's reputation is based on service, but lately I've been losing my patience with the customers. The store is busy from the second we open until we close. Many of the customers are rude, pushy, and demanding. Others expect me to be a tour guide, restaurant reviewer, medical consultant, and even a baby-sitter. I feel like I'm ready to explode.

Beliefs and Self-Talk
1. I'm sick of working with the public. People are really obnoxious!

2. The customers should be more patient and polite instead of treating me like a servant.

3. This work is driving me crazy! If I keep working here, I'm going to become as rude as the customers.

4. I can't quit: I could never find another job that pays this well.

Reappraising Irrational Beliefs
1. It's an overgeneralization to say that *all* people are obnoxious. Actually, most of the customers are fine. Some are even very nice. About 10 percent of them cause most of the trouble. Recognizing that most people are OK leaves me feeling less bitter.

2. It's true that obnoxious customers *should* be more polite, but it's unrealistic to expect that everybody will behave the way they ought to. After all, it's not a perfect world.

3. By saying that the customers are driving me crazy, I suggest that I have no control over the situation. I'm an adult, and I am able to keep a grip on myself. I may not like the way some people behave, but it's my choice how to respond to them.

4. I'm not helpless. If the job is too unpleasant, I can quit. I probably wouldn't find another job that pays

as well as this one, so I have to choose which is more important: money or peace of mind. It's my choice.

Situation 2: Meeting My Girlfriend's Family

Activating Event
Tracy and I are talking about marriage—maybe not soon, but eventually. Her family is very close, and they want to meet me. I'm sure I'll like them, but I am not sure what they will think about me. I was married once before, at a young age. It was a big mistake, and it didn't last. Furthermore, I was laid off two months ago, and I'm between jobs. The family is coming to town next week, and I am very nervous about what they will think of me.

Beliefs and Self-Talk
1. They've *got* to like me! This is a close family, and I'm doomed if they think I'm not right for Tracy.

2. No matter how sensibly I act, all they'll think of is my divorce and unemployment.

3. Maybe the family is right. Tracy deserves the best, and I'm certainly not that!

Reappraising Irrational Beliefs
1. The family's approval is definitely important. Still, my relationship with Tracy doesn't depend on it. She's already said that she's committed to me, no matter what they think. The sensible approach is to say I *want* their approval, but I don't *need* it.

2. I'm expecting the absolute worst if I think that I'm doomed no matter what happens when we meet. There is a chance that they will dislike me, but there's also a chance that things will work out fine. There's no point in dwelling on catastrophes.

3. Just because I've had an imperfect past doesn't mean I'm wrong for Tracy. I've learned from my past mistakes, and I am committed to living a good life. I know I can be the kind of husband she deserves, even though I'm not perfect.

Communication Scenarios
Go to your Premium Website for Looking Out/Looking In, *access "Communication Scenarios" and then select either "Rational Thinking: Annoying Customers" or "Rational Thinking: Meeting My Girlfriend's Family" to watch and analyze dramatized versions of the scenarios described here.*

✔+ SKILL BUILDER

Rational Thinking

1. Return to the diary of irrational thoughts you recorded on page 150. Dispute the self-talk in each case, and write a more rational interpretation of the event.

2. Now try out your ability to think rationally on the spot. You can do this by acting out the scenes listed in step 4. You'll need three players for each one: a subject, the subject's "little voice"—his or her thoughts—and a second party.

3. Play out each scene by having the subject and second party interact while the "little voice" stands just behind the subject and says what the subject is probably thinking. For example, in a scene where the subject is asking an instructor to reconsider a low grade, the little voice might say, "I hope I haven't made things worse by bringing this up. Maybe he'll lower the grade after rereading the test. I'm such an idiot! Why didn't I keep quiet?"

4. Whenever the little voice expresses an irrational thought, the observers who are watching the skit should call out, "Foul." At this point the action should stop while the group discusses the irrational thought and suggests a more rational line of self-talk. The players should then replay the scene with the little voice speaking in a more rational way.

Here are some scenes (of course, you can invent others as well):

a. Two people are just beginning their first date.
b. A potential employee has just begun a job interview.
c. A teacher or boss is criticizing the subject for showing up late.
d. A student and instructor run across each other in the supermarket.

✔+ MAKING THE GRADE

Summary

Emotions have several dimensions. They are signaled by internal physiological changes, manifested by nonverbal reactions, and defined in most cases by cognitive interpretations. We can use this information to make choices about whether or not to verbalize our feelings.

There are several reasons why people do not verbalize many of the emotions they feel. Some people have personalities that are less prone toward emotional expression. Culture and gender also have an effect on the emotions we do and don't share with others. Social rules and roles discourage the expression of some feelings, particularly negative ones. Fear of consequences leads people to withhold expression of some emotions. Finally, contagion can lead us to experience emotions that we might not otherwise have had.

Because total expression of emotions is not appropriate for adults, several guidelines help define when and how to express emotions effectively. Expanding your emotional vocabulary, becoming more self-aware, and expressing mixed feelings are important. Recognizing the difference between feeling, thinking, and acting, as well as accepting responsibility for feelings instead of blaming them on others, lead to better reactions. Choosing the proper time and place to share feelings is also important, as is choosing the best channel for expressing emotions.

Whereas some emotions are facilitative, others are debilitative and inhibit effective functioning. Many of these debilitative emotions are biological reactions rooted in the amygdala portion of the brain, but their negative impact can be altered through rational thinking. It is often possible to communicate more confidently and effectively by identifying troublesome emotions, identifying the activating event and self-talk that triggered them, and reappraising any irrational thoughts with a more logical analysis of the situation.

Key Terms

debilitative emotions (141)
emotional contagion (131)
emotion labor (130)
facilitative emotions (141)
fallacy of approval (146)

fallacy of catastrophic expectations (149)
fallacy of causation (148)
fallacy of helplessness (149)
fallacy of overgeneralization (147)

fallacy of perfection (145)
fallacy of shoulds (147)
reappraisal (124)
rumination (142)
self-talk (145)

Online Resources

Now that you have read this chapter, use your Premium Website for *Looking Out/ Looking In* for quick access to the electronic resources that accompany this text. Your Premium Website gives you access to:

- **Study tools** that will help you assess your learning and prepare for exams (*digital glossary, key term flash cards, review quizzes*).

- **Activities and assignments** that will help you hone your knowledge, understand how theory and research applies to your own life (*Invitation to Insight*), consider ethical challenges in interpersonal communication (*Ethical Challenge*), and build your interpersonal communication skills throughout the course (*Skill Builder*). If requested, you can submit your answers to your instructor.

- **Media resources** that will allow you to watch and critique news video and videos of interpersonal communication situations (*In Real Life, interpersonal video simulations*) and download a chapter review so you can study when and where you'd like (*Audio Study Tools*).

This chapter's key terms and search terms for additional reading are featured in this end-of-chapter section, and you can find this chapter's Invitation to Insight, Ethical Challenge, Skill Builder, and In Real Life activities in the body of the chapter.

Search Terms

When searching online databases to research topics in this chapter, use the following terms (along with this chapter's key terms) to maximize the chances of finding useful information:

affect

communication apprehension

feelings

intrapersonal communication

rational-emotive therapy

shyness

Film and Television

You can see the communication principles described in this chapter portrayed in the following films:

THE SIGNIFICANCE OF EXPRESSING EMOTIONS

Garden State (2004) Rated R

Andrew Largeman (Zach Braff) is living an emotionally numb life, due in part to the belief that he may have been responsible for a paralyzing injury to his mother. When his mother dies, Andrew returns home to New Jersey for the first time in nine years—and he confronts the ghosts of his past.

While home, Andrew meets a young woman named Sam (Natalie Portman) and falls for her quirky charm. With the help of Sam and some of his friends, Andrew realizes that he must acknowledge and purge the pain he's been carrying. Andrew also discovers that the road to emotional health runs through his father, Gideon (Ian Holm), who holds Andrew responsible for the breach between them. Gideon represses his own feelings of anger and pain, and epitomizes the approach to life from which Andrew needs to escape.

Andrew ultimately tells his father that even negative feelings are better than suppressed ones: "What I want more than anything in the world is for it to be okay with you for me to feel something again, even if it's pain. . . ." By the movie's end, Andrew is transformed. He discovers that confronting pain can lead to joy, and that the road to emotional health is most easily traveled with loving companions.

DEBILITATIVE AND FACILITATIVE EMOTIONS

The Upside of Anger (2005) Rated R

Terry Ann Wolfmeyer (Joan Allen) becomes embittered when her husband disappears, apparently having skipped the country with his Swedish secretary. Terry and her four daughters act out their anger in a variety of unproductive ways, including chronic drinking, eating disorders, drug use, poor relational choices, passive aggression, and emotional withdrawal. Many words of anger go unspoken or are said behind closed doors—or come spewing out during alcoholic rages.

Ultimately the characters realize their resentment is eating them alive, both personally and relationally, and they begin to choose facilitative rather than debilitative responses to the issues in their lives. With help from neighbor Denny Davies (Kevin Costner)—who is dealing with problems of his own—they come to a place of wholeness and restoration after several years of upheaval. By the film's end, the Wolfmeyers recognize that they, not the event, were responsible for the many negative emotions they experienced.

Yes Man (2008) Rated PG-13

Carl Allen (Jim Carrey) is a man of many emotions—most of them negative. He's been depressed and lonely since a recent divorce, and he regularly rejects his friends' attempts to get him out of the house. His pattern is to say "no" to every invitation that comes his way—until he attends a motivational seminar that convinces him he needs to say "yes." To everything. Allen's new approach leads to a host of counterintuitive choices, many of which are risky and dangerous (and of course amusing). The adventures that follow help him experience happiness, contentment, and love that otherwise might have escaped him. But feeling obligated to say "yes" comes with a price. Allen wrestles with some of the debilitative emotions described in this chapter as he subscribes to the fallacies of approval, shoulds, and helplessness. Ultimately, Allen realizes there's a time for yes and a time for no. He also learns that sound choices based on rational thinking are the best route to happiness.

LANGUAGE:
Barrier and Bridge

After studying the topics in this chapter, you should be able to:

1. Analyze a real or potential misunderstanding in terms of semantic or pragmatic rules.

2. Describe how principles presented in the section of this chapter titled "The Impact of Language" operate in your life.

3. Construct a message at the optimal level of specificity or vagueness for a given situation.

4. Recast "you" statements into "I" or "we" statements to reflect your responsibility for the content of messages.

5. Rephrase disruptive statements in less inflammatory terms.

6. In a given situation, analyze how gender and/or cultural differences may affect the quality of interaction.

Now the whole world had one language and a common speech.

As men moved eastward, they found a plain in Shinar and settled there.

They said to each other, "Come, let's make bricks and bake them thoroughly." They used brick instead of stone, and tar for mortar.

Then they said, "Come, let us build ourselves a city, with a tower that reaches to the heavens, so that we may make a name for ourselves and not be scattered over the face of the whole earth."

But the Lord came down to see the city and the tower that the men were building.

The Lord said, "If as one people speaking the same language they have begun to do this, then nothing they plan to do will be impossible for them.

Come, let us go down and confuse their language so they will not understand each other."

So the Lord scattered them from there over all the earth, and they stopped building the city.

That is why it was called Babel—because there the Lord confused the language of the whole world.

—*Genesis 11:1–9*

Kunsthistorisches Museum, Wien oder KHM, Wien

*T*he problems that began with Babel continue on today. Sometimes it seems as if none of us speaks the same language. Yet, despite its frustrations and challenges, language is clearly a marvelous tool. It is the gift that allows us to communicate in a way that no other animals appear to match. Without language, we would be more ignorant, ineffectual, and isolated.

In this chapter we explore the nature of language, looking at how to take advantage of its strengths and minimize its weaknesses. After a quick explanation of the symbolic nature of language, we examine the sources of most misunderstandings. We then move beyond the challenges of simply understanding one another and explore how the language we use affects the climate of interpersonal relationships. Finally, we broaden our focus even more to look at how linguistic practices shape the attitudes of entire cultures.

> I was meeting a friend in a bar, and as I went in, I noted two pretty girls looking at me. "Nine," I heard one whisper as I passed. Feeling pleased with myself, I swaggered over to my buddy and told him a girl had just rated me a nine out of ten.
>
> "I don't want to ruin it for you," he said, "but when I walked in, they were speaking German."
>
> —*Richard Mogridge*

Language Is Symbolic

In the natural world, signs have a direct connection with the things they represent. For example, smoke is a sign that something's burning, and a high fever is a sign of illness. There's nothing arbitrary about the relationship between natural signs and the things they represent. Nobody made them up, and they exist independent of human opinions.

In human language, the connection between signs and the things they represent isn't so direct. Instead, language is *symbolic*: There's only an arbitrary connection between words and the ideas or things to which they refer. For example, there is nothing particularly fivelike in the number five. The word represents the number of fingers on your hand only because English speakers agree that it does. To a speaker of French, the symbol "cinq" would convey the same meaning; to a computer programmer, the same value would be represented by the coded symbol "00110101."

Even sign language, as "spoken" by most hearing-impaired people, is symbolic in nature and not the pantomime it might seem. Because this form of communication is symbolic and not literal, hundreds of sign languages around the world have evolved independently whenever significant numbers of hearing-impaired people are in contact.[1] These distinct languages include American Sign Language, British Sign Language, French Sign Language, Danish Sign Language, Chinese Sign Language—even Australian Aboriginal and Mayan Sign Languages.

The symbolic nature of language is a blessing. It enables us to communicate in ways that wouldn't otherwise be possible: about ideas, reasons, the past, the future, and things not present. Without symbolic

"What part of oil lamp next to double squiggle over ox don't you understand?"

It's difficult to catch every equivocal statement and clarify it while speaking. For this reason, the responsibility for interpreting statements accurately rests in large part with the receiver. Feedback of one sort or another—for example, the kind of perception checking introduced in Chapter 3 and the paraphrasing described in Chapter 7—can help clear up misunderstandings.

Despite its obvious problems, equivocal language has its uses. (See the On the Job sidebar on this page for some work-related examples.) As Chapter 9 describes in detail, there are times when using language that is open to several interpretations can be useful. It helps people get along by avoiding the kind of honesty and clarity that can embarrass both the speaker and listener. For example, if a friend proudly shows you a newly completed painting and asks your opinion about it, you might respond equivocally by saying, "Gee, it's really unusual. I've never seen anything like it," instead of giving a less ambiguous but more hurtful response such as "This may be the ugliest thing I've ever seen!"

RELATIVE LANGUAGE **Relative words** gain their meaning by comparison. For example, do you attend a large or small school? This depends on what you compare it to. Alongside a huge state university, your school may not seem big, but compared with

ON THE JOB

Strategic Ambiguity

In most of the English-speaking world, phrases like "Don't beat around the bush" and "Get to the point" reflect the belief that speaking directly is important. Vague language is often seen as a sign of poor communication and perhaps questionable ethics.

Even in normally low-context cultures like the United States and Canada, there are times when indirect speech helps communicators achieve useful goals in an ethically sound way.[a] The first is to *promote harmony*. A boss trying to improve the climate between feuding employees can probably get them to agree that "we can find better ways to handle this problem." The feuding employees may not agree on much else, so this agreement can provide common ground that will increase the odds of cooperation on tougher issues.

Another function of strategic ambiguity is to *save face* by softening the blow of difficult messages. One observer describes how indirectness works in high-context countries, where vague speech is an art form:

When they say "I'd like to reflect on your proposal a while," . . . it means "You are dead wrong, and you'd better come up with a better idea very soon . . . ." It seems to me that such indirectness in interpersonal communication is a virtue; it is just as efficient, and it is certainly more mature and polite than the affront, "You are dead wrong."[b]

A third function of strategic ambiguity is to make a point indirectly that can't be expressed overtly. Here is a humorous letter of reference "endorsing" a former employee who was fired for being a slow, lazy, unmotivated worker.

John Doe is definitely a man to watch: You won't find many people like him. You'll be lucky to get John to work for you. I don't think he could have done a better job for us if he had tried. No salary would be too much for him.

One risk of strategically ambiguous speech is the chance of misunderstandings. As a sender, one measure of communication competence is the ability to understand when and how to create ambiguous messages that are likely to be understood as intended. And competent receivers have the skill to read between the lines and get the intended meaning of vague messages. These skills can enhance the career of skilled communicators.

a small college, it may seem quite large. Relative words such as *fast* and *slow*, *smart* and *stupid*, *short* and *long* are clearly defined only through comparison.

Some relative terms are so common that we mistakenly assume they have a clear meaning. For instance, if a friend told you it's "likely" she'll show up at your party tonight, what are the chances she's going to come? In one study, students were asked to assign percentages to such terms as *doubtful*, *toss-up*, *likely*, *probable*, *good chance*, and *unlikely*.[5] There was a tremendous variation in the meaning of most of these terms. For example, the responses for *probable* ranged from 0 to 99 percent. *Good chance* fell between 35 and 90 percent, whereas *unlikely* fell between 0 and 40 percent.

One way to make words more measurable is to turn them into numbers. Healthcare practitioners have learned that patients often use vague descriptions when describing their pain: "It hurts a little"; "I'm pretty sore." The use of a numeric pain scale can give a more precise response—and lead to a better diagnosis.[6] When patients are asked to rank their pain from 1–10, with 10 being the most severe pain they've ever experienced, the number 7 is much more concrete and specific than "it aches a bit." The same technique can be used when asking people to rate anything from the movies they've seen to their job satisfaction.

STATIC EVALUATION   "Mark is a nervous guy." "Karen is short-tempered." "You can always count on Wes." Statements that contain or imply the word *is* lead to the mistaken assumption that people are consistent and unchanging—an incorrect belief known as **static evaluation**. Instead of labeling Mark as permanently and totally nervous, it would be more accurate to outline the particular situations in which he behaves nervously. The same goes for Karen, Wes, and the rest of us: We are more changeable than the way static, everyday language describes us.

ABSTRACTION   When it comes to describing problems, goals, appreciation, and requests, some language is more specific than others. **Abstract language** is vague in nature, whereas **behavioral language**—as its name implies—refers to specific things that people say or do. The **"abstraction ladder"** in Figure 5.1 illustrates how the same phenomenon can be described at various levels of specificity and abstraction. Notice how the ladder's bottom-rung description is more concrete and behavioral, and thus is probably clearer than the top-rung's abstract injunction to develop a "better attitude."

We use higher-level abstractions all the time. For instance, rather than saying, "Thanks for washing the dishes," "Thanks for vacuuming the

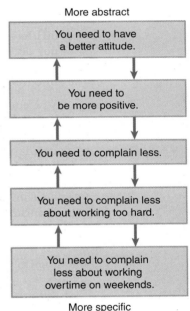

Figure 5.1
Abstraction Ladder

"Be honest with me, Roger. By 'mid-course correction' you mean divorce, don't you."

rug," or "Thanks for making the bed," it's easier to say, "Thanks for cleaning up." In such everyday situations, abstractions are a useful kind of verbal shorthand.

Although verbal shorthand like this can be useful, highly abstract language can lead to blanket judgments and stereotyping: "Marriage counselors are worthless," "Skateboarders are delinquents," or "Men are no good." Overly abstract expressions like these can cause people to *think* in generalities, ignoring uniqueness. As you learned in Chapter 3, stereotyping can injure interpersonal relationships, because it categorizes and evaluates people in ways that may not be accurate.

Overly abstract language can lead to serious problems. For instance, accusations of sexual assault can arise because one person claims to have said "no" when the other person insists that no such refusal was ever conveyed. In response to this sort of disagreement, specific rules of sexual conduct have become more common in work and educational settings. Perhaps the best-known code of this type was the one developed at Ohio's Antioch College. The code uses low-level abstractions to minimize the chances of anyone claiming confusion about a partner's willingness. For example, the code states:

> If sexual contact and/or conduct is not mutually and simultaneously initiated, then the person who initiates sexual contact/conduct is responsible for getting verbal consent of the other individual(s) involved.

> If one person wants to initiate moving to a higher level of sexual intimacy, that person is responsible for getting verbal consent of the other person(s) involved before moving to that level.

> If someone has initially consented but then stops consenting during a sexual interaction, she/he should communicate withdrawal verbally and/or through physical resistance. The other individual(s) must stop immediately.[7]

✓+ SKILL BUILDER

Down-to-Earth Language

You can appreciate the value of nonabstract language by translating the following into behavioral terms:

1. An abstract goal for improving your interpersonal communication (e.g., "be more assertive" or "stop being so sarcastic").

2. A complaint you have about another person (e.g., that he or she is "selfish" or "insensitive").

3. A request for someone to change (e.g., "I wish you'd be more punctual" or "Try to be more positive").

4. An appreciation you could share with another person (e.g., "Thanks for being so helpful" or "I appreciate your patience").

In each case, describe the person or persons involved, the circumstances in which the behavior occurs, and the precise behaviors involved. What differences can you expect when you use behavioral descriptions like the ones you have created here?

Some critics have ridiculed rules like these as being unrealistically legalistic and chilling for romantic relationships. Whatever its weaknesses, the Antioch code illustrates how low-level abstractions can reduce the chance of a serious misunderstanding. Specific language may not be desirable or necessary in many situations, but in an era when misinterpretations can lead to accusations of physical assault, it does seem to have a useful place. You can better understand the value of behavioral descriptions by looking at the examples in Table 5.1. Notice how much more clearly they explain the speaker's thoughts than do the vaguer terms.

Table 5.1
Abstract vs. Behavioral Descriptions

	Abstract Description	Behavioral Description			Remarks
		Who Is Involved	**In What Circumstances**	**Specific Behaviors**	
Problem	I talk too much.	People I find intimidating	When I want them to like me	I talk (mostly about myself) instead of giving them a chance to speak or asking about their lives.	Behavioral description more clearly identifies behaviors to change.
Goal	I want to be more constructive.	My roommate	When we talk about household duties	Instead of finding fault with her ideas, suggest alternatives that might work.	Behavioral description clearly outlines how to act, abstract description doesn't.
Appreciation	"You've really been helpful lately."	(Deliver to fellow worker)	"When I've had to take time off work because of personal problems . . ."	" . . . you took my shifts without complaining."	Give both abstract and behavioral descriptions for best results.
Request	"Clean up your act!"	(Deliver to target person)	"When we're around my family . . ."	" . . . please don't tell jokes that involve sex."	Behavioral description specifies behavior.

UNDERSTANDING STRUCTURE: SYNTACTIC RULES

Syntactic rules govern the grammar of a language. You can appreciate how syntax contributes to the meaning of a statement by considering two versions of a letter:

Version 1

Dear John:

I want a man who knows what love is all about. You are generous, kind, thoughtful. People who are not like you admit to being useless and inferior. You have ruined me for other men. I yearn for you. I have no feelings whatsoever when we're apart. I can be forever happy—will you let me be yours?

Mary

Version 2

Dear John:

I want a man who knows what love is. All about you are generous, kind, thoughtful people, who are not like you. Admit to being useless and inferior. You have ruined me. For other men, I yearn. For you, I have no feelings whatsoever. When we're apart, I can be forever happy. Will you let me be?

Yours,

Mary

Semantic rules don't explain why these letters send virtually opposite messages. There's no ambiguity about the meaning of the words they contain: "love," "kind," "thoughtful," and so on. The opposite meanings of the letters came from their different syntax.

Although most of us aren't able to describe the syntactic rules that govern our language, it's easy to recognize their existence when they are violated. A humorous example is the way the character Yoda speaks in the *Star Wars* movies. Phrases such as "the dark side are they" or "your father he is" often elicit a chuckle because they bend syntactical norms. Sometimes, however, apparently ungrammatical speech is simply following a different set of syntactic rules, reflecting regional or co-cultural dialects. Linguists believe it is crucial to view such dialects as *different* rather than *deficient* forms of English.[8]

UNDERSTANDING CONTEXT: PRAGMATIC RULES

Semantic and syntactic problems don't account for all misunderstandings.[9] To appreciate a different type of communication challenge, imagine how a young female employee might struggle to make sense of her older male boss's statement "You look very pretty today." She almost certainly would understand the meaning of the words, and the syntax is perfectly clear. Still, the boss's message could be interpreted in several ways. Was the remark a simple compliment? A come-on? Did it contain the suggestion that she didn't look nice on other days?

If the boss and employee share the same interpretation of the message, their communication would be smooth. But if they bring different perspectives to interpreting it, a problem exists. Table 5.2 shows several ways in which different perspectives of the boss and employee would lead to their attaching different meanings to the same words.

"I never said 'I love you.' I said 'I love ya.' Big difference!"

In situations like this one, we rely on **pragmatic rules** to decide how to interpret messages in a given context. Pragmatic rules govern the way speech operates in everyday interaction. You can't look up pragmatic rules in any dictionary. They are almost always unstated, but they are just as important as semantic and syntactic rules in helping us make sense of one another's messages.

The best way to appreciate how pragmatic rules operate is to think of communication as a kind of cooperative game. Like all games, success depends on all of the players

Table 5.2

Pragmatic Rules Govern the Use and Meaning of a Statement

	Boss	Employee
Statement	"You look very nice today."	
Self-Concept "Who am I?" "Who is s/he?"	Friendly guy	Woman determined to succeed on own merits
Episode "What's going on in this exchange?"	Casual conversation	Possible come-on by boss?
Relationship "Who are we to one another?"	Boss who treats employees like family members	Subordinate employee, dependent on boss's approval for advancement
Culture "What does my background say about the meaning here?"	Euro-American, raised in United States	Latina, raised in South America

Adapted from W. B. Pearce and V. Cronen (1980). Communication, Action, and Meaning. *New York: Praeger; and E. M. Griffin (2009).* A First Look at Communication Theory, *7th ed. New York: McGraw-Hill.*

understanding and following the same set of rules. This is why communication scholars use the term *coordination* to describe the way conversation operates when everyone involved uses the same set of pragmatic rules.[10]

Some pragmatic rules are shared by most people in a culture. In the United States and Canada, for instance, competent communicators understand that the question "How's it going?" usually isn't really a request for information. Anyone familiar with the rules

✔+ INVITATION TO INSIGHT

Your Linguistic Rules

To what extent do linguistic rules affect your understanding of and relationships with others? Explore this question by following these steps:

1 Recall a time when you encountered someone whose speech violated the syntactic rules that you are used to. What was your impression of this person? To what degree was this impression influenced by her or his failure to follow familiar linguistic rules? Consider whether this impression was or was not valid.

2 Recall at least one misunderstanding that arose when you and another person followed different semantic rules. Use hindsight to consider

whether this misunderstanding (and others like it) could be avoided. If semantic misunderstandings can be minimized, explain what approaches might be useful.

3 Identify at least two pragmatic rules that govern the use of language in one of your relationships. Share these rules with other students. Do they use language in the same way as you and your relational partner?

of conversation knows that the proper answer is something like "Pretty good. How's it going with you?" Likewise, most people understand the pragmatic rule that says that "Would you like a drink?" means "Would you like an alcoholic beverage?" whereas "Would you like something to drink?" is a more open-ended question.

Besides following cultural rules, people in individual relationships create their own sets of pragmatic rules. Consider the use of humor: The teasing and jokes you exchange with gusto with one friend might be considered tasteless or offensive in another relationship.[11] For instance, imagine an email message typed in CAPITAL LETTERS and filled with CURSE WORDS, INSULTS, NAME-CALLING, and EXCLAMATION MARKS!!! How would you interpret such a message? An outside observer may consider this an example of "flaming" and be appalled, when in fact the message might be a fun-loving case of "verbal jousting" between buddies.[12] If you have a good friend whom you call by a less-than-tasteful nickname as a term of endearment, then you understand the concept. Keep in mind, however, that those who aren't privy to your relationship's pragmatic rules are likely to misunderstand you, so you'll want to be wise about when and where to use these personal codes.

The Impact of Language

So far we have focused on language only as a medium for helping communicators understand one another. But along with this important function, language can shape our perceptions of the world around us and reflect the attitudes we hold toward one another.

NAMING AND IDENTITY

"What's in a name?" Juliet asked rhetorically. If Romeo had been a social scientist, he would have answered "A great deal."

Research has demonstrated that names are more than just a simple means of identification: They shape the way others think of us, the way we view ourselves, and the way we act. For more than a century, researchers have studied the impact of rare and unique names on the people who bear them.[13] Early studies claimed that people with unusual names suffered everything from psychological and emotional disturbance to failure in college. More recent studies have shown that people often have negative appraisals not only of unusual names, but also of unusual name spellings.[14] (See the reading on page 171.) Of course, what makes a name (and its spelling) unusual changes with time. In 1900, the twenty most popular names for baby girls included Bertha, Mildred, and Ethel. By 2008, the top twenty names included Madison, Ava, and Chloe—names that would have been highly unusual a century earlier.[15]

Names are one way to shape and reinforce a child's personal identity, as the reading on page 171 suggests. Naming a baby after a fam-

Naming a child is not easy for parents in America who come from non-European backgrounds, from cultures where Ashutosh, Chae-Hyun and Naeem are common names. We have to ask ourselves a number of important questions. How will the child's foreign name sound to American ears? (That test ruled out Shiva, my family deity; a Jewish friend put her foot down.) Will it provoke bullies to beat him up on the school playground? (That was the end of Karan, the name of a warrior from the *Mahabharata,* the Hindu epic. A boy called "Karen" wouldn't stand a chance.) Will it be as euphonic in New York as it is in New Delhi? (That was how Sameer failed to get off the ground. "Like a bagel with a schmear!" said one ruthless well-wisher.)

—*Tunku Varadarajan*

On Naming Baby

A rose by any other name may smell as sweet, but would Rose by another name grow up to be the same person?

Most parents who give their children exotic names are striving for individuality. There are certain advantages to being the only Shalice Jadzia Washington in the school, or on the payroll. Unusual names also don't hold a lot of predispositions that common names do. Danelle Duran named her son Ukiah in part because it was the only name everyone could agree to; no one associated the name with jocks, hicks or nerds, she said.

Unique names can have serious consequences, however. They are harder to pronounce, which can be frustrating, especially for younger children and for teachers coping with a new class at the beginning of the school year. On a more serious note, studies have shown that people tend to negatively judge people with unusual names solely on the basis of the name.

"A very general finding is that people don't react well to things that are new and unusual. They aren't as comfortable with it, and that applies to names," said Dr. Albert Mehrabian, author of *The Name Game*[a] and *The Baby Name Report Card*.[b] For over a decade, Mehrabian has studied how a name changes perceptions of a person's morality, cheerfulness, success and even masculinity or femininity. Compared to names standard for our culture, unusual names are rated dramatically lower in all

© Josh Gosfield/Corbis

categories—even a change of spelling in a common name will negatively affect someone's scores, he said. "I know a lot of people don't like to hear that, because they think they're being creative. They think they're making their kids (individual), but blue hair is unusual. But is it desirable?"

Even bearers of unusual names warn parents not to give their kids "kick-me-in-the-head" names, which will easily lead to teasing in the schoolyard. Regina Koske, a teacher at a private school in California, remembers two of her students, Strawberry and Justice, who had especially hard times. "The other students laughed and teased Strawberry constantly and said things like, 'I'm going to eat you.' Every time we said the Pledge of Allegiance and got to '. . . and justice for all,' many kids would repeat 'And Justice?' and laugh. After a time, (they) got used to the unusual name and it wasn't unusual any more. However, every time that child enters a new group of peers, he or she will once again have to deal with the stigma of a particularly unusual name."

Even as adults, an unusual name may lead to ridicule. Contrary to the "Boy Named Sue" idea that a nonstandard name will strengthen a child in adulthood, Mehrabian said he's found that the more unusual a person's name is, the harder it is for them to adjust.

Karina L. Fabian

ily member (e.g., "Junior" or "Trey") can create a connection between the youngster and his or her namesake. Name choice can also be a powerful way to make a statement about cultural identity. For example, in recent decades a large percentage of names given to African American babies have been distinctively black.[16] In California, more than 40 percent of black girls born recently have names that not a single white baby born in the entire state was given. Researchers suggest that distinctive names like these are a symbol of solidarity with the African American community.

Conversely, choosing a less distinctive name can be a way of integrating the baby into the majority culture. Whether common or unusual, the impact of names recedes after communicators become more familiar with one another.[17]

The importance of names in defining identity applies to membership in groups. For example, the term *African American* has become the label of choice for people who, in earlier times, would probably have been called "colored," "Negro," "Afro-American," or "black."[18] Each label has its own connotations, which is why naming is so important. In one study, white subjects with a variety of political beliefs said they would be more likely to vote for a candidate who talked about the concerns of "blacks" than one who talked about the concerns of "African Americans."[19] Clearly, the terms used to label social groups can shape the way members of those groups regard themselves and the way others regard them. Some terms may seem familiar and thus innocuous, but their impact on both the namers and those being named can have subtle but profound effects.

AFFILIATION

Besides shaping an individual's identity, speech can build and demonstrate solidarity with others. Research has demonstrated that communicators are attracted to others whose style of speaking is similar to theirs.[20] Likewise, communicators who want to show affiliation with one another adapt their speech in a variety of ways, including their choice of vocabulary, rate of talking, number and placement of pauses, and level of politeness.[21] Adolescents who all adopt the same vocabulary of slang words and speech mannerisms illustrate the principle of linguistic solidarity.

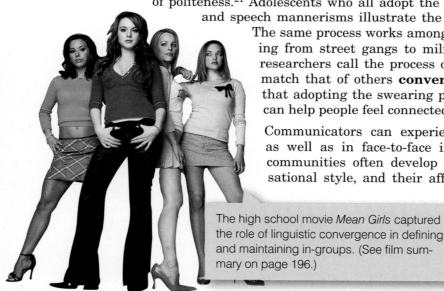

The same process works among members of other groups, ranging from street gangs to military personnel. Communication researchers call the process of adapting one's speech style to match that of others **convergence**. One study even showed that adopting the swearing patterns of bosses and coworkers can help people feel connected on the job.[22]

Communicators can experience convergence in cyberspace as well as in face-to-face interactions. Members of online communities often develop a shared language and conversational style, and their affiliation with each other can be seen in increased uses of the pronoun "we."[23] On a larger scale, IM and email users create and use shortcuts that mark them as Internet-savvy. If you know what ROTFL, IMHO, and JK mean, you're probably part of that group. (For the uninitiated, those acronyms mean "rolling on the floor laughing," "in my humble opinion," and "just kidding.") Interestingly, IMers may find that their cyberlanguage creeps into everyday conversations.[24] (Have you ever said "LOL" instead of the words "laughing out loud"—or instead of actually laughing out loud?)

The high school movie *Mean Girls* captured the role of linguistic convergence in defining and maintaining in-groups. (See film summary on page 196.)

Paramount/The Kobal Collection

When two or more people feel equally positive about one another, their linguistic convergence will be mutual. But when communicators want or need approval, they often adapt their speech to accommodate the other person's style, trying to say the "right thing" or speak in a way that will help them fit in. We see this process when immigrants who want to gain the rewards of material success in a new culture strive to master the host language. Likewise, employees who seek advancement tend to speak more like their superiors, superiors adopt the speech style of managers, and managers converge toward their bosses.

The principle of speech accommodation works in reverse, too. Communicators who want to set themselves apart from others adopt the strategy of **divergence**, speaking in a way that emphasizes their differences from others. For example, members of an ethnic group, even though fluent in the dominant language, might use their own dialect as a way of showing solidarity with one another—a sort of "us against them" strategy. The same behavior can occur across ethnic lines, such as teens who adopt the slang of particular subcultures to show divergence with adults and convergence with their peers.[25] Of course, communicators need to be careful about when to—and when not to—converge their language with others. Most of us can remember the embarrassment of hearing a parent using youthful slang and thinking, "You're too old to be saying that—quit trying to sound like us." On a more serious level, using ethnic/racial epithets when you're not a member of that in-group can be inappropriate and even offensive. One of the pragmatic goals of divergence is the creation of norms about who has the "right" to use certain words and who does not. (The film *The N-Word*, described at the end of this chapter, offers a good discussion of this topic.)

POWER

Communication researchers have identified several language patterns that add to or detract from a speaker's power to influence others. Notice the difference between these two statements:

> "Excuse me, sir. I hate to say this, but I . . . uh . . . I guess I won't be able to turn in the assignment on time. I had a personal emergency, and . . . well . . . it was just impossible to finish it by today. I'll have it on your desk on Monday, OK?"

> "I won't be able to turn in the assignment on time. I had a personal emergency, and it was impossible to finish it by today. I'll have it on your desk Monday."

Whether or not the professor finds the excuse acceptable, it's clear that the tone of the second one is more confident, whereas the tone of the first is apologetic and uncertain. Table 5.3 identifies several **powerless speech mannerisms** illustrated in the statements you just read. Some studies have shown that speakers whose talk is free of these mannerisms are rated as more competent, dynamic, and attractive than speakers who sound powerless.[26] Powerful speech can help candidates in job interviews. Employers rate applicants who use a powerful style as more competent and employable than candidates who speak less forcefully.[27] One study revealed that even a single type of powerless speech mannerism can make a person appear less authoritative or socially attractive.[28]

Powerful speech that gets the desired results in mainstream North American and European cultures doesn't succeed everywhere with everyone.[29] In Japan, saving face for others is an important goal, so communicators there tend to speak in ambiguous terms and use hedge words and qualifiers.

Powerful speech is one way—but not the only way—to get what you want.

© age fotostock/SuperStock

Table 5.3
Examples of Powerless Language

Hedges	"I'm *kinda* disappointed . . ."
	"I *think* we should . . ."
	"I *guess* I'd like to . . ."
Hesitations	"*Uh*, can I have a minute of your time?"
	"*Well*, we could try this idea . . ."
	"I wish you would—*er*—try to be on time."
Intensifiers	"I'm *really* glad to see you."
	"I'm not *very* hungry."
Polite forms	"Excuse me, *sir* . . ."
Tag questions	"It's about time we got started, *isn't it*?"
	"*Don't you think* we should give it another try?"
Disclaimers	"*I probably shouldn't say this, but* . . ."
	"*I'm not really sure, but* . . ."
Rising inflections	(See the reading on page 222 in Chapter 6.)

In most Japanese sentences, the verb comes at the end of the sentence so that the "action" part of the sentence can be postponed. Traditional Mexican culture, with its strong emphasis on cooperation, also uses hedging to smooth over interpersonal relationships. By not taking a firm stand with their speech language, Mexicans avoid making others feel ill at ease. The Korean culture represents yet another people who prefer "indirect" (e.g., "perhaps," "could be") over "direct" speech.

Even in cultures that value assertiveness, language that is *too* powerful may intimidate or annoy others. Consider these two different approaches to handling a common situation:

> "Excuse me. My baby is having a little trouble getting to sleep. Would you mind turning down the music just a little?"

> "My baby can't sleep because your music is too loud. Please turn it down."

The more polite, if less powerful, approach would probably produce better results than the stronger statement. How can this fact be reconciled with the research on powerful language? The answer lies in the tension between the potentially opposing goals of getting immediate results and developing positive relationships. If you come across as too powerful, you may get what you're seeking in the short term but alienate the other person in ways that will make your relationship more difficult in the long term. Furthermore, a statement that is *too* powerful can convey relational messages of disrespect and superiority, which are just as likely to antagonize others as to gain their compliance.

In some situations, polite, less apparently powerful forms of speech can even enhance a speaker's effectiveness.[30] For example, a boss might say to a secretary, "Would you mind retyping this letter?" In truth, both the boss and secretary know that this is an order and not a request, but the questioning form is more considerate and leaves the secretary feeling better about the boss.[31] The importance of achieving both content and relational goals helps explain why a mixture of powerful speech and polite speech is usually most effective.[32]

DISRUPTIVE LANGUAGE

Not all linguistic problems come from misunderstandings. Sometimes people understand one another perfectly and still wind up in a conflict. Of course, not all disagreements can, or should be, avoided. But eliminating three linguistic habits from your communication repertoire can minimize the kind of disagreements that don't need to happen, allowing you to save your energy for the unavoidable and important disagreements.

FACT–OPINION CONFUSION   Factual statements are claims that can be verified as true or false. By contrast, opinion statements are based on the speaker's beliefs. Unlike factual statements, they can never be proved or disproved. Consider a few examples of the difference between factual and opinion statements:

Fact	*Opinion*
You forgot my birthday.	You don't care about me.
You keep interrupting me.	You're a control freak.
You tell a lot of ethnic jokes.	You're a bigot.

Bitching It Out (Out with Bitching)

Different words hold different taboos for different people. I personally don't care when people swear or reference things I've only read about on Urban Dictionary. I don't feel much remorse when I use the word "lame" when referring to that Friday night I spent watching *High School Musical* by myself. But I abhor "the B word." Let me explain why.

©iStockphoto.com/-Vladimir-

Some say that bitch is an insult for both genders. That's actually what makes the word so chauvinist. The most frequently used version of bitch directed at women makes us think of a boss who is abrasive or a girl who always gets what she wants. The term takes on new meaning when it's used to describe men. While a woman who is a bitch is generally at the top of some social or economic hierarchy, the same term applied to a man means he is weak or subordinate (i.e., "a little bitch"). Even the height of power for a woman is a low place for men. At least, that's what the word implies.

The word bitch has attached itself to empowered women. If you disagree, think of the biggest, well, bitch you know. Consider describing her to someone else. What other term could you use? The word automatically comes with a superficial gender-biased archetype of power. To phase out its usage would be to help phase out the idea that women in power have different leadership capabilities than men.

Of course, bitch is used in other ways. For example, one can bitch about something. I find that the verb tags along with the noun's oppressive meaning. Bitching is nagging. For women it's expected, for men it shows weakness. Again, the word reinforces the gender divide. It's also a popularized term—especially visible in hip-hop and rap music—for women in general. To say that this slang definition is harmless is ridiculous. I like to think my sex is composed of more than "hoes and tricks." But that's another discussion.

The only usage I don't find fault with seems to be bitchin', as in cool. That doesn't refer to any one sex. If we all try to make a conscious effort to let go of such troublesome vocabulary choices, we can make an impact in escaping their disappointing societal implications. And that's pretty bitchin'.

Alice Stanley

When factual and opinion statements are set side by side like this, the difference is clear. In everyday conversation, however, we often present our opinions as if they were facts, and in doing so we invite an unnecessary argument. For example:

"That was a dumb thing to say!"

"Spending that much on a pair of shoes is a waste of money!"

"You can't get a fair shake in this country unless you're a white male."

Notice how much less antagonistic each statement would be if it were prefaced by a qualifier that takes responsibility for the opinion such as "I believe . . . ," "In my opinion . . . ," or "It seems to me. . . ." We'll discuss the importance of responsible "I" language later in this chapter.

FACT–INFERENCE CONFUSION   Problems also arise when we confuse factual statements with inferential statements—conclusions arrived at from an interpretation of evidence.

Arguments often result when we label our inferences as facts:

A: *Why are you mad at me?*

B: *I'm not mad at you. Why have you been so insecure lately?*

A: *I'm not insecure. It's just that you've been so critical.*

B: *What do you mean, "critical"? I haven't been critical. . . .*

Instead of trying to read the other person's mind, a far better course is to use the skill of perception checking that you learned in Chapter 3: Identify the observable behaviors (facts) that have caught your attention and describe one or more possible

---

✔+ INVITATION TO INSIGHT

Conjugating "Irregular Verbs"

The technique is simple: Just take an action or personality trait and show how it can be viewed either favorably or unfavorably, according to the label it's given. For example:

I'm casual.
You're a little careless.
He's a slob.

Or try this one:

I'm thrifty.
You're money conscious.
She's a tightwad.

1   Try a few conjugations yourself, using the following statements:
    a.   I'm tactful.
    b.   I'm conservative.

    c.   I'm quiet.
    d.   I'm relaxed.
    e.   My child is high-spirited.
    f.   I have high self-esteem.

2   Now recall at least two situations in which you used emotive language as if it was a description of fact and not an opinion. A good way to recall these situations is to think of a recent disagreement and imagine how the other people involved might have described it differently than you.

interpretations that you have drawn from them. After describing this train of thought, ask the other person to comment on the accuracy of your interpretation.

> "When you didn't return my phone call (*fact*), I got the idea that you're mad at me (*interpretation*). Are you?" (*question*)

> "You've been asking me whether I still love you a lot lately (*fact*), and that makes me think you're feeling insecure (*inference*). Or maybe I'm behaving differently. What's on your mind?" (*question*)

EMOTIVE LANGUAGE **Emotive language** seems to describe something but actually announces the speaker's attitude toward it. If you approve of a friend's roundabout approach to a difficult subject, you might call her "tactful"; if you don't approve of it, you might accuse her of "beating around the bush." Whether the approach is good or bad is more a matter of opinion than of fact, although this difference is obscured by emotive language.

You can appreciate how emotive words are really editorial statements when you consider these examples:

If you approve, say	*If you disapprove, say*
thrifty	cheap
traditional	old-fashioned
extrovert	loudmouth
cautious	cowardly
progressive	radical
information	propaganda
military victory	massacre
eccentric	crazy

The best way to avoid arguments involving emotive words is to describe the person, thing, or idea you are discussing in neutral terms and to label your opinions as such.

Instead of saying "Quit making sexist remarks," say "I really don't like it when you call us 'girls' instead of 'women.'" Not only are nonemotive statements more accurate, but also they have a much better chance of being well received by others.

THE LANGUAGE OF RESPONSIBILITY

Besides providing a way to make the content of a message clear or obscure, language reflects the speakers' willingness to take responsibility for their beliefs and feelings. This acceptance or rejection of responsibility says a great deal about the speaker and can shape the tone of a relationship. To see how, read on.

"My hand is doing this movement . . ."

"Is it doing the movement?"

"I am moving my hand like this . . . and now the thought comes to me that . . ."

"The thought 'comes' to you?"

"I have the thought."

"You have it?"

"I think. Yes. I think that I use 'it' very much, and I am glad that by noticing it

I can bring it all back to me."

"Bring it back?"

"Bring myself back. I feel thankful for this."

"This?"

"Your idea about the 'it.'"

"My idea?"

"I feel thankful towards you."

—*Claudio Naranjo*

"IT" STATEMENTS. Notice the difference between the sentences of each set:

"It bothers me when you're late."

"I'm worried when you're late."

"It's nice to see you."

"I'm glad to see you."

"It's a boring class."

"I'm bored in the class."

As their name implies, **"it" statements** replace the personal pronoun *I* with the less immediate word *it*. By contrast, **"I" language** clearly identifies the speaker as the source of a message. Communicators who use "it" statements avoid responsibility for ownership of a message, attributing it instead to some unidentified source. This habit isn't just imprecise; more important, it is an unconscious way to avoid taking a position.

"BUT" STATEMENTS Statements that take the form "X-but-Y" can be confusing. A closer look at **"but" statements** explains why. In each sentence, the word *but* cancels the thought that precedes it:

"You're really a great person, but I think we ought to stop seeing each other."

"You've done good work for us, but we're going to have to let you go."

"This paper has some good ideas, but I'm giving it a D grade because it's late."

These "buts" often are a strategy for wrapping the speaker's real but unpleasant message between more palatable ideas in a psychological sandwich. This approach can be a face-saving strategy worth using at times. When the goal is to be absolutely clear, however, the most responsible approach is to deliver the positive and negative messages separately so they both get heard.

QUESTIONS Some questions are sincere requests for information. Other questions, though, are a linguistic way to avoid making a declaration.

"What are we having for dinner?" may hide the statement "I want to eat out" or "I want to get a pizza."

"How many textbooks are assigned in that class?" may hide the statement "I'm afraid to get into a class with too much reading."

"Are you doing anything tonight?" can be a less risky way of saying, "I want to go out with you tonight."

"Do you love me?" safely replaces the statement "I love you," which may be too embarrassing, too intimate, or too threatening to say directly.

Sometimes being indirect can be a tactful way to approach a topic that would be difficult to address head on. When used unnecessarily, though, being indirect can be a way to avoid speaking for yourself. See Chapter 9 for more details about the value and risks of indirect communication.

"I" AND "YOU" LANGUAGE We've seen that "I" language is a way of accepting responsibility for a message. In contrast, **"you" language** expresses a judgment of the other person. Positive judgments ("You look great today!") rarely cause problems, but notice how each of the following critical "you" statements implies that the subject of the complaint is doing something wrong:

"You left this place a mess!"

"You didn't keep your promise!"

"You're really crude sometimes!"

Despite its name, "you" language doesn't have to contain the pronoun you, which is often implied rather than stated outright:

"That was a stupid joke!" ("Your jokes are stupid.")

"Don't be so critical!" ("You're too negative.")

"Mind your own business!" ("You're too nosy.")

Whether the judgment is stated outright or implied, it's easy to see why "you" language can arouse defensiveness. A "you" statement implies that the speaker is qualified to judge the target—not an idea that most listeners are willing to accept, even when the judgment is correct.

Fortunately, "I" language provides a more accurate and less provocative way to express a complaint.[33] "I" language shows that the speaker

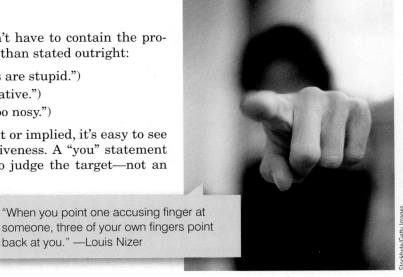

"When you point one accusing finger at someone, three of your own fingers point back at you." —Louis Nizer

Stockbyte/Getty Images

takes responsibility for the complaint by describing his or her reaction to the other's behavior without making any judgments about its worth.

A complete "I" statement has four elements. It describes

1. the other person's behavior
2. your interpretations
3. your feelings
4. the consequences that the other person's behavior has for you

These elements can appear in any order. A few examples of "I" statements illustrate how they sound in everyday conversation:

"I get embarrassed (*feeling*) when you talk about my bad grades in front of our friends (*behavior*). I'm afraid they'll think I'm stupid (*interpretation*). That's why I got so worked up last night (*consequence*)."

"When you didn't pick me up on time this morning (*behavior*), I was late for class, and I wound up getting chewed out by the professor (*consequences*). It seemed to me that my being on time didn't seem important to you. That's why I got so mad (*feeling*)."

"I haven't been very affectionate (*consequence*) because you've hardly spent any time with me in the past few weeks (*behavior*). I'm not sure if you're avoiding me, or if you're just busy (*interpretations*). I'm confused (*feeling*) about how you feel about me, and I want to clear it up."

When the risks of being misunderstood or getting a defensive reaction are high, it's a good idea to include all four elements in your "I" message. In some cases, however, only one or two of them will get the job done:

"I went to a lot of trouble fixing this dinner, and now it's cold. Of course I'm mad!" (*The behavior is obvious.*)

"I'm worried because you haven't called me up." (*"Worried" is both a feeling and a consequence.*)

Even the best "I" statement won't work unless it's delivered in the right way. If your words are nonjudgmental, but your tone of voice, facial expression, and posture all

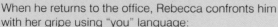

✔+ IN REAL LIFE

"I" and "You" Language on the Job

For some time, Rebecca has been frustrated by her fellow worker Tom's frequent absences from the job. She hasn't spoken up because she likes Tom and also because she doesn't want to sound like a complainer. Lately, though, Tom's absences have become longer and more frequent. Today he extended his half-hour lunch an extra 45 minutes. When he returns to the office, Rebecca confronts him with her gripe using "you" language:

Jason Harris/©Cengage Learning

Rebecca: Where have you been? You were due back at 12:30, and it's almost 1:30 now.

Tom: (*Surprised by Rebecca's angry tone, which she has never used before with him*) I had a few errands to run. What's the problem?

Rebecca: We all have errands to run, Tom. But it's not fair for you to do yours on company time.

Tom: (*Feeling defensive after hearing Rebecca's accusation*) I don't see why you have to worry about

how I do my job. Beth [their boss] hasn't complained, so why should you worry?

Rebecca: Beth hasn't complained because all of us have been covering for you. You should appreciate what a tight spot we're in, making excuses every time you come in late or leave early. (*Again, Rebecca uses "you" language to tell Tom how he should think and act.*)

Tom: (*Now too defensive to consider Rebecca's concerns*) Hey, I thought we all covered for one another here. What about the time last year when I worked late for a week so you could go to your cousin's wedding in San Antonio?

Rebecca: That's different! Nobody was lying then. When you take off, I have to make up stories about where you are. You're putting me in a very difficult spot, Tom, and it's not fair. You can't count on me to keep covering for you.

Tom: (*Feeling guilty, but too angry from Rebecca's judgments and threat to acknowledge his*

send "you" messages, a defensive response is likely to follow. The best way to make sure that your actions match your words is to remind yourself that your goal is to describe your thoughts, feelings, and wants, and to explain how the other's behavior affects you—not to act like a judge and jury.

Some readers have reservations about using "I" language, despite its theoretical appeal. The best way to overcome questions about this communication skill is to answer them.

- *"I get too angry to use 'I' language."* It's true that when you're angry the most likely reaction is to lash out with a judgmental "you" message. But it's probably smarter to keep quiet until you've thought about the consequences of what you might say than to blurt out something you'll regret later. It's also important to note that there's plenty of room for expressing anger with "I" language. It's just that you own the feeling as yours ("You bet I'm mad at you!") instead of distorting it into an attack ("That was a stupid thing to do!").

- *"Even with 'I' language, the other person gets defensive."* Like every communication skill described in this book, "I" language won't always work. You may be so upset or irritated that your judgmental feelings contradict your words. Even if

mistakes) Fine. I'll never ask you for a favor again. Sorry to put you out.

Rebecca may have succeeded in reducing Tom's lateness, but her choice of "you" language left him feeling defensive and angry. The climate in the office is likely to be more strained—hardly the outcome Rebecca was seeking. Here's how she could have handled the same issue using "I" language to describe her problem instead of blaming Tom.

Rebecca: Tom, I need to talk to you about a problem. *(Notice how Rebecca identifies the problem as hers instead of attacking Tom.)*

Tom: What's up?

Rebecca: You know how you come in late to work sometimes or take long lunch hours?

Tom: *(Sensing trouble ahead and sounding wary)* Yeah?

Rebecca: Well, I need to tell you that it's putting me in a tight spot. *(Rebecca describes the problem in behavioral terms and then goes on to express her feeling.)* When Beth asks where you are, I don't want to say you're not here because that might get you in trouble. So sometimes I make excuses or even lie. But Beth is sounding

suspicious of my excuses, and I'm worried about that.

Tom: *(Feeling defensive because he knows he's guilty but also sympathetic to Rebecca's position)* I don't want you to get in trouble. It's just that I've got to take care of a lot of personal business.

Rebecca: I know, Tom. I just want you to understand that it's getting impossible for me to cover for you.

Tom: Yeah, OK. Thanks for helping out.

Notice how "I" language made it possible for Rebecca to confront Tom honestly but without blaming or attacking him personally. Even if Tom doesn't change, Rebecca has gotten the problem off her chest, and she can feel proud that she did so in a way that didn't sound ugly or annoying.

Communication Scenarios

To see and analyze video examples of "I" language in action, go to your Premium Website for Looking Out/Looking In, *access "In Real Life Communication Scenarios," and then click on " 'I' and 'You' Language on the Job."*

you deliver a perfectly worded "I" statement with total sincerity, the other person might be so defensive or uncooperative that nothing you say will make matters better. But using "I" language will almost certainly *improve* your chances for success, with little risk that this approach will make matters worse.

- *"'I' language sounds artificial."* "That's not the way I talk," you might object. Much of the awkwardness that comes with first using "I" language is due to its novelty. As you become more used to making "I" statements, they will sound more and more natural—and become more effective.

One of the best ways to overcome your initial awkwardness is to practice making "I" statements in a safe way: by trying them out in a class, writing them in letters, and delivering them to receptive people on relatively minor issues. After your skills and confidence have grown, you will be ready to tackle really challenging situations in a way that sounds natural and sincere.

Despite its obvious advantages, even the best-constructed and delivered "I" message won't always succeed. As author and "I" language advocate Thomas Gordon acknowledges, "Nobody welcomes hearing that his behavior is causing someone a problem, no matter how the message is phrased."[34] Furthermore, "I" language in large doses can start to sound egotistical. Research shows that self-absorbed people, also known as "conversational narcissists," can be identified by their constant use of first-person singular pronouns.[35] For this reason, "I" language works best in moderation.

"WE" LANGUAGE   One way to avoid overuse of "I" language is to consider the pronoun *we*. **"We" language** implies that the issue is the concern and responsibility of both the speaker and receiver of a message. Consider a few examples:

"We need to figure out a budget that doesn't bankrupt us."

"I think we have a problem. We can't seem to talk about money without fighting."

"We aren't doing a very good job of keeping the place clean, are we?"

It's easy to see how "we" language can help build a constructive climate. It suggests a kind of "we're in this together" orientation that reflects the transactional nature of communication. People who use first-person plural pronouns signal their closeness, commonality, and cohesiveness with others.[36] For example, couples who use

✔+ SKILL BUILDER

Practicing "I" Language

You can develop your skill at delivering "I" messages by following these steps:

1. Visualize situations in your life when you might have sent each of the following messages:

   You're not telling me the truth!

   You think only of yourself!

   Don't be so touchy!

   Quit fooling around!

   You don't understand a word I'm saying!

2. Write alternatives to each statement using "I" language.

3. Think of three "you" statements you might make to people in your life. Transform each of these statements into "I" language and rehearse them with a classmate.

Table 5.4

Pronoun Use and Its Effects

	Advantages	Disadvantages	Tips
"I" language	Takes responsibility for personal thoughts, feelings, and wants. Less defense-provoking than evaluative "you" language.	Can be perceived as egotistical, narcissistic, and self-absorbed.	Use "I" messages when other person doesn't perceive a problem. Combine "I" with "we" language.
"We" language	Signals inclusion, immediacy, cohesiveness, and commitment.	Can speak improperly for others.	Combine with "I" language. Use in group settings to enhance unity. Avoid when expressing personal thoughts, feelings, and wants.
"You" language	Signals other-orientation, particularly when the topic is positive.	Can sound evaluative and judgmental, particularly during confrontations.	Use "I" language during confrontations. Use "you" language when praising or including others.

"we" language are more satisfied than those who rely more heavily on "I" and "you" language.[37] Chapters 10 and 11 offer detailed advice on the value of achieving a "we" orientation.

On the other hand, "we" statements aren't always appropriate. Sometimes using this pronoun sounds presumptuous, because it suggests that you are speaking for the other person as well as yourself. It's easy to imagine someone responding to your statement "We have a problem . . ." by saying "Maybe you have a problem, but don't tell me I do!"

Given the pros and cons of both "I" language and "we" language, what advice can we give about the most effective pronouns to use in interpersonal communication? Researchers have found that "I/we" combinations (e.g., "I think that we . . ." or "I would like to see us . . .") have a good chance of being received favorably.[38] Because too much of any pronoun comes across as inappropriate, combining pronouns is generally a good idea. If your "I" language reflects your position without being overly self-absorbed, your "you" language shows concern for others without judging them, and your "we" language includes others without speaking for them, you will probably come as close as possible to the ideal use of pronouns. Table 5.4 summarizes the advantages and disadvantages of each type of language and offers suggestions for approaches that have a good chance of success.

Gender and Language

So far we have discussed language use as if it were identical for both sexes. Some popular writers and researchers believe that men and women speak in distinct ways, as if they are from different cultures.[39] Other scholars suggest that the differences are few and mostly not significant.[40] What are the similarities and differences between male and female language use?

CONTENT

The first research on conversational topics and gender was conducted more than two generations ago. Despite the changes in male and female roles since then, the results of several studies are remarkably similar.[41] In these studies, women and men ranging in age from 17 to 80 described the range of topics each discussed with friends of the same sex. Certain topics were common to both men and women: work, movies, and television. Both men and women tended to reserve discussions of sex and sexuality for members of the same sex.

The differences between the men and women in these studies were more striking than the similarities. Female friends spent much more time discussing personal and domestic subjects, relationship problems, family, health and reproductive matters, weight, food and clothing, men, and other women. Men, on the other hand, were more likely to discuss music, current events, sports, business, and other men. Both men and women were equally likely to discuss personal appearance, sex, and dating in same-sex conversations. True to one common stereotype, women were more likely to gossip about close friends and family. By contrast, men spent more time gossiping about sports figures and media personalities. Women's gossip was no more derogatory than men's.

These differences can lead to frustration when men and women try to converse with one another. Researchers report that *trivial* is the word often used by both men and women to describe topics discussed by the opposite sex. "I want to talk about important things," a woman might say, "like how we're getting along. All he wants to do is talk about the news or what we'll do this weekend." Likewise, some men complain that women ask for and offer more details than necessary and focus too often on feelings and emotions.

REASONS FOR COMMUNICATING

Both men and women, at least in the dominant cultures of North America, use language to build and maintain social relationships. Regardless of the sex of the communicators, the goals of almost all ordinary conversations include making the

Computer Program Detects Author Gender

A new computer program can tell whether a book was written by a man or a woman. The simple scan of key words and syntax is around 80 percent accurate.[a]

The program's success seems to confirm the stereotypical perception of differences in male and female language use. Crudely put, men talk more about objects, and women more about relationships. Female writers use more pronouns (I, you, she, their, myself), say the program's developers, Moshe Koppel, and colleagues. Males prefer words that identify or determine nouns (a, the, that) and words that quantify them (one, two, more).

So this article would already, through sentences such as this, have probably betrayed its author as male: there is a prevalence of plural pronouns (they, them), indicating the male tendency to categorize rather than personalize.

If I were female, the researchers imply, I'd be more likely to write sentences like this, which assume that you and I share common knowledge or engage us in a direct relationship.

Philip Ball, *Nature*

conversation enjoyable by being friendly, showing interest in what the other person says, and talking about topics that interest the other person.[42] *How* men and women accomplish these goals is often different, though. Although most communicators try to make their interaction enjoyable, men are more likely than women to emphasize making conversation fun. Their discussions involve a greater amount of joking and good-natured teasing.

By contrast, women's discussions tend to involve feelings, relationships, and personal problems.[43] In fact, communication researcher Julia Wood flatly states that "for women, talk *is* the essence of relationships."[44] When members of a group of women were surveyed to find out what kinds of satisfaction they gained from talking with their friends, the most common theme mentioned was a feeling of empathy—"To know you're not alone," as some put it.[45] Whereas men commonly described same-sex conversations as something they *liked*, women described their same-sex conversations as a kind of contact they *needed*. The characteristically female orientation for relational communication is supported by studies of married couples showing that wives spend proportionately more time than husbands communicating in ways that help maintain their relationship.[46]

CONVERSATIONAL STYLE

Women tend to behave somewhat differently in conversations than do men, although the differences aren't as dramatic as you might imagine.[47] For instance, the popular myth that women are more talkative than men doesn't hold up under scientific scrutiny—researchers have found that men and women speak roughly the same number of words per day.[48]

Women do ask more questions in mixed-sex conversations than do men—nearly three times as many, according to one study. Other research has revealed that in mixed-sex conversations, men interrupt women far more than the other way around. Men are also more likely than women to use judgmental adjectives ("Reading can be a drag"), directives ("Think of some more"), and "I" references ("I have a lot to do").[49] Women are more likely to use intensive adverbs ("He's *really* interested"), emotional references ("If he really cared about you . . ."), uncertainty verbs ("It seems to me . . ."), and contradictions ("It's cold, but that's okay"). Differences like these show that men's speech is characteristically more direct, succinct, and task-oriented. By contrast, women's speech is more typically indirect, elaborate, and focused on relationships.

Women typically use statements showing support for the other person, demonstrations of equality, and efforts to keep the conversation going.[50] With these goals, it's not surprising that traditionally female speech often contains statements of sympathy and empathy: "I've felt just like that myself," "The same thing happened to me!" Women are also inclined to ask questions that invite the other person to share information: "How did you feel about that?" "What did you do next?" The importance of nurturing a relationship also explains why female speech is often somewhat tentative. Saying, "This is just my opinion . . ." is less likely to put off a conversational partner than a more definite "Here's what I think . . ."

"Sometimes I think he can understand every word we're saying."

An accommodating style isn't always a disadvantage. One study revealed that women who spoke tentatively were actually more persuasive with men than those who used more powerful speech.[51] However, this tentative style was less effective in persuading women. This study suggests that women who are willing and able to be flexible in their approach can persuade both other women and men.

NONGENDER VARIABLES

Despite the differences identified previously, the link between gender and language use isn't as clear-cut as it might seem. Several research reviews have found that the ways women and men communicate are much more similar than different. For example, one analysis of more than twelve hundred research studies found that only 1 percent of variance in communication behavior resulted from gender difference.[52] According to this research review, there is no significant difference between male speech and female speech in areas such as use of profanity, use of qualifiers ("I guess" or "This is just my opinion"), tag questions, and vocal fluency.[53]

Another study compared women's and men's use of "stance" words—the expression of attitude, emotion, certainty, doubt, and commitment—by analyzing 900,000 words of informal conversation in social and work settings.[54] There were no differences between the sexes in their use of many types of words—for example, opinion and attitude words (e.g., "amazing," "happy," "funny," and "interesting"), certainty, doubt, and factuality words (e.g., "of course," "right?," and "sure"), emphatic words (e.g., "absolutely" and "never"), and hedges (e.g., "almost" and "usually"). Only expletives (e.g., "cool," "damn," and "wow") had a significant difference between men and women. (Men use more of them.)

Some on-the-job research shows that male and female supervisors in similar positions behave the same way and are equally effective. In light of this research showing considerable similarities between the sexes and the relatively minor differences, one communication scholar suggests that the "Men Are from Mars, Women Are from Venus" metaphor should be replaced by the notion that "Men Are from North Dakota, Women Are from South Dakota."[55]

A growing body of research explains some of the apparent contradictions between the similarities and differences between male speech and female speech. Research has revealed other factors that influence language use as much or more than does gender.[56] For example, social philosophy plays a role. Feminist wives talk longer than their partners, whereas nonfeminist wives speak less than their partners. In addition, cooperative or competitive orientations of speakers have more influence on how they interact than does their gender.[57] The speaker's occupation also influences speaking style. For example, male day-care teachers' speech to their students resembles the language of female teachers more closely than it resembles the language of fathers at home.

To the degree that women use less-powerful language, there may be two explanations. The first involves their historical role in society at large: Powerless speech may reflect the relative lack of power held by women. If this explanation is valid, the male-female differences in powerful speech and powerless speech are likely to diminish as our society treats both sexes the same. A second, equally compelling explanation for the finding that women use less-powerful language comes from scholars who point out that what powerless speech loses in potency it gains by building rapport between speaker and receiver.[58] Because women have historically been more concerned with building harmonious relationships, it follows that typically feminine speech will sound less powerful. Toward that end, so-called powerless speech is actually *quite* powerful when it comes to building and maintaining relationships.

Another powerful force that influences the way individual men and women speak is their gender role. Recall the gender roles described in Chapter 3 (pages 98–99): masculine, feminine, and androgynous. Remember that these gender roles don't necessarily line up neatly with biological sex. There are "masculine" females, "feminine" males, and androgynous communicators who combine traditionally masculine and feminine characteristics. These gender roles can influence a communicator's style more than his or her biological sex. For example, one study revealed that masculine subjects used significantly more dominance language than did either feminine or androgynous subjects.[59] Feminine subjects expressed slightly more submissive behaviors and more equivalence behaviors than did the androgynous subjects, and their submissiveness and equivalence were much greater than those of the masculine subjects, regardless of their biological sex. And in gay and lesbian relationships, the conversational styles of partners reflect power differences in the relationship (e.g., who is earning more money) more than the biological sex of the communicators.[60]

What should we conclude about similarities and differences in the way men and women speak? While there are differences in male and female speech patterns, they may not be as great as some popular books suggest—and some of them may not result from biological sex at all. In practical terms, the best approach is to recognize that differences in communication style—whether they come from biological sex, gender, culture, or individual factors—present both challenges and opportunities. We need to take different styles into account, but not exaggerate or use them to stigmatize one another.

✔+ INVITATION TO INSIGHT

Exploring Gender Differences in Communication

Some pop-culture writers have claimed that the communication styles of men and women are so different that "men are from Mars, women are from Venus." Most researchers believe the differences aren't nearly so dramatic. One argues metaphorically that "men are from North Dakota, women are from South Dakota." Based on the research described in these pages and your personal experience, which approach seems more accurate to you? If your answer is "neither" or "both," create another geographical metaphor to describe your experience.

Culture and Language

Anyone who has tried to translate ideas from one language to another knows that conveying the same meaning isn't always easy.[61] Sometimes the results of a bungled translation can be amusing. For example, the American manufacturers of Pet milk unknowingly introduced their product in French-speaking markets without realizing that the word *pet* in French means "to break wind."[62] Likewise, the English-speaking representative of a U.S. soft drink manufacturer naively drew laughs from Mexican customers when she offered free samples of Fresca soda pop. In Mexican slang, the word *fresca* means "lesbian."

LOOKING AT DIVERSITY

Zarina Kolah: Training Non-Native Customer Service Reps

I train representatives in India to give phone support to customers of large American computer manufacturers. If you call for help with your laptop or desktop PC, you may find yourself speaking with one of the men and women I have helped train.

Our representatives are all smart, educated people. Many have university degrees in engineering and other technical fields. They have studied English in school for several years, but they need to learn the "soft skills" to give the kind of service U.S. customers want and deserve.

Many of the soft skills our reps learn involve speaking and understanding everyday English. That can be quite different from what's taught in Indian schools. For example, we have to teach our reps the meaning of phrases like "Let's touch base," "bottom line" and "yada yada."

One way our reps learn everyday American speech is by watching television programs like Oprah and CNN news. The speech in these shows is much closer to everyday language than what's been taught in Indian schools. Also, we train our reps in American traditions and cultural life. That way, when a caller says "Happy Thanksgiving" or asks "How about those Yankees?" our reps will know what to say.

Understanding Standard English can be challenging enough for our reps, but regional or ethnic accents can be even harder. Think about how different the same statements sound when spoken by a Texan, someone with a Hispanic accent, or a native Chinese English speaker. Our reps have to understand them all.

When Indian call centers began serving customers in the United States and Canada, many reps took on Western-sounding names instead of using their real ones. Samik became Sam, Patel was Pat, and Kalyani identified herself as Kate. Nowadays most call centers prefer that their reps use their own names, as customers realize that the reps are in India and would rather have a conversation that reflects this fact.

Language skills are obviously important. But we never forget that the most important "soft skills" are the ones that show we value our customers: politeness, empathy, patience, a sense of humor, and above all, helpfulness. That's true in any language.

Even choosing the right words during translation won't guarantee that non-native speakers will use an unfamiliar language correctly. For example, Japanese insurance companies warn their policyholders who are visiting the United States to avoid their cultural tendency to say "excuse me" or "I'm sorry" if they are involved in a traffic accident.[63] In Japan, apologizing is a traditional way to express goodwill and maintain social harmony, even if the person offering the apology is not at fault. But in the United States an apology can be taken as an admission of fault and result in Japanese tourists being wrongly held responsible for accidents.

Difficult as it may be, translation is only a small part of the differences in communication between members of different cultures. Differences in the way language is used and the worldview that a language creates make communicating across cultures a challenging task.

VERBAL COMMUNICATION STYLES

Using language is more than just choosing a particular group of words to convey an idea. Each language has its own unique style that distinguishes it from others. Matters like the amount of formality or informality, precision or vagueness, and brevity or detail are major ingredients in speaking competently. And when a communicator tries to use the verbal style from one culture in a different one, problems are likely to arise.[64]

One way in which verbal styles vary is in their *directness*. Anthropologist Edward Hall identified two distinct cultural ways of using language.[65] **Low-context cultures** generally value using language to express thoughts, feelings, and ideas as directly as possible. Low-context communicators look for the meaning of a statement in the words spoken. By contrast, **high-context cultures** value using language to maintain social harmony. Rather than upset others by speaking directly, high-context communicators learn to discover meaning from the context in which a message is delivered: the nonverbal behaviors of the speaker, the history of the relationship, and the general social rules that govern interaction between people. Table 5.5 summarizes some key differences between the way low- and high-context cultures use language.

North American culture falls toward the low-context end of the scale. Residents of the United States and Canada value straight talk and grow impatient with "beating around the bush." By contrast, most Asian and Middle Eastern cultures fall toward the high-context end of the scale. In many Asian cultures, for example, maintaining harmony is important, so communicators will avoid speaking directly if that would threaten another person's face. For this reason, Japanese and Koreans are less likely than Americans to offer a clear "no" to an undesirable request. Instead they will probably use roundabout expressions like "I agree with you in principle, but . . ." or "I sympathize with you. . . ."

The same sort of clash between directness and indirectness can aggravate problems between straight-talking, low-context Israelis, who value speaking directly, and Arabs, whose high-context culture stresses smooth interaction. It's easy to imagine how the clash of cultural styles could lead to misunderstandings and conflicts between Israelis and their Palestinian neighbors. Israelis could view the Palestinians as evasive, whereas the Palestinians could view the Israelis as insensitive and blunt.

It's worth noting that even generally straight-talking residents of the United States raised in the low-context Euro-American tradition often rely on context to make their

> What mattered to Abu was the music of the sentence . . . in general, it was the poetics, the music of things that tossed his confetti . . .
>
> Everywhere, the Arabic alphabet wiggled and popped . . . with outbursts of linguistic jazz, notations from the DNA songbook, energetic markings as primal as grunts and as modern as the abstract electricity of synthesizer feedback.
>
> —*Tom Robbins*, Skinny Legs and All

Table 5.5

Low- and High-Context Communication Styles

Low Context	High Context
Majority of information carried in explicit cues (time, place, relationship). Less reliance on explicit verbal messages.	Important information carried in contextual verbal messages, with less focus on the situational context.
Self-expression valued. Communicators state opinions and desires directly and strive to persuade others to accept their own viewpoint.	Relational harmony valued and maintained by indirect expression of opinions. Communicators abstain from saying "no" directly.
Clear, eloquent speech considered praiseworthy. Verbal fluency admired.	Communicators talk "around" the point, allowing the other to fill in the missing pieces. Ambiguity and use of silence admired.

✔+ INVITATION TO INSIGHT

High- and Low-Context Communication

Check your knowledge of high- and low-context communication styles with a self-test and sample dialogues available through your Premium Website for *Looking Out/Looking In.* Click "next page" for further explanations, examples, and exercises that illustrate these direct and indirect communication styles.

point. When you decline an unwanted invitation by saying "I can't make it," it's likely that both you and the other person know that the choice of attending isn't really beyond your control. If your goal was to be perfectly clear, you might say, "I don't want to get together." As Chapter 9 explains in detail, we often equivocate precisely because we want to obscure our true thoughts and feelings.

Besides their degrees of clarity and vagueness, another way in which language styles can vary across cultures is whether they are *elaborate* or *succinct*. Speakers of Arabic, for instance, commonly use language that is much richer and more expressive than that of most communicators who use English. Strong assertions and exaggerations that would sound ridiculous in English are a common feature of Arabic. This contrast in linguistic styles can lead to misunderstandings between people from different backgrounds. As one observer put it:

> First, an Arab feels compelled to overassert in almost all types of communication because others expect him [or her] to. If an Arab says exactly what he [or she] means without the expected assertion, other Arabs may still think that he [or she] means the opposite. For example, a simple "no" by a guest to the host's requests to eat more or drink more will not suffice. To convey the meaning that he [or she] is actually full, the guest must keep repeating "no" several times, coupling it with an oath such as "By God" or "I swear to God." Second, an Arab often fails to realize that others, particularly foreigners, may mean exactly what they say even though their language is simple. To the Arabs, a simple "no" may mean the indirectly expressed consent and encouragement of a coquettish woman. On the other hand, a simple consent may mean the rejection of a hypocritical politician.[66]

Succinctness is most extreme in cultures where silence is valued. In many Native American cultures, for example, the favored way to handle ambiguous social situations is to remain quiet.[67] When you contrast this silent style to the talkativeness that is common in mainstream American cultures when people first meet, it's easy to imagine how the first encounter between an Apache or Navajo and an Anglo might feel uncomfortable to both people.

A third way in which languages differ from one culture to another involves *formality* and *informality*. The informal approach that characterizes relationships in countries like the United States, Canada, Australia, and the Scandinavian countries is quite different from the great concern for using proper speech in many parts of Asia and Africa. Formality isn't so much a matter of using correct grammar as of defining social position. In Korea, for example, the language reflects the Confucian system of relational hierarchies.[68] It has special vocabularies for different sexes, for different

Language and Heritage

© Jose Luis Pelaez, Inc./Blend Images/Corbis

"Mi'ja, it's me. Call me when you wake up." It was a message left on my phone machine from a friend. But when I heard that word mi'ja, a pain squeezed my heart. My father was the only one who ever called me this. Because his death is so recent, the word overwhelmed me and filled me with grief.

Mi'ja (MEE-ha) from *mi hija* (me ee-HA). The words translate as "my daughter." Daughter, my daughter, daughter of mine: They're all stiff and clumsy, and have nothing of the intimacy and warmth of the word *mi'ja*—"daughter of my heart," maybe. Perhaps a more accurate translation of *mi'ja* is "I love you." Sometimes a word can be translated into more than a meaning. In it is the translation of a worldview, a way of looking at things, and, yes, even a way of accepting what others might not perceive as beautiful. *Urraca,* for example, instead of "grackle." Two ways of looking at a black bird. One sings, the other cackles. Or, *tocayola,* your name-twin, and therefore, your friend. Or the beautiful *estrenar,* which means to wear something for the first time. There is no word in English for the thrill and pride of wearing something new.

Spanish gives me a way of looking at myself and the world in a new way. For those of us living between worlds, our job in the universe is to help others see with more than their eyes during this period of chaotic transition.

Sandra Cisneros

levels of social status, for different degrees of intimacy, and for different types of social occasions. For example, there are different degrees of formality for speaking with old friends, nonacquaintances whose background one knows, and complete strangers. One sign of being a learned person in Korea is the ability to use language that recognizes these relational distinctions. When you contrast these sorts of distinctions with the casual friendliness that many North Americans use even when talking with complete strangers, it's easy to see how a Korean might view communicators in the United States as boorish and how an American might view communicators in Korea as stiff and unfriendly.

LANGUAGE AND WORLDVIEW

Different linguistic styles are important, but there may be even more-important differences that separate speakers of various languages. For almost 150 years, theorists have put forth the notion of **linguistic relativism**: that the worldview of a culture is shaped and reflected by the language its members speak.[69] The best-known example of linguistic relativism is the notion that Eskimos have a large number of words (estimated at everything from seventeen to one hundred) for what we simply call "snow." Different terms are used to describe conditions like a driving blizzard, crusty ice, and light powder. This example suggests how linguistic relativism operates. The need to survive in an Arctic environment led Eskimos to make distinctions that would be unimportant to residents of warmer environments, and after the language makes these distinctions, speakers are more likely to see the world in ways that match the broader vocabulary.

Even though there is some doubt that Eskimos really have so many words for snow,[70] other examples do seem to support the principle of linguistic relativism.[71] For instance, bilingual speakers seem to think differently when they change languages. In one study, French American people were asked to interpret a series of pictures. When they described the pictures in French, their descriptions were far more romantic and emotional than when they described the pictures in English. Likewise, when students in Hong Kong were asked to complete a values test, they expressed more traditional Chinese values when they answered in Cantonese than when they answered in English. In Israel, both Arab and Jewish students saw greater distinctions between their group and "outsiders" when using their native language than when they used English, a neutral tongue for them. Examples like these, and like those in the reading on page 191, show the power of language to shape cultural identity—sometimes for better and sometimes for worse.

"The Eskimos have eighty-seven words for snow and not one for malpractice."

The best-known declaration of linguistic relativism is the **Sapir-Whorf hypothesis**, formulated by Edward Sapir and Benjamin Whorf.[72] Following Sapir's theory, Whorf observed that the language spoken by Hopi Native Americans represents a view of reality that is dramatically different from that of more familiar tongues. For example, the Hopi language makes no distinction between nouns and verbs. Therefore, the people who speak it describe the entire world as being constantly in process. Whereas in English we use nouns to characterize people or objects as being fixed or constant, Hopi view them more as verbs, constantly changing. In this sense English represents much of the world rather like a snapshot camera, whereas Hopi language represents the world more like a motion picture.

Some languages contain terms that have no English equivalents.[73] For example, consider a few words in other languages that have no English equivalents:

nemawashi (Japanese): The process of informally feeling out all of the people involved with an issue before making a decision.

lagniappe (French/Creole): An extra gift given in a transaction that wasn't expected by the terms of a contract.

lao (Mandarin): A respectful term used for older people, showing their importance in the family and in society.

dharma (Sanskrit): Each person's unique, ideal path in life and knowledge of how to find it.

koyaanisquatsi (Hopi): Nature out of balance; a way of life so crazy it calls for a new way of living.

After words like these exist and become a part of everyday life, the ideas that they represent are easier to recognize. But even without such words, each of the ideas just listed is still possible to imagine. Thus, speakers of a language that includes the notion of *lao* would probably treat its older members respectfully, and those who are familiar with *lagniappe* might be more generous. Despite these differences, it is possible to follow these principles without knowing or using these words. Although language may shape thoughts and behavior, it doesn't dominate them absolutely.

Summary

Language is both a marvelous communication tool and the source of many interpersonal problems. Every language is a collection of symbols, governed by a variety of rules: semantic, syntactic, and pragmatic. Because of its symbolic nature, language is not a precise vehicle: Meanings rest in people, not in words themselves.

Language both reflects and shapes the perceptions of its users. Terms used to name people influence the way the people are regarded. The terms used to name speakers and the language they use reflect the level of affiliation of a speaker toward others. Language patterns also reflect and shape a speaker's perceived power.

When used carelessly, language can lead to a variety of interpersonal problems. The level of precision or vagueness of messages can affect a receiver's understanding of them. Both precise messages and vague, equivocal ones have their uses in interpersonal relationships, and a competent communicator has the ability to choose the optimal level of precision for the situation at hand. Some language habits—such as confusing facts with opinions or inferences and using emotive terms—can lead to unnecessary disharmony in interpersonal relationships. Language also acknowledges or avoids the speaker's acceptance of responsibility for his or her positions, and competent communicators know how to use "I" and "we" language to accept the optimal level of responsibility and relational harmony.

The relationship between gender and language is a complex one. There are some differences in the ways men and women speak. The content of their conversations varies, as do their reasons for communicating and their conversational styles. However, not all differences in language use can be accounted for by the speaker's biological sex. Gender roles, occupation, social philosophy, and orientation toward problem solving also influence people's use of language.

Different languages often shape and reflect the views of a culture. Low-context cultures like the United States use language primarily to express feelings and ideas as directly and unambiguously as possible. High-context cultures such as Japan and Saudi Arabia, however, avoid specificity in order to promote social harmony. Some cultures value brevity and the succinct use of language, whereas others value elaborate forms of speech. In some societies formality is important, whereas in others informality is important. Beyond these differences, there is evidence to support linguistic relativism—the notion that language exerts a strong influence on the worldview of the people who speak it.

Key Terms

abstraction ladder (165)
abstract language (165)
behavioral language (165)
"but" statements (178)
convergence (172)
divergence (173)
emotive language (177)
equivocal language (162)

high-context cultures (189)
"I" language (178)
"it" statements (178)
linguistic relativism (191)
low-context cultures (189)
powerless speech manner-
    isms (173)
pragmatic rules (168)

relative words (164)
Sapir-Whorf hypothesis (192)
semantic rules (162)
static evaluation (165)
syntactic rules (167)
"we" language (182)
"you" language (179)

Online Resources

Now that you have read this chapter, use your Premium Website for *Looking Out/ Looking In* for quick access to the electronic resources that accompany this text. Your Premium Website gives you access to:

- **Study tools** that will help you assess your learning and prepare for exams (*digital glossary, key term flash cards, review quizzes*).

- **Activities and assignments** that will help you hone your knowledge, understand how theory and research applies to your own life (*Invitation to Insight*), consider ethical challenges in interpersonal communication (*Ethical Challenge*), and build your interpersonal communication skills throughout the course (*Skill Builder*). If requested, you can submit your answers to your instructor.

- **Media resources** that will allow you to watch and critique news video and videos of interpersonal communication situations (*In Real Life, interpersonal video simulations*) and download a chapter review so you can study when and where you'd like (*Audio Study Tools*).

This chapter's key terms and search terms for additional reading are featured in this end-of-chapter section, and you can find this chapter's Invitation to Insight, Skill Builder, and In Real Life activities in the body of the chapter.

Search Terms

When searching online databases to research topics in this chapter, use the following terms (along with this chapter's key terms) to maximize the chances of finding useful information:

ambiguity
general semantics
language & languages

miscommunication
pragmatics

semantics
sociolinguistics

Film and Television

You can see the communication principles described in this chapter portrayed in the following films:

THE IMPORTANCE OF LANGUAGE

Nell (1994) Rated PG-13

The Miracle Worker (1962) Not Rated

Nell is the story of a young woman (played by Jodie Foster) raised in virtual isolation in the backwoods of North Carolina. When her mother dies, Nell is discovered and cared for by small-town doctor Jerry Lovell (Liam Neeson) and big-city psychologist Paula Olsen (Natasha Richardson). Much of the film centers on conflicts within and between Lovell and Olsen as they try, from differing perspectives, to understand and help Nell.

At first Nell's utterances sound like gibberish to Lovell and Olsen. But they soon discover that, in her isolation, she learned a strange version of English as spoken by her mother (a stroke victim who read to Nell from the King James Version of the Bible) and her twin sister (with whom Nell shared a secret linguistic code). Now that both the mother and sister have died, Nell's linguistic isolation is as profound as her physical distance from the rest of the world.

Nell's story is reminiscent in many ways of Helen Keller's early childhood as described in the well-known film *The Miracle Worker*. Both Nell and Helen were intelligent young women, misunderstood and misdiagnosed by "experts" who assumed that their lack of ability to communicate was a sign of limited mental abilities. Both were cut off from the rest of the world until they developed the ability to communicate with others by a shared language system.

The Miracle Worker and *Nell* are by no means identical tales. Helen Keller's story is biographical, while Nell's is a work of fiction. Furthermore, the films' different conclusions show that linguistic skill is no guarantee of living happily ever after. While learning to communicate through sign language opened the door to live a rich and productive life for Helen Keller, Nell found the "civilized world" a less hospitable place. Despite their differences, both movies offer profound insights into the potential and power of language in the human experience.

CULTURAL RULES FOR LANGUAGE

The N-Word (2004) Not Rated

It is possibly the most inflammatory word in American culture—so much so that the letter "N" is substituted for the actual word in most public discussions of the term. But as this documentary shows, the "N-word" has many and varied meanings, ranging from a degrading slur to a term of endearment. A host of scholars and celebrities (including Chris Rock, Whoopi Goldberg, George Carlin, Ice Cube, and Quincy Jones) discuss and debate when, where, how, by whom, and even whether the "N-word" should be used.

The film offers a vivid illustration of how pragmatic rules and linguistic convergence/divergence operate in interpersonal and intercultural communication. It also shows how failing to know and abide by cultural meanings and rules can lead to significant misunderstandings and conflict.

LINGUISTIC CONVERGENCE

Mean Girls (2004) Rated PG-13

Cady Heron (Lindsay Lohan) was raised in African bush country by her zoologist parents. Back in the United States, Cady has her first experience in formal schooling when she enrolls at North Shore High. She soon learns that high school social life can be every bit as vicious as anything she witnessed among the primates. Her new school is rife with social cliques, including the high-status Plastics and the geeky Mathletes.

At the urging of her unpopular friends Janis (Lizzy Caplan) and Damian (Daniel Franzese), Cady infiltrates the Plastics to get information so they can demolish the prestige of the popular girls. For Cady, part of fitting in is to learn and use the vocabulary of the in-group Plastics. In an early conversation with these popular girls, their leader Regina (Rachel McAdams) exclaims to Cady, "Shut up!" Unfamiliar with the slang use of this term, Cady replies, "I didn't say anything." Soon Cady speaks Plastic fluently, tossing about words like "fetch" (cool), "word vomit" (babbling), and the self-explanatory "fugly."

In an interesting example of linguistic convergence, the more Cady "talks the talk" of being a Plastic, the more her values and behaviors become like theirs. By movie's end, she makes some important decisions about herself and her friends—including the decision not to talk or act like a "mean girl."

GENDER AND LANGUAGE

When Harry Met Sally (1989) Rated R

Harry Burns (Billy Crystal) and Sally Albright (Meg Ryan) are strangers who get together for purely functional reasons: a cross-country car ride in which they share gas costs and driving. She sizes him up as crude and insensitive; he views her as naive and obsessive. By the time they finish their journey, they are glad to part ways.

But the car ride is just the start of their relationship—and the beginning of a look at male and female communication styles. In their conversations, Harry and Sally often exhibit communication patterns similar to those found in gender-related research. For instance, Harry tends to treat discussions as debates. He regularly tells jokes and enjoys having the first and last word. He rarely asks questions but is quick to answer them. Harry self-discloses with his buddy Jess (Bruno Kirby) but only while watching a football game or taking swings at a batting cage.

Sally, on the other hand, self-discloses with her female friends at restaurants, by phone, while shopping—just about any place. She regularly asks questions of Harry but seems troubled by his competitive answers and approach to sex (Sally: "So you're saying that a man can be friends with a woman he finds unattractive?" Harry: "No, you pretty much want to nail them too."). In the language of Deborah Tannen, Sally's communication is about "rapport" while Harry's is about "report."

The story ends with a strong sense of hope for cross-sex communication. This is due in part to Harry's learning to "speak a different language." The rancor of his early interactions with Sally softens when he expresses empathy (much to her surprise) in a chance bookstore meeting. By the movie's end, he offers warm and detailed descriptions of why he enjoys being with and around her. Clearly they are friends as well as lovers, which seems to make their communication stronger. It also helps them fulfill a goal of most movies: the ending suggests they have a good chance to live "happily ever after."

NONVERBAL COMMUNICATION:
Messages beyond Words

✔+ MAKING THE GRADE

Here are the topics discussed in this chapter:

After studying the topics in this chapter, you should be able to:

1. Explain the defining characteristics of nonverbal communication as described on pages 201–210.

2. List and offer examples of each type of nonverbal message introduced in this chapter.

3. In a given situation, recognize your own nonverbal behavior and its relational significance.

4. Monitor and manage your nonverbal cues in ways that achieve your goals.

5. Share appropriately your interpretation of another's nonverbal behavior with that person.

Ranald Mackechnie/Stone/Getty Images

What's going on in the photo above? You don't need to be a mind reader to recognize that many unspoken messages are being expressed here. Some social scientists have argued that 93 percent of the emotional impact of a message comes from nonverbal sources. Others have reasoned more convincingly that the figure is closer to 65 percent.[1] Whatever the precise figure, the point remains: Nonverbal communication plays an important role in how we make sense of one another's behavior. In the following pages you'll become acquainted with the field of nonverbal communication— the way we express ourselves, not by what we say but rather by what we do.

> What you are speaks so loudly I cannot hear what you say.
>
> —*Ralph Waldo Emerson*

We need to begin our study of nonverbal communication by defining that term. At first this might seem like a simple task: If *non* means "not" and *verbal* means "words," then *nonverbal communication* means "communicating without words." In fact, this literal definition isn't completely accurate. For instance, most communication scholars do not define American Sign Language as nonverbal even though the messages are unspoken. On the other hand, you'll soon read that certain aspects of the voice aren't really verbal, although they are vocal. (Can you think of any? Table 6.1 will help.)

For our purposes, we'll define **nonverbal communication** as "messages expressed by nonlinguistic means." This rules out sign languages and written words, but it includes messages transmitted by vocal means that don't involve language—the sighs, laughs, and other assorted noises we alluded to earlier. In addition, our definition allows us to explore the nonlinguistic dimensions of the spoken word—volume, rate, pitch, and so

Table 6.1

Types of Communication

	Vocal Communication	Nonvocal Communication
Verbal Communication	Spoken words	Written words
Nonverbal Communication	Tone of voice, sighs, screams, vocal quality, pitch, loudness, etc.	Gestures, movement, appearance, facial expression, touch, etc.

"Types of Communication," adapted from Together: Communicating Interpersonally, *by J. Stewart and G. D'Angelo. ©1980 Addison-Wesley. Used courtesy McGraw-Hill Inc.*

on. It also encompasses more abstract factors such as physical appearance, the environment in which we communicate, how close or far we stand from each other, and the way we use time. And of course, it includes the features most people think of when they consider nonverbal communication: body language, gestures, facial expression, and others.

Characteristics of Nonverbal Communication

The definition in the preceding paragraph only hints at the richness of nonverbal communication. In the following pages, we'll look at characteristics that are true of all the many forms and functions of nonverbal communication.

NONVERBAL SKILLS ARE VITAL

It's hard to overemphasize the importance of effective nonverbal expression and the ability to read and respond to others' nonverbal behavior.[2] Nonverbal encoding and decoding skills are a strong predictor of popularity, attractiveness, and socioemotional well-being.[3] Good nonverbal communicators are more persuasive than people who are less skilled, and they have a greater chance of success in settings ranging from careers to poker games to romance. Nonverbal sensitivity is a major part of the "emotional intelligence" described in Chapter 4, and researchers have come to recognize that it is impossible to study spoken language without paying attention to its nonverbal dimensions.[4]

ALL BEHAVIOR HAS COMMUNICATIVE VALUE

Suppose you tried not to communicate any messages at all. What would you do? Stop talking? Close your eyes? Curl up into a ball? Leave the room? You can probably see that even these behaviors communicate messages—that you're avoiding contact. One study demonstrated this fact.[5] When communicators were told not to express nonverbal clues, others viewed them as dull, withdrawn, uneasy, aloof, and deceptive. This impossibility of not communicating is extremely important to understand, because it means that each of us is a kind of transmitter that cannot be shut off. No matter what we do, we give off information about ourselves.[6]

Writer [to movie producer Sam Goldwyn]: Mr. Goldwyn, I'm telling you a sensational story. I'm only asking for your opinion, and you fall asleep.

Goldwyn: Isn't sleeping an opinion?

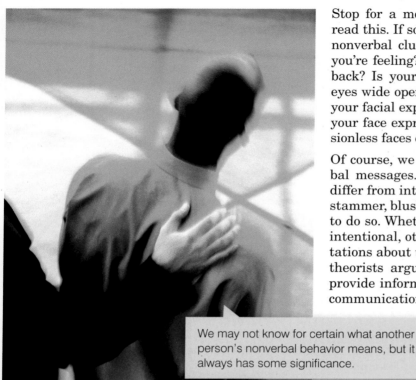

We may not know for certain what another person's nonverbal behavior means, but it always has some significance.

Laurence Monneret/Stone/Getty Images

Stop for a moment, and examine yourself as you read this. If someone were observing you now, what nonverbal clues would that person get about how you're feeling? Are you sitting forward or reclining back? Is your posture tense or relaxed? Are your eyes wide open, or do they keep closing? What does your facial expression communicate? Can you make your face expressionless? Don't people with expressionless faces communicate something to you?

Of course, we don't always intend to send nonverbal messages. Unintentional nonverbal behaviors differ from intentional ones.[7] For example, we often stammer, blush, frown, and sweat without meaning to do so. Whether or not our nonverbal behavior is intentional, others recognize it and make interpretations about us based on their observations. Some theorists argue that unintentional behavior may provide information but that it shouldn't count as communication.[8] We draw the boundaries of nonverbal communication more broadly, suggesting that even unconscious and unintentional behavior conveys messages, and thus is worth studying as communication.

NONVERBAL COMMUNICATION IS PRIMARILY RELATIONAL

Some nonverbal messages serve utilitarian functions. For example, a police officer directs the flow of traffic, and a team of street surveyors uses hand motions to coordinate its work. But nonverbal communication more commonly expresses the kinds of relational (rather than content) messages discussed in Chapter 1 and the kinds of identity messages that you read about in Chapter 2.[9]

Consider, for example, the role of nonverbal communication in *identity management*.[10] Chapter 2 discussed how we strive to create an image of ourselves as we want others to view us. Nonverbal communication plays an important role in this process—in many cases more important than verbal communication. For instance, think what happens when you attend a party where you are likely to meet strangers you would like to get to know better. Instead of projecting your image verbally ("Hi! I'm attractive, friendly, and easygoing"), you behave in ways that will present this identity. You might smile a lot and perhaps try to strike a relaxed pose. It's also likely that you dress carefully—even if the image involves looking as though you hadn't given a lot of attention to your appearance.

Along with identity management, nonverbal communication allows us to *define the kinds of relationships we want to have with others*. Think about the wide range of ways you could behave when greeting another person. You could wave, shake hands, nod, smile, clap the other person on the back, give a hug, or avoid all contact. Each one of these decisions would send a message about the nature of your relationship with the other person.

Nonverbal communication performs a third valuable social function: *conveying emotions* that we may be unwilling or unable to express—or ones that we may not even be aware of. In fact, nonverbal communication is much better suited to expressing attitudes and feelings than ideas. You can prove this by imagining how you could express each item on the following list nonverbally:

a.   You're tired.
b.   You're in favor of capital punishment.
c.   You're attracted to another person in the group.
d.   You think prayer in the schools should be allowed.
e.   You're angry at someone in the room.

This experiment shows that, short of charades, nonverbal messages are much better at expressing attitudes (a, c, and e) than other sorts of messages (b and d). Among other limitations, nonverbal messages can't convey:

>   Simple matters of fact ("The book was written in 1997.")
>   The past or future tenses ("I was happy yesterday"; "I'll be out of town next week.")
>   An imaginary idea ("What would it be like if . . .")
>   Conditional statements ("If I don't get a job, I'll have to move out.")

As technology develops, an increasing number of Internet and phone messages will include both visual and vocal dimensions, making communication richer and enhancing understanding.[11] At present, most text, instant, and email messages offer fewer nonverbal cues about the speaker's feelings than do face-to-face encounters, or even telephone voice conversations. Of course, this makes these messages ripe for misunderstandings. Probably the biggest problems arise from joking remarks being taken as serious statements. To solve this, electronic text correspondents have developed a series of symbols—often called *emoticons*—that can be inserted to simulate nonverbal dimensions of a message.[12]

As you read in Chapter 5, text-based messages can also use linguistic shortcuts and acronyms to indicate nonverbal responses, such as <frown> or "WEG" for "wicked evil grin." Of course, it's important to understand that these markers are also identity-management tools, as discussed in Chapter 2. Do writers actually grin when writing

Proposed Smirking Ban Raises Eyebrows

SAN FRANCISCO (Reuters)—A raised eyebrow, loud guffaw, smirk or other facial expressions could all be banned in future political debate under new rules proposed for the city council in Palo Alto, California.

In a bid to improve civility in the town's public discourse, a committee on the city council has spent hours debating guidelines for its own behavior.

"Do not use body language or other nonverbal methods of expression, disagreement or disgust," a new list of proposed conduct rules reads.

Another rule calls for council members to address each other with titles followed by last names, a formality not always practiced in laidback California.

"I don't want to muzzle my colleagues," councilwoman Judy Kleinberg, who headed the committee that drafted the rules, told the *San Jose Mercury News.* But, she added: "I don't think the people sitting around the cabinet with the president roll their eyes."

<grin>, and do they really scream and swear while typing $%*@!—or are they simply trying to create an impression of how they think and feel? Toward that end, emoticons and shortcuts like these may be helpful, but they clearly aren't an adequate substitute for the rich mixture of nonverbal messages that flows in face-to-face exchanges. That fact explains why the International Academy of Digital Arts & Sciences offered a $10,000 grant to the person or group that devises "a viable way to infuse digital communication with the same individuality and unspoken cues common in face-to-face interactions."[13]

NONVERBAL COMMUNICATION SERVES MANY FUNCTIONS

Just because this chapter focuses on nonverbal communication, don't get the idea that our words and our actions are unrelated. Quite the opposite is true: Verbal and nonverbal communication are interconnected elements in every act of communication. (See Table 6.2 for a comparison of verbal and nonverbal communication.) Nonverbal behaviors can operate in several relationships with verbal behaviors.

REPEATING   If someone asked you for directions to the nearest drugstore, you might say, "North of here about two blocks," **repeating** your instructions nonverbally by pointing north. This sort of repetition isn't just decorative: People remember comments accompanied by gestures more than those made with words alone.[14]

COMPLEMENTING   Even when it doesn't repeat language, nonverbal behavior can reinforce what's been said. **Complementing** nonverbal behaviors match the thoughts and emotions the communicator is expressing linguistically. You can appreciate the value of this function by imagining the difference between saying "thank you" with a sincere facial expression and tone of voice, and saying the same words in a deadpan manner.

SUBSTITUTING   When a friend asks "What's up?" you might shrug your shoulders instead of answering in words. Many facial expressions operate as substitutes for speech. It's easy to recognize expressions that function like verbal interjections and say "gosh," "really?", "oh, please!", and so on.[15] Nonverbal **substituting** can be useful when communicators are reluctant to express their feelings in words. Faced with a message you find disagreeable, you might sigh, roll your eyes, or yawn when speaking out would not be appropriate. Likewise, a parent who wants a child to stop being disruptive at a party can flash a glare across the room without saying a word (and what child doesn't know the power of "the look" from Mom or Dad?).

Table 6.2

Some Differences between Verbal and Nonverbal Communication

	Verbal Communication	Nonverbal Communication
Complexity	One dimension (words only)	Multiple dimensions (voice, posture, gestures, distance, etc.)
Flow	Intermittent (speaking and silence alternate)	Continuous (it's impossible to not communicate nonverbally)
Clarity	Less subject to misinterpretation	More ambiguous
Impact	Has less impact when verbal and nonverbal cues are contradictory	Has stronger impact when verbal and nonverbal cues are contradictory
Intentionality	Usually deliberate	Often unintentional

ACCENTING Just as we use italics to emphasize an idea in print, we use nonverbal devices to emphasize oral messages. Pointing an accusing finger adds emphasis to criticism (as well as probably creating defensiveness in the receiver). **Accenting** certain words with the voice ("It was *your* idea!") is another way to add nonverbal emphasis.

REGULATING Nonverbal behaviors can serve a **regulating** function by influencing the flow of verbal communication.[16] For example, parties in a conversation often unconsciously send and receive turn-taking cues through the way they use their voice.[17] When you are ready to yield the floor, the unstated rule is this: Create a rising vocal intonation pattern, then use a falling intonation pattern or draw out the final syllable of the clause at the end of your statement. Finally, stop speaking. If you want to maintain your turn when another speaker seems ready to cut you off, you can suppress the attempt by taking an audible breath, using a sustained intonation pattern (because rising and falling patterns suggest the end of a statement), and avoiding any

> Both deliberate behavior (like the "thumbs-up" sign) and unintentional cues (like facial expressions) can complement, contradict, or substitute for spoken messages.

pauses in your speech. We can also regulate conversations nonverbally by nodding (indicating "I understand" or "keep going"), looking away (signaling a lack of attention), or moving toward the door (communicating a desire to end the conversation). Of course, most of us have learned the hard way that nonverbal signals like these don't guarantee that the other party will pay attention to, interpret, or respond to them in the ways we had hoped.

CONTRADICTING People often express **contradicting** messages in their verbal and nonverbal behaviors. A common example of this sort of **mixed message** is the experience we've all had of hearing someone with a red face and bulging veins yelling, "Angry? No, I'm not angry!" In situations like these, we tend to believe the nonverbal message instead of the words.[18] A humorous illustration of this concept can be seen in the Cingular cell phone commercial "Mother Love" (available on popular video sites). A mother and daughter appear to be having an argument with raised voices, flailing arms, and scowling faces. Upon listening to their words, however, it turns out they're slinging compliments and praise at each other, including the

> I suppose it was something you said that caused me to tighten and pull away. And when you asked, "What is it?" I, of course, said, "Nothing." Whenever I say, "Nothing," You may be very certain there is something. The something is a old, hard lump of Nothing.
>
> —*Lois Wyse*

phrases "I really like it!" and "I love you!" What makes the commercial amusing is that their verbal and nonverbal messages don't match—and it's easy to believe they're angry rather than happy, no matter what their words say.

Even though some of the ways in which people contradict themselves are subtle, mixed messages have a strong impact. As we grow older, we become better at interpreting these mixed messages. Children between the ages of six and twelve use a speaker's words to make sense of a message. But as adults, we rely more on nonverbal cues to form many impressions. For example, audiences put more emphasis on

She dresses in flags
comes on
like a mack truck
she paints
her eyelids green
and her mouth
is a loud speaker
rasping out
profanity
at cocktail parties
she is everywhere
like a sheep dog
working a flock
nipping at your sleeve

spilling your drink
bestowing
wet sloppy kisses
but i
have received
secret messages
carefully written
from the shy
quiet woman
who hides
in this
bizarre
gaudy castle

—*Ric Masten*

nonverbal cues than on words to decide whether speakers are honest.[19] They also use nonverbal behaviors to judge the character of speakers as well as their competence and composure, and differences in nonverbal behaviors influence how much listeners are persuaded by a speaker.[20] Even the slightest contradiction in verbal and nonverbal messages may suggest that a speaker is being deceptive, as we'll describe in the following section.

NONVERBAL COMMUNICATION OFFERS DECEPTION CLUES

When message-senders are telling lies, their nonverbal behavior sometimes gives them away. Inadvertent signals of deception—often called **leakage**—can come through a variety of nonverbal channels. Some of these channels are more revealing than others. Facial expressions offer important information,[21] but deceivers also pay more attention to monitoring these cues in an attempt to maintain a "poker face." More reliable is pupil dilation, a physiological response that can't easily be controlled.[22] The voice also offers a variety of leakage clues.[23] In one experiment, subjects who were encouraged to be deceitful made more speech errors, spoke for shorter periods of time, and had a lower rate of speech than did others who were encouraged to express themselves honestly. Another experiment revealed that the pitch of a liar's voice tends to be higher than that of a truth teller. Liars leak nonverbal cues of deception in some situations more than others. Table 6.3 outlines some conditions under which leakage is more likely.

A variety of self-help books and seminars claim that liars can be easily identified by monitoring their nonverbal cues, but scientific research doesn't support that notion. Communication scholars Judee Burgoon and Tim Levine have studied deception

"I knew the suspect was lying because of certain telltale discrepancies between his voice and non-verbal gestures. Also his pants were on fire."

Table 6.3

Leakage of Nonverbal Cues to Deception

Deception cues are more likely when the deceiver
Wants to hide emotions being felt at the moment
Feels strongly about the information being hidden
Feels apprehensive or guilty about the deception
Gets little enjoyment from being deceptive
Has not had time to rehearse the lie in advance
Knows there are severe punishments for being caught

Based on P. Ekman (2001). Telling Lies. New York: Norton.

detection for years. In their review of decades of research on the subject, they came up with what they call "Deception Detection 101"—three findings that have been repeatedly supported in studies.[24] They are:

- We are accurate in detecting deception only slightly more than half the time—in other words, only a shade better than what we could achieve with a coin flip.

- We overestimate our abilities to detect other's lies—in other words, we're not as good at catching deception as we think we are.

- We have a strong tendency to judge others' messages as truthful—in other words, we want to believe people wouldn't lie to us (which biases our ability to detect deceit).

As one writer put it, "There is no unique telltale signal for a fib. Pinocchio's nose just doesn't exist, and that makes liars difficult to spot."[25] Moreover, some popular prescriptions about liars' nonverbal behaviors simply aren't accurate. For instance, conventional wisdom suggests that liars avert their gaze and fidget more than nonliars. Research, however, shows just the opposite: Liars often sustain *more* eye contact and fidget *less*, in part because they believe that to do otherwise might look deceitful.[26]

Popular characterizations of "scientific" lie detection aren't helpful, either. One experiment found that viewers who watched the television show *Lie to Me* (described on pages 232–233) were actually *worse* at detecting lies than nonviewers, in part because the show focused on nonverbal cues and ignored important verbal content.[27] While it's possible to make some generalizations about the nonverbal tendencies of liars, caution should be exercised in making evaluations of others' truth-telling based on limited and ambiguous nonverbal cues.

NONVERBAL COMMUNICATION IS AMBIGUOUS

You learned in Chapter 5 that verbal messages are open to multiple interpretations, but nonverbal messages are even more ambiguous. Consider the example of a wink: In one study, college students interpreted this nonverbal signal as

In the TV show *Lie to Me,* Dr. Cal Lightman and his colleagues uncover deception by monitoring nonverbal cues. But is it really that simple?

meaning a variety of things, including an expression of thanks, a sign of friendliness, a measure of insecurity, a sexual come-on, and an eye problem.[28]

Even the most common nonverbal behavior can be ambiguous. Imagine two possible meanings of silence from a normally talkative friend. Or suppose that a much-admired person with whom you've worked suddenly begins paying more attention to you than ever before. What could some possible meanings of this behavior be? Although nonverbal behavior can be very revealing, it can have so many possible meanings that it's impossible to be certain which interpretation is correct.

The ambiguous nature of nonverbal behavior becomes clear in the area of courtship and sexuality. Does a kiss mean "I like you a lot" or "I want to have sex"? Does pulling away from a romantic partner mean "Stop now" or "Keep trying"? Communication researchers explored this question by surveying one hundred college students about sexual consent in twelve dating scenarios in order to discover under what conditions verbal approaches (for example, "Do you want to have sex with me?") were considered preferable to nonverbal indicators (such as kissing as an indicator of a desire to have sex).[29] In every scenario, verbal consent was seen as less ambiguous than nonverbal consent. This doesn't mean that romantic partners don't rely on nonverbal signals; many of the respondents indicated that they interpret nonverbal cues (such as kissing) as signs of sexual willingness. However, nonverbal cues were far less likely to be misunderstood when accompanied by verbal cues. The conclusions of this research seem obvious: Verbal messages are clearer than nonverbal messages in matters of sexual consent. Just because they are clearer, however, doesn't mean that they are practiced. As you read in the previous chapter (pages 162–170), using clearer and less ambiguous verbal messages can reduce the chances of many unfortunate misunderstandings.

Some people have more difficulty decoding nonverbal signals than do others. For instance, young boys often miss the emotional messages that others send them nonverbally, such as when a teacher attempts to express displeasure through arched eyebrows.[30] For people with a syndrome called nonverbal learning disorder (NVLD), reading facial expressions, tone of voice, and other cues is dramatically more difficult.[31] Because of a processing deficit in the right hemisphere of the brain, people with NVLD have trouble making sense of many nonverbal cues. Humor or sarcasm can be especially difficult to understand for people—especially children—with NVLD. For example,

Safeway Clerks Object to "Service with a Smile" Policy

Twelve Safeway employees have filed grievances over the supermarket chain's smile-and-make-eye-contact rule, complaining that they are being propositioned by shoppers who mistake company-required friendliness for flirting.

Under Safeway's "Superior Service" policy, employees are expected to anticipate customers' needs, take them to items they cannot find, make selling suggestions, thank them by name if they pay by check or credit card and offer to carry out their groceries.

Richelle Roberts, a produce clerk, said she is hit on every day by men who think she is coming on to them. Another produce worker, who spoke on condition of anonymity, said she has hidden in a back room to avoid customers who have harassed her, propositioned her and followed her to her car.

San Francisco Chronicle

Proceed with Caution if Using Hand Signals

A drivers' group has developed a guide to gestures that motorists can give one another on the road, but the one you're most familiar with is not among them.

The National Motorists Association, whose mission includes "the enhancement of motorist-to-motorist communication," has developed signals that drivers can use to deliver such messages as "I'm sorry," "Danger ahead," "Pull over to let me pass" and "There is a problem with your car."

Traffic experts, however, urge drivers to use caution in flashing signals to another driver who may mistake one finger for another.

Earlier this month, a motorist on the Ventura Freeway was shot after giving an obscene gesture to a driver who flashed her headlights—the generally accepted signal for prodding slower vehicles to move over. Several years ago an off-duty California Highway Patrol officer, who flashed his headlights in frustration at a pickup driver who cut him off on the freeway, was pursued for several miles and then fatally shot.

And in multicultural Los Angeles, one man's "thumbs up" might mean an insult to another. Or be misinterpreted as a gang sign.

Los Angeles Times

. . . if they learn the right way to introduce themselves to an unfamiliar adult (by shaking hands and saying "pleased to meet you") they may attempt the same response in a group of children where it might be viewed as odd or "nerdy." When peers do give them subtle feedback, such as raised eyebrows, they miss the information completely and therefore cannot modify their behavior next time.[32]

✔+ INVITATION TO INSIGHT

Reading "Body Language"

This exercise that will both increase your skill in observing nonverbal behavior and show you the dangers of being too sure that you're a perfect reader of body language. You can try the exercise either in or out of class, and the period of time over which you do it is flexible, from a single class period to several days. In any case, begin by choosing a partner, and then follow these directions:

1 For the first period of time (however long you decide to make it), observe the way your partner behaves. Notice movements, mannerisms, postures, style of dress, and so on. To remember your observations, jot them down. If you're doing this exercise out of class over an extended period of time, there's no need to let your observations interfere with whatever you'd normally be doing: Your only job here is to compile a list of your partner's behaviors. In this step you should be careful *not to interpret* your partner's behaviors; just record what you see.

2 At the end of the time period, share what you've seen with your partner, who should do the same with you.

3 For the next period of time, your job is not only to observe your partner's behavior but also to *interpret* it. This time in your conference you should tell your partner what you thought his or her behaviors revealed. For example, does careless dressing suggest oversleeping, loss of interest in appearance, or the desire to feel more comfortable? If you noticed frequent yawning, did you think this meant boredom, fatigue after a late night, or sleepiness after a big meal? Don't feel bad if your guesses weren't all correct. Remember that nonverbal clues tend to be ambiguous. You may be surprised how checking out the nonverbal clues you observe can help build a relationship with another person.

Even for those of us who don't suffer from NVLD, the ambiguity of nonverbal behavior can be frustrating. The perception-checking skill you learned in Chapter 3 can be a useful tool for figuring out what meanings you can accurately attach to confusing cues.

Influences on Nonverbal Communication

The way we communicate nonverbally is influenced to a certain degree by biological sex and to a great degree by the way we are socialized. To learn more about these influences, read on.

GENDER

It's easy to identify stereotypical differences in male and female styles of nonverbal communication. Just think about exaggerated caricatures of macho men and delicate women that appear from time to time. Many jokes, as well as humorous films and plays, have been created around the results that arise when characters try to act like members of the opposite sex.

Although few of us behave like stereotypically masculine or feminine movie characters, there are recognizable differences in the way men and women look and act. Some of the most obvious differences are physiological: height, depth and volume of the voice, and so on. Other differences are rooted more in socialization. In general, females are usually more nonverbally expressive, and they are better at recognizing others' nonverbal behavior.[33] More specifically, research shows that, compared to men, women:

- Smile more
- Use more facial expression
- Use more head, hand, and arm gestures (but less expansive gestures)
- Touch others more
- Stand closer to others
- Are more vocally expressive
- Make more eye contact[34]

After looking at differences like these, it might seem as if men and women communicate in radically different ways. In fact, men's and women's nonverbal communication is more similar than different in many respects.[35] Differences like the ones described in the preceding paragraph are noticeable, but they are outweighed by the similar rules we follow in areas such as making eye contact, posture, gestures, and so on. You can prove this by imagining what it would be like to use radically different nonverbal rules: standing only an inch away from others, sniffing strangers, or tapping the forehead of someone when you want his or her attention. While biological sex and cultural norms certainly have an influence on nonverbal style, they aren't as dramatic as the *Men Are from Mars, Women Are from Venus* thesis suggests.

CULTURE

Cultures have different nonverbal languages as well as verbal ones.[36] Fiorello LaGuardia, legendary mayor of New York from 1933 to 1945, was fluent in English, Italian, and Yiddish. Researchers who watched films of his campaign speeches found that they could tell with the sound turned off which language he was speaking by noticing the changes in his nonverbal behavior.[37]

Some nonverbal behaviors have different meanings from culture to culture. The "OK" gesture made by joining the tips of thumb and forefinger to form a circle is a cheery affirmation to most Americans, but it has less positive meanings in other parts of the world.[38] In France and Belgium it means "You're worth zero." In Greece and Turkey it is a vulgar sexual invitation, usually meant as an insult. Given this sort of cross-cultural ambiguity, it's easy to imagine how an innocent tourist might wind up in serious trouble.

> The men walked hand-in-hand, laughing sleepily together under blinding vertical glare. Sometimes they put their arms round each other's necks; they seemed to like to touch each other, as if it made them feel good to know the other man was there. It wasn't love; it didn't mean anything we could understand.
>
> —*Graham Greene*, Journey without Maps

Even though we recognize that differences exist in the nonverbal rules of different cultures, subtle differences can damage relationships without the parties ever recognizing exactly what has gone wrong. Anthropologist Edward Hall points out that, whereas Americans are comfortable conducting business at a distance of roughly four feet, people from the Middle East stand much closer.[39] It is easy to visualize the awkward advance-and-retreat pattern that might occur when two diplomats or businesspeople from these cultures meet. The Middle Easterner would probably keep moving forward to close the gap, whereas the American would continually back away. Both would feel uncomfortable, probably without knowing why.

Like distance, patterns of eye contact vary around the world.[40] A direct gaze is considered appropriate, if not imperative, for speakers seeking power in Latin America, the Arab world, and southern Europe. Asians, Indians, Pakistanis, and northern Europeans, however, gaze at a listener peripherally or not at all.[41] In either case, deviations from the norm are likely to make a listener uncomfortable.

The use of time depends greatly on culture.[42] Some cultures (e.g., North American, German, and Swiss) tend to be **monochronic**, emphasizing punctuality, schedules, and completing one task at a time. Other cultures (e.g., South American, Mediterrannean, and Arab) are more **polychronic**, with flexible schedules in which multiple tasks are pursued at the same time.[43] One psychologist discovered the difference between North and South American attitudes when teaching at a university in Brazil.[44] He found that some Brazilian students arrived halfway through a two-hour class and that most of them stayed put and kept asking questions when the class was scheduled to end. A half-hour after the official end of the class, the psychologist finally closed off discussion, because there was no indication that the students intended to leave. This flexibility of time is quite different from what is common in most North American colleges!

As Table 6.4 shows, differences in cultural rules can lead to misunderstandings. For example, observations have shown that black women in all-black groups are nonverbally more expressive and interrupt one another more than white women in all-white

The Boston Red Sox's David Ortiz bows to teammate Daisuke Matsuzaka after the Japanese pitcher's victory. Cultural sensitivity to nonverbal rules can enhance relationships.

AP Images

Table 6.4

Cultural Differences in Nonverbal Communication Can Lead to Misunderstandings

Behaviors that have one meaning for members of the same culture or co-culture can be interpreted differently by members of other groups.

Behavior	Probable In-Group Perception	Possible Out-Group Perception
Avoidance of direct eye contact (Latino/a)	Used to communicate attentiveness or respect	A sign of inattentiveness; direct eye contact is preferred
Aggressively challenging a point with which one disagrees (African American)	Acceptable means of dialogue; not regarded as verbal abuse or a precursor to violence	Arguments are viewed as inappropriate and a sign of potential imminent violence
Use of finger gestures to beckon others (Asian)	Appropriate if used by adults for children, but highly offensive if directed at adults	Appropriate gesture to use with both children and adults
Silence (Native American)	Sign of respect, thoughtfulness, and/or uncertainty/ambiguity	Interpreted as boredom, disagreement, or refusal to participate
Touch (Latino/a)	Normal and appropriate for interpersonal interactions	Deemed appropriate for some intimate or friendly interactions; otherwise perceived as a violation of personal space
Public display of intense emotions (African American)	Accepted and valued as measure of expressiveness; appropriate in most settings	Violates expectations for self-controlled public behaviors; inappropriate in most public settings
Touching or holding hands of same-sex friends (Asian)	Acceptable in behavior that signifies closeness in platonic relationships	Perceived as inappropriate, especially for male friends

From Interracial Communication Theory into Practice *(with InfoTrac College Edition), 1st ed., by M. P. Orbe and T. M. Harris ©2001. Reprinted with permission of Wadsworth, an imprint of Wadsworth Group, a division of Thomson Learning.*

groups. This doesn't mean that black women always feel more intensely than their white counterparts. A more likely explanation is that the two groups follow different cultural rules. One study found that in racially mixed groups both black and white women moved closer to each others' style.[45] This nonverbal convergence shows that skilled communicators can adapt their behavior when interacting with members of other cultures or subcultures in order to make the exchange smoother and more effective.

Scott Adams/United Features

✔+ INVITATION TO INSIGHT

Gestures Around the World

Before reading any further, take an online quiz to check your understanding of how nonverbal communication can operate in different cultures around the world. Go to your Premium Website for *Looking Out/Looking In* to access the link to this site.

Despite the many cultural differences, some nonverbal behaviors have the same meanings around the world. Smiles and laughter are universal signals of positive emotions, for example, whereas sour expressions are universal signals of displeasure.[46] Charles Darwin believed that expressions like these are the result of evolution, functioning as survival mechanisms that allowed early humans to convey emotional states before the development of language. The innateness of some facial expressions becomes even clearer when we examine the behavior of children who are born with impaired hearing and sight.[47] Despite a lack of social learning, these children often display a broad range of expression. They smile, laugh, and cry in ways that are similar to those of seeing and hearing children. In other words, nonverbal behavior—like much of our communication—is influenced by both our genetic heritage and our culture.

Types of Nonverbal Communication

Keeping the characteristics of nonverbal communication in mind, let's look at some of the ways we communicate in addition to words.

BODY MOVEMENT

The first area of nonverbal communication we'll discuss is the broad field of **kinesics**, or body position and motion. In this section we'll explore the role that body orientation, posture, gestures, facial expressions, and eye contact play in our relationships with one another.

BODY ORIENTATION We'll start with **body orientation**—the degree to which we face toward or away from someone with our body, feet, and head. To understand how this kind of physical positioning communicates nonverbal messages, imagine that you and a friend are in the middle of a conversation when a third person approaches and wants to join you. You're not especially glad to see this person, but you don't want to sound rude by asking him to leave. By turning your body slightly away from the intruder, you can make your feelings very clear. The nonverbal message here is "We're interested in each other right now and don't want to include you in our conversation." The general rule is that facing someone directly signals your interest and facing away signals a desire to avoid involvement.

> Fie, fie upon her! There's language in her eyes, her cheek, her lip. Nay, her foot speaks; her wanton spirits look out at every joint and motive in her body.
>
> —*William Shakespeare,* Troilus and Cressida

You can learn a good deal about how people feel by observing the way people position themselves. The next time you're in a crowded place where people can choose whom to face directly, try noticing who seems to be included in the action and who is being subtly shut out. And in the same way, pay attention to your own body orientation. You may be surprised to discover that you're avoiding a certain person without being conscious of it or that at times you're "turning your back" on people altogether. If this is the case, it may be helpful to figure out why.

POSTURE   Another way we communicate nonverbally is through our **posture**. To see if this is true, stop reading for a moment and notice how you're sitting. What does your position say nonverbally about how you feel? Are there any other people near you now? What messages do you get from their present posture? By paying attention to the postures of those around you, as well as your own, you'll find another channel of nonverbal communication that can furnish information about how people feel about themselves and one another.

An indication of how much posture communicates is shown by our language. It's full of expressions that link emotional states with body postures:

> I won't take this lying down! (Nor will I stand for it!)
> I feel the weight of the world on my shoulders.
> He's a real slouch in the office (but he's no slouch on the basketball court).
> She's been sitting on that project for weeks.

Posture may be the least ambiguous type of nonverbal behavior. In one study, 176 computer-generated mannequin figures were created, and observers were asked to assign emotions to particular postural configurations. The raters had more than 90 percent agreement on postures that were connected with anger, sadness, and happiness.[48] Some postures seem easier to interpret than others. Disgust was the emotion that was hardest to identify from body posture, and some raters thought that surprise and happiness had similar postural configurations.

Tension and relaxation offer other postural keys to feelings. We take relaxed postures in nonthreatening situations and tighten up in threatening situations.[49] Based on this observation, we can tell a good deal about how others feel simply by watching how tense or loose they seem to be. For example, tenseness is a way of detecting status differences: The lower-status person is generally the more rigid, tense-appearing one, whereas the higher-status person is more relaxed.

GESTURES   **Gestures**—movements of the hands and arms—are an important type of nonverbal communication. In fact, they are so basic to our nature that many people who have been sight-impaired from birth use them.[50] Some social scientists claim that a language of gestures was the first form of human communication, preceding speech by tens of thousands of years.[51]

The most common forms of gestures are what social scientists call **illustrators**—movements that accompany speech but don't stand on their own.[52] For instance, if someone on a street corner asked you how to get to a restaurant across town, you might offer street names and addresses—but all the while, you'd probably point with your fingers and gesture with your hands to illustrate how to get there. Remove the words from your directions and it's unlikely that the other person would ever find the restaurant. Think also of people who like to "talk with their hands," gesturing vigorously even when they're conversing on the phone and can't be seen by the other party. Research shows that North Americans use illustrators more often when they

✔+ IN REAL LIFE

Recognizing Nonverbal Cues

You can appreciate how nonverbal cues reflect attitudes by reading the following transcript twice. The first time, imagine that Kim's nonverbal behavior signals that she is glad to meet Stacy, and looking forward to getting to know her better. For your second reading, imagine that Kim feels just the opposite: She is put off by Stacy, and feels uncomfortable around her.

Think about all the ways Kim's nonverbal behaviors might change, depending on her attitude toward Stacy. Even though she speaks the same words, imagine how her posture, gestures, facial expressions, voice, and her use of distance might differ, and how these nonverbal cues would reflect her feelings about her new neighbor.

©Cengage Learning

Stacy: Hi. I'm new here. Just moved in to Unit 14 yesterday. My name's Stacy. *(Extends her hand, ready to shake.)*

Kim: Hi! I'm Kim. I'm your next-door neighbor in number 12.

Stacy: Great! This looks like a nice place.

Kim: It is. Everybody's friendly, and we all get along really well.

Stacy: *(Glancing down at a magazine in Kim's mail.)* Hmmm. *American Songwriter.* Are you a musician?

Kim: Yeah, I'm a singer-songwriter. Mostly acoustic. I play around town. Nothing too big yet, but I'm hoping . . .

Stacy: *(Excitedly)* Whoa! I'm a musician too!

Kim: Really!

Stacy: Yeah. I play rhythm guitar with The Festering Sores. Have you heard of us?

Kim: Yeah, I think so.

Stacy: Well, you'll have to come hear us some time. And maybe we could even jam together, since we're both guitarists.

Kim: That would be interesting!

Stacy: Wow! I can already tell I'm going to like it here. Hey . . . what's the attitude around here about pets?

Kim: They're pretty strict about the "No dogs or cats" policy.

Stacy: No problem! Jezebel isn't either.

Kim: Well, what *is* Jezebel?

Stacy: *(Proudly)* She's a green iguana. A real beauty.

Kim: You're kidding, right?

Stacy: Nope. You'll probably meet her one of these days. In fact, she's kind of a runaway, so you might find her in your place if you leave the door open. Especially when the weather cools down. *(Semi-kidding)* She really likes to snuggle up to a warm body.

Kim: Well, I'm more of a bird person, so . . .

Stacy: She makes friends with everybody. You'll love her!

Kim: Look, I've gotta run. I'm already late for a practice session.

Stacy: I'll see you around. Really glad we're gonna be neighbors!

Kim: Me too.

To see and analyze a video of Stacy and Kim's interactions, go to your Premium Website for Looking Out/Looking In, *access "In Real Life Communication Scenarios," and then click on "Recognizing Nonverbal Cues."*

ON THE JOB

Nonverbal Communication in Job Interviews

The old adage "You never get a second chance to make a first impression" is never truer than in job interviews. The impression you make in the first few minutes of this crucial conversation can define the way a prospective employer views you—and thus the path of your career. Research highlights the vital role that nonverbal communication plays in shaping how interviewers regard job applicants.[a]

Here's a look at three specific behaviors that have been the subject of studies on employment interviewing:

- *Handshaking.* In American culture, most professional interactions begin with a handshake. As simple as this ritual might seem, research shows that the quality of a handshake is related to interviewer hiring recommendations. Handshakes should be firm and energetic without being overpowering—and this holds true for both men and women.[b]

- *Attire/Appearance.* Being well dressed and properly groomed is basic to interview success. Business-appropriate appearance enhances perceptions of

a candidate's credibility and social skills. A rule of thumb is that it's better to err on the side of formality than casualness, and that conservative colors and fashion are preferable to being flashy.[c]

- *Smiling.* While it may seem obvious, one study found that "authentically smiling interviewees were judged to be more suitable and were more likely to be short-listed and selected for the job."[d] The word "authentically" is important—judges in the study made negative appraisals of plastered-on smiles that didn't seem genuine. The key is to smile naturally and regularly, exhibiting a friendly and pleasant demeanor.

It's easy to imagine how other nonverbal cues discussed in this chapter (e.g., eye contact, posture, tone of voice, etc.) are vital in making a good impression in a job interview. For more information, consult the myriad books and websites devoted to employment interviewing. You can also visit your school's career development center or perhaps even take a course in interviewing. In every case, you'll be coached that what you do and how you look is as important as what you say in a job interview.

---

are emotionally aroused—trying to explain ideas that are difficult to put into words when they are furious, horrified, agitated, distressed, or excited.[53] Studies also show that it is easier to comprehend and learn a second language when it is accompanied by illustrators and other nonverbal cues.[54]

A second type of gestures is **emblems**—deliberate nonverbal behaviors that have a precise meaning, known to virtually everyone within a cultural group. Unlike illustrators, emblems can stand on their own and often function as replacements for words. For example, all North Americans know that a head nod means "yes," a head shake means "no," a wave means "hello" or "goodbye," and a hand to the ear means "I can't hear you." And almost every Westerner over the age of seven knows the meaning of a raised middle finger. It's important to remember, however, that the meanings of emblems like these are not universal. For instance, the "thumbs-up" sign means "good" in the United States but is an obscene gesture in Iraq and several other countries.[55]

A third type of gestures is **adaptors**—unconscious

Unlike illustrators that must accompany speech, emblems can stand on their own, substituting for spoken messages.

© JupiterImages/Brand X/Alamy

bodily movements in response to the environment. For instance, shivering when it's cold and folding your arms to get warmer are examples of adaptors. Of course, sometimes we cross our arms when we're feeling "cold" toward another person—and thus adaptors can reveal the climate of our relationships. In particular, self-touching behaviors—sometimes called **manipulators**—are often a sign of discomfort, such as fiddling with your hands or rubbing your arms during an interview.[56] But not *all* fidgeting signals uneasiness. People also are likely to engage in self-touching when relaxed. When they let down their guard (either alone or with friends), they will be more likely to fiddle with an earlobe, twirl a strand of hair, or clean their fingernails. Whether or not the fidgeter is hiding something, observers are likely to interpret these behaviors as a signal of dishonesty. Because not all fidgeters are dishonest, it's important not to jump to conclusions about the meaning of adaptors.

Actually, *too few* gestures may be as significant an indicator of mixed messages as *too many*.[57] Limited gesturing may signal a lack of interest, sadness, boredom, or low enthusiasm. Illustrators also decrease whenever someone is cautious about speaking. For these reasons, a careful observer will look for either an increase or a decrease in the usual level of gestures.

FACE AND EYES   The face and eyes are probably the most noticed parts of the body, but this doesn't mean that their nonverbal messages are the easiest to read. The face is a tremendously complicated channel of expression for several reasons.

First, it's difficult to describe the number and kind of expressions we produce with our face and eyes. Researchers have found that there are at least eight distinguishable positions of the eyebrows and forehead, eight of the eyes and lids, and ten for the lower face.[58] When you multiply this complexity by the number of emotions we feel, you can see why it's almost impossible to compile a dictionary of facial expressions and their corresponding emotions.

Second, facial expressions are difficult to understand because of the speed with which they can change. For example, slow-motion films show **microexpressions** fleeting across a subject's face in as short a time as it takes to blink an eye.[59.] Also, it seems that different emotions show most clearly in different parts of the face: happiness and surprise in the eyes and lower face; anger in the lower face, brows, and forehead; fear and sadness in the eyes; and disgust in the lower face.

> It was terribly dangerous to let your thoughts wander when you were in any public place or within range of a telescreen. The smallest thing could give you away. A nervous tic, an unconscious look of anxiety, a habit of muttering to yourself—anything that carried with it the suggestion of abnormality, of having something to hide. In any case, to wear an improper expression on your face (to look incredulous when a victory was announced, for example) was itself a punishable offense. There was even a word for it in Newspeak: facecrime, it was called.
>
> —*George Orwell*, 1984

Despite the complex way in which the face shows emotions, you can still pick up clues by watching faces carefully. One of the easiest ways is to look for expressions that seem too exaggerated to be true. For instance, genuine facial expressions usually last no longer than five seconds—anything more and we start to doubt they are real (contestants in pageants with smiles plastered on their faces often come across as "fake" or "plastic").[60] Another way to detect feelings is to watch others' expressions when they aren't likely to be thinking about their appearance. We've all had the experience of glancing into another car while stopped in a traffic jam, or of looking around at a sporting event and seeing expressions that the wearer would probably never show in more guarded moments.

The Look of a Victim

Little Red Riding Hood set herself up to be mugged. Her first mistake was skipping through the forest to grandma's house. Her second mistake was stopping to pick flowers. At this point, as you might remember in the story, the mean heavy wolf comes along and begins to check her out. He observes, quite perceptively, that she is happy, outgoing, and basically unaware of any dangers in her surrounding environment. The big bad wolf catches these nonverbal clues and splits to grandma's house. He knows that Red is an easy mark. From this point we all know what happens.

Body movements and gestures reveal a lot of information about a person. Like Little Red Riding Hood, pedestrians may signal to criminals that they are easy targets for mugging by the way they walk. When was the last time you assessed your "muggability rating"? In a recent study two psychologists set out to identify those body movements that characterized easy victims. They assembled "muggability ratings" of sixty New York pedestrians from the people who may have been the most qualified to judge—prison inmates who had been convicted of assault.

The researchers unobtrusively videotaped pedestrians on weekdays between 10:00 A.M. and 12:00 P.M. Each pedestrian was taped for 6 to 8 seconds, the approximate time it takes for a mugger to size up an approaching person. The judges (prison inmates) rated the "assault potential" of the sixty pedestrians on a 10-point scale. A rating of 1 indicated someone was "a very easy rip-off," of 2, "an easy dude to corner." Toward the other end of the scale, 9 meant a person "would be heavy; would give you a hard time," and 10 indicated that the mugger "would avoid it, too big a situation, too heavy." The results revealed several body movements that characterized easy victims: "Their strides were either very long or very short; they moved awkwardly, raising their left legs with their left arms (instead of alternating them); on each step they tended to lift their whole foot up and then place it down (less muggable sorts took steps in which their feet rocked from heel to toe). Overall, the people rated most muggable walked as if they were in conflict with themselves; they seemed to make each move in the most difficult way possible."

Loretta Malandro and Larry Barker

LOOKING AT DIVERSITY

Annie Donnellon: Blindness and Nonverbal Cues

Photo courtesy of Annie Donnellon

I have been blind since birth, so I've never had access to many of the nonverbal cues that sighted people use. In fact, I think that "sightlings" (a pet name for my friends who are sighted) take for granted how much of their meaning comes through nonverbal channels. When I recently took an interpersonal communication course, the material on nonverbal communication was in some ways a foreign language to me.

For instance, I felt a bit left out when the class discussed things like body movement, eye contact, and facial expressions. I understand how these cues work, but I haven't experienced many of them myself. I have never "stared someone down" or "shot a look" at anyone (at least not intentionally!). While I know that some people "talk with their hands," that's something I've never witnessed and rarely do.

When the subject turned to paralanguage, I was back on familiar territory. I listen very carefully to the way people speak to figure out what they're thinking and feeling. My family and friends tell me I'm more tuned in to these issues than most sightlings are. It's typical for me to ask "Are you okay today?" when friends send messages that seem mixed. They may say everything's fine, but their voice often tells a different story.

I'm a singer and performer, and some of my biggest frustrations have come from well-meaning teachers who coach me on my nonverbals. I remember one acting instructor asking me, "How do you think your character would express herself nonverbally in this scene?" and I thought to myself "I have no idea." People who are sighted may think that anger cues like clenched fists, rigid posture, or shrugged shoulders are "natural" expressions, but I believe that many of them are learned by watching others.

Let me pass along some keys that can help make communication smoother and more effective. It's important to mention your name when starting a conversation with people who are blind: Don't assume they can figure out who you are from your voice. At the end of a conversation, please say that you're leaving. I often feel embarrassed when I'm talking to someone, only to find out that they walked away mid-sentence.

Most important: Clue in visually-impaired people when something is going on that they can't see. Often at my sorority meetings, something will happen that everyone is laughing about, but I'm left out of the loop because I can't see the nonverbal cues. Over the years my friends and family have learned that whispering a quick description of the events helps me feel more a part of the interaction.

The interpersonal course I took was an enriching experience for me, my professor, and my classmates. I think we learned a lot from each other—especially about the vital and complex role of nonverbal communication in interpersonal relationships.

The eyes can send several kinds of messages. Meeting someone's glance with your eyes is usually a sign of involvement, whereas looking away is often a sign of a desire to avoid contact. This principle has a practical application in commerce: Customers leave larger tips when their servers (whether male or female) maintain eye contact with them.[61] Research also shows that communicators who make direct eye contact are far more likely to get others to comply with their requests than are those who make evasive glances.[62]

Another kind of message the eyes communicate is a positive or negative attitude.[63] When someone looks toward us with the proper facial expression, we get a clear message that the looker is interested in us—hence the expression "making eyes." At the same time, when our long glances toward someone else are avoided, we can be pretty sure that the other person isn't as interested in a relationship as we are. (Of course, there are all sorts of courtship games in which the receiver of a glance pretends not to notice any message by glancing away, yet signals interest with some other part of the body.) The eyes can also communicate both dominance and submission.[64] We've all played the game of trying to stare down somebody, and there are times when downcast eyes are a sign of giving in.

Even the pupils of our eyes communicate. Researchers measured the amount of pupil dilation while showing various types of pictures to men and women.[65] The results of the experiment were interesting: A person's eyes grow larger in proportion to the degree of interest in an object. For example, men's pupils grew about 18 percent larger when looking at pictures of a naked woman, and women's pupils grew 20 percent larger when looking at pictures of a naked man. Interestingly enough, the greatest increase in pupil size occurred when women looked at a picture of a mother and an infant.

VOICE

The voice is another channel of nonverbal communication. Social scientists use the term **paralanguage** to describe nonverbal, vocal messages. The way a message is spoken can give the same word or words many meanings. For example, note how many meanings come from a single sentence just by shifting the emphasis from one word to another:

This is a fantastic communication book. (Not just any book, but *this* one in particular.)

This is a *fantastic* communication book. (This book is superior, exciting.)

This is a fantastic *communication* book. (The book is good as far as communication goes; it may not be so great as literature or drama.)

This is a fantastic communication *book*. (It's not a play or album; it's a book.)

An entire sentence isn't required to see the impact that emphasis and intonation can have on meaning. Consider the word "dude," which has been the subject of a well-known Bud Light commercial (available on popular video sites), cartoons such as the one on this page, and even a scholarly article.[66] Every time a word like this is uttered, it means something different based on how it's said. (Consider how many meanings you can create for words such as "fine" or "really" simply by altering your paralanguage.)

There are many other ways we communicate paralinguistically through tone, rate, pitch, volume—even through pauses. Consider two types of pauses that can lead to communication snags. The first is the *unintentional pause*—those times when people stop to collect their thoughts before deciding how best to continue their verbal message. It's no surprise that liars tend to have more unintentional pauses than truth-tellers, as they often make up stories on the fly.[67] When people pause at length after being asked a delicate question ("Did you like the gift I bought you?"), it might mean they're buying time to come up with a face-saving—and perhaps less-than-honest—response.

A second type of pause is the *vocalized pause*. These range from disfluencies such as "um," "er," and "uh" to filler words that are used habitually such as "like," "okay," and "ya know." Research shows that vocalized pauses reduce a person's perceived credibility[68] and negatively affect perceptions of candidates in job interviews.[69] When Caroline Kennedy was considering running for the Senate in 2009, her press tour interviews were filled with vocalized pauses. In one case she used "ya know" 142 times in a single interview with *The New York Times*. Although this wasn't the reason she decided not to run for office, many commentators noted that it certainly didn't help her professional image.[70]

> A pause in the wrong place, an intonation misunderstood, and a whole conversation went awry.
>
> —*E. M. Forster,* A Passage to India

Researchers have identified the power of paralanguage through the use of content-free speech—ordinary speech that has been electronically manipulated so that the words are unintelligible, but the paralanguage remains unaffected. (Hearing a foreign language that you don't understand has the same effect.) Subjects who hear content-free speech can consistently recognize the emotion being expressed as well as identify its strength.[71] Young children respond to the paralanguage of adults, warming up to those who speak warmly and shying away from those who speak in a less friendly manner.[72]

Paralanguage can affect behavior in many ways, some of which are rather surprising. Researchers have discovered that communicators are most likely to comply with requests delivered by speakers whose rate was similar to their own: People who spoke rapidly responded most favorably to rapid talkers, whereas slow speakers preferred others whose rate was also slow.[73] Besides complying with same-rate speakers, listeners also feel more positively about people who speak at their own rate.

Sarcasm is one instance in which we use both emphasis and tone of voice to change a statement's meaning to the opposite of its verbal message. Experience this reversal yourself with the following three statements. First say them literally, and then say them sarcastically.

"Thanks a lot!"

"I really had a wonderful time on my blind date."

"There's nothing I like better than lima beans."

As they do with other nonverbal messages, people often ignore or misinterpret the vocal nuances of sarcasm. Members of certain groups—children, people with weak intellectual skills, and poor listeners—are more likely to misunderstand sarcastic messages than others.[74] In one study, children younger than age ten lacked the linguistic sophistication to tell when a message was sarcastic.[75]

Besides reinforcing or contradicting messages, some vocal factors influence the way a speaker is perceived by others. For example, communicators

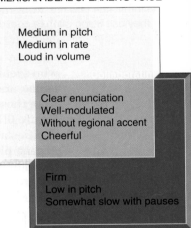

MEXICAN IDEAL SPEAKER'S VOICE

Medium in pitch
Medium in rate
Loud in volume

Clear enunciation
Well-modulated
Without regional accent
Cheerful

Firm
Low in pitch
Somewhat slow with pauses

U.S. IDEAL SPEAKER'S VOICE

Figure 6.1

A Comparison of the Ideal Speakers' Voice Types in Mexico and the United States

Adapted from "Communicative Power: Gender and Culture as Determinants of the Ideal Voice," in *Women and Communicative Power: Theory, Research and Practice,* edited by Carol A. Valentine and Nancy Hoar. ©1988 by SCA. Reprinted by permission.

dren in institutions—picking a baby up, carrying it around, and handling it several times each day. At one hospital that began

of nonverbal communication can have both risks and rewards.

✔+ INVITATION TO INSIGHT

The Rules of Touch

Like most types of nonverbal behavior, touching is governed by cultural and social rules. Imagine that you are writing a guidebook for visitors from another culture. Describe the rules that govern touching in the following relationships. In each case, describe how the gender of the participants also affects the rules.

1 An adult and a five-year-old child

2 An adult and a twelve-year-old

3 Two good friends

4 Boss and employee

this practice, the death rate for infants fell from between 30 and 35 percent to below 10 percent.[87]

Contemporary research confirms the relationship between touch and health. Studies at the University of Miami School of Medicine's Touch Research Institute have shown that premature babies grow faster and gain more weight when they are massaged.[88] The same institute's researchers demonstrated that massage can help premature children gain weight, help colicky children to sleep better, improve the mood of depressed adolescents, and boost the immune function of cancer and HIV patients. Research shows that touch between therapists and clients has the potential to encourage a variety of beneficial changes: more self-disclosure, client self-acceptance, and more positive client–therapist relationships.[89]

APPEARANCE

Whether or not we're aware of the fact, how we look sends messages to others. There are two dimensions to appearance: physical attractiveness and clothing.

PHYSICAL ATTRACTIVENESS The importance of physical attractiveness has been emphasized in the arts for centuries. More recently, social scientists have begun to measure the degree to which physical attractiveness affects interaction between people.[90] For example, females who are perceived as attractive have more dates, receive higher grades in college, persuade males with greater ease, and receive lighter court sentences. Both men and women whom others perceive as attractive are rated as being more sensitive, kind, strong, sociable, and interesting than their less fortunate brothers and sisters. Physical attractiveness is also an asset in the professional world, affecting hiring, promotion, and performance evaluation decisions.[91]

The influence of physical attractiveness begins early in life.[92] Preschoolers were shown photographs of children their own age and asked to choose potential friends and enemies. The researchers found that children as young as three agreed as to who was attractive and unattractive. Furthermore, the children valued their attractive counterparts—both of the same and the opposite sex—more highly. Teachers also are affected by students' attractiveness. Physically attractive students are usually judged more favorably—as being more intelligent, friendly, and popular—than their less attractive counterparts.[93] Teacher-student assessments work in both directions—research shows that physically attractive professors receive higher evaluations from their students.[94]

Fortunately, attractiveness is something we can control without having to call a plastic surgeon. If you aren't totally gorgeous or handsome, don't despair: Evidence suggests that, as we get to know more about people and like them, we start to regard them as better looking.[95] Moreover, we view others as beautiful or ugly not just on the basis of their "original equipment" but also on the basis of how they use that equipment. Posture, gestures, facial expressions, and other behaviors can increase the physical attractiveness of an otherwise unremarkable person. Exercise can improve the way each of us looks. Finally, the way we dress can make a significant difference in the way others perceive us, as you'll now see.

CLOTHING   Besides being a means of protecting us from the elements, clothing is a means of communicating nonverbally. One writer has suggested that clothing conveys at least ten types of messages to others:[96]

- Economic background
- Economic level
- Educational background
- Educational level
- Level of sophistication
- Level of success
- Moral character
- Social background
- Social position
- Trustworthiness

Research shows that we do make assumptions about people based on their clothing. Communicators who wear special clothing often gain persuasiveness. For example, experimenters dressed in uniforms resembling police officers were more successful than those dressed in civilian clothing in requesting pedestrians to pick up litter and in persuading them to lend a dime to an overparked motorist.[97] Likewise, solicitors wearing sheriff's and nurse's uniforms increased the level of contributions to law enforcement and health care campaigns.[98]

Uniforms aren't the only kind of clothing that carries influence. In one study, a male and a female were stationed in a hallway so that anyone who wished to go by had to avoid them or pass between them. In one condition the couple wore "formal daytime dress"; in the other, they wore "casual attire." Passersby behaved differently toward the couple, depending on the style of clothing: They responded positively with the well-dressed couple and negatively with the casually dressed couple.[99]

Similar results in other situations show the influence of clothing. Pedestrians were more likely to return lost coins to people dressed in high-status clothing than to those dressed in

Harley Schwadron/Wall Street Journal/Cartoon Features Syndicate

"Tell me about yourself, Kugelman—your hopes, dreams, career path, and what that damn earring means."

TIME

Social scientists use the term **chronemics** to describe the study of how humans use and structure time. The way we handle time can express both intentional and unintentional messages.[114] For instance, in a culture that values time highly, waiting can be an indicator of status. "Important" people (whose time is supposedly more valuable than that of others) may be seen by appointment only, whereas it is acceptable to intrude without notice on lesser beings. A related rule is that low-status people must never make high-status people wait. It would be a serious mistake to show up late for a job interview, whereas the interviewer might keep you cooling your heels in the lobby. Important people are often whisked to the head of a restaurant or airport line, while presumably less-exalted masses are forced to wait their turn.

Time can be a marker not only of power and status, but also of relationships. Research shows that the amount of time spent with a relational partner sends important messages about valuing that person.[115] In one study analyzing twenty nonverbal behaviors, "spending time together" was the most powerful predictor of both relational satisfaction and perceived interpersonal understanding.[116] Time is also measured and valued in mediated communication. Studies show that the length of time it takes for someone to respond to email messages or to postings in virtual groups has a strong correlation with perceptions of that person.[117] As you might guess, quick responses get positive appraisals, while tardy or neglected replies can have an adverse effect on trust and effectiveness in virtual groups.[118]

between salespeople and customers and between people who work together. We use the far range of social distance—seven to twelve feet—for more formal and impersonal situations. Sitting at this distance signals a far different and less relaxed type of conversation than would pulling a chair around to the boss's side of the desk and sitting only three or so feet away.

- **Public distance** is Hall's term for the farthest zone, running outward from twelve feet. The closer range of public distance is the one that most teachers use in the classroom. In the farther ranges of public space—twenty-five feet and beyond—two-way communication is almost impossible. In some cases, it's necessary for speakers to use public distance because of the size of their audience, but we can assume that anyone who voluntarily chooses to use it when he or she could be closer is not interested in having a dialogue.

Choosing the optimal distance can have a powerful effect on how we regard others and how we respond to them. For example, students are more satisfied with teachers who reduce the distance between themselves and their classes. They also are more satisfied with a course itself, and they are more likely to follow a teacher's instructions.[106] Likewise, medical patients are more satisfied with physicians who operate at the closer end of the social distance zone.[107]

TERRITORIALITY Whereas personal space is the invisible bubble we carry around as an extension of our physical being, **territory** remains stationary. Any geographical area such as a work area, room, house, or other physical space to which we assume some kind of "rights" is our territory. What's interesting about territoriality is that

✔+ MAKING THE GRADE

Summary

Nonverbal communication consists of messages expressed by nonlinguistic means such as body movement, vocal characteristics, touch, appearance, physical space, physical environment, and time.

Nonverbal skills are vital for competent communicators. Nonverbal communication is pervasive; in fact, it is impossible to not send nonverbal messages. Although many nonverbal behaviors are universal, their use is affected by both culture and gender. Most nonverbal communication reveals attitudes and feelings, in contrast to verbal communication, which is better suited to expressing ideas. Nonverbal communication serves many functions. It can repeat, complement, substitute for, accent, regulate, and contradict verbal communication. When presented with conflicting verbal and nonverbal messages, communicators are more likely to rely on the nonverbal ones. For this reason, nonverbal cues are important in detecting deception. It's necessary to exercise caution in interpreting such cues, however, because nonverbal communication is ambiguous.

Key Terms

accenting (205)
adaptors (216)
body orientation (213)
chronemics (229)
complementing (204)
contradicting (205)
emblems (216)
gestures (214)
haptics (222)
illustrators (214)
intimate distance (227)

kinesics (213)
leakage (206)
manipulators (217)
microexpression (217)
mixed message (205)
monochronic (211)
nonverbal communication (200)
paralanguage (220)

personal distance (227)
polychronic (211)
posture (214)
proxemics (226)
public distance (228)
regulating (205)
repeating (204)
social distance (227)
substituting (204)
territory (228)

Online Resources

Now that you have read this chapter, use your Premium Website for *Looking Out/ Looking In* for quick access to the electronic resources that accompany this text. Your Premium Website gives you access to:

- **Study tools** that will help you assess your learning and prepare for exams (*digital glossary, key term flash cards, review quizzes*).

- **Activities and assignments** that will help you hone your knowledge, understand how theory and research applies to your own life (*Invitation to Insight*), consider ethical challenges in interpersonal communication (*Ethical Challenge*), and build your interpersonal communication skills throughout the course (*Skill Builder*). If requested, you can submit your answers to your instructor.

- **Media resources** that will allow you to watch and critique news video and videos of interpersonal communication situations (*In Real Life, interpersonal video simulations*) and download a chapter review so you can study when and where you'd like (*Audio Study Tools*).

This chapter's key terms and search terms for additional reading are featured in this end-of-chapter section, and you can find this chapter's Invitation to Insight and In Real Life activities in the body of the chapter.

Search Terms

When searching online databases to research topics in this chapter, use the following terms (along with this chapter's key terms) to maximize the chances of finding useful information:

body language	gaze	physical attractiveness
eye contact	personal space	vocalics
facial expression		

Film and Television

You can see the communication principles described in this chapter portrayed in the following films and television programs:

NONVERBAL COMMUNICATION IN EVERYDAY LIFE

Seinfeld (1989–1998) Not Rated

In this popular television series, familiar characters Jerry, George, Elaine, and Kramer regularly monitor, discuss, and poke fun at people's nonverbal communication traits. Fans of the show remember "The Close Talker" (who infringes on others' personal and intimate space), "The Low Talker" (who whispers everything she says), and "The High Talker" (whose vocal pitch is far higher than normal for a man). Other disputes occur over George's unintentional winking, the size of Elaine's head, Jerry's puffy shirt, and Kramer's body tan. The writers of the show clearly understood that people pay a great deal of attention to nonverbal communication cues.

NONVERBAL IDENTITY MANAGEMENT

Hitch (2005) Rated PG

Alex "Hitch" Hitchens (Will Smith) is a New York "date doctor" who teaches men how to romance the women of their dreams. His latest client is Albert Brenneman (Kevin James), a nerdy accountant who needs to improve his style to win the affections of the wealthy and beautiful Allegra Cole (Amber Valletta).

Hitch coaches Albert on a variety of nonverbal behaviors, including how to walk, stand, and dance, so that Albert can attract his dream woman. Despite the importance of self-presentation, Hitch's own love life (or lack thereof) shows that romantic success depends on more than manipulating a few nonverbal cues.

PERSONALITY EXPRESSION VIA NONVERBAL COMMUNICATION

Freaky Friday (2003) Rated PG

In the remake of this Disney classic, Tess Coleman (Jamie Lee Curtis) and her teenage daughter Annabell (Lindsay Lohan) wake up to discover that they inhabit one another's bodies and lives. The film is a light and humorous lesson in empathy. Mother, daughter, and viewers all are reminded that the world looks very different depending on one's point of view.

One of the easiest ways to remember "who's who" during the movie is to monitor the characters' nonverbal cues. Although viewers see Tess's body, it's clear that it's being inhabited by a teenage girl if you watch her mannerisms and facial expressions and listen to her vocal tone, rate, and pitch. Similarly, when Tess inhabits her daughter's body, she suddenly engages in a variety of adult behaviors—such as adjusting her teen friend's blouse so it shows less midriff (something only a mother would do).

Although body-switching only happens in the movies, *Freaky Friday* illustrates that nonverbal mannerisms can tell us lot about a person's age, status, and roles.

DETECTING DECEPTION

Lie to Me (2009–) Rated TV-14

Dr. Cal Lightman (Tim Roth) is a deception-detection expert who studies facial expressions and involuntary body language to determine if someone is lying. His ability to spot and analyze deceivers is amazing—in fact, he seems to know more about the liars than they know about themselves.

Many of Lightman's conclusions are based on the studies of renowned social scientist Paul Ekman, who serves as a consultant for the show. Ekman's years of research offer compelling evidence that liars do indeed sometimes send unconscious nonverbal cues that "leak" how they really think and feel.

But some words of caution are in order for fans of the show. For starters, most of Lightman's conclusions come from analyzing slow-motion recordings—something few people have access to in their daily conversations. Second, many nonverbal cues have multiple meanings and are not necessarily indicators of deceit (just because liars often rub their eyes doesn't mean that an eye-rubber is telling a fib). Finally, Lightman (and Ekman) have far more training at analyzing nonverbal communication than the normal person. Their ability to detect deception is clearly the exception, not the norm.

Lie to Me should best be seen as an entertaining look at how social science gives experts some insights into detecting deceit. However, it would be unwise to use it as a layperson's guide for analyzing and judging the nonverbal behavior of friends and family. If you accuse someone of lying based on a few nonverbal cues, your chances of being right are only about 50 percent—and those aren't good odds when it could jeopardize a relationship.

Note: The website http://www.truthaboutdeception.com offers a thorough, current, scholarly, and easy-to-read review of issues related to deception and its detection.

MASCULINE AND FEMININE NONVERBAL BEHAVIORS

Boys Don't Cry (1999) Rated R

This film recounts the sad life and tragic death of Brandon Teena (Hilary Swank), a popular teen who charms the girls in his small Nebraska town and convinces his male buddies that he is a regular guy. In fact, he was born female and chose to change genders after moving to a new town. Brandon's ability to portray both male and female behaviors highlights the gender differences in nonverbal communication.

LISTENING:
More Than Meets the Ear

After studying the topics in this chapter, you should be able to:

1. Identify the situations in which you listen mindfully and those when you listen mindlessly, and evaluate the appropriateness of each style in a given situation.

2. Identify the circumstances in which you listen ineffectively, and the poor listening habits you use in these circumstances.

3. Identify the response styles (listed on pages 247–261) that you commonly use when listening to others.

4. Demonstrate a combination of listening styles you could use to respond effectively in a given situation.

I have just
wandered back
into our conversation
and find
that you
are still
rattling on
about something
or other
i think i must
have been gone

at least
twenty minutes
and you
never missed me
now this might say
something
about my acting ability
or it might say
something about
your sensitivity
one thing

troubles me tho
when it
is my turn
to rattle on
for twenty minutes
which I
have been known to do
have you
been missing too.
　　　—*Ric Masten*

nano/iStockphoto

Ric Masten's poem on this page shows that there's more to listening than gazing politely at a speaker and nodding your head. As you will soon learn, listening is a demanding and complex activity—and just as important as speaking in the communication process.

If we use frequency as a measure, then listening easily qualifies as the most important kind of communication. We spend more time listening to others than in any other type of communication. One study (summarized in Figure 7.1) revealed that college students spend about 11 percent of their communicating time writing, 16 percent speaking, 17 percent reading, but more than 55 percent listening.[1] On the job, listening is just as important. Studies show that most employees of major corporations in North America spend about 60 percent of each workday listening to others.[2]

Besides being the most frequent form of communication, listening is at least as important as speaking in terms of making relationships work. In committed relationships, listening to personal information in everyday conversations is considered a vital ingredient of satisfaction.[3] In one survey, marital counselors identified "failing to take the other's perspective when listening" as one of the most frequent communication problems in the couples with whom they worked.[4] When a group of adults was asked what communication skills were most important in family and social settings, listening was ranked first.[5]

The *International Journal of Listening* devoted an entire issue to exploring various contexts in which listening skills are crucial, including education,[6] health care,[7] religion,[8] and the business world.[9] The On the Job box on page 238 explores in detail the vital role listening plays in the workplace.

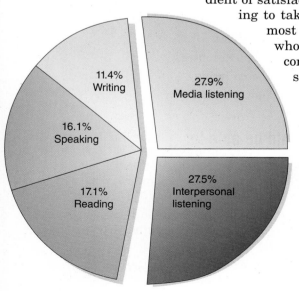

Figure 7.1

Time Devoted to Communication Activities

Source: R. Emanuel, J. Adams, K. Baker, E. K. Daufin, C. Ellington, E. Fitts, J. Himsel, L. Holladay, & D. Okeowo (2008). "How College Students Spend Their Time Communicating." *International Journal of Listening, 22,* 13–28.

This chapter will explore the nature of listening. After defining listening, we will examine the elements that make up the listening process and look at challenges that come with becoming a better listener. Finally, you will read about a variety of listening response styles that you can use to better understand and even help others.

> Listening, not imitation, may be the sincerest form of flattery.
>
> —*Dr. Joyce Brothers*

Listening Defined

So far we've used the term *listening* as if it needs no explanation. Actually, there's more to this concept than you might think. We will define **listening**—at least the interpersonal type—as the process of making sense of others' spoken messages. Because listening is a response to speech, there's obviously a nonverbal dimension as well. As you read in Chapter 6, the way a statement is expressed can affect its meaning. So a good listener pays attention to paralanguage, facial expression, and a host of other nonverbal cues. We'll focus now on explaining what is—and isn't—involved in listening to others.

HEARING VERSUS LISTENING

People often think of hearing and listening as the same thing, but they are quite different. *Hearing* is the process in which sound waves strike the eardrum and cause vibrations that are transmitted to the brain. (You'll read more about hearing in the following section.) *Listening* occurs when the brain reconstructs these electrochemical impulses into a representation of the original sound and then gives them meaning. Barring illness, injury, or cotton plugs, you can't stop hearing.[10] Your ears will pick up sound waves and transmit them to your brain whether you want them to or not.

Listening, however, isn't automatic. As the cartoon on page 239 shows, people hear all the time without listening. Sometimes we automatically and unconsciously block out irritating sounds, such as a neighbor's lawnmower or the roar of nearby traffic. We also stop listening when we find a subject unimportant or uninteresting. Boring stories, TV commercials, and nagging complaints are common examples of messages we may tune out.

MINDLESS LISTENING

When we move beyond hearing and start to listen, researchers note that we process information in two very different ways—sometimes referred to as the *dual-process theory*.[11] Social scientists use the terms "mindless" and "mindful" to describe these different ways of listening.[12] **Mindless listening** occurs when we react to others' messages automatically and routinely, without much mental investment. Words like "superficial" and "cursory" describe mindless listening better than terms like "ponder" and "contemplate."

While the term *mindless* may sound negative, this sort of low-level information processing is a potentially valuable type of communication, because it frees us to focus our minds on messages that require our careful attention.[13] Given the number of messages to which we're exposed, it's impractical to listen carefully and thoughtfully 100 percent

ON THE JOB

Listening in the Workplace

Being an effective speaker is important in career success, but good listening skills are just as vital. A study examining the link between listening and career success revealed that better listeners rose to higher levels in their organizations.[a] When human resource executives across the country were asked to identify skills of the ideal manager, the ability to listen effectively ranked at the top of the list.[b] In problem-solving groups, effective listeners are judged as having the most leadership skills.[c] Listening is just as important in careers that involve cold facts as in ones that involve lots of one-on-one interaction. For example, in a survey of over 90,000 accountants, effective listening was identified as the most important communication skill for professionals entering that field.[d] When a diverse group of senior executives was asked what skills are most important on the job, listening was identified more often than any other skill, including technical competence, computer knowledge, creativity, and administrative talent.[e]

Just because businesspeople believe listening is important doesn't mean they do it well. A survey in which 144 managers were asked to rate their listening skills illustrates this point. Astonishingly, not one of the managers described himself or herself as a "poor" or "very poor" listener, whereas 94 percent rated themselves as "good" or "very good."[f] The favorable self-ratings contrasted sharply with the perceptions of the managers' subordinates, many of whom said their boss's listening skills were weak. Of course, managers aren't the only people whose listening needs work—all of us could stand to improve our skills.

of the time. It's also unrealistic to devote your attention to long-winded stories, idle chatter, or remarks you've heard many times before. The only realistic way to manage the onslaught of messages is to be "lazy" toward many of them. In situations like these, we forego careful analysis and fall back on the schemas—and sometimes the stereotypes—described in Chapter 3 to make sense of a message. If you stop right now and recall the messages you have heard today, it's likely that you processed most of them mindlessly.

MINDFUL LISTENING

By contrast, **mindful listening** involves giving careful and thoughtful attention and responses to the messages we receive. You tend to listen mindfully when a message is important to you, and also when someone you care about is speaking about a matter that is important to him or her. Think of how your ears perk up when someone starts talking about your money ("The repairs will cost me how much?"), or how you tune in carefully when a close friend tells you about the loss of a loved one. In situations like these, you want to give the message sender your complete and undivided attention.

Sometimes we respond mindlessly to information that deserves—and even demands—our mindful attention. Ellen Langer's determination to study mindfulness began when her grandmother complained about headaches coming from a "snake crawling around" beneath her skull. The doctors quickly diagnosed the problem as senility—after all, they reasoned, senility comes with old age and makes people talk nonsense. In fact, the grandmother had a brain tumor that eventually took her life. The event made a deep impression on Langer:

For years afterward I kept thinking about the doctors' reactions to my grandmother's complaints, and about our reactions to the doctors. They went through the motions of diagnosis, but were not open to what they were hearing. Mindsets about senility interfered. We did not question the doctors; mindsets about experts interfered.[14]

Most of our daily decisions about whether to listen mindfully don't have life-and-death consequences, but the point should be clear: There are times when we need to consciously and carefully listen to what others are telling us. That kind of mindful listening will be the focus of the remainder of this chapter.

Elements in the Listening Process

By now, you can begin to see that there is more to listening than sitting quietly while another person speaks. In truth, listening is a process that consists of five elements: hearing, attending, understanding, responding, and remembering.

HEARING

As we have already discussed, **hearing** is the physiological dimension of listening. It occurs when sound waves strike the ear at a certain frequency and loudness. Hearing is influenced by a variety of factors, including background noise. If there are other loud noises, especially at the same frequency as the message we are trying to hear, we find it difficult to sort out the important signals from the background. Hearing is also affected by auditory fatigue, a temporary loss of hearing caused by continuous exposure to the same tone or loudness. If you spend an evening at a loud party, you may have trouble hearing well, even after getting away from the crowd. If you are exposed to loud noise often enough, permanent hearing loss can result—as many rock musicians and fans can attest.

For many communicators, the challenge of hearing is even more difficult as a result of physiological problems. In the United States alone, more than 22 million people communicate with some degree of hearing impairment.[15] One study revealed that, on any given day, one-fourth to one-third of the children in a typical classroom did not hear normally.[16] As a competent communicator, you need to recognize when you may be speaking to someone with a hearing loss and adjust your approach accordingly.

Zits Partnership/King Features

ATTENDING

Whereas hearing is a physiological process, **attending** is a psychological one and is part of the process of selection described in Chapter 3. We would go crazy if we attended to every sound we hear, so we filter out some messages and focus on others. Needs, wants, desires, and interests determine what is attended to. Not surprisingly, research shows that we attend most carefully to messages when there's a payoff for doing so.[17] If you're planning to see a movie, you'll listen to a friend's description more carefully than you would have otherwise. And when you want to get better acquainted with others, you'll pay careful attention to almost anything they say, in hopes of improving the relationship.

Surprisingly, attending doesn't help just the listener: It also helps the message sender. Participants in one study viewed brief movie segments and then described them to listeners who varied in their degree of attentiveness to the speakers. Later on, the researchers tested the speakers' long-term recall of details from the movie segments. Those who had recounted the movie to attentive listeners remembered more details of the film.[18]

Igor Kopelnitsky/Getty Images

UNDERSTANDING

Understanding occurs when we make sense of a message. It is possible to hear and attend to a message without understanding it at all. And, of course, it's possible to misunderstand a message. Communication researchers use the term **listening fidelity** to describe the degree of congruence between what a listener understands and what the message sender was attempting to communicate.[19] This chapter describes the many reasons why we misunderstand others—and why they misunderstand us. It also outlines skills that will help you improve your understanding of others.

RESPONDING

Responding to a message consists of giving observable feedback to the speaker. Although listeners don't always respond visibly to a speaker, research suggests they should do so more often. One study of 195 critical incidents in banking and medical settings showed that a major difference between effective and ineffective listening was the kind of feedback offered.[20] Good listeners show they are attentive by nonverbal behaviors such as keeping eye contact and reacting with appropriate facial expressions—which was of particular importance to children in one study who were asked to evaluate "good" versus "bad" listeners.[21] Verbal behavior—answering questions and exchanging ideas, for example—also demonstrates attention. It's easy to imagine how other responses would signal less effective listening. A slumped posture, bored expression, and yawning send a clear message that you are not tuned in to the speaker.

Adding responsiveness to our listening model demonstrates a fact that we discussed in Chapter 1: Communication is *transactional* in nature. Listening isn't just a passive activity. As listeners, we are active participants in a communication transaction. At the same time we receive messages, we also send them. Responding is such an integral part of good listening that we'll devote an entire section to listening responses at the end of this chapter.

LOOKING AT DIVERSITY

Bonnie Motsch: Learning to Listen in Prison

Photo courtesy of Bonnie Motsch.

I'm an inmate in the Indiana Department of Correction. Like many of the prisoners here, my penal status has sometimes led to rocky relationships with family members and friends. Some visits and phone calls have turned into yelling matches that made a bad situation worse.

A while ago, I signed up for a program in our prison that teaches communication skills. One skill we learned was the "Speaker-Listener" technique for handling difficult discussions. It gave us guidelines like paraphrasing, not interrupting, and trying to understand the other person's side.

These communication skills have done wonders for my father and me. Most of our conversations used to be yelling matches where each of us tried to talk

longest, loudest, and get in the last word. Now that we're using the new techniques, we're actually hearing, listening, and understanding each other in ways we never have before. We also have a new respect for one another's ideas and opinions.

I'm not the only prisoner who has benefited from this training. One of my friends in the program says that she and her mother are communicating much better these days. My friend has learned techniques not only for listening better, but also for expressing her thoughts and feelings more effectively. Her mother is much less defensive and listens more openly to my friend's concerns than she did in the past.

I can honestly say that if I had known about these listening skills earlier in life, I probably would not have veered so far from the path my family laid out for me. I'm guessing a lot of my fellow inmates would say the same thing.

REMEMBERING

Remembering is the ability to recall information. If we don't remember a message, listening is hardly worth the effort. Research suggests that most people remember only about 50 percent of what they hear immediately after hearing it.[22] Within 8 hours, the 50 percent remembered drops to about 35 percent. After two months, the average recall is only about 25 percent of the original message. Given the amount of information we process every day—from teachers, friends, the radio, TV, and other sources—the residual message (what we remember) is a small fraction of what we hear. Although the tendency to forget information is common, there are ways to improve your retention and recall. You'll learn some of those ways later in this chapter. For now, though, you can begin to get a sense of how tough it is to listen effectively by trying the exercise on the next page.

The Challenge of Listening

It's easy to acknowledge that listening is important and to describe the steps in the listening process. What's difficult is to actually become a better listener. This section will describe the challenges that listeners must face and overcome to become more effective communicators. We'll look at various types of ineffective listening, then we'll explore the many reasons we don't listen better. As you read this material, think to yourself, "How many of these describe *me*?" The first step to becoming a better listener is to recognize areas that need improvement.

✔+ INVITATION TO INSIGHT

Listening Breakdowns

You can overcome believing in some common myths about listening by recalling specific instances when

1 You heard another person's message but did not attend to it.

2 You attended to a message but forgot it almost immediately.

3 You attended to and remembered a message but did not understand it accurately.

4 You understood a message but did not respond sufficiently to convey your understanding to the sender.

5 You failed to remember some or all of an important message.

TYPES OF INEFFECTIVE LISTENING

Your own experience will probably confirm the fact that poor listening is all too common. Although a certain amount of ineffective listening is inescapable and sometimes even understandable, it's important to be aware of these types of problems so you can avoid them when listening well really counts.

PSEUDOLISTENING Whereas mindless listening may be a private matter, **pseudolistening** is an imitation of the real thing—an act put on to fool the speaker. Pseudolisteners give the appearance of being attentive: They look you in the eye; they may even nod and smile. But the show of attention is a polite façade because their minds are somewhere else. Paradoxically, pseudolistening can take more effort than simply tuning out the other person.

STAGE-HOGGING Stage-hogs (sometimes called "conversational narcissists") try to turn the topic of conversations to themselves instead of showing interest in the speaker.[23] One **stage-hogging** strategy is a "shift-response"—changing the focus of the conversation from the speaker to the narcissist: "You think your math class is tough? You ought to try my physics class!" Interruptions are another hallmark of stage-hogging. Besides preventing the listener from learning potentially valuable information, they can damage the relationship between the interrupter and the speaker. For example, applicants who interrupt the questions of employment interviewers are likely to be rated less favorably than applicants who wait until the interviewer has finished speaking before they respond.[24]

SELECTIVE LISTENING Selective listeners respond only to the parts of your remarks that interest them, rejecting everything else. Sometimes **selective listening** is legitimate, as when we screen out radio commercials and music and keep an ear cocked for a weather report or an announcement of the time. Selective listen-

"Someday, you'll act like you understand."

ing is less appropriate in personal settings, when your obvious inattention can be a slap in the face to the other person.

INSULATED LISTENING Insulated listeners are almost the opposite of their selective cousins just described. Instead of looking for specific information, these people avoid it. Whenever a topic arises that they'd rather not deal with, those who use **insulated listening** simply fail to hear or acknowledge it. You remind them about a problem, and they'll nod or answer you—and then promptly ignore or forget what you've just said.

DEFENSIVE LISTENING Defensive listeners take others' remarks as personal attacks. The teenager who perceives her parents' questions about her friends and activities as distrustful snooping uses **defensive listening**, as do touchy parents who view any questioning by their children as a threat to their authority and parental wisdom. As Chapter 10 will suggest, it's fair to assume that many defensive listeners are suffering from shaky presenting images and avoid admitting it by projecting their own insecurities onto others.

AMBUSHING Ambushers listen carefully to you, but only because they're collecting information that they'll use to attack what you say. The technique of a cross-examining prosecution attorney is a good example of **ambushing**. Needless to say, using this kind of strategy will justifiably initiate defensiveness in the other person.

INSENSITIVE LISTENING Those who use **insensitive listening** respond to the superficial content in a message but miss the more important emotional information that may not be expressed directly. "How's it going?" an insensitive listener might ask. When you reply by saying "Oh, okay I guess" in a dejected tone, he or she responds "Well, great!" Insensitive listeners tend to ignore the nonverbal cues described in Chapter 6 and lack the empathy described in Chapter 3.

> **Bore**, n. A person who talks when you wish him to listen.
>
> **Conversation**, n. A fair for the display of the minor mental commodities, each exhibitor being too intent upon arrangement of his own wares to observe those of his neighbor.
>
> **Egotist**, n. A person of low taste more interested in himself than me.
>
> **Heaven**, n. A place where the wicked cease from troubling you with talk of their personal affairs, and the good listen with attention while you expound your own.
>
> —*Ambrose Bierce,* The Devil's Dictionary

WHY WE DON'T LISTEN BETTER

After thinking about the styles of ineffective listening described previously, most people begin to see that they listen carefully only a small percentage of the time. Sad as it may be, it's impossible to listen well *all* of the time, for several reasons that we'll outline here.

MESSAGE OVERLOAD It's especially difficult to focus on messages—even important ones—when you are bombarded by information. Face-to-face messages come from friends, family, work, and school. Personal media—text messages, phone calls, emails, and instant messages—demand your attention. Along with these personal channels, we are awash in messages from the mass media. This deluge of communication has made the challenge of attending tougher than at any time in human history.[25]

In *The Devil Wears Prada*, the domineering boss Miranda Priestly (Meryl Streep) is a model of ineffective listening. (See film summary on page 266.)

PREOCCUPATION Another reason we don't always listen carefully is that we're often wrapped up in personal concerns that seem more important than the messages that others are sending. It's difficult to pay attention to someone else when you're worrying about an upcoming exam or thinking about the great time you plan to have over the next weekend.

> Everybody's talkin' at me, I don't hear a word they're sayin'.
>
> —*Fred Neil*

RAPID THOUGHT Listening carefully is also difficult for a physiological reason. Although we're capable of understanding speech at rates of up to 600 words per minute, the average person only speaks between 100 and 150 words per minute.[26] Thus, we have mental "spare time" while someone is talking. The temptation is to use this time in ways that don't relate to the speaker's ideas: thinking about personal interests, daydreaming, planning a rebuttal, and so on. The trick is to use this spare time to understand the speaker's ideas better, rather than to let your attention wander.

EFFORT Listening effectively is hard work. The physical changes that occur during careful listening show the effort it takes: The heart rate quickens, respiration increases, and body temperature rises.[27] Notice that these changes are similar to the body's reaction to physical effort. This is no coincidence, because listening carefully to a speaker can be just as taxing as a workout—which is why some people choose not to make the effort.[28] If you've come home exhausted after an evening of listening intently to a friend in need, you know how draining the process can be.

EXTERNAL NOISE The physical world in which we live often presents distractions that make it difficult to pay attention to others. Consider, for example, how the efficiency of your listening decreases when you are seated in a crowded, hot, stuffy room, surrounded by others talking next to you and traffic noises outside. It's not surprising that noisy classrooms often make learning difficult for students.[29] In such circumstances, even the best intentions aren't enough to ensure clear understanding.

Bright-eyed college students in lecture halls aren't necessarily listening to the professor, the American Psychological Association was told yesterday.

If you shot off a gun at sporadic intervals and asked the students to encode their thoughts and moods at that moment, you would discover that:

- About 20 percent of the students, men and women, are pursuing erotic thoughts.
- Another 20 percent are reminiscing about something.
- Only 20 percent are actually paying attention to the lecture; 12 percent actively listen. The others are worrying, daydreaming, thinking about lunch or—surprise—religion (8 percent).

This confirmation of the lecturer's worst fears was reported by Paul Cameron, an assistant professor at Wayne State University in Detroit. Cameron's results were based on a nine-week course in introductory psychology for 85 college sophomores. A gun was fired 21 times at random intervals, usually when Cameron was in the middle of a sentence.

—The San Francisco Sunday Examiner and Chronicle

FAULTY ASSUMPTIONS We often make faulty assumptions that lead us to believe we're listening attentively when quite the opposite is true. When the subject is a familiar one, it's easy to tune out because you think you've heard it all before. A related problem arises when you assume that a speaker's thoughts are too simple or too obvious to deserve careful attention, when in fact they do. At other times just the opposite occurs: You think that another's comments are too complex to be understood (as in some lectures), so you give up trying to make sense of them.

LACK OF APPARENT ADVANTAGES It often seems that there's more to gain by speaking than by listening. When business consultant Nancy Kline asked some of her clients

Despite the advantages of understanding others, there are many reasons why we don't listen better.

ballyscanlon/Getty Images

why they interrupted their colleagues, these are the reasons she heard:

My idea is better than theirs.

If I don't interrupt them, I'll never get to say my idea.

I know what they are about to say.

They don't need to finish their thoughts since mine are better.

Nothing about their idea will improve with further development.

It is more important for me to get recognized than it is to hear their idea.

I am more important than they are.[30]

Even if some of these thoughts are true, the egotism behind them is stunning. Furthermore, nonlisteners are likely to find that the people they cut off are less likely to treat their ideas with respect. Like defensiveness, listening is often reciprocal. You get what you give.

LACK OF TRAINING   Even if we want to listen well, we're often hampered by a lack of training. A common but mistaken belief is that listening is like breathing—an activity that people do well naturally. "After all," the common belief goes, "I've been listening since I was a child. I don't need to study the subject in school." The truth is that listening is a skill much like speaking: Virtually everybody does it, though few people do it well. Unfortunately, there is no connection between how competently most communicators *think* they listen and how competent they really are in their ability to understand others.[31] The good news is that listening can be improved through instruction and training.[32] Despite this fact, the amount of time spent teaching listening is far less than that spent on other types of communication. Table 7.1 reflects this upside-down arrangement.

HEARING PROBLEMS   Sometimes a person's listening ability suffers from a physiological hearing problem. In such cases, both the person with the problem and others can become frustrated at the ineffective communication that results. One survey explored the feelings of adults who have spouses with hearing loss. Nearly two-thirds of the respondents said they feel annoyed when their partner can't hear them clearly. Almost one-quarter said that beyond just being annoyed, they felt ignored, hurt, or

Table 7.1
Comparison of Communication Activities

	Listening	Speaking	Reading	Writing
Learned	First	Second	Third	Fourth
Used	Most	Next to most	Next to least	Least
Taught	Least	Next to least	Next to most	Most

sad. Many of the respondents believe their spouses are in denial about their condition, which makes the problem even more frustrating.[33] If you suspect that you or someone you know suffers from a hearing loss, it's wise to have a physician or audiologist perform an examination.

MEETING THE CHALLENGE OF LISTENING BETTER

After reading the last few pages, you might decide that listening well is next to impossible. Fortunately, with the right combination of attitude and skill, you can indeed listen better. The following guidelines will show you how.

TALK LESS   Zeno of Citium put it most succinctly: "We have been given two ears and but a single mouth, in order that we may hear more and talk less." If your true goal is to understand the speaker, avoid the tendency to hog the stage and shift the conversation to your ideas. Talking less doesn't mean you must remain completely silent. As you'll soon read, giving feedback that clarifies your understanding and seeks new information is an important way to understand a speaker. Nonetheless, most of us talk too much when we're claiming to understand others. Other cultures, including many Native American ones, value listening at least as much as talking.[34] You can appreciate the value of this approach by trying the exercise below.

To be heard, there are times you must be silent.—Chinese proverb

© Corbis Super RF/Alamy

GET RID OF DISTRACTIONS   Some distractions are external: ringing telephones, radio or television programs, friends dropping in, and so on. Other distractions are internal: preoccupation with your own problems, an empty stomach, and so on. If the information you're seeking is really important, do everything possible to eliminate the internal and external distractions that interfere with careful listening. This might mean turning off the TV, shutting off your cell phone, or moving to a quiet room where you won't be bothered by the lure of

✔+ INVITATION TO INSIGHT

Speaking and Listening with a "Talking Stick"

Explore the benefits of talking less and listening more by using a "Talking Stick." This exercise is based on the Native American tradition of "council." Gather a group of people in a circle, and designate a particular object as the talking stick. (Almost any manageable object will do.) Participants then pass the object around the circle. Each person may speak

    a.   When holding the stick
    b.   For as long as he or she holds the stick
    c.   Without interruption from anyone else in the circle

When a member is through speaking, the stick passes to the left, and the speaker surrendering the stick must wait until it has made its way around the circle before speaking again.

After each member of the group has had the chance to speak, discuss how this experience differed from more common approaches to listening. Decide how the desirable parts of this method could be introduced into everyday conversations.

the computer, the work on your desk, or the food on the counter. (See the reading on page 248 for an example of removing distractions from business meetings.)

DON'T JUDGE PREMATURELY   Most people would agree that it's essential to understand a speaker's ideas before judging them. However, all of us are guilty of forming snap judgments, evaluating others before hearing them out. This tendency is greatest when the speaker's ideas conflict with our own. Conversations that ought to be exchanges of ideas turn into verbal battles, with the "opponents" trying to ambush one another in order to win a victory. It's also tempting to judge prematurely when others criticize you, even when those criticisms may contain valuable truths and when understanding them may lead to a change for the better. Even if there is no criticism or disagreement, we tend to evaluate others based on sketchy first impressions, forming snap judgments that aren't at all valid. The lesson contained in these negative examples is clear: Listen first. Make sure you understand. *Then* evaluate.

"You haven't been listening. I keep telling you that I don't want a product fit for a king."

LOOK FOR KEY IDEAS   It's easy to lose patience with long-winded speakers who never seem to get to the point—or *have* a point, for that matter. Nonetheless, most people do have a central idea. By using your ability to think more quickly than the speaker can talk, you may be able to extract the central idea from the surrounding mass of words you're hearing. If you can't figure out what the speaker is driving at, you can always use a variety of response skills, which we'll examine now.

Types of Listening Responses

Of the five components of listening (hearing, attending, understanding, responding, and remembering), *responding* lets us know how well others are tuned in to what we're saying. Think for a moment of someone you consider a good listener. Why did you choose that person? It's probably because of the way she or he responds while you are speaking: making eye contact and nodding when you're talking, staying attentive while you're telling an important story, reacting with an exclamation when you say something startling, expressing empathy and support when you're hurting, and offering another perspective or advice when you ask for it.[35]

> The greatest compliment that was ever paid me was when one asked me what I thought, and attended to my answer.
>
> —Henry David Thoreau

The rest of this chapter will describe a variety of response styles. We'll begin by describing responses that are focused on gathering more information to better understand the speaker. By chapter's end, our focus will be on listening responses that offer a speaker our assessment and direction.

PROMPTING

In some cases, the best response a listener can give is a small nudge to keep the speaker talking. **Prompting** involves using silences and brief statements of encouragement to

Meetings Going "Topless"

As the capital of information technology, Silicon Valley may have more gadgets per capita than any other place on the planet. Yet, even here, "always on" can be a real turnoff.

Frustrated by workers so plugged in that they tuned out in the middle of business meetings, a growing number of companies are going "topless," as in no laptops allowed. Also banned from some conference rooms: BlackBerrys, iPhones and other devices on which so many people have come to depend.

Over the years, companies have come up with innovative ways to keep meetings from sucking up time. Some remove chairs and force people to stand. Others get everyone to drink a glass of water beforehand.

But as laptops got lighter and smart phones even smarter, people discovered a handy diversion—making more eye contact with their screens than one another. The practice became so pervasive that Todd Wilkens, who runs a San

JamesGdesign/iStockphoto

Francisco design firm, waged a "personal war against CrackBerry."

"In this age of wireless Internet and mobile e-mail devices, having an effective meeting or working session is becoming more and more difficult," he wrote on his company blog in November. "Laptops, Blackberries, Sidekicks, iPhones and the like keep people from being fully present. Aside from just being rude, partial attention generally leads to partial results."

Wilkens' firm, Adaptive Path, now encourages everyone to leave their laptops at their desks. His colleague, Dan Saffer, coined the term "topless" as in laptop-less. Mobile and smart phones must be stowed on a counter or in a box during meetings.

"All of our meetings got a lot more productive," Wilkens said.

Jessica Guynn, *Los Angeles Times*

draw others out. Besides helping you to better understand the speaker, prompting can also help others clarify their thoughts and feelings. Consider this example:

Pablo: *Julie's dad is selling a complete computer system for only $600, but if I want it, I have to buy it now. He's got another interested buyer. It's a great deal, but buying it would wipe out my savings. At the rate I spend money, it would take me a year to save up this much again.*

Tim: *Uh-huh.*

Pablo: *I wouldn't be able to take that ski trip over winter break . . . but I sure could save time with my schoolwork . . . and do a better job, too.*

Tim: *That's for sure.*

Pablo: *Do you think I should buy it?*

Tim: *I don't know. What do you* think?

Pablo: *I just can't decide.*

Tim: *(Silence)*

Pablo: *I'm going to do it. I'll never get a deal like this again.*

In cases like this, your prompting can be a catalyst to help others find their own answers. Prompting will work best when it's done sincerely. Your nonverbal behaviors—eye contact, posture, facial expression, tone of voice—have to show that you are concerned with the other person's problem. Mechanical prompting is likely to irritate instead of help.

QUESTIONING

It's easy to understand why **questioning** has been called "the most popular piece of language."[36] Asking for information can help both the person doing the asking and the one providing answers.

Questioning can help you, the asker, in at least three ways. Most obviously, the answers you get can fill in facts and details that will sharpen your understanding ("Did he give you any reasons for doing that?" "What happened next?"). Also, by asking questions you can learn what others are thinking and feeling ("What's on your mind?" "Are you mad at me?"), as well as what they might want ("Are you asking me to apologize?").

Besides being useful to the person doing the asking, questions can also be a tool for the one who answers. As people in the helping professions know, questions can encourage self-discovery. Playing counselor can be a dangerous game, but there are times when you can use questions to encourage others to explore their thoughts and feelings. "So, what do you see as your options?" may prompt an employee to come up with creative problem-solving alternatives. "What would be your ideal solution?" might help a friend get in touch with various wants and needs. Most importantly, encouraging discovery rather than dispensing advice indicates you have faith in others' ability to think for themselves. This may be the most important message that you can communicate as an effective listener.

Despite their apparent benefits, not all questions are equally helpful. Whereas **sincere questions** are aimed at understanding others, **counterfeit questions** are aimed at sending a message, not receiving one. Counterfeit questions come in several varieties:

- *Questions that trap the speaker.* When your friend says, "You didn't like that movie, did you?", you're being backed into a corner. It's clear that your friend disapproves, so the question leaves you with two choices: You can disagree and defend your position, or you can devalue your reaction by lying or equivocating—"I guess it wasn't perfect." Consider how much easier it would be to respond to the sincere question, "What did you think of the movie?"

From *Communication: The Transfer of Meaning* by Don Fabun.

- *A tag question.* Phrases like "did you?" or "isn't that right?" at the end of a question can be a tip-off that the asker is looking for agreement, not information. Although some tag questions are genuine requests for confirmation, counterfeit ones are used to coerce agreement: "You said you'd call at 5 o'clock, but you forgot, didn't you?" Similarly, leading questions that begin with "Don't you" (such as, "Don't you think he would make a good boss?") direct others toward a desired response. As a simple solution, changing "Don't you?" to "Do you?" makes the question less leading.

- *Questions that make statements.* "Are you *finally* off the phone?" is more of a statement than a question—a fact unlikely to be lost on the targeted person. Emphasizing certain words can also turn a question into a statement: "You lent money to *Tony*?" We also use questions to offer advice. The person who asks "Are you going to stand up to him and give him what he deserves?" clearly has stated an opinion about what should be done.

- *Questions that carry hidden agendas.* "Are you busy Friday night?" is a dangerous question to answer. If you say "No," thinking the person has something fun in mind, you won't like hearing, "Good, because I need some help moving my piano." Obviously, such questions are not designed to enhance understanding: They are setups for the proposal that follows. Other examples include, "Will you do me a favor?" and "If I tell you what happened, will you promise not to get mad?" Wise communicators answer questions that mask hidden agendas cautiously, with responses like "It depends" or "Let me hear what you have in mind before I answer."

- *Questions that seek "correct" answers.* Most of us have been victims of questioners who want to hear only a particular response. "Which shoes do you think I should wear?" can be a sincere question—unless the asker has a predetermined preference. When this happens, the asker isn't interested in listening to contrary opinions, and "incorrect" responses get shot down. Some of these questions may venture into delicate territory. "Honey, do you think I look fat?" can be a request for a "correct" answer.

- *Questions based on unchecked assumptions.* "Why aren't you listening to me?" assumes that the other person isn't paying attention. "What's the matter?" assumes that something is wrong. As Chapter 3 explains, perception checking is a much better way of checking out assumptions. As you recall, a perception check offers a description and interpretations, followed by a sincere request for clarification: "When you kept looking over at the TV, I thought you weren't listening to me, but maybe I was wrong. Were you paying attention?"

PARAPHRASING

For all its value, questioning won't always help you understand or help others. As the cartoon on page 249 shows, questions can even lead to greater confusion. For another example, consider what might happen when you ask for directions to a friend's home. Suppose that you've received these instructions: "Drive about a mile and then turn left at the traffic signal." Now imagine that a few common problems exist in this simple message. First, suppose that your friend's idea of "about a mile" differs from yours: Your mental picture of the

> The reality of the other person is not in what he reveals to you, but in what he cannot reveal to you. Therefore, if you would understand him, listen not to what he says but rather to what he does not say.
>
> —*Kahlil Gibran*

distance is actually closer to 2 miles, whereas your friend's is closer to 300 yards. Next, consider that "traffic signal" really means "stop sign"; after all, it's common for us to think one thing and say another. Keeping these problems in mind, suppose that you tried to verify your understanding of the directions by asking, "After I turn at the signal, how far should I go?" to which your friend replies that the house is the third from the corner. Clearly, if you parted after this exchange, you would encounter a lot of frustration before finding the elusive residence.

Because questioning doesn't always provide the information you need, consider another kind of listening response—one that would tell you whether you understood what had already been said before you asked additional questions. This type of feedback involves restating in your own words the message you thought the speaker just sent, without adding anything new. Statements that reword the listener's interpretation of a message are commonly termed **paraphrasing** or *active listening*. If the listener in the preceding scenario had offered this paraphrase—"You're telling me to drive down to the traffic light by the high school and turn toward the mountains, is that it?"—it probably would have led the speaker to clarify the message.

The key to success in paraphrasing is to restate the other person's comments in your own words as a way of cross-checking the information. If you simply repeat the other person's comments verbatim, you will sound foolish—and you still might well be misunderstanding what has been said. Notice the difference between simply parroting a statement and true paraphrasing:

Speaker:	*I'd like to go, but I can't afford it.*
Parroting:	*You'd like to go, but you can't afford it.*
Paraphrasing:	*So if we could find a way to pay for you, you'd be willing to come. Is that right?*
Speaker:	*You look awful!*
Parroting:	*You think I look terrible.*
Paraphrasing:	*Sounds like you think I've put on too much weight.*

There are two levels at which you can paraphrase messages. The first involves paraphrasing *factual information* that will help you understand the other person's ideas more clearly. At the most basic level, this sort of reflecting can prevent frustrating mixups: "So you want to meet *this* Tuesday, not next week, right?"

You can also paraphrase *personal information*: "So my joking makes you think I don't care about your problem." This sort of nondefensive response may be difficult when you are under attack, but it can short-circuit defensive arguments. Chapter 10 will explain in more detail how to use paraphrasing when you're being criticized.

Paraphrasing personal information can also be a tool for helping others, as the In Real Life transcript on pages 252–253 shows.[37] Reflecting the speaker's thoughts and feelings (instead of judging or analyzing, for example) shows your involvement and concern. The nonevaluative nature of paraphrasing encourages the problem-holder to discuss the matter further. Reflecting thoughts and feelings allows the problem-holder to unload more of the concerns he or she has been carrying around, often leading to the relief that comes from catharsis. Finally, paraphrasing helps the problem-holder to sort out the problem. The clarity that comes from this sort of perspective can make it possible to find solutions that weren't apparent before. These features make paraphrasing a vital skill in the human services professions, leadership training, and even hostage negotiation.[38]

✔+ IN REAL LIFE

Paraphrasing on the Job

This conversation between two coworkers shows how paraphrasing can help people solve their own problems. Notice how Jill comes to a conclusion without Mark's advice. Notice also how the paraphrasing sounds natural when combined with sincere questions and other helping styles.

Jill: I've had the strangest feeling about John (*their boss*) lately.

Mark: What's that? (*A simple question invites Jill to go on*)

Jill: I'm starting to think maybe he has this thing about women—or maybe it's just about me.

Mark: You mean he's coming on to you? (*Mark paraphrases what he thinks Jill has said*)

Jill: Oh, no, not at all! But it seems like he doesn't take women—or at least me—seriously. (*Jill corrects Mark's misunderstanding and explains herself*)

Mark: What do you mean? (*Mark asks another simple question to get more information*)

Jill: Well, whenever we're in a meeting or just talking around the office and he asks for ideas, he always seems to pick men. He gives orders to women—men, too—but he never asks the women to say what they think.

Jason Harris/©Cengage Learning

Mark: So you think maybe he doesn't take women seriously, is that it? (*Mark paraphrases Jill's last statement*)

Jill: He sure doesn't seem interested in their ideas. But that doesn't mean he's a total woman-hater. I know he counts on some women in the office. Teresa has been here forever, and he's always saying he couldn't live without her. And when Brenda got the new computer system up and running last month, I know he appreciated that. He gave her a day off and told everybody how she saved our lives.

Mark: Now you sound confused. (*Reflects her apparent feeling*)

Jill: I am confused. I don't think it's just my imagination. I mean I'm a good producer, but he has never—not once—asked me for my ideas about how to improve sales or anything. And I can't remember a

Effective paraphrasing is a skill that takes time to develop. You can make your paraphrasing sound more natural by taking any of three approaches, depending on the situation:

1. Change the speaker's wording:

   Speaker: *Bilingual education is just another failed idea of bleeding-heart liberals.*

   Paraphrase: *Let me see if I've got this right. You're mad because you think bilingual ed sounds good, but it doesn't work?*

2. Offer an example of what you think the speaker is talking about:

   Speaker: *Lee is such a jerk. I can't believe the way he acted last night.*

   Paraphrase: *You think those jokes were pretty offensive, huh?*

3. Reflect the underlying theme of the speaker's remarks:

   Paraphrase: *You keep reminding me to be careful. Sounds like you're worried that something might happen to me. Am I right?*

time when he's asked any other women. But maybe I'm overreacting.

Mark: You're not positive whether you're right, but I can tell that this has you concerned. (*Mark paraphrases both Jill's central theme and her feeling*)

Jill: Yes. But I don't know what to do about it.

Mark: Maybe you should . . . (*Starts to offer advice but catches himself and decides to ask a question instead*) So what are your choices?

Jill: Well, I could just ask him if he's aware that he never asks women's opinions. But that might sound too aggressive and angry.

Mark: And you're not angry? (*Tries to clarify how Jill is feeling*)

Jill: Not really. I don't know whether I should be angry because he's not taking ideas seriously, or whether he just doesn't take my ideas seriously, or whether it's nothing at all.

Mark: So you're mostly confused. (*Reflects Jill's apparent feeling again*)

Jill: Yes! I don't know where I stand with John, and not being sure is starting to get to me. I wish I knew what he thinks of me. Maybe I could just tell him I'm confused about what is going on here and ask him

to clear it up. But what if it's nothing? Then I'll look insecure.

Mark: (*Mark thinks Jill should confront the boss, but he isn't positive that this is the best approach, so he paraphrases what Jill seems to be saying*) And that would make you look bad.

Jill: I'm afraid maybe it would. I wonder if I could talk it over with anybody else in the office and get their ideas . . .

Mark: . . . see what they think . . .

Jill: Yeah. Maybe I could ask Brenda. She's easy to talk to, and I do respect her judgment. Maybe she could give me some ideas about how to handle this.

Mark: Sounds like you're comfortable with talking to Brenda first. (*Paraphrases*)

Jill: (*Warming to the idea*) Yes! Then if it's nothing, I can calm down. But if I do need to talk to John, I'll know I'm doing the right thing.

Mark: Great. Let me know how it goes.

Communication Scenarios

To see and analyze video examples of paraphrasing in action, go to your Premium Website for Looking Out/Looking In, access "In Real Life Communication Scenarios," and then click on "Paraphrasing on the Job."

Paraphrasing won't always be accurate. But expressing your restatement *tentatively* gives the other person a chance to make a correction. (Note how the examples end with questions in an attempt to confirm if the paraphrase was accurate.)

Because it's an unfamiliar way of responding, paraphrasing may feel awkward at first; but if you start by paraphrasing occasionally and then gradually increase the frequency of such responses, you can begin to learn the benefits. You can begin practicing paraphrasing by trying the Skill Builder on page 254.

There are several factors to consider before you decide to paraphrase:

1. *Is the issue complex enough?* If you're fixing dinner, and someone wants to know when it will be ready, it would be exasperating to hear, "You're interested in knowing when we'll be eating."
2. *Do you have the necessary time and concern?* Paraphrasing can take a good deal of time. Therefore, if you're in a hurry, it's wise to avoid starting a conversation you won't be able to finish. Even more important than time is concern. Paraphrasing that comes across as mechanical or insincere reflecting can do more harm than good.[39]

✔+ SKILL BUILDER

Paraphrasing Practice

This exercise will help you see that it is possible to understand someone who disagrees with you, without arguing or sacrificing your point of view.

1. Find a partner. Designate one person as *A* and the other as *B*.

2. Find a subject on which you and your partner apparently disagree—a current events topic, a philosophical or moral issue, or perhaps simply a matter of personal taste.

3. Person *A* begins by making a statement on the subject. Person *B*'s job is then to paraphrase the statement. *B*'s job is simply to understand here, and doing so in no way should signify agreement or disagreement with *A*'s remarks.

4. *A* then responds by telling *B* whether her response was accurate. If there was some misunderstanding, *A* should make the correction, and *B* should feed back her new understanding of the statement. Continue this process until you're both sure that *B* understands *A*'s statement.

5. Now it's *B*'s turn to respond to *A*'s statement and for *A* to help the process of understanding by correcting *B*.

6. Continue this process until each partner is satisfied that she has explained herself fully and has been understood by the other person.

7. Now discuss the following questions:
   a. How did your understanding of the speaker's statement change after you used active listening?
   b. Did you find that the gap between your position and that of your partner narrowed as a result of active listening?
   c. How did you feel at the end of your conversation? How does this feeling compare to your usual feeling after discussing controversial issues?
   d. How might your life change if you used paraphrasing at home? At work? With friends?

3. *Can you withhold judgment?* Use paraphrasing only if you are willing to focus on the speaker's message without injecting your own judgments. It can be tempting to rephrase others' comments in a way that leads them toward the position you think is best without ever clearly stating your intentions.

4. *Is your paraphrasing in proportion to other responses?* Paraphrasing can become annoying when it's overused. This is especially true if you suddenly add this approach to your style. A far better way to use paraphrasing is to gradually introduce it into your repertoire.

SUPPORTING

There are times when other people want to hear more than a reflection of how *they* feel: They would like to know how *you* feel for and about them. **Supporting** reveals a listener's solidarity with the speaker's situation. One scholar describes supporting as "expressions of care, concern, affection, and interest, especially during times of stress or upset."[40]

There are several types of support:

Empathizing	"I can understand why you'd be upset about this." "Yeah, that class was tough for me, too."
Agreement	"You're right—the landlord is being unfair." "Sounds like the job is a perfect match for you."

Offers to help	"I'm here if you need me." "I'd be happy to study with you for the next test if you'd like."
Praise	"Wow—you did a fantastic job!" "You're a terrific person, and if she doesn't recognize it, that's her problem!"
Reassurance	The worst part seems to be over. It will probably get easier from here." "I'm sure you'll do a great job."

There's no question about the value of receiving comfort and support in the face of personal problems. One survey showed that "comforting ability" was among the most important communication skills a friend could have.[41] The value of receiving support with personal problems is clear when big problems arise, but research shows that the smaller, everyday distresses and upsets can actually take a bigger toll on mental health and physical well-being.[42] The research is clear: Receiving emotional support during times of stress is good for one's health.[43]

It's easy to identify what effective support *doesn't* sound like. Some scholars have called these messages "cold comfort."[44] See Table 7.2 on this page for real cold-comfort messages found in an online discussion. As these examples suggest, you're probably *not* being supportive if you:

- *Deny others the right to their feelings.* Consider the stock remark "Don't worry about it." Although it may be intended as a reassuring comment, the underlying message is that the speaker wants the person to feel differently. The irony is that the suggestion probably won't work—after all, it's unlikely that people can or will stop worrying just because you tell them to do so. Research about such responses is clear: "Messages that explicitly acknowledge, elaborate, and legitimize the feelings and perspective of a distressed person are perceived as more helpful messages

Table 7.2
Cold Comfort: Messages That Don't Help

Don't take it so hard. She was a slut anyway.
That's nothing! Want to hear how I got dumped?
I don't know what you ever saw in him anyway. He's ugly. You can do much better.
You know you had this coming—you were overdue for payback.
She/he was way too young (old) for you.
You can't have everything you want in this life.
Now that it's finally over, I can tell you she's been cheating on you, dude!
He was just using you for sex.
She was always a jerk about you behind your back. Who needs that?
Now we'll have more time to hang out together, just like we used to!
I'm so glad that this happened to you. I heard a story once about a guy whose significant other left him, and he begged and begged and begged for her to come back. Finally she did, and 20 years later she was a drug addict and committed suicide and left him with nothing but heartache. So you never know what you're saved from.

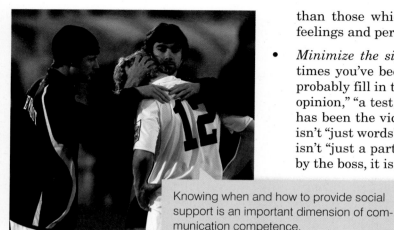

Knowing when and how to provide social support is an important dimension of communication competence.

AP Images

than those which only implicitly recognize or deny the feelings and perspective of the other."[45]

- *Minimize the significance of the situation.* Consider the times you've been told, "Hey, it's only _____." You can probably fill in the blank in a variety of ways: "a job," "her opinion," "a test," "puppy love," "a party." To someone who has been the victim of verbal abuse, the hurtful message isn't "just words"; to a child who didn't get an invitation, it isn't "just a party"; to a worker who has been chewed out by the boss, it isn't "just a job."

- *Focus on "then and there" rather than "here and now."* Although it is sometimes true that "you'll feel better tomorrow," it sometimes isn't. Even if the prediction that "ten years from now you won't remember her name" proves correct, it provides little comfort to someone experiencing heartbreak today.

- *Cast judgment.* It usually isn't encouraging to hear "You know, it's your own fault— you really shouldn't have done that" after you've confessed to making a poor decision. As you'll learn in Chapter 10, evaluative and condescending statements are more likely to engender defensiveness than to help people change for the better.

- *Focus on yourself.* It can be tempting to talk at length about a similar experience you've encountered ("I know exactly how you feel. Something like that happened to me. . . ."). While your intent might be to show empathy, research shows that such messages aren't perceived as helpful because they draw attention away from the distressed person.[46]

- *Defend yourself.* When your response to others' concerns is to defend yourself ("Don't blame me; I've done my part"), it's clear that you are more concerned with yourself than with supporting the other person.

How often do people fail to provide appropriate supportive responses? One survey of mourners who had recently suffered from the death of a loved one reported that 80 percent of the statements made to them were unhelpful.[47] Nearly half of the "helpful" statements were advice: "You've got to get out more." "Don't question God's will." Despite their frequency, these suggestions were helpful only 3 percent of the time. The next most frequent response was reassurance, such as "She's out of pain now." Like advice, this kind of support was helpful only 3 percent of the time. Far more helpful were expressions that acknowledged the mourner's feelings. (See the reading on page 257 for further discussion on allowing people to grieve.)

When handled correctly, supporting responses *can* be helpful. Guidelines for effective support include:

1. *Recognize that you can support another person's struggles without approving of his or her decisions.* Suppose, for instance, that a friend has decided to quit a job that you think she should keep. You could still be supportive by saying, "I know you've given this a lot of thought and that you're doing what you think is best." Responses like this can provide face-saving support without compromising your principles.[48]

Let Mourners Grieve

After a recent death in my family, I received a number of condolence cards that tried to talk me out of my grief. "You should be happy you have your memories," wrote one friend. "You should feel lucky you got to be with your father in the hospital." Lucky? Happy? You've got to be kidding!

I was 25 when I lost my father last fall. He was only 58, and his death from bone cancer was slow and excruciating. When I cry for my father, I cry for his suffering; I cry because he worked long, grueling hours to save for a retirement he never got to enjoy. I cry because my mother is alone. I cry because I have so much of my life ahead of me, and my father will miss everything. If I marry, if I have children, he won't be there. My grief is profound: I am mourning the past, present and future. I resent the condolence cards that hurry me through my grief, as if it were a dangerous street at night.

Why don't people say "I am sorry for your loss" anymore? Why don't people accept that after a parent's death, there will be years of grief? People seem to worry that if they encourage me to grieve openly, I will fall apart. I won't. On the contrary, if you allow me to be sad, I will be a stronger, more effective person.

Our society needs to rethink the way we communicate with mourners—especially since so many people are in mourning these days. Everyone wants mourners to "snap out of it" because observing another's anguish isn't easy to do. Here's my advice: let mourners mourn.

Before I lost my father, I was just as guilty of finding the silver lining of people's grief. If someone told me she lost her mother, I might say something like "She was sick for a very long time. It's good she's not suffering anymore." When a mourner hears nothing but these "silver linings," she begins to wonder why she can't find the good in the situation the way everyone else can. People want her to smile and agree that it's going to be OK, but she can't.

Condolences are some of the most difficult words to write or say. So it's natural that we freeze with writer's block when faced with such an immense task. Here are my basic guidelines for mastering the Art of the Condolence:

- Always begin directly and simply. "I am so sorry about your mother's death."

- It's better to ask "How are you?" or "How are you feeling?" instead of telling someone how she should feel.

- Never give advice about how someone should get through the loss. Some mourners go to parties; others stay home with the shades drawn. Be open to the mourner's individual needs. Be open to the possibility that these needs will change day by day.

- If you want to offer something upbeat, share a funny anecdote or memory about the deceased that might bring a smile to the mourner's face.

Grieving is private, but it can be public, too. We need to stop being afraid of public mourning. We need to be open to mourners. We need to look each other in the eye, and say "I am so sorry."

Jess Decoury Hinds

---

2. *Monitor the other person's reaction to your support.* If it doesn't seem to help, consider other types of responses that let him or her explore the issue.
3. *Realize that support may not always be welcome.* In one survey, some people reported occasions when social support wasn't necessary because they felt capable of handling the problem themselves.[49] Many regarded uninvited support as an intrusion, and some said it left them feeling more nervous than before. The majority of respondents expressed a preference for being in control of whether their distressing situation should be discussed with even the most helpful friend.

ANALYZING

When **analyzing**, the listener offers an interpretation of a speaker's message. Analyses like these are probably familiar to you:

Yesterday a friend related something that someone had done to her. I told her why I thought the person acted the way he had and she became very upset and started arguing with me. Now, the reason is clear. I had been listening to her words and had paid no attention to her feelings. Her words had described how terribly this other person had treated her, but her emotions had been saying, "Please understand how I felt. Please accept my feeling the way I did." The last thing she wanted to hear from me was an explanation of the other person's behavior.

—Hugh Prather

"I think what's really bothering you is . . ."
"She's doing it because . . ."
"I don't think you really meant that."
"Maybe the problem started when she . . ."

Interpretations are often effective ways to help people with problems to consider alternative meanings—meanings they would have never thought of without your help. Sometimes a clear analysis will make a confusing problem suddenly clear, either suggesting a solution or at least providing an understanding of what is occurring.

In other cases, an analysis can create more problems than it solves. There are two potential problems with analyzing. First, your interpretation may not be correct, in which case the speaker may become even more confused by accepting it. Second, even if your analysis is correct, telling it to the problem-holder might not be useful. There's a chance that it will arouse defensiveness (because analysis implies superiority). Even if it doesn't, the person may not be able to understand your view of the problem without working it out personally.

How can you know when it's helpful to offer an analysis? There are several guidelines to follow:

- *Offer your interpretation as tentative rather than as absolute fact.* There's a big difference between saying "Maybe the reason is . . ." or "The way it looks to me . . ." and insisting, "This is the truth."

- *You ought to be sure that the other person will be receptive to your analysis.* Even if you're completely accurate, your thoughts won't help if the problem-holder isn't ready to consider them.

- *Be sure that your motive for offering an analysis is truly to help the other person.* It can be tempting to offer an analysis to show how brilliant you are or even to make the other person feel bad for not having thought of the right answer in the first place. Needless to say, an analysis offered under such conditions isn't helpful.

I've learned that it is best to give advice in only two circumstances: When it is requested and when it is a life-threatening situation.

—Andy Rooney

ADVISING

When we are approached with another's problem, a common tendency is to respond with **advising**: to help by offering a solution.[50] Advice can sometimes be helpful, as long as it's given in a respectful, caring way.[51]

Despite its apparent value, advice has its limits. Research has shown that it is actually *unhelpful* at least as often as it's helpful.[52] Studies on advice-giving offer the following important considerations when trying to help others[53]:

- *Is the advice needed?* If the person has already taken a course of action, giving advice after the fact ("I can't believe you got back together with him") is rarely appreciated.

✔+ INVITATION TO INSIGHT

When Advising Does and Doesn't Work

To see why advising can be tricky business, follow these steps:

1 Recall an instance when someone gave you advice that proved helpful. See how closely that advising communication followed the guidelines in the bulleted list on pages 258–260.

2 Now recall an instance when someone gave you advice that *wasn't* helpful. See whether that

person violated any of the guidelines in the bulleted list on pages 258–260.

3 Based on your insights here, describe how you can advise (or not advise) others in a way that is truly helpful.

- *Is the advice wanted?* People generally don't value unsolicited advice. It's usually best to ask if the speaker is interested in hearing your counsel. Remember that sometimes people just want a listening ear, not solutions to their problems.

- *Is the advice given in the right sequence?* Advice is more likely to be received after the listener first offers supporting, paraphrasing, and questioning responses to better understand the speaker and the situation.

- *Is the advice coming from an expert?* If you want to offer advice about anything from car purchasing to relationship managing, it's important to have experience and success in those matters. If you *don't* have expertise, it's a good idea to offer the speaker supportive responses, then encourage that person to seek out expert counsel.

- *Is the advisor a close and trusted person?* Although sometimes we seek out advice from people we don't know well (perhaps because they have expertise), in most

cases we value advice given within the context of a close and ongoing interpersonal relationship.

- *Is the advice offered in a sensitive, face-saving manner?* No one likes to feel bossed or belittled, even if the advice is good. Remember that messages have both content and relational dimensions, and sometimes the unstated relational messages when giving advice ("I'm smarter than you"; "You're not bright enough to figure this out yourself") will keep people from hearing counsel.[54]

JUDGING

A **judging** response evaluates the sender's thoughts or behaviors in some way. The judgment may be favorable—"That's a good idea" or "You're on the right track now"—or unfavorable—"An attitude like that won't get you anywhere." But in either case it implies that the person doing the judging is in some way qualified to pass judgment on the speaker's thoughts or actions.

Sometimes negative judgments are purely critical. How many times have you heard such responses as "Well, you asked for it!" or "I *told* you so!" or "You're just feeling sorry for yourself"? Although responses like these can sometimes serve as a verbal slap that brings problem-holders to their senses, they usually make matters worse.

In other cases, negative judgments are less critical. These involve what we usually call *constructive criticism*, which is intended to help the problem-holder improve in the future. This is the sort of response given by friends about everything from the choice

✔+ INVITATION TO INSIGHT

What Would You Say?

1 In each situation below, describe what you would say in response to the problem being shared:

a. My family doesn't understand me. Everything I like seems to go against their values, and they just won't accept my feelings as being right for me. It's not that they don't love me—they do. But they don't accept me.

b. I've been pretty discouraged lately. I just can't get a good relationship going with any guys. I've got plenty of male friends, but that's always as far as it goes. I'm tired of being just a pal. . . . I want to be more than that.

c. (Child to parents) I hate you guys! You always go out and leave me with some stupid sitter. Why don't you like me?

d. I don't know what I want to do with my life. I'm tired of school, but there aren't any good jobs around. I could just drop out for a while, but that doesn't really sound very good, either.

e. Things really seem to be kind of lousy in my marriage lately. It's not that we fight much, but all the excitement seems to be gone. We're in a rut, and it keeps getting worse. . . .

f. I keep getting the idea that my boss is angry at me. It seems as if lately he hasn't been joking around very much, and he hasn't said anything at all about my work for about three weeks now. I wonder what I should do.

2 After you've written your response to each of these messages, imagine the probable outcome of the conversation that would have followed. If you've tried this exercise in class, you might have two group members role-play each response. Based on your idea of how the conversation might have gone, decide which responses were productive and which were unproductive.

of clothing to jobs to friends. Another common setting for constructive criticism occurs in school, where instructors evaluate students' work to help them master concepts and skills. But whether it's justified or not, even constructive criticism runs the risk of arousing defensiveness, because it may threaten the self-concept of the person at whom it is directed (we'll discuss this further in Chapter 10).

Judgments have the best chance of being received when two conditions exist:

1. *The person with the problem should have requested an evaluation from you.* Occasionally an unsolicited evaluation may bring someone to his or her senses, but more often an unsolicited evaluation will trigger a defensive response.
2. *The intent of your judgment should be genuinely constructive and not designed as a put-down.* If you are tempted to use judgments as a weapon, don't fool yourself into thinking that you are being helpful. Often the statement "I'm telling you this for your own good . . ." simply isn't true.

Now that you're aware of all the possible listening responses, try the exercise on page 260 to see how you might use them in everyday situations.

CHOOSING THE BEST LISTENING RESPONSE

By now you can see that there are many ways to respond as a listener. Research shows that, in the right circumstances, *all* response styles can help others accept their situation, feel better, and have a sense of control over their problems.[55] But there is enormous variability in which style will work with a given person.[56] This fact explains why communicators who use a wide variety of response styles are usually more effective than those who use just one or two styles.[57] However, there are other factors to consider when choosing how to respond to a speaker.

GENDER Research shows that men and women differ in the ways they listen and respond to others.[58] Women are more likely than men to give supportive responses when presented with another person's problem,[59] are more skillful at composing such messages,[60] and are more likely to seek out such responses from listeners.[61] By contrast, men are less skillful at providing emotional support to those who are distressed,[62] and they're more likely to respond to others' problems by offering advice or by diverting the topic. In a study of helping styles in sororities and fraternities, researchers found that sorority women frequently respond with emotional support when asked to help; also, they rated their sisters as being better at listening nonjudgmentally and on comforting and showing concern for them. Fraternity men, on the other hand, fit the stereotypical pattern of offering help by challenging their brothers to evaluate their attitudes and values.[63]

The temptation when hearing these facts is to conclude that in times of distress, women want support and men want advice—but research doesn't bear that out. Numerous studies show that both men and women prefer and want supportive, endorsing messages in difficult situations.[64] The fact that women are more adept at creating and delivering such messages explains why both males and females tend to seek out women listeners when they want emotional support. When it comes to gender, it's important to remember that while men and women sometimes use different response styles, they all need a listening ear.

THE SITUATION Sometimes people need your advice. At other times, people need encouragement and support, and in still other cases your analysis or judgment will be most helpful. And, as you have seen, sometimes your probes and paraphrasing can

They Aid Customers by Becoming Good Listeners

Do you need someone to listen to your troubles?

Have your hair done. Beauty salon chairs may be to today's women what conversation-centered backyard fences were to their grandmothers and psychiatrists' couches are to their wealthier contemporaries.

"We are not as family-oriented as our ancestors were," says counselor-trainer Andy Thompson. "They listened to and helped each other. Now that we have become a society of individuals isolated from one another by cars, telephones, jobs and the like, we have had to find other listeners." Community training program director for Crisis House, Thompson has designed and is conducting human relations training sessions for workers to whom customers tend to unburden their woes most frequently—cosmetologists, bartenders and cabdrivers.

"People can definitely help others just by letting them talk," he said. "Relatives, friends or spouses who listen do a lot to keep the mental health of this country at a reasonable rate. Workers in situations that encourage communications can make the same meaningful contribution."

Thompson explained that his training is not meant to replace, or be confused with, professional treatment or counseling. His students fill a gap between family and professionals.

"There are not enough psychiatrists or psychologists to go around," he said. "And some professionals become so technical that their help doesn't mean much to persons who just need someone who will let them get problems and questions out in the open where they can look at them."

Thompson's first course of training, completed recently, was for cosmetologists. The human relations training

© Dale Kennington/SuperStock

program attempts to make the most of these built-in assets by using a method Thompson calls "reflective listening."

"The purpose is to let the customer talk enough to clarify her own thinking," he said. "We are not interested in having cosmetologists tell women what to do, but to give them a chance to choose their own course of action.

"There is a tendency among listeners to try to rescue a person with problems and pull them out of negative situations. People don't really want that. They just want to discuss what is on their minds and reach their own conclusions."

Cosmetologists are taught to use phrases that aid customers in analyzing their thoughts. Some of the phrases are, "You seem to think . . ." "You sound like . . ." "You appear to be . . ." "As I get it, you . . ." and "It must seem to you that . . ." There also are barriers to conversation that the cosmetologists are taught to avoid.

"A constant bombardment of questions can disrupt communications," Thompson said. "Commands will have the same effect. Many of them are impossible to follow anyway."

"How many can respond to orders to 'Stop feeling depressed,' 'Don't be so upset,' or 'Don't think about it.' "

"The same applies to negative criticism, 'That's dumb,' for instance; and evaluations, such as 'Oh, you're just confused.' "

"Comments that seem threatening—'You had better stop feeling sad,' as an example—will end a conversation as quickly as changing the subject or not paying attention."

San Diego *Union*

help people find their own answers. In other words, a competent communicator needs to analyze the situation and develop an appropriate response.[65] As a rule of thumb, it's often wise to begin with responses that seek understanding and offer a minimum of direction, such as prompting, questioning, paraphrasing, and supporting. Once you've gathered the facts and demonstrated your interest and concern, it's likely that the speaker will be more receptive to (and perhaps even ask for) your analyzing, advising, and evaluating responses.[66]

THE OTHER PERSON   Besides considering the situation, you should also consider the other person when deciding which style to use. Some people are able to consider advice thoughtfully, whereas others use advice to avoid making their own decisions. Many communicators are extremely defensive and aren't capable of receiving analysis or judgments without lashing out. Still others aren't equipped to think through problems clearly enough to profit from paraphrasing and probing. Sophisticated listeners choose a style that fits the person. One way to determine the most appropriate response is to ask the speaker what she or he wants from you. A simple question such as "Are you looking for my advice, or do you just want a listening ear right now?" can help you give others the kinds of responses they're looking for.

ETHICAL CHALLENGE

Unconditional Positive Regard

Carl Rogers was the best-known advocate of paraphrasing as a helping tool. As a psychotherapist, Rogers focused on how professionals can help others, but he and his followers were convinced that the same approach can work in all interpersonal relationships.

Rogers used several terms to describe his approach. Sometimes he labeled it "nondirective," sometimes "client-centered," and at other times "person-centered." All of these terms reflect his belief that the best way to help another is to offer a supportive climate in which the people seeking help can find their own answers. Rogers believed that advising, judging, analyzing, and questioning are not the best ways to help others solve their problems. Instead, Rogers and his followers were convinced that people are basically good and that they can improve without receiving any guidance from others, after they accept and respect themselves.

An essential ingredient for person-centered helping is what Rogers called "unconditional positive regard." This attitude requires the helper to treat the speaker's ideas respectfully and nonjudgmentally. Unconditional positive regard means accepting others for who they are, even when you don't approve of their posture toward life. Treating a help-seeker with unconditional positive regard doesn't oblige you to agree with everything the help-seeker thinks, feels, or does, but it does oblige you to suspend judgment about the rightness or wrongness of the help-seeker's thoughts and actions.

A person-centered approach to helping places heavy demands on the listener. At the skill level, it demands an ability to reflect the speaker's thoughts and feelings perceptively and accurately. Even more difficult, though, is the challenge of listening and responding without passing judgment on the speaker's ideas or behavior.

Unconditional positive regard is especially hard when we are faced with the challenge of listening and responding to someone whose beliefs, attitudes, and values differ profoundly from our own. This approach requires the helper to follow the scriptural injunction of loving the sinner while hating the sin. One of the best models of this approach is illustrated in the movie *Dead Man Walking*. (See the description of this movie on page 267.)

For a better understanding of unconditional positive regard, see the following works of Carl Rogers: On Becoming a Person *(Boston: Houghton Mifflin, 1961);* Carl Rogers on Personal Power *(New York: Delacorte Press, 1977); "A Theory of Therapy, Personality and Interpersonal Relationships, as Developed in the Client-Centered Framework," in S. Koch (Ed.),* Psychology: A Study of Science *(New York: McGraw-Hill, 1959).*

YOUR PERSONAL STYLE   Finally, consider yourself when deciding how to respond. Most of us reflexively use one or two response styles. You may be best at listening quietly, offering a prompt from time to time. Or perhaps you are especially insightful and can offer a truly useful analysis of the problem. Of course, it's also possible to rely on a response style that is unhelpful. You may be overly judgmental or too eager to advise, even when your suggestions aren't invited or productive. As you think about how to respond to another's messages, consider both your strengths and weaknesses and adapt accordingly.

✔+ MAKING THE GRADE

Summary

Listening is the most common—and perhaps the most overlooked—form of communication. There is a difference between hearing and listening, and there is also a difference between mindless and mindful listening. Listening, defined as the process of making sense of others' spoken messages, consists of five elements: hearing, attending, understanding, responding, and remembering.

Several responding styles masquerade as listening but actually are only poor imitations of the real thing. We listen poorly for a variety of reasons. Some reasons have to do with the tremendous number of messages that bombard us daily and with the personal preoccupations, noise, and rapid thoughts that distract us from focusing on the information we are exposed to. Another set of reasons has to do with the considerable effort involved in listening carefully and the mistaken belief that there are more rewards in speaking than in listening. A few listeners fail to receive messages because of physical hearing defects; others listen poorly because of lack of training. Some keys to better listening are to talk less, reduce distractions, avoid making premature judgments, and seek the speaker's key ideas.

Listening responses are the primary way we evaluate whether and how others are paying attention to us. Some listening responses put a premium on gathering information and providing support; these include prompting, questioning, paraphrasing, and supporting. Other listening responses focus more on providing direction and evaluation: analyzing, advising, and judging. The most effective communicators use a variety of these styles, taking into consideration factors such as gender, the situation at hand, the person with the problem, and their own personal style.

Key Terms

advising (258)
ambushing (243)
analyzing (257)
attending (240)
counterfeit questions (249)
defensive listening (243)
hearing (239)
insensitive listening (243)
insulated listening (243)

judging (260)
listening (237)
listening fidelity (240)
mindful listening (238)
mindless listening (237)
paraphrasing (251)
prompting (247)
pseudolistening (242)

questioning (249)
remembering (241)
responding (240)
selective listening (242)
sincere questions (249)
stage-hogging (242)
supporting (254)
understanding (240)

Online Resources

Now that you have read this chapter, use your Premium Website for *Looking Out / Looking In* for quick access to the electronic resources that accompany this text. Your Premium Website gives you access to:

- **Study tools** that will help you assess your learning and prepare for exams (*digital glossary, key term flash cards, review quizzes*).

- **Activities and assignments** that will help you hone your knowledge, understand how theory and research applies to your own life (*Invitation to Insight*), consider ethical challenges in interpersonal communication (*Ethical Challenge*), and build your interpersonal communication skills throughout the course (*Skill Builder*). If requested, you can submit your answers to your instructor.

- **Media resources** that will allow you to watch and critique news video and videos of interpersonal communication situations (*In Real Life, interpersonal video simulations*) and download a chapter review so you can study when and where you'd like (*Audio Study Tools*).

This chapter's key terms and search terms for additional reading are featured in this end-of-chapter section, and you can find this chapter's Invitation to Insight, Ethical Challenge, Skill Builder, and In Real Life activities in the body of the chapter.

Search Terms

When searching online databases to research topics in this chapter, use the following terms (along with this chapter's key terms) to maximize the chances of finding useful information:

attention
communication fidelity
compassion

comprehension
conversation

empathy
memory

Film and Television

You can see the communication principles described in this chapter portrayed in the following films and television programs:

THE IMPORTANCE OF LISTENING

CSI and *Law & Order* (2000– and 1990–) Both Rated TV-14

The crime shows *CSI* and *Law & Order* have become a fixture of television programming. In their many forms, these franchises have one thing in common: Their main characters must engage in active listening to do their jobs effectively. Sometimes a lawyer uses prompting and support to draw out a difficult confession. Other times a private investigator asks probing questions and offers analyzing responses to arrive at important conclusions. In still other instances, a police officer carefully attends to and remembers specific details during a testimony, which later helps solve a case. And in a variety of situations, the characters offer advising and judging responses to their clients, colleagues, and coworkers. Watch an episode of one of these programs and see how many of the listening responses from pages 247–261 you can observe. Chances are, you'll find quite a few.

INEFFECTIVE LISTENING

The Devil Wears Prada (2006) Rated PG-13

Miranda Priestly (Meryl Streep) is every employee's nightmare. She's a self-centered, domineering, hard-driven boss who treats the people who work for her like slaves. Priestly offers a tour de force of every poor listening habit. She attends only to things that matter to her ("The details of your incompetence do not interest me") and does so insensitively ("Bore someone else with your questions"). Pseudolistening, defensive listening, and stage-hogging? She does them all. She also interrupts, rolls her eyes when she doesn't like what she's hearing, and walks out on her subordinates in mid-conversation. Priestly may be a successful businesswoman, but she fails on many other counts—especially as a listener.

SUPPORTIVE LISTENING

In Treatment (2008–) Rated TV-MA

This HBO series follows therapist Paul (Gabriel Byrne) as he meets with a variety of clients. They include a young doctor with a confused romantic life, a cocky fighter pilot who left sixteen Iraqi children dead in a bombing mission, a teenage gymnast who may have attempted suicide, and a couple struggling to keep their marriage alive. Weekly episodes also track Paul's visits with his own therapist (Dianne Wiest).

Paul's therapeutic manner includes all of the listening responses described in this chapter. His genuine regard for each client and his skill shows that these response styles don't need to sound formulaic, and that they can indeed be helpful.

Dead Man Walking (1995) Rated R

Sister Helen Prejean (Susan Sarandon) is a nun who serves in an inner-city neighborhood. She receives a letter from death row inmate Matthew Poncelet (Sean Penn) and decides to visit him in prison. He fits the profile for everything she is not: uneducated, angry, bigoted, rude, and insecure. Nonetheless, Sister Helen agrees to help Poncelet appeal his murder conviction and death sentence—and her world turns upside down.

Sister Helen's highest goal is to get Matthew to take responsibility for his actions and to come to peace with God, the murder victims' parents, and himself. She does this not by pushing or persuading, but by giving him her time and her ear. In their early meetings, Prejean comes with no agenda; she tells Poncelet, "I'm here to listen. Whatever you want to talk about is fine with me." She asks open-ended questions and allows Poncelet to arrive at his own conclusions. He admits to being surprised that she "didn't come down here preaching fire and brimstone," so he slowly opens his life to her.

As time goes on, Sister Helen comes to realize that Poncelet is, indeed, guilty of the awful crimes for which he has been convicted. Her pain is obvious as she confronts the grieving families of his victims, none of whom can understand or accept why she is willing to help a murderer. What they don't appreciate is that she never wavers in her abhorrence for his deeds, but she remains steadfast in separating her hate for the crime from her concern and love for Poncelet. As such, she provides viewers with proof that unconditional positive regard can be achieved, and can heal.

COMMUNICATION AND RELATIONAL DYNAMICS

After studying the topics in this chapter, you should be able to:

1. Identify factors that have influenced your choice of relational partners.
2. Use Knapp's model to describe the nature of communication in the various stages of a relationship.
3. Describe the dialectical tensions in a given relationship, how they influence communication, and the most effective strategies for managing them.
4. Describe the possible strategies for repairing a given relational transgression.
5. Identify the content and relational dimensions of communication in a given transaction.
6. Describe how metacommunication can be used to improve the quality of a given relationship.

those who are offensive but different. One likely reason is that such people threaten our self-esteem, causing us to fear that we may be as unappealing as they are. In such circumstances, the reaction is often to put as much distance as possible between ourselves and this threat to our ideal self-image.

"We have a terrific relationship."

"I'm looking for a better relationship."

In the *Star Trek* sagas, hotheaded Kirk and emotionless Spock find that their differing styles complement each other, leading to a strong personal and professional friendship.

PARAMOUNT/BAD ROBOT/THE KOBAL COLLECTION

COMPLEMENTARITY

The familiar saying that "opposites attract" seems to contradict the principle of similarity we just described. In truth, though, both are valid. Differences strengthen a relationship when they are *complementary*—when each partner's characteristics satisfy the other's needs. Research suggests that attraction to partners who have complementary temperaments might be rooted in biology.[15] Individuals, for instance, are often likely to be attracted to each other when one partner is dominant and the other passive.[16] Relationships also work well when the partners agree that one will exercise control in certain areas ("You make the final decisions about money") and the other will exercise control in different areas ("I'll decide how we ought to decorate the place"). Strains occur when control issues are disputed.

When successful and unsuccessful couples are compared over a twenty-year period, it becomes clear that partners in successful marriages are similar enough to satisfy each other physically and mentally but different enough to meet each other's needs and keep the relationship interesting. Successful couples find ways to keep a balance between their similarities and differences, adjusting to the changes that occur over the years. We'll have more to say about balancing similarities and differences later in this chapter.

RECIPROCAL ATTRACTION

We like people who like us—usually.[17] The power of reciprocal attraction is especially strong in the early stages of a relationship. At that time we are attracted to people who we believe are attracted to us. Conversely, we will probably not care for people who either attack or seem indifferent toward us.

It's no mystery why reciprocal liking builds attractiveness. People who approve of us bolster our feelings of self-esteem. This approval is rewarding in its own right, and it can also confirm a presenting self-concept that says, "I'm a likable person."

You can probably think of cases where you haven't liked people who seemed to like you. For example, you might think the other person's supposed liking is counterfeit— an insincere device to get something from you. At other times the liking may not fit with your own self-concept. When someone says you're good-looking, intelligent, and kind, but you believe you're ugly, stupid, and mean, you may choose to disregard the flattering information and remain in your familiar state of unhappiness. Groucho Marx summarized this attitude when he said he would never join any club that would consider having him as a member.

COMPETENCE

We like to be around talented people, probably because we hope their skills and abilities will rub off on us. We are uncomfortable around those who are *too* competent, however, probably because we look bad by comparison. Given these contrasting attitudes, it's no surprise that people are generally attracted to those who are talented but who have visible flaws that show that they are human, just like us.[18] There are some qualifications to this principle. People with especially high or low self-esteem find "perfect" people more attractive than those who are competent but flawed, and some studies suggest that women tend to be more impressed by uniformly superior people of both sexes, whereas men tend to be more impressed by desirable but "human" subjects. On the whole, though, the principle stands: The best way to gain the liking of others is to be good at what you do but to admit your mistakes.

DISCLOSURE

Revealing important information about yourself can help build liking.[19] Sometimes the basis of this liking comes from learning about how we are similar, either in experiences ("I broke off an engagement myself") or in attitudes ("I feel nervous with strangers, too"). Self-disclosure also builds liking because it is a sign of regard. When people share private information with you, it suggests that they respect and trust you—a kind of liking that we've already seen increases attractiveness. Disclosure plays an even more important role as relationships develop beyond their earliest stages.

Not all disclosure leads to liking. Research shows that the key to satisfying self-disclosure is *reciprocity*: getting back an amount and kind of information equivalent to that which you reveal.[20] A second important ingredient in successful self-disclosure is *timing*. It's probably unwise to talk about your sexual insecurities with a new acquaintance or express your pet peeves to a friend at your birthday party. Finally, for the sake of self-protection, it's important to reveal personal information only when you are sure the other person is trustworthy.[21] Chapter 9 contains more information on the subject of self-disclosure.

PROXIMITY

As common sense suggests, we are likely to develop relationships with people we interact with frequently.[22] In many cases, proximity leads to liking. For instance, we're more likely to develop friendships with close neighbors than with distant ones, and chances are good that we'll choose a mate with whom we cross paths often. Facts like these are understandable when we consider that proximity allows us to get more information about other people and benefit from a relationship with them. Also, people in close proximity may be more similar to us than those who are not close; for example, if we live in the same neighborhood, odds are we share the same socioeconomic status. As the reading on page 274 shows, the Internet provides a new means for creating closeness, as users are able to experience "virtual proximity" in cyberspace.[23]

Familiarity can also breed contempt. Evidence to support this fact comes from police blotters as well as university laboratories. Thieves frequently prey on nearby victims,

A Geek Love Story

Courtesy of Rhonda Lillie

Rhonda Lillie fiddles with a tiny camera on her computer, aiming its lens at her smiling face and curly blond hair. She'll spend the next four hours here, at this wooden desk in her parents' house in Oxnard, Calif. "Hey, babe," she calls out, eyes fixed on the camera. On the screen, her fiancé, Paul Hawkins, grins back, reclining in a T shirt and black boots.

Lillie and Hawkins met four years ago atop a waterfall overlooking a lush green valley—the kind of magical tableau you find only in romance novels, or in sophisticated virtual universes. The two had stumbled upon each other in Second Life, the 3-D computer world where nearly a million people log in regularly, communicating via digital representations of themselves, or avatars.

Hawkins's avatar was tall (*very* tall: 7 feet 8), with darkened eyes and a towering white Mohawk. But it was his boots that caught Lillie's eye: black, ornamented, dazzling. "The most intricate boots I'd ever seen," she says. Lillie, whose own avatar is porcelain-skinned, with white or black hair depending on her mood, was thunderstruck. "Heart Wishbringer" (that's her avatar's name) and "Joe Stravinsky" (that's his) spent the next three weeks online together, chatting for hours via IM. Then, before they'd ever seen or heard each other's real voices, they got "married" in Second Life, like 43,000 other couples, typing their vows while their avatars stood atop the waterfall where they first met. Then Heart and Joe stripped down to their naked digital bodies and swam in the crisp pool of water below.

The couple has been inseparable ever since—at least in a sense. In the real world, there are oceans between them.

Lillie lives in California; Hawkins in Wales. In four years, Lillie and Hawkins have seen each other in the flesh just three times. Their life as a couple exists almost entirely online.

Physical intimacy is out, but they use the technology to fake it as best they can. They hold hands. They kiss. Sometimes they have virtual sex. (It's possible—though they say watching their avatars knock boots is more comic than erotic.) Outside of Second Life, they use Webcams and Skype, the online voice-video-chat system, to peer into each other's worlds, even when they're just doing daily chores. At night, they hookup headphones, so that even while they sleep, they can hear each other breathing.

They know their relationship sounds odd—and, they admit, it's far from ideal. But beneath all the high-tech gadgetry, behind the Webcams and avatars, is an ordinary—if admittedly geeky—romance between two ordinary people. The only thing extraordinary about Rhonda Lillie and Paul Hawkins's life together is that, at any other moment in history, it would've been impossible.

Lillie and Hawkins say they've shared things with each other that they've never told anyone else, and that it's the deepest bond either has felt. Some of that surely has to do with their detachment; but had they met in real life, it might not have been possible. In one survey of gamers in online relationships, 60 percent said they didn't think their unions would've formed in real life because a physical attribute would've turned them off.

There are still plenty of folks who think of the Internet as chilly and perverse, but a competing sense of that universe as warm and humane, an instrument of fulfillment, is finding flower as successive generations grow up wired. "The Internet has an amazing capacity to allow people to self-sort—to find and engage with like-minded others," says Harvard Law professor Cass Sunstein, who has written on politics in the information age. "That will have impacts for courtship and dating that go beyond anything we've ever seen."

Jessica Bennett

even though the risk of being recognized is greater. Spousal and child abuse are distressingly common. Most aggravated assaults occur within the family or among close neighbors. Within the law, the same principle holds: You are likely to develop strong personal feelings of either like or dislike regarding others you encounter frequently.

REWARDS

Some social scientists have argued that all relationships—both impersonal and personal—are based on a semi-economic model called *social exchange theory*.[24] This model suggests that we often seek out people who can give us rewards that are greater than or equal to the costs we encounter in dealing with them. According to social exchange theory, relationships suffer when one partner feels "underbenefited."[25]

Rewards may be tangible (a nice place to live, a high-paying job) or intangible (prestige, emotional support, companionship). Costs are undesirable outcomes: unpleasant work, emotional pain, and so on. A simple formula captures the social exchange theory of why we form and maintain relationships:

$$\text{Rewards} - \text{Costs} = \text{Outcome}$$

According to social exchange theorists, we use this formula (often unconsciously) to decide whether dealing with another person is a "good deal" or "not worth the effort," based on whether the outcome is positive or negative.

At its most blatant level, an exchange approach seems cold and calculating, but in some types of relationships it seems quite appropriate. A healthy business relationship is based on how well the parties help one another, and some friendships are based on an informal kind of barter: "I don't mind listening to the ups and downs of your love life, because you rescue me when the house needs repairs." Even close relationships have an element of exchange. Friends and lovers often tolerate each other's quirks, because the comfort and enjoyment they get make the less-than-pleasant times worth accepting. In more serious cases, social exchange explains why some people stay in abusive relationships. Sadly, these people often report that they would rather be in a bad relationship than have no relationship at all.

"I'd like to buy everyone a drink. All I ask in return is that you listen patiently to my shallow and simplistic views on a broad range of social and political issues."

At first glance, the social exchange approach seems to present a view of relationships that is very different from one based on the need to seek intimacy. In fact, the two approaches aren't incompatible. Seeking intimacy of any type—whether emotional, physical, or even intellectual—has its costs, and our decision about whether to "pay" those costs is, in great measure, made by considering the likely rewards. If the costs of seeking and maintaining an intimate relationship are too great or the payoffs are not worth the effort, we may decide to withdraw.

Relational Development and Maintenance

So far we have looked at some factors that influence why we are attracted to certain people. In the following pages, we'll examine the kinds of communication that we use to start, maintain, and end relationships.

MODELS OF RELATIONAL DEVELOPMENT

Your own experience demonstrates that relational beginnings are a unique time. How does communication change as we spend time with others and get to know them? Communication scholars have different perspectives on this question. To learn two major perspectives, read on.

DEVELOPMENTAL MODELS One of the best-known models of relational stages was developed by communication researcher Mark Knapp. It breaks the rise and fall of relationships into ten stages, contained in the two broad phases of "coming together" and "coming apart."[26] Other researchers have suggested that any model of relational communication ought to contain a third phase of **relational maintenance**—communication aimed at keeping relationships operating smoothly and satisfactorily.[27] Figure 8.1 shows how Knapp's ten stages fit into this three-phase view of relational communication.

This model seems most appropriate for describing communication between romantic partners, but in many respects it works well for other types of close relationships.[28] As you read the following section, consider how the stages could describe a long-term friendship, a couple in love, or even business partners.

Initiating The goals in the first stage of a relationship are to show that you are interested in making contact and that you are the kind of person worth talking to. Communication during this **initiating** stage is usually brief, and it generally follows conventional formulas: handshakes, remarks about innocuous subjects like the weather, and friendly expressions. These kinds of behavior may seem superficial and meaningless, but they are a way of signaling that we're interested in building some kind of relationship with the other person. They allow us to say without saying, "I'm a friendly person, and I'd like to get to know you."

Initiating relationships—especially romantic ones—can be particularly difficult for people who are shy. As the Looking at Diversity profile on page 278 illustrates,

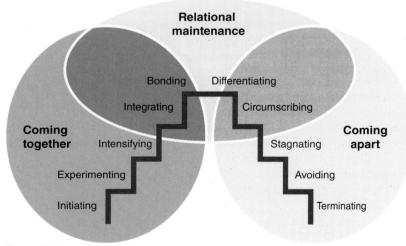

Figure 8.1
Stages of Relational Development

Adapted from *Interpersonal Communication and Human Relationships,* 2nd edition by Mark L. Knapp and Anita L. Vangelisti. Published by Allyn and Bacon, Boston, MA. Copyright © 1992 by Pearson Education. Adapted by permission of the publisher.

making contact via the Internet can be helpful in cases like this. One study of an online dating service found that participants who identified themselves as shy expressed a greater appreciation for the system's anonymous, non-threatening environment than did more outgoing users.[29] The researchers found that many shy users employed the online service specifically to help overcome their inhibitions about initiating relationships in face-to-face settings.

Experimenting After we have made contact with a new person, the next stage is to decide whether we are interested in pursuing the relationship further. This involves *uncertainty reduction*—the process of getting to know others by gaining more information about them.[30] A usual part of uncertainty reduction is the search for common ground, and it involves the conversational basics such as "Where are you from?" or

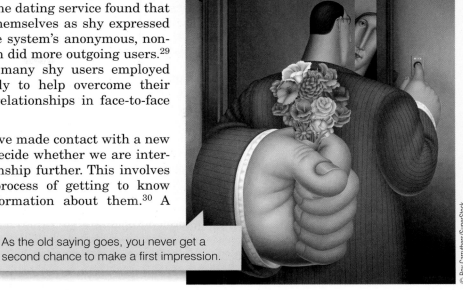

As the old saying goes, you never get a second chance to make a first impression.

© Roy Carruthers/SuperStock

"What's your major?" From there we look for other similarities: "You're a runner, too? How many miles do you do a week?"

The hallmark of the **experimenting** stage is small talk. Even though we may dislike it, we tolerate the ordeal of small talk because it serves several functions. First, it is a useful way to find out what interests we share with the other person. It also provides a way to audition the other person—to help us decide whether a relationship is worth pursuing. In addition, small talk is a safe way to ease into a relationship. You haven't risked much as you decide whether to proceed further.

The willingness to pursue relationships with strangers is partly a matter of personal style. Some people are outgoing and others are shy, but culture also shapes behavior toward newcomers, especially those from a different background. Research suggests that members of high-context cultures are more cautious in their first encounters with strangers and make more assumptions about them based on their backgrounds than do members of low-context cultures.[31] This fact might explain why people from certain backgrounds appear reserved or even unfriendly, when in fact they are simply operating by a set of rules different from those common in low-context North America.

For communicators who are interested in one another, the move from initiating to experimenting seems to occur even more rapidly in cyberspace than in person. One study found that people who develop relationships via email begin asking questions about attitudes, opinions, and preferences more quickly than those engaged in face-to-face contact.[32] It probably helps that emailers can't see each other's nonverbal reactions; they don't have to worry about blushing, stammering, or looking away if they realize that they asked for too much information too quickly.

Intensifying In the **intensifying** stage, the kind of truly interpersonal relationship defined in Chapter 1 begins to develop. Several changes in communication patterns occur during intensifying. The expression of feelings toward the other becomes more common. Dating couples use a wide range of communication strategies to describe their feelings of attraction.[33] About one-quarter of the time they express their feelings directly, openly discussing the state of the relationship. More often they use less direct methods of communication: spending an increasing amount of time together, asking for support from one another, doing favors for the partner, giving tokens of affection, hinting and flirting, expressing feelings nonverbally, getting to know the partner's friends and family, and trying to look more physically attractive. In developing friendships, intensifying can include participating in shared activities, hanging out with mutual friends, or taking trips together.[34]

The intensifying stage is usually a time of relational excitement and even euphoria. For romantic partners, it's often filled with starstruck gazes, goosebumps, and daydreaming. As a result, it's a stage that's regularly depicted in movies and romance novels—after all, we love to watch lovers in love. The problem, of course, is that the stage doesn't last forever. Sometimes romantic partners who stop feeling goosebumps begin to question whether they're still in love. Although it's possible that they're not, it's also possible that they've simply moved on to a different stage in their relationship—integrating.

Integrating As a relationship strengthens, the parties begin to take on an identity as a social unit. In romantic relationships, invitations begin to come addressed to the couple. Social circles merge. The partners begin to take on each other's commitments: "Sure, we'll spend Thanksgiving with your family." Common property may begin to be designated—our apartment, our car, our song.[35] Partners develop unique, ritualistic

LOOKING AT DIVERSITY

Matt DeLanoy: Stuttering and Relationship Building

Photo courtesy of Matt DeLanoy

Meeting people can be hard for anybody, but it's especially tough for me because I stutter. The first words out of my mouth in a new situation are usually the most awkward. After I'm comfortable with the other person and the setting, I tend to stutter less—or I just don't worry about it as much.

I enjoy meeting strangers in Internet chat rooms where my stuttering isn't an issue. Many of them become friends over time. On the computer, I can say what I want, the way I want, without worrying about how the words will come out.

I'm okay with my stuttering—it's part of who I am, and I've learned to live with it. But before I phone an Internet friend for the first time, I usually tell them about my stuttering so they aren't surprised. Holding back this kind of personal information can become a problem. I have an Internet friend who was hitting it off with a guy in one of our chat rooms. She kept asking him to phone her and he kept turning her down, and none of us could figure out why. He finally confessed that he was deaf, and all of us were mad that he hadn't told us sooner. It's not like he had to announce

"I'm deaf" the first time he got in the chat room, and nobody had a problem with his deafness. But hiding that kind of information for too long is a bad idea. It's better to trust people than keep a secret.

I've learned over the years that cyber-communication is more similar to face-to-face communication than some people think. For instance, in chat rooms our interaction is in "real time"—not delayed like it is when e-mailing. Because of this, I can often sense when others are uncomfortable with a subject, or perhaps even being deceptive, simply by noticing pauses as they are writing their messages. I can also tell a lot from the words and phrases people use, such as whether they know the "lingo" of the Internet, or if their language suddenly becomes more or less formal while they're cyber-chatting.

Most of my communication still takes place in person, so I've had to learn how to manage my stuttering. When I get stuck on a certain word, the best thing for me to do is stop, take a breath, and choose a different word. When that happens, what I need most from others is patience. Most of all, I want people to know that my stuttering doesn't mean I'm unable or unwilling to communicate—it just means I sometimes need to find different ways to make it work.

ways of behaving.[36] Close friends may even begin to speak alike, using personal idioms and sentence patterns.[37] In this sense, the **integrating** stage is a time when individuals give up some characteristics of their old selves and develop shared identities.

As we become more integrated with others, our sense of obligation to them grows.[38] We feel obliged to provide a variety of resources, such as class notes and money, whether or not the other person asks for them. Surprisingly, although integration is characterized by more relational solidarity, partners make fewer straightforward requests than they did in earlier relational stages. In dating relationships, for example, there is a curvilinear relationship (shown in Figure 8.2) between the relational stage and the number of explicit requests.[39] This pattern isn't as surprising as it might at first seem: As partners become better acquainted, their knowledge of each other makes overt requests less necessary. But later, as the relationship inevitably begins to change, the need for more explicit statements of wants and needs will increase again.

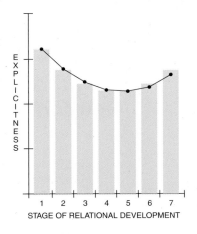

Figure 8.2
Explicitness of Requests Varies across Relational Stages

Adapted from D. H. Solomon (1997). "A Developmental Model of Intimacy and Date Request Explicitness." *Communication Monographs, 64,* 99–118.

Bonding During the **bonding** stage, the parties make symbolic public gestures to show the world that their relationship exists. What constitutes a bonded, committed relationship isn't always easy to define.[40] Terms such as *common-law, cohabitation,* and *life partners* have been used to describe relationships that don't have the full support of custom and law but still involve an implicit or explicit bond. Nonetheless, given the importance of bonding in validating relationships and taking them to another level, it's not surprising that the gay and lesbian communities are striving to have legally sanctioned and recognized marriages.

For our purposes here, we'll define bonded relationships as those involving a significant measure of public commitment. These can include engagement or marriage, sharing a residence, a public ceremony, or a written or verbal pledge. The key is that bonding is the culmination of a developed relationship—the "officializing" of a couple's integration. We'll talk more about the role of commitment in relationships later in this chapter.

Bonding marks a turning point in a relationship. Up to now the relationship may have developed at a steady pace. Experimenting gradually moved into intensifying and then into integrating. Now, however, there is a spurt of commitment. The public display and declaration of exclusivity make this a distinct stage in the relationship.

Relationships don't have to be romantic to achieve bonding. Consider, for example, the contracts that formalize a business partnership or the initiation ceremony in a fraternity or sorority. As one author notes, even friendships can achieve bonding with acts that "officialize" the relationship:

> Some Western cultures have rituals to mark the progress of a friendship and to give it public legitimacy and form. In Germany, for example, there's a small ceremony called *Duzen,* the

Bonding is marked by public expressions of commitment.

Masterfile (Royalty-Free Div.)

ON THE JOB

Memorable Messages: Initiating Company Newcomers

Getting off to a good start is just as important on the job as it is in romances or friendships. Scholars use the terms *assimilation* and *socialization* to describe how employees are integrated into their organizations. Not surprisingly, communication plays a major role in the socialization process. When helpful information is plentiful, new employees grow more satisfied with and committed to their jobs in the long run.[a]

In one study, researchers explored the nature of socialization messages.[b] While orientation sessions, handbooks, emails, and memos were useful, new employees reported that the most valuable messages often come via informal conversations—over 90 percent of which took place in face-to-face settings.

Many of the helpful messages were about professional behavior and office rules ("It's crucial to be punctual"; "Be careful when you challenge the boss"). Office politics also came into play ("Always be nice to the secretary Nadine because she's the gateway to the supervisor"). Not all of the messages were warnings; some were warm and welcoming ("It's one big family here"; "We're glad they hired you"). Regardless of the specific content, virtually all of the messages were perceived as positive, supportive, and designed to help the recipient, the company, or both.

It's important to remember the importance of messages—both large and small, deliberate and offhand—in building a happy, effective work team. As a newcomer, it's wise to seek the counsel and support of your colleagues. As a veteran, it's important to help rookies get off to a good start.

---

name itself signifying the transformation in the relationship. The ritual calls for the two friends, each holding a glass of wine or beer, to entwine arms, thus bringing each other physically close, and to drink up after making a promise of eternal brotherhood with the word *Bruderschaft*. When it's over, the friends will have passed from a relationship that requires the formal *Sie* mode of address to the familiar *du*.[41]

Differentiating Bonding is the peak of what Knapp calls the "coming together" phase of relational development, but people in even the most committed relationships need to assert their individual identities. This **differentiating** stage is the point where the "we" orientation that has developed shifts, and more "me" messages begin to occur. Instead of talking about "our" weekend plans, differentiating conversations focus on what "I" want to do. Relational issues that were once agreed upon (such as "You'll be the breadwinner and I'll manage the home") may now become points of contention: "Why am *I* stuck at home when I have better career potential than *you*?" The root of the term *differentiating* is the word *different*, suggesting that change plays an important role in this stage.

Differentiating is likely to occur when a relationship begins to experience the first, inevitable feelings of stress. This need for autonomy and change needn't be a negative experience, however. People need to be individuals as well as parts of a relationship, and differentiation is a necessary step toward autonomy. Think, for instance, of young adults who want to forge their own unique lives and identity, even while maintaining their relationships with their parents.[42] As the model on page 276 illustrates, differentiating is often a part of normal relational maintenance, in which partners manage the inevitable changes that come their way. The key to successful differentiating is maintaining a commitment to the relationship while creating the space for being an individual as well. (This is a challenge that we will discuss in more detail later in this chapter when we discuss dialectical tensions in relationships.)

Circumscribing So far we have been looking at the growth of relationships. Although some reach a plateau of development, going on successfully for as long as a lifetime, others pass through several stages of decline and dissolution.

In the **circumscribing** stage, communication between members decreases in quantity and quality. Restrictions and restraints characterize this stage. Rather than discuss a disagreement (which requires energy on both sides), members opt for withdrawal—either mental (silence or daydreaming and fantasizing) or physical (where people spend less time together). Circumscribing doesn't involve total avoidance, which may come later. Rather, it involves a shrinking of interest and commitment—the opposite of what occurred in the integrating stage.

Stagnating If circumscribing continues, the relationship enters the **stagnating** stage. The excitement of the intensifying stage is long gone, and the partners behave toward each other in old, familiar ways without much feeling. No growth occurs. The relationship is a hollow shell of its former self. We see stagnation in many workers who have lost enthusiasm for their job yet continue to go through the motions for years. The same sad event occurs for some couples who unenthusiastically have the same conversations, see the same people, and follow the same routines without any sense of joy or novelty.

Avoiding When stagnation becomes too unpleasant, parties in a relationship begin to create physical distance between each other. This is the **avoiding** stage. Sometimes they do it indirectly under the guise of excuses ("I've been sick lately and can't see you"); sometimes they do it directly ("Please don't call me; I don't want to see you now"). In either case, by this point the relationship's future is in doubt.

The deterioration of a relationship from bonding through circumscribing, stagnating, and avoiding isn't inevitable. One of the key differences between marriages that end in separation and those that are restored to their former intimacy is the communication that occurs when the partners are unsatisfied.[43] Unsuccessful couples deal with their problems by avoidance, indirectness, and less involvement with each other. By contrast, couples who repair their relationship communicate much more directly. They confront each other with their concerns (sometimes with the assistance of a counselor) and spend time and effort negotiating solutions to their problems.

Terminating Not all relationships end. Many career partnerships, friendships, and marriages last for a lifetime once they've been established. But many do deteriorate and reach the final stage of **terminating**. Characteristics of this stage include summary dialogues of where the relationship has gone and the desire to dissociate. The relationship may end with a cordial dinner, a note left on the kitchen table, a phone call, or a legal document. Depending on each person's feelings, this stage can be quite short, or it may be drawn out over time.

Relationships don't always move toward termination in a straight line. Rather, they take a back-and-forth pattern, where the trend is toward dissolution.[44] Regardless of how long it takes, termination doesn't have to be totally negative. Understanding each other's investments in the relationship and needs for personal growth may dilute the hard feelings. In fact, many relationships aren't so much terminated as redefined. A divorced couple, for example, may find new, less intimate ways to relate to each other.

©2008 Harry Bliss. Distributed by Tribune Media Services, Inc.   10/9

www.harrybliss.com

Harry Bliss

"We'll always have Facebook."

In romantic relationships, the best predictor of whether the parties will be friends after reaching the terminating stage is whether they were friends before their emotional involvement.[45] The way the couple splits up also makes a difference. It's no surprise to find that friendships are most possible when communication during the breakup is positive: expressions that there are no regrets for time spent together and other attempts to minimize hard feelings. When communication during termination is negative (manipulative, complaining to third parties), friendships are less likely.

After termination, couples often engage in "grave-dressing"—retrospective attempts to explain why the relationship failed.[46] The narrative each partner creates about "what went wrong" has an impact on how the couple will get along after their breakup (imagine the difference between saying and hearing "We just weren't right for each other" versus "He was too selfish and immature for a committed relationship").[47]

While Knapp's model offers insights into relational stages, it doesn't describe the ebb and flow of communication in every relationship. For instance, Knapp suggests that movement among stages is generally sequential, so that relationships typically progress from one stage to another in a predictable manner as they develop and deteriorate. One study found that many terminated friendships did follow a pattern similar to the one described by Knapp and pictured in Pattern One of Figure 8.3.[48] However, several other patterns of development and deterioration were also identified, as seen in Patterns Two through Five. In other words, not all relationships begin, progress, decline, and end in the same linear fashion.

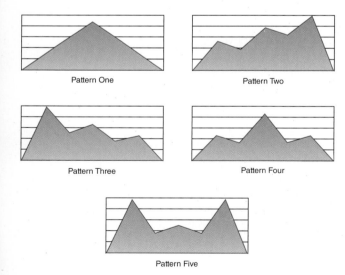

Pattern One

Pattern Two

Pattern Three

Pattern Four

Pattern Five

Figure 8.3
Patterns of Relational Development and Deterioration

Adapted from A. Johnson, E. Wittenberg, M. Haigh, S. Wigley, J. Becker, K. Brown, & E. Craig (2004). "The Process of Relationship Development and Deterioration: Turning Points in Friendships that Have Terminated." *Communication Quarterly, 52*, 54–67.

Finally, Knapp's model suggests that a relationship exhibits only the most dominant traits of just one of the ten stages at any given time, but elements of other stages are usually present. For example, two lovers deep in the throes of integrating may still do their share of experimenting ("Wow, I never knew that about you!") and have differentiating disagreements ("Nothing personal, but I need a weekend to myself"). Likewise, family members who spend most of their energy avoiding each other may have an occasional good spell in which their former closeness briefly intensifies. The notion that relationships can experience features of both "coming together" and "coming apart" at the same time is explored in the following section on relational dialectics.

DIALECTICAL PERSPECTIVES Not all theorists agree that stage-related models like the one described in the preceding pages are the best way to explain interaction in relationships. Some suggest that communicators grapple with the same kinds of challenges whether a relationship is

✔+ INVITATION TO INSIGHT

Your Relational Stage

You can gain a clearer appreciation of the accuracy and value of relational stages by answering the following questions:

1 If you are in a relationship, describe its present stage and the behaviors that characterize your communication in this stage. Give specific examples to support your assessment.

2 Discuss the trend of the communication in terms of the stages described on pages 276–282. Are you likely to remain in the present stage, or do you anticipate movement to another stage? Which one? Explain your answer.

3 Describe your level of satisfaction with the answer to question 2. If you are satisfied, describe what you can do to increase the likelihood that the relationship will operate at the stage you described. If you are not satisfied, discuss what you can do to move the relationship toward a more satisfying stage.

4 Because both parties define a relationship, define your partner's perspective. Would she or he say that the relationship is at the same stage as you describe it? If not, explain how your partner would describe it. What does your partner do to determine the stage at which your relationship operates? (Give specific examples.) How would you like your partner to behave in order to move the relationship to or maintain it at the stage you desire? What can you do to encourage your partner to behave in the way you desire?

5 Now consider a relationship (friendship or romance) you have been in that has terminated. Which of the five graphs on page 282 best describes the development and decline of that relationship? If none of the graphs matches your experience, develop a new graph to illustrate your relationship's pattern.

brand new or decades old. They argue that communicators seek important but inherently incompatible goals throughout virtually all of their relationships. The struggle to achieve these goals creates **dialectical tensions**: conflicts that arise when two opposing or incompatible forces exist simultaneously. Communication scholars have identified several dialectical forces that make successful communication challenging.[49] They suggest that the struggle to manage these dialectical tensions creates the most powerful dynamics in relational communication. In the following pages, we will discuss three powerful dialectical tensions.

Connection versus Autonomy No one is an island. Recognizing this fact, we seek out involvement with others. But, at the same time, we are unwilling to sacrifice our entire identity to even the most satisfying relationship. The conflicting desires for connection and autonomy are embodied in the **connection-autonomy dialectic**. Research on relational breakups demonstrates the consequences for relational partners who can't find a way to manage these very different personal needs.[50] Some of the most common reasons for relational breakups involve failure of partners to satisfy each other's needs for connection: "We barely spent any time together," "She/he wasn't committed to the relationship," "We had different needs." But other relational complaints involve excessive demands for connection: "I was feeling trapped," "I needed freedom." Perhaps not surprisingly, some research suggests that men value autonomy in relationships more than women do, whereas women tend to value connection and commitment.[51]

The levels of connection and autonomy that we seek can change over time. In his book *Intimate Behavior*, Desmond Morris suggests that each of us repeatedly goes through three stages: "Hold me tight," "Put me down," and "Leave me alone."[52] This cycle becomes apparent in the first years of life, when children move from the "hold-me-tight" stage that characterizes infancy into a new "put-me-down" stage of exploring the world by crawling, walking, touching, and tasting. The same three-year-old who insists "I can do it myself" in August may cling to parents on the first day of preschool in September. As children grow into adolescents, the "leave-me-alone" orientation becomes apparent. Teenagers who used to happily spend time with their parents now may groan at the thought of a family vacation or even the notion of sitting down at the dinner table each evening. As adolescents move into adulthood, they typically grow closer to their families again.[53]

> Love one another, but make not a bond of love: Let it rather be a moving sea between the shores of your souls.
>
> Fill each other's cup but drink not from one cup.
>
> Give one another of your bread but eat not of the same loaf.
>
> Sing and dance together and be joyous, but let each one of you be alone. Even as the strings of a lute are alone though they quiver with the same music.
>
> —*Kahlil Gibran,* The Prophet

In adult relationships, the same cycle of intimacy and distance repeats itself. In marriages, for example, the "hold-me-tight" bonds of the first year are often followed by a desire for autonomy. This desire can manifest itself in several ways, such as wanting to make friends or engage in activities that don't include the spouse or the need to make a career move that might disrupt the relationship. As the discussion of relational stages earlier in this chapter explained, this movement from connection to autonomy may lead to the breakup of relationships, but it can also be part of a cycle that redefines the relationship in a new form that can recapture or even surpass the intimacy that existed in the past.

In accounts of relational turning points, both men and women in heterosexual romantic pairs cite the connection-autonomy dialectic as one of the most significant factors affecting their relationship.[54] This dialectical tension is crucial in negotiating turning points related to commitment, conflict, disengagement, and reconciliation.

Managing the tension between connection and autonomy is also important at the end of a relationship, as partners seek ways to salvage the positive parts of their relationship (if only the good memories) and take steps toward their new independence.[55] Even at the end of life, the connection-autonomy dialectic comes into play. When a loved one is in an extended period of declining health, the partner often feels torn between the desire to stay close and the need to let go. This tension is especially poignant when one partner suffers from a condition like Alzheimer's disease and becomes mentally absent while physically present.[56]

Openness versus Privacy As Chapter 1 explained, disclosure is one characteristic of interpersonal relationships. Yet, along with the need to disclose, we have an equally important drive to maintain some space between ourselves and others. These conflicting needs create the **openness-privacy dialectic**.

Even the strongest interpersonal relationships require some distance. Lovers may go through periods of much sharing and periods of relative withdrawal. Likewise, they experience periods of passion and then periods of little physical contact. Friends have times of high disclosure when they share almost every feeling and idea and then disengage for days, months, or even longer.

What do you do in an intimate relationship when a person you care about asks an important question that you don't want to answer? "Do you think I'm attractive?" "Are you having a good time?" Your commitment to honesty may compel you toward a candid response, but your concern for the other person's feelings and a desire for privacy may lead you to be less than completely honest. Partners use a variety of strategies to gain privacy from each other.[57] For example, they may confront the other person directly and explain that they don't want to continue a discussion, or they may be less direct and offer nonverbal cues, change the topic, or leave the room. This dialectic raises so many communication challenges that Chapter 9 explores it in depth.

Predictability versus Novelty Stability is an important need in relationships, but too much of it can lead to feelings of staleness. The **predictability-novelty dialectic** reflects this tension. Humorist Dave Barry exaggerates only slightly when he talks about the boredom that can come when husbands and wives know each other too well:

> After a decade or so of marriage, you know *everything* about your spouse, every habit and opinion and twitch and tic and minor skin growth. You could write a seventeen-pound book solely about the way your spouse *eats*. This kind of intimate knowledge can be very handy in certain situations—such as when you're on a TV quiz show where the object is to identify your spouse from the sound of his or her chewing—but it tends to lower the passion level of a relationship.[58]

"And do you, Rebecca, promise to make love only to Richard, month after month, year after year, and decade after decade, until one of you is dead?"

Although too much familiarity can lead to the risk of boredom and stagnation, nobody wants a completely unpredictable relational partner. Too many surprises can threaten the foundations upon which the relationship is based ("You're not the person I married!").

The challenge for communicators is to juggle the desire for predictability with the desire for novelty that keeps the relationship fresh and interesting. People differ in their desire for predictability and novelty, so there is no optimal mixture of the two. As you will read shortly, people can use several strategies to manage these contradictory drives.

Managing Dialectical Tensions Although all of the dialectical tensions play an important role in managing relationships, some occur more frequently than others. In one study, young married couples reported that connection-autonomy was the most frequent tension (30.8 percent of all reported contradictions).[59] Predictability-novelty was second (21.7 percent). Least common was openness-privacy (12.7 percent).

Managing the dialectical tensions outlined in these pages presents communication challenges. There are many ways to meet these challenges, and some work better than others.[60]

- *Denial.* In the strategy of denial, communicators respond to one end of the dialectical spectrum and ignore the other. For example, a couple caught between the conflicting desires for predictability and novelty might find their struggle for change too difficult to manage and choose to follow predictable, if unexciting, patterns of relating to each other.

- *Disorientation*. In this strategy, communicators feel so overwhelmed and helpless that they are unable to confront their problems. In the face of dialectical tensions, they might fight, freeze, or even leave the relationship. Two people who discover soon after the honeymoon that a "happily ever after" conflict-free life isn't realistic might become so terrified that they would come to view their marriage as a mistake.

- *Alternation*. Communicators who use this strategy choose one end of the dialectical spectrum at some times and the other end at other times. Friends, for example, might manage the connection-autonomy dialectic by alternating between times when they spend a large amount of time together and other times when they live independent lives.

- *Segmentation*. Partners who use this tactic compartmentalize different areas of their relationship. For example, a couple might manage the openness-privacy dialectic by sharing almost all their feelings about mutual friends with each other, but keeping certain parts of their past romantic histories private. Segmentation is the most frequently used method for stepchildren to manage openness-privacy tensions with their nonresident parents.[61] In the "Zits" cartoon on this page, Jeremy realizes he has forgotten to use his usual approach of segmentation to manage the openness-privacy dialectic with his inquisitive parents.

- *Balance*. Communicators who try to balance dialectical tensions recognize that both forces are legitimate and try to manage them through compromise. As Chapter 11 points out, compromise is inherently a situation in which everybody loses at least a little of what he or she wants. A couple caught between the conflicting desires for predictability and novelty might seek balance by compromising with a lifestyle that is neither as predictable as one wants nor as surprise-filled as the other wants—not an ideal outcome.

- *Integration*. With this strategy, communicators simultaneously accept opposing forces without trying to diminish them. Communication researcher Barbara Montgomery describes a couple who accept the needs for both predictability and novelty by devising a "predictably novel" approach: Once a week they would do something together that they had never done before.[62] In a similar way, some stepfamilies manage the tension between the "old family" and the "new family" by adapting and blending their family rituals.[63]

- *Recalibration*. Communicators can respond to dialectical challenges by reframing them so that the apparent contradiction disappears. For example, a change in

Zits Partnership/King Features

thinking can transform your attitude from loving someone *despite* your differences to loving him or her *because* of those differences.[64] Or consider how two people who each felt hurt by each other's unwillingness to share parts of his or her past might redefine the secrets as creating an attractive aura of mystery instead of being a problem to be solved. The desire for privacy would still remain, but it would no longer compete with a need for openness about every aspect of the past.

- *Reaffirmation*. This strategy acknowledges that dialectical tensions will never disappear. Instead of trying to make them go away, reaffirming communicators accept—or even embrace—the challenges that the tensions present. The metaphorical view of relational life as a kind of roller coaster reflects this strategy, and communicators who use reaffirmation view dialectical tensions as part of the ride.

✔+ INVITATION TO INSIGHT

Your Dialectical Tensions

Describe how each of the dialectical tensions described in these pages operates in one of your important relationships. Which incompatible goals do you and your relational partner(s) seek? Which of the strategies described on pages 285–287 do you use to manage these tensions? Are you satisfied with this strategy, or can you suggest better strategies?

CHARACTERISTICS OF RELATIONSHIPS

Whether you analyze a relationship in terms of stages or dialectical tensions, two characteristics are true of every interpersonal relationship. As you read about each, consider how it applies to your own experience.

RELATIONSHIPS ARE CONSTANTLY CHANGING Relationships are certainly not doomed to deteriorate, but even the strongest ones are rarely stable for long periods. In fairy tales a couple may live "happily ever after," but in real life this sort of equilibrium is less common. Consider a husband and wife who have been married for some time. Although they have formally bonded, their relationship will probably shift from one dimension of a relational dialectic to another, and forward or backward along the spectrum of stages. Sometimes the partners will feel the need to differentiate from each other, and at other times they will need to seek intimacy. Sometimes they will feel secure in the predictable patterns they have established, and at other times one or both will feel hungry for novelty. The relationship may become circumscribed or even stagnant. From this point the marriage may fail, but this fate isn't certain. With effort, the partners may move from the stage of stagnating to experimenting, or from circumscribing to intensifying.

Communication theorist Richard Conville describes the constantly changing, evolving nature of relationships as a cycle in which partners move through a series of stages, returning to ones they previously encountered, although at a new level[65] (see Figure 8.4). In this cycle, partners move from security (integration, in Knapp's

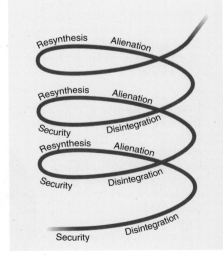

Figure 8.4
A Helical Model of Relational Cycles

terminology) to disintegration (differentiating) to alienation (circumscribing) to resynthesis (intensifying, integrating) to a new level of security. This process is constantly repeating.

RELATIONSHIPS ARE AFFECTED BY CULTURE   Many of the qualities that shape personal relationships are universal.[66] For example, social scientists have found that communication in all cultures has both the content and relational dimensions described on pages 293–294 in this chapter, that the same facial expressions signal the same emotions in all cultures, and that the distribution of power is a factor in every human society. Males in all cultures (in fact, in all species of mammals) are likely to invest less emotionally in sexual relationships, and are typically more competitive.

Although the general elements of relationships are universal, the particulars often differ from one culture to another. Consider, for example, how the Western notion of romance and marriage is reflected in the model of relational stages described on pages 276–282. The notion that bonding only follows after experimenting, intensifying, and integrating doesn't apply everywhere.[67] Indeed, in some cultures, the bride and groom may meet only weeks, days, or even minutes before they become husband and wife. Research shows that these relationships can be both successful and satisfying.[68] (See the reading on this page for a perspective on Indian courtship patterns.)

A variety of differences—profound, but not always apparent—can make relationships between people from different cultures challenging.[69] For example, deciding how much (or how little) to share what's on your mind is a challenge in any relationship. This decision can be especially tricky when the cultural rules about self-disclosure vary.

Technology and Indian Marriage: A Match Made in Heaven

Some 18 months ago in southern India, the parents of a software engineer working in Chennai began to despair of finding him a suitable bride. They were, truth to tell, rather picky: "Our requirement is a suitable Hindu Nadar girl of Sivakasi/Madurai side origin, preferably employed as a software engineer in Chennai, age between 21 to 24, height 5 feet 2 inches to 5 feet 6 inches and sufficiently good-looking." She also had to speak Tamil.

There was, however, a happy ending. They ventured online, to a website called Bharatmatrimony.com, which now flaunts their story. They identified a girl, received a message from her father, matched horoscopes and, having introduced the happy couple to each other, will celebrate the wedding next month.

Online marriage-broking is one of the successes of Indian e-business, used by the single looking for "love matches" as well as by their parents and siblings. So complex are the requirements of Indians seeking a partner that the Internet might have been designed to meet their needs. Bharatmatrimony's boss, Janakiram Murugavel, says that language is the biggest criterion. His site is divided into 15 linguistic sections. Then comes status and caste, which divides Indians at birth into thousands of groups. About 70% of his customers want to marry within their caste. Most still also use astrology. Bharatmatrimony offers an online horoscope service.

Economist

©Ken Seet/Corbis

(Chapter 9 addresses this subject in detail.) Low-context cultures such as the United States value directness, whereas high-context ones like Japan consider tact far more important. The titles of two self-help books offer a revealing peek at the mindset of these approaches. One American self-help book is titled *How to Say No without Feeling Guilty*,[70] while the Japanese counterpart is titled *16 Ways to Avoid Saying No*.[71] It's easy to see how differing notions of appropriateness could lead to challenges in intercultural relationships.

When challenges arise out of cultural differences, the kinds of intercultural competence described in Chapter 1 (pages 32–34) become especially important. Motivation, tolerance for ambiguity, open-mindedness, knowledge of others' practices, and skill at adapting to others' communication styles are likely to make communication more smooth and relationships more satisfying.

RELATIONSHIPS REQUIRE MAINTENANCE   Just as gardens need tending, cars need tune-ups, and bodies need exercise, relationships need ongoing maintenance to keep them successful and satisfying.[72] Communication accounts for as much as 80 percent of the difference between satisfying and unsatisfying relationships, so it's important to explore the nature of maintenance-related interaction.[73]

What kinds of communication help maintain relationships? Researchers have identified five strategies that couples use to keep their interaction satisfying.[74]

- *Positivity*. Keeping the relational climate polite and upbeat, and also avoiding criticism. (Chapter 10 addresses this topic in detail.)

- *Openness*. Talking directly about the nature of the relationship and disclosing your personal needs and concerns. (Chapter 9 describes the challenges of finding the optimal amount of self-disclosure.)

- *Assurances*. Letting the other person know—both verbally and nonverbally—that he or she matters to you, and that you are committed to the relationship.

- *Social networks*. Providing support and relief that helps relational partners understand and appreciate one another.

- *Sharing tasks*. Helping one another take care of life's chores and obligations makes life easier and reaffirms the value of the relationship.

These maintenance strategies aren't only for romantic relationships. One study analyzed college students' email to see which strategies they used.[75] With family and friends, two strategies were used most: openness ("Things have been a little crazy for me lately") and social networks ("How are you and Sam? Hopefully good"). With romantic partners, however, assurances ("This is just a little email to say I love you") was the most-used maintenance device. The study shows not only that different relationships call for different types of maintenance, but also that email can be a helpful tool for maintaining interpersonal relationships.

Every type of relationship can benefit from these maintenance strategies, but social scientists have found that some communicators are more likely than others to use them. For example, a twelve-year research program at the Universities of Washington and California explored relational patterns of same-sex couples.[76] While all types of couples—straight, gay, and lesbian—have about the same levels of relational satisfaction, gay and lesbian partners seem to be better at maintaining a positive tone by using some of the maintenance strategies outlined earlier. For example, compared to straight couples, gay and lesbian partners are more upbeat in the face of conflict. They

✔+ INVITATION TO INSIGHT

Maintaining Your Relationships

How well are you maintaining your important relationships through constructive communication? Choose one relationship that matters to you: with family members, friends, or a romantic partner. Analyze the degree to which you and the others involved use the maintenance strategies listed on page 289 to keep the relationship strong and satisfying. What steps could you take to improve matters?

tend to take disagreements less personally; use fewer controlling, hostile tactics; and get less emotionally aroused when problems arise.

RELATIONSHIPS REQUIRE COMMITMENT   Some common statements suggest the central role commitment plays in our ongoing interactions with others: "I'm looking for a committed relationship." "Our relationship didn't work because my partner wasn't committed." "I'm just not ready for commitment."

Relational commitment involves a promise—sometimes implied, and sometimes explicit—to remain in a relationship, and to make that relationship successful. Commitment is important in every type of interpersonal relationship, whether it's a friendship ("Friends for life!"), family ("We're always here for you"), a close-knit working team ("I've got you covered"), or a romantic relationship ("Till death do us part").

As these examples suggest, commitment is both formed and reinforced through communication. Table 8.1 spells out commitment indicators in romantic relationships. You can probably imagine how similar indicators of commitment would operate in other sorts of close relationships.

As Table 8.1 suggests, words alone aren't a surefire measure of true commitment. Deeds are also important. Simply saying "You can count on me" doesn't guarantee loyalty. But without language, commitment may not be clear. For this reason, the kinds of bonding ceremonies described on pages 279–280 are an important way to recognize and cement loyalty.

Table 8.1

Major Indicators of a Committed Romantic Relationship

Providing affection
Providing support
Maintaining integrity
Sharing companionship
Making an effort to communicate regularly
Showing respect
Creating a relational future
Creating a positive relational atmosphere
Working on relationship problems together
Reassuring one's commitment

Source: D. J. Weigel (2008). "Mutuality and the Communication of Commitment in Romantic Relationships." Southern Communication Journal, 73, 24–41.

REPAIRING DAMAGED RELATIONSHIPS

Sooner or later, even the strongest relationships hit a bumpy patch. Some problems arise from outside forces: work, finances, competing relationships, and so on. At other times, problems arise from differences and disagreements within your relationship. Chapter 11 offers guidelines for dealing with these sorts of challenges.

A third type of relational problem comes from **relational transgressions**, when one partner violates the explicit or implicit terms of the relationship, letting the other one down in some important way.[77]

TYPES OF RELATIONAL TRANSGRESSIONS Table 8.2 lists some types of relational transgressions. Violations like these fall into different categories.[78]

Minor versus Significant Some of the items listed in Table 8.2 aren't inherently transgressions, and in small doses they can actually aid relationships. For instance, a *little* distance can make the heart grow fonder, a *little* jealousy can be a sign of affection, and a *little* anger can start the process of resolving a gripe. In large and regular doses, however, these acts become serious transgressions that can damage personal relationships.

Social versus Relational Some transgressions violate *social rules* shared by society at large. For example, almost everyone would agree that ridiculing or humiliating a friend or family member in public is a violation of a fundamental social rule regarding saving others' face. Other rules are *relational* in nature—unique norms constructed by the parties involved. For instance, some families have a rule stating "If I'm going to be more than a little bit late, I'll let you know so you don't worry." Once such a rule exists, failure to honor it feels like a violation, even though outsiders might not view it as such.

Deliberate versus Unintentional Some transgressions are unintentional. You might reveal something about a friend's past without realizing that this disclosure would be embarrassing. Other violations, though, are intentional. In a fit of anger, you might purposely lash out with a cruel comment, knowing that it will hurt the other person's feelings.

Table 8.2
Some Types of Relational Transgressions

Lack of Commitment	Failure to honor important obligations (e.g., financial, emotional, task-related)
	Self-serving dishonesty
	Unfaithfulness
Distance	Physical separation (beyond what is necessary)
	Psychological separation (avoidance, ignoring)
Disrespect	Criticism (especially in front of third parties)
Problematic Emotions	Jealousy
	Unjustified suspicion
	Rage
Aggression	Verbal hostility
	Physical violence

One-time versus Incremental The most obvious transgressions occur in a single episode: an act of betrayal, a verbal assault, or stalking out in anger. But more subtle transgressions can occur over time. Consider emotional withdrawal: Everybody has times of needing isolation, and we usually give one another the space to do just that. But if the withdrawal slowly becomes pervasive, it becomes a violation of the fundamental rule in most relationships that partners should be available to one another.

STRATEGIES FOR RELATIONAL REPAIR Research confirms the commonsense notion that a first step toward repairing a transgression is to talk about the violation.[79] Chapter 10 offers tips for sending clear, assertive messages when you believe you've been wronged: "I was really embarrassed when you yelled at me in front of everybody last night." In other cases, you might be responsible for the transgression and want to raise it for discussion: "What did I do that you found so hurtful?" "Why was my behavior a problem for you?" Asking questions like these—and listening nondefensively to the answers—can be an enormous challenge. Chapter 7 offered guidelines for listening, and Chapter 10 provides tips about how to manage criticism.

The best chance for righting a wrong is taking responsibility for your transgression.[80] It isn't easy to apologize, especially in Western cultures where saving one's own face is a strong concern.[81] But not expressing regret can be worse than saying "I'm sorry." Participants in one study reported that they had more remorse over apologies they didn't offer than about those they did.[82] There's another benefit of seeking forgiveness: Research shows that transgressors who have been forgiven are less likely to repeat their offenses than those who have not received forgiveness.[83]

For the best chance of repairing damaged relationships, an apology requires three elements:

1. An explicit acknowledgment that the transgression was wrong: "I acted like a selfish jerk."
2. A sincere apology: "I'm really sorry. I feel awful for letting you down."
3. Some type of compensation: "If I act that way again, you can call me on it."[84]

An apology will only be convincing if the speaker's nonverbal behaviors match his or her words. Even then, it may be unrealistic to expect immediate forgiveness. Sometimes, especially with severe transgressions, expressions of regret and promises of new behavior need to be demonstrated over time before the aggrieved party accepts them as genuine.[85]

✔+ INVITATION TO INSIGHT

Your Relational Transgressions

1 Identify transgressions you have made in one important relationship. Describe whether these transgressions were minor or significant, social or relational, deliberate or unintentional, and one-time or incremental. (If you think the relationship can handle it, consider asking the "victim" of your transgression to describe your behavior and its effects.)

2 Consider (or ask the other person) whether it's necessary to repair your transgression. Examine the strategies described on page 292, and decide how you could put them into action.

FORGIVING TRANSGRESSIONS Many people think of forgiveness as a topic for theologians and philosophers. However, social scientists have found that forgiving others has both personal and relational benefits. On a personal level, forgiveness has been shown to reduce emotional distress and aggression,[86] as well as to improve cardiovascular functioning.[87] Interpersonally, extending forgiveness to lovers, friends, and family can help restore damaged relationships.[88]

Research suggests that the most effective conversations about forgiveness contain two elements:

"I said I'm sorry."

1. An explicit statement: "I can't forget what you did, but I believe your apology and I accept it."
2. A discussion of the implications of the transgression and the future of the relationship: "I have to be honest. It's going to take time before I can trust you again."[89]

Not surprisingly, some transgressions are harder to forgive than others. One study of dating partners found that sexual infidelity and breaking up with the partner were the two least forgivable offenses.[90] It's significant to note that being emotionally unfaithful can be as distressing as sexual infidelity.[91]

Even when a sincere apology is offered, forgiving others can be difficult. Research shows that one way to improve your ability to forgive is to recall times when you have mistreated or hurt others in the past—in other words, to remember that you, too, have wronged others and needed their forgiveness.[92] Knowing that it's in our own best interest to be forgiving, communication researcher Douglas Kelley encourages us to remember these words from R. P. Walters: "When we have been hurt we have two alternatives: be destroyed by resentment, or forgive. Resentment is death; forgiving leads to healing and life."[93]

Communicating about Relationships

By now you understand that relationships are complex, dynamic, and important. But what kinds of messages do we exchange as we communicate in those relationships?

CONTENT AND RELATIONAL MESSAGES

In Chapter 1, you read that every message has a *content* and a *relational* dimension. The most obvious component of most messages is their content—the subject being discussed. The content of such statements as "It's your turn to do the dishes" or "I'm busy Saturday night" is obvious.

Content messages aren't the only thing being exchanged when two people communicate. In addition, almost every message—both verbal and nonverbal—has a second, relational dimension, which makes statements about how the parties feel toward one another.[94] As you'll read in the following section, these relational messages deal with one or more social needs, most commonly affinity, immediacy, respect, and control. Consider the two examples we just mentioned:

"You say 'off with her head,' but what I'm hearing is, 'I feel neglected.'"

- Imagine two ways of saying "It's your turn to do the dishes": one that is demanding and another that is matter-of-fact. Notice how the different nonverbal messages make statements about how the sender views control in this part of the relationship. The demanding tone says, in effect, "I have a right to tell you what to do around the house," whereas the matter-of-fact tone suggests, "I'm just reminding you of something you might have overlooked."

- You can easily visualize two ways to deliver the statement "I'm busy Saturday night": one with little affinity and the other with much affinity.

Notice that in each of these examples the relational dimension of the message was never discussed. In fact, most of the time we aren't conscious of the many relational messages that bombard us every day. Sometimes we are unaware of relational messages because they match our belief about the amount of respect, control, and affection that is appropriate. For example, you probably wouldn't be offended if your boss told you to do a certain job, because you agree that supervisors have the right to direct employees. In other cases, however, conflicts arise over relational messages, even though content is not disputed. If your boss delivered the order in a condescending, sarcastic, or abusive tone of voice, you probably would be offended. Your complaint wouldn't be with the order itself, but rather with the way it was delivered. "I may work for this company," you might think, "but I'm not a slave or an idiot. I deserve to be treated like a human being."

How are relational messages communicated? As the boss–employee example suggests, they are usually communicated nonverbally (which includes tone of voice). To test this fact for yourself, imagine how you could act while saying, "Can you help me for a minute?" in a way that communicates each of the following relationships:

superiority   friendliness   sexual desire

helplessness   aloofness   irritation

Although nonverbal behaviors are a good source of relational messages, they are ambiguous. The sharp tone that you receive as a personal insult might be a result of fatigue, and the interruption that you assume is an attempt to ignore your ideas might be a sign of pressure that has nothing to do with you. Before you jump to conclusions about relational clues, it's a good idea to check them out verbally, using the perception-checking skills described in Chapter 3.

TYPES OF RELATIONAL MESSAGES

The number and variety of content messages are almost infinite, ranging from black holes to doughnut holes, from rock and roll to *Rock of Ages*. But unlike the range of content messages, there is a surprisingly narrow range of relational messages. Virtually all of them fit into one of four categories: affinity, immediacy, respect, or control.

AFFINITY An important kind of relational communication involves **affinity**—the degree to which people like or appreciate one another.[95] Not surprisingly, affection is the most important ingredient in romantic relationships.[96] Not all affinity messages are positive, though: A glare or an angry word shows the level of liking just as clearly as a smile or profession of love.

IMMEDIACY **Immediacy** refers to the degree of interest and attention that we feel toward and communicate to others. Not surprisingly, immediacy is an important element of relationships.[97] A great deal of immediacy comes from nonverbal behavior, such as eye contact, facial expression, tone of voice, and the distance we put between ourselves and others.[98] Immediacy can also come from our language. For example, saying "we have a problem" is more immediate than saying "you have a problem." Chapters 5 and 6 discuss nonverbal and verbal immediacy in more detail.

Immediacy isn't the same thing as affinity: It's possible to like someone without being immediate with them. For instance, you can convey liking with a high degree of immediacy, such as with a big hug and kiss or by shouting "I really like you!" You can also imagine situations where you like someone but operate with a low degree of immediacy. (Picture a quiet, pleasant evening at home where you and another person each read or work comfortably but independently.) You can also imagine communicating dislike in high- and low-immediacy ways.

The most obvious types of immediacy involve positive feelings, but it's possible to express disapproval and disliking with either high or low intensity. Imagine, for instance, the difference between mild and extreme ways—both verbal and nonverbal—of letting a friend know that you are unhappy about something he or she has done.

Highly immediate communication certainly has its value, but there are also times when a low degree of intensity is desirable. It would be exhausting to interact with full intensity all the time. It would also be inappropriate to communicate with high immediacy in cultures that frown upon such behaviors, particularly in public settings. In most cases, the key to relational satisfaction is to create a level of immediacy that works for you and the other person.

RESPECT At first glance, respect might seem identical to affinity, but the two attitudes are different.[99] Whereas affinity involves liking, **respect** involves esteem. It's possible to like others without respecting them. For instance, you might like—or even probably love—your two-year-old cousin without respecting her. In the same way, you might have a great deal of affection for some friends, yet not respect the way they behave. The reverse is also true: It's possible to respect people you don't like. You might hold an acquaintance in high esteem for being a hard worker, honest, talented, or clever, yet not particularly enjoy that person's company.

Respect is an extremely important ingredient in good relationships. In fact, it is a better predictor of relational satisfaction than liking, or even loving.[100] Your own experience will show that being respected is sometimes more important than being liked. Think about occasions in school when you were offended because an instructor or fellow students didn't seem to take your comments or questions seriously. The same principle holds on the job, where having your opinions count often means more than being popular. Even in more personal relationships, conflicts often focus on the issue of respect. Being taken seriously is a vital ingredient of self-esteem.

CONTROL A final dimension of relational communication involves **control**—the degree to which the parties in a relationship have the power to influence one another. Some types of control involve *conversation*—who talks the most, who interrupts whom, and who changes the topic most often.[101] Another dimension of control involves *decisions*: Who has the power to determine what will happen in the relationship? What will we do Saturday night? Shall we use our savings to fix up the house or to take a vacation? How much time should we spend together and how much should we spend apart?

Relational problems arise when the people involved don't have similar ideas about the distribution of control. If you and a friend each push for your own idea, problems are likely to arise. (It can also be difficult when neither person wants to make a decision: "What do you want to do tonight?" "I don't know . . . why don't you decide." "No, *you* decide.")

Most healthy relationships handle the distribution of control in a flexible way. Rather than clinging to the lopsidedness of one-up/one-down relationships or the unrealistic equality of complete shared responsibility, partners shift between one-up, one-down, and straight-across roles. John may handle the decisions about car repairs and menu planning, as well as taking the spotlight at parties with their friends. Mary manages the finances and makes most of the decisions about childcare, as well as controlling the conversation when she and John are alone. When a decision is very important to one partner, the other willingly gives in, knowing that the favor will be returned later. When issues are important to both partners, they try to share power equally. But when an impasse occurs, each will make concessions in a way that keeps the overall balance of power equal.

METACOMMUNICATION

Not all relational messages are nonverbal. Social scientists use the term **metacommunication** to describe messages that people exchange, verbally or nonverbally, about their relationship.[102] In other words, metacommunication is communication about communication. Whenever we discuss a relationship with others, we are metacommunicating: "I hate it when you use that tone of voice," or "I appreciate how honest you've been with me." Verbal metacommunication is an essential ingredient in successful relationships. Sooner or later it becomes necessary to talk about what is going on between you and the other person. The ability to focus on the kinds of issues described in this chapter can keep the relationship on track.

Metacommunication is an important method for resolving conflicts in a constructive manner. It provides a way to shift discussion from the content level to relational questions, where the problem often lies. For example, consider the conversation between Macon and Muriel in the In Real Life sidebar on page 297. Imagine how the discussion might have been more productive if they had focused on the relational issue of Macon's commitment to Muriel and her son. By sticking to the content level—the boy's math skill—Macon avoided the kind of metacommunication that is often necessary to keep relationships healthy.

Metacommunication isn't just a tool for handling problems. It is also a way to reinforce the satisfying aspects of a relationship: "I really appreciate it when you compliment me about my work in front of the boss." Comments like this serve two functions.

✔+ IN REAL LIFE

Content and Relational Messages

Both content and relational communication are important, but when each person in a conversation focuses on a different level, problems are likely to arise. In this excerpt from Anne Tyler's novel *The Accidental Tourist,* Muriel tries to turn Macon's content-related remark about her son into a discussion about the future of their relationship. Until Macon and Muriel agree about whether they will focus on content or relational issues, they are likely to remain at an uncomfortable impasse.

"I don't think Alexander's getting a proper education," he said to her one evening.

"Oh, he's okay."

"I asked him to figure what change they'd give back when we bought the milk today, and he didn't have the faintest idea. He didn't even know he'd have to subtract."

"Well, he's only in second grade," Muriel said.

"I think he ought to switch to a private school."

"Private schools cost money."

"So? I'll pay."

She stopped flipping the bacon and looked over at him. "What are you saying?" she asked.

"Pardon?"

"What are you saying, Macon? Are you saying you're committed?"

Macon cleared his throat. He said, "Committed."

"Alexander's got ten more years of school ahead of him. Are you saying you'll be around for all ten years?"

"Um . . ."

"I can't just put him in a school and take him out again with every passing whim of yours."

He was silent.

"Just tell me this much," she said. "Do you picture us getting married sometime? I mean when your divorce comes through?"

He said, "Oh, well, marriage, Muriel . . ."

"You don't, do you. You don't know what you want. One minute you like me and the next you don't. One minute you're ashamed to be seen with me and the next you think I'm the best thing that ever happened to you."

He stared at her. He had never guessed that she read him so clearly.

"You think you can just drift along like this, day by day, no plans," she said. "Maybe tomorrow you'll be here, maybe you won't. Maybe you'll just go on back to Sarah. Oh yes! I saw you at Rose's wedding. Don't think I didn't see how you and Sarah looked at each other."

Macon said, "All I'm saying is—"

"All I'm saying," Muriel told him, "is take care what you promise my son. Don't go making him promises you don't intend to keep."

"But I just want him to learn to subtract!" he said.

First, they let others know that you value their behavior; second, they boost the odds that others will continue the behavior in the future.

Despite the benefits of metacommunication, bringing relational issues out in the open does have its risks. Your desire to focus on the relationship might look like a bad omen—"Our relationship isn't working if we have to keep talking it over."[103] Furthermore, metacommunication does involve a certain degree of analysis ("It seems like you're angry with me"), and some people resent being analyzed. These cautions don't mean that verbal metacommunication is a bad idea. They do suggest, though, that this tool needs to be used carefully.

Summary

People form interpersonal relationships for a variety of reasons. Some reasons involve the degree of interpersonal attraction that communicators feel for one another. Attraction can come from physical appearance, perceived similarity, complementarity, reciprocal attraction, perceived competence, disclosure of personal information, proximity, and rewards.

Two models offer somewhat different perspectives on how communication operates in the development and maintenance of interpersonal relationships. A stage-related model characterizes communication as exhibiting different characteristics as people come together and draw apart. A dialectical model characterizes communicators in every stage as being driven by the need to manage a variety of mutually incompatible needs. Both models share a variety of characteristics, such as the fact that relationships are constantly changing, are affected by culture, and require both maintenance and commitment. When relationships become damaged by transgressions, repair strategies and forgiveness become important skills for both parties.

Communication occurs on two levels: content and relational. Relational communication can be both verbal and nonverbal. Relational messages usually refer to one of four dimensions of a relationship: affinity, immediacy, respect, or control. Metacommunication consists of messages that refer to the relationship between the communicators.

Key Terms

affinity (295)
avoiding (281)
bonding (279)
circumscribing (281)
connection-autonomy dialectic (283)
control (295)
dialectical tensions (283)
differentiating (280)
experimenting (277)

immediacy (295)
initiating (276)
integrating (279)
intensifying (277)
metacommunication (296)
openness-privacy dialectic (284)
predictability-novelty dialectic (285)

relational commitment (290)
relational maintenance (276)
relational transgressions (291)
respect (295)
stagnating (281)
terminating (281)

Online Resources

Now that you have read this chapter, use your Premium Website for *Looking Out/ Looking In* for quick access to the electronic resources that accompany this text. Your Premium Website gives you access to:

- **Study tools** that will help you assess your learning and prepare for exams (*digital glossary, key term flash cards, review quizzes*).

- **Activities and assignments** that will help you hone your knowledge, understand how theory and research applies to your own life (*Invitation to Insight*), consider ethical challenges in interpersonal communication (*Ethical Challenge*), and build your interpersonal communication skills throughout the course (*Skill Builder*). If requested, you can submit your answers to your instructor.

- **Media resources** that will allow you to watch and critique news video and videos of interpersonal communication situations (*In Real Life, interpersonal video simulations*) and download a chapter review so you can study when and where you'd like (*Audio Study Tools*).

This chapter's key terms and search terms for additional reading are featured in this end-of-chapter section, and you can find this chapter's Invitation to Insight and In Real Life activities in the body of the chapter.

Search Terms

When searching online databases to research topics in this chapter, use the following terms (along with this chapter's key terms) to maximize the chances of finding useful information:

apologizing	interpersonal attraction	relational dialectics theory
attractiveness	interpersonal communication	relational satisfaction
forgiveness	interpersonal relations	

Film and Television

You can see the communication principles described in this chapter portrayed in the following films and television programs:

RELATIONAL ATTRACTION

TV Reality Shows

Beginning with *The Real World* in the 1990s, many so-called reality shows have allowed viewers to watch people create, maintain, and end interpersonal relationships in televised episodes. Some of these programs (such as *The Bachelor / Bachelorette* and *Blind Date*) are matchmaking contests in which participants select relational partners. Physical attractiveness plays an important role in initial attraction in these shows, but increased proximity and disclosure allow participants to assess the costs and rewards of an ongoing relationship with their selected partners.

Other reality shows (such as *Survivor* and *Big Brother*) pit participants against each other, with each person vying to not be voted off the show by fellow contestants. In many cases, alliances form based on similarities (women versus men; older participants versus younger ones) and proximity (allied teammates spend more time with each other and often—but not always—grow to like each other). Competence is also a factor in that participants are attracted to those who perform well in the shows' survival contests. And complementarity plays a role when participants' differing talents create "odd bedfellow" partnerships. Although reality shows don't always match most people's real worlds, the interpersonal relationships that develop on these programs often mirror what happens in everyday life.

Waitress (2007) Rated PG-13

Jenna (Keri Russell) is a small-town waitress who creates delicious pies for the customers at Joe's Diner. Unfortunately, she feels stuck in an unhappy marriage to a controlling and abusive husband. Social exchange theory explains why Jenna stays in the relationship, and it also describes why she wants to get out. She is not alone: Virtually every character in the film makes relational choices based on rewards, costs, and comparisons with alternatives. For the folks who frequent Joe's Diner, social exchange is as much a part of their everyday lives as are Jenna's scrumptious pies.

DEVELOPMENTAL MODELS

50 First Dates (2004) Rated PG-13

When Henry Roth (Adam Sandler) meets Lucy Whitmore (Drew Barrymore) for the first time, they hit it off and make plans to see each other the following day. At their next encounter, Lucy has no memory of having met Henry. It turns out that several years earlier Lucy suffered a head injury that causes her, as she sleeps at night, to forget everything that has happened since the day of her accident.

This fictional premise offers an in-depth look at the relational stages of initiating, experimenting, and intensifying—the stages in which Henry and Lucy are stuck. Henry woos Lucy each day with a variety of techniques, some of which work better than others. After a bevy of "first dates," avowed bachelor Henry realizes he needs and wants relational commitment—so he develops a creative method to move the relationship to the integrating and bonding stages.

50 First Dates, like the movie *Groundhog Day*, metaphorically illustrates that relationships can sometimes get stuck in ruts, and that personal growth by one or both parties can be a key for moving relationships forward.

The Break-Up (2006) Rated PG-13

This tragicomedy chronicles the disintegration of the relationship between Brooke Meyers (Jennifer Aniston) and Gary Grobowski (Vince Vaughn) in ways that closely

Intimacy has several dimensions. The first dimension is *physical*. Even before birth, the fetus experiences a physical closeness with its mother that will never happen again, "floating in a warm fluid, curling inside a total embrace, swaying to the undulations of the moving body and hearing the beat of the pulsing heart."[6] As they grow up, fortunate children are continually nourished by physical intimacy: being rocked, fed, hugged, and held. As we grow older, the opportunities for physical intimacy are less regular but still possible and important. Some, but by no means all, physical intimacy is sexual—and it's not always connected with a close relationship. One study revealed that more than half of sexually active teens had partners that they weren't dating, and the majority of the repondents expressed no desire to establish a dating relationship.[7] (See the reading on page 306 for more about "friends with benefits.")

A second dimension of intimacy comes from *intellectual* sharing. Not every exchange of ideas counts as intimacy, of course. Talking about next week's midterm with your professor or classmates isn't likely to forge strong relational bonds. But when you engage another person in an exchange of important ideas, a kind of closeness develops that can be powerful and exciting.

A third dimension of intimacy is *emotional*: exchanging important feelings. Sharing personal information can both reflect and create feelings of closeness. Surprisingly, this sort of personal communication needn't happen in face-to-face encounters. One study revealed that almost two-thirds of a randomly selected group of email users said they had formed a personal relationship with someone they met for the first time through an Internet newsgroup.[8] The electronic friends characterized their relationships in ways that sound remarkably similar to traditional friendships: interdependence (for instance, "We would go out of our way to help each other"), breadth ("Our communication ranges over a wide variety of topics"), depth ("I feel I could confide in this person about almost anything"), and commitment ("I am very committed to maintaining this relationship").

If we define intimacy as being close to another person, then *shared activities* is a fourth dimension that can achieve intimacy. Shared activities can include everything from working side by side at a job to meeting regularly for exercise workouts. When partners spend time together, they can develop unique ways of relating that transform the relationship from an impersonal one to an interpersonal one. For example, both friendships and romantic relationships are often characterized by several forms of play. Partners invent private codes, fool around by acting like other people, tease one another, and play games—everything from having punning contests to arm wrestling.[9] Not all shared activities create and express intimacy, but the bond that comes from experiencing significant events with another person is too frequent and significant to ignore. Companions who have endured physical challenges together—in athletics or emergencies, for example—form a bond that can last a lifetime.

Most teammates agree that working together can create bonds of intimacy unlike any other.

AP Images

Some intimate relationships exhibit all four dimensions: physical, intellectual, emotional, and shared activities. Other intimate relationships exhibit only one or two.

Friends With Benefits, and Stress Too

To some, it may seem like an ideal relationship, less stressful than an affair, longer lived than a fling or that elusive one-night stand. You can even sit around in your sweats and watch "Friends" reruns together, feeling vaguely reassured.

Yet relationships in which close friends begin having sex come with their own brand of awkwardness, according to the first study to explore the dynamics of such pairs, often called friends with benefits, or F.W.B.[a]

The relationships tend to have little romantic passion, but stir the same fears that stalk lovers: namely, that one person will fall harder than the other.

Paradoxically, and perhaps predictably, the study suggests, these physical friendships often occlude one of the emotional arteries of real friendship, openness. Friends who could once talk about anything now have an unstated taboo topic—the relationship itself. In every conversation, there is innuendo; in every room, an elephant.

The research, conducted among Michigan State University students, confirmed that "friends with benefits" have become a cultural signature of today's college and postcollege experience.

Image Source/Getty

"The study really adds to the little we know about these relationships," said Paul Mongeau, a professor of communication at Arizona State University. "One of the most interesting things I get from it," he said, "is this sense that people in these relationships are afraid to develop feelings for the other person, because those feelings might be unreciprocated."

The study surveyed 125 young men and women and found that 60 percent reported having had at least one friend with benefits. One-tenth of these relationships went on to become full-scale romances, the study found. About a third stopped the sex and remained friends, and one in four eventually broke it off—the sex and the friendship. The rest continued as friends-with-benefits relationships.

Dr. Mongeau said the study seemed to have captured the dissonant, circular thinking that characterized what it felt like for a friendship to enter treacherous territory.

"There's clearly a strong desire to be with this other person, who fills important needs," he added. "But at the same time, it's as if I'm saying, 'O.K., I'm not going to get passionately involved—because then it's at risk of being a real romance.' "

Benedict Carey, *The New York Times*

Some relationships aren't intimate in any way. Acquaintances, roommates, and coworkers may never become intimate. In some cases, even family members develop smooth but relatively impersonal relationships.

Not even the closest relationships always operate at the highest level of intimacy. At times you might share all of your thoughts or feelings with a friend, family member, or lover; at other times you might withdraw. You might freely share your feelings about one topic and stay more aloof about another one. The same principle holds for physical intimacy, which waxes and wanes in most relationships.

Although no relationship is *always* intimate, living without *any* sort of intimacy is hardly desirable. For example, people who fear intimacy in dating relationships anticipate less satisfaction in a long-term relationship and report feeling more distant from even longtime dating partners. A great deal of evidence supports the conclusion that fear of intimacy can cause major problems in both creating relationships and sustaining them.[10]

MASCULINE AND FEMININE INTIMACY STYLES

Until recently, most social scientists believed that women are better than men at developing and maintaining intimate relationships.[11] This view grew from the assumption that the disclosure of personal information is the most important ingredient of intimacy. Most research *does* show that women (taken as a group) are somewhat more willing than men to share their thoughts and feelings, although the differences aren't as dramatic as some people might think.[12] In terms of the amount and depth of information exchanged, female–female relationships are at the top of the disclosure list. Male–female relationships come in second, whereas male–male relationships involve less disclosure than any other type. At every age, women disclose more than men, and the information they disclose is more personal and more likely to involve feelings. Although both sexes are equally likely to reveal negative information, men are less likely to share positive feelings.[13]

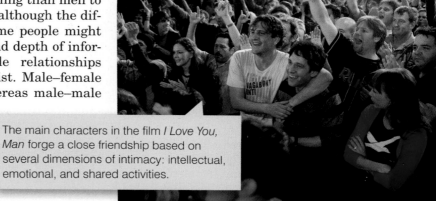

The main characters in the film *I Love You, Man* forge a close friendship based on several dimensions of intimacy: intellectual, emotional, and shared activities.

DREAMWORKS SKG/THE KOBAL COLLECTION

Throughout the mid-1980s, many social scientists interpreted the relative lack of male self-disclosure as a sign that men are unwilling or even unable to develop close relationships. Some argued that the female trait of disclosing personal information and feelings makes women more "emotionally mature" and "interpersonally competent" than men. The title of one book captured this attitude of female superiority and male deficiency: *The Inexpressive Male: A Tragedy of American Society*.[14] Personal-growth programs and self-help books urged men to achieve closeness by learning to open up and share their feelings.

But scholarship conducted in the past two decades has shown that emotional expression isn't the *only* way to develop close relationships. Unlike women, who value personal talk, men grow close to one another by doing things together. In one study, more than 75 percent of the men surveyed said that their most meaningful experiences with friends came from activities other than talking.[15] They reported that, through shared activities, they "grew on one another," developed feelings of interdependence, showed appreciation for one another, and demonstrated mutual liking. Likewise, men regarded practical help as a measure of caring. Research like this shows that, for many men, closeness grows from activities that don't depend heavily on disclosure: A friend is a person who does things *for* you and *with* you.

The same pattern holds in communication between fathers and their sons. Whereas mothers typically express their love toward sons directly through words and nonverbal behaviors like hugs and kisses, fathers are less likely to be so direct with their young adult sons.[16] Instead, they often show their sons affection by doing favors and helping the sons with tasks and challenges.

Actually, biological sex isn't most significant in shaping how men express intimacy. Rather, it's the *gender role* that a particular man adopts. Recall that Chapter 3 explained how both men and women can adopt a gender role—masculine, feminine, or androgynous—that may or may not match their biological sex. Applying this range of styles to intimacy reveals that masculine men are most likely to express caring via helping behaviors and shared activities.[17] Men whose communication style includes some stereotypically feminine elements are more likely to express affection more directly, especially to other men.

The difference between male and female measures of intimacy helps explain some of the stresses and misunderstandings that can arise between the sexes. For example, a woman who looks for emotional disclosure as a measure of affection may overlook an "inexpressive" man's efforts to show he cares by doing favors or spending time together. Fixing a leaky faucet or taking a hike may look like ways to avoid getting close, but to the man who proposes them, they may be measures of affection and bids for intimacy. Likewise, differing ideas about the timing and meaning of sex can lead to misunderstandings. Whereas many women think of sex as a way to express intimacy that has already developed, men are more likely to see it as a way to *create* that intimacy.[18] In this sense, the man who encourages sex early in a relationship or after a fight may not be just a testosterone-crazed lecher: He may view the shared activity as a way to build closeness. By contrast, the woman who views personal talk as the pathway to intimacy may resist the idea of physical closeness before the emotional side of the relationship has been discussed.

As always, it's important to realize that generalizations don't apply to every person. Also, notions of what constitutes appropriate male behavior are changing.[19] For example, one analysis of prime-time television sitcoms revealed that male characters who disclose personal information generally receive favorable responses from other characters.[20] Researchers also note that a cultural shift is occurring in North America in which fathers are becoming more affectionate with their sons than they were in previous generations—although some of that affection is still expressed through shared activities.[21]

CULTURAL INFLUENCES ON INTIMACY

Historically, the notions of public and private behavior have changed dramatically.[22] What would be considered private behavior in modern terms was quite public at times in the past. For example, in sixteenth-century Germany, a new husband and wife were expected to consummate their marriage upon a bed carried among witnesses who would validate the marriage![23] Conversely, at the same time in England as well as in colonial America, the customary level of communication between spouses was rather formal: not much different from the way acquaintances or neighbors spoke to one another.

Even today, the notion of intimacy varies from one culture to another. In one study, researchers asked residents of Britain, Japan, Hong Kong, and Italy to describe their use of thirty-three rules that governed interaction in social relationships.[24] The rules governed a wide range of communication behaviors: everything from using humor to shaking hands to managing money. The results showed that the greatest differences between Asian and European cultures focused on the rules for dealing with intimacy: showing emotions, expressing affection in public, conducting sexual activity, respecting privacy, and so on.

Self-disclosure is especially high in mainstream North American society. In fact, people from the United States are more disclosing than members of any culture studied.[25] They are likely to disclose more about themselves to acquaintances and even strangers. One British travel book captured this tendency to disclose personal information with this tongue-in-cheek description:

> Sit next to an American on an airplane and he will immediately address you by your first name, ask "So how do you like it in the States?," explain his recent divorce in intimate detail, invite you home for dinner, offer to lend you money, and wrap you in a warm hug on parting. This does not necessarily mean he will remember your name the next day.[26]

> The locker room had become a kind of home to me . . . I relax, my concerns lost among relationships that are warm and real, but never intimate, lost among the constants of an athlete's life. The lines of communication are clear and simple. . . . We are at ease in the setting of satin uniforms and shower nozzles.
>
> —*Bill Bradley*

Not all Americans are equally disclosing. Within U.S. culture, intimacy varies from one group to another. For example, working-class African American men are much more disclosing than their white counterparts.[27] By contrast, upwardly mobile black men communicate more like white men with the same social agenda, disclosing less with their male friends.

In some collectivist cultures such as Taiwan and Japan, there is an especially great difference in the way people communicate with members of their in-groups (such as family and close friends) and with their outgroups.[28] They generally do not reach out to outsiders, often waiting until they are properly introduced before entering into a conversation. After they are introduced, they address outsiders with a degree of formality.

✔+ INVITATION TO INSIGHT

Your IQ (Intimacy Quotient)

What is the level of intimacy in your important relationships? Find out by following these directions.

1 Identify the point on each scale below that best describes one of your important relationships.

a. Your level of physical intimacy

1	2	3	4	5
low				high

b. Your amount of emotional intimacy

1	2	3	4	5
low				high

c. The extent of your intellectual intimacy

1	2	3	4	5
low				high

d. The degree of shared activities in your relationship

1	2	3	4	5
low				high

2 Now answer the following questions:

a. What responses to each dimension of intimacy seem most significant to you?

b. Are you satisfied with the intimacy profile outlined by your responses?

c. If you are not satisfied, what steps can you take to change your degree of intimacy?

They go to extremes to hide unfavorable information about in-group members from outsiders, on the principle that one doesn't air dirty laundry in public.

By contrast, members of more individualistic cultures like the United States and Australia make fewer distinctions between personal relationships and casual ones. They act more familiar with strangers and disclose more personal information, making them excellent "cocktail party conversationalists." Social psychologist Kurt Lewin captured the difference nicely when he noted that Americans are easy to meet but difficult to get to know, whereas Germans are difficult to meet but easy to get to know.[29]

Cultural differences in intimacy are becoming less prominent as the world becomes more connected through the media, travel, and technology. For instance, romance and passionate love were once seen as particularly American concepts of intimacy. Recent evidence shows, however, that men and women in a variety of cultures—individualist and collectivist, urban and rural, rich and poverty-stricken—may be every bit as romantic as Americans. These studies suggest that the large differences that once existed between Western and Eastern cultures may be fast disappearing.[30]

INTIMACY IN MEDIATED COMMUNICATION

A few decades ago, it would have been difficult to conceive that the words "computer" and "intimacy" could be positively linked. Computers were viewed as impersonal machines that couldn't transmit important features of human communication, such as facial expression, tone of voice, and touch. However, as Chapters 1 and 2 described, researchers now know that mediated communication can be just as personal as face-to-face interaction. In fact, studies show that relational intimacy may develop *more* quickly through mediated channels than in face-to-face communication,[31] and that IM-ing, blogging, Facebooking, and so on enhance verbal, emotional, and social intimacy in interpersonal relationships.[32]

Your own experience probably supports these claims. The relative anonymity of chat rooms, blogs, and online dating services provides a freedom of expression that might not occur in face-to-face meetings,[33] giving relationships a chance to get started. In addition, instant messaging, emailing, and text messaging offer more constant contact with friends, family, and partners than might otherwise be possible.[34] The potential for developing and maintaining intimate relationships via computer is captured well by one user's comment (which has a fun double meaning): "I've never clicked this much with anyone in my life."[35]

This doesn't mean that all cyber-relationships are (or will become) intimate. Just as in face-to-face relationships, communicators choose varying levels of self-disclosure with their cyberpartners, including the way they manage their privacy settings on social network sites.[36] Some online relationships are relatively impersonal; others are highly interpersonal. In any case, mediated communication is an important component in creating and maintaining intimacy in contemporary relationships.

THE LIMITS OF INTIMACY

It's impossible to have a close relationship with everyone you know—nor is that necessarily desirable. Social psychologist Roy Baumeister makes a compelling case that, on average, most people want four to six close, important relationships in their lives at any given time.[37] While fewer than four such relationships can lead to a sense of social deprivation, he argues that more than six leads to diminishing returns: "It is possible that people simply do not have the time or energy to pursue emotional closeness with more than a half dozen people."

Lonely Gay Teen Seeking Same

Stephen Simpson/Getty

When he was 15, a youth I will refer to by only his first name, Jeffrey, finally admitted to himself that he was gay. Jeffrey knew of no homosexuals in his high school or in his small town in the heart of the South.

It was around this time that Jeffrey first typed the words "gay" and "teen" into a search engine on the computer he'd gotten several months before and was staggered to find himself aswirl in a teeming online gay world, replete with resource centers, articles, advice columns, personals, chat rooms, message boards, porn sites and—most crucially—thousands of closeted and anxious kids like himself. That discovery changed his life.

"The Internet is the thing that has kept me sane," he told me. "I live constantly in fear. I can't be my true self. My mom complains: 'I can see you becoming more detached from us. You're always spending time on the computer.' But the Internet is my refuge."

Jeffrey's computer is in his bedroom, garrisoned inside a thicket of codes and passwords. While he uses the Internet to communicate with high-school friends, he has separate screen names and instant messaging services for these activities. This way, no one from his "straight life" can track his forays into the online gay world.

A brainy, ebullient kid, Jeffrey is an excellent student, active in high-school government, with a number of close friends. He took a girl as his date to homecoming earlier this fall. But his free time belongs largely to the disembodied gay life he pursues online—from 8:30 p.m. to 2 a.m. during the school year, and for even longer stretches in summertime.

For homosexual teenagers with computer access, the Internet has, quite simply, revolutionized the experience of growing up gay. Isolation and shame persist among gay teenagers, of course, but now, along with the inhospitable families and towns in which many find themselves marooned, there exists a parallel online community—real people like them in cyberspace. Gay teenagers surfing the Net can find Web sites packed with information about homosexuality and about local gay support groups and counseling services, along with coming-out testimonials from young people around the world.

"The Internet is an inferior substitute for real-live human beings," says Kevin Jennings, executive director of the Gay, Lesbian and Straight Education Network, a national organization working to end antigay bias in schools. "But it's frankly better than nothing, which is what gay youth have had before."

Online boyfriends and girlfriends were common among the gay teenagers I spoke with. In some cases, the relationships had a sexual component, but what startled me was the level of closeness and intimacy teenagers derived from these cyber relationships. Jeffrey explained how he and C. sustained that intimacy without ever meeting. "We were in search of things we could do and share that were very personal and very intimate," he said. "We'd come up with little nicknames and little jokes between ourselves." They planned to attend the same college, he said, and had even discussed marriage and the adoption of children.

Jeffrey told me once, speaking of his relationship with C.: "I think it's almost like an accelerated relationship. You can't go out to the movies, so there's nothing to fill the space. You have to talk. It creates this intimacy between you; it draws you closer. Our relationship isn't based on looks or financial status or anything physical. There's no space fillers, because you can't just sit there for 15 minutes and not say anything."

Jennifer Egan

Even if we could seek intimacy with everyone we encountered, few of us would want that much closeness. Consider the range of everyday contacts that don't require any sort of intimacy. Some are based on economic transactions (the people at work or the shopkeeper you visit several times a week), some are based on group membership (church or school), some on physical proximity (neighbors, carpooling), and some grow

ON THE JOB

Romance in the Workplace

Mixing work with pleasure can be risky business, especially when it comes to romance. As you read on pages 273–274, proximity often leads to attraction. When coworkers spend many hours interacting with one another, it's no surprise that workplace romances are relatively common. Research on the topic has produced these findings[a]:

- 40 percent of employees in one survey said they had had an office romance at some point in their careers.

- 76 percent of employees in another study said that workplace romances are far more frequent than they were ten years ago.

- 70 percent of human resource professionals said their company had no official verbal or written policy on workplace romance.

Companies that do have policies about office romances discourage them. "Dating on the job is like eating at your desk: Invariably, it's going to get messy," said one researcher. "Workplace romances can seem terrific up front, but if they explode—and they usually do—that shrapnel can land in the workplace and be very distracting."

On a more positive note, 34 percent of people who said they dated a coworker ended up marrying that person. Human resource professionals suggest that if you're going to have a romantic relationship with a coworker, you should know and follow company policies. It's also important to be subtle and discrete about your romance—especially in the office and on company time.

out of third-party connections (mutual friends, child care). Simply engaging in conversational give-and-take with both strangers and acquaintances can be enjoyable.

Some scholars have pointed out that an obsession with intimacy can actually lead to *less* satisfying relationships.[38] People who consider intimate communication as the only kind worth pursuing place little value on relationships that don't meet this standard. This can lead them to regard interaction with strangers and casual acquaintances as superficial, or at best as the groundwork for deeper relationships. When you consider the pleasure that can come from polite but distant communication, the limitations of this view become clear. Intimacy is definitely rewarding, but it isn't the only way of relating to others.

Self-Disclosure in Relationships

One way by which we judge the strength of our relationships is the amount of information we share with others. "We don't have any secrets," some people proudly claim. Opening up certainly is important. As you read in Chapter 1, one ingredient in qualitatively interpersonal relationships is disclosure. Given the obvious importance of self-disclosure, we need to look closer at the subject. Just what is it? When is it desirable? How can it best be done?

The best place to begin is with a definition. **Self-disclosure** is the process of deliberately revealing information about oneself that is significant and would

Radius Images/Jupiter Images

LOOKING AT DIVERSITY

Lexie Lopez-Mayo: Culture, Gender, and Self-Disclosure

Photo courtesy of Lexie Lopez-Mayo

I was born in Mexico and have lived in the U.S. since I was ten. One of the things I've noticed about my Latin friends and family is that we tend to be more expressive and disclosing than many of my Euro-American friends. Of course there are exceptions to that rule, but overall I think people from my cultural background tend to reveal a lot. If we think it, we say it; if we feel it, we express it.

But culture isn't the only issue. Gender also plays a role. In my experience, Latin men easily express positive emotions, but they often hide negative feelings such as hurt and sadness. There's a strong cultural norm for Latinos to be tough, not admit failure, or show weakness—in other words, to be "macho."

I have other opportunities to see how culture and gender affect communication. My husband, who is African-American, is generally a laid-back, quiet kind of guy. However, when he's around his African-American buddies, he's much less reserved and much more disclosing. His language, volume, and mannerisms all change and he becomes a lot more expressive.

And of course, personality plays a role in communication. I know quiet Latinas and disclosing Latinos, so culture doesn't always dictate how people express themselves. In the end, I think the way people communicate is influenced by who they are, where they're from, and whom they're with. In my case, I'm a highly expressive Latina who will tell just about anybody what I think, feel, and want!

not normally be known by others. Let's look closer at this definition. Self-disclosure must be *deliberate*. If you accidentally mention to a friend that you're thinking about quitting a job, or if your facial expression reveals irritation you wanted to hide, that information doesn't qualify as self-disclosure. Besides being deliberate, the information must also be *significant*. Volunteering trivial facts, opinions, or feelings—that you like fudge, for example—hardly counts as disclosure. The third requirement is that the information being disclosed is *not known by others*. There's nothing noteworthy about telling others that you are depressed or elated if they already know that. Table 9.1 describes some characteristics of self-disclosure in personal relationships.

Table 9.1
Characteristics of Self-Disclosure

Characteristic	Comments
Usually occurs in dyads	One-on-one disclosures are usually more comfortable than more public revelations.
Incremental	Small disclosures build confidence to reveal more important information later.
Relatively scarce	Most common early in relationships and at crucial times later. Not frequent in mature relationships (where partners know each other well).
Best in context of positive relationships	Most productive when delivered in a constructive manner, even if the information is difficult. Positive relationships have the strength to handle such revelations.

DEGREES OF SELF-DISCLOSURE

Although our definition of self-disclosure is helpful, it doesn't reveal the important fact that not all self-disclosure is equally revealing—that some disclosing messages tell more about us than others.

Social psychologists Irwin Altman and Dalmas Taylor describe two ways in which communication can be more or less disclosing.[39] Their model of **social penetration** is pictured in Figure 9.1. The first dimension of self-disclosure in this model involves the **breadth** of information volunteered—the range of subjects being discussed. For example, the breadth of disclosure in your relationship with a fellow worker will expand as you begin revealing information about your life away from the job as well as on-the-job information. The second dimension of self-disclosure is the **depth** of information volunteered, the shift from relatively impersonal messages to more personal ones.

Depending on the breadth and depth of information shared, a relationship can be casual or intimate. In a casual relationship the breadth may be great, but not the depth. A more intimate relationship is likely to have high depth in at least one area. The most intimate relationships are those in which disclosure is great in both breadth and depth. Altman and Taylor see the development of a relationship as a progression from the periphery of their model to its center, a process that typically occurs over time. Each of your personal relationships probably has a different combination of breadth of subjects and depth of disclosure. Figure 9.2 pictures a student's self-disclosure in one relationship.

What makes the disclosure in some messages deeper than others? One way to measure depth is by how far it goes on two of the dimensions that define self-disclosure. Some revelations are certainly more *significant* than others. Consider the difference

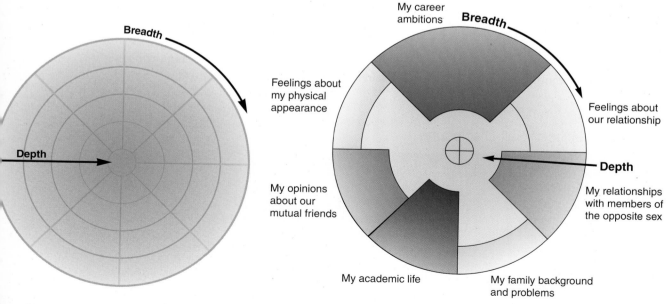

Figure 9.1
Social Penetration Model

Figure 9.2
Sample Model of Social Penetration

between saying "I love my family" and "I love you." Other revelations qualify as deep disclosure because they are *private*. Sharing a secret that you've told to only a few close friends is certainly a revealing act of self-disclosure, but it's even more revealing to divulge information that you've never told anyone.

Another way to measure the depth of disclosure is to look at the types of information we share.

CLICHÉS   **Clichés** are ritualized, stock responses to social situations—virtually the opposite of self-disclosure: "How are you doing?" "Fine!" "We'll have to get together soon."

Although they sound superficial, clichés can also serve as codes for messages we don't usually express directly, such as "I want to acknowledge your presence" (for instance, when two acquaintances walk past each other). Additional unstated messages often contained in clichés are "I'm interested in talking if you feel like it" or "Let's keep the conversation light and impersonal; I don't feel like disclosing much about myself right now." Accompanied by a different set of nonverbal cues, a cliché can say, "I don't want to be impolite, but you'd better stay away from me for now." Whatever valuable functions they may serve, it's clear that clichés don't qualify as self-disclosure.

FACTS   Not all facts qualify as self-disclosure. They must fit the criteria of being intentional, significant, and not otherwise known:

> "This isn't my first try at college. I dropped out a year ago with terrible grades."
> "I'm practically engaged." (*On meeting a stranger while away from home*)
> "That idea that everyone thought was so clever wasn't really mine. I read it in a book last year."

Facts like these can be meaningful in themselves, but they also have a greater significance in a relationship. Disclosing important information suggests a level of trust and commitment to the other person that signals a desire to move the relationship to a new level.

OPINIONS   Still more revealing is the level of opinions:

> "I used to think abortion was no big deal, but lately I've changed my mind."
> "I really like Karen."
> "I don't think you're telling me what's on your mind."

Opinions like these usually reveal more about a person than facts alone. If you know where the speaker stands on a subject, you can get a clearer picture of how your relationship might develop. Likewise, every time you offer a personal opinion, you are giving others information about yourself.

FEELINGS   The fourth level of self-disclosure—and usually the most revealing one—is the realm of feelings. At first glance, feelings might appear to be the same as opinions, but there is a big difference. As we saw, "I don't think you're telling me what's on your mind" is an opinion. Now notice how much more we learn about the speaker by looking at three different feelings that might accompany this statement:

> "I don't think you're telling me what's on your mind, *and I'm suspicious*."
> "I don't think you're telling me what's on your mind, *and I'm angry*."
> "I don't think you're telling me what's on your mind, *and I'm hurt*."

The difference between these four levels of communication suggests why relationships can be frustrating. Sometimes the communicators might never get to the levels of personal opinions and feelings. At other times communicators can spend too much time at these more personal levels. Just as a diet of rich foods can become unappealing if carried to excess, too much personal information can also become unappealing. Another sort of problem occurs when two communicators want to disclose on different levels. If one person is willing to deal only with facts and perhaps an occasional opinion, and the other insists on revealing personal feelings, the results are likely to be uncomfortable for both.

A MODEL OF SELF-DISCLOSURE

One way to look at the important part that self-disclosure plays in interpersonal communication is by means of a device called the **Johari Window**.[40] (The window takes its name from the first names of its creators, Joseph Luft and Harry Ingham.) Imagine a frame like Figure 9.3 that contains everything there is to know about you: your likes and dislikes, your goals, your secrets, your needs—everything.

Of course, you aren't aware of everything about yourself. Like most people, you're probably discovering new things about yourself all the time. To represent this, we can divide the frame containing everything about you into two parts: the part you know about and the part you do not know about, as in Figure 9.4.

We can also divide this frame containing everything about you in another way. In this division, one part represents the things about you that others know, and the second part represents the things about you that you keep to yourself. Figure 9.5 represents this view.

When we impose these two divided frames one atop the other, we have a Johari Window. By looking at Figure 9.6, you can see everything about you divided into four parts.

Figure 9.3

Figure 9.4

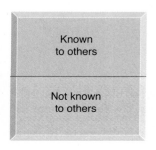

Figure 9.5

	Known to self	Not known to self
Known to others	1 OPEN	2 BLIND
Not known to others	3 HIDDEN	4 UNKNOWN

Figure 9.6

✔+ INVITATION TO INSIGHT

Building a Johari Window

You can use the Johari Window model to examine the level of self-disclosure in your own relationships.

1 Use the format described in this section to draw two Johari Windows representing the relationship between you and one other person. Remember to reverse one of the windows so that your open area and that of the other person face each other.

2 Describe which parts of yourself you keep in the hidden area. Explain your reasons for doing so. Describe the advantages or disadvantages or both of not disclosing these parts of yourself.

3 Look at the blind area of your model. Is this area large or small because of the amount of feedback (much or little) that you get from your partner or because of your willingness to receive the feedback that is offered?

4 Explain whether you are satisfied with the results illustrated by your answers. If you are not satisfied, explain what you can do to remedy the problem.

Part 1 represents the information of which both you and the other person are aware. This part is your *open area*. Part 2 represents the *blind area*: information of which you are unaware but of which the other person is aware. You learn about information in the blind area primarily through feedback from others. Part 3 represents your *hidden area*: information that you know but aren't willing to reveal to others. Items in this hidden area become public primarily through self-disclosure, which is the focus of this chapter. Part 4 represents information that is *unknown* to both you and others. At first the unknown area seems impossible to verify. After all, if neither you nor others know what it contains, how can you be sure it exists? We can deduce its existence because we are constantly discovering new things about ourselves. It is not unusual to discover, for example, that you have an unrecognized talent, strength, or weakness.

BENEFITS AND RISKS OF SELF-DISCLOSURE

Occasionally we may blurt out a piece of revealing personal information, but most of the time our decision to self-disclose is conscious and deliberate. Communication researchers use the term **privacy management** to describe the choices people make to reveal or conceal information about themselves.[41] Those decisions are often made by weighing the pros and cons of self-disclosing. What are the risks and benefits of opening up?

BENEFITS OF SELF-DISCLOSURE   There are several reasons why people choose to share personal information. As you read about each of them, see which apply to you.

Catharsis Sometimes you might disclose information in an effort to "get it off your chest." In a moment of candor you might, for instance, reveal your regrets about having behaved badly in the past. Catharsis can provide mental and emotional relief—when handled properly.[42] Later in this chapter you'll read guidelines for disclosing that increase the odds that you can achieve catharsis in a way that helps, instead of harming relationships.

Reciprocity A well-documented conclusion from research is that one act of self-disclosure begets another.[43] There is no guarantee that your self-disclosures will

"Bob, as a token of my appreciation for this wonderful lunch I would like to disclose to you my income-tax returns for the past four years."

trigger self-disclosures by others, but your own honesty can create a climate that makes others feel safer and perhaps even obligated to match your level of honesty. Sometimes revealing personal information will cause the other person to do so. It's easy to imagine how telling a partner how you feel about the relationship ("I've been feeling bored lately . . .") would generate the same degree of candor ("You know, I've felt the same way!"). Reciprocity doesn't always occur on a turn-by-turn basis. Telling a friend today about your job-related problems might help her feel comfortable opening up to you later about her family history, when the time is right for this sort of disclosure.

Self-Clarification Sometimes you can clarify your beliefs, opinions, thoughts, attitudes, and feelings by talking about them with another person. This sort of "talking the problem out" occurs with psychotherapists, but it also goes on with others, all the way from good friends to bartenders or hairdressers.

Self-Validation If you disclose information ("I think I did the right thing . . .") with the hope of obtaining the listener's agreement, you are seeking validation of your behavior—confirmation of a belief that you hold about yourself. On a deeper level, this sort of self-validating disclosure seeks confirmation of important parts of your self-concept. Self-validation through self-disclosure is an important part of the "coming out" process through which gay people recognize their sexual preference and choose to integrate this knowledge into their personal, family, and social lives.[44]

Identity Management Sometimes we reveal personal information to make ourselves more attractive. Some observers have made this point bluntly, asserting that self-disclosure has become another way of marketing ourselves.[45] Consider two people on their first date. It's not hard to imagine how one or both partners might share personal information to appear more sincere, interesting, sensitive, or interested in the other person. The same principle applies in other situations. A salesperson might say "I'll be honest with you . . ." primarily to show that she is on your side, and a new acquaintance might talk about the details of his past to seem more friendly and likable.

he stripped
the dark circles
of mystery off
revealed his eyes
and thus
he waited
exposed
and I

did sing the song
around
until I found
the chorus
that speaks of windows
looking out means looking in
my friend
   —Ric Masten

Secret Website Gets a Million Hits a Week

When Tina Malament was 17, she felt isolated and alone. Suffering from anorexia, depression, and suicidal thoughts, she lashed out at everyone close to her.

It took an intervention from family and friends for her to realize starving herself to be thin wasn't worth it. Over the next few years, she became serious about her recovery, and she took heart from a blog called PostSecret, where strangers mail in postcards to be posted online every Sunday. On the postcards, people anonymously share their secrets—funny secrets, happy secrets, and secrets filled with anguish, remorse, and pain. It is a place where people can release the secrets that suffocate them. About 1 million people visit the site each week.

The secrets posted on the site vary widely. One reads, "My mom won't tell me who my real father is. I wonder if she told him about me." Another reads: "I am so much bigger than the life I am leading."

Malament, now 21 and living in Colorado, sent in her own secret as well. She took a picture of herself standing in front of another postcard, which had a cupcake crossed out on it. She put her hands across the postcard and wrote across the picture that she was going to win her fight with anorexia. Although her secret wasn't posted, she found the process of making and sending it therapeutic, and the idea that someone else might read it and get something out of it encouraging.

PostSecret's ability to help people inspired Malament to start her own project. When she was a freshman at American University she made a T-shirt with a message about anorexia. On the front was a statistic about anorexics who die from the disorder. The back read: "I refuse to become a statistic." She wore the shirt around campus and eventually to a PostSecret event. At the end she stood up and told her story. Afterward six girls approached her crying and told her how much her story had affected them. They also asked her to make them T-shirts.

Courtney R. Brooks

Relationship Maintenance and Enhancement A large body of research supports the role of self-disclosure in relational success.[46] For example, there is a strong relationship between the quality of self-disclosure and marital satisfaction.[47] The same principle applies in other personal relationships. The bond between grandparents and grandchildren, for example, grows stronger when the honesty and depth of sharing between them are high.[48]

Social Influence Revealing personal information may increase your control over the other person and sometimes over the situation in which you and the other person find yourselves. For example, an employee who tells the boss that another firm has made overtures probably will have an increased chance of getting raises and improvements in working conditions.

Although most of the preceding motives might strike you as being manipulative, they often aren't premeditated. There are cases, however, when an act of self-disclosure is calculated to achieve a desired result. Of course, if a disclosure's hidden motive ever becomes clear to the receiver, the results can be negative.

The motives for disclosing vary from one situation to another, depending on several factors. The strongest factor in why we disclose seems to be how well we know the other person.[49] When the target of disclosure is a friend, the most important reason that people give for disclosing is relationship maintenance and enhancement. In other words, we disclose to friends in order to strengthen the relationship. The second important reason is self-clarification—to sort out confusion to understand ourselves better.

With strangers, reciprocity becomes the most common reason for disclosing. We offer information about ourselves to strangers to learn more about them, so that we can

✔+ INVITATION TO INSIGHT

PostSecret

The website PostSecret allows people to anonymously divulge confidential information about themselves (see the reading on page 319 for a description). Visit the website at http://postsecret.blogspot.com and analyze some of the postcards you find there, using these concepts from the chapter:

1 *Benefits of self-disclosure* (pages 317–320): What are the potential benefits of creating this postcard and sending it to PostSecret? What might be the benefits of actually disclosing this secret without hiding your identity, perhaps to the person(s) involved, a trusted friend, or a counselor?

2 *Risks of self-disclosure* (pages 320–321): Why do you think this person chose to disclose this information anonymously? What risks would

be involved in sharing the information directly with others? Do the risks outweigh the potential benefits?

3 *Ethics of evasion* (page 333): Is there a moral obligation to reveal this information, or do you believe it's acceptable to keep this secret?

4 Using this secret as a case study, explain the role you believe privacy management should play in interpersonal relationships.

decide whether and how to continue the relationship. The second-most common reason is impression formation. In other words, we often reveal information about ourselves to strangers to make ourselves look good. This information is usually positive, at least in the early stages of a friendship.

RISKS OF SELF-DISCLOSURE   While the benefits of disclosing are certainly important, opening up can also involve risks that make the decision to disclose a difficult and sometimes painful one.[50] The risks of self-disclosure fall into several categories.[51]

Rejection   John Powell summed up the risks of disclosing in answering the question that forms the title of his book, *Why Am I Afraid to Tell You Who I Am?*: "I am afraid to tell you who I am, because, if I tell you who I am, you may not like who I am, and that's all I have."[52] The fear of disapproval is powerful. Sometimes it is exaggerated and illogical, but there are real dangers in revealing personal information:

A: *I'm starting to think of you as more than a friend. To tell the truth, I love you.*

B: *I think we should stop seeing one another.*

Negative Impression   Even if disclosure doesn't lead to total rejection, it can create a negative impression.

A: *I've been thinking that we should get another dog.*

B: *To tell you the truth, I really don't like dogs. I haven't said so before because I know how much you love them.*

A: *Really? I can't imagine living with somebody who doesn't love dogs as much as I do.*

Decrease in Relational Satisfaction   Besides affecting others' opinions of you, disclosure can lead to a decrease in the satisfaction that comes from a relationship.

A: *I need to tell you something. I really don't like it when you want to cuddle so much.*

B: *But I want to be close to you. . . .*

Loss of Influence Another risk of disclosure is a potential loss of influence in the relationship. Once you confess a secret weakness, your control over how the other person views you can be diminished.

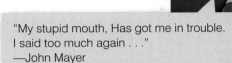

"My stupid mouth, Has got me in trouble. I said too much again . . ."
—John Mayer

Dave Robertson/Masterfile

A: (Manager to employee)
I'd like to give you the weekend off, but to tell you the truth, I don't get to make any judgment calls around here. My boss makes all the decisions. In fact, he doesn't respect my opinions at all.

B: *No kidding. I guess I know who to ask when I want to get anything done around here.*

Hurting the Other Person Even if revealing hidden information leaves you feeling better, it might hurt others—cause them to be upset, for example. It's probably easy to imagine yourself in a situation like this:

A: *I'm so ugly! I can't think of anything that will change the way I look.*

B: *Neither can I.*

GUIDELINES FOR SELF-DISCLOSURE

By now it should be clear that deciding when and how much personal information to disclose is not a simple matter. The following guidelines can help you choose the level of self-disclosure that is appropriate in a given situation.

DO YOU HAVE A MORAL OBLIGATION TO DISCLOSE? Sometimes we are morally obliged to disclose personal information. For example, surveys reveal that a majority of HIV-positive patients believe they have a duty to reveal their status to healthcare providers and partners, even when doing so risks their pride, dignity, and being stigmatized.[53] Despite this prevailing belief, two decades of research has shown that 40 percent of persons testing positive for HIV did not reveal this result to their sexual partners.[54]

IS THE OTHER PERSON IMPORTANT TO YOU? There are several ways in which someone might be important to you. Perhaps you have an ongoing relationship deep enough so that sharing significant parts of yourself justifies keeping your present level of togetherness intact. Or perhaps the person to whom you're considering disclosing is someone with whom you've previously related on a less personal level. But now you see a chance to grow closer, and disclosure may be the path toward developing that personal relationship.

ARE THE AMOUNT AND TYPE OF DISCLOSURE APPROPRIATE? It is usually a mistake to share too much information too soon. Research shows that in most relationships the process of disclosure is gradual.[55] At first, most of the information that is exchanged is relatively superficial. As the parties move into the intensifying,

"Since we're both being honest, I should tell you I have fleas."

integrating, and bonding stages of the relationship, the rate of disclosure begins to grow—but not in all situations. Most conversations—even among friends—focus on everyday, mundane topics and disclose little or no personal information.[56] Even partners in intimate relationships rarely talk about personal information.[57] One good measure of happiness is how well the level of disclosure matches the expectations of communicators. If we get what we believe is a reasonable amount of candor from others, we are satisfied. If they tell us too little—or too much—we become less satisfied.

Besides being moderate in amount, self-disclosure should consist of positive information as well as negative information. Hearing nothing but a string of dismal confessions or complaints can be discouraging. In fact, people who disclose an excess of negative information are often considered "negatively adjusted."[58]

Finally, when considering the appropriateness of disclosure in any relationship, timing is also important. If the other person is tired, preoccupied, or in a bad mood, it may be best to postpone an important conversation.

IS THE RISK OF DISCLOSING REASONABLE?

Take a realistic look at the potential risks of self-disclosure. Even if the probable benefits are great, opening yourself up to almost certain rejection may be asking for trouble. On the other hand, knowing that your partner is trustworthy and supportive makes the prospect of disclosing more reasonable.

Revealing personal thoughts and feelings can be especially risky on the job.[59] The politics of the workplace sometimes requires communicators to keep feelings to themselves in order to accomplish both personal and organizational goals. You might, for example, find the opinions of a boss or customer personally offensive but decide to bite your tongue rather than risk losing your job or goodwill for the company.

In anticipating risks, be sure that you are realistic. It's sometimes easy to indulge in catastrophic expectations and imagine all sorts of disastrous consequences when in fact such horrors are unlikely to occur.

IS THE DISCLOSURE RELEVANT TO THE SITUATION AT HAND?

The kind of disclosure that is often a characteristic of highly personal relationships usually isn't appropriate in less personal settings. For instance, a study of classroom communication revealed that sharing all feelings—both positive and negative—and being completely honest resulted in less cohesiveness than did a "relatively" honest climate in which pleasant but superficial relationships were the norm.[60]

Even in personal relationships—with close friends, family members, and so on—constant disclosure isn't a useful goal. Even during a phase of high disclosure, sharing everything about yourself isn't necessarily constructive. Usually the subject of appropriate self-disclosure involves the relationship rather than personal information. Furthermore, it is usually most constructive to focus your disclosure about the relationship on the "here and now" as opposed to "there and then." "How am I feeling now?" "How are we doing now?" These are appropriate topics for sharing personal thoughts and feelings. At times it's relevant to bring up the past, but only as it relates to what's going on in the present.

The characters in *The Breakfast Club* bared their souls during a Saturday detention session. Their self-disclosure helped forge new relationships, but we're left wondering whether all these confessions could come back to haunt them when they return to their cliques on Monday.

UNIVERSAL/THE KOBAL COLLECTION

WILL THE EFFECT BE CONSTRUCTIVE?

Self-disclosure can be a vicious tool if it's not used carefully. As Chapter 11 explains, every person has a psychological "beltline." Below that beltline are areas about which the person is extremely sensitive. Below-the-belt jabs are a powerful way to disable another person, though usually at great cost to the relationship. It's important to consider the effects of your candor before opening up to others. Comments such as "I've always thought you were pretty unintelligent" or "Last year I made love to your best friend" may sometimes resolve old business and thus be constructive, but they also can be devastating—to the listener, to the relationship, and to your self-esteem.

IS THE SELF-DISCLOSURE CLEAR AND UNDERSTANDABLE?

When you are expressing yourself to others, it's important that you reveal yourself in a way that's intelligible. This means using the guidelines for clear language outlined in Chapter 5. For instance, it's far better to describe another's behavior by saying, "When you don't answer my phone calls or drop by to visit anymore . . ." than to complain vaguely, "When you avoid me. . . ."

IS THE SELF-DISCLOSURE RECIPROCATED?

The amount of personal information you reveal will usually depend on how much the other person reveals. As a rule, disclosure is a two-way street. For example, couples are happiest when their levels of openness are roughly equal.[61]

There are a few times when one-way disclosure is acceptable. Most of them involve formal, therapeutic relationships in which a client approaches a trained professional with the goal of resolving a problem. For instance, you wouldn't necessarily expect to hear about your doctor's personal ailments during a physical checkup—although it's been known to happen, sometimes to the chagrin of the patient.[62]

✔+ SKILL BUILDER

Appropriate Self-Disclosure

Use the guidelines on pages 321–323 to develop one scenario where you might reveal a self-disclosing message. Create a message of this type, and use the information in this chapter to discuss the advantages and disadvantages of sharing this message.

✔+ IN REAL LIFE

Appropriate and Inappropriate Self-Disclosure

Ramon has been working in an entry-level sales job for almost a year after graduating from the university. He likes the company, but he is growing frustrated at his lack of advancement. After much thought, he decides to share his concerns with his boss, Julie. Notice that Ramon's self-disclosure has the potential to enhance or jeopardize personal goals and relationships, depending on how well it follows the guidelines on pages 321–323.

Jason Harris/©Cengage Learning

Ramon: Do you have a few minutes to talk?

Julie: Sure, no problem. Come on in.

Ramon: Do you mind if we close the door?

Julie: *(Looking a bit surprised)* Sure.

Ramon: I'd like to talk to you about the future.

Julie: The future?

Ramon: Well, it's been over a year since I started to work here. One of the things you told me in the interview back then was that people move up fast here . . .

Julie: Well, . . .

Ramon: . . . and I'm confused because I've been doing pretty much the same work since I was hired.

Julie: Well, we do think a lot of your work.

Ramon: I'm glad to hear that. But I'm starting to wonder how much of a chance I'll have to grow with this company. *(Ramon is disclosing his concerns about career advancement—a very appropriate topic to raise with his boss. There is some risk in this sort of disclosure, but given Ramon's apparently good standing with his boss, it seems reasonable.)*

Julie: I can understand that you're anxious about taking on more responsibility. I can tell you that you've got a good shot at advancing, if you can just hang in there for a little while.

Ramon: *(Impatiently)* That sounds good, but I've been waiting—longer than I expected to. I'm starting to wonder if some of the things I've heard around here are true.

Julie: *(Suspiciously)* What kinds of things are you talking about, Ramon?

Ramon: Well, Bill and Latisha were telling me about some people who left here because they didn't get the promotions they were promised. *(Ramon discloses information that was told to him*

Alternatives to Self-Disclosure

Although self-disclosure plays an important role in interpersonal relationships, it isn't the only type of communication available. To understand why complete honesty isn't always an easy or ideal choice, consider some familiar dilemmas:

A new acquaintance is much more interested in becoming friends than you are. She invites you to a party this weekend. You aren't busy, but you don't want to go. What would you say?

Your boss asks you what you think of his new wardrobe. You think it's cheap and flashy. Would you tell him?

You're attracted to your best friend's mate, who has confessed that s/he feels the same way about you. You both agreed that you won't act on your feelings and that even bringing up the subject would make your friend feel terribly insecure. Now

in confidence, jeopardizing the standing of two coworkers with Julie.)

Julie: *(Firmly)* Ramon, I'm sure you understand that I can't talk about personnel decisions involving former employees. I can tell you that we try to give people all the challenges and rewards they deserve, though it can take a while.

Ramon: A year seems like more than "a while." I'm starting to think this company is more interested in having somebody with a Hispanic name on the payroll than giving me a real shot at promotion. *(Ramon's concern may be legitimate, but the sarcastic tone of his disclosure isn't constructive.)*

Julie: Look: I probably shouldn't be saying this, but I'm as frustrated as you are that it's taking so long to get a promotion arranged for you. I can tell you that there will be some personnel changes soon that will give you a good chance to make the kinds of changes you want. I think you can expect to see some changes in the next six weeks. *(Julie offers two items of self-disclosure that encourage Ramon to reciprocate.)*

Ramon: That's really good to hear! I have to tell you that I've started to think about other career options. Not because I want to leave here, but because I just can't afford to stand still. I really need to start bringing home more money. I don't want to be one of those losers who still can't

afford to buy his own house by the time he's forty. *(Ramon makes a big mistake disclosing his opinion about home ownership—a topic that has no relevance to the discussion at hand.)*

Julie: Gee, I'm still renting . . .

Ramon: Oh, I didn't mean that the way it sounded . . . *(But the damage from the inappropriate disclosure is already done.)*

Julie: Anyway, I'm glad you let me know about your concerns. I hope you can hang in there for just a little while longer.

Ramon: Sure. Six weeks, huh? I'll keep an eye on the calendar!

After the conversation, Julie still thinks Ramon is a candidate for promotion, but some of his inappropriate disclosures have left her with doubts about his maturity and good judgment, which she didn't have before they spoke. Julie makes a mental note to keep an eye on Ramon and to reconsider the amount of responsibility she gives him until he has demonstrated the ability to share his personal feelings and concerns more constructively.

Communication Scenarios

To see and analyze a video of the conversation between Ramon and Julie, go to your Premium Website for Looking Out/Looking In, *access "In Real Life Communication Scenarios," and then click on "Appropriate and Inappropriate Self-Disclosure."*

your friend has asked whether you're attracted at all to the mate. Would you tell the truth?

You've just been given a large, extremely ugly painting as a gift by a relative who visits your home often. How would you respond to the question, "Where will you put it?"

Situations like these highlight some of the issues that surround deceptive communication. Our moral education and common sense lead us to abhor anything less than the truth. Ethicists point out that the very existence of a society seems based on a foundation of truthfulness.[63] Although honesty is desirable in principle, it can have potentially unpleasant consequences. It's tempting to avoid situations where self-disclosure would be difficult, but examples like the preceding ones show that evasion isn't always possible. Research and personal experience show that communicators—even those with the best intentions—aren't always completely honest when they find themselves in situations in which honesty would be uncomfortable.[64] Four common alternatives to self-disclosure are silence, lying, equivocating, and hinting. We will look closer at each one.

SILENCE

One alternative to self-disclosure is to keep your thoughts and feelings to yourself. You can get a sense of how much you rely on silence instead of disclosing by keeping a record of when you do and don't express your opinions. You're likely to find that withholding thoughts and feelings is a common approach for you. Silence can be in the best interest of both you and the other person. Telling the whole truth may be honest, but it can jeopardize you, the other person, and your relationship. (See the risks of self-disclosure outlined on pages 320–321.)

As the Ethical Challenge on page 332 shows, many ethicists argue that silence isn't necessarily dishonorable, especially when total candor is likely to cause pain. Most thoughtful communicators would keep quiet rather than blurt out unsolicited opinions like "You look awful" or "You talk too much." Social scientists have found that people often make distinctions between "lies of omission" and "lies of commission"—and that saying nothing (omission) is usually judged less harshly than telling an outright lie (commission).[65]

LYING

To most of us, lying appears as a breach of ethics. Although lying to gain unfair advantage over an unknowing victim seems clearly wrong, another kind of mistruth—the "benevolent lie"—isn't so easy to dismiss as completely unethical. A **benevolent lie** is defined (at least by the teller) as unmalicious, or even helpful, to the person to whom it is told. Whether or not they are innocent, benevolent lies are quite common, both in face-to-face and mediated relationships.[66] In several studies spanning four decades, a significant majority of people surveyed acknowledge that even in their closest relationships, there are times when lying is justified.[67] In one study, 130 subjects were asked to keep track of the truthfulness of their everyday conversational statements.[68] Only 38.5 percent of these statements—slightly more than one-third—proved to be totally honest. In another experiment, subjects recorded their conversations over a two-day period and later counted their own deceptions. The average lie rate: three fibs for every ten minutes of conversation.[69]

REASONS FOR LYING   What reasons do people give for being deceitful? When subjects in one study were asked to provide a lie-by-lie account of their reasons for concealing or distorting the truth, five major reasons emerged[70]:

1. *To save face.* More than half of the lies were justified as a way to prevent embarrassment. Such lying is often given the approving label "tact" and is used "when it would be unkind to be honest, but dishonest to be kind."[71] Sometimes a face-saving lie protects the recipient, as when you pretend to remember someone at a party in order to save that person from the embarrassment of being forgotten. At other times a lie protects the teller from humiliation. You might, for instance, cover up your mistakes by blaming them on outside forces: "You didn't receive the check? It must have been delayed in the mail."

We may have been taught that lying is wrong, but less-than-truthful communication is common in even the closest relationships.

Boden/Ledingham/Masterfile

2. *To avoid tension or conflict.* Sometimes it seems worthwhile to tell a small lie to prevent a large conflict. You might, for example, say you're not annoyed at a friend's teasing in order to prevent the hassle that would result if you expressed your annoyance. It's often easier to explain your behavior in dishonest terms than to make matters worse. You might avoid further tension by saying, "I'm not mad at you; it's just been a tough day."

> The injunction against bearing false witness, branded in stone and brought down by Moses from the mountaintop, has always provoked ambivalent, conflicting emotions. On the one hand, nearly everyone condemns lying. On the other, nearly everyone does it every day. How many of the Ten Commandments can be broken so easily and with so little risk of detection over the telephone?
>
> —*Paul Gray*

3. *To guide social interaction.* Sometimes we lie to make everyday relationships run smoothly. You might, for instance, pretend to be glad to see someone you actually dislike or fake interest in a dinner companion's boring stories to make a social event pass quickly. Children who aren't skilled or interested in these social lies are often a source of embarrassment for their parents.

4. *To expand or reduce relationships.* Some lies are designed to make relationships grow: "You're going downtown? I'm headed that way. Can I give you a ride?" In one study, a majority of college students (both men and women) willingly lied to improve their chances of getting a date with an attractive partner. Their exaggerations and untruths covered a wide range of topics, including their attitudes about love, personality traits, income, past relationships, career skills, and intelligence—all in the direction of making themselves more similar to the attractive prospects.[72]

   Sometimes we tell untruths to *reduce* interaction with others: "I really have to go. I should be studying for a test tomorrow." At other times people lie to end a relationship entirely: "You're really great, but I'm just not ready to settle down yet."

5. *To gain power.* Sometimes we tell lies to show that we're in control of a situation. Turning down a last-minute request for a date by claiming you're busy can be one way to put yourself in a one-up position, saying in effect, "Don't expect me to sit around waiting for you to call." Lying to get confidential information—even for a good cause—also falls into the category of lying to gain power.

This five-part scheme isn't the only way to categorize lies. The taxonomy outlined in Table 9.2 is more complicated and covers some types of lies that don't fit into the previous categories. Exaggerations, for example, are lies told to boost the effect of a story. In exaggerated tales the fish grow larger, hikes grow longer and more strenuous, and so on. The stories may be less truthful, but they become more interesting—at least to the teller.

Most people think that benevolent lies are told for the benefit of the recipient. In the study cited earlier, the majority of subjects claimed that such lying is "the right thing to do." Other research paints a less flattering picture of who benefits most from lying. One study found that two out of every three lies are told for "selfish reasons."[73] A look at Table 9.2 seems to make this figure too conservative. Of the 322 lies recorded, 75.8 percent were for the benefit of the liar. Less than 22 percent were for the benefit of the person hearing the lie, whereas a mere 2.5 percent were intended to aid a third party.

Before we become totally cynical, however, the researchers urge a charitable interpretation. After all, most intentional communication behavior—truthful or not—is designed to help the speaker achieve a goal. Therefore, it's unfair to judge benevolent

Table 9.2

Types of Lies and Their Frequency

	Benefit Self	Benefit Other	Benefit Third Party
Basic Needs	68	1	1
A. Acquire resources	29	0	0
B. Protect resources	39	1	1
Affiliation	128	1	6
A. Positive	65	0	0
1. Initiate interaction	8	0	0
2. Continue interaction	6	0	0
3. Avoid conflict	48	0	0
4. Obligatory acceptance	3	0	0
B. Negative	43	1	3
1. Avoid interaction	34	1	3
2. Leave-taking	9	0	0
C. Conversational control	20	0	3
1. Redirect conversation	3	0	0
2. Avoid self-disclosure	17	0	3
Self-Esteem	35	63	1
A. Competence	82	6	0
B. Taste	0	18	1
C. Social desirability	27	19	0
Other	13	5	0
A. Dissonance reduction	3	5	0
B. Practical joke	2	0	0
C. Exaggeration	8	0	0

From "White Lies in Interpersonal Communication: A Taxonomy and Preliminary Investigation of Social Motivations" (1984). Western Journal of Speech Communication, 48, 315.

lies more harshly than other types of messages. If we define selfishness as the extent to which some desired resource or interaction is denied to the person hearing the lie or to a third party, then only 111 lies (34.5 percent) can be considered truly selfish. This figure may be no worse than the degree of selfishness in honest messages.

EFFECTS OF LIES What are the consequences of discovering you've been lied to? In an interpersonal relationship, the discovery can be traumatic. As we grow closer to others, our expectations about their honesty grow stronger. After all, discovering that you've been lied to requires you to redefine not only the lie you just discovered, but also many of the messages you previously took for granted. Was last week's compliment really sincere? Was your joke really funny, or was the other person's laughter a put-on? Does the other person care about you as much as he or she claimed?

Research has shown that lying does, in fact, threaten relationships.[74] Not all lies are equally devastating, however. Research suggests that a liar's motives make a significant difference in whether the deception is perceived as acceptable by others.[75] If a lie

Is Misleading Your Spouse Fraud or Tact?

When their marriage of more than a decade ended in divorce, Anaheim banker Ronald Askew sued his ex-wife for fraud because she admittedly concealed the fact that she had never felt sexually attracted to him. On Wednesday, an Orange County jury agreed, and ordered Bonnette Askew to pay her ex-husband $242,000 in damages.

© Lou Brooks

"I'm astonished by this verdict and I've looked at divorce in 62 societies," said Helen Fisher, an American Museum of Natural History anthropologist who authored the recent book *Anatomy of Love: The Natural History of Monogamy, Adultery and Divorce.*

Bonnette Askew, 45, acknowledged in court that she had never been sexually attracted to her husband. But she said she always loved him and noted that their marriage was not sexless and that they had two children together.

She first admitted her lack of sexual desire for him during a joint therapy session in 1991. "I guess he confused sex with love," Bonnette Askew said, adding that she concealed her lack of desire because she "didn't want to hurt his male ego."

But Ronald Askew, 50, said his lawsuit had more to do with honesty and integrity than sex. He felt deceived, especially because he said he repeatedly asked her before their marriage to be honest with him and reveal any important secrets.

If Ronald Askew believes total honesty is the foundation of good marriages, Fisher has a message for him: "Grow up."

"Since when is anyone truly honest with anyone?" Fisher said. "Did this man really want her to say: 'You're short, fat and you're terrible in bed'? Much of the world is amazed at what they see as brutal honesty in America. She was operating on an entirely different set of social values, which much of the world operates on—delicacy as opposed to brutal honesty."

Maria Cone

---

appears to be self-serving and exploitive, it will most likely be treated as a relational transgression. On the other hand, if a mistruth seems aimed at sparing another's feelings, the chances of being forgiven increase.

Feelings like dismay and betrayal are greatest when the relationship is most intense, when the importance of the subject is high, and when there is previous suspicion that the other person isn't being completely honest. Of these three factors, the importance of the information lied about proved to be the key factor in provoking a relational crisis. We may be able to cope with "misdemeanor" lying, but "felonies" are a grave threat. In fact, the discovery of major deception can lead to the end of the relationship. More than two-thirds of the subjects in one study reported that their relationship had ended because they discovered a lie. Furthermore, they attributed the breakup directly to the lie.

The lesson here is clear: Lying about major parts of your relationship can have the gravest consequences. If preserving a relationship is important, honesty—at least about important matters—really does appear to be the best policy.

EQUIVOCATING

Lying isn't the only alternative to self-disclosure. When faced with the choice between lying and telling an unpleasant truth, communicators can—and often do—equivocate. As Chapter 5 explained, *equivocal language* has two or more equally plausible meanings. Sometimes people send equivocal messages without meaning to, resulting in confusion. "I'll meet you at the apartment" could refer to more than one place. But at other times we are deliberately vague. For instance, when a friend asks what you think of an awful outfit, you could say "It's really unusual—one of a kind!" Likewise, if you are too angry to accept a friend's apology but don't want to appear petty, you might say, "Don't worry about it." One humorous set of suggestions shows how equivocation can help a reluctant business contact provide ambiguous references for an incompetent job applicant:

> For a lazy worker: "You will be lucky to get this person to work for you."
>
> For someone with no talent: "I recommend this candidate with no qualifications."
>
> For a candidate who should not be hired under any circumstances: "Waste no time hiring this person."

The value of equivocation becomes clear when you consider the alternatives. Consider the dilemma of what to say when you've been given an unwanted present—an ugly painting, for example—and the giver asks what you think of it. How can you respond? On one hand, you need to choose between telling the truth and lying. On the other hand, you have a choice of whether to make your response clear or vague. Figure 9.7 displays these choices. After considering the choices, it's clear that the first—an equivocal, true response—is far preferable to the others in several respects.

- *It spares the receiver from embarrassment.* For example, rather than flatly saying "No" to an unappealing invitation, it may be kinder to say, "I have other plans"— even if those plans are to stay home and watch TV.

- *It can save face for both the sender and receiver.* Because equivocation is often easier to take than the cold, hard truth, it spares the teller from feeling guilty. It's less taxing on the conscience to say "I've never tasted anything like this" than to say "This meal tastes terrible," even though the latter comment is more precise. Few people want to lie, and equivocation provides an alternative to deceit.

  A study by communication researcher Sandra Metts and her colleagues shows how equivocation can save face in difficult situations.[76] Several hundred college students were asked how they would turn down unwanted sexual overtures from a person whose feelings were important to them: either a close friend, a prospective date, or a dating partner. The majority of students chose a diplomatic reaction ("I just don't think I'm ready for this right now") as being more face-saving and comfortable than a direct statement ("I just don't feel sexually attracted to you"). The diplomatic reaction seemed sufficiently clear

Equivocal

OPTION I: (Equivocal, True Message) "What an unusual painting! I've never seen anything like it!"	OPTION II: (Equivocal, False Message) "Thanks for the painting. I'll hang it as soon as I can find just the right place."
OPTION III: (Clear, True Message) "It's just not my kind of painting. I don't like the colors, the style, or the subject."	OPTION IV: (Clear, False Message) "What a beautiful painting! I love it."

True ... False

Clear

Figure 9.7

Dimensions of Truthfulness and Equivocation

From J. Bavelas, et al. (1990). *Equivocal Communication.* Newbury Park, CA: Sage.

to get the message across but not so blunt as to embarrass or even humiliate the other person.

- *It provides an alternative to lying.* If a potential employer asks about your grades during an interview, you would be safe saying "I had a B average last semester," even though your overall grade average is closer to C. The statement isn't a complete answer, but it is honest as far as it goes. As one team of researchers put it, "equivocation is neither a false message nor a clear truth, but rather an alternative used precisely when both of these are to be avoided."[77]

Given these advantages, it's not surprising that most people will usually choose to equivocate rather than tell a lie. In a series of experiments, subjects chose among telling a face-saving lie, telling the truth, and equivocating. Only 6 percent chose the lie, and only between 3 and 4 percent chose the hurtful truth. By contrast, more than 90 percent chose the equivocal response.[78] People *say* they prefer truth telling to equivocating, but given the choice, they prefer to finesse the truth.[79]

HINTING

Hints are more direct than equivocal statements. Whereas an equivocal statement isn't necessarily aimed at changing others' behavior, a hint does aim to get a desired response from others.[80]

Direct Statement	***Face-Saving Hint***
I'm too busy to continue with this conversation.	I know you're busy; I better let you go.
Please don't smoke in here because it's bothering me.	I'm pretty sure that smoking isn't permitted here.
I'd like to invite you out for lunch, but I don't want to risk a "no" answer.	Gee, it's almost lunchtime. Have you ever eaten at that new Italian restaurant around the corner?

As Emily Dickinson's poem on this page suggests, hinting can spare others discomfort that comes with the undiluted truth. The face-saving value of hints explains why communicators are more likely to be indirect than fully disclosing when they deliver a potentially embarrassing message.[81] The success of a hint depends on the other person's ability to pick

Tell all the Truth but tell it slant—

Success in Circuit lies

Too bright for our infirm Delight

The Truth's superb surprise

—*Emily Dickinson*

ETHICAL CHALLENGE

Must We Always Tell the Truth?

"Is there really a Santa Claus?"

"Am I talking too much?"

"Isn't this the cutest baby you've ever seen?"

"Was it good for you?"

Questions like these often seem to invite answers that are less than totally honest. The research summarized on pages 326–327 reveals that, at one time or another, virtually everyone avoids telling the complete truth. Sometimes we remain silent, sometimes we tell benevolent lies, and sometimes we equivocate. We seem to be caught between the time-honored commandment "Thou shall not lie" and the fact that everybody *does* seem to bend the truth, if only for altruistic reasons. What, then, are the ethics of honesty?

Philosopher Immanuel Kant had a clear answer: We may be able to evade unpleasant situations by keeping quiet, but we must always tell the complete truth when there is no way to avoid speaking up. He said that "truthfulness in statements which cannot be avoided is the formal duty of an individual . . . however great may be the disadvantage accruing to himself or another." Kant's unbending position didn't make any exception for lies or equivocations told in the best interests of the receiver. In his moral code, lying is wrong—period.

Kant's unbending position grows from his *categorical imperative:* the dictum that the morality of an action is determined by whether it could be practiced universally. At one level, the categorical imperative demands that we ask, "What if everybody lied?" Because it would be intolerable—even impossible— to function in a world in which everyone lied, we have an ethical obligation to refrain from lying, even once.

Not all ethicists have shared Kant's rigid standards of truth telling. Utilitarian philosophers claim that the way to determine the morality of a behavior is to explore whether it leads to the greatest happiness for the greatest number of people. Philosopher Sissela Bok

adopts this stance when she argues that the morality (or immorality) of an untruth can be calculated only by comparing its effect to that of telling the unvarnished truth. She offers some circumstances in which deception may be justified: doing good, avoiding harm, and protecting a larger truth.

Despite her tolerance for some lies, Bok doesn't consider benign falsehoods to be just as acceptable as the truth. Her *principle of veracity* asserts that "truthful statements are preferable to lying in the absence of special considerations." In other words, she encourages truth telling whenever possible. Of course, the phrase "whenever possible" is open to interpretation, and Bok is realistic enough to recognize that liars are prone to self-deceptive justifications. For this reason, she tempers her utilitarian position with a *test of publicity.* She suggests that we ask how others would respond if they knew that we were being untruthful. If most disinterested observers with all the facts supported untruthful speech as the best course, then it passes the test of publicity.

Submit your case for avoiding the truth to a "court of self-disclosure":

1. Recall recent situations in which you have used each of the following evasive approaches: lying, equivocating, and hinting.

2. Write an anonymous description of each situation, including a justification for your behavior, on a separate sheet of paper. Submit the cases to a panel of "judges" (most likely fellow students), who will evaluate the morality of these decisions.

Read Kant's own words on truth telling in the following works: "On a Supposed Right to Lie from Altruistic Motives," in Lewis White Beck, trans. and ed., Critique of Practical Reason and Other Writings in Moral Philosophy *(Chicago: University of Chicago Press, 1964); and H. J. Paton, trans.,* Groundwork of the Metaphysics of Morals *(New York: Harper Torchbooks, 1964). Bok's arguments are detailed in her book* Lying: Moral Choice in Public and Private Life *(New York: Vintage, 1979). See also Charles Fried's essay "The Evil of Lying," in* Right and Wrong *(Cambridge, MA: Harvard University Press, 1978).*

up the unexpressed message. Your subtle remarks might go right over the head of an insensitive receiver—or one who chooses not to respond. If this happens, you may decide to be more direct. If the costs of a direct message seem too high, however, you can withdraw without risk.

THE ETHICS OF EVASION

It's easy to see why people choose hints, equivocations, and benevolent lies instead of complete self-disclosure. These strategies provide a way to manage difficult situations that is easier than the alternatives for both the speaker and the receiver of the message. In this sense, successful liars, equivocators, and hinters can be said to possess a certain kind of communicative competence. On the other hand, there are certainly times when honesty is the right approach, even if it's painful. At times like these, evaders could be viewed as lacking the competence or the integrity to handle a situation most effectively.

Are hints, benevolent lies, and equivocations ethical alternatives to self-disclosure? Some of the examples in these pages suggest that the answer is a qualified "yes." Many social scientists and philosophers agree. As the Ethical Challenge on page 332 shows, some argue that the morality of a speaker's *motives* for lying, not the lie itself, ought to be judged, and others ask whether the *effects* of a lie will be worth the deception.

Another measure of the acceptability of some lies is the fact that most people are willing to accept them without challenging the person who they know is lying. In fact, there are some circumstances when lies are judged as *more* appropriate than the undiluted truth.[82] For example, there are times when we are likely to not challenge statements that we know are untruthful, such as the following:[83]

- When we expect others tell a fib. *(You listen with amusement to a friend's or relative's tall tales, even though you know they are exaggerations.)*

- When the lie is mutually advantageous. *(A fellow employee's self-serving account of a job mix-up might get you off the hook, too.)*

- When a lie helps us avoid embarrassment. *(You assure your host that a meal was delicious, even though it tasted awful.)*

- When the lie helps us avoid confronting an unpleasant truth. *(A family acts as if there is nothing wrong when they know that one member is an alcoholic.)*

- When we have asked the other person to lie. *(One partner tells the other: "If you're ever unfaithful to me, I don't want to know about it.")*

In light of these facts, perhaps the right questions to ask are whether an indirect message is truly in the interests of the receiver and whether this sort of evasion is the only, or the best, way to behave in a given situation.

Summary

Intimacy in interpersonal relationships has four dimensions: physical, intellectual, emotional, and shared activities. Both gender and culture affect the way intimacy is expressed. Intimacy can occur in mediated communication as well as in face-to-face interaction. Not all relationships are intimate; communicators must make choices about when, where, and with whom they will be intimate.

An important issue in interpersonal relationships is the appropriate type and degree of self-disclosure: honest, revealing messages about the self that are intentionally directed toward others. Several factors govern whether a communicator will be judged as being a high- or low-level discloser. The social penetration model describes two dimensions of self-disclosure: breadth and depth. Disclosure of feelings is usually more revealing than disclosure of opinions, and disclosure of opinions is usually more revealing than disclosure of facts. Clichés are the least revealing.

The Johari Window model is a useful way to illustrate self-disclosure. A window representing a single person can illustrate the amount of information that an individual reveals to others, hides, is blind to, and is unaware of. Communicators disclose personal information for a variety of reasons and benefits: catharsis, reciprocity, self-clarification, self-validation, identity management, relationship maintenance and enhancement, and social influence. The risks of self-disclosure include the possibility of rejection, making a negative impression, a decline in relational satisfaction, a loss of influence, and hurting the other person.

Four alternatives to revealing personal facts, feelings, and opinions are silence, lying, equivocating, and hinting. Nonmalicious benevolent lies serve a variety of functions: saving face for the sender or receiver, avoiding tension or conflict, guiding social interaction, managing relationships, and gaining power. Equivocal messages are an attractive alternative to lies and direct honesty. Hints, which are more direct than equivocal statements, are used primarily to avoid embarrassment. Lies, equivocations, and hints may be ethical alternatives to self-disclosure; however, whether they are depends on the speaker's motives and the effects of the deception.

Key Terms

benevolent lie (326)
breadth (314)
clichés (315)

depth (314)
intimacy (305)
Johari Window (316)

privacy management (317)
self-disclosure (312)
social penetration (314)

Online Resources

Now that you have read this chapter, use your Premium Website for *Looking Out/ Looking In* for quick access to the electronic resources that accompany this text. Your Premium Website gives you access to:

- **Study tools** that will help you assess your learning and prepare for exams (*digital glossary, key term flash cards, review quizzes*).

- **Activities and assignments** that will help you hone your knowledge, understand how theory and research applies to your own life (*Invitation to Insight*), consider ethical challenges in interpersonal communication (*Ethical Challenge*), and build your interpersonal communication skills throughout the course (*Skill Builder*). If requested, you can submit your answers to your instructor.

- **Media resources** that will allow you to watch and critique news video and videos of interpersonal communication situations (*In Real Life, interpersonal video simulations*) and download a chapter review so you can study when and where you'd like (*Audio Study Tools*).

This chapter's key terms and search terms for additional reading are featured in this end-of-chapter section, and you can find this chapter's Invitation to Insight, Ethical Challenge, Skill Builder, and In Real Life activities in the body of the chapter.

Search Terms

When searching online databases to research topics in this chapter, use the following terms (along with this chapter's key terms) to maximize the chances of finding useful information:

deception	personal relationships	social networks
honesty	self-presentation	truthfulness
identity management		

Film and Television

You can see the communication principles described in this chapter portrayed in the following films:

THE NEED FOR INTIMACY

About a Boy (2002) Rated PG-13

Bachelor Will Freeman (Hugh Grant) prides himself on being free of any emotional commitments. "I'm on my own," Will proclaims. "There's just me. I'm not putting myself first, because there isn't anybody else there." Marcus (Nicholas Hoult), who is twelve, also has little intimacy in his life, but not by choice. His bad haircut, nerdy clothing, and visible love for his mother make him a constant target of teasing by the kids at school. Marcus has no friends, but plenty of pluck and determination.

A series of events leads Will into Marcus's life, where both decide they can use each other for their own devices. Marcus wants Will to marry his mother; Will wants Marcus to feign the role of his son to help Will score points with single mothers. Neither plan works—but in the process, Will and Marcus slowly creep inside each other's lives. The intimacy they experience as friends changes both of them for the better. Ultimately they learn that, indeed, no person is meant to be an island.

INTIMACY AND SELF-DISCLOSURE IN FAMILY RELATIONSHIPS

Transamerica (2006) Rated R

A week before surgery that will finally complete her transformation from a man to a woman, Bree Osbourne (Felicity Huffman) discovers that, as a young man, he fathered a son who is now seventeen years old. Before authorizing the surgery, Bree's therapist insists that Bree must meet and come to terms with the son.

Bree reluctantly travels to New York, where she discovers that Toby (Kevin Zegers) is a street hustler. Understandably hesitant to reveal her true identity, Bree presents herself as a Christian missionary dedicated to helping sex workers live a more healthy life. She offers to drive Toby to Los Angeles, where he hopes to become a porn star. During their cross-country trip, parent and child find points of connection. Still, Bree cannot bring herself to disclose her true identity until events force her to reveal the truth.

While Bree's secret is far more explosive than most, her struggle to protect her most precious and private feelings while honoring relational obligations is familiar and touching.

THE PROCESS OF SELF-DISCLOSURE

I've Loved You So Long (2008) Rated PG-13

Juliette (Kristin Scott Thomas) is a shell of her former self. Released from prison after serving fifteen years for an unspeakable crime, she reluctantly agrees to be taken in by her younger sister's family. She struggles to merge back into society, and to keep

IMPROVING COMMUNICATION CLIMATES

10

✔+ MAKING THE GRADE

Here are the topics discussed in this chapter:

After studying the topics in this chapter, you should be able to:

1. Identify confirming, disagreeing, and disconfirming messages and patterns in your own important relationships, and describe their consequences.

2. Describe how the messages you identified in the previous objective either threaten or honor the self (face) of the communicators involved.

3. Use Gibb's categories and the assertive message format to create messages that are likely to build supportive rather than defensive communication climates.

4. Create appropriate nondefensive responses to real or hypothetical criticisms.

as a sign of affection within the context of your personal relationship. Likewise, a comment that the sender might have meant to be helpful ("I'm telling you this for your own good . . .") could easily be regarded as a disconfirming attack.

What makes some messages more confirming than others? Table 10.1 outlines the levels of message confirmation that are described in the following pages.

In the TV show *Everybody Loves Raymond*, the Barone family exchanges messages ranging from highly confirming to highly disconfirming (see the summary on page 373).

same pattern held for other kinds of messages: avoidance begat avoidance, analysis begat analysis, and so on. Table 10.2 on page 346 illustrates some reciprocal communication patterns that have the potential to create positive and negative spirals.

*P*ersonal relationships are a lot like the weather. Some are fair and warm, whereas others are stormy and cold; some are polluted, and others healthy. Some relationships have stable climates, whereas others change dramatically—calm one moment and turbulent the next. You can't measure the interpersonal climate by looking at a thermometer or glancing at the sky, but it's there nonetheless. Every relationship has a feeling, a pervasive mood that colors the interactions of the participants.

Although we can't change the external weather, we *can* change an interpersonal climate. This chapter will explain the forces that make some relationships pleasant and others unpleasant. You will learn what kinds of behavior contribute to defensiveness and hostility and what kinds lead to more positive feelings. After reading these pages, you will have a better idea of the climate in each of your important relationships—and

on a negative-to-positive scale. We will do just
that in this section...

Table 10.3

The Gibb Categories of Defensive and Supportive Behaviors

Defensive Behaviors	Supportive Behaviors
1. Evaluation	1. Description
2. Control	2. Problem Orientation
3. Strategy	3. Spontaneity
4. Neutrality	4. Empathy
5. Superiority	5. Equality
6. Certainty	6. Provisionalism

Source: Jack Gibb

statements, which they are likely to interpret as indicating a lack of regard. One form of evaluation is "you" language, described in Chapter 5.

Unlike evaluative "you" language, **description** focuses on the *speaker's* thoughts and feelings instead of judging the other person. Descriptive messages often are expressed in "I" language, which tends to provoke less defensiveness than "you" language.[31] Contrast the following evaluative "you" claims with their descriptive "I" counterparts:

> ***Evaluation:*** "*You don't know what you're talking about!*"
>
> ***Description:*** "*I don't understand how you came up with that idea.*"
>
> ***Evaluation:*** "*This place is a mess!*"
>
> ***Description:*** "*When you don't clean up, I have to either do it or live with your mess. That's why I'm mad!*"
>
> ***Evaluation:*** "*Those jokes are disgusting!*"
>
> ***Description:*** "*When you tell those off-color jokes, I get really embarrassed.*"

Note how each of the descriptive statements focuses on the speaker's thoughts and feelings without judging the other person. Despite its value, descriptive language isn't the only element necessary for success. Its effectiveness depends in part on when, where, and how the language is used. You can imagine how each of the preceding descriptive statements would go over if said in front of a room full of bystanders or in a whining tone of voice. Even the best timing and delivery of a descriptive message won't guarantee success. Some people will react defensively to anything you say or do. Nonetheless, it's easy to see that describing how the other person's behavior affects you is likely to produce better results than judgmentally attacking the other person.

CONTROL VERSUS PROBLEM ORIENTATION A second defense-provoking message involves some attempt to control another. **Controlling communication** occurs when a sender seems to be imposing a solution on the receiver with lit-

Evaluative "you" language (see pages 179–182) is a recipe for triggering defensiveness.

tle regard for the receiver's needs or interests. The object of control can involve almost anything: where to eat dinner, what TV program to watch, whether to remain in a relationship, or how to spend a large sum of money. Whatever the situation, people who act in controlling ways create a defensive climate. None of us likes to feel that our ideas are worthless and that nothing we say will change other people's determination to have their way—yet this is precisely the attitude that a controller communicates. Whether it is done through words, gestures, tone of voice, or some other channel, the controller generates hostility wherever he or she goes. The unspoken message that such behavior communicates is "I know what's best for you, and if you do as I say, we'll get along."

In contrast, in **problem orientation** communicators focus on finding a solution that satisfies both their needs and those of the others involved. The goal here isn't to win at the expense of your partner, but rather to work out some arrangement in which everybody feels like a winner. Chapter 11 has a great deal to say about win-win problem-solving as a way to find problem-oriented solutions.

Here are some examples of how some controlling and problem-orientation messages might sound:

Controlling:	*"You need to stay off the phone for the next two hours."*
Problem orientation:	*"I'm expecting some important calls. Can we work out a way to keep the line open?"*
Controlling:	*"There's only one way to handle this problem . . ."*
Problem orientation:	*"Looks like we have a problem. Let's work out a solution we can both live with."*

STRATEGY VERSUS SPONTANEITY   Gibb uses the word **strategy** to characterize defense-arousing messages in which speakers hide their ulterior motives. The words *dishonesty* and *manipulation* capture the essence of strategy. Even if the motives of strategic communication are honorable, the victim of such deception who discovers the attempt to deceive is likely to feel offended at being played for a naive sucker.

Spontaneity is the behavior that contrasts with strategy. Spontaneity simply means being honest with others rather than manipulating them. What it doesn't mean is blurting out what you're thinking as soon as an idea comes to you. As we discussed in Chapter 9, there are appropriate (and inappropriate) times for self-disclosure. You would undoubtedly threaten others' presenting selves if you were "spontaneous" about every opinion that crossed your mind. Gibb's notion of spontaneity involves setting aside hidden agendas that others both sense and resist. These examples illustrate the difference:

Strategy:	*"What are you doing Friday after work?"*
Spontaneity:	*"I have a piano I need to move Friday after work. Can you give me a hand?"*
Strategy:	*"Tom and Judy go out to dinner every week."*
Spontaneity:	*"I'd like to go out to dinner more often."*

This is a good place to talk about larger issues regarding the Gibb model. First, Gibb's emphasis on being direct is better suited for a low-context culture like the United States, which values straight talk, than for high-context cultures. Second, there are

---

under.... ...., ...

Use Meaningless but Weighty-Sounding Words and Phrases
Memorize this list:

Let me put it this way
In terms of
Vis-a-vis
Per se
As it were
Qua
So to speak

ously right and you are spectacularly wrong. Bring Hitler up subtly. Say, "That sounds suspiciously like something Adolf Hitler might say," or "You certainly do remind me of Adolf Hitler."

So that's it. You now know how to out-argue anybody. Do not try to pull any of this on people who generally carry weapons.

Dave Barry

ways in which each of the communication approaches Gibb labels as "supportive" can be used to exploit others and, therefore, violate the spirit of positive climate building. For instance, consider spontaneity. Although it sounds paradoxical at first, spontaneity can be a strategy, too. Sometimes you'll see people using honesty in a calculating way, being just frank enough to win someone's trust or sympathy. This "leveling" is probably the most defense-arousing strategy of all, because once you have learned someone is using frankness as a manipulation, you are less likely to trust that person in the future.

NEUTRALITY VERSUS EMPATHY   Gibb uses the term **neutrality** to describe a fourth behavior that arouses defensiveness. Probably a better descriptive word would be *indifference*. A neutral attitude is disconfirming because it communicates a lack of concern and implies that the welfare of the other person isn't very important to you. This perceived indifference is likely to promote defensiveness, because people do not like to think of themselves as worthless, and they'll protect a self-concept that regards them as worthwhile.

LOOKING AT DIVERSITY

Abdel Jalil Elayyadi: Promoting Understanding after 9/11

Photo courtesy of Abdel Jalil Elayyadi

I grew up in Morocco and moved to the United States when I was 19. I love the U.S. and have many wonderful friends here—but communicating with strangers became more difficult after the September 11 terrorist attacks in 2001. The fact that I'm an Arab Muslim created a tense climate between some Americans and me since that fateful day.

The good news is that people who knew me before 9/11 have been very supportive. In fact, because they know how I conduct my life—peacefully, morally, responsibly—their immediate reaction to the events of that day was, "How can this be? Muslims don't believe in killing innocent lives." I was happy to learn that my relationship with them made a difference in how they understood the Muslim faith.

Unfortunately, things are different with those who didn't know me before 9/11. I feel as if I'm easily stereotyped and misunderstood by people who prejudge me because of my religion and nationality. When I encounter people who think that all Muslims are terrorists who hate Americans, I try to do three things to change the defensive climate:

First, I quickly explain that Muslims are peace-loving people who abhor the taking of innocent life. I want them to know that I completely agree with their disdain for the terrorists. That builds a bridge of trust that allows us to keep talking.

Second, I try to use examples to help them understand how the 9/11 terrorists don't represent most Muslims or Arabs. I ask them how they would feel if Arabs judged Americans by the acts of Timothy McVeigh, or Christians by the acts of the Ku Klux Klan. This usually helps them view Muslims in a different and more accurate light.

Finally, the more we talk, the more we focus on things we have in common and beliefs we share. The goal is to discover that we are not enemies simply because we have different religions or nationalities—and in fact, there is no reason we can't be friends.

What do these conversations accomplish? In some cases, not a lot—because there are a few people who prefer to keep their prejudices rather than change them. But in other cases, I think I've made a difference, however small, in promoting peace and understanding in the world.

talking loudly and slowly, not listening, and varying speaking pitch convey a patronizing attitude.

Here are two examples of the difference between superiority and equality:

> *Superior:*   "You don't know what you're talking about."
>
> *Equal:*   "I see it a different way."
>
> *Superior:*   "No, that's not the right way to do it!"
>
> *Equal:*   "If you want, I can show you a way that has worked for me."

There are certainly times when we communicate with others who possess talents or knowledge lesser than ours, but even then it isn't necessary to communicate an attitude of superiority. Gibb found ample evidence that many people who have superior skills and talents are capable of projecting feelings of **equality** rather than superiority. Such people convey that, although they may have greater talent in certain areas, they see others as having just as much worth as human beings.

CERTAINTY VERSUS PROVISIONALISM   Have you ever run into people who are positive they're right, who know that theirs is the only or proper way of doing

✔+ INVITATION TO INSIGHT

How Critical Are You?

You can get a sense of how critical you are by taking a short online test at RateYourself.com. Besides receiving your own score, you can compare your results with the average ratings of other quiz-takers.

You can find the link to this site through your Premium Website for *Looking Out/ Looking In*.

something, who insist that they have all the facts and need no additional information? If you have, you've met individuals who project the defense-arousing behavior that Gibb calls **certainty**. Communicators who regard their own opinions with certainty while disregarding the ideas of others demonstrate a lack of regard and respect. It's likely that the receiver will take the certainty as a personal affront and react defensively.

In contrast to certainty is **provisionalism**, in which people may have strong opinions but are willing to acknowledge that they don't have a corner on the truth and will change their stance if another position seems more reasonable. Consider these examples that contrast certain and provisional approaches:

"I understand completely. I like good movies, and you like bad movies."

Certain:	*"That will never work!"*
Provisional:	*"I think you'll run into problems with that approach."*
Certain:	*"You don't know what you're talking about!"*
Provisional:	*"I've never heard anything like that before. Where did you hear it?"*

There is no guarantee that using Gibb's supportive, confirming approach to communication will build a positive climate. The other person may simply not be receptive. But the chances for a constructive relationship will be greatest when communication consists of the

The need to be right—the sign of a vulgar mind.

—*Albert Camus*

supportive approach described here. Besides boosting the odds of getting a positive response from others, supportive communication can leave you feeling better in a variety of ways: more in control of your relationships, more comfortable, and more positive toward others.

Saving Face

Gibb's categories of supportive communication offer useful guidelines for reducing defensiveness. In the following pages, you will learn some specific ways to use these approaches when you need to deliver challenging messages.

✔+ INVITATION TO INSIGHT

Defensiveness Feedback

1. Approach an important person in your life and request some help in learning more about yourself. Inform the other person that your discussion will probably take at least an hour, so make sure that both of you are prepared to invest the necessary amount of time.

2. Begin by explaining all twelve of the Gibb behaviors to your partner. Be sure to give enough examples so that each category is clearly understood.

3. When your explanation is complete and you've answered all of your partner's questions, ask him or her to tell you which of the Gibb categories you use. Seek specific examples so that you are certain to understand the feedback fully. (Because you are requesting an evaluation, be prepared for a little defensiveness on your own part at this point.) Inform your partner that you are interested in discovering both the defense-arousing and the supportive behaviors you use and that you are sincerely interested in receiving a candid answer. (*Note:* If you don't want to hear the truth from your partner, don't try this exercise.)

4. As your partner speaks, record the categories that he or she lists in sufficient detail for both of you to be sure that you have understood the comments.

5. When you have finished your list, show it to your partner. Listen to your partner's reactions, and make any corrections that are necessary to reflect an accurate understanding of the comments. When your list is accurate, have your partner sign it to indicate that you have understood it clearly.

6. In a concluding statement note:
   a. How you felt as your partner was describing you
   b. Whether you agree with the evaluation
   c. What effect your use of the Gibb categories has on your relationship with your partner

THE ASSERTIVE MESSAGE FORMAT

As you've already seen, an essential ingredient in building a supportive climate is to avoid attacking others—to preserve their face. At the same time, you need to share your legitimate concerns when problems arise in a relationship.

The next few pages will describe a method for speaking your mind in a clear, direct, yet nonthreatening assertive way that expresses your needs, thoughts, and feelings clearly and directly without judging or dictating to others. This **assertive message format** builds on the perception-checking skill you learned in Chapter 3 and the "I" language approach you learned in Chapter 5. This new skill works for a variety of messages: your hopes, problems, complaints, and appreciations.[33] Whereas perception checking and "I" statements have three elements, a complete assertive message has five parts: behavior, interpretation, feeling, consequence, and intention. We'll examine each part one by one and then discuss how to combine them in your everyday communication.

BEHAVIOR As you read in Chapter 5, a behavioral description describes the raw material to which you react. A behavioral description should be *objective*, describing an event without interpreting it. Two examples of behavioral descriptions might look like this:

Example 1

"One week ago John promised me that he would ask my permission before smoking in the same room with me. Just a moment ago he lit up a cigarette without asking for my OK."

Example 2

"Chris has acted differently over the last week. I can't remember her laughing once since the holiday weekend. She hasn't dropped by my place like she usually does, hasn't suggested we play tennis, and hasn't returned my phone calls."

Notice that both statements describe only facts. The observer hasn't attached any meaning.

INTERPRETATION   An **interpretation statement** describes the meaning you've attached to the other person's behavior. The important thing to realize about interpretations is that they are *subjective*. As you learned via the skill of perception checking (see Chapter 3), we can attach more than one interpretation to any behavior. For example, look at these two different interpretations of each of the preceding descriptions:

Example 1

Interpretation A: "John must have forgotten about our agreement that he wouldn't smoke without asking me first. I'm sure he's too considerate to go back on his word on something he knows I feel strongly about."

Interpretation B: "John is a rude, inconsiderate person. After promising not to smoke around me without asking, he's just deliberately done so. This shows that he cares only about himself. In fact, I bet he's deliberately doing this to drive me crazy!"

Example 2

Interpretation A: "Something must be bothering Chris. It's probably her family. She'll probably just feel worse if I keep pestering her."

Interpretation B: "Chris is probably mad at me. It's probably because I kidded her about losing so often at tennis. I'd better leave her alone until she cools off."

After you become aware of the difference between observable behavior and interpretation, some of the reasons for communication difficulties become clear. Many problems

✔+ SKILL BUILDER

Behaviors and Interpretations

1. Tell two other group members several interpretations that you have recently made about other people in your life. For each interpretation, describe the behavior on which you based your interpretations.

2. With your partners' help, consider some alternate interpretations of the behavior that might be as plausible as your original one.

3. After considering the alternate interpretations, decide
   a. which one was most reasonable.
   b. how you might share that interpretation (along with the behavior) with the other person involved in a tentative, provisional way.

occur when a sender fails to describe the behavior on which an interpretation is based. For instance, imagine the difference between hearing a friend say

"You are a tightwad!" (*No behavioral description*)

versus explaining

"When you never offer to pay me back for the coffee and snacks I often buy you, I think you're a tightwad." (*Behavior plus interpretation*)

The first speaker's failure to specify behavior would probably confuse the receiver, who has no way of knowing what prompted the speaker's remarks. This failure to describe behavior also reduces any chance that the receiver will change the offensive behavior, which, after all, is unknown to that person. In Gibb's terms, these examples show the difference between evaluation and description.

Just as important as specifying behavior is the need to label an interpretation as such instead of presenting it as a matter of fact—or what Gibb would describe as the difference between certainty and provisionalism. Consider the difference between saying

"It's obvious that if you cared for me you'd write more often." (*Interpretation presented as fact*)

versus

"When I didn't get a letter or even a postcard from you, I thought that you didn't care for me." (*Interpretation made clear*)

FEELING Reporting behavior and sharing your interpretations are important, but **feeling statements** add a new dimension to a message. For example, consider the difference between saying

"When you laugh at me (*behavior*), I think you find my comments foolish (*interpretation*), and *I feel embarrassed.*"

versus

"When you laugh at me, I think you find my comments foolish, and *I feel angry.*"

It's important to recognize that some statements *seem* as if they're expressing feelings but are actually interpretations or statements of intention. For instance, it's not

✔+ SKILL BUILDER

Name the Feeling

Add a feeling that you would be likely to have to each of the following messages:

1. I felt _____ when I found out you didn't invite me on the camping trip. You said you thought I wouldn't want to go, but I have a hard time accepting that.

2. I felt _____ when you offered to help me move. I know how busy you are.

3. When you tell me you still want to be a friend but you want to "lighten up a little," I get the idea you're tired of me, and I feel _____.

4. You told me you wanted my honest opinion about your paintings, and then when I tell you what I think, you say I don't understand them. I'm _____.

How would the impact of each message be different if it didn't include a feeling statement?

accurate to say "I feel like leaving" (really an intention) or "I feel you're wrong" (an interpretation). Statements like these obscure the true expression of feelings.

CONSEQUENCE A **consequence statement** explains what happens as a result of the situation you've described so far. There are three types of consequences:

- What happens to you, the speaker
  "When I didn't get the phone message yesterday (*behavior*), I didn't know that my doctor's appointment was delayed and that I would end up sitting in the office for an hour when I could have been studying or working (*consequences*). It seems to me that you don't care enough about how busy I am to even write a simple note (*interpretation*), and that's why I'm so mad (*feeling*)."

- What happens to the person you're addressing
  "When you have four or five drinks at a party after I've warned you to slow down (*behavior*), you start to act strange: You make crude jokes that offend everybody, and on the way home you drive poorly (*consequences*). For instance, last night you almost hit a phone pole while you were backing out of the driveway (*more behavior*). I don't think you realize how differently you act (*interpretation*), and I'm worried (*feeling*) about what will happen if you don't drink less."

- What happens to others
  "You probably don't know because you couldn't hear her cry (*interpretation*), but when you rehearse your lines for the play without closing the doors (*behavior*), the baby can't sleep (*consequence*). I'm especially concerned (*feeling*) about her because she's had a cold lately."

Consequence statements are valuable for two reasons. First, they help you understand more clearly why you are bothered or pleased by another's behavior. Just as important, telling others about the consequences of their actions can clarify for them the results of their behavior. As with interpretations, we often think that others should be aware of consequences without being told, but the fact is that they often aren't. By explicitly stating consequences, you can be sure that you or your message leaves nothing to the listener's imagination.

When you are stating consequences, it's important simply to describe what happens without moralizing. For instance, it's one thing to say, "When you didn't call to say you'd be late, I stayed up worrying," and another to rant on, "How can I ever trust you? You're going to drive me crazy!" Remember that it's perfectly legitimate to express your thoughts and feelings, but it's important to label them as such. And when you want to request change from someone, you can use intention statements, which we'll now describe.

INTENTION **Intention statements** are the final element of the assertive message format. They can communicate three kinds of messages:

- Where you stand on an issue
  "When you call us 'girls' after I've told you we want to be called 'women' (*behavior*), I get the idea you don't appreciate how important the difference is to us (*interpretation*) and how demeaning it feels (*feeling*). Now I'm in an awkward spot: Either I have to keep bringing the subject up, or else drop it and feel bad (*consequence*). I want you to know how much this bothers me (*intention*)."

- Requests of others
  "When I didn't hear from you last night (*behavior*), I thought you were mad at me (*interpretation*). I've been thinking about it ever since (*consequence*), and I'm still worried (*feeling*). I'd like to know whether you are angry (*intention*)."

- Descriptions of how you plan to act in the future
  "I've asked you to repay the twenty-five dollars I lent you three times now (*behavior*). I'm getting the idea that you've been avoiding me (*interpretation*), and I'm pretty angry about it (*feeling*). I want you to know that unless we clear this up now, you shouldn't expect me ever to lend you anything again (*intention*)."

As in the preceding cases, we are often motivated by one single intention. Sometimes, however, we act from a combination of intentions, which may even be in conflict with each other. When this happens, our conflicting intentions often make it difficult for us to reach decisions:

"I want to be truthful with you, but I don't want to violate my friend's privacy."

"I want to continue to enjoy your friendship and company, but I don't want to get too attached right now."

"I want to have time to study and get good grades, but I also want to have a job with some money coming in."

✔+ IN REAL LIFE

The Assertive Message Format

consequence for other

©Cengage Learning

While the elements of the assertive message format don't vary, the way they sound will depend on the situation and your personal style. Here are a few examples to show how this approach can operate in real life.

You can appreciate the value of the assertive approach by imagining how different the likely outcome would be if each message had been delivered in a blaming, aggressive way . . . or not at all.

To a Neighbor

I had an awful scare just now (*feeling*). I was backing out of the driveway, and Angela (*neighbor's toddler*) wandered right behind my car (*behavior*). Thank God I saw her, but she is so small, and it would have been easy to miss her. I can't bear to think what might have happened if I hadn't seen her (*consequences for others*). I know how hard it is to keep an eye on little kids (*interpretation*), but I really hope you can keep her inside unless you're watching her (*intention*).

To a Friend

I just checked my Facebook account and saw that you tagged me in your photos from the party last weekend (*behavior*). I told you before that I'm trying to get a good job, and I'm afraid those kinds of pictures could blow my chance (*consequence for you*). I know you like to post lots of pictures, and you probably think I'm overreacting (*interpretations*). Anyway, this is a big deal for me. So I need you to remember not to post any pictures that you think would embarrass me. If you aren't sure about a photo, just ask me (*intention*).

To a Boss

I've got a favor to ask (*intention*). Last month I told you I wanted to work extra hours, and I know you're doing me a favor by giving me more shifts (*interpretation*). But it would really help if you could give me a couple of days' advance notice instead of telling me the night before you want me to work (*clarifies intention*). That way I can say "yes" to the extra shifts (*consequence for boss*). It would also cause a lot less stress for me (*feeling*).

To an Auto Mechanic

I need to tell you that I'm pretty unhappy (*feeling*). When I dropped the car off yesterday, you told me it would definitely be ready today by noon. Now it's 12:30 and it isn't done (*behavior*). I'm going to be late for an important meeting (*consequence for you*). I know you aim to please (*interpretation*), but you have to understand that I can't bring my car to you unless I can count on it being ready when you promise (*consequence for other*).

USING THE ASSERTIVE MESSAGE FORMAT Before you try to deliver messages by using the clear message format, there are a few points to remember.

1. *The elements may be delivered in mixed order.* As the examples on the preceding pages show, it's sometimes best to begin by stating your feelings. At other times you can start by sharing your intentions or interpretations or by describing consequences.
2. *Word the message to suit your personal style.* Instead of saying, "I interpret your behavior to mean . . ." you might choose to say "I think . . ." or "It seems to me . . ." or perhaps "I get the idea . . ."

    In the same way, you can express your intentions by saying, "I hope you'll understand (or do) . . ." or perhaps, "I wish you would . . ." The words that you choose should sound authentic in order to reinforce the genuineness of your statement.

Putting Your Message Together

1. Join with two other class members. Each person in turn should share a message that he or she might want to send to another person, being sure to include behavior, interpretation, feeling, consequence, and intention statements in the message.

2. The others in the group should help the speaker by offering feedback about how the message could be made clearer if there is any question about the meaning.

3. After the speaker has composed a satisfactory message, he or she should practice actually delivering it by having another group member play the role of the intended receiver. Continue this practice until the speaker is confident that he or she can deliver the message effectively.

4. Repeat this process until each group member has had a chance to practice delivering a message.

3. *When appropriate, combine two elements in a single phrase.* The statement ". . . and ever since then I've been wanting to talk to you" expresses both a consequence and an intention. In the same way, saying, ". . . and after you said that, I felt confused" expresses a consequence and a feeling. Whether you combine elements or state them separately, the important point is to be sure that each one is present in your statement.

4. *Take your time delivering the message.* It isn't always possible to deliver messages such as the ones here all at one time, wrapped up in neat paragraphs. It will often be necessary to repeat or restate one part before the other person understands what you're saying. As you've already read, there are many types of psychological and physical noise that make it difficult for us to understand each other. In communication, as in many other activities, patience and persistence are essential.

Now try your hand at combining all these elements in the exercise above.

RESPONDING NONDEFENSIVELY TO CRITICISM

The world would be a happier place if everyone communicated supportively and assertively. But how can you respond nondefensively when others send aggressive messages that don't match the prescriptions outlined in this chapter? Despite your best intentions, it's difficult to be reasonable when you're being attacked. Being attacked is hard enough when the criticism is clearly unfair, but it's often even harder when the criticism is on target. Despite the accuracy of your critic, the tendency is either to counterattack aggressively with a barrage of verbal aggression or to withdraw nonassertively.

© moodboard/Corbis

Because neither of these counterattacks is likely to resolve a dispute, we need alternative ways of behaving. There are two such ways. Despite their apparent simplicity, they have proven to be among the most valuable skills many communicators have learned.[34]

SEEK MORE INFORMATION The response of seeking more information makes good sense when you realize that it's foolish to respond to a critical attack until you understand what the other person has said. Even attacks that on first consideration appear to be totally unjustified or foolish often prove to contain at least a grain of truth and sometimes much more.

Many readers object to the idea of asking for details when they are criticized. Their resistance stems from confusing the act of *listening open-mindedly* to a speaker's comments with *accepting* the comments. After you realize that you can listen to, understand, and even acknowledge the most hostile comments without necessarily accepting them, it becomes much easier to hear another person out. If you disagree with a person's criticism, you will be in a much better position to explain yourself after you understand the criticism. On the other hand, after carefully listening to the person's criticism, you might just see that it is valid, in which case you have learned some valuable information about yourself. In either case, you have everything to gain and nothing to lose by paying attention to the critic.

Of course, after one has spent years instinctively resisting criticism, learning to listen to the other person will take some practice. To make matters clearer, here are several ways in which you can seek additional information from your critics.

Ask for Specifics Often the vague attack of a critic is virtually useless even if you sincerely want to change. Abstract attacks such as "You're being unfair" or "You never help out" can be difficult to understand. In such cases it is a good idea to request more specific information from the sender. "What do I *do* that's unfair?" is an important question to ask before you can judge whether the attack is correct. "When haven't I helped out?" you might ask before agreeing with or disagreeing with the attack.

If you have already asked for specifics and are still accused of reacting defensively, the problem may be in the *way* you ask. Your tone of voice and facial expression, posture, and other nonverbal clues can give the same words radically different connotations. For example, think of how you could use the words "Exactly what are you talking about?" to communicate either a genuine desire to know or your belief that the speaker is crazy. It's important to request specific information only when you genuinely want to learn more from the speaker because asking under any other circumstances will make matters only worse.

Guess about Specifics On some occasions even your sincere and well-phrased requests for specific information won't meet with success. Sometimes your critics won't be able to define precisely the behavior they find offensive. At these times, you'll hear such comments as "I can't tell you exactly what's wrong with your sense of humor—all I can say is that I don't like it." At other times, your critics may know the exact behaviors they don't like, but for some reason seem to get a perverse satisfaction out of making you struggle to figure it out. At times like this, you hear such comments as, "Well, if you don't know what you did to hurt my feelings, I'm certainly not going to tell you!"

Needless to say, failing to learn the specifics of another's criticism when you genuinely want to know can be frustrating. In instances like these, you can often learn more clearly what is bothering your critic by *guessing* at the specifics of a criticism. In a sense you become both detective and suspect, the goal being to figure out exactly what "crime" you have committed. Like the technique of asking for specifics, guessing must

> Nothing is weaker than water;
>
> Yet, for attacking what is hard and tough,
>
> Nothing surpasses it, nothing equals it.
>
> The principle, that what is weak overcomes what is strong,
>
> And what is yielding conquers what is resistant, is known to everyone.
>
> Yet few utilize it profitably in practice . . .
>
> *—Lao Tzu*, Tao Te Ching

be done with goodwill if it's to produce satisfying results. You need to convey to the critic that for both your sakes you're truly interested in finding out what is the matter. After you have communicated this intention, the emotional climate generally becomes more comfortable because, in effect, both you and the critic are seeking the same goal.

Here are some typical questions you might hear from someone guessing about the specifics of another's criticism:

> "So you object to the language I used in writing the paper. Was my language too formal?"

> "Okay, I understand that you think the outfit looks funny. What's so bad? Is it the color? Does it have something to do with the fit? The fabric?"

> "When you say that I'm not doing my share around the house, do you mean that I haven't been helping enough with the cleaning?"

Paraphrase the Speaker's Ideas Another strategy is to draw out confused or reluctant speakers by paraphrasing their thoughts and feelings and using the active listening skills described in Chapter 7. Paraphrasing is especially good in helping others solve their problems; and because people generally criticize you because your behavior creates some problem for them, the strategy is especially appropriate at such times.

One advantage of paraphrasing is that you don't have to guess about the specifics of your behavior that might be offensive. By clarifying or amplifying what you understand critics to be saying, you'll learn more about their objections. A brief dialogue between a disgruntled customer and an especially talented store manager using paraphrasing might sound like this:

> **Customer:** *The way you people run this store is disgusting! I just want to tell you that I'll never shop here again.*

> **Manager:** (Reflecting the customer's feeling) *It seems that you're quite upset. Can you tell me your problem?*

> **Customer:** *It isn't my problem; it's the problem your salespeople have. They seem to think it's a great inconvenience to help a customer find anything around here.*

> **Manager:** *So you didn't get enough help locating the items you were looking for, is that it?*

> **Customer:** *Help? I spent twenty minutes looking around in here before I even talked to a clerk. All I can say is that it's a hell of a way to run a store.*

> **Manager:** *So what you're saying is that the clerks seemed to be ignoring the customers?*

> **Customer:** *No. They were all busy with other people. It just seems to me that you ought to have enough help around to handle the crowds that come in at this hour.*

> **Manager:** *I understand now. What frustrated you most was the fact that we didn't have enough staff to serve you promptly.*

> **Customer:** *That's right. I have no complaint with the service I get after I'm waited on, and I've always thought you had a good selection here. It's just that I'm too busy to wait so long for help.*

> **Manager:** *Well, I'm glad you brought this to my attention. We certainly don't want loyal customers going away mad. I'll try to see that it doesn't happen again.*

This conversation illustrates two advantages of paraphrasing. First, the critic often reduces the intensity of the attack after he or she realizes that the complaint is being heard. Often criticism grows from the frustration of unmet needs, which in this case was partly a lack of attention. As soon as the manager genuinely demonstrated interest in the customer's plight, the customer began to feel better and was able to leave the store relatively calm. Of course, this sort of reflective listening won't always mollify your critic, but even when it doesn't, there's still another benefit that makes the strategy worthwhile. In the sample conversation, for instance, the manager learned some valuable information by taking time to understand the customer. The manager discovered that there were certain times when the number of employees was insufficient to help the crowd of shoppers and also that the delays at these times seriously annoyed at least some shoppers, thus threatening a loss in business. This knowledge is certainly important, and by reacting defensively to the customer's complaint, the manager would not have learned from it.

> Placing the blame is a bad habit, but taking the blame is a sure builder of character.
>
> —O. A. Battista

Ask What the Critic Wants Sometimes your critic's demand will be obvious:

"Turn down that music!"

"I wish you'd remember to tell me about phone messages."

"Would you clean up your dirty dishes now?"

At other times, however, you'll need to do some investigating to find out what the critic wants from you:

> **Alex:** *I can't believe you invited all those people over without asking me first!*
>
> **Barb:** *Are you saying you want me to cancel the party?*
>
> **Alex:** *No, I just wish you'd ask me before you make plans.*
>
> **Cynthia:** *You're so critical! It sounds like you don't like anything about this paper.*
>
> **Donna:** *But you asked for my opinion. What do you expect me to do when you ask?*
>
> **Cynthia:** *I want to know what's wrong, but I don't just want to hear criticisms. If you think there's anything good about my work, I wish you'd tell me that, too.*

This last example illustrates the importance of accompanying your questions with the right nonverbal behavior. It's easy to imagine two ways in which Donna could have nonverbally supported her response, "What do you expect me to do when you ask?" One would show a genuine desire to clarify what Cynthia wanted, whereas the other would have been clearly hostile and defensive. As with all the styles in this section, your responses to criticism have to be sincere to work.

Ask about the Consequences of Your Behavior As a rule, people criticize your behavior only when some need of theirs is not being met. One way to respond to this kind of criticism is to find out exactly what troublesome consequences your behavior has for them. You'll often find that behaviors that seem perfectly legitimate to you cause some difficulty for your critic; after you have understood this, criticisms that previously sounded foolish take on a new meaning.

Neighbor A: *You say that I ought to have my cat neutered. Why is that important to you?*

Neighbor B: *Because at night he picks fights with my cat, and I'm tired of paying the vet's bills.*

Worker A: *Why do you care whether I'm late to work?*

Worker B: *Because when the boss asks, I feel obligated to make up some story so you won't get in trouble, and I don't like to lie.*

Husband: *Why does it bother you when I lose money at poker? You know I never gamble more than I can afford.*

Wife: *It's not the cash itself. It's that when you lose, you're in a grumpy mood for two or three days, and that's no fun for me.*

ETHICAL CHALLENGE

Nonviolence: A Legacy of Principled Effectiveness

Among the most familiar and challenging biblical injunctions is Christ's mandate, "If someone strikes you on one cheek, turn to him the other. . . ."

The notion of meeting aggression with nonviolence is an ancient one. The Taoist doctrine of *wu-wei,* promulgated over twenty-four hundred years ago in China, advocates nonaction in the face of an attack. In ancient India, the principle of *ahimsa*—nonharming—was shared by Buddhists, Jains, and many Hindus. In the West, some Greek stoics advocated nonaction in the face of threats.

Pacifism has a moral foundation, but by the nineteenth century it was used as a potent strategy for achieving political goals. In the United States, abolitionist William Lloyd Garrison advocated the use of nonviolence to protest slavery. On both sides of the Atlantic, the suffragette movement used nonviolent resistance as a tool to secure rights for women. In czarist Russia, Count Leo Tolstoy led a pacifist movement rejecting war and advocating civil disobedience as a tool for inhibiting violence.

In the twentieth century, nonviolence proved to be a powerful tool for political change. Mahatma Gandhi was demonstrably the most successful practitioner of this tool, first in South Africa and later in India, where his approach of *satyagraha* (truth-force) played a decisive role in the 1947 withdrawal of imperial Britain from India. In the 1950s and 1960s, Martin Luther King, Jr. and his followers used nonviolence to demonstrate the evils of racial segregation, contributing to the passage of groundbreaking civil rights laws.

The effectiveness of nonviolence in achieving social change can also be effective in interpersonal situations. Nonconfrontational strategies provide communicators with an approach that is both principled and pragmatic.

For more information on nonviolent strategies, see Peter Ackerman and Christopher Kruegler, Strategic Nonviolent Conflict: The Dynamics of People Power in the Twentieth Century *(Westport, CT: Praeger, 1994); and Robert L. Holmes, ed.,* Nonviolence in Theory and Practice *(Belmont, CA: Wadsworth, 1990).*

Ask What Else Is Wrong It might seem crazy to invite more criticism, but sometimes asking about other complaints can uncover the real problem:

> **Raul:** *Are you mad at me?*
>
> **Tina:** *No. Why are you asking?*
>
> **Raul:** *Because the whole time we were at the picnic you hardly spent any time talking to me. In fact, it seemed like whenever I came over to where you were, you went off somewhere else.*
>
> **Tina:** *Is anything else wrong?*
>
> **Raul:** *Well, I've been wondering lately if you're tired of me.*

This example shows that asking if anything else bothers your critic isn't just an exercise in masochism. If you can keep your defensiveness in check, probing further can lead the conversation to issues that are the source of the critic's real dissatisfaction.

Sometimes soliciting more information from a critic isn't enough. What do you do, for instance, when you fully understand the other person's criticism and still feel a defensive response on the tip of your tongue? You know that if you try to defend yourself, you'll wind up in an argument; on the other hand, you simply can't accept what the other person is saying about you. The solution to such a dilemma is outrageously simple and is discussed in the following section.

AGREE WITH THE CRITIC But, you protest, how can you honestly agree with criticisms that you don't believe are true? The following pages will answer this question by showing that in virtually every situation you can honestly accept the other person's point of view

> Love your enemies, for they tell you your faults.
>
> —*Benjamin Franklin*

while still maintaining your own position. To see how this can be so, you need to realize that there are two different types of agreement you can use in almost any situation.

Agree with the Facts This is the easiest type of agreement to understand, though not always to practice. Research suggests that it is also highly effective in restoring a damaged reputation with a critic.[35] You agree with your critic when the accusation is factually correct:

"You're right, I am angry."

"I suppose I *was* being defensive."

"Now that you mention it, I did get pretty sarcastic."

Agreeing with the facts seems sensible when you realize that certain facts are indisputable. If you agree to be somewhere at 4:00 and don't show up until 5:00, you are tardy, no matter how good your explanation for tardiness. If you've broken a borrowed object, run out of gas, or failed to finish a job you started, there's no point in denying it. In the same way, if you're honest, you may have to agree with many interpretations of your behavior even when they're not flattering. You do get angry, act foolishly, fail to listen, and behave inconsiderately. After you rid yourself of the myth of perfection, it's much easier to acknowledge these truths.

If many criticisms aimed at you are accurate, why is it so difficult to accept them without being defensive? The answer to this question lies in a confusion between

✔+ IN REAL LIFE

Responding Nondefensively to Criticism

Defending yourself—even when you're right—isn't always the best approach. This dialogue shows the importance of using self-control and thinking before responding when you are being criticized. The employee realizes that arguing won't change her boss's mind, so she decides to reply as honestly as she can without becoming defensive.

Jason Harris/©Cengage Learning

Boss: How'd things go while I was out?

Employee: Pretty well, except for one thing. Mr. Macintosh—he said you knew him—came in and wanted to buy about $200 worth of stuff. He wanted me to charge him wholesale, and I asked him for his tax resale number, just like you told me. He said he didn't have it, so I told him he'd have to pay retail. He got pretty mad.

Boss: He's a good customer. I hope you gave him the discount.

Employee: (*Beginning to sound defensive*) Well, I didn't. You told me last week that the law said we had to charge full price and sales tax unless the customer had a resale number.

Boss: Oh, my gosh! Didn't Macintosh tell you he had a number?

Employee: (*Becoming more defensive*) He did, but he didn't have it with him. I didn't want to get you mad at me for breaking the law.

Boss: (*Barely concealing her exasperation*) Well, customers don't always have their resale numbers memorized. Macintosh has been coming here for years, and we just fill in his number on the records later.

Employee: (*Deciding to respond nondefensively instead of getting into an argument that she knows she can't win*) I can see why it looks like I gave Mr. Macintosh a hard time. You don't ask him for the number, and I insisted on having it. (*Agrees with the boss's perception*)

Boss: Yes! There's a lot of competition in this business, and we have to keep our customers happy—especially the good ones—or we'll lose them. Macintosh drives across town to do business with us. There are places right near him. If we jerk him around he'll go there, and we'll lose a good customer.

Employee: That's true. (*Agrees with the fact that it is important to keep customers happy*) And I want to know how to treat customers right. But I'm confused about how to handle people who want a discount and don't have resale numbers. What should I do? (*Asks what the boss wants*)

Boss: Well, you need to be a little flexible with good customers.

Employee: How should I do that? (*Asks for specifics*)

agreeing with the *facts* and accepting the *judgment* that so often accompanies them. Most critics don't merely describe the action that offends them; they also evaluate it, and it's this evaluation that we resist:

> "It's silly to be angry."
> "You have no reason for being defensive."
> "You were wrong to be so sarcastic."

It's evaluations like these that we resent. By realizing that you can agree with—and even learn from—the descriptive part of many criticisms and still not accept the accompanying evaluations, you'll often have a response that is both honest and nondefensive.

Boss: Well, it's OK to trust people who are regulars.

Employee: So I don't need to ask regular customers for their resale numbers. I should look them up later? (*Paraphrases to clarify boss's ambiguous directions to "trust" regular customers*)

Boss: That's right. You've got to use your head in business!

Employee: (*Ignores the indirect accusation about not "using her head," recognizing that there's no point in defending herself*) OK, so when regular customers come in, I won't even ask them for their resale numbers . . . right? (*Paraphrases again to be sure she has the message correct; the employee has no desire to get criticized again about this matter*)

Boss: No, go ahead and ask for the number. If they have it, we won't have to look it up later. But if they don't have the number, just say OK and give them the discount.

Employee: Got it. I only have one question: How can I know who the regular customers are? Should I take their word for it? (*Asks for specifics*)

Boss: Well, you'll get to know most of them after you've been here a while. But it's OK to trust them until then. If they say they're regulars, just take their word for it. You've got to trust people sometimes, you know!

Employee: (*Ignores the fact that the boss originally told her not to trust people but rather to insist on getting their number; decides instead to agree with the boss*) I can see how important it is to trust good customers.

Boss: Right.

Employee: Thanks for clearing up how to handle the resale numbers. Is there anything else I ought to know so things will run smoothly when you're not in the store? (*Asks if anything else is wrong*)

Boss: I don't think so. (*Patronizingly*) Don't get discouraged; you'll catch on. It took me twenty years to build this business. Stick with it, and some day you could be running a place like this.

Employee: (*Trying to agree with her boss without sounding sarcastic*) That would be great.

The employee's refusal to act defensively turned what might have been a scolding into a discussion about how to handle a business challenge in the future. The employee might not like the boss's patronizing attitude and contradictory directions, but her communication skill kept the communication climate positive—probably the best possible outcome for this situation.

Communication Scenarios

To see and analyze a video of this conversation, go to your Premium Website for Looking Out/Looking In, *access "In Real Life Communication Scenarios," and then click on "Responding Nondefensively to Criticism."*

Of course, in order to reduce defensiveness, your agreements with the facts must be honest ones admitted without malice. It's humiliating to accept descriptions that aren't accurate, and maliciously manipulatively pretending to accept these leads only to trouble. You can imagine how unproductive the conversation given earlier would have been if the manager had spoken the same words in a sarcastic tone. Agree with the facts only when you can do so sincerely. Though this won't always be possible, you'll be surprised at how often you can use this simple response.

Agree with the Critic's Perception Agreeing with your critics may be fine when you acknowledge that the criticisms are justified, but how can you agree when they seem to be completely unjustified? You've listened carefully and asked questions to make sure you understand the criticisms, but the more you listen, the more positive you are that the critics are totally out of line. Even in these cases there is a way of agreeing—this time not with the critics' conclusions but with their right to see things their way.

A: *I don't believe that you've been all the places you were just describing. You're probably just making all this up to impress us.*

B: *Well, I can see how you might think that. I've known people who lie to get approval.*

C: *I want to let you know right from the start that I was against hiring you for the job. I think you got it because you're a woman.*

D: *I can understand why you'd believe that with all the antidiscrimination laws on the books. I hope that after I've been here for a while, you'll change your mind.*

E: *I don't think you're being totally honest about your reason for wanting to stay home. You say it's because you have a headache, but I think you're avoiding Mary.*

F: *I can see why that would make sense to you because Mary and I got into an argument the last time we were together. All I can say is that I do have a headache.*

"When will he be able to sit up and take criticism?"

One key to feeling comfortable with acknowledging accurate criticism is to understand that *agreeing* with a critic doesn't necessarily oblige you to *apologize*. Sometimes you aren't responsible for the behavior that your critic finds objectionable, in which case an explanation might be more appropriate than an apology:

"I know I'm late. There was an accident downtown, and the streets are jammed." (*Spoken in an explanatory, nondefensive tone*)

In other cases, your behavior might be understandable, if not perfect. When this happens, you can acknowledge the validity of the criticism without apologizing:

"You're right. I *did* lose my temper. I've had to remind you three or four times, and I guess I finally used up all my patience." (*Again, delivered as an explanation, not a defense or counterattack*)

In still other cases, you can acknowledge your critic's right to see things differently than you without backing off from your position.

"I can understand why you think I'm overreacting. I know this doesn't seem as important to you as it does to me. I hope you can understand why I think this is such a big deal."

Apologizing is fine if you can do so sincerely; but you will be able to agree with critics more often if you understand that doing so doesn't require you to grovel.

Some critics don't seem to deserve the kinds of respectful responses outlined here. They seem more interested in attacking you than explaining themselves. Before you counterattack these hostile critics, ask yourself whether a defensive response will be worth the consequences.

✔+ SKILL BUILDER

Coping with Criticism

Take turns practicing nondefensive responses with a partner:

1. Choose one of the following criticisms, and brief your partner on how it might be directed at you:
   a. You're so selfish sometimes. You think only of yourself.
   b. Don't be so touchy!
   c. You say you understand me, but you don't really.
   d. I wish you'd do your share around here.
   e. You're so critical!

2. As your partner criticizes you, answer with the appropriate response from the preceding pages. As you do so, try to adopt an attitude of genuinely wanting to understand the criticism and finding parts that you can sincerely agree with.

3. Ask your partner to evaluate your response. Does it follow the forms described in the previous pages? Does it sound sincere?

4. Replay the same scene, trying to improve your response.

✔+ MAKING THE GRADE

Summary

Every relationship has a communication climate. Positive climates are characterized by confirming messages, which make it clear that the parties value one another. Negative climates are usually disconfirming. In one way or another, messages in disconfirming relationships convey indifference or hostility. Disagreeing messages have some combination of confirmation and disconfirmation. Communication climates develop early in a relationship, from both verbal and nonverbal messages. After they are created, reciprocal messages create either positive or negative spirals in which the frequency and intensity of either positive or negative messages are likely to grow.

Defensiveness hinders effective communication. Most defensiveness occurs when people try to protect key parts of a presenting self-image that they believe is under attack. Using the supportive behaviors defined by Jack Gibb when expressing potentially threatening messages can reduce the likelihood of triggering defensive reactions in others. In addition, we can share our thoughts and feelings with others in face-saving ways by using the assertive message format. A complete, clear message describes the behavior in question, at least one interpretation, the speaker's feelings, the consequences of the situation, and the speaker's intentions in making the statement.

When faced with criticism by others, it is possible to respond nondefensively by attempting to understand the criticism and by agreeing with either the facts or the critic's perception.

Key Terms

aggressiveness (344)
ambiguous response (343)
argumentativeness (344)
assertive message format (356)
certainty (355)
communication climate (340)
complaining (344)
confirming communication (341)
consequence statement (359)
controlling communication (350)
de-escalatory conflict spiral (347)

defensiveness (348)
description (350)
disagreeing messages (343)
disconfirming communication (341)
empathy (352)
equality (354)
escalatory conflict spiral (346)
evaluation (349)
face-threatening act (348)
feeling statement (358)
Gibb categories (349)
impersonal response (343)
impervious response (342)

incongruous response (343)
intention statement (359)
interpretation statement (357)
interrupting response (342)
irrelevant response (342)
neutrality (352)
problem orientation (351)
provisionalism (355)
spiral (345)
spontaneity (351)
strategy (351)
superiority (352)
tangential response (343)

Online Resources

Now that you have read this chapter, use your Premium Website for *Looking Out/ Looking In* for quick access to the electronic resources that accompany this text. Your Premium Website gives you access to:

- **Study tools** that will help you assess your learning and prepare for exams (*digital glossary*, *key term flash cards*, *review quizzes*).

- **Activities and assignments** that will help you hone your knowledge, understand how theory and research applies to your own life (*Invitation to Insight*), consider ethical challenges in interpersonal communication (*Ethical Challenge*), and build your interpersonal communication skills throughout the course (*Skill Builder*). If requested, you can submit your answers to your instructor.

- **Media resources** that will allow you to watch and critique news video and videos of interpersonal communication situations (*In Real Life*, *interpersonal video simulations*) and download a chapter review so you can study when and where you'd like (*Audio Study Tools*).

This chapter's key terms and search terms for additional reading are featured in this end-of-chapter section, and you can find this chapter's Invitation to Insight, Ethical Challenge, Skill Builder, and In Real Life activities in the body of the chapter.

Search Terms

When searching online databases to research topics in this chapter, use the following terms (along with this chapter's key terms) to maximize the chances of finding useful information:

assertiveness
cognitive dissonance

communication patterns
criticism

defense mechanisms
supportive communication

Film and Television

You can see the communication principles described in this chapter portrayed in the following films and television programs:

CONFIRMING AND DISCONFIRMING COMMUNICATION

Everybody Loves Raymond (1996–2005) Rated TV-G

The title character of this situation comedy is sportswriter Raymond Barone (Ray Romano), but fans of the show know that the central character in the family's communication patterns is his mother Marie (Doris Roberts). The messages she sends, both verbally and nonverbally, clearly communicate how she feels about each family member.

In Marie's eyes, Ray can do no wrong, so she lavishes him with acknowledgment and endorsement. On the other hand, her husband Frank (Peter Boyle) and daughter-in-law Debra (Patricia Heaton) often can do no right in Marie's eyes, so she sends them messages filled with arguing, complaining, and even aggression. Her other son Robert (Brad Garrett), who lives in Raymond's shadow, gets heavy doses of impervious, irrelevant, and impersonal communication—almost as if he doesn't exist.

What keeps the family relatively sane is that they call each other on the carpet when these patterns get out of hand. They repair the communication climate just in time to start back in on each other the following episode.

Antwone Fisher (2002) Rated PG-13

Antwone Fisher (Derek Luke) is an angry young sailor. A shipboard fight lands him in the office of base psychiatrist Jerome Davenport (Denzel Washington), whose job is to help Antwone manage his temper. After several sessions of stubborn silence, Antwone reveals that he was abandoned at birth by his imprisoned mother. He never knew his father, who was murdered two months before he was born. Raised by a cruel foster family, Antwone feels rootless and angry at the world. Davenport becomes a father figure to Antwone and assures him of his value and worth. On Davenport's advice, Antwone travels home to Cleveland in search of his roots.

The movie, based on a true story, is a powerful example of how being ignored is the ultimate form of disconfirmation. The fact that Antwone's mother never sought him out during or after her imprisonment communicated to Antwone that his existence didn't matter. When he finally tracks her down and confronts her with the pain of his abandonment, she sits in guilty silence and doesn't respond (it appears she is emotionally incapable of doing so). The good news is that his father's family—who didn't even know Antwone existed before he shows up on their doorstep—gives him a royal welcome home. The movie offers hope for turning around a tough life through the confirmation and love of people who care.

COMMUNICATION SPIRALS

Changing Lanes (2002) Rated R

Gavin Banek (Ben Affleck) and Doyle Gipson (Samuel L. Jackson) are strangers who literally meet by accident. Both are running late for court appointments when their cars collide. Gipson wants to exchange insurance information and file an accident report; Banek only cares about getting to court on time. Banek hands Gipson a blank check and drives away yelling "Better luck next time"—leaving Gipson stranded in the middle of the road with a disabled car.

This event begins a negative spiral that quickly spins out of control. Gipson sends Banek a fax with the phrase "Better luck next time" scrawled on an important document that Banek accidentally left with Gipson. Banek retaliates by finding ways to ruin Gipson's credit rating. Gipson counterattacks and so does Banek—and in one day's time, these two men wreak havoc on each other's lives. *Changing Lanes* offers a sobering look at how the ineffective handling of a communication episode between strangers can lead to a destructive communication spiral.

DEFENSIVE COMMUNICATION CLIMATES

Doubt (2008) Rated PG-13

The emotional climate at St. Nicholas parochial school varies depending on who is in the room. When it's Sister James (Amy Adams), the mood is calm and respectful. When parish priest Father Flynn (Philip Seymour Hoffman) is in charge, his jovial personality inspires a mood of fun and intellectual curiosity. But whenever the severe principal Sister Aloysius (Meryl Streep) is around, students duck and cover to avoid (or at least survive) her suspicion and wrath.

Sister Aloysius distrusts all things modern, including Father Flynn's progressive attitudes. When the priest summons a young student to the rectory alone, she jumps to the worst possible interpretation of his motives and behavior. In the unfolding drama, Sister Aloysius demonstrates many of Gibb's defense-arousing styles of communication. She is evaluative, dogmatic, strategic, and indifferent to Father Flynn's desires to touch the hearts and minds of his students. As the film ends, though, we learn why the story is titled *Doubt*.

Office Space (1999) Rated R

Peter Gibbons (Ron Livingston) hates his job—with good reason. He works for a computer firm that treats its employees like cogs in a machine. The company is top-heavy with impersonal managers who bombard their supervisees with memos and pounce on the smallest infractions of office policy. As a result, the employees lack motivation and feel little commitment to the organization. They also feel defensive any time they are approached by a manager.

Peter's boss is Bill Lumbergh (Gary Cole), who on the surface talks a good game. He doesn't raise his voice or use abusive language when correcting Peter; in fact, he offers suggestions in positive terms ("If you could go ahead and make sure to do that from now on, that would be great"). Unfortunately, he delivers these messages in a syrupy tone of voice that reeks of condescension. Moreover, Lumbergh doesn't listen or respond to his employees, nor does he ask for their input or participation. He simply delivers monologues and walks away. In Gibb's terms, Lumbergh uses control, neutrality, and superiority (and most of the other defense-provoking components as well)—and the result is that Peter and the other employees hide when they see the boss coming their way.

Office Space is a good example of a toxic communication climate. For anyone who has had the misfortune of working in a dysfunctional organization, the movie will probably elicit a chuckle, because the office communication will look and sound all too familiar.

GIVING AND RECEIVING CRITICISM

American Idol (2002–) Rated TV-G

The popular television show *American Idol* requires contestants to perform songs not only in front of millions of TV viewers and a live audience, but also before a panel of judges who publicly critique the performers and their talents (or lack thereof). Receiving criticism is always a face-threatening process, but particularly so when a huge audience is listening in.

It's interesting to watch how the *Idol* judges offer their criticisms and how the contestants respond. When the verdict is negative, some judges are curt and evaluative ("That was awful!") or broad and vague ("That didn't work"). The most helpful criticisms focus on specific behaviors and suggestions for change ("I think you need a song in a lower range—you seemed to be straining for the high notes").

Of course, performers don't always respond well to suggestions. Many quickly defend themselves ("I thought I did just fine") or shift the blame ("I didn't choose the song"). Others follow principles described in this chapter, such as seeking more information or agreeing with the critic, hoping to improve their next performance. Shows like *American Idol* are designed for entertainment, not education—but from a communication perspective, they offer valuable lessons about giving and receiving criticism.

11

MANAGING INTERPERSONAL CONFLICTS

After studying the material in this chapter, you should be able to:

1. Identify the conflicts in your important relationships and how satisfied you are with the way they have been handled.

2. Describe your personal conflict styles, evaluate their effectiveness, and suggest alternatives as appropriate.

3. Identify the relational conflict styles, patterns of behavior, and conflict rituals that define a given relationship.

4. Demonstrate how you could use the win-win approach in a given conflict.

*F*or most people, conflict has about the same appeal as a trip to the dentist. A quick look at a thesaurus offers a clue about the distasteful nature of conflict. Synonyms for the term include *battle, brawl, clash, competition, discord, disharmony, duel, fight, strife, struggle, trouble,* and *violence.*

Even the metaphors we use to describe our conflicts show that we view conflict as something to be avoided.[1] We often talk about conflict as a kind of war: "He shot down my arguments." "Okay, fire away." "Don't try to defend yourself!" Other metaphors suggest that conflict is explosive: "Don't blow up!" "I needed to let off steam." "You've got a short fuse." Sometimes conflict seems like a kind of trial, in which one party accuses another: "Come on, admit you're guilty." "Stop accusing me!" "Just listen to my case." Language that suggests that conflict is a mess is also common: "Let's not open this can of worms." "That's a sticky situation." "Don't make such a stink!" Even the metaphor of a game implies that one side has to defeat the other: "That was out of bounds." "You're not playing fair." "I give up; you win!"

Despite images like these, the truth is that conflict *can* be constructive. With the right set of communication skills, conflict can be less like a struggle and more like a kind of dance in which partners work together to create something that would be impossible without their cooperation. You may have to persuade the other person to become your partner rather than your adversary, and you may be clumsy at first, but with enough practice and goodwill, you can work together instead of at cross-purposes.

The attitude you bring to your conflicts can make a tremendous difference between success and failure. One study revealed that college students in close romantic relationships who believed that conflicts are destructive were most likely to neglect or quit the relationship and less likely to seek a solution than couples who had less-negative attitudes.[2] Of course, attitudes alone won't always guarantee satisfying solutions to conflicts—but the kinds of skills you will learn in this chapter can help well-intentioned partners handle their disagreements constructively.

The Nature of Conflict

Before focusing on how to solve interpersonal problems constructively, we need to look briefly at the nature of conflict. What is it? Why is it an inevitable part of life? How can it be beneficial?

CONFLICT DEFINED

Before reading further, make a list of the interpersonal conflicts in your life. They probably involve many different people, revolve around very different subjects, and take many different forms. Some become loud, angry arguments. Others may be expressed in calm, rational discussions. Still others might simmer along most of the time with brief but bitter flare-ups.

Whatever form they may take, all interpersonal conflicts share certain characteristics. William Wilmot and Joyce Hocker provide a thorough definition when they define **conflict** as "an expressed struggle between at least two interdependent parties who perceive incompatible goals, scarce resources, and interference from the other party in achieving their goals."[3] A closer look at the key parts of this definition will help you recognize how conflict operates in your life.

EXPRESSED STRUGGLE A conflict can exist only when both parties are aware of a disagreement. For instance, you may be upset for months because a neighbor's loud stereo keeps you awake at night, but no conflict exists between the two of you until the neighbor learns of your problem. Of course, the expressed struggle doesn't have to be verbal. A dirty look, the silent treatment, and avoiding the other person are all ways of expressing yourself. One way or another, both parties must know that a problem exists before they're in conflict.

PERCEIVED INCOMPATIBLE GOALS

All conflicts look as if one party's gain would be another's loss. For instance, consider the neighbor whose stereo keeps you awake at night. Doesn't somebody have to lose? If the neigh-

> Personal experience may suggest otherwise, but with skill and the right attitude, conflicts can be constructive.

Christina Kennedy/Getty Images

bor turns down the noise, she loses the enjoyment of hearing the music at full volume, but if the neighbor keeps the volume up, you're still awake and unhappy.

The goals in this situation really aren't completely incompatible; there are solutions that allow both parties to get what they want. For instance, you could achieve peace and quiet by closing your windows or getting the neighbor to close hers. You might use a pair of earplugs, or perhaps the neighbor could get a set of earphones, allowing the music to be played at full volume without bothering anyone. If any of these solutions prove workable, the conflict disappears. Unfortunately, people often fail to see mutually satisfying solutions to their problems. As long as they *perceive* their goals to be mutually exclusive, a conflict exists.

PERCEIVED SCARCE RESOURCES Conflicts also exist when people believe there isn't enough of something to go around. The most obvious example of a scarce resource is money—a cause of many conflicts. If a worker asks for a raise in pay and the boss would rather keep the money or use it to expand the business, the two parties are in conflict.

Time is another scarce commodity. As authors and family men, we writers of this textbook constantly face struggles about how to use the limited time we have at home. Should we work on this book? Chat with our wives? Spend time with our children? Enjoy the luxury of being alone? With only twenty-four hours in a day, we're bound to wind up in conflicts with our families, editors, students, and friends—all of whom want more of our time than we have to give.

INTERDEPENDENCE However antagonistic they might feel, the parties in conflict are usually dependent on each other. The welfare and satisfaction of one depend on the actions of another. If not, then even in the face of scarce resources and incompatible goals, there would be no need for conflict. Interdependence exists between conflicting nations, social groups, organizations, friends, and lovers. In each case, if the two parties didn't need each other to solve the problem, they would go their separate ways. One of the first steps toward resolving a conflict is to take the attitude that "we're all in this together."

INTERFERENCE FROM THE OTHER PARTY

No matter how much one person's position may differ from another's, a full-fledged conflict won't occur until the participants act in

> We struggled together, knowing. We prattled, pretended, fought bitterly, laughed, wept . . . nagged, supported, gave, took, demanded. . . . Will I ever find someone to battle with as we battled, love as we loved, share with as we shared, challenge as we challenged, forgive as we forgave?
>
> —*Vian Catrell*

ways that prevent one another from reaching their goals. For example, you might let some friends know that you object to their driving after drinking too much alcohol, but the conflict won't escalate until you act in ways that prevent them from getting behind the wheel. Likewise, a parent–child dispute about what clothing and music are appropriate will blossom into a conflict when the parents try to impose their position on the child.

CONFLICT IS NATURAL

Every relationship of any depth at all has conflict.[4] No matter how close, how understanding, how compatible you and other people are, there will be times when your ideas or actions or needs or goals won't match. You like rap music, but your companion likes classical; you want to date other people, but your partner wants to keep the relationship exclusive; you think a paper that you've written is fine, but your instructor wants it changed; you like to sleep late on Sunday mornings, but your housemate likes to get up early and exercise loudly. There's no end to the number and kinds of disagreements possible.

College students who have kept diaries of their relationships report that they take part in about seven arguments per week. Most have argued with the other person before, often about the same topic.[5] In another survey, 81 percent of the respondents acknowledged that they had conflicts with friends.[6] Even the 19 percent who claimed that their friendships were conflict-free used phrases like "push and pull" or "little disagreements" to describe the tensions that inevitably occurred. Among families, conflict can be even more frequent. Researchers recorded dinner conversations for fifty-two families and found an average of 3.3 "conflict episodes" per meal.[7]

At first this might seem depressing. If problems are inevitable in even the best relationships, does this mean that you're doomed to relive the same arguments, the same hurt feelings, over and over? Fortunately, the answer to this question is a definite "no." Even though conflict is part of a meaningful relationship, you can change the way you deal with it.

CONFLICT CAN BE BENEFICIAL

Because it is impossible to avoid conflicts, the challenge is to handle them well when they do arise. Effective communication during conflicts can actually keep good relationships strong. People who use the constructive skills described in this chapter are more satisfied with their relationships[8] and with the outcomes of their conflicts.[9]

> Not everything that is faced can be changed, but nothing can be changed until it is faced.
>
> —*James Baldwin*

Perhaps the best evidence of how constructive conflict skills can benefit a relationship focuses on communication between husbands and wives. More than twenty years of research shows that couples in both happy and unhappy marriages have conflicts, but that they manage conflict in very different ways.[10] One nine-year study revealed that unhappy couples argue in ways that we have catalogued in this book as destructive.[11] They are more concerned with defending themselves than with being problem oriented; they fail to listen carefully to each other, have little or no empathy for their partners, use evaluative "you" language, and ignore each other's nonverbal relational messages.

Many satisfied couples think and communicate differently when they disagree. They view disagreements as healthy and recognize that conflicts need to be faced.[12] Although they may argue vigorously, they use skills like perception checking to find out what the other person is thinking, and they let each other know that they understand the other side of the argument.[13] They are willing to admit their mistakes, both contributing to a harmonious relationship and helping to solve the problem at hand.

In the following pages, we'll review communication skills that can make conflicts constructive, and introduce still more skills that you can use to resolve the inevitable conflicts you face. Before doing so, however, we need to examine how individuals behave when faced with a dispute.

Conflict Styles

Most people have default styles of handling conflict. (See Figure 11.1.) These habitual styles work sometimes, but they may not be effective in all situations. What styles do you typically use to deal with conflict? Find out by thinking about how two hypothetical characters—Paul and Lucia—manage a problem.

Paul and Lucia have been running partners for over a year. Three times every week, they spend an hour or more together working out. The two runners are equally matched, and they enjoy challenging one another to cover longer distances at a quicker pace. During their time on the road, the friends have grown quite close. Now they often talk about personal matters that they don't share with anyone else.

Recently, Lucia has started to invite some of her friends along on the runs. Paul likes Lucia's friends, but they aren't strong athletes, so the outings become a much less satisfying workout. Also, Paul fears losing the special one-on-one time that he and Lucia have had. Paul shared his concerns with Lucia, but she dismissed them. "I don't see what the problem is," she replied. "We still get plenty of time on the road, and you said you like my friends." "But it isn't the same," replied Paul.

This situation has all the elements of a conflict: expressed struggle (their differences are in the open and they still disagree), seemingly incompatible goals and interference (Lucia wants to run with her friends; Paul wants to run with just Lucia), apparently scarce resources (they only have so much time for running), and interdependence (they enjoy one another's company and run better together than separately).

Here are five ways Paul and Lucia could handle the matter. Each represents one approach to managing conflict:

- They could say "Let's just forget it" and stop running together.

- Paul could give in, sacrificing his desire for one-on-one conversations and challenging runs. Or Lucia could give in, sacrificing her other friendships to maintain her friendship with Paul.

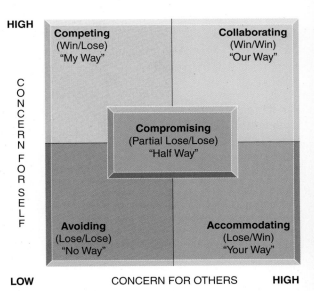

Figure 11.1
Conflict Styles

Adapted from W. W. Wilmot & J. L. Hocker (2010). *Interpersonal Conflict,* 8th ed. New York: McGraw-Hill.

- One or the other could issue an ultimatum: "Either we do it my way, or we stop running together."

- They could compromise, inviting friends along on some runs but excluding them on other days.

- Lucia and Paul could brainstorm ways they could run with her friends and still get their workouts and one-on-one time with each other.

These approaches represent the five styles depicted in Figure 11.1, each of which is described in the following paragraphs.

AVOIDING (LOSE-LOSE)

Avoiding occurs when people nonassertively ignore or stay away from conflict. Avoidance can be physical (steering clear of a friend after having an argument) or conversational (changing the topic, joking, or denying that a problem exists). It can be tempting to avoid conflict, but research suggests that this approach has its costs: Partners of "self-silencers" report more frustration and discomfort when dealing with the avoiding partner than with those who face conflict more construcively.[14]

Avoidance reflects a pessimistic attitude about conflict under the belief that there is no good way to resolve the issue at hand. Some avoiders believe it's easier to put up with the status quo than to face the problem head-on and try to solve it. Other avoiders believe it's better to quit (on either the topic or the relationship) than to keep facing the same issues without hope of solution. In either case, avoiding often results in *lose-lose* outcomes in which none of the parties get what they want.

In the case of Paul and Lucia, avoiding means that, rather than struggling with their disagreement, they just stop running together. Although it means they'll no longer be fighting, it also means they'll both lose a running partner and an important component of their friendship (and maybe their friendship altogether). This solution illustrates how avoiding can produce lose-lose results.

Although avoiding may keep the peace temporarily, it typically leads to unsatisfying relationships.[15] Chronic misunderstandings, resentments, and disappointments pile up and contaminate the emotional climate. For this reason, we can say that avoiders have a low concern both for their own needs and for the interests of the other person, who is also likely to suffer from unaddressed issues (see Figure 11.1).

Are there genuinely nice, sweet people in this world? Yes, absolutely yes, and they get angry as often as you and I. They must—otherwise they would be full of vindictive feelings and slush, which would prevent genuine sweetness.

—*Theodore Isaac Rubin*

© Bettmann/Corbis

Despite its obvious shortcomings, avoiding isn't always a bad idea.[16] You might choose to avoid certain topics or situations if the risk of speaking up is too great, such as triggering an embarrassing fight in public, or even risking physical harm. You might also avoid a conflict if the relationship it involves isn't worth the effort. Even in close relationships, though, avoidance has its logic. If the issue is temporary or minor, you might let it pass. These reasons help explain why the communication of many happily married couples is characterized by "selectively ignoring" the other person's minor flaws.[17] This doesn't mean that a key to successful relationships is avoiding *all* conflicts. Instead, it suggests that it's smart to save energy for the truly important ones.

ACCOMMODATING (LOSE-WIN)

Accommodating occurs when you allow others to have their way rather than asserting your own point of view. Figure 11.1 depicts accommodators as having low concern for themselves and high concern for others, resulting in *lose-win*, "we'll do it your way" outcomes. In our hypothetical scenario, Paul could accommodate Lucia by letting her friends join in on their runs, even though it means less of a physical challenge and quality time with Lucia—or Lucia could accommodate Paul by running with just him.

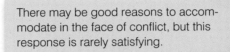

There may be good reasons to accommodate in the face of conflict, but this response is rarely satisfying.

The motivation of an accommodator plays a significant role in this style's effectiveness. If accommodation is a genuine act of kindness, generosity, or love, then chances are good that it will enhance the relationship. Most people appreciate those who "take one for the team," "treat others as they want to be treated," or "lose the battle to win the war." However, people are far less appreciative of those who habitually use this style to play the role of "martyr, bitter complainer, whiner, or saboteur."[18]

We should pause here to mention the important role that culture plays in perceptions of conflict styles. People from high-context, collectivist backgrounds (such as many Asian cultures) are likely to regard avoidance and accommodation as face-saving and noble ways to handle conflict.[19] In low-context, individualist cultures (such as the United States), avoidance and accommodation are often viewed less positively. For instance, think of the many unflattering terms that Americans use for people who give up or give in during conflicts ("pushover," "yes man," "doormat," "spineless"). As you will read later in this chapter, collectivist cultures have virtuous words and phrases to describe these same traits. The point here is that all conflict styles have value in certain situations, and that culture plays a significant role in determining how each style is valued.

COMPETING (WIN-LOSE)

The flip side of accommodating is **competing**. This *win-lose* approach to conflict involves high concern for self and low concern for others. As Figure 11.1 shows, competition seeks to resolve conflicts "my way." If Lucia and Paul each tried to force the other to concede, one of them might prevail, but at the other's expense.

People resort to competing when they perceive a situation as being an either-or one: Either I get what I want or you get what you want. The most clear-cut examples of win-lose situations are certain games such as baseball or poker, in which the rules require a winner and a loser. Some interpersonal issues seem to fit into this win-lose framework: two coworkers seeking a promotion to the same job, or a couple who disagrees on how to spend their limited money.

"Well, if it doesn't matter who's right and who's wrong, why don't I be right and you be wrong?"

There are cases when competing can enhance a relationship. One study revealed that some men and women in satisfying dating relationships use competition to enrich their interaction.[20] For example, some found satisfaction by competing in play (who's the better racquetball player?), in achievement (who gets the better job offer?), and in altruism (who's more romantic?). These satisfied couples developed a shared narrative (see Chapter 3) that defined competition as a measure of regard, quite different from conflict that signaled a lack of appreciation and respect. Of course, it's easy to see how these arrangements could backfire if one partner became a gloating winner or a sore loser. Feeling like you've been defeated can leave you wanting to get even, creating a downward competitive spiral that degrades to a *lose-lose* relationship.[21]

Power is the distinguishing characteristic in win-lose problem solving, because it is necessary to defeat an opponent to get what one wants. The most obvious kind of power is physical. Some parents threaten their children with warnings such as "Stop misbehaving, or I'll send you to your room." Adults who use physical power to deal with each other usually aren't so blunt, but the legal system is the implied threat: "Follow the rules, or we'll lock you up."

Real or implied force isn't the only kind of power used in conflicts. People who rely on authority of many types engage in win-lose methods without ever threatening physical coercion. In most jobs, supervisors have the authority to assign working hours, job promotions, and desirable or undesirable tasks and, of course, to fire an unsatisfactory employee. Teachers can use the power of grades to coerce students to act in desired ways. Even the usually admired democratic system of majority rule is a win-lose method of resolving conflicts. However fair it may seem, with this system one group is satisfied and the other is defeated.

The dark side of competition is that it often breeds aggression.[22] Sometimes aggression is obvious, but at other times it can be more subtle. To understand how, read on.

DIRECT AGGRESSION   **Direct aggression** occurs when a communicator expresses a criticism or demand that threatens the face of the person at whom it is directed. Communication researcher Dominic Infante identified several types of direct aggression: character attacks, competence attacks, physical appearance attacks, maledictions (wishing the other ill fortune), teasing, ridicule, threats, swearing, and nonverbal emblems.[23]

Direct aggression can have a severe impact on the target. Recipients can feel embarrassed, inadequate, humiliated, hopeless, desperate, or depressed.[24] These results can lead to decreased effectiveness in personal relationships, on the job, and in families.[25] There is a significant connection between verbal aggression and physical aggression,[26] but even if the attacks never lead to blows, the psychological effects can be devastating. For example, siblings who were teased by a brother or sister report less satisfaction and trust than those whose relationships were relatively free of this sort of aggression,[27] and high school teams with aggressive coaches lose more games than those whose coaches are less aggressive.[28]

PASSIVE AGGRESSION   **Passive aggression** occurs when a communicator expresses hostility in an obscure or manipulative way. As the Ethical Challenge on page 386

As the TV show's title suggests, *Hell's Kitchen* chef Gordon Ramsay's communication style is heavy on aggression.

Granada/Fox-TV/The Kobal Collection/ Ecclesine, Patrick

explains, this behavior has been termed **crazymaking**. It occurs when people have feelings of resentment, anger, or rage that they are unable or unwilling to express directly. Instead of keeping these feelings to themselves, a crazymaker sends aggressive messages in subtle, indirect ways, thus maintaining the front of kindness. This amiable façade eventually crumbles, leaving the crazymaker's victim confused and angry at having been fooled. The targets of the crazymaker can either react with aggressive behavior of their own or retreat to nurse their hurt feelings. In either case, passive aggression seldom has anything but harmful effects on a relationship.[29] In our scenario, Lucia could take a passive-aggressive approach to Paul's desire to keep their workouts exclusive by showing up late to run, just to annoy him. Paul could become passive-aggressive by agreeing to include Lucia's friends, then pouring on the speed and leaving them behind.

Aggressive behavior can punish the attacker as well as the victim. Men who view conversations as contests and partners as opponents are 60 percent more apt to die earlier than those who are less aggressive.[30] Newly married couples whose disagreements are marked by sarcasm, interruptions, and criticism suffer a drop in the effectiveness of their immune systems.[31]

COMPROMISING (PARTIAL LOSE-LOSE)

A **compromise** gives both people at least some of what they want, although both sacrifice part of their goals. People usually settle for a compromise when it seems that partial satisfaction is the best they can hope for. In the case of Paul and Lucia, they could strike a halfway deal by alternating workouts with and without her friends. Unlike avoidance, where both parties lose because they don't address their problem, compromisers actually negotiate a solution that gives them some of what they want, but also leaves everybody losing something.

Compromising is sometimes touted as an effective way to handle conflicts. As Diamond Rio vocalist Marty Roe sings, "There ain't no road too long when we meet in the middle." Compromise may be better than losing everything, but there are times when this approach hardly seems ideal. One observer has asked why it is that if someone says, "I will compromise my values," we view the action unfavorably, yet we favorably view parties in a conflict who compromise to reach a solution.[32] Although compromises may be the best obtainable result in some conflicts, it's important to realize that both people in a conflict can often work together to find much better solutions. In such cases *compromise* is a negative word.

Most of us are surrounded by the results of bad compromises. Consider a common example: the conflict between one person's desire to smoke cigarettes and another's need for clean air. The win-lose outcomes of this issue are obvious: either the smoker abstains, or the nonsmoker gets polluted lungs—neither option is very satisfying. But

ETHICAL CHALLENGE

Dirty Fighting with Crazymakers

Psychologist George Bach uses the term *crazymakers* to describe passive-aggressive behavior. His term reflects the insidious nature of indirect aggression, which can confuse and anger a victim who may not even be aware of being victimized. Although a case can be made for using all of the other approaches to conflict described in this chapter, it is difficult to find a justification for passive-aggressive crazymaking.

The following categories represent a nonexhaustive list of crazymaking. They are presented here as a warning for potential victims, who might choose to use perception checking, "I" language, assertion, or other communication strategies to explore whether the user has a complaint that can be addressed in a more constructive manner.

The Avoider Avoiders refuse to fight. When a conflict arises, they leave, fall asleep, pretend to be busy at work, or keep from facing the problem in some other way. Because avoiders won't fight back, this strategy can frustrate the person who wants to address an issue.

The Pseudoaccommodator Pseudoaccommodators pretend to give in and then continue to act in the same way.

The Guiltmaker Instead of expressing dissatisfaction directly, guiltmakers try to make others feel responsible for causing pain. A guiltmaker's favorite line is "It's okay; don't worry about me . . ." accompanied by a big sigh.

The Mind Reader Instead of allowing their partners to express feelings honestly, mind readers go into character analysis, explaining what the partner really means or what's wrong with the partner. By behaving this way, mind readers refuse to handle their own feelings and leave no room for their partners to express themselves.

The Trapper Trappers play an especially dirty trick by setting up a desired behavior for their partners and then, when it's met, attacking the very behavior they requested. An example of this technique is for the trapper to say, "Let's be totally honest with each other," and then attack the partner's self-disclosure.

The Crisis Tickler Crisis ticklers almost bring what's bothering them to the surface but never quite come out and express themselves. Instead of admitting concern about the finances, they innocently ask, "Gee, how much did that cost?", dropping a rather obvious hint but never really dealing with the crisis.

The Gunnysacker These people don't share complaints as they arise. Instead, they put their resentments into a psychological gunnysack, which after a while begins to bulge with both large and small gripes. Then, when the sack is about to burst, the gunnysacker pours out all the pent-up aggressions on the overwhelmed and unsuspecting victim.

The Trivial Tyrannizer Instead of honestly sharing their resentments, trivial tyrannizers do things they know will get their partners' goat—leaving dirty dishes in the sink, clipping fingernails in bed, belching out loud, turning up the television too loud, and so on.

The Beltliner Everyone has a psychological "beltline," and below it are subjects too sensitive to be approached without damaging the relationship. Beltlines may have to do with physical characteristics, intelligence, past behavior, or deeply ingrained personality traits that a person is trying to overcome. In an attempt to "get even" or hurt their partners, beltliners will use intimate knowledge to hit below the belt, where they know it will hurt.

The Joker Because they are afraid to face conflicts squarely, jokers kid around when their partners want to be serious, thus blocking the expression of important feelings.

The Withholder Instead of expressing their anger honestly and directly, withholders punish their partners by keeping back something—courtesy, affection, good cooking, humor, sex. As you can imagine, this is likely to build up even greater resentments in the relationship.

The Benedict Arnold These characters get back at their partners by sabotage, by failing to defend them from attackers, and even by encouraging ridicule or disregard from outside the relationship.

For more information about crazymaking, see G. Bach & Peter Wyden (1968). The Intimate Enemy. *New York: Avon; and G. Bach (1971).* Aggression Lab: The Fair Fight Manual. *Dubuque, IA: Kendall-Hunt.*

a compromise in which the smoker gets to enjoy only a rare cigarette or must retreat outdoors and in which the nonsmoker still must inhale some fumes or feel like an ogre is hardly better. Both sides have lost a considerable amount of both comfort and goodwill. Of course, the costs involved in other compromises are even greater. For example, if a divorced couple compromises on child care by haggling over custody and then grudgingly agree to split the time with their children, it's hard to say that anybody has won.

Some compromises do leave both parties satisfied. You and the seller might settle on a price for a used car that is between what the seller was asking and what you wanted to pay. Although neither of you got everything you wanted, the outcome would still leave both of you satisfied. Likewise, you and your companion might agree to see a film that is the second choice for both of you in order to spend an evening together. As long as everyone is satisfied with an outcome, compromise can be an effective way to resolve conflicts. When compromises are satisfying and successful, it might be more accurate to categorize them as the final style we'll discuss: collaborating.

COLLABORATING (WIN-WIN)

Collaborating seeks *win-win* solutions to conflict. Collaborators show a high degree of concern for both themselves and others. Rather than trying to solve problems "my way" or "your way," their focus is on "our way." In the best case, collaborating can lead to a win-win outcome, where everybody gets what they want.

If Lucia and Paul were to collaborate, they might determine that the best way for both of them to get what they want is to continue their one-on-one workouts, but invite Lucia's friends to join in for a few miles at the end of each run. They might schedule other, less-challenging workouts that include the friends. Or they might find other ways to get together with Lucia's friends that are fun for both of them.

> Let us begin anew, remembering on both sides that civility is not a sign of weakness.
>
> —*John F. Kennedy*

The goal of collaboration is to find a solution that satisfies the needs of everyone involved. Not only do the partners avoid trying to win at the other's expense, but they also believe that by working together, it is possible to find a solution that goes beyond a mere compromise and allows all parties to reach their goals. Consider a few examples:

- A newly married husband and wife find themselves arguing frequently over their budget. The husband enjoys buying impractical and enjoyable items for himself and for the house, whereas the wife fears that such purchases will ruin their carefully constructed budget. Their solution is to set aside a small amount of money each month for "fun purchases." The amount is small enough to be affordable yet gives the husband a chance to escape from their spartan lifestyle. The wife is satisfied with the arrangement, because the luxury money is now a budget category by itself, which gets rid of the out-of-control feeling that comes when her husband makes unexpected purchases. The plan works so well that the couple continues to use it even after their income rises, by increasing the amount devoted to luxuries.

- Marta, a store manager, hates the task of rescheduling employee work shifts to accommodate their social and family needs. She and her staff develop an

ON THE JOB

Leaving on a Good Note

In an ideal world, employees would love their jobs and stay happily employed forever. In reality, though, that rarely happens. Some people leave for positive reasons such as career advancement or new opportunities. Many, however, quit because of workplace conflicts.[a]

Some conflicts arise when workers don't get enough information to do their jobs, and others come from conflicting demands (e.g., "Work faster, but don't make any mistakes").[b] Sometimes the reasons for leaving are darker, such as bullying by coworkers or bosses.[c]

Whatever the reasons for quitting, these strategies will help you leave on the best possible terms[d]:

- *Leave before you lose your cool.* Waiting until your situation is intolerable may cause you to blow up and say things you'll regret later. Once the writing is on the wall, it's smart to move on.

- *Tell your boss first.* Management will be insulted if they hear about your departure plans through the grapevine. When you explain your reasons directly to the boss, you can control the information he or she hears, rather than risking misunderstandings and misinformation.

- *Don't trash the company.* Even if you have been treated poorly, be careful about criticizing the organization or its personnel. It's a small world, and you may need the goodwill of these people in the future.

- *Finish on a strong note.* Make sure to do an exemplary job during your final days and weeks. The impression you leave can influence the references you get later, as well as the attitudes of supervisors and colleagues you may encounter again during your career.

arrangement in which employees arrange schedule swaps on their own and notify her in writing after they are made.

- Wendy and Kathy are roommates who have different study habits. Wendy likes to do her work in the evenings, which leaves her days free for other things, but Kathy feels that nighttime is party time. The solution they worked out is that Monday through Wednesday evenings Wendy studies at her boyfriend's place while Kathy does anything she wants; Thursday and Sunday, Kathy agrees to keep things quiet around the house.

The point here isn't that these solutions are the correct ones for everybody with similar problems. The win-win method doesn't work that way. Different people might have found other solutions that suit them better. Collaboration gives you a way of creatively finding just the right answer for your unique problem—and that answer might be one that neither party thought of or expected before collaborating. By generating win-win solutions, you can tailor-make a way of resolving your conflicts that everyone can live with comfortably. Later in this chapter, you'll learn a specific process for arriving at collaborative solutions to problems.

WHICH STYLE TO USE?

Collaborating might seem like the ideal approach to solving problems, but it's an oversimplification to imagine that there is a single "best" way.[33] Generally speaking, win-win approaches are preferable to win-lose and lose-lose solutions. But we've already seen that there are times when avoiding, accommodating, competing, and compromising are appropriate. Table 11.1 lists some of the issues to consider when deciding which style to use when facing a conflict. As you decide which approach to use, consider several factors:

1. *The Relationship.* When someone else clearly has more power than you, accommodating may be the best approach. If the boss tells you to fill that order "Now!", it may be smart to do so without comment. A more assertive response ("I'm still tied up with the job you gave me yesterday") might be reasonable, but it could also cost you your job.

2. *The Situation.* Different situations call for different conflict styles. After haggling over the price of a car for hours, it might be best to compromise by simply splitting the difference. In other cases, though, it may be a matter of principle for you to "stick to your guns" and attempt to get what you believe is right.

3. *The Other Person.* Win-win is a fine ideal, but sometimes the other person isn't willing or able to collaborate. You probably know communicators who are so competitive that they put winning on even minor issues ahead of the well-being of your relationship. In such cases, your efforts to collaborate may have a low chance of success.

4. *Your Goals.* Sometimes your overriding concern may be to calm down an enraged or upset person. Accomodating an outburst from your crotchety and sick neighbor, for example, is probably better than standing up for yourself and triggering a stroke. In still other cases, your moral principles might compel an aggressive

> What counts in making a happy marriage is not so much how compatible you are, but how you deal with incompatibility.
>
> —Leo Tolstoy

Table 11.1

Factors to Consider When Choosing the Most Appropriate Conflict Style

Avoiding (lose-lose)	Accommodating (lose-win)	Competing (win-lose)	Compromising (partial lose-lose)	Collaborating (win-win)
When the issue is of little importance	When you discover you are wrong	When there is not enough time to seek a win-win outcome	To achieve quick, temporary solutions to complex problems	When the issue is too important for a compromise
When the costs of confrontation outweigh the benefits	When the issue is more important to the other person than it is to you	When the issue is not important enough to negotiate at length	When opponents are strongly committed to mutually exclusive goals	When a long-term relationship between you and the other person is important
To cool down and gain perspective	When the long-term cost of winning isn't worth the short-term gain	When the other person is not willing to cooperate	When the issues are moderately important but not enough for a stalemate	To merge insights with someone who has a different perspective on the problem
	To build up credits for later conflicts	When you are convinced that your position is right and necessary	As a backup mode when collaboration doesn't work	To develop a relationship by showing commitment to the concerns of both parties
	To let others learn by making their own mistakes	To protect yourself against a person who takes advantage of noncompetitive people		To come up with creative and unique solutions to problems

Adapted from W. W. Wilmot & J. L. Hocker (2010). Interpersonal Conflict, 8th ed. New York: McGraw-Hill.

✔+ INVITATION TO INSIGHT

Your Conflict Style

Assess your conflict style by taking the self-test at the website for the Peace and Justice Support Network of the Mennonite Church. This instrument measures the way you deal with issues in both "calm" and "stormy" situations. Go to your Premium Website for *Looking Out/Looking In* to access a link to this site.

statement even though it might not get you what you originally sought: "I've had enough of your racist jokes. I've tried to explain why they're so offensive, but you obviously haven't listened. I'm leaving!"

Conflict in Relational Systems

So far we have focused on individual conflict styles. Even though the style you choose in a conflict is important, your style isn't the only factor that will determine how a conflict unfolds. In reality, conflict is relational: Its character usually is determined by the way the parties interact with each other.[34] You might, for example, be determined to handle a conflict with your neighbor assertively, only to be driven to aggression by his uncooperative nature—or even to avoidance by his physical threats. Likewise, you might plan to hint to a professor that you are bothered by her apparent indifference, but wind up discussing the matter in an open, assertive way in reaction to her constructive response. Examples like these suggest that conflict doesn't depend on just individual choice. Rather, it depends on how the partners interact. When two or more people are in a long-term relationship, they develop their own **relational conflict style**—a pattern of managing disagreements. The mutual influence that parties have on each other is so powerful that it can overcome our disposition to handle conflicts in the manner that comes most easily to one or the other.[35] As we will soon see, some relational conflict styles are constructive, whereas others can make life miserable and threaten relationships.

COMPLEMENTARY, SYMMETRICAL, AND PARALLEL STYLES

Partners in interpersonal relationships—and impersonal ones, too—can use one of three styles to manage their conflicts. In relationships with a **complementary conflict style**, the partners use different but mutually reinforcing behaviors. In a **symmetrical conflict style**, both partners use the same behaviors. In a **parallel conflict style**, both partners shift between complementary and symmetrical patterns from one issue to another. Table 11.2 illustrates how the same conflict can unfold in very different ways, depending on whether the partners' communication is symmetrical or complementary. A parallel style would alternate between these two patterns, depending on the situation.

Research shows that a complementary "fight-flight" style is common in many unhappy marriages. One partner—most commonly the wife—addresses the conflict directly, whereas the other—usually the husband—withdraws.[36] It's easy to see how this pattern can lead to a cycle of increasing hostility and isolation, because each partner punctuates the conflict differently, blaming the other for making matters worse. "I withdraw because she's so critical," a husband might say. The wife wouldn't organize the sequence in the same way, however. "I criticize because he withdraws" would be her perception.

Complementary styles aren't the only ones that can lead to problems. Some distressed marriages suffer from destructively symmetrical communication. If both partners treat each other with matching hostility, one threat or insult leads to another in an escalatory spiral. If the partners both withdraw from each other instead of facing their problems, a de-escalatory spiral results, in which the satisfaction and vitality ebb from the relationship, leaving it a shell of its former self.

As Table 11.2 shows, both complementary and symmetrical behaviors can produce "good" results as well as "bad" results. If the complementary behaviors are positive, then a positive spiral results and the conflict stands a good chance of being resolved. This is the case in Example 2 in Table 11.2, where the boss is open to hearing the employee's concerns, listening willingly as the employee talks. Here, a complementary talk-listen pattern works well.

Symmetrical styles can also be beneficial. The clearest example of constructive symmetry occurs when both parties communicate assertively, listening to each other's concerns and working together to resolve them. The potential for this sort of solution occurs in Example 3, in the parent–teenager conflict. With enough mutual respect and careful listening, both the parents and their teenager can understand one another's concerns and very possibly find a way to give both parties what they want.

INTIMATE AND AGGRESSIVE STYLES

Another way to look at conflict styles is to examine the interaction between intimacy and aggression. The following scheme was originally used to describe communication between couples, but it also works well for other types of relationships.

Table 11.2
Complementary and Symmetrical Conflict Styles

Situation	Complementary Styles	Symmetrical Styles
Example 1: Wife upset because husband is spending little time at home.	Wife complains; husband withdraws, spending even less time at home. (Destructive)	Wife complains. Husband responds angrily and defensively. (Destructive)
Example 2: Female employee offended when male boss calls her "sweetie."	Employee objects to boss, explaining her reasons for being offended. Boss apologizes for his unintentional insult. (Constructive)	Employee maliciously "jokes" about boss at company party. (Destructive)
Example 3: Parents uncomfortable with teenager's new friends.	Parents express concerns. Teen dismisses them, saying "There's nothing to worry about." (Destructive)	Teen expresses discomfort with parents' protectiveness. Parents and teen negotiate a mutually agreeable solution. (Constructive)

- *Nonintimate-Aggressive.* These partners fight but are unsuccessful at satisfying important content and relational goals. In some relationships, aggression is expressed directly: "Forget it. I'm not going to another stupid party with your friends. All they do is gossip and eat." In other relationships, indirect aggression is the norm: (*Sarcastically*) "Sure, I'd *love* to go to another party with your friends." Neither of these approaches is satisfying, because there are few rewards to justify the costs of the unpleasantness.

- *Nonintimate-Nonaggressive.* The parties avoid conflicts—and each other—instead of facing issues head-on: "You won't be coming home for the holidays? Oh, well, I guess that's okay. . . ." Relationships of this sort can be quite stable, but because this pattern of communication doesn't confront and resolve problems, the vitality and satisfaction can decline over time.

- *Intimate-Aggressive.* This pattern combines aggression and intimacy in a manner that might seem upsetting to outsiders but that can work well in some relationships. Lovers may argue like cats and dogs, but then make up just as intensely. Coworkers might argue heatedly about how to get the job done, but cherish their association.

- *Intimate-Nonaggressive.* This sort of relationship has a low amount of attacking or blaming. Partners may confront each other directly or indirectly, but one way or another they manage to prevent issues from interfering with their relationship.

The pattern that partners choose may reveal a great deal about the kind of relationship they have chosen. Communication researcher Mary Ann Fitzpatrick identified three types of couples, which she descriptively labeled as "separates," "independents," and "traditionals."[37] Further research revealed that partners in each type of relationship approached conflict in a different manner.[38] Separates and independents tended to avoid conflict. Traditionals, by contrast, spent the most time focusing on their interaction. They also felt most secure about their relationships. They expressed negative emotions frequently but also sought and revealed a large amount of personal information. Satisfied

✔+ INVITATION TO INSIGHT

Understanding Conflict Styles

You can gain a clearer idea of how conflict styles differ by completing the following exercise:

1 Join a partner, and choose one of the following conflicts to work on. If you prefer, you may substitute a conflict of your own.
   a. Roommates disagree about the noise level in their apartment.
   b. Parents want their college sophomore son or daughter to stay home for the winter vacation. The son or daughter wants to travel with friends.
   c. One person in a couple wants to spend free time socializing with friends. The other wants to stay at home together.

2 Role-play the conflict four times, reflecting each of the following styles:
   a. Nonintimate-Aggressive
   b. Nonintimate-Nonaggressive
   c. Intimate-Aggressive
   d. Intimate-Nonaggressive

3 After experiencing each of these styles, determine which of them characterizes the way conflict is managed in one of your interpersonal relationships. Are you satisfied with this approach? If not, describe what style would be more appropriate.

traditional couples fit the intimate-nonaggressive pattern, communicating more positive and less negative information than independents.

Findings like this suggest that there's no single "best" relational conflict style.[39] Some families or couples may fight intensely but love one another just as strongly. Others might handle issues more rationally and calmly. Even a nonintimate-nonaggressive style can work well when there's no desire to have an interpersonal relationship. You might, for example, be willing to accommodate the demands of an eccentric professor for a semester because rolling with the punches gets you the education you are seeking without provoking a confrontation that could be upsetting and costly.

"I'm not yelling *at* you, I'm yelling *with* you."

CONFLICT RITUALS

When people have been in a relationship for some time, their communication often develops into **conflict rituals**—usually unacknowledged but very real patterns of interlocking behavior.[40] Consider a few common rituals:

- A young child interrupts her parents, demanding to be included in their conversation. At first the parents tell the child to wait, but she whines and cries until the parents find it easier to listen than to ignore the fussing.

- A couple fights. One partner leaves. The other accepts the blame for the problem and begs forgiveness. The first partner returns, and a happy reunion takes place. Soon they fight again.

- A boss flies into rage when the pressure builds at work. Recognizing this, the employees avoid him as much as possible. When the crisis is over, the boss compensates for his outbursts by being especially receptive to employee requests.

- Roommates have a blowout over housekeeping responsibilities. One roommate gives the other "the silent treatment" for several days, then begins picking up around the house without admitting being wrong.

There's nothing inherently wrong with the interaction in many rituals, especially when everybody involved accepts them as ways of managing conflict.[41] Consider the preceding examples. In the first, the little girl's whining may be the only way she can get the parents' attention. In the second, both partners might use the fighting as a way to blow off steam, and both might find that the joy of a reunion is worth the grief of the separation. In the third, the ritual might work well for the boss (as a way of releasing pressure) and for employees (as a way of getting their requests met). And in the fourth, at least the house gets cleaned—eventually.

Rituals can cause problems, though, when they become the *only* way relational partners handle their conflicts. As you learned in Chapter 1, competent communicators have a large repertoire of behaviors, and they are able to choose the most effective response for a given situation. Relying on one ritual pattern to handle all conflicts is no more effective than using a screwdriver to handle every home repair or putting the same seasoning on every dish you cook. Conflict rituals may be familiar and

✔+ INVITATION TO INSIGHT

Your Conflict Rituals

Describe two conflict rituals in one of your important relationships. One of your examples should consist of a positive ritual and the other of a negative ritual. For each example, explain:

1 A subject that is likely to trigger the conflict (such as, money, leisure time, affection)

2 The behavior of one partner that initiates the ritual

3 The series of responses by both partners that follows the initiating event

4 How the ritual ends

Based on your description, explain an alternative to the unsatisfying ritual, and describe how you might be able to change the way you manage the conflict in a more satisfying way.

comfortable, but they aren't always the best way to resolve the various conflicts that are part of any relationship.

Variables in Conflict Styles

By now you can see that every relational system is unique. The communication patterns in one family, business, or classroom are likely to be very different from those in any other. But along with the differences that arise in individual relationships, two powerful variables affect the way people manage conflict: gender and culture. We will now look at each of these variables and see how they affect how conflict is managed.

GENDER

Men and women often approach conflicts differently. Even in childhood, males are more likely to be aggressive, demanding, and competitive, whereas females are more likely to be cooperative. Studies of children from preschool to early adolescence have shown that boys try to get their way by ordering one another around: "Lie down." "Get off my steps." "Gimme your arm." By contrast, girls are more likely to make proposals for action, beginning with the word "Let's": "Let's go find some." "Let's ask her, 'Do you have any bottles?' " "Let's move these out first."[42] Whereas boys tell each other what role to take in pretend play ("Come on, be a doctor"), girls more commonly ask each other what role they want ("Will you be the patient for a few minutes?") or make a joint proposal ("We can both be doctors"). Furthermore, boys often make demands without offering an explanation ("Look, man. I want the wire cutters right now."). By contrast, girls often give reasons for their suggestions ("We gotta clean 'em first . . . 'cause they got germs.").

Adolescent girls use aggression in conflicts, but their methods are usually more indirect than those of boys. Whereas teenage boys often engage in verbal showdowns, and may even engage in physical fights, teenage girls typically use gossip, backbiting, and social exclusion.[43] This is not to suggest that girls' aggression is any less destructive than boys'. The film *Mean Girls* (based on the book *Queen Bees and Wannabes*[44]) offers a vivid depiction of just how injurious these indirect assaults can be on the self-concepts and relationships of young women.

Gender differences in dealing with conflict often persist into adulthood. One survey of college students revealed that men and women viewed conflicts in contrasting ways.[45] Regardless of their cultural background, female students described men as being concerned with power and more interested in content than relational issues. Phrases used to describe male conflict styles included: "The most important thing to males in conflict is their egos." "Men don't worry about feelings." "Men are more direct." By contrast, women were described as being more concerned with maintaining the relationship during a conflict. Phrases used to describe female conflict styles included: "Women are better listeners." "Women try to solve problems without controlling the other person." "Females are more concerned with others' feelings." When the actual conflict behaviors of both sexes are observed, women turn out to be more assertive than men about expressing their ideas and feelings, and men are more likely to withdraw from discussing issues.[46]

These sorts of differences don't mean that men are incapable of forming good relationships. Instead, their notions of what makes a good relationship are different. (See the commentary about the TV show *30 Rock* on page 408.) For some men, friendship and aggression aren't mutually exclusive. In fact, many strong male relationships are built around competition (e.g., at work or in athletics). Women can be competitive, too, but they also are more likely to use logical reasoning and bargaining than aggression.[47] When men communicate with women, they become less aggressive and more cooperative than they are in all-male groups.

In contrast with the "Men Are from Mars, Women Are from Venus" view of conflict, a look at the entire body of research on gender and conflict suggests that the differences in how the two sexes handle conflict are relatively small, and sometimes different from the stereotypical picture of aggressive men and passive women.[48] It would appear that people may *think* there are greater differences in male and female ways of handling conflicts than there actually are.[49] People who assume that men are aggressive and women accommodating may notice behavior that fits these stereotypes ("See how much he bosses her around. A typical man!"). On the other hand, behavior that doesn't fit these stereotypes (accommodating men, pushy women) goes unnoticed.

Where men and women do have characteristically different conflict styles, the reasons may have little to do with gender. The situation at hand has a greater influence on shaping the way a person handles conflict.[50] For example, both men and women are more likely to respond aggressively when attacked by the other person. (Recall the discussion of defensive spirals in Chapter 10.) In fact, researchers exploring how married couples handle disagreements found that the importance of gender in determining conflict style is "dwarfed" by the behavior of the other person.[51]

What, then, can we conclude about the influence of gender on conflict? Research has demonstrated that there are, indeed, some small but measurable differences in the two sexes. But, although men and women may have characteristically different conflict styles, the individual style of each communicator—regardless of gender—and the nature of the relationship are more important than gender in shaping the way he or she handles conflict.

CULTURE

The way in which people manage conflict varies tremendously depending on their cultural background. The straight-talking, assertive approach that characterizes many North Americans is not the universal norm.[52]

Perhaps the most important cultural factor in shaping attitudes toward conflict is an orientation toward individualism or collectivism.[53] In individualistic cultures like the United States, the goals, rights, and needs of each person are considered important, and most people would agree that it is an individual's right to stand up for himself or herself. By contrast, collectivist cultures (more common in Latin America and Asia) consider the concerns of the group to be more important than those of any individual. In these cultures, the kind of assertive behavior that might seem perfectly appropriate to a North American would be regarded as rude and insensitive.

Another factor that distinguishes the assertiveness that is so valued by North Americans and northern Europeans is the difference between high- and low-context cultural styles.[54] Recall from our discussion in Chapter 6 that low-context cultures like the United States place a premium on being direct and literal. By contrast, high-context cultures like Japan value self-restraint and avoid confrontation. Communicators in these cultures derive meaning from a variety of unspoken rules, such as context, social conventions, and hints. Preserving and honoring the face of the other person is a prime goal, and communicators go to great lengths to avoid any communication that might risk embarrassing a conversational partner. For this reason, what seems like "beating around the bush" to an American would be polite to an Asian. In Japan, for example, even a simple request like "close the door" would be too straightforward.[55] A more indirect statement such as "It is somewhat cold today" would be more appropriate. To take a more important example, Japanese are reluctant to say "no" to a request. A more likely answer would be "let me think about it for a while," which anyone familiar with Japanese culture would recognize as a refusal.

When indirect communication is a cultural norm, it is unreasonable to expect more straightforward approaches to succeed. When people from different cultures face a conflict, their habitual communication patterns may not mesh smoothly. The challenge faced by an American husband and his Taiwanese wife illustrates this sort of problem. The husband would try to confront his wife verbally and directly (as is typical in the United States), leading her to either become defensive or withdraw completely from the discussion. She, on the other hand, would attempt to indicate her displeasure by changes in mood and eye contact (typical of Chinese culture) that were either not noticed or uninterpretable by her husband. Thus, neither "his way" nor "her way" was working, and they could not see any realistic way to "compromise."[56]

The film character Borat Sagdiyev claimed to visit the United States to bring "cultural learnings" back to his own country. But his colossal insensitivity created conflict wherever he traveled. (For more about *Borat*, see page 409.)

It isn't necessary to look at Asia to encounter cultural differences in conflict. Americans visiting Greece, for example, often think they are witnessing an argument when they are overhearing a friendly conversation.[57] A comparative study of American and Italian nursery schoolchildren showed that one of the Italian children's favorite pastimes was a kind of heated debating that Italians call *discussione* but that Americans would call arguing. Likewise, research has shown that the conversations of working-class Jewish speakers of eastern European origin used arguments as a means of being sociable.

Within the United States, the ethnic background of communicators also plays a role in their ideas about conflict. When members of a group of African American, Mexican American, and Anglo American college

LOOKING AT DIVERSITY

Marilynn Jorgensen: Conflict and Cultural Style

Marilynn Jorgensen conducts workshops around the world for Six Seconds, an international organization that helps clients improve performance by dealing effectively with the emotion-related side of work.

Used with permission of Marilynn Jorgensen.

I work with clients from a variety of cultures. At one recent workshop in Dubai, we hosted attendees from countries including Sweden, India, Brazil, Germany, China, Iraq, Iran, Israel, South Africa, Poland, Japan, and Canada.

People all around the world have the same powerful emotions: pride, concern, fear, and anger. But the way they *deal* with those emotions is often shaped by their background. For example, some cultures deal with conflict head on, while others handle it much more indirectly. Some cultures are open to change, while others resist changing communication patterns that have been practiced for centuries.

When working with people from a different background, a lot of behavior can seem odd, disturbing, or even offensive. "Why won't she speak up?" one person might think. "Why is he so loud and aggressive?" the other might wonder.

A major part of my training is to help people from different cultural backgrounds slow down when they encounter others with different conflict styles so they don't overreact. Instead of responding before you understand the other person's personal style and cultural background, it's better to adopt an attitude of curiosity. Be an observer and a listener: Try to find out how that stranger feels, and why. Get in the habit of saying "Please help me understand . . ." Being genuinely interested in the other person is a sign of respect, and that's very disarming. Once you understand why people are behaving as they do, their "strange" actions usually make more sense.

Techniques like these won't resolve every conflict, but they can make working together more smooth, satisfying, and productive.

students were asked about their views regarding conflict, some important differences emerged.[58] For example, Anglo Americans seem more willing to accept conflict as a natural part of relationships, whereas Mexican Americans describe the short- and long-term dangers of conflict. Anglos' willingness to experience conflicts may be part of their individualistic, low-context communication style of speaking directly and avoiding uncertainty. It's not surprising that people from more collective, high-context cultures that emphasize harmony among people with close relationships tend to handle conflicts in less direct ways. With differences like these, it's easy to imagine how two friends, lovers, or fellow workers from different cultural backgrounds might have trouble finding a conflict style that is comfortable for them both.

Despite these differences, it's important to realize that culture isn't the only factor that influences the way people approach conflict or how they behave when they disagree. Some research suggests that our approach to conflict may be part of our biological makeup.[59] Furthermore, scholarship suggests that a person's self-concept is more powerful than his or her culture in determining conflict style.[60] For example, an assertive person raised in an environment that downplays conflict is still likely to be more aggressive than an unassertive person who grew up in a culture where conflicts are common. You might handle conflicts calmly in a job where rationality and civility are the norm, but shriek like a banshee at home if that's the way you and a relational partner handle conflicts. Finally, the way each of us deals with conflict is a matter of personal choice. We can choose to follow unproductive patterns, or we can choose more constructive approaches.

Constructive Conflict Skills

The collaborative, win-win conflict style described earlier in this chapter has many advantages over win-lose and lose-lose approaches. Why, then, is it so rarely used? There are three reasons. The first is lack of awareness. Some people are so used to competition that they mistakenly think that winning requires them to defeat their "opponent."

Even when they know better, another reason prevents many people from seeking win-win solutions. Conflicts are often emotional affairs, in which people react combatively without stopping to think of better alternatives. Because this kind of emotional reflex prevents constructive solutions, it's often necessary to stop yourself from speaking out aggressively during a conflict and starting an escalating spiral of defensiveness. The time-honored advice of "counting to ten" applies here. After you've thought about the matter, you'll be able to *act* constructively instead of *reacting* in a way that's likely to produce a lose-lose outcome.

A third reason win-win solutions are rare is that they require the other person's cooperation. It's difficult to negotiate constructively with someone who insists on trying to defeat you. In this case, use your best persuasive skills to explain that by working together you can find a solution that satisfies both of you.

Despite these challenges, it is definitely possible to become better at resolving conflicts. In the following pages, we will outline a method to increase your chances of being able to handle your conflicts in a collaborative, win-win manner. As you read the following steps, try to imagine yourself applying them to a problem that's bothering you now.

IDENTIFY YOUR PROBLEM AND UNMET NEEDS

Before you speak out, it's important to realize that the problem that is causing conflict is yours. Whether you want to return an unsatisfactory piece of merchandise, complain to noisy neighbors because your sleep is being disturbed by their barking dog, or request a change in working conditions from your employer, the problem is yours. Why? Because in each case you are the person who "owns" the problem—the one who is dissatisfied. You are the one who has paid for the unsatisfactory merchandise; the merchant who sold it to you has the use of your good money. You are the one who is losing sleep as a result of your neighbors' dog; they are content to go on as before. You are the one who is unhappy with your working conditions, not your employer.*

Realizing that the problem is yours will make a big difference when the time comes to approach the other party. Instead of feeling and acting in an evaluative way, you'll be more likely to state your problem in a descriptive way, which will not only be more accurate but also reduce the chance of a defensive reaction.

---

*Of course, others involved in the conflict may have problems of their own. For instance, the merchant, the noisy neighbors, and your employer may all be bothered by your requests. But the fact remains that the reason you are speaking up about these matters is because you are dissatisfied. Thus, the problem is at least initially yours.

After you realize that the problem is yours, the next step is to identify the unmet needs that make you dissatisfied. For instance, in the barking dog example, your need may be to get some sleep or to study without interruptions. In the case of a friend who teases you in public, your need would probably be to avoid embarrassment.

Sometimes the task of identifying your needs isn't as simple as it first seems. Behind the apparent content of an issue is often a relational need. Consider this example: A friend hasn't returned some money you lent long ago. Your apparent need in this situation might be to get the money back. But a little thought will probably show that this isn't the only, or even the main, thing you want. Even if you were rolling in money, you'd probably want the loan repaid because of a more important need: *to avoid feeling victimized by your friend's taking advantage of you.*

As you'll soon see, the ability to identify your real needs plays a key role in solving interpersonal problems. For now, the point to remember is that before you voice your problem to your partner, you ought to be clear about which of your needs aren't being met.

MAKE A DATE

Destructive fights often start because the initiator confronts a partner who isn't ready. There are many times when a person isn't in the right frame of mind to face a conflict, perhaps owing to fatigue, being in too much of a hurry to take the necessary time, being upset over another problem, or not feeling well. At times like these, it's unfair to "jump" a person without notice and expect to get full attention for your problem. If you do persist, you'll probably have an ugly fight on your hands.

"Is this a good time to have a big fight?"

After you have a clear idea of the problem, approach your partner with a request to try to solve it. For example, "Something's been bothering me. Can we talk about it?" If the answer is "yes," you're ready to go further. If it isn't the right time to confront your partner, find a time that's agreeable to both of you.

DESCRIBE YOUR PROBLEM AND NEEDS

Your partner can't possibly meet your needs without knowing why you're upset and what you want. Therefore, it's up to you to describe your problem as specifically as possible. The best way to deliver a complete, accurate message is to use the assertive message format discussed in Chapter 10. Notice how well this approach works in the following examples:

Example 1

"I have a problem. It's about your leaving dirty clothes around the house after I've told you how much it bothers me (*behavior*). It's a problem because I have to run around like crazy and pick things up whenever guests come, which is no fun at all (*consequence*). I'm starting to think that either you're not paying attention to my requests or you're trying to drive me crazy (*thoughts*), and either way I'm getting more and more resentful (*feeling*). I'd like to find some way to have a neat place without my having to be a maid or a nag."

Example 2

"I have a problem. When you drop by without calling ahead, and I'm studying (*behavior*), I don't know whether to visit or ask you to leave (*thought*). Either way, I get uncomfortable (*feeling*), and it seems like whatever I do, I lose: Either I have to put you off or get behind in my work (*consequences*). I'd like to find a way to get my studying done and still socialize with you (*intention*)."

Example 3

"Something is bothering me. When you tell me you love me and yet spend almost all your free time with your other friends (*behavior*), I wonder whether you mean it (*thought*). I get insecure (*feeling*), and then I start acting moody (*consequence*). I need some way of finding out for sure how you feel about me (*intention*)."

> Our marriage used to suffer from arguments that were too short.
>
> Now we argue long enough to find out what the argument is about.
>
> —Hugh Prather

After stating your problem and describing what you need, it's important to make sure that your partner has understood what you've said. As you can remember from the discussion of listening in Chapter 7, there's a good chance—especially in a stressful conflict—that your words will be misinterpreted.

It's usually unrealistic to insist that your partner paraphrase your statement, and fortunately there are more tactful and subtle ways to make sure that you've been understood. For instance, you might try saying, "I'm not sure I expressed myself very well just now—maybe you should tell what you heard me say so I can be sure I got it right." In any case, be absolutely sure that your partner understands your whole message before going any further. Legitimate agreements are tough enough without getting upset about a conflict that doesn't even exist.

CONSIDER YOUR PARTNER'S POINT OF VIEW

After you have made your position clear, it's time to find out what your partner needs to feel satisfied about this issue. There are two reasons why it's important to discover your partner's needs. First, it's fair: Your partner has just as much right as you to feel satisfied, and if you expect help in meeting your needs, it's reasonable that you behave in the same way. But in addition to fairness, there's another practical reason for concerning yourself with what your partner wants. Just as an unhappy partner will make it hard for you to become satisfied, a happy partner will be more likely to cooperate in letting you reach your goals. Thus, it's in your own self-interest to discover and meet your partner's needs.

You can learn about your partner's needs simply by asking about them, "Now I've told you what I want and why. Tell me what you need to feel okay about this." After your partner begins to talk, your job is to use the listening skills discussed earlier in this book to make sure that you understand.

NEGOTIATE A SOLUTION

Now that you and your partner understand each other's needs, the goal becomes finding a way to meet them. This is done by developing as many potential solutions as possible and then evaluating them to decide which one best meets everyone's needs.

Probably the best description of the win-win approach was written by Thomas Gordon in his book *Parent Effectiveness Training*.[61] The following steps are a modification of this approach.

1. *Identify and define the conflict.* We've discussed identifying and defining the conflict in the preceding pages. These consist of discovering each person's problem and needs, setting the stage for meeting all of them.
2. *Generate a number of possible solutions.* In this step, the partners work together to think of as many means as possible to reach their stated ends. The key concept here is quantity: It's important to generate as many ideas as you can think of without worrying about which ones are good or bad. Write down every thought that comes up, no matter how unworkable. Sometimes a far-fetched idea will lead to a more workable one.
3. *Evaluate the alternative solutions.* This is the time to talk about which solutions will work and which ones won't. It's important for all parties to be honest about their willingness to accept an idea. If a solution is going to work, everyone involved has to support it.
4. *Decide on the best solution.* Now that you've looked at all the alternatives, pick the one that looks best to everyone. It's important to be sure that everybody understands the solution and is willing to try it out. Remember that your decision doesn't have to be final, but it should look potentially successful.

Negotiating a solution usually lacks the fireworks of more volatile approaches—and can produce more satisfying results.

Masterfile (Royalty-Free Div.)

FOLLOW UP THE SOLUTION

You can't be sure that the solution will work until you try it. After you've tested it for a while, it's a good idea to set aside some time to talk over its progress. You may find that you need to make some changes or even rethink the whole problem. The idea is to keep on top of the problem, to keep using creativity to solve it.

As you think about applying this method, it is important to keep two points in mind. First, realize the importance of following every step. Each one is essential to the success of your encounter, and skipping one or more steps can lead to misunderstandings that might cause the conversation to degenerate into a negative spiral. After you have practiced the method several times and are familiar with it, this type of problem solving will become almost second nature. You will then be able to approach your conflicts without following this step-by-step approach. But for the time being, try to be patient and trust the value of the pattern.

You can expect and prepare for a certain amount of resistance from the other person. As Figure 11.2 on page 402 shows, when a step doesn't meet with success, simply move back and repeat the preceding ones as necessary.

Win-win solutions aren't always possible. There will be times when even the best-intentioned people simply won't be able to find a way of meeting all their needs. In times like these, the process of negotiation has to include some compromises, but even then the preceding steps haven't been wasted. The genuine desire to learn what the other person wants and to try to satisfy those wants will build a climate of goodwill

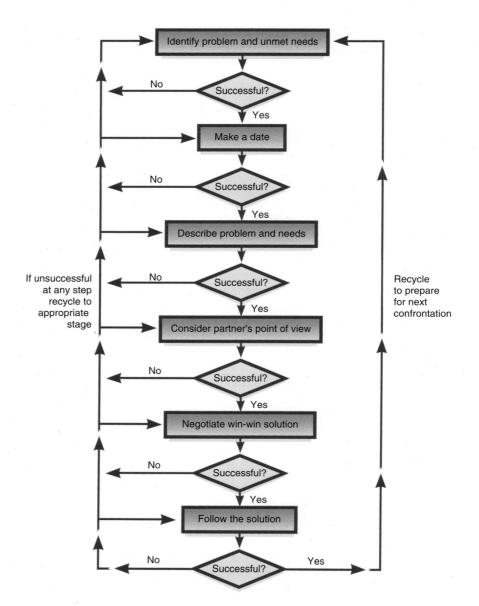

Figure 11.2
Flow Chart of the Win-Win Negotiation Process

Adapted from Rory Remer and Paul deMesquita, "Teaching and Learning Skills of Interpersonal Confrontation," in *Intimates in Conflict: A Communication Perspective* edited by Cahn ©1990 p. 227.

that can help you find the best solution to the present problem and also improve your relationship in the future.

Constructive Conflict: Questions and Answers

After learning about win-win negotiating, people often express doubts about how well it can work. "It sounds like a good idea," they say, "but . . ." Three questions arise more than any others, and they deserve an answer.

ISN'T THE WIN-WIN APPROACH TOO GOOD TO BE TRUE?

Research shows that seeking mutual benefit is not just a good idea—it actually works. In fact, the win-win approach produces better results than a win-lose approach. In a series of experiments, researchers presented subjects with a bargaining situation called "prisoner's dilemma," in which they could choose either to cooperate or betray a confederate.[62] There are three types of outcomes in prisoner's dilemma: One partner can win big by betraying a confederate, both can win by cooperating, or both can lose by betraying each other. Although cynics might assume that the most effective strategy is to betray a partner (a win-lose approach), researchers found that cooperation is actually the best hard-nosed strategy. Players who demonstrated their willingness to support the other person and not hold grudges did better than those using a more competitive approach.

There are certainly some conflicts that can't be resolved with win-win approaches. Only one suitor can marry the prince or princess, and only one person can be hired for the advertised job. Furthermore, it's impossible to reach a win-win solution when your partner refuses to cooperate. Most of the time, however, good intentions and creative thinking can lead to outcomes that satisfy everyone's needs.

ISN'T THE WIN-WIN APPROACH TOO ELABORATE?

The win-win approach is detailed and highly structured. In everyday life, you may rarely use every step. Sometimes the problem at hand won't justify the effort, and at other times you and your partner might not need to be so deliberate to take care of the problem. Nonetheless, while learning to use the approach, try to follow all of the steps carefully. After you have become familiar with and skillful at using them all, you will be able to use whichever ones prove necessary in a given situation. For important issues, you are likely to find that every step of the win-win approach is important. If this process seems time-consuming, just consider the time and energy that will likely be required if you don't resolve the issue at hand.

ISN'T WIN-WIN NEGOTIATING TOO RATIONAL?

Frustrated readers often complain that the win-win approach is so sensible that only a saint could use it successfully. "Sometimes I'm so angry that I don't care about being supportive or empathetic or anything else," they say. "I just want to blow my top!"

At times like this, you might need to temporarily remove yourself from the situation so you don't say or do something you'll later regret. You might feel better confiding in a third party. Or you might blow off steam with physical exercise. There are even cases when an understanding partner might allow you to have what has been called a "Vesuvius"—an uncontrolled, spontaneous explosion. Before you blow your top, though, be sure that your partner understands what you're doing and realizes that whatever you say doesn't call for a response. Your partner should let you rant and rave for as long as

✔+ IN REAL LIFE

Win-Win Problem Solving

Jason Harris/ ©Cengage Learning

It is 7:15 a.m. on a typical school day. Chris enters the kitchen and finds the sink full of dirty dishes. It was her roommate Terry's turn to do them. She sighs in disgust and begins to clean up, slamming pots and pans.

Terry: Can't you be a little more quiet? I don't have a class till 10:00, and I want to catch up on sleep.

Chris: (*Expressing her aggression indirectly in a sarcastic tone of voice*) Sorry to bother you. I was cleaning up last night's dinner dishes.

Terry: (*Misses the message*) Well, I wish you'd do it a little more quietly. I was up late studying last night, and I'm beat.

Chris: (*Decides to communicate her irritation more directly, if aggressively*) Well, if you'd done the dishes last night, I wouldn't have had to wash them now.

Terry: (*Finally realizes that Chris is mad at her, responds defensively*) I was going to do them when I got up. I've got two midterms this week, and I was studying until midnight last night. What's more important, grades or a spotless kitchen?

Chris: (*Perpetuating the growing defensive spiral*) I've got classes, too, you know. But that doesn't mean we have to live like pigs!

Terry: (*Angrily*) Forget it. If it's such a big deal, I'll never leave another dirty dish!

Chris and Terry avoid each other as they get ready for school. During the day, Chris realizes that attacking Terry will only make matters worse. She decides on a more constructive approach that evening.

Chris: That wasn't much fun this morning. Want to talk about it?

Terry: I suppose so. But I'm going out to study with Kim and Alisa in a few minutes.

Chris: (*Realizing that it's important to talk at a good time*) If you have to leave soon, let's not get into it now. How about talking when you get back?

Terry: Okay, if I'm not too tired.

Chris: Or we could talk tomorrow before class.

Terry: Okay.

Later that evening Terry and Chris continue their conversation.

Chris: (*Defines the issue as her problem by using the assertive message format*) I hated to start the day with a fight. But I also hate having to do the dishes when it's not my turn (*behavior*). It doesn't seem fair for me to do my job and yours (*interpretation*), and that's why I got so mad (*feeling*) and nagged at you (*consequence*).

Terry: But I was studying! You know how much I have to do. It's not like I was partying.

Chris: (*Avoids attacking Terry by sincerely agreeing with the facts and explaining further why she was upset*) I know. It wasn't just doing the dishes that got me upset. It seems like there have been a lot of times when I've done your jobs and mine, too.

Terry: (*Defensively*) Like when?

Chris: (*Gives specific descriptions of Terry's behavior*) Well, this was the third time this week that I've done the dishes when it's your turn, and I can think of a couple of times lately when I've had to clean up your stuff before people came over.

Terry: I don't see why it's such a big deal. If you just leave the stuff there, I'll clean it up.

Chris: (*Still trying to explain herself, she continues to use "I" language*) I know you would. I guess it's harder for me to put up with a messy place than it is for you.

Terry: Yeah. If you'd just relax, living together would be a lot easier!

Chris: (*Resenting Terry's judgmental accusation that the problem is all hers*) Hey, wait a second! Don't blame the whole thing on me. It's just that we have different standards. It looks to you like I'm too hung up on keeping the place clean . . .

Terry: Right.

Chris: . . . and if we do it your way, then I'd be giving up. I'd have to either live with the place messier than I like it or clean everything up myself. Then I'd get mad at you, and things would be pretty tense around here. (*Describes the unpleasant consequences of not solving the problem in a mutually satisfactory way*)

Terry: I suppose so.

Chris: We need to figure out how to take care of the apartment in a way that we can both live with. (*Describes the broad outline of a win-win solution*)

Terry: Yeah.

Chris: So what could we do?

Terry: (*Sounding resigned*) Look, from now on I'll just do the dishes right away. It isn't worth arguing about.

Chris: Sure it is. If you're sore, the apartment may be clean, but it won't be worth it.

Terry: (*Skeptically*) Okay, what do you suggest?

Chris: Well, I'm not sure. You don't want the pressure of having to clean up right away, and I don't want to have to do my jobs and yours, too. Right?

Terry: Yeah. (*Still sounding skeptical*) So what are we going to do—hire a housekeeper to clean up?

Chris: (*Refusing to let Terry sidetrack the discussion*) That would be great if we could afford it. How about using paper plates? That would make cleaning up from meals easier.

Terry: Yeah, but there would still be pots and pans.

Chris: Well, it's not a perfect fix, but it might help a little. (*Goes on to suggest other ideas*) How about cooking meals that don't take a lot of work to clean up—maybe more salads and less fried stuff that sticks to pans. That would be a better diet, too.

Terry: Yeah. I do hate to scrub crusty frying pans. But that doesn't do anything about your wanting the living room picked up all the time, and I bet I still wouldn't keep the kitchen as clean as you like it. Keeping the place super clean just isn't as big a deal to me as it is for you.

Chris: That's true, and I don't want to have to nag you! (*Clarifies the end she's seeking*) You know, it's not really cleaning up that bothers me. It's doing more than my share of work. I wonder if there's a way I could be responsible for keeping the kitchen clean and picking up if you could do something else to keep the workload even.

Terry: Are you serious? I'd love to get out of doing the dishes! You mean you'd do them . . . and keep the place picked up . . . if I did something else?

Chris: As long as the work was equal and you really did your jobs without me having to remind you.

Terry: What kind of work would you want me to do?

Chris: How about cleaning up the bathroom?

Terry: Forget it. That's worse than doing the dishes.

Chris: Okay. How about cooking?

Terry: That might work, but then we'd have to eat together all the time. It's nice to do our own cooking when we want to. It's more flexible that way.

Chris: Okay. But what about shopping? I hate the time it takes, and you don't mind it that much, do you?

Terry: You mean shop for groceries? You'd trade that for cleaning the kitchen?

Chris: Sure. And picking up the living room. It takes an hour each time we shop, and we make two trips every week. Doing the dishes would be much quicker.

Terry: All right!

The plan didn't work perfectly. At first Terry put off shopping until all the food was gone, and Chris took advantage by asking Terry to run other errands during her shopping trips. But their new arrangement proved much more successful than the old arrangement. The apartment was cleaner and the workload more even, which satisfied Chris. Terry was less the object of Chris's nagging, and she had no kitchen chores, which made her happier. Just as important, the relationship between Chris and Terry was more comfortable—thanks to win-win problem solving.

Communication Scenarios

To see and analyze a video of the interactions between Chris and Terry, go to your Premium Website for Looking Out/Looking In, *access "In Real Life Communication Scenarios," and then click on "Win-Win Problem Solving."*

you want without getting defensive or "tying in." Then when your eruption subsides, you can take steps to work through whatever still troubles you.

IS IT POSSIBLE TO CHANGE OTHERS?

Readers often agree that win-win problem solving would be terrific—if everyone had read *Looking Out/Looking In* and understood the method. "How can I get the other person to cooperate?" the question goes. Though you won't always be able to gain your partner's cooperation, a good job of selling can do the trick most of the time. The key lies in showing that it's in your partner's self-interest to work together with you: "Look, if we can't settle this, we'll both feel miserable. But if we can find an answer, think how much better off we'll be." Notice that this sort of explanation projects both the favorable consequences of cooperating and the unfavorable consequences of competing.

You can also boost the odds of getting your partner's cooperation by modeling the communication skills described in this book. You've read that defense-arousing behavior is reciprocal, but so is supportive communication. If you can listen sincerely, avoid evaluative attacks, and empathize with your partner's concerns, for example, there's a good chance that you'll get the same kind of behavior in return. And even if your cooperative attitude doesn't succeed, you'll gain self-respect from knowing that at least you behaved honorably and constructively.

✔+ MAKING THE GRADE

Summary

Conflict is a fact of life in every interpersonal relationship. The way in which conflicts are handled plays a major role in the quality of a relationship. When managed constructively, conflicts can lead to stronger and more satisfying interaction; but when they are handled poorly, relationships will suffer.

Communicators can respond to conflicts in a variety of ways: avoiding, accommodating, competing, compromising, or collaborating. Each of these approaches can be justified in certain circumstances. The way a conflict is handled is not always the choice of a single person, because the parties influence each other as they develop a relational conflict style. This style may be complementary, symmetrical, or parallel; it can involve a combination of intimate and aggressive elements; and it can involve constructive or destructive rituals. Besides being shaped by the relationship, a conflict style is also shaped by a person's gender and cultural background.

In most circumstances a collaborative, win-win outcome is the ideal, and it can be achieved by following the guidelines outlined on pages 398–402.

Key Terms

accommodating (383)
avoiding (382)
collaborating (387)
competing (383)
complementary conflict style (390)

compromising (385)
conflict (378)
conflict ritual (393)
crazymaking (385)
direct aggression (384)

parallel conflict style (390)
passive aggression (384)
relational conflict style (390)
symmetrical conflict style (390)

Online Resources

Now that you have read this chapter, use your Premium Website for *Looking Out/ Looking In* for quick access to the electronic resources that accompany this text. Your Premium Website gives you access to:

- **Study tools** that will help you assess your learning and prepare for exams (*digital glossary*, *key term flash cards*, *review quizzes*).

- **Activities and assignments** that will help you hone your knowledge, understand how theory and research applies to your own life (*Invitation to Insight*), consider ethical challenges in interpersonal communication (*Ethical Challenge*), and build your interpersonal communication skills throughout the course (*Skill Builder*). If requested, you can submit your answers to your instructor.

- **Media resources** that will allow you to watch and critique news video and videos of interpersonal communication situations (*In Real Life*, *interpersonal video simulations*) and download a chapter review so you can study when and where you'd like (*Audio Study Tools*).

This chapter's key terms and search terms for additional reading are featured in this end-of-chapter section, and you can find this chapter's Invitation to Insight, Ethical Challenge, and In Real Life activities in the body of the chapter.

Search Terms

When searching online databases to research topics in this chapter, use the following terms (along with this chapter's key terms) to maximize the chances of finding useful information:

competition
conflict management
culture conflict

interpersonal conflict
negotiation

problem solving
social conflict

Film and Television

You can see the communication principles described in this chapter portrayed in the following films and television shows:

DYSFUNCTIONAL CONFLICT

American Beauty (1999) Rated R

From outside, Lester and Carolyn Burnham (Kevin Spacey and Annette Bening) look like the perfect couple: attractive, with good jobs and an immaculate suburban home. But we soon learn that their life isn't as good as it seems. The Burnhams' relationship with their daughter Jane (Thora Birch) is superficial. Carolyn is in denial about Lester's midlife crisis, and she ignores his pleas to recapture their lost love. As the film relentlessly moves toward a stunning conclusion, we are presented with a portrait of American family members who alternate between avoidance and aggression without demonstrating any apparent skill at managing the serious conflicts that face them.

CONFLICT STYLES

30 Rock (2006–)

TV comedy producer Liz Lemon (Tina Fey) and her boss Jack Donaghy (Alec Baldwin) are "frienemies." They obviously value their relationship, yet they constantly struggle over both work-related issues and personal matters. Jack obviously enjoys provoking Liz—not out of malice, but because he relishes conflict. By contrast, Liz is an accommodator: Keeping everyone around her happy is her goal, and she'll punish herself to keep the peace.

Many episodes of this popular series revolve around the complications that arise from Jack's confrontational style and Liz's obsession with harmony. The results are amusing, but in real life each character would profit from adopting some of the other's approach.

Up for Grabs (2005) Not Rated

When baseball slugger Barry Bonds pounded his record-setting seventy-third homerun into the arcade at San Francisco's PacBell Park, two fans claimed to have recovered the ball. This documentary records the struggle over that piece of sports memorabilia, which at the time was estimated to be worth $1 million. This real-life farce illustrates how the desire to win at any cost can produce surprising, and often disappointing, results.

CULTURE AND CONFLICT

Borat (2008) Rated R

This over-the-top mockumentary chronicles the misadventures of Kazakhstani TV personality Borat Sagdiyev (Sacha Baron Cohen) as he travels across the United States to learn about American culture. One critic aptly described Borat as the "village idiot for the global village." His efforts to reach out to Americans are stunningly incompetent and offensive. Viewers who appreciate the satire in this film recognize that the outrageousness pictured is less about Borat's shocking but fictional prejudices than about how those attitudes go unchallenged by the Americans he meets.

The Joy Luck Club (1993) Rated R

This film tells a series of stories involving four Chinese women and their daughters. The mothers all flee difficult situations in China to start new lives in the United States, where they raise their daughters with a mixture of Chinese and American styles. Many of the movie's conflicts are rooted in cultural value clashes.

The mothers were raised in the high-context, collectivist environment of China, where open conflict is discouraged, and individual needs (particularly of women) are submerged for the larger good. To achieve their goals, the mothers use a variety of indirect and passive-aggressive methods. Their daughters, raised in the United States, adopt a more low-context, direct form of communication. They are also more assertive and aggressive in their conflict styles, particularly when dealing with their mothers.

The daughters have a harder time dealing with the men in their lives. For example, Rose (Rosalind Chao) begins her relationship with Ted (Andrew McCarthy) very assertively, telling him candidly what she thinks and how she feels about him (he is charmed by her directness). They marry, and she becomes an accommodator, constantly submerging her needs for his. Rather than liking Rose's accommodating, Ted comes to despise it. He exhorts her to be more assertive: "Once in a while, I would like to hear what you want. I'd like to hear your voice, even if we disagree." He then suggests that they separate.

Several of the stories have happy endings. In Rose's case, she fights for her rights with Ted—and ultimately they reconcile. In fact, each woman in the movie takes a stand on an important issue in her life, and most of the outcomes are positive. The women in *The Joy Luck Club* learn to both embrace and reject aspects of their cultural heritage as they attempt to manage their conflicts effectively.

ENDNOTES

CHAPTER ONE

1. K. D. Williams (2001). *Ostracism: The Power of Silence* (pp. 7–11). New York: Guilford.

2. J. B. Ross & M. M. McLaughlin (Eds.) (1949). *A Portable Medieval Reader*. New York: Viking.

3. S. Schachter (1959). *The Psychology of Affiliation* (pp. 9–10). Stanford, CA: Stanford University Press.

4. UPI, *Wisconsin State Journal*, September 7, 1978.

5. J. McCain (1999). *Faith of My Fathers* (p. 212). New York: Random House.

6. A. Gawande (March 30, 2009). "Hellhole." *The New Yorker*, 36–45.

7. Three articles in the *Journal of the American Medical Association* 267 (January 22/29, 1992) discuss the link between psychosocial influences and coronary heart disease: R. B. Case, A. J. Moss, N. Case, M. McDermott, & S. Eberly. "Living Alone after Myocardial Infarction" (pp. 515–519); R. B. Williams, J. C. Barefoot, R. M. Califf, T. L. Haney, W. B. Saunders, D. B. Pryon, M. A. Hlatky, I. C. Siegler, & D. B. Mark. "Prognostic Importance of Social and Economic Resources among Medically Treated Patients with Angiographically Documented Coronary Artery Disease" (pp. 520–524); and R. Ruberman. "Psychosocial Influences on Mortality of Patients with Coronary Heart Disease" (pp. 559–560). See also J. T. Cacioppo, J. M. Ernst, M. H. Burleson, M. K. McClintock, W. B. Malarkey, L. C. Hawkley, R. B. Kowalewski, A. Paulsen, J. A. Hobson, K. Hugdahl, D. Spiegel, & G. G. Berntson (2000). "Lonely Traits and Concomitant Physiological Processes: The MacArthur Social Neuroscience Studies." *International Journal of Psychophysiology, 35*, 143–154.

8. S. Cohen, W. J. Doyle, D. P. Skoner, B. S. Rabin, & J. M. Gwaltney (1997). "Social Ties and Susceptibility to the Common Cold." *Journal of the American Medical Association, 277*, 1940–1944.

9. C. H. Kroenke, L. D. Kubzansky, E. S. Schernhammer, M. D. Holmes, & I. Kawachi (2006). "Social Networks, Social Support, and Survival After Breast Cancer Diagnosis." *Journal of Clinical Oncology, 24*, 1105–1111; H. Litwin & S. Shiovitz-Ezra (2006). "Network Type and Mortality Risk in Later Life." *Gerontologist, 46*, 735–743; C. F. Mendes de Leon (2005). "Why Do Friendships Matter For Survival?" *Journal of Epidemiology and Community Health, 59*, 538–539.

10. W. D. Rees and S. G. Lutkins (1967). "Mortality of Bereavement." *British Medical Journal, 4*, 13.

11. O. Ybarra, O. E. Burnstein, P. Winkielman, M. C. Keller, M. Manis, E. Chan, & J. Rodriguez (2008). "Mental Exercising Through Simple Socializing: Social Interaction Promotes General Cognitive Functioning." *Personality and Social Psychology Bulletin, 34,* 248–259.

12. "Defensiveness and High Blood Pressure" (1997). *Harvard Heart Letter, 4,* 8.

13. K. Floyd & S. Riforgiate (2006). "Human Affection Exchange: XII. Affectionate Communication Is Related to Diurnal Variation in Salivary Free Cortisol." *Western Journal of Communication, 75*, 351–368.

14. R. Shattuck (1980). *The Forbidden Experiment: The Story of the Wild Boy of Aveyron* (p. 37). New York: Farrar, Straus & Giroux.

15. R. B. Rubin, E. M. Perse, & C. A. Barbato (1988). "Conceptualization and Measurement of Interpersonal Communication Motives." *Human Communication Research, 14*, 602–628.

16. E. Diener & M. E. P. Seligman (2002). "Very Happy People." *Psychological Science, 13*, 81–84.

17. D. Kahneman, A. B. Krueger, D. A. Schkade, N. Schwartz, & A. A. Stone (n.d.). "A Daily Measure." *Science, 306*, 1645.

18. U. S. Rehman & A. Holtzworth-Munroe (2007). "A Cross-Cultural Examination of the Relation of Marital Communication Behavior to Marital Satisfaction." *Journal of Family Psychology, 21*, 759–763.

19. J. Rochmis (2000). "Humans Do Many Things." *Wired Magazine* online. Retrieved July 24, 2009, at http://www.wired.com/culture/lifestyle/news/2000/02/34387.

20. M. McPherson, L. Smith-Lovin, & M. E. Brashears (2006). "Social Isolation in America: Changes in Core Discussion Networks over Two Decades." *American Sociological Review, 71*, 353–375. See also M. McPherson, L. Smith-Lovin, & M. E. Brashears (2008). "The Ties That Bind Are Fraying." *Contexts, 7*, 32–36.

21. H. T. Reis & S. L. Gable (2003). "Toward a Positive Psychology of Relationships." In C. L. Keyes & J. Haidt (Eds.), *Flourishing: The Positive Person and the Good Life* (pp. 129–159). Washington, DC: American Psychological Association.

22. "Harper's Index" (December 1994). *Harper's*, 13.

23. L. B. Mauksch, D. C. Dugdale, S. Dodsonb, & R. Epstein (2007). "Relationship, Communication, and Efficiency in the Medical Encounter." *Archives of Internal Medicine, 168*, 1387–1395; F. Holmes (2007). "If You Listen, The Patient Will Tell You the Diagnosis." *International Journal of Listening, 21*, 156–161.

24. *Sentinel Event Statistics* (2008). Oakbrook Terrace, IL: Joint Commission on the Accreditation of Healthcare Organizations.

25. W. Levinson, D. Roter, & J. P. Mullooly (1997). "Physician-Patient Communication: The Relationship with Malpractice Claims Among Primary Care Physicians and Surgeons." *Journal of the American Medical Association, 277*, 553–59. See also H. P. Rodriguez, A. C. Rodday, R. E. Marshall, K. L. Nelson, W. H. Rogers, & D. G. Safran (2008). "Relation of Patients' Experiences with Individual Physicians to Malpractice Risk." *International Journal for Quality in Health Care, 20*, 5–12.

26. A. H. Maslow (1968). *Toward a Psychology of Being.* New York: Van Nostrand Reinhold.

27. P. Mychalcewycz (February 12, 2009). "Breaking Up Via Text Message Becoming Commonplace, Poll Finds." Retrieved July 24, 2009, at http://www.switched.com/2009/02/12/breaking-up-via-text-message-becoming-commonplace-poll-finds/.

28. See, for example, R. K. Shelly (1997). "Sequences and Cycles in Social Interaction." *Small Group Research, 28,* 333–356.

29. See R. Buck & C. A. VanLear (2002). "Verbal and Nonverbal Communication: Distinguishing Symbolic, Spontaneous, and Pseudo-Spontaneous Nonverbal Behavior." *Journal of Communication, 52,* 522–541; and T. Clevenger, Jr. (1991). "Can One Not Communicate? A Conflict of Models." *Communication Studies, 42,* 340–353. For a detailed rationale of the position argued in this section, see G. H. Stamp & M. L. Knapp (1990). "The Construct of Intent in Interpersonal Communication." *Quarterly Journal of Speech, 76,* 282–299.

30. For a thorough discussion of communication difficulties, see N. Coupland, H. Giles, & J. M. Wiemann (Eds.) (1991). *Miscommunication and Problematic Talk.* Newbury Park, CA: Sage.

31. J. P. Dillard, D. H. Solomon, & M. T. Palmer (1999). "Structuring the Concept of Relational Communication." *Communication Monographs, 66,* 49–65; and P. Watzlawick, J. Beavin, & D. Jackson (1967). *Pragmatics of Human Communication.* New York: Norton.

32. For a similar list of characteristics, see J. C. McCroskey & V. P. Richmond (1996). *Fundamentals of Human Communication: An Interpersonal Perspective.* Prospect Heights, IL: Waveland.

33. A. Sillars (1998). "(Mis)Understanding." In B. H. Spitzberg & W. R. Cupach (Eds.), *The Dark Side of Close Relationships.* Mahwah, NJ: Erlbaum.

34. B. Keysar & A. S. Henley (2002). "Speakers' Overestimation of Their Effectiveness." *Psychological Science, 13,* 207–212.

35. S. Wu & B. Keysar (2007). "The Effect of Information Overlap on Communiction Effectiveness." *Cognitive Science, 31,* 169–181.

36. See, for example, W. G. Powers & P. L. Witt (2008). "Expanding the Framework of Communication Fidelity Theory." *Communication Quarterly, 56,* 247–267.

37. J. C. McCroskey & L. Wheeless (1976). *Introduction to Human Communication* (p. 5). Boston: Allyn and Bacon. See also D. H. Cloven & M. E. Roloff (1991). "Sense-Making Activities and Interpersonal Conflict: Communicative Cures for the Mulling Blues." *Western Journal of Speech Communication, 55,* 134–158; and D. Stiebel (1997). *When Talking Makes Things Worse! Resolving Problems When Communication Fails.* Kansas City, MO: Andrews and McMeel.

38. M. V. Redmond (1995). "Interpersonal Communication: Definitions and Conceptual Approaches." In M. V. Redmond (Ed.), Interpersonal Communication: *Readings in Theory and Research* (pp. 4–11). Fort Worth, TX: Harcourt Brace.

39. See, for example, G. R. Miller & M. Steinberg (1975). Between People: *A New Analysis of Interpersonal Communication.* Chicago: SRA; and J. Stewart & C. Logan (1998). *Together: Communicating Interpersonally,* 5th ed. New York: McGraw-Hill.

40. For further discussion of the characteristics of impersonal and interpersonal communications, see A. P. Bochner (1984). "The Functions of Human Communication in Interpersonal Bonding." In C. C. Arnold & J. W. Bowers (Eds.), *Handbook of Rhetorical and Communication Theory* (p. 550). Boston: Allyn and Bacon; S. Trenholm & A. Jensen (1992). *Interpersonal Communication,* 2nd ed. (pp. 27–33). Belmont, CA: Wadsworth; and J. Stewart & G. D'Angelo (1998). *Together: Communicating Interpersonally,* 5th ed. (p. 5). New York: McGraw-Hill.

41. J. Wood (1997). *Relational Communication,* 2nd ed. Belmont, CA: Wadsworth.

42. K. J. Gergen (1991). *The Saturated Self: Dilemmas of Identity in Contemporary Life* (p. 158). New York: Basic Books.

43. M. Daum (March 7, 2009). "The Age of Friendaholism." *Los Angeles Times,* B13.

44. L. Rainie & J. Anderson (2008). *The Future of the Internet III: How Experts See It.* Washington, DC: Pew Internet & American Life Project.

45. UCLA Internet Report (2000). "Surveying the Digital Future." UCLA Center for Communication Policy.

46. "Surveying the Digital Future: Year Four," op. cit.

47. B. Wellman, A. Smith, A. Wells, & T. Kennedy (2008). *Networked Families.* Washington, DC: Pew Internet & American Life Project.

48. See, for example, J. Boase, J. B. Horrigan, B. Wellman, & L. Rainie (January 2006). *The Strength of Internet Ties.* Washington, DC: Pew Internet & American Life Project; A. Lenhart, M. Madden, & P. Hitlin (July 2005). *Teens and Technology: Youth are Leading the Transition to a Fully Wired and Mobile Nation.* Washington, DC: Pew Internet & American Life Project; and J. Boase & B. Wellman (2006). "Personal Relationships: On and Off the Internet." In D. Perlman & A. L. Vangelisti (Eds.), *The Cambridge Handbook of Personal Relationships.* New York: Cambridge University Press.

49. L. M. Atheunis, P. M. Valkenburg, & J. Peter (2007). "Computer-Mediated Communication and Interpersonal Attraction: An Experimental Test of Two Explanatory Hypotheses." *CyberPsychology & Behavior, 10,* 831–835.

50. A. J. Flanagin (2005). "IM Online: Instant Messaging Use Among College Students." *Communication Research Reports, 22,* 175–187.

51. J. Boase, J. B. Horrigan, B. Wellman, & L. Rainie (January 2006). *The Strength of Internet Ties.* Washington, DC: Pew Internet & American Life Project.

52. M. Dainton & B. Aylor (2002). "Patterns of Communication Channel Use in the Maintenance of Long-Distance Relationships." *Communication Research Reports, 19,* 118–129.

53. M. Marriott (1998). "The Blossoming of Internet Chat." *New York Times* online. Retrieved July 24, 2009, at http://www.nytimes.com/1998/07/02/technology/the-blossoming-of-internet-chat.html?pagewanted=2.

54. D. Tannen (May 16, 1994). "Gender Gap in Cyberspace." *Newsweek*, 52–53.

55. D. Kirkpatrick (March 23, 1992). "Here Comes the Payoff from PCs." *Fortune*, 93–102.

56. K. S. Surinder & R. B. Cooper (2003). "Exploring the Core Concepts of Media Richness Theory: The Impact of Cue Multiplicity and Feedback Immediacy on Decision Quality." *Journal of Management Information Systems, 20*, 263–299.

57. J. Walther & A. Ramirez (2010). "New Technologies and New Directions in Online Relating." In S. W. Smith & S. R. Wilson (Eds.), *New Directions in Interpersonal Communication Research* (pp. 264–284). Los Angeles: Sage.

58. A. Ramirez & S. Zhang (2007). "When Online Meets Offline: The Effect of Modality Switching on Relational Communication." *Communication Monographs, 74*, 287–310.

59. S. A. Watts (2007). "Evaluative Feedback: Perspectives on Media Effects." *Journal of Computer-Mediated Communication, 12*. Retrieved June 1, 2009, at http://jcmc.indiana.edu/vol12/issue2/watts.html.

60. For a thorough review of this topic, see B. H. Spitzberg & W. R. Cupach (1989). *Handbook of Interpersonal Competence Research*. New York: Springer-Verlag.

61. For a thorough discussion of the nature of communication competence, see B. H. Spitzberg & W. R. Cupach (2002). "Interpersonal Skills." In M. L. Knapp & J. A. Daly (Eds.), *Handbook of Interpersonal Communication,* 3rd ed. Thousand Oaks, CA: Sage.; and S. R. Wilson & C. M. Sabee (2003). "Explicating Communicative Competence as a Theoretical Term." In J. O. Greene & B. R. Burleson (Eds.), *Handbook of Communication and Social Interaction Skills.* Mahwah, NJ: Erlbaum.

62. B. H. Spitzberg (1991). "An Examination of Trait Measures of Interpersonal Competence." *Communication Reports, 4*, 22–29.

63. B. H. Spitzberg (2000). "What Is Good Communication?" *Journal of the Association for Communication Administration, 29*, 103–119.

64. L. K. Guerrero, P. A. Andersen, P. F. Jorgensen, B. H. Spitzberg, & S. V. Eloy (1995). "Coping with the Green-Eyed Monster: Conceptualizing and Measuring Communicative Responses to Romantic Jealousy." *Western Journal of Communication, 59*, 270–304.

65. See B. J. O'Keefe (1988). "The Logic of Message Design: Individual Differences in Reasoning about Communication." *Communication Monographs, 55*, 80–103.

66. See, for example, A. D. Heisel, J. C. McCroskey, & V. P. Richmond (1999). "Testing Theoretical Relationships and Non-Relationships of Genetically-Based Predictors: Getting Started with Communibiology." *Communication Research Reports, 16*, 1–9; and J. C. McCroskey & M. J. Beatty (2000). "The Communibiological Perspective: Implications for Communication in Instruction." *Communication Education, 49*, 1–6.

67. J. Ayres & T. Hopf (1993). *Coping with Speech Anxiety.* Norwood, NJ: Ablex. See also M. Allen, J. Bourhis, T. Emmers-Sommer, & E. Sahlstein (1998). "Reducing Dating Anxiety: A Meta-Analysis." *Communication Reports, 11*, 49–55.

68. M. A. deTurck & G. R. Miller (1990). "Training Observers to Detect Deception: Effects of Self-Monitoring and Rehearsal." *Human Communication Research, 16*, 603–620.

69. R. B. Rubin, E. M. Perse, & C. A. Barbato (1988). "Conceptualization and Measurement of Interpersonal Communication Motives." *Human Communication Research, 14*, 602–628.

70. S. P. Morreale & J. C. Pearson (2008). "Why Communication Education Is Important: The Centrality of the Discipline in the 21st Century." *Communication Education, 57*, 224–240.

71. D. Hemple (in press). "Invitational Capacity." In F. van Emeren & P. Houtlosser, *The Practice of Argumentation.* Amsterdam: John Benjamins.

72. D. O. Braithwaite & N. Eckstein (2003). "Reconceptualizing Supportive Interactions: How Persons with Disabilities Communicatively Manage Assistance." *Journal of Applied Communication Research, 31*, 1–26.

73. B. R. Burleson (2007). "Constructivism: A General Theory of Communication Skill." In B. B. Whaley & W. Samter (Eds.), *Explaining Communication: Contemporary Theories and Exemplars* (pp. 105–128). Mahwah, NJ: Erlbaum.

74. D. B. Wackman, S. Miller, & E. W. Nunnally (1976). *Student Workbook: Increasing Awareness and Communication Skills* (p. 6). Minneapolis, MN: Interpersonal Communication Programs.

75. B. R. Burleson and S. E. Caplan (1998). "Cognitive Complexity." In J. C. McCroskey, J. A. Daly, M. M. Martin, & M. J. Beatty (Eds.), *Communication and Personality: Trait Perspectives* (pp. 233–286). Creskill, NJ: Hampton Press.

76. J. M. Wiemann & P. M. Backlund (1980). "Current Theory and Research in Communication Competence." *Review of Educational Research, 50*, 185–199; and S. G. Lakey & D. J. Canary (2002). "Actor Goal Achievement and Sensitivity to Partner as Critical Factors in Understanding Interpersonal Communication Competence and Conflict Strategies." *Communication Monographs, 69*, 217–235. See also M. V. Redmond (December 1985). "The Relationship between Perceived Communication Competence and Perceived Empathy." *Communication Monographs, 52*, 377–382; and M. V. Redmond (1989). "The Functions of Empathy (Decentering) in Human Relations." *Human Relations, 42*, 593–605.

77. Research summarized in D. E. Hamachek (1987). *Encounters with the Self*, 2nd ed. (p. 8.). Fort Worth, TX: Holt, Rinehart and Winston. See also J. A. Daly, A. L. Vangelisti, & S. M. Daughton (1995). "The Nature and Correlates of Conversational Sensitivity." In M. V. Redmond (Ed.), *Interpersonal Communication: Readings in Theory and Research.* Fort Worth, TX: Harcourt Brace.

78. D. A. Dunning & J. Kruger (December 1999). "Unskilled and Unaware of It: How Difficulties in Recognizing One's Own Incompetence Lead to Inflated Self-Assessments." *Journal of Personality and Social Psychology, 77,* 1121–1134.

79. Adapted from the work of R. P. Hart as reported by M. L. Knapp (1984). In *Interpersonal Communication and Human Relationships* (pp. 342–344). Boston: Allyn and Bacon. See also R. P. Hart & D. M. Burks (1972). "Rhetorical Sensitivity and Social Interaction." *Speech Monographs, 39,* 75–91; and R. P. Hart, R. E. Carlson, & W. F. Eadie (1980). "Attitudes toward Communication and the Assessment of Rhetorical Sensitivity." *Communication Monographs, 47,* 1–22.

80. See Y. Y. Kim (1991). "Intercultural Communication Competence: A Systems-Theoretic View." In S. Ting-Toomey & F. Korzenny (Eds.), *Cross-Cultural Interpersonal Communication.* Newbury Park, CA: Sage; and G. M. Chen & W. J. Sarosta (1996). "Intercultural Communication Competence: A Synthesis." In B. R. Burleson & A. W. Kunkel (Eds.), *Communication Yearbook 19.* Thousand Oaks, CA: Sage.

81. J. K. Burgoon & N. E. Dunbar (2000). "An Interactionist Perspective on Dominance-Submission: Interpersonal Dominance as a Dynamic, Situationally Contingent Social Skill." *Communication Monographs, 67,* 96–121.

82. M. J. Collier (1996). "Communication Competence Problematics in Ethnic Relationships." *Communication Monographs, 63,* 314–336.

83. L. Chen (1997). "Verbal Adaptive Strategies in U.S. American Dyadic Interactions with U.S. American or East-Asian Partners." *Communication Monographs, 64,* 302–323.

84. See, for example, C. Hajek & H. Giles (2003). "New Directions in Intercultural Communication Competence: The Process Model." In B. R. Burleson & J. O. Greene (Eds.), *Handbook of Communication and Social Interaction Skills.* Mahwah, NJ: Erlbaum; and S. Ting-Toomey & L. C. Chung (2005). *Understanding Intercultural Communication.* Los Angeles: Roxbury.

85. M. Kalliny, K. Cruthirds, & M. Minor (2006). "Differences between American, Egyptian and Lebanese Humor Styles: Implications for International Management." *International Journal of Cross-Cultural Management, 6,* 121–134.

86. L. A. Samovar & R. E. Porter (2004). *Communication Between Cultures,* 5th ed. Belmont, CA: Wadsworth.

87. J. W. Kassing (1997). "Development of the Intercultural Willingness to Communicate Scale." *Communication Research Reports, 14,* 399–407.

88. J. K. Burgoon, C. R. Berger, & V. R. Waldron (2000). "Mindfulness and Interpersonal Communication." *Journal of Social Issues, 56,* 105–128.

89. C. R. Berger (1979). "Beyond Initial Interactions: Uncertainty, Understanding, and the Development of Interpersonal Relationships." In H. Giles & R. St. Clair (Eds.), *Language and Social Psychology* (pp. 122–144). Oxford: Blackwell.

90. L. J. Carrell (1997). "Diversity in the Communication Curriculum: Impact on Student Empathy." *Communication Education, 46,* 234–244.

CHAPTER TWO

1. R. F. Baumeister (2005). *The Cultural Animal: Human Nature, Meaning, and Social Life.* New York: Oxford University Press; and R. F. Baumeister, J. D. Campbell, J. I. Krueger, & K. D. Vohs (2003). "Does High Self-Esteem Cause Better Performance, Interpersonal Success, Happiness, or Healthier Lifestyles?" *Psychological Science in the Public Interest, 4,* 1–44.

2. K. D. Vohs & T. F. Heatherton (2004). "Ego Threats Elicits Different Social Comparison Process Among High and Low Self-Esteem People: Implications for Interpersonal Perceptions." *Social Cognition, 22,* 168–191.

3. W. Soldz & G. E. Vaillant (1999). "The Big Five Personality Traits and the Life Course: A 45-Year Longitudinal Study." *Journal of Research in Personality, 33,* 208–232.

4. For a summary of research on heritability of personality, see W. Wright (1998). *Born That Way: Genes, Behavior, Personality.* New York: Knopf.

5. C. E. Schwartz, C. I. Wright, L. M. Shin, J. Kagan, & S. L. Rauch (June 20, 2003). "Inhibited and Uninhibited Infants 'Grown Up': Adult Amygdalar Response to Novelty." *Science,* 1952–1953.

6. J. G. Cole & J. C. McCroskey (2000). "Temperament and Socio-Communicative Orientation." *Communication Research Reports, 17,* 105–114.

7. A. D. Heisel, J. C. McCroskey, & V. P. Richmond (1999). "Testing Theoretical Relationships and Non-Relationships of Genetically-Based Predictors: Getting Started with Communibiology." *Communication Research Reports, 16,* 1–9.

8. Cole & McCroskey, op. cit.

9. C. J. Wigley (1998). "Verbal Aggressiveness." In J. C. McCroskey, J. A. Daly, M. M. Martin, & M. J. Beatty (Eds.), *Personality and Communication: Trait Perspectives.* New York: Hampton.

10. J. C. McCroskey, A. D. Heisel, & V. P. Richmond (2001). "Eysenck's Big Three and Communication Traits: Three Correlational Studies." *Communication Monographs, 68,* 360–366.

11. R. R. McCrae & P. T. Costa (1987). "Validation of the Five-Factor Model of Personality across Instruments and Observers." *Journal of Personality and Social Psychology, 52,* 81–90.

12. R. R. McCrae & P. T Costa., Jr. (1997). "Personality Trait Structure as a Human Universal." *American Psychologist, 52,* 509–516.

13. C. Dweck (2008). "Can Personality Be Changed? The Role of Beliefs in Personality and Change." *Current Directions in Psychological Science, 6,* 391–394.

14. S. Begney (December 1, 2008). "When DNA is Not Destiny." *Newsweek, 152,* 14.

15. C. H. Cooley (1912). *Human Nature and the Social Order.* New York: Scribner's.

16. C. Jaret, D. Reitzes, & N. Shapkina (2005). "Reflected Appraisals and Self-Esteem." *Sociological Perspectives, 48*, 403–419.

17. S. Salimi, S. Mirzamani, & M. Shahiri-Tabarestani (2005). "Association of Parental Self-Esteem and Expectations with Adolescents' Anxiety about Career and Education." *Psychological Reports, 96*, 569–578; A. L. Vangelisti & L. P. Crumley (1998). "Reactions to Messages that Hurt: The Influence of Relational Contexts." *Communication Monographs, 65*, 173–196.

18. L. Leets & Sunwolf (2004). "Being Left Out: Rejecting Outsiders and Communicating Group Boundaries in Childhood and Adolescent Peer Groups." *Journal of Applied Communication Research, 32*, 195–223.

19. A. Sillars, A. Koerner, & M. A. Fitzpatrick (2005). "Communication and Understanding in Parent-Adolescent Relationships." *Human Communication Research, 31*, 107–128.

20. T. Adler (October 1992). "Personality, Like Plaster, Is Pretty Stable over Time." *APA Monitor*, 18.

21. J. D. Brown, N. J. Novick, K. A. Lord, & J. M. Richards (1992). "When Gulliver Travels: Social Context, Psychological Closeness, and Self-Appraisals." *Journal of Personality and Social Psychology, 62*, 717–734.

22. M. Krcmar, S. Giles, & D. Helme (2008). "Understanding the Process: How Mediated and Peer Norms Affect Young Women's Body Esteem." *Communication Quarterly, 56*, 111–130.

23. P. N. Myers & F. A. Biocca (1992). "The Elastic Body Image: The Effect of Television Advertising and Programming on Body Image Distortions in Young Women." *Journal of Communication, 42*, 108–134.

24. C. M. Strong (2005). "The Role of Exposure to Media Idealized Male Physiques on Men's Body Image." *Dissertation Abstracts International, 65*, 4306.

25. K. N. Kubric & R. M. Chory (2007). "Exposure to Television Makeover Programs and Perceptions of Self." *Communication Research Reports, 24*, 283–291.

26. D. Grodin & T. R. Lindolf (1995). *Constructing the Self in a Mediated World*. Newbury Park, CA: Sage.

27. M. Han (2003). "Body Image Dissatisfaction and Eating Disturbance among Korean College Female Students: Relationships to Media Exposure, Upward Comparison, and Perceived Reality." *Communication Studies, 34*, 65–78; and K. Harrison & J. Cantor (1997). "The Relationship Between Media Consumption and Eating Disorders." *Journal of Communication, 47*, 40–67.

28. L. J. Carrell & S. C. Willmington (1996). "A Comparison of Self-Report and Performance Data in Assessing Speaking and Listening Competence." *Communication Reports, 9*, 185–191.

29. D. Meyers (May 1980). "The Inflated Self." *Psychology Today, 14*, 16.

30. A. B. Canton & K. H. Teigen. "Better Than Average and Better With Time: Relative Evaluations of Self and Others in the Past, Present, and Future." *European Journal of Social Psychology, 38*, 343–353.

31. N. Ellison, R. Heino, & J. Gibbs (2006). "Managing Impressions Online: Self-Presentation Processes in the Online Dating Environment." *Journal of Computer-Mediated Communication 11*: Article 2. Retrieved September 11, 2006, from http://jcmc.indiana.edu/vol11/issue2/ellison.html.

32. E. D. Sturman & M. Mongrain (2008). "The Role of Personality in Defeat: A Revised Social Rank Model." *European Journal of Personality, 22*, 55–79; J. D. Brown & T. A. Mankowski (1993). "Self-Esteem, Mood, and Self-Evaluation: Changes in Mood and the Way You See You." *Journal of Personality and Social Psychology, 64*, 421–430.

33. M. A. Gara, R. L. Woolfolk, B. D. Cohen, & R. B. Goldston (1993). "Perception of Self and Other in Major Depression." *Journal of Abnormal Psychology, 102*, 93–100.

34. L. C. Miller, L. L. Cooke, J. Tsang, & F. Morgan (1992). "Should I Brag? Nature and Impact of Positive and Boastful Disclosures for Women and Men." *Human Communication Research, 18*, 364–399.

35. B. Bower (August 15, 1992). "Truth Aches: People Who View Themselves Poorly May Seek the 'Truth' and Find Despair." *Science News*, 110–111; and W. B. Swann (2005). "The Self and Identity Negotiation." *Interaction Studies, 6*, 69–83.

36. W. W. Wilmot (1995). *Relational Communication* (pp. 35–54). New York: McGraw-Hill.

37. J. Servaes (1989). "Cultural Identity and Modes of Communication." In J. A. Anderson (Ed.), *Communication Yearbook 12* (p. 396). Newbury Park, CA: Sage.

38. A. Bharti (1985). "The Self in Hindu Thought and Action." In *Culture and Self: Asian and Western Perspectives*. New York: Tavistock.

39. S. Bochner (1994). "Cross-Cultural Differences in the Self Concept: A Test of Hofstede's Individualism/Collectivism Distinction." *Journal of Cross-Cultural Psychology, 25*, 273–283.

40. W. B. Gudykunst & S. Ting-Toomey (1988). *Culture and Interpersonal Communication*. Newbury Park, CA: Sage.

41. L. A. Samovar & R. E. Porter (1991). *Communication between Cultures* (p. 91). Belmont, CA: Wadsworth.

42. D. Klopf (1984). "Cross-Cultural Apprehension Research: A Summary of Pacific Basin Studies." In J. Daly & J. McCroskey (Eds.), *Avoiding Communication: Shyness, Reticence, and Communication Apprehension*. Beverly Hills, CA: Sage.

43. S. Ting-Toomey (1988). "A Face-Negotiation Theory." In Y. Kim & W. Gudykunst (Eds.), *Theory in Interpersonal Communication*. Newbury Park, CA: Sage.

44. L. C. Lederman (1993). "Gender and the Self." In L. P. Arliss & D. J. Borisoff (Eds.), *Women and Men Communicating: Challenges and Changes* (pp. 41–42). Fort Worth, TX: Harcourt Brace.

45. For more examples of gender-related labels, see A. Wittels (1978). *I Wonder . . . A Satirical Study of Sexist Semantics*. Los Angeles: Price Stern Sloan.

46. M. Knox, J. Funk, R. Elliott, & E. G. Bush (2000). "Gender Differences in Adolescents' Possible Selves." *Youth and Society, 31,* 287–309.

47. J. Robins and R. W. Robins (1993). "A Longitudinal Study of Consistency and Change in Self-Esteem from Early Adolescence to Early Childhood." *Child Development, 64,* 909–923.

48. C. J. Smith, J. A. Noll, & J. B. Bryant (1999). "The Effect of Social Context on Gender Self-Concept." *Sex Roles, 40,* 499–512.

49. Dweck, C. S. (2006). *Mindset: The New Psychology of Success.* New York: Random House.

50. J. Kolligan, Jr. (1990). "Perceived Fraudulence as a Dimension of Perceived Incompetence." In R. J. Sternberg & J. Kolligen, Jr. (Eds.), *Competence Considered.* New Haven, CT: Yale University Press. See also A. L. Vangelisti, S. D. Corbin, A. E. Lucchetti, & R. J. Sprague (1999). "Couples' Concurrent Cognitions: The Influence of Relational Satisfaction on the Thoughts Couples Have as They Converse." *Human Communication Research, 25,* 370–398.

51. B. Zimmerman, A. Bandura, & M. Martinez-Pons (1992). "Self-Motivation for Academic Attainment: The Role of Self-Efficacy Beliefs and Personal Goal Setting." *American Educational Research Journal, 29,* 663–676.

52. G. Downey & S. I. Feldman (1996). "Implications of Rejection Sensitivity for Intimate Relationships." *Journal of Personality and Social Psychology, 70,* 1327–1343.

53. P. D. MacIntyre & K. A Thivierge (1995). "The Effects of Speaker Personality on Anticipated Reactions to Public Speaking." *Communication Research Reports, 12,* 125–133.

54. C. L. Kleinke, T. R. Peterson, & T. R. Rutledge (1998). "Effects of Self-Generated Facial Expressions on Mood." *Journal of Personality and Social Psychology, 74,* 272–279.

55. R. Rosenthal & L. Jacobson (1968). *Pygmalion in the Classroom.* New York: Holt, Rinehart and Winston.

56. P. D. Blank (Ed.) (1993). *Interpersonal Expectations: Theory, Research, and Applications.* Cambridge, UK: Cambridge University Press.

57. R. M. Perloff, B. Bonder, G. B. Ray, E. B. Ray, & L. A. Siminoff (2006). "Doctor-Patient Communication, Cultural Competence, and Minority Health." *American Behavioral Scientist, 49,* 835–852.

58. For a thorough discussion of this subject, see M. E. P. Seligman (1993). *What You Can Change and What You Can't.* New York: Knopf.

59. C. M. Shaw & R. Edwards (1997). "Self-Concepts and Self-Presentations of Males and Females: Similarities and Differences." *Communication Reports, 10,* 55–62.

60. C. M. Scotton (1983). "The Negotiation of Identities in Conversation: A Theory of Markedness and Code Choice." *International Journal of Sociological Linguistics, 44,* 119–125.

61. E. Goffman (1959). *The Presentation of Self in Everyday Life.* Garden City, NY: Doubleday; and E. Goffman (1971). *Relations in Public.* New York: Basic Books.

62. J. Stewart & C. Logan (1998). *Together: Communicating Interpersonally,* 5th ed. (p. 120). New York: McGraw-Hill.

63. M. R. Leary & R. M. Kowalski (1990). "Impression Management: A Literature Review and Two-Component Model." *Psychological Bulletin, 107,* 34–47.

64. V. Brightman, A. Segal, P. Werther, & J. Steiner (1975). "Ethological Study of Facial Expression in Response to Taste Stimuli." *Journal of Dental Research, 54,* 141.

65. N. Chovil (1991). "Social Determinants of Facial Displays." *Journal of Nonverbal Behavior, 15,* 141–154.

66. See, for example, R. A. Giacalone & P. Rosenfeld (Eds.) (1991). *Applied Impression Management: How Image-Making Affects Managerial Decisions.* Newbury Park, CA: Sage.

67. D. Morier & C. Seroy (1994). "The Effect of Interpersonal Expectancies on Men's Self-Presentation of Gender Role Attitudes to Women." *Sex Roles, 31,* 493–504.

68. M. Leary, J. B. Nezlek, & D. Downs, et al. (1994). "Self-Presentation in Everyday Interactions: Effects of Target Familiarity and Gender Composition." *Journal of Personality and Social Psychology, 67,* 664–673.

69. M. Snyder (1987). *Public Appearances, Private Realities: The Psychology of Self-Monitoring.* New York: W. H. Freeman.

70. The following discussion is based on material in D. E. Hamachek (1992). *Encounters with the Self,* 3rd ed. (pp. 24–26). Fort Worth, TX: Harcourt.

71. C. N. Wright, A. Holloway, & M. E. Roloff (2007). "The Dark Side of Self-Monitoring: How High Self-Monitors View Their Romantic Relationships." *Communication Reports, 20,* 101–114.

72. For a more detailed discussion of identity-related goals, see S. Metts & E. Grohskopf (2003). "Impression Management: Goals, Strategies, and Skills." In J. O. Greene and B. R. Burleson (Eds.), *Handbook of Communication and Social Skills.* Mahwah, NJ: Erlbaum.

73. L. M. Coleman & B. M. DePaulo (1991). "Uncovering the Human Spirit: Moving beyond Disability and 'Missed' Communications." In N. Coupland, H. Giles, & J. M. Wiemann (Eds.), *"Miscommunication" and Problematic Talk* (pp. 61–84). Newbury Park, CA: Sage.

74. P. M. Valkenburg & J. Peter (2008). "Adolescents' Identity Experiments on the Internet: Consequences for Social Competence and Self-Concept Unity." *Communication Research, 35,* 208–231.

75. J. W. Vander Zanden (1984). *Social Psychology,* 3rd ed. (pp. 235–237). New York: Random House.

76. D. Brouwer (1998). "The Precarious Visibility Politics of Self-Stigmatization: The Case of HIV/AIDS Tattoos." *Text and Performance Quarterly, 18,* 114–136.

77. P. B. O'Sullivan (2000). "What You Don't Know Won't Hurt Me: Impression Management Functions of

Communication Channels in Relationships." *Communication Monographs, 26,* 403–432. See also S. B. Barnes (2003). *Computer-Mediated Communication: Human-to-Human Communication across the Internet* (pp. 136–162). Boston: Allyn and Bacon.

78. J. Sanderson (2008). "The Blog is Serving Its Purpose: Self-Presentation Strategies on 38Pitches.com." *Journal of Computer-Mediated Communication, 13,* 912–936.

79. J. R. Suler (2002). "Identity Management in Cyberspace." *Journal of Applied Psychoanalytic Studies, 4,* 455–459.

80. J. L. Gibbs, N. B. Ellison, & R. D. Heino (2006). "Self-Presentation in Online Personals: The Role of Anticipated Future Interaction, Self-Disclosure, and Perceived Success in Internet Dating." *Communication Research, 33,* 1–26.

81. See, for example, D. Chandler (n.d.). "Personal Home Pages and the Construction of Identities on the Web." Retrieved May 8, 2006, from http://www.aber .ac.uk/~dgc/webident.html.

82. R. Bennett (April 4, 2008). "Revealed: Secrets of Choosing an Online Dating Name." *Times Online.* Retrieved July 24, 2009, from http://technology.timesonline.co.uk/ tol/news/tech_and_web/the_web/article3677778.ece.

83. O'Sullivan, op. cit.

CHAPTER THREE

1. The graphic demonstrations of factors influencing perception in this and the following paragraph are borrowed from D. Coon & J. Mitterer (2010). *Introduction to Psychology*, 12th ed. Belmont, CA: Cengage Wadsworth.

2. G. W. Allport (1958). *The Nature of Prejudice* (p. 185). New York: Doubleday Anchor.

3. M. Allen (1998). "Methodological Considerations When Examining a Gendered World." In D. Canary and K. Dindia (Eds.), *Handbook of Sex Differences and Similarities in Communication* (pp. 427–444). Mahwah, NJ: Erlbaum.

4. B. Allen (1995). "Diversity and Organizational Communication." *Journal of Applied Communication Research, 23,* 143–155. See also R. Buttny (1997). "Reported Speech in Talking Race on Campus." *Human Communication Research, 23,* 477–506; and P. C. Hughes & J. R. Baldwin (2002). "Communication and Stereotypical Impressions." *Howard Journal of Communications, 13,* 113–128.

5. R. M. Perloff, B. Bonder, G. B. Ray, E. B. Ray, & L. A. Siminoff (2006). "Doctor-Patient Communication, Cultural Competence, and Minority Health: Theoretical and Empirical Perspectives." *American Behavioral Scientist, 49,* 835–852; M. N. Oliver, M. A. Goodwin, R. S. Gotler, & K. C. Strange (2001). "Time Use in Clinical Encounters: Are African-American Patients Treated Differently?" *Journal of the National Medical Association, 93,* 380–385.

6. J. Oetzel (1998). "The Effects of Self-Construals and Ethnicity on Self-Reported Conflict Styles." *Communication Reports, 11,* 133–144.

7. N. Nishizawa (2004). "The 'Self' of Japanese Teenagers: Growing Up in the Flux of a Changing Culture and Society." *Dissertation Abstracts International, 65,* 2642.

8. M. L. Inman & R. S. Baron (1996). "Influence of Prototypes on Perceptions of Prejudice." *Journal of Personality and Social Psychology, 70,* 727–739.

9. P. Watzlawick, J. Beavin, & D. D. Jackson (1967). *Pragmatics of Human Communication* (p. 65). New York: Norton.

10. V. Manusov (1993). "It Depends on Your Perspective: Effects of Stance and Beliefs about Intent on Person Perception." *Western Journal of Communication, 57,* 27–41.

11. T. Adler (June 1992). "Enter Romance, Exit Objectivity." *APA Monitor,* 18.

12. K. Floyd & M. T. Morman (2000). "Reacting to the Verbal Expression of Affection in Same-Sex Interaction." *Southern Communication Journal, 65,* 287–299.

13. C. Edwards, A. Edwards, Q. Qingmei, & S. T. Wahl (2007). "The Influence of Computer-Mediated Word-of-Mouth Communication on Student Perceptions of Instructors and Attitudes Toward Learning Course Content." *Communication Education, 56,* 255–277.

14. J. K. Alberts, U. Kellar-Guenther, & S. R. Corman (1996). "That's Not Funny: Understanding Recipients' Responses to Teasing." *Western Journal of Communication, 60,* 337–357. See also R. Edwards, R. Bello, F. Brandau-Brown, & D. Hollems (2001). "The Effects of Loneliness and Verbal Aggressiveness on Message Interpretation." *Southern Communication Journal, 66,* 139–150.

15. See T. N. Bradbury & F. D. Fincham (1990). "Attributions in Marriage: Review and Critique." *Psychological Bulletin, 107,* 3–33; and V. Manusov (1990). "An Application of Attribution Principles to Nonverbal Behavior in Romantic Dyads." *Communication Monographs, 57,* 104–118.

16. C. L. M. Shaw (1997). "Personal Narrative: Revealing Self and Reflecting Other." *Human Communication Research, 24,* 302–319.

17. J. K. Kellas (2005). "Family Ties: Communicating Identity Through Jointly Told Family Stories." *Communication Monographs, 72,* 365–389.

18. J. Flora & C. Segrin (2000). "Relationship Development in Dating Couples: Implications for Relational Satisfaction and Loneliness." *Journal of Social and Personal Relationships, 17,* 811–825.

19. L. A. Baxter & G. Pittman (2001). "Communicatively Remembering Turning Points of Relational Development in Heterosexual Romantic Relationships." *Communication Reports, 14,* 1–17.

20. S. L. Murray, J. G. Holmes, & D. W. Griffin (2004). "The Benefits of Positive Illusions: Idealization and the Construction of Satisfaction in Close Relationships."

In *Close Relationships: Key Readings* (pp. 317–338). Philadelphia: Taylor & Francis. See also J. M. Martz, J. Verette, X. B. Arriaga, L. F. Slovik, C. L. Cox, & C. E. Rosbult (1998). "Positive Illusion in Close Relationships." *Personal Relationships*, 5, 159–181.

21. J. C. Pearson (1996). "Positive Distortion: 'The Most Beautiful Woman in the World.' " In K. M. Galvin & P. Cooper (Eds.), *Making Connections: Readings in Interpersonal Communication* (p. 177). Beverly Hills, CA: Roxbury.

22. For a detailed description of how the senses affect perception, see N. Ackerman (1990). *A Natural History of the Senses.* New York: Random House.

23. J. Piaget (1952). *The Origins of Intelligence in Children.* New York: International Universities Press.

24. K. Alaimo, C. M. Olson, & E. A. Frongillo (2001). "Food Insufficiency and American School-Aged Children's Cognitive, Academic, and Psychosocial Development." *Pediatrics, 108*, 44–53.

25. M. Maguire (2005). "Biological Cycles and Cognitive Performance." In A. Esgate et al., *An Introduction to Applied Cognitive Psychology* (pp. 137–161). New York: Psychology Press. See also C. Cooper & C. McConville (1990). "Interpreting Mood Scores: Clinical Implications of Individual Differences in Mood Variability." *British Journal of Medical Psychology, 63*, 215–225.

26. For descriptions of various psychological disorders and their treatments, visit the National Institute of Mental Health website at http://www.nimh.nih.gov/.

27. J. W. Bagby (1957). "A Cross-Cultural Study of Perceptual Predominance in Binocular Rivalry." *Journal of Abnormal and Social Psychology, 54,* 331–334.

28. E. T. Hall (1969). *The Hidden Dimension* (p. 160). New York: Doubleday Anchor.

29. H. Giles, N. Coupland, & J. M. Wiemann (1992). "Talk Is Cheap . . . But 'My Word Is My Bond': Beliefs about Talk." In K. Bolton & H. Kwok (Eds.), *Sociolinguistics Today: International Perspectives.* London: Routledge & Kegan Paul.

30. R. Steves (May–September 1996). "Culture Shock." *Europe Through the Back Door Newsletter, 50,* 20.

31. A. Fadiman (1997). *The Spirit Catches You and You Fall Down* (p. 33). New York: Farrar, Straus, and Giroux.

32. P. Andersen, M. Lustig, & J. Anderson (1987). *Changes in Latitude, Changes in Attitude: The Relationship between Climate, Latitude, and Interpersonal Communication Predispositions.* Paper presented at the annual convention of the Speech Communication Association, Boston; P. Andersen, M. Lustig, & J. Andersen (1988). *Regional Patterns of Communication in the United States: Empirical Tests.* Paper presented at the annual convention of the Speech Communication Association, New Orleans.

33. V. Manusov, M. R. Winchatz, & L. M. Manning (1997). "Acting Out of Our Minds: Incorporating Behavior Into Models of Stereotype-Based Expectancies for Cross-Cultural Interactions." *Communication Monographs, 64,* 119–139.

34. J. B. Becker, K. J. Berkley, N. Geary, E. Hampson, J. P. Herman, & E. Young (2007). *Sex Differences in the Brain: From Genes to Behavior.* New York: Oxford University Press.

35. D. F. Halpern (2000). *Sex Differences in Cognitive Abilities*, 3rd ed. Mahwah, NJ: Lawrence Erlbaum.

36. See S. A. Rathus (1993). *Psychology*, 5th ed. (pp. 640–643). Fort Worth, TX: Harcourt Brace Jovanovich; and C. Wade & C. Tavris (1987). *Psychology* (pp. 488–490). New York: Harper & Row.

37. S. L. Bem (1985). "Androgyny and Gender Schema Theory: A Conceptual and Empirical Integration." In T. B. Sonderegger (Ed.), *Nebraska Symposium on Motivation: Psychology and Gender.* Lincoln: University of Nebraska Press.

38. V. Swami & A. Furnham (2008). "Is Love Really So Blind?" *The Psychologist, 21*, 108–111.

39. G. C. Gonzaga, M. G. Haselton, J. Smurda, M. Davies, & J. C. Poore (2008). "Love, Desire, and the Suppression of Thoughts of Romantic Alternatives." *Evolution and Human Behavior, 29*, 119–126.

40. D. Hamachek (1992). *Encounters with the Self*, 3rd ed. Fort Worth, TX: Harcourt Brace Jovanovich.

41. For a review of these perceptual biases, see Hamachek, *Encounters with the Self.* See also Bradbury & Fincham, op. cit. For an example of the self-serving bias in action, see R. Buttny (1997). "Reported Speech in Talking Race on Campus." *Human Communication Research, 23*, 477–506.

42. S. L. Young (2004). "What the _____ Is Your Problem?: Attribution Theory and Perceived Reasons for Profanity Usage During Conflict." *Communication Research Reports, 21*, 338–347.

43. K. Dion, E. Berscheid, & E. Walster (1972). "What Is Beautiful Is Good." *Journal of Personality and Social Psychology, 24*, 285–290.

44. L. Watkins & L. Johnston (2000). "Screening Job Applicants: The Impact of Physical Attractiveness and Application Quality." *International Journal of Selection and Assessment, 8*, 76–84.

45. T. Dougherty, D. Turban, & J. Collander (1994). "Confirming First Impressions in the Employment Interview." *Journal of Applied Psychology, 79*, 659–665.

46. G. I. Cook, R. L. Marsh, & J. L. Hicks (2003). "Halo and Devil Effects Demonstrate Valenced-Based Influences on Source-Mentoring Decisions." *Consciousness and Cognition, 12*, 257–278.

47. C. I. Marek, M. B. Wanzer, & J. L. Knapp (2004). "An Exploratory Investigation of the Relationship between Roommates' First Impressions and Subsequent Communication Patterns." *Communication Research Reports, 21*, 210–220.

48. B. Keysar (2007). "Communication and Miscommunication: The Role of Egocentric Processes." *Intercultural Pragmatics, 4*, 71–84.

49. See, for example, A. Sillars, W. Shellen, A. McIntosh, & M. Pomegranate (1997). "Relational Characteristics of

Language: Elaboration and Differentiation in Marital Conversations." *Western Journal of Communication, 61,* 403–422.

50. J. B. Stiff, J. P. Dillard, L. Somera, H. Kim, & C. Sleight (1988). "Empathy, Communication, and Prosocial Behavior." *Communication Monographs, 55,* 198–213.

51. This research is described by D. Goleman (2006). In *Social Intelligence.* New York: Bantam. See also J. Decety, K. Michalska, & Y. Aktsuki (2008). "Who Caused the Pain? An fMRI Investigation of Empathy and Intentionality in Children." *Neuropsychologia, 46,* 2607–2614.

52. Goleman, op cit.

53. M. Davis (1994). "The Heritability of Characteristics Associated with Dispositional Empathy." *Journal of Personality, 62,* 369–391.

54. B. Burleson, J. Delia, & J. Applegate (1995). "The Socialization of Person-Centered Communication: Parental Contributions to the Social-Cognitive and Communication Skills of Their Children." In M. A. Fitzpatrick & A. Vangelisti (Eds.), *Perspectives in Family Communication.* Thousand Oaks, CA: Sage.

55. D. M. Tucker, P. Luu, & D. Derryberry (2005). "Love Hurts: The Evolution of Empathic Concern Through the Encephalization of Nociceptive Capacity." *Development and Psychopathology, 17,* 699–713.

56. S. Wu & B. Keysar (2007). "Cultural Effects on Perspective Taking." *Psychological Science, 18,* 600–606.

57. R. Martin (1992). "Relational Cognition Complexity and Relational Communication in Personal Relationships." *Communication Monographs, 59,* 150–163. See also B. R. Burleson & S. E. Caplan (1998). "Cognitive Complexity." In J. C. McCroskey, J. A. Daly, M. M. Martin, and M. J. Beatty (Eds.), *Communication and Personality: Trait Perspectives* (pp. 233–286). Creskill, NY: Hampton Press.

58. Burleson & Caplan, op. cit., p. 22.

59. B. R. Burleson (1989). "The Constructivist Approach to Person-Centered Communication: Analysis of a Research Exemplar." In B. Dervin, L. Grossberg, B. J. O'Keefe, & E. Wartella (Eds.), *Rethinking Communication: Paradigm Exemplars* (pp. 33–72). Newbury Park, CA: Sage.

60. B. D. Sypher & T. Zorn (1986). "Communication-Related Abilities and Upward Mobility: A Longitudinal Investigation." *Human Communication Research, 12,* 420–431.

61. Joireman, J. (2004). "Relationships Between Attributional Complexity and Empathy." *Individual Differences Research, 2,* 197–202.

62. L. Medvene, K. Grosch, & N. Swink (2006). "Interpersonal Complexity: A Cognitive Component of Person-Centered Care." *The Gerontologist, 46,* 220–226.

63. P. Rockwell (2007). "The Effects of Cognitive Complexity and Communication Apprehension on the Expression and Recognition of Sarcasm." In A. M. Columbus (Ed.), *Advances in Psychology Research, 49,* 185–196. Hauppauge, NY: Nova Science Publishers.

64. C. Little, J. Packman, M. H. Smaby, & C. D. Maddux (2005). "The Skilled Counselor Training Model: Skills Acquisition, Self-Assessment, and Cognitive Complexity." *Counselor Education & Supervision, 44,* 189–200.

65. P. Reps (1967). "Pillow Education in Rural Japan." In *Square Sun, Square Moon.* New York: Tuttle.

CHAPTER FOUR

1. D. Goleman (1995). *Emotional Intelligence: Why It Can Matter More Than I.Q.* New York: Bantam. See also D. Goleman (2006). *Social Intelligence: The New Science of Human Relationships.* New York: Bantam.

2. A. Carmeli, M. Yitzhak-Halevy, & J. Weisberg (2009). "The Relationship Between Emotional Intelligence and Psychological Wellbeing." *Journal of Managerial Psychology, 24,* 66–78.

3. L. Smith, P. C. Heaven, & J. Ciarrochi (2008). "Trait Emotional Intelligence, Conflict Communication Patterns, and Relationship Satisfaction." *Personality and Individual Differences, 44,* 1314–1325.

4. S. Planalp, J. Fitness, & B. Fehr (2006). "Emotion in Theories of Close Relationships." In A. L. Vangelisti & D. Perlman (Eds.), *The Cambridge Handbook of Personal Relationships* (pp. 369–384). New York: Cambridge University Press; R. F. Baumeister (2005). *The Human Animal.* New York: Oxford University Press.

5. G. M. Rochman & G. M. Diamond (2008). "From Unresolved Anger to Sadness: Identifying Physiological Correlates." *Journal of Counseling Psychology, 55,* 96–105.

6. J. M. Gottman & N. Silver (1999). *The Seven Principles for Making Marriages Work.* New York: Three Rivers Press.

7. P. Ekman, R. W. Levenson, & W. V. Friesen (September 16, 1983). "Autonomic Nervous System Activity Distinguishes among Emotions." *Science, 221,* 1208–1210.

8. C. L. Kleinke, T. R. Peterson, & T. R. Rutledge (1998). "Effects of Self-Generated Facial Expressions on Mood." *Journal of Personality and Social Psychology, 74,* 272–279.

9. S. Valins (1966). "Cognitive Effects of False Heart-Rate Feedback." *Journal of Personality and Social Psychology, 4,* 400–408.

10. P. Zimbardo (1977). *Shyness: What It Is, What To Do about It* (p. 53). Reading, MA: Addison-Wesley.

11. K. N. Ochsner & J. J. Gross (2008). "Cognitive Emotion Regulation: Insights From Social Cognitive and Affective Neuroscience." *Current Directions in Psychological Science, 17,* 153–158.

12. J. C. Wallace, B. D. Edwards, A. Shull, & D. M. Finch (2009). "Examining the Consequences in the Tendency to Suppress and Reappraise Emotions on Task-Related Job Performance." *Human Performance, 22,* 23–43; S. A. Moore, L. A. Zoellner, & N. Mollenholt (2008). "Are Expressive Suppression and Cognitive Reappraisal Associated with Stress-Related Symptoms?" *Behaviour Research and Therapy, 46,* 993–1000; J. B. Nezlek & P. Kuppens (2008). "Regulating Positive and Negative

Emotions in Daily Life." *Journal of Personality, 76,* 561–580.

13. R. Plutchik (1980). *Emotion: A Psychoevolutionary Synthesis.* New York: Harper & Row; P. R. Shaver, S. Wu, & J. C. Schwartz (1992). "Cross-Cultural Similarities and Differences in Emotion and its Representation: A Prototype Approach." In M. S. Clark (Ed.), *Emotion* (pp. 175–212). Newbury Park, CA: Sage.

14. P. Ekman (1999). "Basic Emotions." In T. Dalgleish & T. Power (Eds.), *The Handbook of Cognition and Emotion* (pp. 45–60). Sussex, UK: John Wiley & Sons; A. Ortony & T. J. Turner (1990). "What's Basic about Basic Emotions?" *Psychological Review, 97,* 315–331.

15. M. Ferrari & E. Koyama (2002). "Meta-Emotions about Anger and Amae: A Cross-Cultural Comparison." *Consciousness and Emotion, 3,* 197–211.

16. Shaver et al., op. cit.

17. Goleman, *Emotional Intelligence,* op. cit.

18. J. M. Gottman, L. F. Katz, & C. Hooven (1997). *Meta-Emotion: How Families Communicate Emotionally.* Mahwah, NJ: Erlbaum.

19. E. S. Lunkenheimer, A. M. Shields, & K. S. Kortina (2007). "Parental Emotion Coaching and Dismissing in Family Interaction." *Social Development, 16,* 232–248.

20. J. C. McCroskey, V. P. Richmond, A. D. Heisel, & J. L Hayhurst (2004). "Eysenck's Big Three and Communication Traits: Communication Traits as Manifestations of Temperament." *Communication Research Reports, 21,* 404–410; J. J. Gross, S. K. Sutton, & T. V. Ketelaar (1998). "Relations between Affect and Personality: Support for the Affect-Level and Affective-Reactivity Views." *Personality and Social Psychology Bulletin, 24,* 279–288.

21. P. T. Costa & R. R. McCrae (1980). "Influence of Extraversion and Neuroticism on Subjective Well-Being: Happy and Unhappy People." *Journal of Personality and Social Psychology, 38,* 668–678.

22. T. Canli, Z. Zhao, J. E. Desmond, E. Kang, J. Gross, & J. D. E. Gabrieli (2001). "An MRI Study of Personality Influences on Brain Reactivity to Emotional Stimuli." *Behavioral Neuroscience, 115,* 33–42.

23. L. Kelly, R. L. Duran, & J. J. Zolten (2001). "The Effect of Reticence on College Students' Use of Electronic Mail to Communicate with Faculty." *Communication Education, 50,* 170–176. See also B. W. Scharlott & W. G. Christ (2001). "Overcoming Relationship-Initiation Barriers: The Impact of a Computer-Dating System on Sex Role, Shyness, and Appearance Inhibitions." *Computers in Human Behavior, 11,* 191–204.

24. C. Goddard (2002). "Explicating Emotions across Languages and Cultures: A Semantic Approach." In S. R. Fussell (Ed.), *The Verbal Communication of Emotions.* Mahwah, NJ: Erlbaum.

25. S. Ting-Toomey (1991). "Intimacy Expressions in Three Cultures: France, Japan, and the United States." *International Journal of Intercultural Relations, 15,* 29–46. See also C. Gallois (1993). "The Language and Communication of Emotion: Universal, Interpersonal, or Intergroup?" *American Behavioral Scientist, 36,* 309–338.

26. J. L. Tsai, B. Knutson, & H. H. Fung (2006). "Cultural Variation in Affect Valuation." *Journal of Personality and Social Psychology, 90,* 288–307.

27. J. W. Pennebaker, B. Rime, & V. E. Blankenship (1996). "Stereotypes of Emotional Expressiveness of Northerners and Southerners: A Cross-Cultural Test of Montesquieu's Hypotheses." *Journal of Personality and Social Psychology, 70,* 372–380.

28. Ibid., p. 176. See also Gallois, op. cit.

29. H. C. Triandis (1994). *Culture and Social Behavior* (p. 169). New York: McGraw-Hill. See also F. M. Moghaddam, D. M. Taylor, & S. C. Wright (1993). *Social Psychology in Cross-Cultural Perspective.* New York: Freeman.

30. S. T. Mortenson (2009). "Interpersonal Trust and Social Skill in Seeking Social Support Among Chinese and Americans." *Communication Research, 36,* 32–53.

31. R. Wilkins & E. Gareis (2006). "Emotion Expression and the Locution 'I Love You': A Cross-Cultural Study." *International Journal of Intercultural Relations, 30,* 51–75.

32. L. K. Guerrero, S. M. Jones, & R. R. Boburka (2006). "Sex Differences in Emotional Communication." In K. Dindia & D. J. Canary (Eds.), *Sex Differences and Similarities in Communication,* 2nd ed. Mahwah, NJ: Erlbaum; S. R. Wester, D. L. Vogel, P. K. Pressly, & M. Heesacker (2002). "Sex Differences in Emotion: A Critical Review of the Literature and Implications for Counseling Psychology." *Counseling Psychologist, 30,* 630–652.

33. J. Swenson & F. L. Casmir (1998). "The Impact of Culture-Sameness, Gender, Foreign Travel, and Academic Background on the Ability to Interpret Facial Expression of Emotion in Others." *Communication Quarterly, 46,* 214–230.

34. T. Canli, J. E. Desmond, Z. Zhao, & J. D. E. Gabrieli (2002). "Sex Differences in the Neural Basis of Emotional Memories." *Proceedings of the National Academy of Sciences, 10,* 10789–10794.

35. J. Merten (2005). "Culture, Gender and the Recognition of the Basic Emotions." *Psychologia: An International Journal of Psychology in the Orient, 48,* 306–316.

36. See, for example, A. W. Kunkel & B. R. Burleson (1999). "Assessing Explanations for Sex Differences in Emotional Support: A Test of the Different Cultures and Skill Specialization Accounts." *Human Communication Research, 25,* 307–340.

37. D. J. Goldsmith & P. A. Fulfs (1999). " 'You Just Don't Have the Evidence': An Analysis of Claims and Evidence in Deborah Tannen's *You Just Don't Understand.*" In M. E. Roloff (Ed.), *Communication Yearbook 22* (pp. 1–49). Thousand Oaks, CA: Sage.

38. D. F. Witmer & S. L. Katzman (1999). "On-Line Smiles: Does Gender Make a Difference in the Use of Graphic Accents?" *Journal of Computer-Mediated Communication, 2* (online, domain name expired).

39. K. Floyd (1997). "Communication Affection in Dyadic Relationships: An Assessment of Behavior and Expectancies." *Communication Quarterly, 45,* 68–80.

40. Ibid.

41. M. S. Clark & E. J. Finkel (2005). "Willingness to Express Emotion: The Impact of Relationship Type, Communal Orientation, and Their Interaction." *Personal Relationships, 12,* 169–180.

42. J. A. Feeney (2005). "Hurt Feelings in Couple Relationships: Exploring the Role of Attachment and Perceptions of Personal Injury." *Personal Relationships, 12,* 253–271.

43. S. E. Snodgrass (1985). "Women's Intuition: The Effect of Subordinate Role on Interpersonal Sensitivity." *Journal of Personality and Social Psychology, 49,* 146–155.

44. S. B. Shimanoff (1984). "Commonly Named Emotions in Everyday Conversations." *Perceptual and Motor Skills, 58,* 514. See also J. M. Gottman (1982). "Emotional Responsiveness in Marital Conversations." *Journal of Communication, 32,* 108–120.

45. J. G. Haybe & S. Metts (2008). "Managing the Expression of Emotion." *Western Journal of Communication, 72,* 374–396; S. B. Shimanoff (1988). "Degree of Emotional Expressiveness as a Function of Face-Needs, Gender, and Interpersonal Relationship." *Communication Reports, 1,* 43–53.

46. C. E. Waugh & B. L. Fredericson (2006). "Nice to Know You: Positive Emotions, Self-Other Overlap, and Complex Understanding in the Formation of a New Relationship." *The Journal of Positive Psychology, 1,* 93–106.

47. C. A. Stearns & P. Stearns (1986). *Anger: The Struggle for Emotional Control in America's History.* Chicago: University of Chicago Press.

48. S. B. Shimanoff (1985). "Rules Governing the Verbal Expression of Emotions between Married Couples." *Western Journal of Speech Communication, 49,* 149–165.

49. S. Duck (1992). "Social Emotions: Showing Our Feelings about Other People." *Human Relationships.* Newbury Park, CA: Sage. See also S. B. Shimanoff (1985). "Expressing Emotions in Words: Verbal Patterns of Interaction." *Journal of Communication, 35,* 16–31.

50. L. B. Rosenfeld (1979). "Self-Disclosure Avoidance: Why I Am Afraid To Tell You Who I Am." *Communication Monographs, 46,* 63–74.

51. L. A. Erbert & K. Floyd (2004). "Affectionate Expressions as Face-Threatening Acts: Receiver Assessments." *Journal of Social and Personal Relationships, 17,* 230–246.

52. E. Hatfield, J. T. Cacioppo, R. L. Rapson, & K. Oatley (1984). *Emotional Contagion.* Cambridge, UK: Cambridge University Press. See also S. Colino (May 30, 2006). "That Look—It's Catching." *The Washington Post,* HE01.

53. Goleman, *Social Intelligence,* op. cit., p. 115.

54. A. B. Bakker (2005). "Flow Among Music Teachers and Their Students: The Crossover of Peak Experiences." *Journal of Vocational Behavior, 66,* 822–833.

55. C. R. Goodman & R. A. Shippy (2002). "Is it Contagious? Affect Similarity Among Spouses." *Aging and Mental Health, 6,* 266–274.

56. P. Belluck (December 5, 2008). "Strangers May Cheer You Up, Study Says." *The New York Times,* A12.

57. E. S. Sullins (1991). "Emotional Contagion Revisited: Effects of Social Comparison and Expressive Style on Mood Convergence." *Personality and Social Psychology Bulletin, 17,* 166–174.

58. C. Anderson, D. Keltner, & O. P. John (May 2003). "Emotional Convergence between People over Time." *Journal of Personality and Social Psychology, 84,* 1054–1068.

59. T. DeAngelis (1992). "Illness Linked with Repressive Style of Coping." *APA Monitor, 23(12),* 14–15.

60. A. W. Seigman & T. W. Smith (1994). *Anger, Hostility, and the Heart.* Hillsdale, NJ: Erlbaum.

61. S. Graham, J. Y. Huang, M. S. Clark, & V. S. Helgeson (2008). "The Positives of Negative Emotions: Willingness to Express Negative Emotions Promotes Relationships." *Personality and Social Psychology Bulletin, 34,* 394–406; E. Kennedy-Moore & J. C. Watson (1999). *Expressing Emotion: Myths, Realities, and Therapeutic Strategies.* New York: Guilford.

62. S. Nelton (February 1996). "Emotions in the Workplace." *Nation's Business,* 25–30.

63. M. W. Kramer & J. A. Hess (2002). "Communication Rules for the Display of Emotions in Organizational Settings." *Management Communication Quarterly, 16,* 66–80.

64. M. Booth-Butterfield & S. Booth-Butterfield (1998). "Emotionality and Affective Orientation." In J. C. McCroskey, J. A. Daly, M. M. Martin, & M. J. Beatty (Eds.), *Communication and Personality: Trait Perspectives.* Creskill, NY: Hampton.

65. L. F. Barrett, J. Gross, T. Christensen, & M. Benvenuto (2001). "Knowing What You're Feeling and Knowing What to Do About It: Mapping the Relation Between Emotion Differentiation and Emotion Regulation." *Cognition and Emotion, 15,* 713–724.

66. D. Grewal & P. Salovey (2005). "Feeling Smart: The Science of Emotional Intelligence." *American Scientist, 93,* 330–339; S. H. Yoo, D. Matsumoto, & J. LeRoux (2006). "The Influence of Emotion Recognition and Emotion Regulation on Intercultural Adjustment." *International Journal of Intercultural Relations, 30,* 345–363.

67. B. J. Bushman, R. F. Baumeister, & A. D. Stack (1999). "Catharsis, Aggression, and Persuasive Influence: Self-Fulfilling or Self-Defeating Prophecies?" *Journal of Personality and Social Psychology, 76,* 367–376.

68. For an extensive discussion of ways to express emotions, see S. R. Fussell (2002). *The Verbal Communication of Emotions.* Mahwah, NJ: Erlbaum.

69. J. M. Honeycutt (2003). *Imagined Interactions: Daydreaming About Communication.* Cresskill, NJ: Hampton Press; J. M. Honeycutt & S. G. Ford (2001). "Mental Imagery and Intrapersonal Communication: A Review of Research on Imagined Interactions (IIs) and Current Developments." *Communication Yearbook 25* (pp. 315–338). Thousand Oaks, CA: Sage.

70. J. Pennebaker (2004). *Writing to Heal: A Guided Journal for Recovering from Trauma and Emotional Upheaval*. Oakland, CA: Harbinger.

71. K. Floyd, A. C. Mikkelson, C. Hesse, & P. M. Pauley (2007). "Affectionate Writing Reduces Total Cholesterol: Two Randomized, Controlled Studies." *Human Communication Research, 33*, 119–142.

72. S. Metts & B. Wood (2008). "Interpersonal Emotional Competence." In M. T. Motley (Ed.), *Studies in Applied Interpersonal Communication* (pp. 267–285). Thousand Oaks, CA: Sage.

73. B. H. Spitzberg (2006). "Preliminary Development of a Model and Measure of Computer-Mediated Communication (CMC) Competence." *Journal of Computer-Mediated Communcation, 11*, article 12. Retrieved September 11, 2006, from http://jcmc.indiana.edu/vol11/issue2/spitzberg.html.

74. P. B. O'Sullivan (2000). "What You Don't Know Won't Hurt Me: Impression Management Functions of Communication Channels in Relationships." *Human Communication Research, 26*, 403–431.

75. T. E. Galovski, L. S. Malta, & E. B. Blanchard (2005). *Road Rage: Assessment and Treatment of the Angry, Aggressive Driver*. Washington, DC: American Psychological Association.

76. S. D. Mallalieu, S. Hanton, & G. Jones (2003). "Emotional Labeling and Competitive Anxiety in Preparation and Competition." *The Sports Psychologist, 17*, 157–174.

77. S. A. McCornack & T. R. Levine (1990). "When Lovers Become Leery: The Relationship between Suspicion and Accuracy in Detecting Deception." *Communication Monographs, 57*, 219–230.

78. J. Bourhis & M. Allen (1992). "Meta-Analysis of the Relationship between Communication Apprehension and Cognitive Performance." *Communication Education, 41*, 68–76.

79. M. L. Patterson & V. Ritts (1997). "Social and Communicative Anxiety: A Review and Meta-Analysis." In B. R. Burleson (Ed.), *Communication Yearbook 20*. Thousand Oaks, CA: Sage.

80. C. L. Rusting & S. Nolen-Hoeksema (1998). "Regulating Responses to Anger." *Journal of Personality and Social Psychology, 74*, 790–803.

81. B. J. Bushman, A. M. Bonacci, W. C. Pedersen, E. A. Vasquez, & N. Miller (2005). "Chewing on It Can Chew You Up: Effects of Rumination on Triggered Displaced Aggression." *Journal of Personality and Social Psychology, 88*, 969–983.

82. For a thorough discussion of how neurobiology shapes feelings, see J. E. LeDoux (1996). *The Emotional Brain*. New York: Simon and Schuster.

83. D. R. Vocate (1994). "Self-Talk and Inner Speech." In D. R. Vocate (Ed.), *Intrapersonal Communication: Different Voices, Different Minds*. Hillsdale, NJ: Erlbaum.

84. J. Ayers, T. Keereetaweep, P. Chen, & P. A. Edwards (1998). "Communication Apprehension and Employment Interviews." *Communication Education, 47*, 1–17.

85. M. Booth-Butterfield & M. R. Trotta (1994). "Attributional Patterns for Expressions of Love." *Communication Reports, 7*, 119–129.

86. A. L. Vangelisti, S. D. Corgin, A. E. Lucchetti, & R. J. Sprague (1999). "Couples' Concurrent Cognitions: The Influence of Relational Satisfaction on the Thoughts Couples Have as They Converse." *Human Communication Research, 25*, 370–398.

87. J. A. Bargh (1988). "Automatic Information Processing: Implications for Communication and Affect." In H. E. Sypher & E. T. Higgins (Eds.), *Communication, Social Cognition, and Affect*. Hillsdale, NJ: Erlbaum.

88. A. Beck (1976). *Cognitive Therapy and the Emotional Disorders*. New York: International Universities Press.

89. S. Metts & W. R. Cupach (1990). "The Influence of Relationship Beliefs and Problem-Solving Relationships on Satisfaction in Romantic Relationships." *Human Communication Research, 17*, 170–185.

90. A. Meichenbaum (1977). *Cognitive Behavior Modification*. New York: Plenum. See also A. Ellis & R. Greiger (1977). *Handbook for Rational-Emotive Therapy*. New York: Springer; and M. Wirga & M. DeBernardi (March 2002)."The ABCs of Cognition, Emotion, and Action." *Archives of Psychiatry and Psychotherapy, 1*, 5–16.

91. A. Chatham-Carpenter & V. DeFrancisco (1997). "Pulling Yourself Up Again: Women's Choices and Strategies for Recovering and Maintaining Self-Esteem." *Western Journal of Communication, 61*, 164–187.

CHAPTER FIVE

1. O. W. Sacks (1989). *Seeing Voices: A Journey into the World of the Deaf* (p. 17). Berkeley: University of California Press.

2. M. Henneberger (January 29, 1999). "Misunderstanding of Word Embarrasses Washington's New Mayor." *New York Times* online. http://www.nyt.com (no longer in database).

3. B. Keysar & A. S. Henly (2002). "Speakers' Overestimation of Their Effectiveness." *Psychological Science, 13*, 207–212. See also R. S. Wyer & R. Adava (2003). "Message Reception Skills in Social Communication." In J. O. Greene & B. R. Burleson (Eds.), *Handbook of Communication and Social Interaction Skills* (pp. 291–355). Mahwah, NJ: Erlbaum.

4. T. L. Scott (November 27, 2000). "Teens before Their Time." *Time*, 22.

5. T. Wallsten (1986). "Measuring the Vague Meanings of Probability Terms." *Journal of Experimental Psychology, 115*, 348–365.

6. W. E. Prentice (2005). *Therapeutic Modalities in Rehabilitation*. New York: McGraw-Hill.

7. Antioch College. "The Antioch College Sexual Offense Policy." Reprinted in *Newsweek*, March 7, 1994, 54, and *Time*, October 11, 1993, 24.

8. W. Wolfram & N. Schilling-Estes (2005). *American English: Dialects and Variation*, 2nd ed. Malden, MA: Blackwell.

9. N. Coupland, J. M. Wiemann, & H. Giles (1991). "Talk as 'Problem' and Communication as 'Miscommunication': An Integrative Analysis." In N. Coupland, J. M. Wiemann, & H. Giles (Eds.), *"Miscommunication" and Problematic Talk*. Newbury Park, CA: Sage.

10. W. B. Pearce & V. Cronen (1980). *Communication, Action, and Meaning*. New York: Praeger. See also V. Cronen, V. Chen, & W. B. Pearce (1988). "Coordinated Management of Meaning: A Critical Theory." In Y. Y. Kim & W. B. Gudykunst (Eds.), *Theories in Intercultural Communication*. Newbury Park, CA: Sage.

11. E. K. E. Graham, M. Papa, & G. P. Brooks (1992). "Functions of Humor in Conversation: Conceptualization and Measurement." *Western Journal of Communication, 56*, 161–183.

12. P. B. O'Sullivan & A. Flanagin (2003). "Reconceptualizing 'Flaming' and Other Problematic Communication." *New Media and Society, 5*, 67–93.

13. N. Christenfeld & B. Larsen (2008). "The Name Game." *The Psychologist, 21*, 210–213.

14. A. Mehrabian (2001). "Characteristics Attributed to Individuals on the Basis of Their First Names." *Genetic, Social, and General Psychology Monographs, 127*, 59–88.

15. Social Security Administration (2009). "America's Parents Vote for Change on Social Security's Most Popular Baby Names List." Retrieved June 17, 2009, at http://www.ssa.gov/pressoffice/pr/baby-names2008-pr.htm.

16. R. G. Fryer & S. D. Levitt (2004). "The Causes and Consequences of Distinctively Black Names." *Quarterly Journal of Economics, 119*, 767–805.

17. C. A. VanLear (1991). "Testing a Cyclical Model of Communicative Openness in Relationship Development." *Communication Monographs, 58*, 337–361.

18. D. Niven & J. Zilber (2000). "Preference for African American or Black." *Howard Journal of Communications, 11*, 267–277.

19. J. Zilber & D. Niven (1995). " 'Black' versus 'African American': Are Whites' Political Attitudes Influenced by the Choice of Racial Labels?" *Social Science Quarterly, 76*, 655–664.

20. See, for example, R. K. Aune & Toshiyuki Kikuchi (1993). "Effects of Language Intensity Similarity on Perceptions of Credibility, Relational Attributions, and Persuasion." *Journal of Language and Social Psychology, 12*, 224–238.

21. H. Giles, J. Coupland, & N. Coupland (Eds.) (1991). *Contexts of Accommodation: Developments in Applied Sociolinguistics*. Cambridge, UK: Cambridge University Press.

22. Y. Baruch and S. Jenkins (2006). "Swearing at Work and Permissive Leadership Culture: When Anti-Social Becomes Social and Incivility Is Acceptable." *Leadership & Organization Development Journal, 28*, 492–507.

23. J. Cassell & D. Tversky (2005). "The Language of Online Intercultural Community Formation." *Journal of Computer-Mediated Communication, 10*, article 2.

24. *NPR Weekend Edition* (February 18, 2006). "OMG: IM Slang is Invading Everyday English." Retrieved September 11, 2006, at http://www.npr.org/templates/story/story.php?storyId=5221618.

25. A. Reyes (2005). "Appropriation of African American Slang by Asian American Youth." *Journal of Sociolinguistics, 9*, 509–532.

26. S. H. Ng & J. J. Bradac (1993). *Power in Language: Verbal Communication and Social Influence* (p. 27). Newbury Park, CA: Sage. See also A. El-Alayli, C. J. Myers, T. L. Petersen, & A. L. Lystad (2008). " 'I Don't Mean to Sound Arrogant, But . . .': The Effects of Using Disclaimers on Person Perception." *Personality and Social Psychology Bulletin, 34*, 130–143.

27. S. Parton, S. A. Siltanen, L. A. Hosman, & J. Langenderfer (2002). "Employment Interview Outcomes and Speech Style Effects." *Journal of Language and Social Psychology, 21*, 144–161.

28. L. A. Hosman (1989). "The Evaluative Consequences of Hedges, Hesitations, and Intensifiers: Powerful and Powerless Speech Styles." *Human Communication Research, 15*, 383–406.

29. L. A. Samovar & R. E. Porter (2001). *Communication between Cultures*, 4th ed. (pp. 58–59). Belmont, CA: Wadsworth.

30. J. Bradac & A. Mulac (1984). "Attributional Consequences of Powerful and Powerless Speech Styles in a Crisis-Intervention Context." *Journal of Language and Social Psychology, 3*, 1–19.

31. J. J. Bradac (1983). "The Language of Lovers, Flovers [sic], and Friends: Communicating in Social and Personal Relationships." *Journal of Language and Social Psychology, 2*, 141–162.

32. D. Geddes (1992). "Sex Roles in Management: The Impact of Varying Power of Speech Style on Union Members' Perception of Satisfaction and Effectiveness." *Journal of Psychology, 126*, 589–607.

33. E. S. Kubany, D. C. Richard, G. B. Bauer, & M. Y. Muraoka (1992). "Impact of Assertive and Accusatory Communication of Distress and Anger: A Verbal Component Analysis." *Aggressive Behavior, 18*, 337–347.

34. T. Gordon (1974). *T.E.T.: Teacher Effectiveness Training* (p. 74). New York: Wyden.

35. R. Raskin & R. Shaw (1988). "Narcissism and the Use of Personal Pronouns." *Journal of Personality, 56*, 393–404; and A. L. Vangelisti, M. L. Knapp, & J. A. Daly (1990). "Conversational Narcissism." *Communication Monographs, 57*, 251–274.

36. A. S. Dreyer, C. A. Dreyer, & J. E. Davis (1987). "Individuality and Mutuality in the Language of Families of Field-Dependent and Field-Independent Children." *Journal of Genetic Psychology, 148*, 105–117.

37. J. M. Honeycutt (1999). "Typological Differences in Predicting Marital Happiness from Oral History Behaviors and Imagined Interactions." *Communication Monographs, 66*, 276–291.

38. R. F. Proctor & J. R. Wilcox (1993). "An Exploratory Analysis of Responses to Owned Messages in Inter-

personal Communication." *ETC: A Review of General Semantics, 50*, 201–220; and A. L. Vangelisti et al., "Conversational Narcissism," op. cit.

39. See, for example, D. Tannen (1990). *You Just Don't Understand: Women and Men in Conversation.* New York: William Morrow; and J. Gray (1992). *Men Are from Mars, Women Are from Venus.* New York: HarperCollins.

40. K. Dindia (2006). "Men Are from North Dakota, Women Are from South Dakota." In K. Dindia and D. J. Canary (Eds.), *Sex Differences and Similarities in Communication: Critical Essays and Empirical Investigations of Sex and Gender in Interaction*, 2nd ed. Mahwah, NJ: Erlbaum; and D. J. Goldsmith & P. A. Fulfs (1999). " 'You Just Don't Have the Evidence': An Analysis of Claims and Evidence in Deborah Tannen's *You Just Don't Understand.*" In M. E. Roloff (Ed.), *Communication Yearbook 22.* Thousand Oaks, CA: Sage.

41. See, for example, A. Haas & M. A. Sherman (1982). "Conversational Topic as a Function of Role and Gender." *Psychological Reports, 51,* 453–454; and B. Fehr (1996). *Friendship Processes.* Thousand Oaks, CA: Sage.

42. R. A. Clark (1998). "A Comparison of Topics and Objectives in a Cross Section of Young Men's and Women's Everyday Conversations." In D. J. Canary & K. Dindia (Eds.), *Sex Differences and Similarities in Communication: Critical Essays and Empirical Investigations of Sex and Gender in Interaction.* Mahwah, NJ: Erlbaum.

43. A. DeCapua, D. Berkowitz, & D. Boxer (2006). "Women Talk Revisited: Personal Disclosures and Alignment Development." *Multilingua, 25,* 393–412.

44. J. T. Wood (1994). *Gendered Lives: Communication, Gender, and Culture* (p. 141). Belmont, CA: Wadsworth.

45. M. A. Sherman & A. Haas (June 1984). "Man to Man, Woman to Woman." *Psychology Today, 17,* 72–73.

46. J. D. Ragsdale (1996). "Gender, Satisfaction Level, and the Use of Relational Maintenance Strategies in Marriage." *Communication Monographs, 63,* 354–371.

47. For a summary of research on differences between male and female conversational behaviors, see H. Giles & R. L. Street Jr. (1985). "Communication Characteristics and Behavior." In M. L. Knapp & G. R. Miller (Eds.), *Handbook of Interpersonal Communication* (pp. 205–261). Beverly Hills, CA: Sage; and A. Kohn (February 1988). "Girl Talk, Guy Talk." *Psychology Today, 22,* 65–66.

48. M. R. Mehl, S. Vazire, N. Ramírez-Esparza, R. B. Slatcher, & J. W. Pennebaker (2007). "Are Women Really More Talkative Than Men?" *Science, 317,* 82.

49. A. Mulac (2006). "The Gender-Linked Language Effect: Do Language Differences Really Make a Difference?" In K. Dindia & D. J. Canary (Eds.), *Sex Differences and Similarities in Communication: Critical Essays and Empirical Investigations of Sex and Gender in Interaction*, 2nd ed. Mahwah, NJ: Erlbaum.

50. Clark, op. cit.

51. L. L. Carli (1990). "Gender, Language, and Influence." *Journal of Personality and Social Psychology, 59,* 941–951.

52. D. J. Canary & K. S. Hause (1993). "Is There Any Reason to Research Sex Differences in Communication?" *Communication Quarterly, 41,* 129–144.

53. C. J. Zahn (1989). "The Bases for Differing Evaluations of Male and Female Speech: Evidence from Ratings of Transcribed Conversation." *Communication Monographs, 56,* 59–74. See also L. M. Grob, R. A. Meyers, & R. Schuh (1997). "Powerful/Powerless Language Use in Group Interactions: Sex Differences or Similarities?" *Communication Quarterly, 45,* 282–303.

54. K. Precht (2008). "Sex Similarities and Differences in Stance in Informal American Conversation." *Journal of Sociolinguistics, 12,* 89–111.

55. K. Dindia, "Men Are from North Dakota, Women Are from South Dakota," op. cit.

56. C. J. Zahn, op. cit.

57. B. A. Fisher (1983). "Differential Effects of Sexual Composition and Interactional Content on Interaction Patterns in Dyads." *Human Communication Research, 9,* 225–238.

58. See, for example, D. Tannen (1994). *Talking from 9 to 5: Women and Men in the Workplace: Language, Sex and Power.* New York: William Morrow; and Wood, op. cit.

59. D. G. Ellis & L. McCallister (1980). "Relational Control Sequences in Sex-Typed and Androgynous Groups." *Western Journal of Speech Communication, 44,* 35–49.

60. S. Steen & P. Schwarz (1995). "Communication, Gender, and Power: Homosexual Couples as a Case Study." In M. A. Fitzpatrick & A. L. Vangelisti (Eds.), *Explaining Family Interactions* (pp. 310–343). Thousand Oaks, CA: Sage.

61. For a thorough discussion of the challenges involved in translation from one language to another, see L. A. Samovar & R. E. Porter (1991). *Communication between Cultures* (pp. 165–169). Dubuque, IA: W. C. Brown.

62. The examples in this paragraph are taken from D. Ricks (1983). *Big Business Blunders: Mistakes in International Marketing* (p. 41). Homewood, IL: Dow Jones-Irwin.

63. N. Sugimoto (March 1991). *"Excuse Me" and "I'm Sorry": Apologetic Behaviors of Americans and Japanese.* Paper presented at the Conference on Communication in Japan and the United States, California State University, Fullerton.

64. A summary of how verbal style varies across cultures can be found in Chapter 5 of W. B. Gudykunst & S. Ting-Toomey (1988). *Culture and Interpersonal Communication.* Newbury Park, CA: Sage.

65. E. Hall (1959). *Beyond Culture.* New York: Doubleday.

66. A. Almaney & A. Alwan (1982). *Communicating with the Arabs.* Prospect Heights, IL: Waveland.

67. K. Basso (1970). "To Give Up on Words: Silence in Western Apache Culture." *Southern Journal of Anthropology, 26,* 213–230.

68. J. Yum (1987). "The Practice of Uye-ri in Interpersonal Relationships in Korea." In D. Kincaid (Ed.),

Communication Theory from Eastern and Western Perspectives. New York: Academic Press.

69. T. Seinfatt (1989). "Linguistic Relativity: Toward a Broader View." In S. Ting-Toomey & F. Korzenny (Eds.), *Language, Communication, and Culture: Current Directions.* Newbury Park, CA: Sage.

70. L. Martin & G. Pullum (1991). *The Great Eskimo Vocabulary Hoax.* Chicago: University of Chicago Press.

71. H. Giles & A. Franklyn-Stokes (1989). "Communicator Characteristics." In M. K. Asante & W. B. Gudykunst (Eds.), *Handbook of International and Intercultural Communication.* Newbury Park, CA: Sage.

72. B. Whorf (1956). "The Relation of Habitual Thought and Behavior to Language." In J. B. Carrol (Ed.), *Language, Thought, and Reality.* Cambridge, MA: MIT Press.

73. H. Rheingold (1988). *They Have a Word for It.* Los Angeles: Jeremy P. Tarcher.

CHAPTER SIX

1. Research summarized by J. K. Burgoon (1994). "Nonverbal Signals." In M. L. Knapp & G. R. Miller (Eds.), *Handbook of Interpersonal Communication* (p. 235). Newbury Park, CA: Sage.

2. For a review of the importance of nonverbal skills in interpersonal communication, see R. E. Riggio (2006). "Nonverbal Skills and Abilities." In V. Manusov & M. L. Patterson (Eds.), *The Sage Handbook of Nonverbal Communication* (pp. 79–86). Thousand Oaks, CA: Sage.

3. Research supporting these claims is cited in J. K. Burgoon & G. D. Hoobler (2002). "Nonverbal Signals." In M. L. Knapp & J. A. Daly (Eds.), *Handbook of Interpersonal Communication*, 3rd ed. Thousand Oaks, CA: Sage.

4. S. E. Jones & C. D. LeBaron (2002). "Research on the Relationship between Verbal and Nonverbal Communication: Emerging Interactions." *Journal of Communication, 52*, 499–521.

5. B. M. DePaulo (1994). "Spotting Lies: Can Humans Learn to Do Better?" *Current Directions in Psychological Science, 3*, 83–86.

6. Not all communication theorists agree with the claim that all nonverbal behavior has communicative value. For a contrasting opinion, see Burgoon, "Nonverbal Signals," pp. 229–232.

7. F. Manusov (Summer 1991). "Perceiving Nonverbal Messages: Effects of Immediacy and Encoded Intent on Receiver Judgments." *Western Journal of Speech Communication, 55*, 235–253. See also R. Buck & C. A. VanLear (2002). "Verbal and Nonverbal Communication: Distinguishing Symbolic, Spontaneous, and Pseudo-Spontaneous Nonverbal Behavior." *Journal of Communication, 52*, 522–541.

8. See, for example, T. Clevenger Jr. (1991). "Can One Not Communicate? A Conflict of Models." *Communication Studies, 42*, 340–353.

9. J. K. Burgoon & B. A. LePoire (1999). "Nonverbal Cues and Interpersonal Judgments: Participant and Observer Perceptions of Intimacy, Dominance, Composure, and Formality." *Communication Monographs, 66*, 105–124. See also Burgoon & Hoobler, op. cit.

10. C. F. Keating (2006). "Why and How the Silent Self Speak Volumes: Functional Approaches to Nonverbal Impression Management." In V. Manusov & M. L. Patterson (Eds.), *The Sage Handbook of Nonverbal Communication* (pp. 321–340). Thousand Oaks, CA: Sage.

11. A. Ramirez & J. K. Burgoon (2004). "The Effect of Interactivity on Initial Interactions: The Influence of Information Valence and Modality and Information Richness on Computer-Mediated Interaction." *Communication Monographs, 71*, 442–447.

12. K. Byron & D. Baldridge (2007). "E-Mail Recipients' Impressions of Senders' Likeability: The Interactive Effect of Nonverbal Cues and Recipients' Personality." *Journal of Business Communication, 44*, 137.

13. "Smile When You Write That" (March 18, 1999). *Los Angeles Times*, C2.

14. E. S. Cross & E. A. Franz (April 2003). *Talking Hands: Observation of Bimanual Gestures as a Facilitative Working Memory Mechanism.* Paper presented at the Cognitive Neuroscience Society 10th Annual Meeting, New York.

15. M. T. Motley (1993). "Facial Affect and Verbal Context in Conversation: Facial Expression as Interjection." *Human Communication Research, 20*, 3–40.

16. J. N. Capella & D. M. Schreiber (2006). "The Interaction Management Function of Nonverbal Cues." In V. Manusov & M. L. Patterson (Eds.), *The Sage Handbook of Nonverbal Communication* (pp. 361–379). Thousand Oaks, CA: Sage.

17. See, for example, K. Drummond & R. Hopper (1993). "Acknowledgment Tokens in Series." *Communication Reports, 6*, 47–53; and H. M. Rosenfeld (1987). "Conversational Control Functions of Nonverbal Behavior." In A. W. Siegman & S. Feldstein (Eds.), *Nonverbal Behavior and Communication*, 2nd ed. Hillsdale, NJ: Erlbaum.

18. H. Giles & B. A. LePoire (2006). "The Ubiquity of Social Meaningfulness of Nonverbal Communication." In V. Manusov & M. L. Patterson (Eds.), *The Sage Handbook of Nonverbal Communication* (pp. xv–xxvii). Thousand Oaks, CA: Sage.

19. J. Hale & J. B. Stiff (1990). "Nonverbal Primacy in Veracity Judgments." *Communication Reports, 3*, 75–83; and J. B. Stiff, J. L. Hale, R. Garlick, & R. G. Rogan (1990). "Effect of Individual Judgments of Honesty and Deceit." *Southern Speech Communication Journal, 55*, 206–229.

20. J. K. Burgoon, T. Birk, & M. Pfau (1990). "Nonverbal Behaviors, Persuasion, and Credibility." *Human Communication Research, 17*, 140–169.

21. P. Ekman (2003). *Emotions Revealed: Recognizing Faces and Feelings to Improve Communication and Emotional Life.* New York: Holt.

22. A. Vrig (2006). "Nonverbal Communication and Deception." In V. Manusov & M. L. Patterson (Eds.), *The Sage Handbook of Nonverbal Communication* (pp. 341–360). Thousand Oaks, CA: Sage.

23. Summarized in L. K. Guerrero & K. Floyd (2006). *Nonverbal Communication in Close Relationships.* Mahwah, NJ: Lawrence Erlbaum. See also B. M. DePaulo (1980). "Detecting Deception Modality Effects." In L. Wheeler (Ed.), *Review of Personality and Social Psychology*, vol. 1. Beverly Hills, CA: Sage; and J. Greene, D. O'Hair, M. Cody, & C. Yen (1985). "Planning and Control of Behavior during Deception." *Human Communication Research, 11*, 335–364.

24. J. K. Burgoon & T. R. Levine (2010). "Advances in Deception Detection." In S. W. Smith & S. R. Wilson (Eds.), *New Directions in Interpersonal Communication Research* (pp. 201–220). Thousand Oaks, CA: Sage.

25. C. Lock (2004). "Deception Detection: Psychologists Try to Learn How to Spot a Liar." *Science News Online, 166*, 72.

26. L. Caso, A. Vrij, S. Mann, & G. DeLeo (2006). "Deceptive Responses: The Impact of Verbal and Non-Verbal Countermeasures." *Legal and Criminological Psychology, 11*, 99–111; A. Vrig (2004). "Why Professionals Fail to Catch Liars and How They Can Improve." *Legal and Criminological Psychology, 9*, 159–181.

27. T. Levine (2009). "To Catch a Liar." *Communication Currents, 4*, 1–2.

28. A. E. Lindsey & V. Vigil (1999). "The Interpretation and Evaluation of Winking in Stranger Dyads." *Communication Research Reports, 16*, 256–265.

29. G. Y. Lim & M. E. Roloff (1999). "Attributing Sexual Consent." *Journal of Applied Communication Research, 27*, 1–23.

30. J. Amos (September 8, 2005). "How Boys Miss Teacher's Reprimand." *BBC News.* Retrieved September 11, 2006, at http://news.bbc.co.uk/1/hi/sci/tech/4227296.stm.

31. B. P. Rourke (1989). *Nonverbal Learning Disabilities: The Syndrome and the Model.* New York: Guilford.

32. E. S. Fudge (n.d.). "Nonverbal Learning Disorder Syndrome?" Retrieved September 11, 2006, at http://www.nldontheweb.org/fudge.htm.

33. J. C. Rosip & J. A. Hall (2004). "Knowledge of Nonverbal Cues, Gender, and Nonverbal Decoding Accuracy." *Journal of Nonverbal Behavior, 28*, 267–286; J. A. Hall (1985). "Male and Female Nonverbal Behavior." In A. W. Siegman & S. Feldstein (Eds.), *Multichannel Integrations of Nonverbal Behavior.* Hillsdale, NJ: Erlbaum.

34. J. A. Hall (2006). "Women and Men's Nonverbal Communication." In V. Manusov & M. L. Patterson (Eds.), *The Sage Handbook of Nonverbal Communication* (pp. 201–218). Thousand Oaks, CA: Sage.

35. D. J. Canary & T. M. Emmers-Sommer (1997). *Sex and Gender Differences in Personal Relationships.* New York: Guilford.

36. D. Matsumoto & S. H. Yoo (2005). "Culture and Applied Nonverbal Communication." In R. S. Feldman & R. E. Riggio (Eds.), *Applications of Nonverbal Communication* (pp. 255–277). Mahwah, NJ: Erlbaum.

37. R. Birdwhistell (1970). *Kinesics and Context*, chapter 9. Philadelphia: University of Pennsylvania Press.

38. P. Ekman, W. V. Friesen, & J. Baer (May 1984). "The International Language of Gestures." *Psychology Today, 18*, 64–69.

39. E. Hall (1969). *The Hidden Dimension.* Garden City, NY: Anchor Books.

40. D. Matsumoto (2006). "Culture and Nonverbal Behavior." In V. Manusov & M. L. Patterson (Eds.), *The Sage Handbook of Nonverbal Communication* (pp. 219–235). Thousand Oaks, CA: Sage.

41. J. B. Bavelas, L. Coates, & T. Johnson (2002). "Listener Responses as a Collaborative Process: The Role of Gaze." *Journal of Communication, 52*, 566–579.

42. R. Levine (1988). "The Pace of Life across Cultures." In J. E. McGrath (Ed.), *The Social Psychology of Time.* Newbury Park, CA: Sage.

43. E. T. Hall & M. R. Hall (1987). *Hidden Differences: Doing Business with the Japanese.* Garden City, NY: Anchor Press.

44. R. Levine & E. Wolff (March 1985). "Social Time: The Heartbeat of Culture." *Psychology Today, 19*, 28–35.

45. M. Booth-Butterfield & F. Jordan (1998). *"Act Like Us": Communication Adaptation among Racially Homogeneous and Heterogeneous Groups.* Paper presented at the Speech Communication Association meeting, New Orleans.

46. P. Eckman (2003). *Emotions Revealed.* New York: Holt.

47. J. Eibl-Eibesfeldt (1972). "Universals and Cultural Differences in Facial Expressions of Emotions." In J. Cole (Ed.), *Nebraska Symposium on Motivation.* Lincoln: University of Nebraska Press.

48. M. Coulson (2004). "Attributing Emotion to Static Body Postures: Recognition Accuracy, Confusions, and Viewpoint Dependence." *Journal of Nonverbal Behavior, 28*, 117–139.

49. A. Mehrabian (1981). *Silent Messages*, 2nd ed. (pp. 47–48, 61–62). Belmont, CA: Wadsworth.

50. J. M. Iverson (1999). "How to Get to the Cafeteria: Gesture and Speech in Blind and Sighted Children's Spatial Descriptions." *Developmental Psychology, 35*, 1132–1142.

51. M. C. Corballis (2002). *From Hand to Mouth: The Origins of Language.* Princeton, NJ: Princeton University Press.

52. P. A. Andersen (2008). *Nonverbal Communication: Forms and Functions*, 2nd ed. (p. 37). Long Grove, IL: Waveland Press.

53. P. Ekman & W. V. Friesen (1969). "The Repertoire of Nonverbal Behavior: Categories, Origins, Usage, and Coding." *Semiotica, 1*, 49–98.

54. A. Sueyoshi & D. M. Hardison (2005). "The Role of Gestures and Facial Cues in Second Language Listening Comprehension." *Language Learning, 55*, 661–699.

55. B. I. Koerner (March 28, 2003). "What Does a 'Thumbs Up' Mean in Iraq?" *Slate.* Retrieved September 11, 2006, at http://www.slate.com/id/2080812.

56. P. Ekman & W. V. Friesen (1974). "Nonverbal Behavior and Psychopathology." In R. J. Friedman & M. N. Katz (Eds.), *The Psychology of Depression: Contemporary Theory and Research.* Washington, DC: J. Winston.

57. P. Ekman (2001). *Telling Lies.* New York: Norton.

58. P. Ekman & W. V. Friesen (1975). *Unmasking the Face: A Guide to Recognizing Emotions from Facial Clues.* Englewood Cliffs, NJ: Prentice-Hall.

59. Ibid., p. 150.

60. E. Krumhuber & A. Kappas (2005). "Moving Smiles: The Role of Dynamic Components for the Perception of the Genuineness of Smiles." *Journal of Nonverbal Behavior, 29*, 3–24.

61. S. F. Davis & J. C. Kieffer (1998). "Restaurant Servers Influence Tipping Behavior." *Psychological Reports, 83*, 223–226.

62. N. Gueguen & C. Jacob (2002). "Direct Look versus Evasive Glance and Compliance With a Request." *Journal of Social Psychology, 142*, 393–396.

63. P. A. Andersen, L. K. Guerrero, & S. M. Jones (2006). "Nonverbal Behavior in Intimate Interactions and Intimate Relationships." In V. Manusov & M. L. Patterson (Eds.), *The Sage Handbook of Nonverbal Communication* (pp. 259–278). Thousand Oaks, CA: Sage.

64. J. K. Burgoon & N. E. Dunbar (2006). "Nonverbal Skills and Abilities." In V. Manusov & M. L. Patterson (Eds.), *The Sage Handbook of Nonverbal Communication* (pp. 279–298). Thousand Oaks, CA: Sage.

65. E. H. Hess & J. M. Polt (1960). "Pupil Size as Related to Interest Value of Visual Stimuli." *Science, 132*, 349–350.

66. S. F. Kiesling (2004). "Dude." *American Speech, 79*, 281–305.

67. L. K. Guerrero & K. Floyd (2006). *Nonverbal Communication in Close Relationships.* Mahwah, NJ: Lawrence Erlbaum.

68. M. Davis, K. A. Markus, & S. B. Walters (2006). "Judging the Credibility of Criminal Suspect Statements: Does Mode of Presentation Matter?" *Journal of Nonverbal Behavior, 30*, 181–198.

69. L. J. Einhorn (1981). "An Inner View of the Job Interview: An Investigation of Successful Communicative Behaviors." *Communication Education, 30*, 217–228.

70. J. Bone (January 23, 2009). "Caroline Kennedy Says No to Senate but May Become London Envoy." Retrieved January 23, 2009, at http://www.timesonline.co.uk.

71. For a summary, see M. L. Knapp & J. A. Hall (2010). *Nonverbal Communication in Human Interaction*, 7th ed. (pp. 344–346). Boston: Cengage.

72. A. R. Trees (2000). "Nonverbal Communication and the Support Process: Interactional Sensitivity in Interactions between Mothers and Young Adult Children." *Communication Monographs, 67*, 239–261.

73. D. Buller & K. Aune (1992). "The Effects of Speech Rate Similarity on Compliance: Application of Communication Accommodation Theory." *Western Journal of Communication, 56*, 37–53. See also D. Buller, B. A. LePoire, K. Aune, & S. V. Eloy (1992). "Social Perceptions as Mediators of the Effect of Speech Rate Similarity on Compliance." *Human Communication Research, 19*, 286–311; and D. B. Buller & R. K. Aune (1988). "The Effects of Vocalics and Nonverbal Sensitivity on Compliance: A Speech Accommodation Theory Explanation." *Human Communication Research, 14*, 301–332.

74. P. A. Andersen (1984). "Nonverbal Communication in the Small Group." In R. S. Cathcart & L. A. Samovar (Eds.), *Small Group Communication: A Reader*, 4th ed. Dubuque, IA: W. C. Brown.

75. M. Harris, S. Ivanko, S. Jungen, S. Hala, & P. Pexman (October 2001). *You're Really Nice: Children's Understanding of Sarcasm and Personality Traits.* Poster presented at the 2nd Biennial Meeting of the Cognitive Development Society, Virginia Beach.

76. K. J. Tusing & J. P. Dillard (2000). "The Sounds of Dominance: Vocal Precursors of Perceived Dominance during Interpersonal Influence." *Human Communication Research, 26*, 148–171.

77. M. Zuckerman & R. E. Driver (1989). "What Sounds Beautiful Is Good: The Vocal Attractiveness Stereotype." *Journal of Nonverbal Behavior, 13*, 67–82.

78. S. H. Ng & J. J. Bradac (1993). *Power in Language: Verbal Communication and Social Influence* (p. 40). Newbury Park, CA: Sage.

79. R. Heslin & T. Alper (1983). "Touch: A Bonding Gesture." In J. M. Wiemann & R. P. Harrison (Eds.), *Nonverbal Interaction* (pp. 47–75). Beverly Hills, CA: Sage.

80. Ibid.

81. J. Burgoon, J. Walther, & E. Baesler (1992). "Interpretations, Evaluations, and Consequences of Interpersonal Touch." *Human Communication Research, 19*, 237–263.

82. C. R. Kleinke (1977). "Compliance to Requests Made by Gazing and Touching Experimenters in Field Settings." *Journal of Experimental Social Psychology, 13*, 218–223.

83. F. N. Willis & H. K. Hamm (1980). "The Use of Interpersonal Touch in Securing Compliance." *Journal of Nonverbal Behavior, 5*, 49–55.

84. A. H. Crusco & C. G. Wetzel (1984). "The Midas Touch: Effects of Interpersonal Touch on Restaurant Tipping." *Personality and Social Psychology Bulletin, 10*, 512–517.

85. M. Lynn & K. Mynier (1993). "Effect of Server Posture on Restaurant Tipping." *Journal of Applied Social Psychology, 23*, 678–685.

86. D. Kaufman & J. M. Mahoney (1999). "The Effect of Waitresses' Touch on Alcohol Consumption in Dyads." *Journal of Social Psychology, 139*, 261–267.

87. H. Bakwin (1949). "Emotional Deprivation in Infants." *Journal of Pediatrics, 35*, 512–521.

88. T. Adler (February 1993). "Congressional Staffers Witness Miracle of Touch." *APA Monitor*, 12–13.

89. M. S. Driscoll, D. L. Newman, & J. M. Seal (1988). "The Effect of Touch on the Perception of Counselors." *Counselor Education and Supervision, 27*, 344–354; and J. M. Wilson (1982). "The Value of Touch in Psychotherapy." *American Journal of Orthopsychiatry, 52*, 65–72.

90. For a summary, see Knapp & Hall, op. cit., pp. 93–132.

91. M. Hosoda, E. F. Stone-Romero, & G. Coats (2003). "The Effects of Physical Attractiveness on Job-Related Outcomes: A Meta-Analysis of Experimental Studies." *Personnel Psychology, 56*, 431–462.

92. K. K. Dion (1973). "Young Children's Stereotyping of Facial Attractiveness." *Developmental Psychology, 9*, 183–188.

93. V. Ritts, M. L. Patterson, & M. E. Tubbs (1992). "Expectations, Impressions, and Judgments of Physically Attractive Students: A Review." *Review of Educational Research, 62*, 413–426.

94. T. C. Riniolo, K. C. Johnson, & T. R. Sherman (2006). "Hot or Not: Do Professors Perceived as Physically Attractive Receive Higher Student Evaluations?" *Journal of General Psychology, 133*, 19–35.

95. K. F. Albada, M. L. Knapp, & K. E. Theune (2002). "Interaction Appearance Theory: Changing Perceptions of Physical Attractiveness Through Social Interaction." *Communication Theory, 12*, 8–40.

96. W. Thourlby (1978). *You Are What You Wear* (p. 1). New York: New American Library.

97. L. Bickman (1974). "The Social Power of a Uniform." *Journal of Applied Social Psychology, 4*, 47–61.

98. S. G. Lawrence & M. Watson (1991). "Getting Others to Help: The Effectiveness of Professional Uniforms in Charitable Fund Raising." *Journal of Applied Communication Research, 19*, 170–185.

99. H. Fortenberry, J. Maclean, P. Morris, & M. O'Connell (1978). "Mode of Dress as a Perceptual Cue to Deference." *The Journal of Social Psychology, 104*, 139–140.

100. L. Bickman (April 1974). "Social Roles and Uniforms: Clothes Make the Person." *Psychology Today, 7*, 48–51.

101. M. Lefkowitz, R. R. Blake, & J. S. Mouton (1955). "Status of Actors in Pedestrian Violation of Traffic Signals." *Journal of Abnormal and Social Psychology, 51*, 704–706.

102. L. E. Temple & K. R. Loewen (1993). "Perceptions of Power: First Impressions of a Woman Wearing a Jacket." *Perceptual and Motor Skills, 76*, 339–348.

103. T. F. Hoult (1954). "Experimental Measurement of Clothing as a Factor in Some Social Ratings of Selected American Men." *American Sociological Review, 19*, 326–327.

104. P. A. Andersen, L. K. Guerrero, & S. M. Jones (2006). "Nonverbal Behavior in Intimate Interactions and Intimate Relationships." In V. Manusov & M. L. Patterson (Eds.), *The Sage Handbook of Nonverbal Communication* (pp. 259–278). Thousand Oaks, CA: Sage.

105. Hall, *The Hidden Dimension*, op. cit.

106. M. Hackman & K. Walker (1990). "Instructional Communication in the Televised Classroom: The Effects of System Design and Teacher Immediacy." *Communication Education, 39*, 196–206. See also J. C. McCroskey & V. P. Richmond (1992). "Increasing Teacher Influence through Immediacy." In V. P. Richmond & J. C. McCroskey (Eds.), *Power in the Classroom: Communication, Control, and Concern*. Hillsdale, NJ: Erlbaum.

107. C. Conlee, J. Olvera, & N. Vagim (1993). "The Relationships among Physician Nonverbal Immediacy and Measures of Patient Satisfaction with Physician Care." *Communication Reports, 6*, 25–33.

108. G. Brown, T. B. Lawrence, & S. L. Robinson (2005). "Territoriality in Organizations." *Academy of Management Review, 30*, 577–594.

109. E. Sadalla (1987). "Identity and Symbolism in Housing." *Environment and Behavior, 19*, 569–587.

110. A. Maslow & N. Mintz (1956). "Effects of Aesthetic Surroundings: Initial Effects of Those Aesthetic Surroundings upon Perceiving 'Energy' and 'Well-Being' in Faces." *Journal of Psychology, 41*, 247–254.

111. J. J. Teven & M. E. Comadena (1996). "The Effects of Office Aesthetic Quality on Students' Perceptions of Teacher Credibility and Communicator Style." *Communication Research Reports, 13*, 101–108.

112. R. Sommer (1969). *Personal Space: The Behavioral Basis of Design*. Englewood Cliffs, NJ: Prentice-Hall.

113. R. Sommer & S. Augustin (2007). "Spatial Orientation in the Cubicle." *Journal of Facilities Management, 5*, 205–214.

114. D. I. Ballard & D. R. Seibold (2000). "Time Orientation and Temporal Variation across Work Groups: Implications for Group and Organizational Communication." *Western Journal of Communication, 64*, 218–242.

115. P. A. Andersen, L. K. Guerrero, & S. M. Jones (2006). "Nonverbal Behavior in Intimate Interactions and Intimate Relationships." In V. Manusov & M. L. Patterson (Eds.), *The Sage Handbook of Nonverbal Communication* (pp. 259–278). Thousand Oaks, CA: Sage.

116. K. I. Egland, M. A. Stelzner, P. A. Andersen, & B. S. Spitzberg (1997). "Perceived Understanding, Nonverbal Communication, and Relational Satisfaction." In J. E. Aitken & L. J. Shedletsky (Eds.), *Intrapersonal Communication Processes* (pp. 386–396). Annandale, VA: Speech Communication Association.

117. J. B. Walther (2006). "Nonverbal Dynamics in Computer-Mediated Communication." In V. Manusov & M. L. Patterson (Eds.), *The Sage Handbook of Nonverbal Communication* (pp. 461–479). Thousand Oaks, CA: Sage.

118. J. B. Walther & U. Bunz (2005). "The Rules of Virtual Groups: Trust, Liking, and Performance in

Computer-Mediated Communication." *Journal of Communication, 55*, 828–846.

CHAPTER SEVEN

1. R. Emanuel, J. Adams, K. Baker, E. K. Daufin, C. Ellington, E. Fitts, J. Himsel, L. Holladay, & D. Okeowo (2008). "How College Students Spend Their Time Communicating." *International Journal of Listening, 22*, 13–28. See also L. Barker, R. Edwards, C. Gaines, K. Gladney, & R. Holley (1981). "An Investigation of Proportional Time Spent in Various Communication Activities by College Students." *Journal of Applied Communication Research, 8*, 101–109.

2. Research summarized in A. D. Wolvin & C. G. Coakley (1981). "A Survey of the Status of Listening Training in Some Fortune 500 Corporations." *Communication Education, 40*, 152–164.

3. K. J. Prager & D. Buhrmester (1998). "Intimacy and Need Fulfillment in Couple Relationships." *Journal of Social and Personal Relationships, 15*, 435–469.

4. A. L. Vangelisti (1994). "Couples' Communication Problems: The Counselor's Perspective." *Journal of Applied Communication Research, 22*, 106–126.

5. A. D. Wolvin (1984). "Meeting the Communication Needs of the Adult Learners." *Communication Education, 33*, 267–271.

6. M. L. Beall, J. Gill-Rosier, J. Tate, & A. Matten (2008). "State of the Context: Listening in Education." *International Journal of Listening, 22*, 123–132.

7. J. Davis, A. Foley, N. Crigger, & M. C. Brannigan (2008). "Healthcare and Listening: A Relationship for Caring." *International Journal of Listening, 22*, 168–175; J. Davis, C. R. Thompson, A. Foley, C. D. Bond, & J. DeWitt (2008). "An Examination of Listening Concepts in the Healthcare Context: Differences Among Nurses, Physicians, and Administrators." *International Journal of Listening, 22*, 152–167.

8. D. C. Schnapp (2008). "Listening in Context: Religion and Spirituality." *International Journal of Listening, 22*, 133–140.

9. J. Flynn, T. Valikoski, & J. Grau (2008). "Listening in the Business Context: Reviewing the State of Research." *International Journal of Listening, 22*, 141–151.

10. A. Fernald (2001). "Hearing, Listening, and Understanding: Auditory Development in Infancy." In G. Bemner & A. Fogel (Eds.), *Blackwell Handbook of Infant Development* (pp. 35–70). Malden, MA: Blackwell.

11. B. R. Burleson (2010). "Explaining Recipient Responses to Supportive Messages: Development and Tests of a Dual-Process Theory." In S. W. Smith & S. R. Wilson (Eds.), *New Directions in Interpersonal Communication Research* (pp. 159–179). Los Angeles: Sage. See also G. D. Bodie & B. R. Burleson (2008). "Explaining Variations in the Effects of Supportive Messages: A Dual-Process Framework." In C. S. Beck (Ed.), *Communication Yearbook 32*. New York: Routledge.

12. E. Langer (1990). *Mindfulness.* Reading, MA: Addison-Wesley. See also J. K. Burgoon, C. R. Berger, & V. R. Waldron (2000). "Mindfulness and Interpersonal Communication." *Journal of Social Issues, 56*, 105–127.

13. Burgoon et al., op. cit.

14. Langer, op. cit., p. 90.

15. S. Kochkin (2005). "MarkeTrak VII: Hearing Loss Population Tops 31 Million." *Hearing Review, 12*, 16–29.

16. C. Flexer (February 1997). "Commonly-Asked Questions about Children with Minimal Hearing Loss in the Classroom." *Hearing Loss*, 8–12.

17. L. R. Smeltzer & K. W. Watson (1984). "Listening: An Empirical Comparison of Discussion Length and Level of Incentive." *Central States Speech Journal, 35*, 166–170.

18. M. Pasupathi, L. M. Stallworth, & K. Murdoch (1998). "How What We Tell Becomes What We Know: Listener Effects on Speakers' Long-Term Memory for Events." *Discourse Processes, 26*, 1–25.

19. W. G. Powers & P. L. Witt (2008). "Expanding the Theoretical Framework of Communication Fidelity." *Communication Quarterly, 56*, 247–267; M. Fitch-Hauser, W. G. Powers, K. O'Brien, & S. Hanson (2007). "Extending the Conceptualization of Listening Fidelity." *International Journal of Listening, 21*, 81–91; W. G. Powers & G. D. Bodie (2003). "Listening Fidelity: Seeking Congruence Between Cognitions of the Listener and the Sender." *International Journal of Listening, 17*, 19–31.

20. M. H. Lewis & N. L. Reinsch, Jr. (1988). "Listening in Organizational Environments." *Journal of Business Communication, 23*, 49–67.

21. M. Imhof (2002). "In the Eye of the Beholder: Children's Perception of Good and Poor Listening Behavior." *International Journal of Listening, 16*, 40–57.

22. L. L. Barker (1971). *Listening Behavior.* Englewood Cliffs, NJ: Prentice-Hall.

23. A. L. Vangelisti, M. L. Knapp, & J. A. Daly (1990). "Conversational Narcissism." *Communication Monographs, 57*, 251–274. See also J. C. McCroskey & V. P. Richmond (1993). "Identifying Compulsive Communicators: The Talkaholic Scale." *Communication Research Reports, 10*, 107–114.

24. K. B. McComb & F. M. Jablin (1984). "Verbal Correlates of Interviewer Empathic Listening and Employment Interview Outcomes." *Communication Monographs, 51*, 367.

25. J. Hansen (2007). *24/7: How Cell Phones and the Internet Change the Way We Live, Work, and Play.* New York: Praeger. See also J. W. Turner amd N. L. Reinsch (2007). "The Business Communicator as Presence Allocator: Multicommunicating, Equivocality, and Status at Work." *Journal of Business Communication, 44*, 36–58.

26. A. Wolvin & C. G. Coakley (1988). *Listening,* 3rd ed. (p. 208). Dubuque, IA: W. C. Brown.

27. R. Nichols (September 1987). "Listening Is a Ten-Part Skill." *Nation's Business, 75*, 40.

28. S. Golen (1990). "A Factor Analysis of Barriers to Effective Listening." *Journal of Business Communication, 27*, 25–36.

29. P. Nelson, K. Kohnert, S. Sabur, & D. Shaw (2005). "Noise and Children Learning Through a Second Language: Double Jeopardy?" *Language, Speech, & Hearing Services in Schools, 36*, 219–229.

30. N. Kline (1999). *Time to Think: Listening to Ignite the Human Mind* (p. 21). London: Ward Lock.

31. L. J. Carrell & S. C. Willmington (1996). "A Comparison of Self-Report and Performance Data in Assessing Speaking and Listening Competence." *Communication Reports, 9*, 185–191.

32. R. G. Nichols, J. I. Brown, & R. J. Keller (2006). "Measurement of Communication Skills." *International Journal of Listening, 20*, 13–17; N. Spinks & B. Wells (1991). "Improving Listening Power: The Payoff." *Bulletin of the Association for Business Communication, 54*, 75–77.

33. "Listen to This: Hearing Problems Can Stress Relationships." (2008). Retrieved at http://www.energizer.com/livehealthy/#listentothis. See also D. N. Shafer (2007). "Hearing Loss Hinders Relationships." *ASHA Leader, 12*, 5–7.

34. D. Carbaugh (1999). " 'Just Listen': 'Listening' and Landscape among the Blackfeet." *Western Journal of Communication, 63*, 250–270.

35. A. M. Bippus (2001). "Recipients' Criteria for Evaluating the Skillfulness of Comforting Communication and the Outcomes of Comforting Interactions." *Communication Monographs, 68*, 301–313.

36. G. Goodman & G. Esterly (1990). "Questions—The Most Popular Piece of Language." In J. Stewart (Ed.), *Bridges Not Walls*, 5th ed. New York: McGraw-Hill.

37. Adapted from B. R. Burleson (1994). "Comforting Messages: Features, Functions, and Outcomes." In J. A. Daly & J. M. Wiemann (Eds.), *Strategic Interpersonal Communication* (p. 140). Hillsdale, NJ: Erlbaum.

38. S. Myers (2000). "Empathic Listening: Reports on the Experience of Being Heard." *Journal of Humanistic Psychology, 40*, 148–173; S. G. Grant (1998). "A Principal's Active Listening Skills and Teachers' Perceptions of the Principal's Leader Behaviors." *Dissertation Abstracts International Section A: Humanities and Social Sciences, 58*, 2933; V. B. Van Hasselt, M. T. Baker, & S. J. Romano (2006). "Crisis (Hostage) Negotiation Training: A Preliminary Evaluation of Program Efficacy." *Criminal Justice and Behavior, 33*, 56–69.

39. See J. Bruneau (1989). "Empathy and Listening: A Conceptual Review and Theoretical Directions." *Journal of the International Listening Association, 3*, 1–20; and K. N. Cissna & R. Anderson (1990). "The Contributions of Carl R. Rogers to a Philosophical Praxis of Dialogue." *Western Journal of Speech Communication, 54*, 137–147.

40. B. R. Burleson (2003). "Emotional Support Skills." In J. O. Greene and B. R. Burleson (Eds.), *Handbook of Communication and Social Interaction Skills* (p. 552). Mahwah, NJ: Erlbaum.

41. B. Burleson & W. Samter (August 1987). *Cognitive Complexity, Communication Skills, and Friendship.* Paper presented at the 7th International Congress on Personal Construct Psychology, Memphis.

42. See, for example, J. Ekenrode (1984). "Impact of Chronic and Acute Stressors on Daily Reports of Mood." *Journal of Personality and Social Psychology, 46*, 907–918; A. D. Kanner, J. C. Coyne, C. Schaefer, & R. S. Lazarus (1981). "Comparison of Two Modes of Stress Measurement: Daily Hassles and Uplifts versus Major Life Events." *Journal of Behavioral Medicine, 4*, 1–39; A. DeLongis, J. C. Coyne, G. Dakof, S. Polkman, & R. S. Lazarus (1982). "Relation of Daily Hassles, Uplifts, and Major Life Events to Health Status." *Health Psychology, 1*, 119–136.

43. E. L. MacGeorge, W. Samter, & S. J. Gillihan (2005). "Academic Stress, Supportive Communication, and Health." *Communication Education, 54*, 365–372; B. R. Burleson (2003). "Emotional Support Skills." In J. O. Greene & B. R. Burleson (Eds.), *Handbook of Communication and Social Interaction Skills* (pp. 551–594). Mahwah, NJ: Erlbaum.

44. D. Hample (2006). "Anti-Comforting Messages." In K. M. Galvin & P. J. Cooper (Eds.), *Making Connections: Readings in Relational Communication*, 4th ed. (pp. 222–227). Los Angeles: Roxbury. See also B. R. Burleson & E. L. MacGeorge (2002). "Supportive Communication." In M. L. Knapp & J. A. Daly (Eds.), *Handbook of Interpersonal Communication*, 3rd ed. Thousand Oaks, CA: Sage.

45. W. Samter, B. R. Burleson, & L. B. Murphy (1987). "Comforting Conversations: The Effects of Strategy Type on Evaluations of Messages and Message Producers." *Southern Speech Communication Journal, 52*, 263–284.

46. B. Burleson (2008). "What Counts as Effective Emotional Support?" In M. T. Motley (Ed.), *Studies in Applied Interpersonal Communication* (pp. 207–227). Thousand Oaks, CA: Sage.

47. M. Davidowitz & R. D. Myrick (1984). "Responding to the Bereaved: An Analysis of 'Helping' Statements." *Death Education, 8*, 1–10. See also H. L. Servaty-Seib & B. R. Burleson (2007). "Bereaved Adolescents Evaluations of the Helpfulness of Support-Intended Statements." *Journal of Social and Personal Relationships, 24*, 207–223.

48. N. Miczo & J. K. Burgoon (2008). "Facework and Nonverbal Behavior in Social Support Interactions Within Romantic Dyads." In M. T. Motley (Ed.), *Studies in Applied Interpersonal Communication* (pp. 245–266). Thousand Oaks, CA: Sage.

49. R. A. Clark & J. G. Delia (1997). "Individuals' Preferences for Friends' Approaches to Providing Support in Distressing Situations." *Communication Reports, 10*, 115–121.

50. E. L. MacGeorge, B. Feng, & E. R. Thompson (2008). " 'Good' and 'Bad' Advice: How to Advise More Effectively." In M. T. Motley (Ed.), *Studies in Applied Interpersonal Communication* (pp. 145–164). Thousand Oaks, CA: Sage. See also C. J. Notarius & L. R. Herrick (1988). "Listener Response Strategies to a Distressed Other." *Journal of Social and Personal Relationships, 5*, 97–108.

51. S. J. Messman, D. J. Canary, & K. S. Hause (2000). "Motives to Remain Platonic, Equity, and the Use of

Maintenance Strategies in Opposite-Sex Friendships." *Journal of Social and Personal Relationships, 17,* 67–94.

52. D. J. Goldsmith & K. Fitch (1997). "The Normative Context of Advice as Social Support." *Human Communication Research, 23,* 454–476. See also D. J. Goldsmith & E. L. MacGeorge (2000). "The Impact of Politeness and Relationship on Perceived Quality of Advice about a Problem." *Human Communication Research, 26,* 234–263; and B. R. Burleson (1992). "Social Support." In M. L. Knapp & J. A. Daly (Eds.), *Handbook of Interpersonal Communication,* 3rd ed. Thousand Oaks, CA: Sage.

53. E. L. MacGeorge, B. Feng, & E. R. Thompson (2008). " 'Good' and 'Bad' Advice: How to Advise More Effectively." In M. T. Motley (Ed.), *Studies in Applied Interpersonal Communication* (pp. 145–164). Thousand Oaks, CA: Sage.

54. Miczo & Burgoon, op. cit.

55. See, for example, R. Silver & C. Wortman (1981). "Coping with Undesirable Life Events." In J. Garber & M. Seligman (Eds.), *Human Helplessness: Theory and Applications* (pp. 279–340). New York: Academic Press; and C. R. Young, D. E. Giles, & M. C. Plantz (1982). "Natural Networks: Help-Giving and Help-Seeking in Two Rural Communities." *American Journal of Community Psychology, 10,* 457–469.

56. Clark & Delia, op. cit.

57. See research cited in B. Burleson (1990). "Comforting Messages: Their Significance and Effects." In J. A. Daly & J. M. Wiemann (Eds.), *Communicating Strategically: Strategies in Interpersonal Communication.* Hillside, NJ: Erlbaum. See also J. L. Chesbro (1999). "The Relationship between Listening Styles and Conversational Sensitivity." *Communication Research Reports, 16,* 233–238.

58. S. L. Sargent & J. B. Weaver (2003). "Listening Styles: Sex Differences in Perceptions of Self and Others." *International Journal of Listening, 17,* 5–18. See also M. Johnston, M. Kirtley, J. B. Weaver, K. Watson, & L. Barker (2000). "Listening Styles: Biological or Psychological Differences?" *International Journal of Listening, 14,* 32–47.

59. W. Samter (2002). "How Gender and Cognitive Complexity Influence the Provision of Emotional Support: A Study of Indirect Effects." *Communication Reports, 15,* 5–17; J. L. Hale, M. R. Tighe, & P. A. Mongeau (1997). "Effects of Event Type and Sex on Comforting Messages." *Communication Research Reports, 14,* 214–220.

60. B. R. Burleson (1982). "The Development of Comforting Communication Skills in Childhood and Adolescence." *Child Development, 53,* 1578–1588.

61. R. Lemieux & M. R. Tighe (2004). "Attachment Styles and the Evaluation of Comforting Responses: A Receiver Perspective." *Communication Research Reports, 21,* 144–153.

62. B. R. Burleson, A. J. Holmstrom, & C. M. Gilstrap (2005). " 'Guys Can't Say That to Guys:' Four Experiments

Assessing the Normative Motivation Account for Deficiencies in the Emotional Support Provided by Men." *Communication Monographs, 72,* 468–501.

63. M. S. Woodward, L. B. Rosenfeld, & S. K. May (1996). "Sex Differences in Social Support in Sororities and Fraternities." *Journal of Applied Communication Research, 24,* 260–272.

64. B. R. Burleson & A. Kunkel (2006). "Revisiting the Different Cultures Thesis: An Assessment of Sex Differences and Similarities in Supportive Communication." In K. Dindia & D. J. Canary (Eds.), *Sex Differences and Similarties in Communication,* 2nd ed. (pp. 137–159). Mawah, NJ: Erlbaum.

65. L. M. Horowitz, E. N. Krasnoperova, & D. G. Tatar (2001). "The Way to Console May Depend on the Goal: Experimental Studies of Social Support." *Journal of Experimental Social Psychology, 37,* 49–61.

66. MacGeorge et al., op. cit. See also R. W. Young & C. M. Cates (2004). "Emotional and Directive Listening in Peer Mentoring." *International Journal of Listening, 18,* 21–33.

CHAPTER EIGHT

1. D. Byrne (1997). "An Overview (and Underview) of Research and Theory Within the Attraction Paradigm." *Journal of Social and Personal Relationships, 17,* 417–431.

2. E. Hatfield & S. Sprecher (1986). *Mirror, Mirror: The Importance of Looks in Everyday Life.* Albany: State University of New York Press.

3. E. Walster, E. Aronson, D. Abrahams, & L. Rottmann (1966). "Importance of Physical Attractiveness in Dating Behavior." *Journal of Personality and Social Psychology, 4,* 508–516.

4. G. W. Lewandowski, A. Aron, & J. Gee (2007). "Personality Goes a Long Way: The Malleability of Opposite-Sex Physical Attractiveness." *Personal Relationships, 14,* 571–585.

5. K. F. Albada (2002). "Interaction Appearance Theory: Changing Perceptions of Physical Attractiveness Through Social Interaction." *Communication Theory, 12,* 8–41.

6. D. Barelds & P. Dijkstra (2009). "Positive Illusions about a Partner's Physical Attractiveness and Relationship Quality." *Personal Relationships, 16,* 263–283.

7. D. Hamachek (1982). *Encounters with Others: Interpersonal Relationships and You.* New York: Holt, Rinehart and Winston.

8. K. A. Yun (2002). "Similarity and Attraction." In M. Allen, N. Burrell, B. M. Eayle, & R. W. Preiss (Eds.), *Interpersonal Communication Research: Advances Through Meta-analysis* (pp. 145–168). Mahwah, NJ: Erlbaum.

9. S. Luo & E. Klohnen (2005). "Assortative Mating and Marital Quality in Newlyweds: A Couple-Centered Approach." *Journal of Personality and Social Psychology, 88,* 304–326. See also D. M. Amodio & C. J.

Showers (2005). "Similarity Breeds Liking Revisited: The Moderating Role of Commitment." *Journal of Social and Personal Relationships, 22*, 817–836.

10. F. E. Aboud & M. J. Mendelson (1998). "Determinants of Friendship Selection and Quality: Developmental Perspectives." In W. M. Bukowski & A. F. Newcomb (Eds.), *The Company They Keep: Friendship in Childhood and Adolescence.* New York: Cambridge University Press.

11. A. M. Ledbetter, E. Griffin, & G. G. Sparks (2007). "Forecasting Friends Forever: A Longitudinal Investigation of Sustained Closeness Between Best Friends." *Personal Relationships, 14*, 343–350.

12. B. R. Burleson & W. Samter (1996). "Similarity in the Communication Skills of Young Adults: Foundations of Attraction, Friendship, and Relationship Satisfaction." *Communication Reports, 9*, 127–139.

13. J. T. Jones, B. W. Pelham, & M. Carvallo (2004). "How Do I Love Thee? Let Me Count the J's: Implicit Egotism and Interpersonal Attraction." *Journal of Personality and Social Psychology, 87*, 665–683.

14. D. Mette & S. Taylor (1971). "When Similarity Breeds Contempt." *Journal of Personality and Social Psychology, 20*, 75–81.

15. H. Fisher (May/June 2007). "The Laws of Chemistry." *Psychology Today, 40*, 76–81.

16. L. Heatherington, V. Escudero, & M. L. Friedlander (2005). "Couple Interaction During Problem Discussions: Toward an Integrative Methodology." *Journal of Family Communication, 5*, 191–207.

17. S. Specher (1998). "Insiders' Perspectives on Reasons for Attraction to a Close Other." *Social Psychology Quarterly, 61*, 287–300.

18. E. Aronson (2004). *The Social Animal*, 9th ed. New York: Bedford, Freeman, & Worth. See Chapter 9: "Liking, Loving, and Interpersonal Sensitivity."

19. K. Dindia (2002). "Self-Disclosure Research: Knowledge Through Meta-Analysis." In M. Allen & R. W. Preiss (Eds.), *Interpersonal Communication Research: Advances Through Meta-analysis* (pp. 169–185). Mahwah, NJ: Erlbaum.

20. Ibid.

21. J. A. Shirley, W. G. Powers, & C. R. Sawyer (2007). "Psychologically Abusive Relationships and Self-Disclosure Orientations." *Human Communication, 10*, 289–301.

22. C. Flora (January/February 2004). "Close Quarters." *Psychology Today, 37*, 15–16.

23. C. Haythornthwaite, M. M. Kazmer, & J. Robbins (2000). "Community Development Among Distance Learners: Temporal and Technological Dimensions." *Journal of Computer-Mediated Communication, 6*, Issue 1, Article 2. Retrieved September 11, 2006, at http://jcmc.indiana.edu/vol6/issue1/haythornthwaite.html.

24. See, for example, M. E. Roloff (1981). *Interpersonal Communication: The Social Exchange Approach.* Beverly Hills, CA: Sage.

25. A. DeMaris (2007). "The Role of Relationship Inequity in Marital Disruption." *Journal of Social and Personal Relationships, 24*, 177–195.

26. M. L. Knapp & A. L. Vangelisti (2006). *Interpersonal Communication and Human Relationships*, 6th ed. Boston: Allyn & Bacon. See also T. A. Avtgis, D. V. West, & T. L. Anderson (1998). "Relationship Stages: An Inductive Analysis Identifying Cognitive, Affective, and Behavioral Dimensions of Knapp's Relational Stages Model." *Communication Research Reports, 15*, 280–287; and S. A. Welch & R. B. Rubin (2002). "Development of Relationship Stage Measures." *Communication Quarterly, 50*, 34–40.

27. K. Dindia (2003). "Definitions and Perspectives on Relational Maintenance Communication." In D. J. Canary and M. Dainton (Eds.), *Maintaining Relationships through Communication.* Mahwah, NJ: Erlbaum.

28. A. J. Johnson, E. Wittenberg, M. Haigh, S. Wigley, J. Becker, K. Brown, & E. Craig (2004). "The Process of Relationship Development and Deterioration: Turning Points in Friendships That Have Terminated." *Communication Quarterly, 52*, 54–67.

29. B. W. Scharlott & W. G. Christ (1995). "Overcoming Relationship-Initiation Barriers: The Impact of a Computer-Dating System on Sex Role, Shyness, and Appearance Inhibitions." *Computers in Human Behavior, 11*, 191–204.

30. C. R. Berger (1987). "Communicating under Uncertainty." In M. E. Roloff & G. R. Miller (Eds.), *Interpersonal Processes: New Directions in Communication Research.* Newbury Park, CA: Sage. See also C. R. Berger & R. J. Calabrese (1975). "Some Explorations in Initial Interaction and Beyond: Toward a Developmental Theory of Interpersonal Communication." *Human Communication Research, 1*, 99–112.

31. W. B. Gudykunst & S. Ting-Toomey (1988). *Culture and Interpersonal Communication* (p. 193). Newbury Park, CA: Sage.

32. L. Pratt, R. L. Wiseman, M. J. Cody, & P. F. Wendt (1999). "Interrogative Strategies and Information Exchange in Computer-Mediated Communication." *Communication Quarterly, 47*, 46–66.

33. J. H. Tolhuizen (1989). "Communication Strategies for Intensifying Dating Relationships: Identification, Use and Structure." *Journal of Social and Personal Relationships, 6*, 413–434.

34. Johnson et al., op. cit.

35. L. A. Baxter (1987). "Symbols of Relationship Identity in Relationship Culture." *Journal of Social and Personal Relationships, 4*, 261–280.

36. C. J. S. Buress & J. C. Pearson (1997). "Interpersonal Rituals in Marriage and Adult Friendship." *Communication Monographs, 64*, 25–46.

37. R. A. Bell & J. G. Healey (1992). "Idiomatic Communication and Interpersonal Solidarity in Friends' Relational Cultures." *Human Communication Research, 18*, 307–335.

38. M. Roloff, C. A. Janiszewski, M. A. McGrath, C. S. Burns, & L. A. Manrai (1988). "Acquiring Resources from Intimates: When Obligation Substitutes for Persuasion." *Human Communication Research, 14*, 364–396.

39. D. H. Solomon (1997). "A Developmental Model of Intimacy and Date Request Explicitness." *Communication Monographs, 64*, 99–118.

40. E. Foster (2008). "Commitment, Communication, and Contending with Heteronormativity: An Invitation to Greater Reflexivity in Interpersonal Research." *Southern Communication Journal, 73*, 84–101.

41. L. Rubin (1985). *Just Friends: The Role of Friendship in Our Lives*. New York: Harper & Row.

42. L. G. Ferdinand (2005). "The Influence of Differentiation of Self and Family of Origin on Individual and Relationship Functioning in Young Adults." *Dissertation Abstracts International: Section B: The Sciences and Engineering, 66*, 1715.

43. J. A. Courtright, F. E. Miller, L. E. Rogers, & D. Bagarozzi (1990). "Interaction Dynamics of Relational Negotiation: Reconciliation versus Termination of Distressed Relationships." *Western Journal of Speech Communication, 54*, 429–453.

44. D. M. Battaglia, F. D. Richard, D. L. Datteri, & C. G. Lord (1998). "Breaking Up Is (Relatively) Easy to Do: A Script for the Dissolution of Close Relationships." *Journal of Social and Personal Relationships, 15*, 829–845.

45. S. Metts, W. R. Cupach, & R. A. Bejllovec (1989). " 'I Love You Too Much to Ever Start Liking You': Redefining Romantic Relationships." *Journal of Social and Personal Relationships, 6*, 259–274.

46. S. Duck (1982). "A Topography of Relationship Disengagement and Dissolution." In S. Duck (Ed.), *Personal Relationships 4: Dissolving Personal Relationships* (pp. 1–30). New York: Academic Press.

47. A. L. Weber, J. H. Harvey, & T. L. Orbuch (1992). "What Went Wrong: Communicating Accounts of Relationship Conflict." In M. L. McLaughlin, M. J. Cody, & S. J. Read (Eds.), *Explaining One's Self to Others: Reason-Giving in a Social Context* (pp. 261–280). Hillsdale, NJ: Erlbaum.

48. Johnson et al., op. cit.

49. See, for example, L. A. Baxter & B. M. Montgomery (1992). *Relating: Dialogues and Dialectics.* New York: Guilford; and W. K. Rawlins (1996). *Friendship Matters: Communication, Dialectics, and the Life Course.* New York: Aldine de Gruyter.

50. Summarized by L. A. Baxter (1994). "A Dialogic Approach to Relationship Maintenance." In D. J. Canary & L. Stafford (Eds.), *Communication and Relational Maintenance.* San Diego, CA: Academic Press. See also E. Sahlstein & T. Dun (2008). " 'I Wanted Time to Myself and He Wanted to be Together All the Time': Constructing Breakups as Managing Autonomy-Connection." *Qualitative Research Reports in Communication, 9*, 37–45.

51. A. P. Buunk (2005). "How Do People Respond to Others with High Commitment or Autonomy in their Relationships?" *Journal of Social and Personal Relationships, 22*, 653–672.

52. D. Morris (1997). *Intimate Behavior* (pp. 21–29). New York: Kodansha Amer Inc.

53. T. D. Golish (2000). "Changes in Closeness between Adult Children and Their Parents: A Turning Point Analysis." *Communication Reports, 13*, 78–97.

54. L. A. Baxter & L. A. Erbert (1999). "Perceptions of Dialectical Contradictions in Turning Points of Development in Heterosexual Romantic Relationships." *Journal of Social and Personal Relationships, 16*, 547–569.

55. E. E. Graham (2003). "Dialectic Contradictions in Postmarital Relationships." *Journal of Family Communication, 3*, 193–215.

56. L. A. Baxter, D. O. Braithwaite, T. D. Golish, & L. N. Olson (2002). "Contradictions of Interaction for Wives of Elderly Husbands with Adult Dementia." *Journal of Applied Communication Research, 30*, 1–20.

57. S. Petronio (2000). "The Boundaries of Privacy: Praxis of Everyday Life." In S. Petronio (Ed.), *Balancing the Secrets of Private Disclosures* (pp. 37–49). Mahwah, NJ: Erlbaum.

58. D. Barry (1990). *Dave Barry Turns 40* (p. 47). New York: Fawcett.

59. D. R. Pawlowski (1998). "Dialectical Tensions in Marital Partners' Accounts of Their Relationships." *Communication Quarterly, 46*, 396–416.

60. E. M. Griffin (2000). *A First Look at Communication Theory*, 4th ed. New York: McGraw-Hill.

61. D. O. Braithwaite & L. Baxter (2006). " 'You're My Parent But You're Not': Dialectical Tensions in Stepchildren's Perceptions About Communicating with the Nonresident Parent." *Journal of Applied Communication Research, 34*, 30–48.

62. B. M. Montgomery (1993). "Relationship Maintenance versus Relationship Change: A Dialectical Dilemma." *Journal of Social and Personal Relationships, 10*, 205–223.

63. D. O. Braithwaite, L. A. Baxter, & A. M. Harper (1998). "The Role of Rituals in the Management of the Dialectical Tension of 'Old' and 'New' in Blended Families." *Communication Studies, 49*, 101–120.

64. See A. Christensen & J. Jacobson (2000). *Reconcilable Differences.* New York: Guilford.

65. R. L. Conville (1991). *Relational Transitions: The Evolution of Personal Relationships* (p. 80). New York: Praeger.

66. For a discussion of similarities across cultures, see D. E. Brown (1991). *Human Universals.* New York: McGraw-Hill.

67. R. R. Hamon & B. B. Ingoldsby (Eds.) (2003). *Mate Selection Across Cultures.* Thousand Oaks, CA: Sage.

68. J. E. Myers, J. Madathil, & L. R. Tingle (2005). "Marriage Satisfaction and Wellness in India and the United States: A Preliminary Comparison of Arranged Marriages and Marriages of Choice."

Journal of Counseling & Development, 83, 183–190; P. Yelsma & K. Athappilly (1988). "Marriage Satisfaction and Communication Practices: Comparisons Among Indian and American Couples." *Journal of Comparative Family Studies, 19*, 37–54.

69. For a detailed discussion of cultural differences that affect relationships, see M. Sun Kim (2002). *Non-Western Perspectives on Human Communication: Implications for Theory and Practice.* Thousand Oaks, CA: Sage.

70. P. Breitman & C. Hatch (2000). *How To Say No Without Feeling Guilty.* New York: Broadway Books.

71. M. Imami (1981). *16 Ways to Avoid Saying No.* Tokyo: The Nihon Keizai Shimbun.

72. D. J. Canary & L. Stafford (1992). "Relational Maintenance Strategies and Equity in Marriage." *Communication Monographs, 59*, 243–267.

73. D. J. Weigel & D. S. Ballard-Reisch (1999). "Using Paired Data to Test Models of Relational Maintenance and Marital Quality." *Journal of Social and Personal Relationships, 16*, 175–191.

74. L. Stafford & D. J. Canary (1991). "Maintenance Strategies and Romantic Relationship Type, Gender, and Relational Characteristics." *Journal of Personality and Social Psychology, 7*, 217–242.

75. A. J. Johnson, M. M. Haigh, J. A. H. Becker, E. A. Craig, & S. Wigley (2008). "College Students' Use of Relational Management Strategies in Email in Long-Distance and Geographically Close Relationships." *Journal of Computer-Mediated Communication, 13*, 381–404.

76. For a description of this ongoing research program, see The Gottman Institute. "Twelve-Year Study of Gay and Lesbian Couples." Retrieved July 28, 2006, at http://www.gottman.com/research.

77. For an overview of this topic, see C. E. Rusbult, P. A. Hannon, S. L. Stocker, & E. J. Finkel (2005). "Forgiveness and Relational Repair." In E. L. Worthington (Ed.), *Handbook of Forgiveness* (pp. 185–206). New York: Routledge.

78. T. M. Emmers-Sommer (2003). "When Partners Falter: Repair After a Transgression." In D. J. Canary & M. Dainton (Eds.), *Maintaining Relationships through Communication* (pp. 185–205). Mahwah, NJ: Erlbaum.

79. K. Dindia & L. A. Baxter (1987). "Strategies for Maintaining and Repairing Marital Relationships." *Journal of Social and Personal Relationships, 4*, 143–158.

80. V. R. Waldron, D. L. Kelley, & J. Harvey (2008). "Forgiving Communication and Relational Consequence." In M. T. Motley (Ed.), *Studies in Applied Interpersonal Communication* (pp. 165–184). Thousand Oaks, CA: Sage.

81. H. S. Park (2009). "Cross-Cultural Comparison of Verbal and Nonverbal Strategies of Apologizing." *Journal of International and Intercultural Communication, 2*, 66–87. See also H. S. Park & X. Guan (2006). "The Effects of National Culture and Face Concerns on Intention to Apologize: A Comparison of U.S. and China." *Journal of Intercultural Communication Research, 35*, 183–204.

82. J. J. Exline, L. Deshea, & V. T. Holeman (2007). "Is Apology Worth the Risk? Predictors, Outcomes, and Ways to Avoid Regret." *Journal of Social & Clinical Psychology, 26*, 479–504.

83. H. M. Wallace, J. J. Exline, & R. F. Baumeister (2008). "Interpersonal Consequences of Forgiveness: Does Forgiveness Deter or Encourage Repeat Offenses?" *Journal of Experimental Social Psychology, 44*, 453–460.

84. D. L. Kelley & V. R. Waldron (2005). "An Investigation of Forgiveness-Seeking Communication and Relational Outcomes." *Communication Quarterly, 53*, 339–358.

85. A. J. Merolla (2008). "Communicating Forgiveness in Friendships and Dating Relationships." *Communication Studies, 59*, 114–131.

86. H. K. Orcutt (2006). "The Prospective Relationship of Interpersonal Forgiveness and Psychological Distress Symptoms Among College Women." *Journal of Counseling Psychology, 53*, 350–361; J. Eaton & C. W. Struthers (2006). "The Reduction of Psychological Aggression Across Varied Interpersonal Contexts Through Repentance and Forgiveness." *Aggressive Behavior, 32*, 195–206.

87. K. A. Lawler, J. W. Younger, R. L. Piferi, et al. (2003). "A Change of Heart: Cardiovascular Correlates of Forgiveness in Response to Interpersonal Conflict." *Journal of Behavioral Medicine, 26*, 373–393.

88. V. R. Waldron & D. L. Kelley (2005). "Forgiving Communication as a Response to Relational Transgressions." *Journal of Social and Personal Relationships, 22*, 723–742.

89. V. R. Waldron & D. L. Kelley (2008). *Communicating Forgiveness.* Thousand Oaks, CA: Sage.

90. G. F. Bachman & L. K. Guerrero (2006). "Forgiveness, Apology, and Communicative Responses to Hurtful Events." *Communication Reports, 19*, 45–56.

91. B. H. Henline, L. K. Lamke, & M. D. Howard (2007). "Exploring Perceptions of Online Infidelity." *Personal Relationships, 14*, 113–128.

92. S. Takaku, B. Weiner, & K. Ohbuchi (2001). "A Cross-Cultural Examination of the Effects of Apology and Perspective-Taking on Forgiveness." *Journal of Language & Social Psychology, 20*, 144–167.

93. D. Kelley (1998). "The Communication of Forgiveness." *Communication Studies, 49*, 255–272.

94. See P. Watzlawick, J. H. Beavin, & D. D. Jackson (1967). *Pragmatics of Human Communication.* New York: Norton; and W. J. Lederer & D. D. Jackson (1968). *The Mirages of Marriage.* New York: Norton.

95. See, for example, R. A. Bell & J. A. Daly (1995). "The Affinity-Seeking Function of Communication." In M. V. Redmond (Ed.), *Interpersonal Communication: Readings in Theory and Research.* Fort Worth, TX: Harcourt Brace.

96. M. Dainton (1998). "Everyday Interaction in Marital Relationships: Variations in Relative Importance and Event Duration." *Communication Reports, 11*, 101–143.

97. S. A. Myers & T. A. Avtgis (1997). "The Association of Socio-Communicative Style and Relational Types on Perceptions of Nonverbal Immediacy." *Communication Research Reports, 14*, 339–349.

98. For a thorough examination of this topic, see Chapter 11: "Nonverbal Immediacy" of V. P. Richmond & J. C. McCroskey (2004). *Nonverbal Behavior in Interpersonal Relationships*, 5th ed. Boston: Allyn and Bacon.

99. T. S. Lim & J. W. Bowers (1991). "Facework: Solidarity, Approbation, and Tact." *Human Communication Research, 17*, 415–450.

100. J. R. Frei & P. R. Shaver (2002). "Respect in Close Relationships: Prototype, Definition, Self-Report Assessment, and Initial Correlates." *Personal Relationships, 9*, 121–139.

101. M. T. Palmer (1989). "Controlling Conversations: Turns, Topics, and Interpersonal Control." *Communication Monographs, 56*, 1–18.

102. Watzlawick et al., op. cit.

103. D. Tannen (1986). *That's Not What I Meant! How Conversational Style Makes or Breaks Your Relations with Others* (p. 190). New York: Morrow.

CHAPTER NINE

1. D. Tannen (1986). *That's Not What I Meant! How Conversational Style Makes or Breaks Relationships* (pp. 17–18). New York: Ballantine. For an extended discussion of Schopenhauer's position, see D. Luepnitz (2003). *Schopenhauer's Porcupines: Intimacy and Its Dilemmas*. New York: Basic Books.

2. K. J. Prager & D. Buhrmester (1998). "Intimacy and Need Fulfillment in Couple Relationships." *Journal of Social and Personal Relationships, 15*, 435–469.

3. C. E. Crowther & G. Stone (1986). *Intimacy: Strategies for Successful Relationships* (p. 13). Santa Barbara, CA: Capra Press.

4. C. Peterson (2006). *A Primer in Positive Psychology*. New York: Oxford.

5. E. Berscheid, M. Schneider, & A. M. Omoto (1989). "Issues in Studying Close Relationships: Conceptualizing and Measuring Closeness." In C. Hendrick (Ed.), *Close Relationships* (pp. 63–91). Newbury Park, CA: Sage.

6. D. Morris (1973). *Intimate Behavior* (p. 7). New York: Bantam.

7. W. D. Manning, P. C. Giordano, & M. A. Longmore (2006). "Hooking Up: The Relationship Contexts of 'Nonrelationship' Sex." *Journal of Adolescent Research, 21*, 459–483.

8. M. R. Parks & K. Floyd (1996). "Making Friends in Cyberspace." *Journal of Communication, 46*, 80–97.

9. L. A. Baxter (1994). "A Dialogic Approach to Relationship Maintenance." In D. Canary & L. Stafford (Eds.), *Communication and Relational Maintenance*. San Diego, CA: Academic Press.

10. A. L. Vangelisti & G. Beck (2007). "Intimacy and the Fear of Intimacy." In L. L'Abate (Ed.), *Low-Cost Approaches to Promote Physical and Mental Health: Theory, Research, and Practice* (pp. 395–414). New York: Springer.

11. J. T. Wood & C. C. Inman (1993). "In a Different Mode: Masculine Styles of Communicating Closeness." *Applied Communication Research, 21*, 279–295; K. Floyd (1995). "Gender and Closeness among Friends and Siblings." *Journal of Psychology, 129*, 193–202.

12. See, for example, K. Dindia (2000). "Sex Differences in Self-Disclosure, Reciprocity of Self-Disclosure, and Self-Disclosure and Liking: Three Meta-Analyses Reviewed." In S. Petronio (Ed.), *Balancing Disclosure, Privacy and Secrecy*. Mahwah, NJ: Erlbaum.

13. See, for example, K. Floyd, op. cit.

14. J. O. Balswick (1988). *The Inexpressive Male: A Tragedy of American Society*. Lexington, MA: Lexington Books.

15. S. Swain (1989). "Covert Intimacy in Men's Friendships: Closeness in Men's Friendships." In B. J. Risman & P. Schwartz (Eds.), *Gender in Intimate Relationships: A Microstructural Approach*. Belmont, CA: Wadsworth.

16. M. T. Morman & K. Floyd (1999). "Affection Communication between Fathers and Young Adult Sons: Individual and Relational-Level Correlates." *Communication Studies, 50*, 294–309.

17. L. Stafford, M. Dainton, & S. Haas (2000). "Measuring Routine and Strategic Relational Maintenance: Scale Revision, Sex versus Gender Roles, and the Prediction of Relational Characteristics." *Communication Monographs, 67*, 306–323.

18. C. K. Reissman (1990). *Divorce Talk: Women and Men Make Sense of Personal Relationships*. New Brunswick, NJ: Rutgers University Press.

19. J. M. Bowman (2008). "Gender Role Orientation and Relational Closeness: Self-Disclosive Behavior in Same-Sex Male Friendships." *Journal of Men's Studies, 16*, 316–330.

20. G. E. Good, M. J. Porter, & M. G. Dillon (2002). "When Men Divulge: Men's Self-Disclosure on Prime Time Situation Comedies." *Sex Roles, 46*, 419–427.

21. M. T. Morman & K. Floyd (2002). "A 'Changing Culture of Fatherhood': Effects of Affectionate Communication, Closeness, and Satisfaction in Men's Relationships With Their Fathers and Their Sons." *Western Journal of Communication, 66*, 395–411.

22. J. Adamopoulos (1991). "The Emergence of Interpersonal Behavior: Diachronic and Cross-Cultural Processes in the Evolution of Intimacy." In S. Ting-Toomey & F. Korzenny (Eds.), *Cross-Cultural Interpersonal Communication*. Newbury Park, CA: Sage. See also G. Fontaine (1990). "Cultural Diversity in Intimate Intercultural Relationships." In D. D. Cahn (Ed.), *Intimates in Conflict: A Communication Perspective*. Hillsdale, NJ: Erlbaum.

23. J. Adamopoulos & R. N. Bontempo (1986). "Diachronic Universals in Interpersonal Structures." *Journal of Cross-Cultural Psychology, 17*, 169–189.

24. M. Argyle & M. Henderson (1985). "The Rules of Relationships." In S. Duck & D. Perlman (Eds.), *Understanding Personal Relationships*. Beverly Hills, CA: Sage.

25. W. B. Gudykunst & S. Ting-Toomey (1988). *Culture and Interpersonal Communication* (pp. 197–198). Newbury Park, CA: Sage.

26. S. Faul (1994). *The Xenophobe's Guide to the Americans* (p. 3). London: Ravette.

27. C. W. Franklin (1992). " 'Hey Home—Yo Bro': Friendship among Black Men." In P. M. Nardi (Ed.), *Men's Friendships*. Newbury Park, CA: Sage.

28. H. C. Triandis (1994). *Culture and Social Behavior* (p. 230). New York: McGraw-Hill.

29. K. Lewin (1936). *Principles of Topological Psychology*. New York: McGraw-Hill.

30. E. Hatfield & R. L. Rapson (2006). "Passionate Love, Sexual Desire, and Mate Selection: Cross-Cultural and Historical Perspectives." In P. Noller & J. A. Feeney (Eds.), *Close Relationships: Functions, Forms and Processes* (pp. 227–243). Hove, England: Psychology Press/ Taylor & Francis.

31. L. B. Hian, S. L. Chuan, T. M. K. Trevor, & B. H. Detenber (2004). "Getting to Know You: Exploring the Development of Relational Intimacy in Computer-Mediated Communication." *Journal of Computer-Mediated Communication, 9*, Issue 3.

32. P. Valkenberg & J. Peter (2009). "The Effects of Instant Messaging on the Quality of Adolescents' Existing Friendships: A Longitudinal Study." *Journal of Communication, 59*, 79–97; H. Ko & F. Kuo (2009). "Can Blogging Enhance Subjective Well-Being Through Self-Disclosure?" *CyberPsychology & Behavior, 12*, 75–79; J. P. Mazer, R. E. Murphy, & C. J. Simonds (2008). "The Effects of Teacher Self-Disclosure via 'Facebook' on Teacher Credibility." *RCA Vestnik (Russian Communication Association)*, 30–37; Y. Hu, J. F. Wood, V. Smith, & N. Westbrook (2004). "Friendships Through IM: Examining the Relationship Between Instant Messaging and Intimacy." *Journal of Computer-Mediated Communication, 10*, Issue 1.

33. L. D. Rosen, et al. (2008). "The Impact of Emotionality and Self-Disclosure on Online Dating versus Traditional Dating." *Computers in Human Behavior, 24*, 2124–2157; A. Ben-Ze'ev (2003). "Privacy, Emotional Closeness, and Openness in Cyberspace." *Computers in Human Behavior, 19*, 451–467.

34. J. Boase, J. B. Horrigan, B. Wellman, & L. Rainie (2006). "The Strength of Internet Ties." *Pew Internet & American Life Project*. Retrieved September 11, 2006, at http://www.pewinternet.org/pdfs/PIP_Internet_ties .pdf.

35. S. Henderson & M. Gilding (2004). " 'I've Never Clicked this Much with Anyone in My Life': Trust and Hyperpersonal Communication in Online Friendships." *New Media & Society, 6*, 487–506.

36. K. Lewis, J. Kaufman, & N. Christakis (2008). "The Taste for Privacy: An Analysis of College Student Privacy Settings in an Online Social Network." *Journal of Computer-Mediated Communication, 14*, 79–100; Z. Tufekei (2008). "Can You See Me Now? Audience and Disclosure Regulation in Online Social Network Sites." *Bulletin of Science, Technology & Society, 28*, 20–36.

37. R. F. Baumeister (2005). *The Cultural Animal: Human Nature, Meaning, and Social Life*. New York: Oxford.

38. See, for example, R. Bellah, W. M. Madsen, A. Sullivan, & S. M. Tipton (1985). *Habits of the Heart: Individualism and Commitment in American Life*. Berkeley, CA: University of California Press; R. Sennett (1974). *The Fall of Public Man: On the Social Psychology of Capitalism*. New York: Random House; and S. Trenholm & A. Jensen (1990). *The Guarded Self: Toward a Social History of Interpersonal Styles*. Paper presented at the Speech Communication Association meeting, San Juan, Puerto Rico.

39. I. Altman & D. A. Taylor (1973). *Social Penetration: The Development of Interpersonal Relationships*. New York: Holt, Rinehart and Winston. See also D. A. Taylor & I. Altman (1987). "Communication in Interpersonal Relationships: Social Penetration Processes." In M. E. Roloff & G. R. Miller (Eds.), *Interpersonal Processes: New Directions in Communication Research*. Newbury Park, CA: Sage.

40. J. Luft (1969). *Of Human Interaction*. Palo Alto, CA: National Press Books.

41. S. Petronio (2007). "Translational Research Endeavors and the Practices of Communication Privacy Management." *Journal of Applied Communication Research, 35*, 218–22.

42. T. D. Affifi & K. Steuber (2009). "The Revelation Risk Model (RRM): Factors that Predict the Revelation of Secrets and the Strategies Used to Reveal Them." *Communication Monographs, 76*, 144–176. See also T. D. Affifi & K. Steuber (2009). "Keeping and Revealing Secrets." *Communication Currents, 4*, 1–2.

43. K. Dindia (2002). "Self-Disclosure Research: Advances Through Meta-Analysis." In M. Allen & R. W. Preiss (Eds.), *Interpersonal Communication Research: Advances Through Meta-Analysis* (pp. 169–185). Mahwah, NJ: Erlbaum; V. J. Derlega & A. L. Chaikin (1975). *Sharing Intimacy: What We Reveal to Others and Why*. Englewood Cliffs, NJ: Prentice-Hall.

44. R. C. Savin-Williams (2001). *Mom, Dad. I'm Gay: How Families Negotiate Coming Out*. Washington, DC: American Psychological Association.

45. H. L. Wintrob (1987). "Self-Disclosure as a Marketable Commodity." *Journal of Social Behavior and Personality, 2*, 77–88.

46. J. A. Hess, A. D. Fannin, & L. H. Pollom (2007). "Creating Closeness: Discerning and Measuring Strategies for Fostering Closer Relationships." *Personal Relationships, 14*, 25–44. A. E. Mitchell, et al. (2008). "Predictors of Intimacy in Couples' Discussions of Relationship Injuries: An Observational Study." *Journal of Family Psychology, 22*, 21–29.

47. S. MacNeil & E. S. Byers (2009). "Role of Sexual Self-Disclosure in the Sexual Satisfaction of Long-Term Heterosexual Couples." *Journal of Sex Research, 46*, 3–14; F. D. Fincham & T. N. Bradbury (1989). "The Impact of Attributions in Marriage: An Individual Difference Analysis." *Journal of Social and Personal Relationships, 6*, 69–85.

48. V. G. Downs (1988). "Grandparents and Grandchildren: The Relationship between Self-Disclosure and Solidarity in an Intergenerational Relationship." *Communication Research Reports, 5*, 173–179.

49. L. B. Rosenfeld & W. L. Kendrick (Fall 1984). "Choosing to Be Open: Subjective Reasons for Self-Disclosing." *Western Journal of Speech Communication, 48*, 326–343.

50. V. Derlega, B. A. Winstead, A. Mathews, & A. L. Braitman (2008). "Why Does Someone Reveal Highly Personal Information? Attributions for and against Self-Disclosure in Close Relationships." *Communication Research Reports, 25*, 115–130; K. G. Niederhoffer & J. W. Pennebaker (2002). "Sharing One's Story: On the Benefits of Writing or Talking About Emotional Experience." In C. R. Snyder & S. J. Lopez (Eds.), *Handbook of Positive Psychology* (pp. 573–583). London: Oxford University Press.

51. K. Greene, V. J. Derlega, & A. Mathews (2006). "Self-Disclosure in Personal Relationships." In A. Vangelisti & D. Perlman (Eds.), *The Cambridge Handbook of Personal Relationships*. New York: Cambridge University Press; L. B. Rosenfeld (2000). "Overview of the Ways Privacy, Secrecy, and Disclosure are Balanced in Today's Society." In S. Petronio (Ed.), *Balancing the Secrets of Private Disclosures* (pp. 3–17). Mahwah, NJ: Erlbaum.

52. J. Powell (1969). *Why Am I Afraid to Tell You Who I Am?* Niles, IL: Argus Communications.

53. R. Agne, T. L. Thompson, & L. P. Cusella (2000). "Stigma in the Line of Face: Self-Disclosure of Patients' HIV Status to Health Care Providers." *Journal of Applied Communication Research, 28*, 235–261; V. J. Derlega, B. A. Winstead, & L. Folk-Barron (2000). "Reasons for and Against Disclosing HIV-Seropositive Test Results to an Intimate Partner: A Functional Perspective." In S. Petronio (Ed.), *Balancing the Secrets of Private Disclosures* (pp. 71–82). Mahwah, NJ: Erlbaum. See also J. P. Caughlin, et al. (2009). "Do Message Features Influence Reactions to HIV Disclosures? A Multiple-Goals Perspective." *Health Communication, 24*, 270–283.

54. M. Allen, et al. (2008). "Persons Living with HIV: Disclosure to Sexual Partners." *Communication Research Reports, 25*, 192–199.

55. K. Dindia, M. A. Fitzpatrick, & D. A. Kenny (1988). *Self-Disclosure in Spouse and Stranger Interaction: A Social Relations Analysis.* Paper presented at the annual meeting of the International Communication Association, New Orleans; and S. W. Duck & D. E. Miell (1991). "Charting the Development of Personal Relationships." In R. Gilmour & S. W. Duck (Eds.), *Studying Interpersonal Interaction* (pp. 133–144). New York: Guilford.

56. S. Duck (1991). "Some Evident Truths about Conversations in Everyday Relationships: All Communications Are Not Created Equal." *Human Communication Research, 18*, 228–267.

57. C. L. Kleinke (1979). "Effects of Personal Evaluations." In *Self-Disclosure.* San Francisco: Jossey-Bass.

58. E. M. Eisenberg & M. G. Witten (1987). "Reconsidering Openness in Organizational Communication." *Academy of Management Review, 12*, 418–428.

59. L. B. Rosenfeld & J. R. Gilbert (1989). "The Measurement of Cohesion and Its Relationship to Dimensions of Self-Disclosure in Classroom Settings." *Small Group Behavior, 20*, 291–301.

60. T. E. Runge & R. L. Archer (December 1981). "Reactions to the Disclosure of Public and Private Self-Information." *Social Psychology Quarterly, 44*, 357–362.

61. L. B. Rosenfeld & G. I. Bowen (1991). "Marital Disclosure and Marital Satisfaction: Direct-Effect versus Interaction-Effect Models." *Western Journal of Speech Communication, 55*, 69–84.

62. S. H. McDaniel, et al. (2007). "Physician Self-Disclosure in Primary Care Visits: Enough About You, What About Me?" *Archives of Internal Medicine, 167*, 1321–1326.

63. A. Jaksa & M. Pritchard (1993). *Communication Ethics: Methods of Analysis*, 2nd ed. (pp. 65–66). Belmont, CA: Wadsworth.

64. D. O'Hair & M. J. Cody (1993). "Interpersonal Deception: The Dark Side of Interpersonal Communication?" In B. H. Spitzberg & W. R. Cupach (Eds.), *The Dark Side of Interpersonal Communication.* Hillsdale, NJ: Erlbaum.

65. M. Spranca, E. Minsk, & J. Baron (1991). "Omission and Commission in Judgement and Choice." *Journal of Experimental Social Psychology, 27*, 76–105.

66. J. F. George & A. Robb (2008). "Deception and Computer-Mediated Communication in Daily Life." *Communication Reports, 21*, 92–103.

67. M. L. Knapp (2006). "Lying and Deception in Close Relationships." In A. Vangelisti & D. Perlman (Eds.), *The Cambridge Handbook of Personal Relationships.* New York: Cambridge University Press.

68. R. E. Turner, C. Edgely, & G. Olmstead (1975). "Information Control in Conversation: Honesty Is Not Always the Best Policy." *Kansas Journal of Sociology, 11*, 69–89.

69. R. S. Feldman, J. A. Forrest, & B. R. Happ (2002). "Self-Presentation and Verbal Deception: Do Self-Presenters Lie More?" *Basic and Applied Social Psychology, 24*, 163–170.

70. B. M. DePaulo, D. A. Kashy, S. E. Kirkendol, & M. M. Wyer (1996). "Lying in Everyday Life." *Journal of Personality and Social Psychology, 70*, 779–795.

71. J. Bavelas (1983). "Situations that Lead to Disqualification." *Human Communication Research, 9*, 130–145.

72. W. C. Rowatt, M. R. Cunningham, & P. B. Druen (1999). "Lying to Get a Date: The Effect of Facial Physical Attractiveness on the Willingness to Deceive

Prospective Dating Partners." *Journal of Social and Personal Relationships, 16*, 209–223.

73. D. Hample (1980). "Purposes and Effects of Lying." *Southern Speech Communication Journal, 46*, 33–47.

74. S. A. McCornack & T. R. Levine (1990). "When Lies Are Uncovered: Emotional and Relational Outcomes of Discovered Deception." *Communication Monographs, 57*, 119–138.

75. J. S. Seiter, J. Bruschke, & C. Bai (2002). "The Acceptability of Deception as a Function of Perceivers' Culture, Deceiver's Intention, and Deceiver-Deceived Relationship." *Western Journal of Communication, 66*, 158–181.

76. S. Metts, W. R. Cupach, & T. T. Imahori (1992). "Perceptions of Sexual Compliance-Resisting Messages in Three Types of Cross-Sex Relationships." *Western Journal of Communication, 56*, 1–17.

77. J. B. Bavelas, A. Black, N. Chovil, & J. Mullett (1990). *Equivocal Communication* (p. 171). Newbury Park, CA: Sage.

78. Ibid.

79. W. P. Robinson, A. Shepherd, & J. Heywood (1998). "Truth, Equivocation/Concealment, & Lies in Job Applications & Doctor-Patient Communication." *Journal of Language & Social Psychology, 17*, 149–164.

80. M. T. Motley (1992). "Mindfulness in Solving Communicators' Dilemmas." *Communication Monographs, 59*, 306–314.

81. S. B. Shimanoff (1988). "Degree of Emotional Expressiveness as a Function of Face-Needs, Gender, & Interpersonal Relationship." *Communication Reports, 1*, 43–53.

82. A. P. Hubbell (May 1999). *"I Love Your Family—They Are Just Like You": Lies We Tell to Lovers & Perceptions of Their Honesty & Appropriateness.* Paper presented at the annual meeting of the International Communication Association, San Francisco. See also S. A. McCornack (1992). "Information Manipulation Theory." *Communication Monographs, 59*, 1–16.

83. P. Andersen (1999). *Nonverbal Communication: Forms & Functions* (pp. 297–298). Mountain View, CA: Mayfield.

CHAPTER TEN

1. J. Veroff, E. Douvan, T. L. Orbuch, & L. K. Acitelli (1998). "Happiness in Stable Marriages: The Early Years." In T. N. Bradbury (Ed.), *The Developmental Course of Marital Dysfunction.* New York: Cambridge University Press.

2. J. Gottman (2006). "Why Marriages Fail." In K. M. Galvin & P. J. Cooper (Eds.), *Making Connections: Readings in Relational Communication*, 4th ed. (pp. 228–236). Los Angeles: Roxbury. See also A. M. Hicks & L. M. Diamond (2008). "How Was Your Day? Couples' Affect When Telling and Hearing Daily Events." *Personal Relationships, 15*, 205–228.

3. C. A. Barbato, E. E. Graham, & E. E. Perse (2003). "Communicating in the Family: An Examination of the Relationship of Family Communication Climate & Interpersonal Communication Motives." *Journal of Family Communication, 3*, 123–148.

4. R. M. Dailey (2006). "Confirmation in Parent-Adolescent Relationships and Adolescent Openness: Toward Extending Confirmation Theory." *Communication Monographs, 73*, 434–458.

5. J. J. Teven, M. M. Martin, & N. C. Neupauer (1998). "Sibling Relationships: Verbally Aggressive Messages & Their Effect on Relational Satisfaction." *Communication Reports, 11*, 179–186.

6. A. L. Vangelisti & S. L. Young (2000). "When Words Hurt: The Effects of Perceived Intentionality on Interpersonal Relationships." *Journal of Social & Personal Relationship, 17*, 393–424.

7. E. Seiberg (1976). "Confirming & Disconfirming Communication in an Organizational Setting." In J. Owen, P. Page, & G. Zimmerman (Eds.), *Communication in Organizations* (pp. 129–149). St. Paul, MN: West.

8. E. Sieberg & C. Larson (1971). *Dimensions of Interpersonal Response.* Paper presented at the meeting of the International Communication Association, Phoenix.

9. S. A. Cox (1999). "Group Communication & Employee Turnover: How Coworkers Encourage Peers to Voluntarily Exit." *Southern Communication Journal, 64*, 181–192.

10. J. M. Gottman & R. W. Levenson (2000). "The Timing of Divorce: Predicting When a Couple Will Divorce over a 14-Year Period." *Journal of Marriage and the Family, 62*, 737–745.

11. A. S. Rancer & T. A. Avtgis (2006). *Argumentative and Aggressive Communication: Theory, Research, and Application.* Thousand Oaks, CA: Sage.

12. J. K. Alberts (1988). "An Analysis of Couples' Conversational Complaints." *Communication Monographs, 55*, 184–197.

13. J. K. Alberts & G. Driscoll (1992). "Containment versus Escalation: The Trajectory of Couples' Conversational Complaints." *Western Journal of Communication, 56*, 394–412.

14. J. M. Gottman & N. Silver (1999). *The Seven Principles for Making Marriage Work.* New York: Random House.

15. A. S. Rancer & T. A. Avtgis (2006). *Argumentative and Aggressive Communication: Theory, Research, and Application.* Thousand Oaks, CA: Sage.

16. F. F. Jordan-Jackson, Y. Lin, A. S. Rancer, & D. A. Infante (2008). "Perceptions of Males and Females' Use of Aggressive Affirming and Nonaffirming Messages in an Interpersonal Dispute: You've Come a Long Way Baby??" *Western Journal of Communication, 72*, 239–258.

17. K. Cissna & E. Seiberg (1995). "Patterns of Interactional Confirmation & Disconfirmation." In M. V. Redmond (Ed.), *Interpersonal Communication: Readings in Theory & Research.* Fort Worth, TX: Harcourt Brace.

18. M. W. Allen (1995). "Communication Concepts Related to Perceived Organizational Support." *Western Journal of Communication, 59*, 326–346.

19. See, for example, R. M. Dailey (2008). "Assessing the Contribution of Nonverbal Behaviors in Displays of Confirmation During Parent-Adolescent Interactions: An Actor-Partner Interdependence Model." *Journal of Family Communication, 8*, 62–91.

20. W. W. Wilmot (1987). *Dyadic Communication* (pp. 149–158). New York: Random House.

21. C. Burggraf & A. L. Sillars (1987). "A Critical Examination of Sex Differences in Marital Communication." *Communication Monographs, 54*, 276–294. See also D. A. Newton & J. K. Burgoon (1990). "The Use & Consequences of Verbal Strategies during Interpersonal Disagreements." *Human Communication Research, 16*, 477–518.

22. J. Gottman (1994). *Why Marriages Succeed or Fail.* New York: Simon & Schuster.

23. J. L. Hocker & W. W. Wilmot (1995). *Interpersonal Conflict*, 4th ed. (p. 34). Dubuque, IA: Brown & Benchmark.

24. Ibid., p. 36.

25. J. M. Gottman & R. W. Levinson (1999). "Rebound for Marital Conflict & Divorce Prediction." *Family Process, 38*, 387–292.

26. K. Domenici & S. Littlejohn (2006). *Facework: Bridging Theory and Practice.* Thousand Oaks, CA: Sage; M. K. Lapinski & F. J. Boster (2001). "Modeling the Ego-Defensive Function of Attitudes." *Communication Monographs, 68*, 314–324.

27. J. A. H. Becker, B. Ellevold, & G. H. Stamp (2008). "The Creation of Defensiveness in Social Interaction II: A Model of Defensive Communication Among Romantic Couples." *Communication Monographs, 75*, 86–110; G. H. Stamp, A. L. Vangelisti, & J. A. Daly (1992). "The Creation of Defensiveness in Social Interaction." *Communication Quarterly, 40*, 177–190.

28. D. R. Turk & J. L. Monahan (1999). " 'Here I Go Again': An Examination of Repetitive Behaviors during Interpersonal Conflicts." *Southern Communication Journal, 64*, 232–244.

29. See, for example, W. R. Cupach & S. J. Messman (1999). "Face Predilections & Friendship Solidarity." *Communication Reports, 12*, 117–124.

30. J. Gibb (September 1961). "Defensive Communication." *Journal of Communication, 11*, 141–148. See also E. Robertson (2005). "Placing Leaders at the Heart of Organizational Communication." *Communication Management, 9*, 34–37.

31. R. F. Proctor & J. R. Wilcox (1993). "An Exploratory Analysis of Responses to Owned Messages in Interpersonal Communication." *ETC: A Review of General Semantics, 50*, 201–220.

32. Research summarized in J. Harwood, E. B. Ryan, H. Giles, & S. Tysoski (1997). "Evaluations of Patronizing Speech & Three Response Styles in a Non-Service-Providing Context." *Journal of Applied Communication Research, 25*, 170–195.

33. Adapted from S. Miller, E. W. Nunnally, & D. B. Wackman (1975). *Alive & Aware: How to Improve Your Relationships through Better Communication.* Minneapolis, MN: International Communication Programs. See also R. Remer & P. deMesquita (1990). "Teaching & Learning the Skills of Interpersonal Confrontation." In D. D. Cahn (Ed.), *Intimates in Conflict: A Communication Perspective.* Hillsdale, NJ: Erlbaum.

34. Adapted from M. Smith (1975). *When I Say No, I Feel Guilty* (pp. 93–110). New York: Dial Press.

35. W. L. Benoit & S. Drew (1997). "Appropriateness & Effectiveness of Image Repair Strategies." *Communication Reports, 10*, 153–163. See also Stamp et al., op. cit.

CHAPTER ELEVEN

1. W. Wilmot & J. L. Hocker (2010). *Interpersonal Conflict*, 8th ed. (pp. 44–56). New York: McGraw-Hill. See also P. M. Buzzanell & N. A. Burrell (1997). "Family & Workplace Conflict: Examining Metaphorical Conflict Schemas & Expressions across Context & Sex." *Human Communication Research, 24*, 109–146.

2. S. Metts & W. Cupach (1990). "The Influence of Relationship Beliefs & Problem-Solving Responses on Satisfaction in Romantic Relationships." *Human Communication Research, 17*, 170–185.

3. Wilmot & Hocker, op. cit., pp. 11–19.

4. For a summary of research detailing the prevalence of conflict in relationships, see W. R. Cupach & D. J. Canary (1997). *Competence in Interpersonal Conflict* (pp. 5–6). New York: McGraw-Hill.

5. W. L. Benoit & P. J. Benoit (1987). "Everyday Argument Practices of Naive Social Actors." In J. Wenzel (Ed.), *Argument & Critical Practices.* Annandale, VA: Speech Communication Association.

6. W. Samter & W. R. Cupach (1998). "Friendly Fire: Topical Variations in Conflict among Same- & Cross-Sex Friends." *Communication Studies, 49*, 121–138.

7. S. Vuchinich (1987). "Starting & Stopping Spontaneous Family Conflicts." *Journal of Marriage and Family, 49*, 591–601.

8. J. M. Gottman (1982). "Emotional Responsiveness in Marital Conversations." *Journal of Communication, 32*, 108–120. See also W. R. Cupach (May 1982). *Communication Satisfaction and Interpersonal Solidarity as Outcomes of Conflict Message Strategy Use.* Paper presented at the International Communication Association conference, Boston.

9. P. Koren, K. Carlton, & D. Shaw (1980). "Marital Conflict: Relations among Behaviors, Outcomes, and Distress." *Journal of Consulting and Clinical Psychology, 48*, 460–468.

10. Wilmot & Hocker, op. cit., p. 37.

11. J. M. Gottman (1979). *Marital Interaction: Experimental Investigations.* New York: Academic Press. See also D. A. Infante, S. A. Myers, & R. A. Buerkel (1994). "Argument and Verbal Aggression in Constructive and Destructive Family and Organizational Disagreements." *Western Journal of Communication, 58*, 73–84.

12. S. E. Crohan (1992). "Marital Happiness & Spousal Consensus on Beliefs about Marital Conflict: A Longitudinal Investigation." *Journal of Science and Personal Relationships, 9,* 89–102.

13. D. J. Canary, H. Weger, Jr., & L. Stafford (1991). "Couples' Argument Sequences and Their Associations with Relational Characteristics." *Western Journal of Speech Communication, 55,* 159–179.

14. M. S. Harper & D. P. Welsh (2007). "Keeping Quiet: Self-Silencing and Its Association with Relational and Individual Functioning among Adolescent Romantic Couples." *Journal of Social and Personal Relationships, 24,* 99–116.

15. J. P. Caughlin & T. D. Golish (2002). "An Analysis of the Association Between Topic Avoidance and Dissatisfaction: Comparing Perceptual and Interpersonal Explanations." *Communication Monographs, 69,* 275–295.

16. J. P. Caughlin & T. D. Arr (2004). "When is Topic Avoidance Unsatisfying? Examining Moderators of the Association Between Avoidance and Dissatisfaction." *Human Communication Research, 30,* 479–513.

17. D. D. Cahn (1992). *Conflict in Intimate Relationships* (p. 100). New York: Guilford.

18. Wilmot & Hocker, op. cit., p. 159.

19. J. G. Oetzel & S. Ting-Toomey (2003). "Face Concerns in Interpersonal Conflict: A Cross-Cultural Empirical Test of the Face Negotiation Theory." *Communication Research, 30,* 599–625; M. U. Dsilva & L. O. Whyte (1998). "Cultural Differences in Conflict Styles: Vietnamese Refugees and Established Residents." *Howard Journal of Communication, 9,* 57–68.

20. S. J. Messman & R. L. Mikesell (2000). "Competition & Interpersonal Conflict in Dating Relationships." *Communication Reports, 13,* 21–34.

21. L. N. Olson & D. O. Braithwaite (2004). " 'If You Hit Me Again, I'll Hit You Back': Conflict Management Strategies of Individuals Experiencing Aggression During Conflicts." *Communication Studies, 55,* 271–285.

22. K. Warren, S. Schoppelrey, & D. Moberg (2005). "A Model of Contagion Through Competition in the Aggressive Behaviors of Elementary School Students." *Journal of Abnormal Child Psychology, 33,* 283–292.

23. D. A. Infante (1987). "Aggressiveness." In J. C. McCroskey & J. A. Daly (Eds.), *Personality & Interpersonal Communication.* Newbury Park, CA: Sage.

24. M. E. Roloff & R. M. Reznick (2008). "Communication During Serial Arguments: Connections with Individuals' Mental and Physical Well-Being." In M. T. Motley (Ed.), *Studies in Applied Interpersonal Communication* (pp. 97–120). Thousand Oaks, CA: Sage.

25. D. A. Infante, A. S. Rancer, & F. F. Jordan (1996). "Affirming & Nonaffirming Style, Dyad Sex, and the Perception of Argumentation and Verbal Aggression in an Interpersonal Dispute." *Human Communication Research, 22,* 315–334.

26. D. A. Infante, T. A. Chandler, & J. E. Rudd (1989). "Test of an Argumentative Skill Deficiency Model of Interspousal Violence." *Communication Monographs, 56,* 163–177.

27. M. M. Martin, C. M. Anderson, P. A. Burant, & K. Weber (1997). "Verbal Aggression in Sibling Relationships." *Communication Quarterly, 45,* 304–317.

28. J. W. Kassing & D. A. Infante (1999). "Aggressive Communication in the Coach-Athlete Relationship." *Communication Research Reports, 16,* 110–120.

29. M. J. Beatty, K. M. Valencic, J. E. Rudd, & J. A. Dobos (1999). "A 'Dark Side' of Communication Avoidance: Indirect Interpersonal Aggressiveness." *Communication Research Reports, 16,* 103–109.

30. B. K. Houston, M. A. Babyak, M. A. Chesney, & G. Black (1997). "Social Dominance and 22-Year All-Cause Mortality in Men." *Psychosomatic Medicine, 59,* 5–12.

31. "Marital Tiffs Spark Immune Swoon" (September 4, 1993). *Science News,* 153.

32. A. C. Filley (1975). *Interpersonal Conflict Resolution* (p. 23). Glenview, IL: Scott, Foresman.

33. D. Canary (2003). "Managing Interpersonal Conflict: A Model of Events Related to Strategic Choices." In J. O. Greene & B. R. Burleson (Eds.), *Handbook of Communication and Social Interaction Skills* (pp. 515–549). Mahwah, NJ: Erlbaum.

34. Hocker & Wilmot, op. cit., pp. 13–16. See also M. L. Knapp, L. L. Putnam, & L. J. Davis (1988). "Measuring Interpersonal Conflict in Organizations: Where Do We Go from Here?" *Management Communication Quarterly, 1,* 414–429.

35. C. S. Burggraf & A. L. Sillars (1987). "A Critical Examination of Sex Differences in Marital Communication." *Communication Monographs, 53,* 276–294.

36. J. Gottman & L. J. Krofoff (1989). "Marital Interaction and Satisfaction: A Longitudinal View." *Journal of Consulting and Clinical Psychology, 67,* 47–52; G. R. Pike & A. L. Sillars (1985). "Reciprocity of Marital Communication." *Journal of Social and Personal Relationships, 2,* 303–324.

37. M. A. Fitzpatrick (1977). "A Typological Approach to Communication in Relationships." In B. Rubin (Ed.), *Communication Yearbook 1.* New Brunswick, NJ: Transaction Books.

38. M. A. Fitzpatrick, J. Fey, C. Segrin, & J. L. Schiff (1993). "Internal Working Models of Relationships and Marital Communication." *Journal of Language and Social Psychology, 12,* 103–131. See also M. A. Fitzpatrick, S. Fallis, & L. Vance (1982). "Multifunctional Coding of Conflict Resolution Strategies in Marital Dyads." *Family Relations, 21,* 61–70.

39. J. Gottman (2006). "Why Marriages Fail." In K. M. Galvin & P. J. Cooper, *Making Connections: Readings in Relational Communication,* 4th ed. Los Angeles: Roxbury.

40. J. Rossel & R. Collins (2006). "Conflict Theory and Interaction Rituals: The Microfoundations of Conflict Theory." In J. H. Turner (Ed.), *Handbook of Sociological Theory* (pp. 509–532). New York: Springer.

41. Cupach & Canary, op. cit., p. 109.

42. Research summarized by D. Tannen (1989). *You Just Don't Understand: Women and Men in Conversation* (pp. 152–157, 162–165). New York: William Morrow.

43. N. H. Hess & E. H. Hagen (2006). *Evolution and Human Behavior, 27,* 231–245; M. K. Underwood (2003). *Social Aggression Among Girls.* New York: Guilford.

44. R. Wiseman (2003). *Queen Bees & Wannabes: Helping Your Daughter Survive Cliques, Gossip, Boyfriends, and Other Realities of Adolescence.* New York: Three Rivers Press.

45. M. J. Collier (1991). "Conflict Competence within African, Mexican, and Anglo-American Friendships." In S. Ting-Toomey & F. Korzenny (Eds.), *Cross-Cultural Interpersonal Communication.* Newbury Park, CA: Sage.

46. D. J. Canary, W. R. Cupach, & S. J. Messman (1995). *Relationship Conflict.* Newbury Park, CA: Sage.

47. See M. J. Papa & E. J. Natalle (1989). "Gender, Strategy Selection, and Discussion Satisfaction in Interpersonal Conflict." *Western Journal of Speech Communication, 52,* 260–272.

48. B. M. Gayle, R. W. Preiss, & M. A. Allen (2001). "A Meta-Analytic Interpretation of Intimate and Non-Intimate Interpersonal Conflict." In M. A. Allen, R. W. Preiss, B. M. Gayle, & N. Burrell (Eds.), *Interpersonal Communication: Advances through Meta-Analysis.* New York: Erlbaum.

49. M. Allen (1998). "Methodological Considerations When Examining a Gendered World." In D. Canary & K. Dindia (Eds.), *Handbook of Sex Differences and Similarities in Communication.* Mahwah, NJ: Erlbaum.

50. Research summarized in Cupach & Canary, op. cit., pp. 63–65.

51. C. S. Burggraf & A. L. Sillars (1987). "A Critical Examination of Sex Differences in Marital Communication." *Communication Monographs, 54,* 276–294.

52. For a more detailed discussion of culture, conflict, and context, see W. B. Gudykunst & S. Ting-Toomey (1988). *Culture and Interpersonal Communication* (pp. 153–160). Newbury Park, CA: Sage.

53. See, for example, J. L. Holt & C. J. DeVore (2005). "Culture, Gender, Organizational Role, and Styles of Conflict Resolution: A Meta-Analysis." *International Journal of Intercultural Relations, 29,* 165–196.

54. See, for example, S. Ting-Toomey (1988). "Rhetorical Sensitivity Style in Three Cultures: France, Japan, and the United States." *Central States Speech Journal, 39,* 28–36.

55. K. Okabe (1987). "Indirect Speech Acts of the Japanese." In L. Kincaid (Ed.), *Communication Theory: Eastern and Western Perspectives* (pp. 127–136). San Diego, CA: Academic Press.

56. G. Fontaine (1991). "Cultural Diversity in Intimate Intercultural Relationships." In D. D. Cahn, *Intimates in Conflict: A Communication Perspective.* Hillsdale, NJ: Erlbaum.

57. The following research is summarized in Tannen, op. cit., p. 160.

58. Collier, op. cit.

59. See, for example, K. J. Beatty & J. C. McCroskey (1997). "It's in Our Nature: Verbal Aggressiveness as Temperamental Expression." *Communication Quarterly, 45,* 466–460.

60. J. G. Oetzel (1998). "Explaining Individual Communication Processes in Homogeneous and Heterogeneous Groups through Individualism-Collectivism and Self-Construal." *Human Communication Research, 25,* 202–224.

61. T. Gordon (1970). *Parent Effectiveness Training* (pp. 236–264). New York: Wyden.

62. R. Axelrod (1984). *The Evolution of Cooperation.* New York: Basic Books.

FEATURE BOX NOTES

CHAPTER ONE, ON THE JOB

a. *Job Outlook 2010* (2009). Bethlehem, PA: National Association of Colleges and Employers.

b. J. L. Winsor, D. B. Curtis, & R. D. Stephens (1997). "National Preferences in Business and Communication Education: An Update." *Journal of the Association for Communication Administration, 3*, 170–179. See also M. S. Peterson (1997). "Personnel Interviewers' Perceptions of the Importance and Adequacy of Applicants' Communication Skills." *Communication Education, 46*, 287–291.

c. F. S. Endicott (1979). *The Endicott Report: Trends in the Employment of College and University Graduates in Business and Industry.* Evanston, IL: Placement Center, Northwestern University.

d. See, for example, N. M. Hindi, D. S. Miller, & S. E. Catt (2004). "Communication and Miscommunication in Corporate America: Evidence from Fortune 200 Firms." *Journal of Organizational Culture, 8*, 13–26.

e. See, for example, A. L. Darling & D. P. Dannels (2003). "Practicing Engineers Talk about the Importance of Talk: A Report on the Role of Oral Communication in the Workplace." *Communication Education, 52*, 1–16.

f. D. A. Nellermoe, T. R. Weirich, & A. Reinstein (1999). "Using Practitioners' Viewpoints to Improve Accounting Students' Communications Skills." *Business Communication Quarterly, 62*, 41–60.

g. "Communication Skills Deemed Vital" (August 22, 1999). *Santa Barbara News-Press*, J1.

h. J. Richman (September 16, 2002). "The News Journal of the Life Scientist." *The Scientist, 16*, 42.

CHAPTER TWO, ON THE JOB

a. P. D. Blank (Ed.) (1993). *Interpersonal Expectations: Theory, Research, and Applications.* Cambridge, UK: Cambridge University Press.

b. C. E. Johnson (2006). *Ethics in the Workplace: Tools and Tactics for Organizational Transformation.* Thousand Oaks, CA: Sage.

c. W. Turk (2009). "Let's Go For Self-Fulfilling Prophecies." *Defense AT&L, 38*, 56–59.

d. D. Eden (1990). *Pygmalion in Management: Productivity as a Self-Fulfilling Prophecy.* New York: Simon & Schuster; D. Eden (1990). "Pygmalion Without Interpersonal Contrast Effects: Whole Groups Gain From Raising Manager Expectations." *Journal of Applied Psychology, 75*, 394–398.

CHAPTER THREE, ON THE JOB

a. P. G. Zimbardo, C. Haney, & W. C. Banks (April 8, 1973). "A Pirandellian Prison." *New York Times Magazine*, 38 ff.

b. K. Burke (1984). *Permanence and Change* (p. 38). Berkeley: University of California Press.

CHAPTER FOUR, ON THE JOB

a. C. Scott & K. K. Myers (2005). "The Socialization of Emotion: Learning Emotion Management at the Fire Station." *Journal of Applied Communication Research, 33*, 67–92.

b. K. I. Miller & J. Koesten (2008). "Financial Feeling: An Investigation of Emotion and Communication in the Workplace." *Journal of Applied Communication Research, 36*, 8–32.

c. S. J. Tracy (2005). "Locking Up Emotion: Moving Beyond Dissonance for Understanding Emotion Labor Discomfort." *Communication Monographs, 72*, 261–283.

CHAPTER FIVE, ON THE JOB

a. E. M. Eisenberg (2007). "Ambiguity as Strategy in Organizational Communication." In *Strategic Ambiguities: Essays on Communication* (pp. 3–24). Thousand Oaks, CA: Sage. See also J. P. & C. A. Strbiak (1997). "The Ethics of Strategic Ambiguity." *The Journal of Business Communication, 34*, 149–159.

b. T. Weiss (1995). "Translation in a Borderless World." *Technical Communication Quarterly, 4*, 407–425.

CHAPTER FIVE, "ON NAMING BABY"

a. A. Mehrabian (1992). *The Name Game: The Decision That Lasts a Lifetime.* New York: Penguin.

b. A. Mehrabian (2005). "Baby Name Report Card: Beneficial and Harmful Baby Names." Retrieved June 17, 2009, at http://www.kaaj.com/psych/namebk.html.

CHAPTER FIVE, "COMPUTER PROGRAM DETECTS AUTHOR GENDER"

a. S. Argamon, M. Koppel, J. W. Pennebaker, & J. Schler (2009). "Automatically Profiling the Author of an Anonymous Text." *Communications of the ACM, 52*, 119–123.

CHAPTER SIX, ON THE JOB

a. C. Goldberg & D. J. Cohen (2004). "Walking the Walk and Talking the Talk: Gender Differences in the Impact of Interviewing Skills on Applicant Assessments." *Group & Organization Management, 29*, 369–384.

b. G. L. Stewart, S. L. Dustin, M. R. Barrick, & T. C. Darnold (2008). "Exploring the Handshake in Employment Interviews." *Journal of Applied Psychology, 93*, 1139–1146.

c. R. E. Riggio & B. Throckmorton (1988). "The Relative Effects of Verbal and Nonverbal Behavior, Appearance, and Social Skills on Evaluation Made in Hiring Interviews." *Journal of Applied Social Psychology, 18*,

331–348; R. Gifford, C. F. Ng, & M. Wilkinson (1985). "Nonverbal Cues in the Employment Interview: Links Between Applicant Qualities and Interviewer Judgments." *Journal of Applied Psychology, 70,* 729–736.

d. E. Krumhuber, A. Manstead, D. Cosker, D. Marshall, & Paul Rosin (2009). "Effects of Dynamic Attributes of Smiles in Human and Synthetic Faces: A Simulated Job Interview Setting." *Journal of Nonverbal Behavior, 33,* 1–15.

CHAPTER SEVEN, ON THE JOB

a. B. D. Sypher, R. N. Bostrom, & J. H. Seibert (1989). "Listening Communication Abilities and Success at Work." *Journal of Business Communication, 26,* 293–303. See also E. R. Alexander, L. E. Penley, & I. E. Jernigan (1992). "The Relationship of Basic Decoding Skills to Managerial Effectiveness." *Management Communication Quarterly, 6,* 58–73.

b. J. L. Winsor, D. B. Curtis, & R. D. Stephens (1999). "National Preferences in Business and Communication Education: An Update." *Journal of the Association for Communication Administration, 3,* 170–179.

c. S. Johnson & C. Bechler (1998). "Examining the Relationship between Listening Effectiveness and Leadership Emergence: Perceptions, Behaviors, and Recall." *Small Group Research, 29,* 452–471.

d. D. Christensen & D. Rees (October 2002). "Communication Skills Needed by Entry-Level Accountants." *The CPA Letter, 82.* Retrieved July 5, 2006, at http://www.aicpa.org/pubs/cpaltr/Oct2002/AUDIT/audit.htm.

e. V. Marchant (June 28, 1999). "Listen Up!" *Time, 153,* 74. See also *Job Outlook 2006,* summarized at http://www.naceweb.org/press/display.asp?year=&prid=235.

f. J. Brownell (1990). "Perceptions of Effective Listeners: A Management Study." *Journal of Business Communication, 27,* 401–415.

CHAPTER EIGHT, ON THE JOB

a. J. H. Waldeck & K. K. Myers (2007). "Organizational Assimilation Theory, Research, and Implications for Multiple Areas of the Discipline: A State of the Art Review." *Communication Yearbook, 31,* 322–367; Z. P. Hart & V. D. Miller (2005). "Context and Message Content During Organizational Socialization: A Research Note." *Human Communication Research, 31,* 295–309; P. E. Madlock & S. M. Horan (2009). "Predicted Outcome Value of Organizational Commitment." *Communication Research Reports, 26,* 40–49.

b. J. K. Barge & D. W. Schlueter (2004). "Memorable Messages and Newcomer Socialization." *Western Journal of Communication, 68,* 233–256.

CHAPTER NINE, "FRIENDS WITH BENEFITS, AND STRESS TOO"

a. M. A. Bisson & T. R. Levine (2009). "Negotiating a Friends With Benefits Relationship." *Archives of Sexual Behavior, 38,* 66–73.

CHAPTER NINE, ON THE JOB

a. Studies summarized in "More Confident, Less Careful: Why Office Romances Are Hard to Manage" (March 21, 2007). Retrieved at http://knowledge.wharton.upenn.edu; and "How To Handle An Office Romance" (August 30, 2007). Retrieved at www.cnn.com.

CHAPTER TEN, ON THE JOB

a. B. Cooil, L. Aksoy, T. L. Keiningham, & K. M. Maryott (2009). "The Relationship of Employee Perceptions of Organizational Climate to Business-Unit Outcomes: An MPLS Approach." *Journal of Service Research, 11,* 277–294; D. Pincus (1986). "Communication Satisfaction, Job Satisfaction, & Job Performance." *Human Communication Research, 12,* 395–419.

b. E. Sopow (2008). "The Communication Climate Change at RCMP." *Strategic Communication Management, 12,* 20–23; J. W. Kassing (2008). "Consider This: A Comparison of Factors Contributing to Employees' Expressions of Dissent." *Communication Quarterly, 56,* 342–355; D. Saunders (2008). "Create an Open Climate for Communication." *Supervision, 69,* 6–8; C. E. Beck & E. A. Beck (1996). "The Manager's Open Door and the Communication Climate." In K. M. Galvin & P. Cooper (Eds.), *Making Connections: Readings in Relational Communication* (pp. 286–290). Los Angeles: Roxbury.

c. D. Goleman (2006). *Social Intelligence* (p. 279). New York: Random House.

d. A. D. Akkirman & D. L. Harris (2005). "Organizational Communication Satisfaction in the Virtual Workplace." *Journal of Management Development, 24,* 397–409.

e. J. Waldvogel (2007). "Greetings and Closings in Workplace Email." *Journal of Computer-Mediated Communication, 12,* 456–477.

CHAPTER TEN, "TYPES OF DEFENSIVE REACTIONS"

a. L. Festinger (1957). *A Theory of Cognitive Dissonance.* Stanford, CA: Stanford University Press.

CHAPTER ELEVEN, ON THE JOB

a. S. Smith (2006). "Quitting Time: Top 10 Reasons People Leave Their Jobs." *Training, 43,* 8.

b. C. Anton (2009). "The Impact of Role Stress on Workers' Behaviour Through Job Satisfaction and Organizational Commitment." *International Journal of Psychology, 44,* 187–194.

c. P. Lutgen-Sandvik (2006). "Take This Job and . . . : Quitting and Other Forms of Resistance to Workplace Bullying." *Communication Monographs, 73,* 406–433.

d. P. Trunk (2006). "9 Tips for Quitting a Job Gracefully." Retrieved August 3, 2009, at http://blog.penelopetrunk.com/2006/08/20/9-tips-for-quitting-a-job-gracefully/.

GLOSSARY

abstraction ladder A range of more to less abstract terms describing an event or object.

abstract language Language that is vague and general rather than concrete and specific. *See also* behavioral language.

accenting Nonverbal behaviors that emphasize part of a verbal message.

accommodating A lose-win conflict style in which the communicator submits to a situation rather than attempts to have his or her needs met.

adaptors Unconscious bodily movements in response to the environment.

advising A listening response in which the receiver offers suggestions about how the speaker should deal with a problem.

affinity The degree to which persons like or appreciate one another.

aggressiveness Verbal attacks that demean others' self-concept and inflict psychological pain.

ambiguous response A disconfirming response with more than one meaning, leaving the other party unsure of the responder's position.

ambushing A style in which the receiver listens carefully in order to gather information to use in an attack on the speaker.

analyzing A listening response in which the receiver offers an interpretation of a speaker's message.

androgynous Possessing both masculine and feminine traits.

argumentativeness Presenting and defending positions on issues while attacking positions taken by others.

assertive message format A direct expression of the sender's needs and thoughts delivered in a way that does not attack the receiver's dignity. A complete assertive message describes behavior, interpretation, feeling, consequence, and intention.

attending The process of filtering out some messages and focusing on others.

attribution The process of attaching meaning to behavior. *See also* interpretation statement.

avoiding (conflict style) A lose-lose conflict style in which the parties ignore the problem at hand.

avoiding (relational stage) A stage of relational deterioration immediately prior to terminating in which the parties minimize contact with one another.

behavioral description An account that refers only to observable phenomena.

behavioral language Language that describes observable behavior. *See also* abstract language.

benevolent lie A lie defined by the teller as not malicious, or even helpful, to the person to whom it is told.

body orientation A type of nonverbal communication characterized by the degree to which we face forward or away from someone.

bonding A stage of relational development in which the parties make symbolic public gestures to show that their relationship exists.

breadth A dimension of self-disclosure involving the range of subjects being discussed.

"but" statement A statement in which the word *but* cancels out the expression that preceded it.

certainty An attitude behind messages that dogmatically implies that the speaker's position is correct and that the other person's ideas are not worth considering. Likely to generate a defensive response.

channel The medium through which a message passes from sender to receiver.

chronemics The study of how humans use and structure time.

circumscribing A stage of relational deterioration in which partners begin to reduce the scope of their contact and commitment to one another.

clichés Ritualized, stock statements delivered in response to a social situation.

co-culture A culture that exists within the larger culture of a country or society, such as subgroups defined by age, race/ethnicity, occupation, sexual orientation, physical disability, religion, avocation, and so on.

cognitive complexity The ability to construct a variety of frameworks for viewing an issue.

cognitive conservatism The tendency to seek and attend to information that conforms to an existing self-concept.

collaborating A conflict management style that seeks win-win solutions.

communication A continuous, transactional process involving participants who occupy different but overlapping environments and create relationships through the exchange of messages, many of which are affected by external, physiological, and psychological noise.

communication climate The emotional tone of a relationship between two or more individuals.

communication competence The ability to accomplish one's personal goals in a manner that maintains a relationship on terms that are acceptable to all parties.

competing A win-lose approach to conflicts that seeks to resolve them in one's own way.

complaining A disagreeing message that directly or indirectly communicates dissatisfaction with another person.

complementary conflict style A relational conflict style in which partners use different but mutually reinforcing behaviors.

complementing Nonverbal behavior that reinforces a verbal message.

compromising An approach to conflict resolution in which both parties attain at least part of what they wanted through self-sacrifice.

confirming communication A message that expresses caring or respect for another person.

conflict An expressed struggle between at least two interdependent parties who perceive incompatible goals, scarce resources, and interference from the other party in achieving their goals.

conflict ritual An unacknowledged repeating pattern of interlocking behavior used by participants in a conflict.

connection-autonomy dialectic The tension between the need for integration and the need for independence in a relationship.

consequence statement An explanation of the results that follow from either the behavior of the person to whom the message is addressed or the speaker's interpretation of the addressee's behavior. Consequence statements can describe what happens to the speaker, the addressee, or others.

content dimension The part of a message that communicates information about the subject being discussed. *See also* relational dimension.

contradicting Nonverbal behavior that is inconsistent with a verbal message.

control The social need to influence others.

controlling communication Messages in which the sender tries to impose some sort of outcome on the receiver, usually resulting in a defensive reaction.

convergence The process of adapting one's speech style to match that of others with whom the communicator wants to identify. *See also* divergence.

counterfeit questions Questions that disguise the speaker's true motives, which do not include a genuine desire to understand the other person. *See also* sincere questions.

crazymaking *See* passive aggression.

debilitative emotions Emotions that prevent a person from functioning effectively.

decode The process in which a receiver attaches meaning to a message.

de-escalatory conflict spiral A communication pattern in which the parties slowly lessen their dependence on one another, withdraw, and become less invested in the relationship. *See also* spiral.

defensive listening A response style in which the receiver perceives a speaker's comments as an attack.

defensiveness The attempt to protect a presenting image a person believes is being attacked.

depth A dimension of self-disclosure involving a shift from relatively nonrevealing messages to more personal ones.

description Gibb's term for language that describes a complaint in behavioral terms rather than being judgmental, thereby creating a supportive communication climate. *See also* evaluation, "I" language.

dialectical tensions Inherent conflicts that arise when two opposing or incompatible forces exist simultaneously.

differentiating A relational stage in which the parties reestablish their individual identities after having bonded together.

direct aggression A criticism or demand that threatens the face of the person at whom it is directed.

disagreeing messages Messages that communicate to the other person, "You are wrong." Includes aggressiveness, complaining, and argumentativeness.

disconfirming communication A message that expresses a lack of caring or respect for another person.

disinhibition The tendency to transmit messages without considering their consequences; occurs more frequently in mediated communication.

divergence Language mannerisms that emphasize a communicator's differences from others. *See also* convergence.

dyad Two individuals communicating. The interaction may or may not be interpersonal in nature.

emblems Deliberate nonverbal behaviors with precise meanings, known to virtually all members of a cultural group.

emotional contagion The process by which emotions are transferred from one person to another.

emotion labor Managing and even suppressing emotions when doing so is both appropriate and necessary.

emotive language Language that conveys the sender's attitude rather than simply offers an objective description.

empathy The ability to project oneself into another person's point of view, so as to experience the other's thoughts and feelings. *See also* sympathy.

encode The process of putting thoughts into symbols, most commonly words.

environment The field of experiences that leads a person to make sense of another's behavior. Environments consist of physical characteristics, personal experiences, relational history, and cultural background.

equality A type of supportive communication described by Gibb, suggesting that the sender regards the receiver as worthy of respect.

equivocal language Ambiguous language that has two or more equally plausible meanings.

escalatory conflict spiral A communication pattern in which one attack leads to another until the initial skirmish escalates into a full-fledged battle. *See also* spiral.

ethnocentrism The attitude that one's own culture is superior to others.

evaluation Gibb's term for judgmental assessments of another person's behavior, thereby increasing the odds of creating a defensive communication climate. *See also* description, "I" language.

experimenting An early stage in relational development, consisting of a search for common ground. If the experimentation is successful, the relationship will progress to intensifying. If not, it may go no further.

face The socially approved identity that a communicator tries to present. *See also* identity management.

face-threatening act Behavior by another that is perceived as attacking an individual's presenting image, or face.

facilitative emotions Emotions that contribute to effective functioning.

fallacy of approval The irrational belief that it is vital to win the approval of virtually every person a communicator deals with.

fallacy of catastrophic expectations The irrational belief that the worst possible outcome will probably occur.

fallacy of causation The irrational belief that emotions are caused by others and not by the person who has them.

fallacy of helplessness The irrational belief that satisfaction in life is determined by forces beyond one's control.

fallacy of overgeneralization Irrational beliefs in which (1) conclusions (usually negative) are based on limited evidence, or (2) communicators exaggerate their shortcomings.

fallacy of perfection The irrational belief that a worthwhile communicator should be able to handle every situation with complete confidence and skill.

fallacy of shoulds The irrational belief that people should behave in the most desirable way.

feeling statement An expression of the sender's emotions that results from interpretation of sense data.

gender role Socially approved ways that men and women are expected to behave.

gestures Motions of the body, usually hands or arms, that have communicative value.

Gibb categories Six sets of contrasting styles of verbal and nonverbal behavior. Each set describes a communication style that is likely to arouse defensiveness and a contrasting style that is likely to prevent or reduce it. Developed by Jack Gibb.

halo effect The power of a first impression to influence subsequent perceptions.

haptics The study of touching.

hearing The physiological dimension of listening.

high-context cultures Cultures that avoid direct use of language, relying on the context of a message to convey meaning.

identity management The communication strategies people use to influence how others view them. *See also* face.

"I" language A statement that clearly identifies the speaker as the source of a message. *See also* "you" language, description.

illustrators Nonverbal behaviors that accompany and support verbal messages.

immediacy The degree of interest and attention that we feel toward and communicate to others.

impersonal communication Behavior that treats others as objects rather than individuals. *See also* interpersonal communication.

impersonal response A disconfirming response that is superficial or trite.

impervious response A disconfirming response that ignores another person's attempt to communicate.

impression management *See* identity management.

incongruous response A disconfirming response in which two messages, one of which is usually nonverbal, contradict each other.

initiating The first stage in relational development, in which the parties express interest in one another.

insensitive listening Failure to recognize the thoughts or feelings that are not directly expressed by a speaker.

instrumental goals Goals aimed at getting others to behave in desired ways.

insulated listening A style in which the receiver ignores undesirable information.

integrating A stage of relational development in which the parties begin to take on a single identity.

intensifying A stage of relational development preceding integrating, in which the parties move toward integration by increasing the amount of contact and the breadth and depth of self-disclosure.

intention statement A description of where the speaker stands on an issue, what he or she wants, or how he or she plans to act in the future.

interpersonal communication In a quantitative sense, communication (usually face-to-face) between two individuals. (*See also* dyad.) In a qualitative sense, communication in which the parties consider one another as unique individuals rather than objects. It is characterized by minimal use of stereotyped labels; unique, idiosyncratic rules; and a high degree of information exchange.

interpretation The process of attaching meaning to sense data.

interpretation statement A statement that describes the speaker's interpretation of the meaning of another person's behavior. *See also* attribution.

interrupting response A disconfirming response in which one communicator interrupts another.

intimacy A state of closeness arising from physical, intellectual, and/or emotional contact, or sometimes from shared activities.

intimate distance One of Hall's four distance zones, ranging from skin contact to 18 inches.

irrelevant response A disconfirming response in which one communicator's comments bear no relationship to the previous speaker's ideas.

"it" statements Statements that replace the personal pronoun "I" with the less immediate word "it," often reducing the speaker's acceptance of responsibility for the statement.

Johari Window A model that describes the relationship between self-disclosure and self-awareness.

judging A listening response in which the receiver evaluates the sender's message either favorably or unfavorably.

kinesics The study of body position and motion.

leakage Nonverbal behaviors that reveal information a communicator does not disclose verbally.

linear communication model A characterization of communication as a one-way event in which a message flows from sender to receiver.

linguistic relativism The notion that the worldview of a culture is shaped and reflected by the language its members speak. *See also* Sapir-Whorf hypothesis.

listening Process that consists of hearing, attending, understanding, responding, and remembering an aural message.

listening fidelity The degree of congruence between what a listener understands and what the message-sender was attempting to communicate.

low-context cultures Cultures that use language primarily to express thoughts, feelings, and ideas as directly as possible.

manipulators A type of nonverbal adaptors involving self-touching behaviors.

mediated communication Communication between individuals that is conducted via technological channels such as email, chat rooms, texting, and instant messaging.

message Information sent from a sender to a receiver.

metacommunication Messages (usually relational) that refer to other messages; communication about communication.

microexpression A brief facial expression.

mindful listening Giving careful and thoughtful attention and responses to the messages we receive.

mindless listening Reacting to others' messages automatically and routinely, without much mental investment.

mixed message Situation in which a person's words are incongruent with his or her nonverbal behavior.

monochronic Behavior emphasizing punctuality, schedules, and completing one task at a time.

narrative The stories used to describe one's personal world.

negotiation The sense-making that occurs between and among people as they influence one another's perceptions and try to achieve a shared perspective. Fourth stage in the perception process.

neutrality A defense-arousing behavior described by Gibb in which the sender expresses indifference toward a receiver.

noise External, physiological, and psychological distractions that interfere with the accurate transmission and reception of a message.

nonverbal communication Messages expressed by other than linguistic means.

openness-privacy dialectic The tension between the need for disclosure and the need for secrecy in a relationship.

organization The second stage in the perception process in which selected information is arranged in some meaningful way.

paralanguage Nonlinguistic means of vocal expression: rate, pitch, tone, and so on.

parallel conflict style A relational conflict style in which the approach of the partners varies from one situation to another.

paraphrasing Restating a speaker's thoughts and/or feelings in the listener's own words.

passive aggression An indirect expression of aggression, delivered in a way that allows the sender to maintain a façade of kindness.

perceived self The person we believe ourselves to be in moments of candor. It may be identical with or different from the presenting and ideal self.

perception checking A three-part method for verifying the accuracy of interpretations, including a description of the sense data, two possible interpretations, and a request for confirmation of the interpretations.

personal distance One of Hall's four distance zones, ranging from 18 inches to 4 feet.

personality A relatively consistent set of traits exhibited by a person across a variety of situations.

pillow method A method for understanding an issue from several perspectives rather than with an egocentric "I'm right and you're wrong" attitude.

polychronic An approach to the use of time that emphasizes flexibility and pursuing multiple tasks.

posture The way in which individuals carry themselves—erect, slumping, and so on.

powerless speech mannerisms Ways of speaking that may reduce perceptions of a communicator's power.

pragmatic rules Linguistic rules that help communicators understand how messages may be used and interpreted in a given context.

predictability-novelty dialectic The tension between the need for stability and the need for change in a relationship.

presenting self The image a person presents to others. It may be identical with or different from the perceived and ideal self.

privacy management The choices people make to reveal or conceal information about themselves.

problem orientation A supportive style of communication described by Gibb in which the communicators focus on working together to solve their problems instead of trying to impose their own solutions on one another.

prompting Using silences and brief statements of encouragement to draw out a speaker.

provisionalism A supportive style of communication described by Gibb in which the sender expresses a willingness to consider the other person's position.

proxemics The study of how people use interpersonal space and distance.

pseudolistening An imitation of true listening in which the receiver's mind is elsewhere.

public distance One of Hall's four distance zones, extending outward from 12 feet.

punctuation The process of determining the causal order of events.

questioning A listening response in which the receiver seeks additional information from the sender.

reappraisal Rethinking the meaning of emotionally charged events in ways that alter their emotional impact.

receiver One who notices and attends to a message.

reference groups Groups against which we compare ourselves, thereby influencing our self-concept and self-esteem.

reflected appraisal The theory that a person's self-concept mirrors the way the person believes others regard him or her.

regulating One function of nonverbal communication, in which nonverbal cues control the flow of verbal communication among individuals.

relational commitment A promise—sometimes implied, and sometimes explicit—to remain in a relationship, and to make that relationship successful.

relational conflict style A pattern of managing disagreements that repeats itself over time in a relationship.

relational dimension The part of a message that expresses the social relationship between two or more individuals. *See also* content dimension.

relational maintenance Communication aimed at keeping relationships operating smoothly and satisfactorily.

relational transgressions One partner's violation of the explicit or implicit terms of the relationship, letting the other one down in some important way.

relative words Words that gain their meaning by comparison.

remembering Ability to recall information.

repeating Nonverbal behaviors that duplicate the content of a verbal message.

respect The social need to be held in esteem by others.

responding Giving observable feedback to the speaker.

richness An abundance of nonverbal cues that add clarity to a verbal message; opposite of leanness.

rumination Dwelling persistently on negative thoughts that, in turn, intensifies negative feelings.

Sapir-Whorf hypothesis Theory of linguistic relativity in which language shapes a culture's perceived reality. *See also* linguistic relativism.

selection The first stage in the perception process in which some data are chosen to attend to and others to ignore.

selective listening A listening style in which the receiver responds only to messages that interest him or her.

self-concept The relatively stable set of perceptions each individual holds of himself or herself.

self-disclosure The process of deliberately revealing information about oneself that is significant and that would not normally be known by others.

self-esteem The part of the self-concept that involves an individual's evaluations of his or her self-worth.

self-fulfilling prophecy An expectation of an event, followed by behaviors based on that expectation, that makes the outcome more likely to occur than would have been the case otherwise.

self-monitoring The process of attending to one's behavior and using these observations to shape the way one behaves.

self-serving bias The tendency to interpret and explain information in a way that casts the perceiver in the most favorable manner.

self-talk The nonvocal process of thinking, sometimes referred to as intrapersonal communication.

semantic rules Rules that govern the meaning of language, as opposed to its structure. *See also* syntactic rules.

sender The creator of a message.

significant others People whose opinion is important enough to affect one's self-concept strongly.

sincere questions Attempts to elicit information that enable the asker to understand the other person. *See also* counterfeit questions.

social comparison Evaluation of oneself in terms of or by comparison to others.

social distance One of Hall's distance zones, ranging from 4 to 12 feet.

social penetration A model that describes relationships in terms of their breadth and depth.

spiral A reciprocal communication pattern in which each person's message reinforces the other's. *See also* de-escalatory conflict spiral, escalatory conflict spiral.

spontaneity A supportive communication behavior described by Gibb in which the sender expresses a message without any attempt to manipulate the receiver.

stage-hogging A listening style in which the receiver is more concerned with making his or her own point than in understanding the speaker.

stagnating A stage of relational deterioration characterized by declining enthusiasm and by standardized forms of behavior.

static evaluation The tendency to view people or relationships as unchanging.

stereotyping Categorizing individuals according to a set of characteristics assumed to belong to all members of a group.

strategy A defense-arousing style of communication described by Gibb in which the sender tries to manipulate or deceive a receiver.

substituting Nonverbal behavior that takes the place of a verbal message.

superiority A defense-arousing style of communication described by Gibb in which the sender states or implies that the receiver is not worthy of respect.

supporting A listening response that demonstrates solidarity with a speaker's situation.

symmetrical conflict style A relational conflict style in which both partners use the same tactics.

sympathy Compassion for another's situation. *See also* empathy.

syntactic rules Rules that govern the ways symbols can be arranged, as opposed to the meanings of those symbols. *See also* semantic rules.

tangential response A disconfirming response that uses the speaker's remark as a starting point for a shift to a new topic.

terminating The concluding stage of relational deterioration, characterized by the acknowledgement of one or both parties that the relationship is over.

territory A stationary area claimed by an individual.

transactional communication model A characterization of communication as the simultaneous sending and receiving of messages in an ongoing, irreversible process.

understanding Occurs when sense is made of a message.

"we" language Statement that implies that the issue is the concern and responsibility of both the speaker and receiver of a message. *See also* "I" language, "you" language.

"you" language A statement that expresses or implies a judgment of the other person. *See also* "I" language.

CREDITS

CHAPTER 1

Pg. 4: From "The Silencing." *Newsweek,* June 18, 1973, p. 42. Copyright © 1973 Newsweek, Inc. All rights reserved. Reprinted by permission.

Pg. 19: From Brad K., "Social Networking, Survival, and Healing." Used by permission of the author.

CHAPTER 2

Pg. 69: From Mark Snyder, "The Many Me's of the Self-Monitor," *Psychology Today* (March 1983): 34. Reprinted with permission from *Psychology Today Magazine*, Copyright © 1983 Sussex Publishers, Inc.

Pg. 71: Ketzel Levine, "Alter Egos in a Virtual World," July 31, 2007, National Public Radio www.npr.org/templates/story/story.php?storyId=12263532

Pg. 74: "Complicated" words and music by Lauren Christy, Graham Edwards, Scott Spock, and Avril LaVigne. Copyright © 2002 Warner-Tamerlane Publishing Corp., Primary Wave Tunes, WB Music Corp., Primary Wave Songs, Almo Music Corp. and Avril LaVigne Publishing Ltd. All rights on behalf of itself and Primary Wave Tunes administered by Warner-Tamerlane Publishing Corp. All rights on behalf of itself and Primary Wave Songs administered by WB Music Corp. All rights reserved.

CHAPTER 3

Pg. 89: "The Magic Wand" by Lynn Manning. Reprinted by permission of the author.

Pg. 94: From *New York Times*, "Fast-Forwarding to Age 85, With Lessons on Offering Better Care for Elderly," National Section, 8/3/2008 Issue, pg. A22. (c) 2008 The New York Times. All rights reserved. Used by permission and protected by the Copyright Laws of the United States. The printing, copying, redistribution, or retransmission of the Material without express written permission is prohibited.

Pg. 104: *Newsweek*, "I'm Not Who You Think I Am," Carol Paik, 2/18/08. Copyright © 2008 Newsweek, Inc. All rights reserved. Reprinted by permission.

CHAPTER 4

Pg. 143: "Emotion," words and music by Barry Gibb and Robin Gibb, (c) 1977 (Renewed) Crompton Songs LLC and Gibb Brothers Music. All rights

for Crompton Songs LLC Administered by Warner-Tamerlane Publishing Corp. All rights reserved. Used by permission.

CHAPTER 5

Pg. 163: From *Conversation and Communication* by J. A. M. Meerloo, p. 83. Copyright © 1993 by International Universities Press, Inc. Reprinted by permission.

Pg. 163: "What Kind of Gone?" by Chris Cagle, 2007/2008, Capitol Records, © Dixie Stars Music (ASCAP), © Sounds Of R P M.

Pg. 177: "Bitching It Out (Out with Bitching)" by Alice Stanley. Copyright © 2009, Alice Stanley. This article originally appeared in The Bygone Bureau, http://bygonebureau.com. Reprinted by permission of the author.

CHAPTER 6

Pg. 202: Lyrics to "When You Say Nothing at All," sung by Alison Krauss. Don Schlitz & Paul Overstreet/ MCA music, Inc., Don Schlitz Music, ASCAP, Scarlet Moon, BMI.

Pg. 205: "Nothing" from *Love Poems for the Very Married* by Lois Wyse. Copyright © 1967 by Lois Wyse, renewed 1995 by Lois Wyse. Reprinted by permission of HarperCollins Publishers.

Pg. 206: Poem "Flags" from *Even As We Speak* by Ric Masten. Copyright (c) Sunflower Ink, Palo Colorado Road, Carmel, CA 93923. Reprinted with permission.

Pg. 212 Table 6.4: From *Interracial Communication Theory into Practice* (with InfoTrac College Edition), 1st ed., by M. P. Orbe and T. M. Harris. Wadsworth, 2001. ©2001 by Mark Orbe.

Pg. 218: From *Introduction to Nonverbal Communication* by L. Malandro and L. Baker, p. 112–113. Copyright © 1982. Used by permission of The McGraw-Hill Companies.

Pg. 219: "Blindness and Nonverbal Cues" by Annie Donnellon. Used with permission of author.

Pg. 227: "Prologue: The Birth of Architecture" copyright © 1976 by Edward Mendelson, William Meredith and Monro K. Spears, Executors of the Estate of W.H. Auden, from *Collected Poems by W.H. Auden*. Used by permission of Random House, Inc.

NAME INDEX

Note: page references followed by *f* refer to figures.

SUBJECT INDEX

relationship development and, 277, 288–89
self-concept as reflection of, 54–56, 55t
self-disclosure and, 34, 288–89, 309–10, 313
stereotyping based on, 86–89, 118

D

deception
  alternatives to self-disclosure and, 324–33
  defensiveness and, 351–52
  lying as, 326–29, 328t, 332, 333
  nonverbal communication and, 206–7, 207t, 232–33
decoding, 10, 10f
defensiveness
  assessment of, 356, 357
  causes of, 348
  communication climate and, 346–47, 348–55, 355–71, 374–75
  criticism and, 261, 355, 362–71, 375
  culture and, 354
  defensive listening, 243
  "I" *versus* "you" language and, 179–82
  listening responses and, 241, 243, 245, 251, 256, 258, 261, 363–67
  nonverbal communication and, 363, 365
  prevention of, 349–55
  saving face and, 348, 355–71
  types of defensive reactions, 349
dialetic tensions, 282–87, 301
disagreeing messages, 343–44
disagreements. *See* conflict
disruptive language, 175–78
distance, personal
  communication climate and, 345
  cultural differences in, 34, 211, 212
  as nonverbal communication, 34, 211, 212, 226–28, 345
  relationships formed based on proximity, 273–74, 312
duty theory, 63

E

effective communication, 14, 25–34, 37, 110, 245, 353
ego boosters/busters, 46
electronic media, 10. *See also* films; mediated communication; television shows
email
  communication climate of, 340
  emotional expression through, 126, 129, 133, 141
  flaming via, 22, 133, 141
  identity management through, 73–74
  as interpersonal communication tool, 19–22, 126
  intimacy and, 310
  language used in, 172
  nonverbal communication and, 21–22, 203–4
  relationship development through, 277, 289, 305
emoticons, 129, 203–4
emotions
  assessment of, 125, 131, 136, 138, 144, 150, 153–54, 358
  common, 135t
  components of, 122–26
  culture and, 124–25, 126–28, 211–12
  denying others right to their, 255–56, 255t
  emotional tone of communication (*See* communication climate)
  facilitative *versus* debilitative, 141–42, 157
  feeling statements, 358–59
  films depicting, 156–57
  golden mean of expression, 139
  guidelines for expressing, 132–41
  influences on expression of, 126–32
  intimacy and, 305
  irrational thinking and, 145–50
  managing difficult, 141–54
  minimizing debilitative, 150–54

nonverbal communication and, 123, 130, 134, 203, 211–12, 217
  rational-emotive thought, 151–54
  reappraisal of, 124, 144–45, 151–52
  recognition of, 125, 134–35, 150
  self-disclosure and, 131, 134, 315–16
  sources of debilitative, 142–45
empathy, 30, 108–16, 119, 254–55, 352
employment. *See* occupation; workplace communication
encoding, 9–10, 10f
endorsement, 345
environment. *See also* culture
  competent communicators' adjustment to, 28
  for emotional expression, 137–39
  identity management through, 72–73
  as nonverbal communication, 228–29
  perception of (*See* perception)
  self-concept as reflection of, 45–49, 54–56, 55t
  in transactional communication model, 11–12, 11f
equality, 352–54
equivocating/equivocal language, 162–64, 329–31
esteem. *See* respect; self-esteem
ethics
  conflict and, 386
  culture and, 33
  duty theory, 63
  empathy and, 111
  evasion and, 326, 332, 333
  honesty *versus* deception, 74, 325, 326, 332, 333
  moral virtue, 139
  self-disclosure and, 321
  strategic ambiguity and, 164
  unconditional positive regard, 263
ethnicity. *See also* culture
  conflict and, 396–97
  intercultural communication and, 32–34
  language and, 173
  multiple identities and, 67

equivocating as means of, 162–64, 330–31
hinting as means of, 331, 333
identity management for, 70
language and, 173–74, 178
listening responses and, 260
lying as means of, 326
perception checking and, 107–8

self-actualization, 9

self-awareness, 30–31, 34, 125, 134–35. *See also* self-monitoring

self-clarification, 318

self-concept. *See also* identity
assessment of, 41, 45, 52
biology and, 43–45
changing, 53–54, 60–62, 78
characteristics of, 49–54
conflict and, 397
culture shaping, 54–56, 55*t*
defensiveness and, 348–49
environment reflecting, 45–49, 54–56, 55*t*
films/television shows depicting, 77–78
influences on, 77
perceptions influenced by, 91
relationships and, 272
resistance to change in, 53–54
self-esteem and, 40–43, 42*t*, 43*f*, 50–51
as self-fulfilling prophecy, 57–60, 62, 78
socialization and, 45–49, 63
subjectivity of, 49–52

self-disclosure
alternatives to, 324–33, 337
assessment of, 316, 317, 320, 323
benefits of, 317–20
characteristics of, 313*t*
culture and, 34, 288–89, 309–10, 313
defined, 312–13
degrees of, 314–16, 314*f*
emotions and, 131, 134, 315–16
equivocating *versus*, 329–31
fear of, 131
films depicting, 336–37
gender and, 307–8, 313
guidelines for, 321–25
hinting *versus*, 331, 333
in interpersonal communication, 18, 24

intimacy and, 307–8, 309–10, 312–24, 336
Johari Window model of, 316–17, 316*f*
lying *versus*, 326–29, 328*t*, 332, 333
relationship development and, 273, 284–85, 286–87, 288–89
risks of, 320–21
silence *versus*, 326, 332

self-esteem
assessment of, 43, 52
gender and, 56–57
as need, 9
relationships and, 272–73
self-concept and, 40–43, 42*t*, 43*f*, 50–51

self-fulfilling prophecy
fallacy of helplessness as, 149
self-concept as, 57–60, 62, 78
stereotypes and, 86–88

self-monitoring, 30–31, 68–70, 134, 150–54

self-serving bias, 101–2

self-talk, 143–45, 151–54

self-validation, 318

semantic rules, 162–67

sender, 9–10, 10*f*. *See also* communicators

senses, 93–94. *See also* hearing; touch

setting, 72–73, 137–38, 139, 228–29. *See also* environment

sex. *See also* gender
gender distinction from, 98
physical intimacy, 305, 306, 308

sexual orientation, 32. *See also* gays and lesbians

shared activities, 305, 307–8

shoulds, fallacy of, 147

significant others, 46–47

sign language, 161, 195, 200

silence, 4–5, 96–97, 190, 326, 332

similarity, 271

social comparison, 47–48, 61

social exchange theory, 275

social influence, 319–20

social isolation, 4–6, 8*f*, 195, 311

socialization, 45–49, 63

social needs, 7–8

social networking, 18–22, 73–74, 310. *See also* mediated communication

social penetration, 314–15, 314*f*

social roles
affiliation and, 172–73, 196
emotions and, 130
impersonal communication and, 17
intercultural communication and, 32
language and, 186–87
listening and, 262
perception and, 85, 98–101
self-concept and, 40, 41

social rules/conventions, 17, 129–30, 291, 308–10

socioeconomics, 88

solitude, 4–6, 8*f*, 195, 311

speech, 201*t*, 204*t*, 236, 236*f*, 246. *See also* language

spouses. *See also* marital communication
abuse of, 274
communication climate between, 341, 345–46, 346*t*
conflict between, 380–81, 385, 387, 390–93
defensiveness of, 346
emotions and, 128–29, 131, 142
listening to, 236
perceptions of, 91–92
relationships between (*See* relationships)
social needs of, 7

static evaluation, 165

status, 228–29

stereotyping, 86–89, 98–99, 99*t*, 118, 166

stimuli
interpretation of, 90–91, 103–8
obvious, 103
organization of, 84–90, 84*f*, 85*f*
physiological, 93–96
selection of, 83–84

strengths, recognizing, 52

subjectivity of self-concept, 49–52

substitution, 204

superiority, 352–54

supporting, 254–57, 263, 266–67

symbolism of language, 161–62

symmetrical conflict style, 390–91

syntactic rules, 167–68